Creating and Sustaining an Information Governance Program

Kris Helge
Rutgers University, USA

Caitlin A. Rookey
Tarrant County College, USA

IGI Global
PUBLISHER of TIMELY KNOWLEDGE

A volume in the Advances in Information Quality and Management (AIQM) Book Series

Published in the United States of America by
IGI Global
Information Science Reference (an imprint of IGI Global)
701 E. Chocolate Avenue
Hershey PA, USA 17033
Tel: 717-533-8845
Fax: 717-533-8661
E-mail: cust@igi-global.com
Web site: http://www.igi-global.com

Library of Congress Cataloging-in-Publication Data

CIP Pending
ISBN: 979-8-3693-0472-3
EISBN: 979-8-3693-0474-7

This book is published in the IGI Global book series Advances in Information Quality and Management (AIQM) (ISSN: 2331-7701; eISSN: 2331-771X)

British Cataloguing in Publication Data
A Cataloguing in Publication record for this book is available from the British Library.

Advances in Information Quality and Management (AIQM) Book Series

Siddhartha Bhattacharyya
RCC Institute of Information Technology, India

ISSN:2331-7701
EISSN:2331-771X

Mission

Acquiring and managing quality information is essential to an organization's success and profitability. Innovation in information technology provides managers, researchers, and practitioners with the tools and techniques needed to create and adapt new policies, strategies, and solutions for information management.

The **Advances in Information Quality and Management (AIQM) Book Series** provides emerging research principals in knowledge society for the advancement of future technological development. This series aims to increase available research publications and emphasize the global response within the discipline and allow for audiences to benefit from the comprehensive collection of this knowledge.

Coverage

- IT Management in Public Organizations
- IT Innovation and Diffusion
- Decision Support and Group Decision Support Systems
- E-Collaboration
- Mobile Commerce
- Human and Societal Issue
- Web Services and Technologies
- Supply Chain Management
- Knowledge Management
- Emerging Technologies Management

IGI Global is currently accepting manuscripts for publication within this series. To submit a proposal for a volume in this series, please contact our Acquisition Editors at Acquisitions@igi-global.com or visit: http://www.igi-global.com/publish/.

The Advances in Information Quality and Management (AIQM) Book Series (ISSN 2331-7701) is published by IGI Global, 701 E. Chocolate Avenue, Hershey, PA 17033-1240, USA, www.igi-global.com. This series is composed of titles available for purchase individually; each title is edited to be contextually exclusive from any other title within the series. For pricing and ordering information please visit http://www.igi-global.com/book-series/advances-information-quality-management/73809. Postmaster: Send all address changes to above address.

Titles in this Series

For a list of additional titles in this series, please visit:
http://www.igi-global.com/book-series/advances-information-quality-management/73809

Reviving and Re-Writing Ethics in Social Research For Commoning the Community
Jahid Siraz Chowdhury (Lincoln University College, Malaysia) Kumarashwaran Vadevelu (Universiti Malaya, Malaysia) Zulkarnain A. Hatta (Lincoln University College, Malaysia) Mahfuz Ashraf (Lincoln Institute of Higher Education, Australia) and Amiya Bhaumik (Lincoln University College, alaysia)
Information Science Reference • © 2024 • 293pp • H/C (ISBN: 9781668485262) • US $245.00

Methodologies and Ethics for Social Sciences Research
Aytekin Demircioğlu (Kastamonu University, Turkey)
Information Science Reference • © 2024 • 345pp • H/C (ISBN: 9798369317266) • US $245.00

Theoretical and Conceptual Frameworks in ICT Research
Agripah Kandiero (Insituto Superior Mutasa (ISMU), Mozambique & Mozambique Institute of Technology, Mozambique & Africa University, Zimbabwe) Stanislas Bigirimana (Africa University, Zimbabwe) and Sabelo Chizwina (University of South Africa, South Africa)
Information Science Reference • © 2024 • 311pp • H/C (ISBN: 9781799896876) • US $215.00

Digital Preservation and Documentation of Global Indigenous Knowledge Systems
Tlou Maggie Masenya (Durban University of Technology, South Africa)
Information Science Reference • © 2023 • 442pp • H/C (ISBN: 9781668470244) • US $285.00

Information Literacy Skills and the Role of Social Media in Disseminating Scholarly Information in the 21st Century
C. Baskaran (Alagappa University, India) and S. Dhanavandan (Central University of Tamil Nadu, India)
Information Science Reference • © 2023 • 236pp • H/C (ISBN: 9781668488058) • US $215.00

Library and Media Roles in Information Hygiene and Managing Information
Collence Takaingenhamo Chisita (Durban University of Technology, South Africa & University of South Africa, South Africa) Alexander Madanha Rusero (University of Johannesburg, South Africa) Ngoako Solomon Marutha (University of South Africa, South Africa) Josiline Phiri Chigwada (Chinhoyi University of Technology, Zimbabwe) and Oluwole Olumide Durodolu (Department of Information Science, University of South Africa, South Africa)
Information Science Reference • © 2022 • 268pp • H/C (ISBN: 9781799887133) • US $215.00

IGI Global
PUBLISHER of TIMELY KNOWLEDGE

701 East Chocolate Avenue, Hershey, PA 17033, USA
Tel: 717-533-8845 x100 • Fax: 717-533-8661
E-Mail: cust@igi-global.com • www.igi-global.com

Kris Helge – To Terri, Andrew, Jason, Jacob, Emelie, and Mom with love for the most important things in life.

Caitlin Rookey -- For Sam and Ben. Thank you for supporting me in everything I do.

Table of Contents

Foreword xvi

Preface xix

Acknowledgment xxiv

Chapter 1
Examining the Public Perception of Law Enforcement: A Twitter User Engagement Analysis With the Dallas Police Department 1
Tereza Raquel Merlo, University of North Texas, USA
Nayana Madali M. Pampapura, University of North Texas, USA
Jason M. Merlo, Texas DPS, USA

Chapter 2
Locating Appropriate Executive Sponsorship and the Information Governance Cadillac as Catalysts for a Successful IG Program 15
Kris Swen Helge, Rutgers University, USA

Chapter 3
Role of Information Security and Protection in the Modern Era 24
Ahmad Tasnim Siddiqui, Sandip University, Nashik, India
Gulshaira Banu Jahangeer, Taif University, Saudi Arabia
Amjath Fareeth Basha, Taif University, Saudi Arabia

Chapter 4
Building Culture for Sustaining Information Governance 36
Jennie Lee Khun, Purdue Global University, USA

Chapter 5
Strategic Information Governance Review: Exploring Data Management for Effective Business Op. Intelligence in a Data-Centric Environment 55
Tereza Raquel Merlo, University of North Texas, USA

Chapter 6
Decentralized Data and Privacy: Exploring the Conflict Between Distributed Ledger Technology and the Right to Be Forgotten Under GDP 74
Akash Bag, Amity University, India
Paridhi Sharma, O.P. Jindal Global University, India
Pranjal Khare, O.P. Jindal Global University, India
Souvik Roy, Adamas University, India

Chapter 7
Navigating the Digital Dilemma: The Right to Be Forgotten, Privacy, and Freedom of Speech in the Age of GDPR 105
Akash Bag, Adamas University, India
Upasana Khattri, O.P. Jindal Global University, India
Aditya Agrawal, O.P. Jindal Global University, India
Souvik Roy, Adamas University, India

Chapter 8
Study of Literature on Quality Management in Manufacturing and Healthcare for Information Governance 133
Balaji Gopalan, CMS Business School, Bangalore, India

Chapter 9
Privacy of Information and Data: Policies, Threats, and Solutions 155
Ali Kavak, Kırıkkale University, Turkey

Chapter 10
Implementing Information Governance in Academic Libraries: An Exploration of Opportunities 188
Amanda Zerangue, University of North Texas Libraries, USA
Kristin Clark, Texas Woman's University Libraries, USA
Adrian Shapiro, Texas Woman's University Libraries, USA

Chapter 11
Spatial Data Infrastructure for Information Governance: The Case Study From Pakistan 203
Munir Ahmad, Survey of Pakistan, Pakistan
Asmat Ali, Survey of Pakistan, Pakistan
Froilan Delute Mobo, Philippine Merchant Marine Academy, Philippines
Hammad Hussain, COMSATS University Islamabad, Wah, Pakistan

Chapter 12
Navigating the Legal Landscape of Information Governance 217
Hemendra Singh, O.P. Jindal Global University, India

Chapter 13
Information Governance for Public Authorities: An Indian Perspective 236
Kirt Agarwal, Dr. B.R. Ambedkar University, Delhi, India
Sneha Hooda, O.P. Jindal Global University, India
Shashank Maheshwari, O.P. Jindal Global University, India

Chapter 14
Tax Authorities Big Data Analytics in Developing Countries: A Case Study of Indonesia............... 259
Susanna Hartanto, Widya Mandala Catholic University, Indonesia

Chapter 15
An Overarching Guide to Data Governance 283
Kritika, Independent Researcher, India

Chapter 16
The Library and Information Science Perspective on Knowledge Management................................ 308
Muhammad Rosyihan Hendrawan, University of Brawijaya, Indonesia
Luh Putu Sri Ariyani, Universitas Pendidikan Ganesha, Indonesia
Aniesa Samira Bafadhal, University of Brawijaya, Indonesia

Compilation of References 325

About the Contributors 358

Index 363

Detailed Table of Contents

Foreword xvi

Preface xix

Acknowledgment xxiv

Chapter 1
Examining the Public Perception of Law Enforcement: A Twitter User Engagement Analysis With the Dallas Police Department 1
Tereza Raquel Merlo, University of North Texas, USA
Nayana Madali M. Pampapura, University of North Texas, USA
Jason M. Merlo, Texas DPS, USA

The emergence of social media platforms has revolutionized communication and interaction across various domains, including law enforcement, and users have increasingly utilized these platforms to express their opinions and consume information. This research chapter focuses on evaluating user responses and behaviors on Twitter presenting an analysis of tweets mentioning the Dallas Police Department. Data analysis is performed to investigate tweet frequency and patterns related to the law enforcement agency. Additionally, sentiment analysis and topic modeling techniques are employed to gain deeper insights into the content and context of user tweets. The research findings reveal that users tend to increase their tweeting activity whenever there is an incident involving the agency. Moreover, the results indicate that users generally express a neutral sentiment towards the law enforcement agency, with their tweets largely reflecting personal opinions. Overall, this study provides valuable insights into user behavior and sentiments concerning the Dallas Police Department, demonstrating the significant role of social media platforms in shaping public perceptions and online interactions with the agency.

Chapter 2
Locating Appropriate Executive Sponsorship and the Information Governance Cadillac as Catalysts for a Successful IG Program.. 15
Kris Swen Helge, Rutgers University, USA

There are many important facets to consider when establishing an information governance (IG) program. Many of these facets include ensuring you have executive sponsorship to support your new IG program, locating a large need in the organization to justify your IG program creation (AKA the grand Cadillac, discussed later in this chapter), securing adequate funding and staff, creating an IG program charter and strategic plan, recruiting organization-wide support through tiered steering committees, procuring efficient technologies, obtaining appropriate IG related education and training, and considering current industry-wide IG trends. However, the two most important aspects one must have in place to initially begin the building and sustainment of an IG program are high level executive sponsorship and a shiny Cadillac or large need in the organization that an IG program can help meet. The first and foremost important facet is the executive sponsor.

Chapter 3
Role of Information Security and Protection in the Modern Era 24
Ahmad Tasnim Siddiqui, Sandip University, Nashik, India
Gulshaira Banu Jahangeer, Taif University, Saudi Arabia
Amjath Fareeth Basha, Taif University, Saudi Arabia

The purpose of information security is to protect data by mitigating the risks associated with it. It refers to preventing unauthorized access to disclosure, destruction, disruption, modification of information and the information that they process, store, and transmit. Every information, especially sensitive or confidential, must be protected. It is essential to consider technology, policies, procedures, and people when implementing an effective information security system. In addition, emerging threats and vulnerabilities need to be monitored, assessed, and adapted continuously. Cybercrime, theft, and espionage are some of the threats we face trying to protect our valuable information assets. The goal of information security is to safeguard valuable information assets against a variety of threats. No matter how information is stored, whether electronically or on paper, it must be protected to ensure privacy, integrity, and availability. This chapter talks about the role of information security in modern days.

Chapter 4
Building Culture for Sustaining Information Governance 36
Jennie Lee Khun, Purdue Global University, USA

The chapter explains what information governance is and why it is important. The problem is identified that organizations know information governance is important but many fail to implement governance or do so poorly. The author questions why companies fail to recognize the benefit of a cultural approach to addressing this critical gap. The chapter introduces the concept that information governance is integral for every organization. The chapter provides insight into hiring, training, professional development, emotional intelligence, and soft skills to build a thriving organization. The chapter explores the need for a positive and dedicated approach to leadership. The chapter explores communication, operational efficiencies, board governance approaches, and examines compliance. Lastly, the chapter explores risk and why organizations must implement a risk management strategy. A conclusion summarizes the need for information governance to build a successful culture that adopts an information governance strategy to be successful.

Chapter 5
Strategic Information Governance Review: Exploring Data Management for Effective Business Op. Intelligence in a Data-Centric Environment 55
Tereza Raquel Merlo, University of North Texas, USA

This book chapter, "Strategic Information Governance: Optimizing Business Operations, Business Intelligence, and Data Management," explores the dynamic intersection of information governance and organizational functionality. Grounded in an exhaustive literature review, it guides businesses in enhancing operations, fortifying business intelligence, and refining data management. From principles to practical applications, the chapter emphasizes the symbiotic relationship between information governance and business operations. It provides actionable insights, empowering businesses to strategically leverage information governance for optimized processes. Addressing the evolving data landscape, it offers proven strategies for aligning governance with efficient data practices, ensuring compliance, security, and accessibility. This chapter is an indispensable resource for decision-makers, providing a comprehensive guide for organizations navigating the complexities of strategic information governance in today's dynamic business environment.

Chapter 6
Decentralized Data and Privacy: Exploring the Conflict Between Distributed Ledger Technology and the Right to Be Forgotten Under GDP 74
Akash Bag, Amity University, India
Paridhi Sharma, O.P. Jindal Global University, India
Pranjal Khare, O.P. Jindal Global University, India
Souvik Roy, Adamas University, India

Our personal information, or "digital footprint," is gathered and used in today's digital age. Digital footprints are kept, unlike snow footprints. There is a large market for this data, which businesses utilize to analyze consumer preferences. Businesses collecting a lot of data in one place pose a privacy risk. Thus, people are worried. Businesses prefer not to utilize intermediaries to manage client data to save money. Therefore, new technology is needed to make online interactions safer and more efficient. We're considering "distributed ledger technology." This technology is interesting because it securely collects, stores, and processes data without central authority. It has data immutability, transparency, and safety. A problem exists. The European GDPR (general data protection regulation) may conflict with this technology. This chapter will examine this tension, focusing on the right to be forgotten, which permits people to delete their data. It will examine how this new technology and existing privacy policies can function together or need tweaking.

Chapter 7
Navigating the Digital Dilemma: The Right to Be Forgotten, Privacy, and Freedom of Speech in the Age of GDPR 105
Akash Bag, Adamas University, India
Upasana Khattri, O.P. Jindal Global University, India
Aditya Agrawal, O.P. Jindal Global University, India
Souvik Roy, Adamas University, India

The 2014 Google Spain lawsuit was a major European Court ruling. It indicated that online name searches yield personal information. Google and other search engine operators must remove or prevent search results that breach privacy rights. The "right to forget" lets users remove their personal information from search engine results. Your internet privacy isn't completely protected. Technology changes quickly, making it hard for laws to stay up. The right to be forgotten is criticized for its deceptive nomenclature and inconsistent application. European websites may remove information, but non-European sites (like the US) may not. This right may also limit free speech. The chapter discusses the "right to be forgotten" from the new GDPR perspective. They are testing whether this right gives internet users more control over their data. It conflicts with privacy and free speech. It's considerably difficult since private firms, whose major objective is to make money, have a say, raising problems about our rights.

Chapter 8
Study of Literature on Quality Management in Manufacturing and Healthcare for Information Governance 133
Balaji Gopalan, CMS Business School, Bangalore, India

The chapter aims to comprehend the best practices of quality management in manufacturing and healthcare services and its relevance to information governance. Quality management principles of quality gurus have contributed significantly to the manufacturing and services sector. Its implementations in manufacturing and health care services provide numerous learning opportunities. Delivery of care processes integrates quality of health and life, lean management, quality assurance, quality implementation, quality control, affordability, and satisfaction with services. These best practices in quality management are relevant across various disciplines of research including information management, psychology, business research, service quality and technology management. The study has explored the challenges of quality management in health care services and manufacturing and integrates studies that may contribute to the subject of quality management and its relevance for information governance.

Chapter 9
Privacy of Information and Data: Policies, Threats, and Solutions 155
Ali Kavak, Kırıkkale University, Turkey

Information and data privacy is a critical issue in modern society to protect the privacy of individuals and institutions, ensure their security, and prevent the misuse of their information. Rapidly developing technology has posed new challenges in ensuring information and data privacy. Technological developments such as big data, artificial intelligence, cloud computing and the internet of things require innovative solutions to protect information and data privacy. Today, with the acceleration of the digitizing world, individuals' and institutions' concerns about information and data privacy are increasing. By addressing information and data privacy through policies, threats and solutions, this study aims to examine new protection-oriented frameworks, policies, and best practices. Aiming to examine coping strategies with technological developments by emphasizing the importance of information and data privacy, this study is original in terms of presenting innovative policies and practices, guiding readers, and providing solutions to current challenges in this field.

Chapter 10
Implementing Information Governance in Academic Libraries: An Exploration of Opportunities 188
Amanda Zerangue, University of North Texas Libraries, USA
Kristin Clark, Texas Woman's University Libraries, USA
Adrian Shapiro, Texas Woman's University Libraries, USA

This chapter focuses on opportunities to implement an information governance framework within an academic library. Due to their mission and breadth of information management activities, academic libraries face numerous challenges in organizing and preserving information and records, and governing data. Implementing information governance strategies, specifically in the areas of records and information management, metadata creation, institutional repositories, digital preservation, and data management will result in well-informed and collaborative policies which protect the library as well as the institution. Developing this skill set within the library requires a culture shift towards transparency, collaboration, and accountability. Additionally, library and information science curricula should reflect the current demands of the academic library landscape and expand course offerings to build information governance competencies.

Chapter 11
Spatial Data Infrastructure for Information Governance: The Case Study From Pakistan................. 203
Munir Ahmad, Survey of Pakistan, Pakistan
Asmat Ali, Survey of Pakistan, Pakistan
Froilan Delute Mobo, Philippine Merchant Marine Academy, Philippines
Hammad Hussain, COMSATS University Islamabad, Wah, Pakistan

By examining the case study of spatial data infrastructure (SDI) implementation in Pakistan and its relationship with information governance, this chapter contributed to a deeper understanding of how effective spatial data management can support information governance objectives. A feasibility study is ongoing to establish NSDI in Pakistan. Moreover, a provincial-level SDI under PULSE is also planned. However, challenges such as the absence of uniform standards, a poor technology setup, and a shortage of qualified manpower are associated with NSDI implementation in Pakistan. By enhancing data quality and consistency and facilitating data sharing & collaboration, NSDI Pakistan would strengthen information governance in Pakistan by supporting decisions as well as policymaking. The findings and recommendations will help policymakers and practitioners in Pakistan, as well as researchers interested in the fields of spatial data infrastructure and information governance, advance their understanding and implementation of these critical concepts.

Chapter 12
Navigating the Legal Landscape of Information Governance 217
Hemendra Singh, O.P. Jindal Global University, India

There has been a massive increase in information volume in the modern business environment. This means that it has become very important to understand the complex relationship between information governance and the legal framework. This chapter aims to explore the various dimensions that define this intersection. It provides a comprehensive examination of general data protection regulation as a global legal framework for information governance. It also examines sector specific regulations, legal implications of information management and real-world cases to see how organizations can proactively address the legal dimensions of information governance. By exploring different dimensions of this intersection, this chapter serves as a strategic guide for organizations that want to strengthen their information governance frameworks.

Chapter 13
Information Governance for Public Authorities: An Indian Perspective... 236
Kirt Agarwal, Dr. B.R. Ambedkar University, Delhi, India
Sneha Hooda, O.P. Jindal Global University, India
Shashank Maheshwari, O.P. Jindal Global University, India

In an era dominated by digital transformation, public authorities globally face a profound challenge in effectively managing and governing the burgeoning volumes of information under their purview. Using specific case study of teacher attendance monitoring system (TAMS) in State of Meghalaya, this chapter seeks to explore the landscape of information governance within the context of public authorities in India. As the country undergoes significant advancements in digital infrastructure and governance, understanding the nuances of information governance becomes imperative for ensuring transparency, accountability, and optimal service delivery. This chapter aims to provide a comprehensive analysis of the current state of information governance in Indian public authorities, identifying key challenges, proposing strategic solutions, and offering insights into the potential impact on public administration and citizen engagement.

Chapter 14
Tax Authorities Big Data Analytics in Developing Countries: A Case Study of Indonesia............... 259
Susanna Hartanto, Widya Mandala Catholic University, Indonesia

Nowadays, most tax authorities in the world are utilizing various technologies, including big data analytics to be more efficient and effective in their works. Utilization of big data analytics and business intelligence by tax authorities in developing countries can be used to help identify the non-compliance taxpayers and support other activities in order to explore potential tax revenues. Directorate General of Taxes, Indonesian Tax Autbority, uses combination of compliance risk management application and business intelligence. There are nine types of compliance risk management applications. Currently, seven types of compliance risk management applications have been launched and used by the directorate general of taxes. The last two compliance risk management applications will be released in the near future. The series of nine compliance risk management applications will be supported by four business intelligence. Those compliance risk management and business intelligence applications will lead directorate general of taxes to be data driven organization.

Chapter 15
An Overarching Guide to Data Governance 283
Kritika, Independent Researcher, India

The advent of advanced technologies like blockchain, cryptocurrency, etc. has posed threats to the humongous data of the organisations at voluminous scale hindering day to day activities of the institution which paves way for governance of data at every level of the organisation defining roles and responsibilities of each and every member. Data governance is one such way of collocating and administering policies, plan of action and calibre for the tacit usage of organisation's structured or unstructured information with the focus on 5 V's—namely, volume, veracity, value, variety, and velocity. The chapter focuses on providing the details of the need of data governance, the tools used, data governance framework, challenges posed to models of data governance and its solution.

Chapter 16
The Library and Information Science Perspective on Knowledge Management................................ 308
Muhammad Rosyihan Hendrawan, University of Brawijaya, Indonesia
Luh Putu Sri Ariyani, Universitas Pendidikan Ganesha, Indonesia
Aniesa Samira Bafadhal, University of Brawijaya, Indonesia

Knowledge management (KM) creates value and competitive advantage via innovation. Library and information science (LIS) developed KM using social epistemology and varied scientific methods. LIS continued to study KM to guarantee its understanding and usage in the organization. KM attitudes and actions must also be agreed upon. This chapter discusses the LIS viewpoint on KM and delivers the fundamental point, which implies that LIS may advance knowledge management. Thus, readers should ask questions about LIS and all of the preceding advances, especially KM. The perception of data, information, and knowledge especially has changed significantly. LIS perspective should be dynamic, and librarianship has individuality and dignity with knowledge managing tradition. LIS and Librarianship roles, especially KM, may help drive these new advancements. Instead of only watching or ignoring improvements, active engagement and additional research are expected to raise LIS roles on KM.

Compilation of References 325

About the Contributors 358

Index 363

Foreword

Between 1980 and early 1990s Larry English, well-known professional and researcher in data quality and governance, labelled as "Father of Information Quality," developed the Total Information Quality (TIQM) system adopting preliminary concepts from predecessors in the field. Larry's work inspired the development of *infonomics* that has been applied to organizations worldwide. The conceptual framework laid by Larry English is based on the understanding that data is valuable and plays a critical role in businesses and the decision-making processes. He advocated for the systematic approach to address issues with data inaccuracies, inconsistencies, quality, factors identified as critical in the improvement of governance of organizational data assets. In an era defined by the incessant flow of information, mastering its legal landscape has become imperative for organizations striving for longevity and prosperity. *Creating and Sustaining an Information Governance Program* serves as a beacon in this tumultuous universe, offering a comprehensive roadmap to comprehend and leverage the intricate interplay between information governance, knowledge production and use, and the legal realm.

Dr Helge executed an exceptional job with the organization of this anthology which comprises sixteen meticulously crafted chapters, each a cornerstone in the edifice of modern information management. At its core, this book acknowledges the pressing need to navigate the legal intricacies of information governance, making it not only relevant but indispensable in today's data-driven economy.

One chapter lays the foundation, dissecting the legal landscape of information governance with precision and clarity. In an era where regulatory compliance is non-negotiable, understanding frameworks like the General Data Protection Regulation (GDPR) is paramount for businesses worldwide. This chapter not only provides strategic insights but also equips organizations to proactively address legal challenges in an increasingly digitized world.

As businesses grapple with the implications of social media engagement, another chapter emerges as a guiding light, offering a nuanced analysis of user behavior on platforms like Twitter. In an age where public perception can make or break an organization, deciphering sentiment and patterns in user interactions with entities like law enforcement agencies is invaluable for reputation management and strategic decision-making, as well as community engagement, safety, and growth.

The significance of spatial data infrastructure (SDI) in information governance cannot be overstated, as elucidated in one chapter in this book. Drawing from a real-world case study in Pakistan, this chapter underscores the transformative potential of effective spatial data management in bolstering governance frameworks. In an era characterized by data-driven decision-making, the insights gleaned from this chapter are indispensable for organizations across sectors grappling with the challenges of data governance and spatial data management.

Academic libraries, often the custodians of vast repositories of information, occupy a unique position in the information ecosystem. A chapter delves into the challenges and opportunities of implementing information governance frameworks within these institutions. As bastions of knowledge dissemination, academic libraries play a pivotal role in shaping the information landscape of tomorrow, making this chapter essential reading for librarians, educators, and policymakers alike.

Privacy of information and data has emerged as a burning issue in contemporary discourse, as expounded in a chapter. With the proliferation of technologies like big data and artificial intelligence, safeguarding individual and institutional privacy has become imperative. This chapter not only examines existing privacy frameworks but also offers innovative solutions to navigate the ever-evolving privacy landscape, making it indispensable for businesses and policymakers seeking to strike a balance between innovation and privacy rights.

An additional chapter conveys how executive sponsorship and organizational alignment are discussed as crucial components of any successful information governance program, particularly in an era characterized by rapid technological change and organizational flux, securing buy-in from senior leadership is essential for the sustainability and effectiveness of governance initiatives. This chapter provides invaluable insights into garnering support and fostering a culture of governance across organizational hierarchies, making it essential reading for executives and governance practitioners alike.

The role of information security in the modern era cannot be overstated, as articulated in the book. In an environment rife with cyber threats and data breaches, safeguarding valuable information assets is imperative for organizational resilience and survival. This chapter not only delves into the intricacies of information security but also offers actionable strategies to mitigate risks and enhance security posture, making it indispensable for businesses seeking to fortify their defenses against cyber threats.

Quality management principles, long heralded in manufacturing and healthcare sectors, find resonance in the realm of information governance, as expounded in this book. Drawing from the best practices of quality gurus, this chapter offers a holistic perspective on integrating quality management principles into governance frameworks. As businesses increasingly rely on data-driven insights to inform decision-making, the insights gleaned from this chapter are invaluable for organizations seeking to optimize their operations and enhance service delivery.

The "right to be forgotten" has emerged as a contentious issue in the era of digital proliferation, as dissected within. From the landmark Google Spain lawsuit to the complexities of compliance with regulations like the GDPR, this chapter navigates the intricate terrain of privacy rights and freedom of expression in the digital age. As businesses grapple with the implications of data retention and deletion, the insights gleaned from this chapter are indispensable for navigating the delicate balance between privacy rights and technological innovation.

Decentralized data technologies, epitomized by distributed ledger technology (DLT), hold immense promise in revolutionizing information governance, as discussed in this text. Yet, the tension between privacy rights and the immutable nature of DLT poses unique challenges for governance practitioners. This chapter offers a nuanced exploration of this tension, offering insights into reconciling privacy concerns with the transformative potential of decentralized data technologies.

At the intersection of information governance and organizational functionality lies the promise of strategic alignment, as elucidated in the text. From optimizing business operations to refining data management practices, this chapter offers actionable insights into leveraging information governance as a strategic asset. In an era defined by data-driven decision-making, the insights gleaned from this chapter are indispensable for organizations seeking to harness the full potential of their information assets.

Finally, this anthology underscores the indispensable role of organizational culture in sustaining information governance initiatives. From fostering a culture of transparency and accountability to nurturing leadership capabilities, this chapter offers a roadmap for building a resilient governance framework. As organizations grapple with the challenges of digital transformation, the insights gleaned from this chapter are essential for fostering a culture of governance that permeates every facet of organizational life.

In summation, *Creating and Sustaining an Information Governance Program* transcends the boundaries of traditional discourse. Dr Helge offers a holistic perspective on the intersection of information governance and the legal, technological, and organizational realms throughout this book. Whether you are a seasoned practitioner, a budding researcher, or a curious enthusiast, this book is an indispensable companion in navigating the complexities of modern information management. Dive in, explore, and embark on a journey towards creating a resilient and sustainable information governance program that stands the test of time, and the most complex technological advances, such as Artificial Intelligence, AI.

Tereza Raquel Merlo
University of North Texas, USA & Merlo Management Consulting, USA

Preface

This book conveys many concepts, programs, and subprograms that provide building blocks for information governance programs. These consist of data governance, data privacy, knowledge management, information security, legal and compliance, information technology, records management, and information management. Various chapters discuss what these programs might look like in differing industries. Some of these industries consist of cultural heritage institutions such as libraries and museums, information technology departments, government entities, the healthcare industry, the automotive industry, and others. Many chapters discuss the importance of how various information governance programs are needed and h0w they can benefit these various industries.

The book also discusses the value of having executive leadership support for the implementation of an information governance program, and the significance of having a "why" to implement information governance. The why may be a recent loss of money due to poor information tracking, a current public request of information or a lawsuit, poor sales, a recent data breach, current information security issues, inefficient sharing of information across an enterprise, or an inability to locate stored digital information in a timely manner. Using these information barriers as a "why" to create an information governance program can ultimately be an information governance officer's Cadillac they need to drive the initial setup of an information governance program.

Information governance is becoming more vital at any organization in the world today. All industries face challenges of attempting to keep PII, PHI, PCI DSS, and other types of private data free of breaches. Also, all industries face barriers of efficiently storing, sharing, deleting, archiving, and retrieving information. Couple these challenges with continuous requests for public information, eDiscovery requirements, attempting to remain compliant with everchanging global data privacy laws and local regulations, and information governance programs prominently become a necessity in any industry. All industries now face varied information challenges – healthcare, automotive, financial, education, government, agriculture, construction, information, leisure and hospitality, oil and gas, the arts, retail, telecommunications, and others.

Since so many industries are affected by data compliance, data privacy, knowledge management, information security, information technology, accessibility, and other information governance related issues; this book is appropriate for many audiences. Any for-profit or non-profit organization looking to establish or maintain an information governance program could benefit from the high-level coverage of many types of information governance challenges and opportunities conveyed in this book. Education audiences could also benefit from this book as it delivers several real-world case studies. Those interested in various global data compliance laws could further benefit from the discussions included in the book. Also, audiences seeking information about various technologies to implement in information governance programs will gain insight in this book.

The chapters in the book convey the following:

Chapter one evaluates user responses and behaviors on Twitter presenting an analysis of tweets mentioning law enforcement. Data analysis is performed to investigate tweet frequency and patterns related to the law enforcement agency. Additionally, sentiment analysis and topic modeling techniques are employed to gain deeper insights into the content and context of user tweets. This study provides valuable insights into user behavior and sentiments concerning law enforcement.

Chapter two examines many important facets to consider when establishing an Information Governance Program. Many of these facets include ensuring you have executive sponsorship to support your new IG Program, locating a large need in the organization to justify your IG Program creation (aka the grand Cadillac), securing adequate funding and staff, creating an IG Program charter and strategic plan, recruiting organization-wide support through tiered steering committees, procuring efficient technologies, obtaining appropriate IG related education and training, and considering current industry-wide IG trends. However, the two most important aspects one must have in place to initially begin the building and sustainment of an IG program are high level executive sponsorship and a shiny Cadillac or large need in the organization that an IG Program can help meet. The most important facet is the executive sponsor.

Chapter three discusses the purpose of information security in protecting data by mitigating the risks associated with it. It refers to preventing unauthorized access to disclosure, destruction, disruption, modification of information and the information that they process, store, and transmit. All information whether sensitive or confidential must be protected. It is essential to consider technology, policies, procedures, and people when implementing an effective information security system. In addition, emerging threats and vulnerabilities need to be monitored, assessed, and adapted continuously. Cybercrime, espionage, and theft are some of the threats that potentially affect valuable information assets. The goal of information security is to safeguard valuable information assets against a variety of threats. No matter how information is stored, whether electronically or on paper, it must be protected to ensure privacy, integrity, and availability. This chapter talks about the role of information security in modern days.

Chapter four explains what information governance is and why it is important. The problem identified is that organizations know information governance is important but many fail to implement governance or do so poorly. The author questions why companies fail to recognize the benefit of a cultural approach to addressing this critical gap. The chapter introduces the concept that information governance is integral for every organization. The chapter provides insight into hiring, training, professional development, emotional intelligence, and soft skills to build a thriving organization. The chapter additionally explores the need for a positive and dedicated approach to leadership. The chapter also explores communication, operational efficiencies, board governance approaches, and examines compliance. Lastly, the chapter discusses risk and why organizations must implement a risk management strategy. A conclusion summarizes the need for information governance to build a successful culture that adopts an information governance strategy to be successful.

Chapter five explores the dynamic intersection of information governance and organizational functionality. Grounded in an exhaustive literature review, it guides businesses in enhancing operations, fortifying business intelligence, and refining data management. From principles to practical applications, the chapter emphasizes the symbiotic relationship between information governance and business operations. It provides actionable insights, empowering businesses to strategically leverage information governance for optimized processes. Addressing the evolving data landscape, it offers proven strategies for aligning governance with efficient data practices, ensuring compliance, security, and accessibility. This chapter is an indispensable resource for decision-makers, providing a comprehensive guide for organizations navigating the complexities of strategic information governance in today's dynamic business environment.

Chapter six discusses personal information, or digital footprints, how they are gathered and used in today's digital age. Digital footprints are kept, unlike snow footprints. There is a large market for this data, which businesses utilize to analyze consumer preferences. Businesses collecting a lot of data in one place pose a privacy risk. Thus, people are worried. Businesses prefer not to utilize intermediaries to manage client data to save money. Therefore, innovative technology is needed to make online interactions safer and more efficient. The author considers Distributed Ledger Technology. This technology is interesting because it securely collects, stores, and processes data without central authority. It has data immutability, transparency, and safety. The European GDPR (General Data Protection Regulation) may conflict with this technology. This chapter will examine this tension, focusing on the right to be forgotten, which permits people to delete their data. It will examine how this recent technology and existing privacy policies can function together or need tweaking.

Chapter seven discusses how the 2014 Google Spain lawsuit was a major European Court ruling. It indicated that online name searches yield personal information. Google and other search engine operators must remove or prevent search results that breach privacy rights. The "right to forget" lets users remove their personal information from search engine results. Your internet privacy is not completely protected. Technology changes quickly, making it hard for laws to remain current. The right to be forgotten is criticized for its nomenclature and inconsistent application. European websites may remove information, but non-European sites (like the US) may not. This right may also limit free speech. The article discusses the "right to be forgotten" from the new GDPR perspective. Some are testing whether this right gives internet users more control over their data. It may conflict with privacy and free speech. It's considerably difficult since private firms, whose major objective is to make money, have a say, raising problems about our rights.

Chapter eight discusses the best practices of quality management in manufacturing and healthcare services and its relevance to information governance. Quality management principles of quality gurus have contributed significantly to the manufacturing and services sector. Its implementations in manufacturing and health care services provide numerous learning opportunities. Delivery of care processes integrates quality of health and life, lean management, quality assurance, quality implementation, quality control, affordability, and satisfaction with services. These best practices in quality management are relevant across various disciplines of research including information management, psychology, business research, service quality and technology management. The study further explores the challenges of quality management in health care services and manufacturing and integrates studies that may contribute to the subject of quality management and its relevance for information governance.

Chapter nine examines how information and data privacy are critical issues in modern society to protect the privacy of individuals and institutions, ensure their security, and prevent the misuse of their information. Rapidly developing technology has posed new challenges in ensuring information and data privacy. Technological developments such as big data, artificial intelligence, cloud computing and the internet of things require innovative solutions to protect information and data privacy. Today, with the acceleration of the digitizing world, individuals' and institutions' concerns about information and data privacy are increasing. By addressing information and data privacy through policies, threats and solutions, this study aims to examine new protection-oriented frameworks, policies, and best practices. Aiming to examine coping strategies with technological developments by emphasizing the importance of information and data privacy, this study is original in terms of presenting innovative policies and practices, guiding readers, and providing solutions to current challenges in this field.

Chapter ten focuses on opportunities to implement an Information Governance framework within an academic library. Due to their mission and breadth of information management activities, academic libraries face numerous challenges in organizing and preserving information and records, and governing data. Implementing information governance strategies, specifically in the areas of records and information management, metadata creation, institutional repositories, digital preservation, and data management will result in well-informed and collaborative policies which protect the library as well as the institution. Developing this skillset within the library requires a culture shift towards transparency, collaboration, and accountability. Additionally, library and information science curricula should reflect the current demands of the academic library landscape and expand course offerings to build information governance competencies.

Chapter eleven presents a case study of Spatial Data Infrastructure (SDI) implementation in Pakistan and its relationship with information governance. The chapter contributes to a deeper understanding of how effective spatial data management can support information governance objectives. A feasibility study is ongoing to establish NSDI in Pakistan. Moreover, a provincial-level SDI under PULSE is also planned. However, challenges such as the absence of uniform standards, a poor technology setup, and a shortage of qualified person-power are associated with NSDI implementation in Pakistan. By enhancing data quality & consistency and facilitating data sharing & collaboration, NSDI Pakistan would strengthen information governance in Pakistan by supporting decisions as well as policymaking. The findings and recommendations will help policymakers and practitioners in Pakistan, as well as researchers interested in the fields of spatial data infrastructure and information governance, advance their understanding and implementation of these critical concepts.

Chapter twelve looks at a massive increase in information volume in the modern business environment. This means that it has become very important to understand the complex relationship between information governance and the legal framework. This chapter aims to explore the various dimensions that define this intersection. It provides a comprehensive examination of General Data Protection Regulation as a global legal framework for information governance. It also examines sector specific regulations, legal implications of information management and real-world cases to see how organizations can proactively address the legal dimensions of information governance. By exploring different dimensions of this intersection, this chapter serves as a strategic guide for organizations that want to strengthen their information governance frameworks.

Chapter thirteen examines an era dominated by digital transformation leading public authorities to globally face a profound challenge in effectively managing and governing the burgeoning volumes of information under their purview. Using specific case study of Teacher Attendance Monitoring System (TAMS) in State of Meghalaya, this research paper seeks to explore the landscape of information governance within the context of public authorities in India. As the country undergoes significant advancements in digital infrastructure and governance, understanding the nuances of information governance becomes imperative for ensuring transparency, accountability, and optimal service delivery. This paper aims to provide a comprehensive analysis of the current state of information governance in Indian public authorities, identifying key challenges, proposing strategic solutions, and offering insights into the potential impact on public administration and citizen engagement.

Chapter fourteen discusses how tax authorities in the world are utilizing various technologies, including big data analytics to be more efficient and effective in their works. Utilization of big data analytics and business intelligence by tax authorities in developing countries can be used to help identify the non-compliance taxpayers and support other activities in order to explore potential tax revenues. Directorate General of Taxes, Indonesian Tax Authority, uses a combination of Compliance Risk Management application and Business Intelligence. There are nine types of Compliance Risk Management applications. Currently, seven types of Compliance Risk Management applications have been launched and used by The Directorate General of Taxes. The last two Compliance Risk Management applications will be released soon. The series of nine Compliance Risk Management applications will be supported by four Business Intelligence. Those Compliance Risk Management and Business Intelligence applications will lead Directorate General of Taxes to be data driven organization.

Chapter fifteen discusses the advent of advanced technologies like blockchain, cryptocurrency etc. and how they posed threats to the humongous data of the organizations at voluminous scale hindering day to day activities of institution. This paved the way for governance of data at every level of the organization defining roles and responsibilities of each and every member. Data governance is one such way of collocating and administering policies, developing a plan of action for the tacit usage of organizations' structured or unstructured information with the focus on the 5 V's, namely, volume, veracity, value, variety, and velocity. The chapter focuses on providing the details of the need of data governance, the tools used, data governance framework, challenges posed to models of data governance and its solution.

Chapter sixteen highlights how Knowledge Management (KM) creates value and competitive advantages via innovations. Library and Information Science (LIS) developed KM using social epistemology and varied scientific methods. LIS continued to study KM to guarantee its understanding and usage in the organization. KM attitudes and actions must also be agreed upon. This chapter discusses the LIS viewpoint on KM and delivers the fundamental point, which implies that LIS may advance knowledge management. Thus, readers should ask questions about LIS and all of the preceding advances, especially KM. The perception of data, information, and knowledge especially has changed significantly. LIS perspective should be dynamic, and librarianship has individuality and dignity with knowledge managing tradition. LIS and Librarianship roles, especially KM, may help drive these new advancements. Instead of only watching or ignoring improvements, active engagement and additional research are expected to raise LIS roles on KM.

Ultimately, this book offers unique perspectives for several pertinent issues for anyone working in, looking to establish, or learning more about information governance programs. The book would benefit global audiences in an endless number of industries. Many topics covered include data privacy, compliance, knowledge management, data governance, information management, accessibility, legal, information technology, records management, and other related information governance realms. This book serves as a vital, modern information tool to help many players in this quickly evolving information governance field.

Kris Helge
Rutgers University, USA

Caitlin A. Rookey
Tarrant County College, USA

Acknowledgment

Kris Helge and Caitlin Rookey would like to acknowledge and thank all the chapter authors of this book who participated in the peer review process. Your efforts and attention to detail enabled the success of this project.

Chapter 1
Examining the Public Perception of Law Enforcement:
A Twitter User Engagement Analysis With the Dallas Police Department

Tereza Raquel Merlo
https://orcid.org/0000-0002-2042-5415
University of North Texas, USA

Nayana Madali M. Pampapura
University of North Texas, USA

Jason M. Merlo
https://orcid.org/0009-0007-4281-7755
Texas DPS, USA

ABSTRACT

The emergence of social media platforms has revolutionized communication and interaction across various domains, including law enforcement, and users have increasingly utilized these platforms to express their opinions and consume information. This research chapter focuses on evaluating user responses and behaviors on Twitter presenting an analysis of tweets mentioning the Dallas Police Department. Data analysis is performed to investigate tweet frequency and patterns related to the law enforcement agency. Additionally, sentiment analysis and topic modeling techniques are employed to gain deeper insights into the content and context of user tweets. The research findings reveal that users tend to increase their tweeting activity whenever there is an incident involving the agency. Moreover, the results indicate that users generally express a neutral sentiment towards the law enforcement agency, with their tweets largely reflecting personal opinions. Overall, this study provides valuable insights into user behavior and sentiments concerning the Dallas Police Department, demonstrating the significant role of social media platforms in shaping public perceptions and online interactions with the agency.

DOI: 10.4018/979-8-3693-0472-3.ch001

INTRODUCTION

Social media platforms are tools that enable individuals to actively create, share, and exchange various types of content, thoughts, interests, and information within virtual communities and networks. Social media use and popularity has significantly expanded over the past couple of decades (Abi-Jaoude Naylor, & Pignatiello, 2020). As reported by Pew Research Center in 2021, 72% of the U.S. public use some kind of social media, with usage being higher among young adults (ages 18-29) than among older people (Social Media Fact Sheet, 2021; Ortiz-Ospina, 2019). According to the latest reports, as of 2023 the U.S. has around 302.35 million social media users which is approximately 90% of the total US population (Ruby, 2023). Per reports, in 2023 Facebook, YouTube, and Instagram are the top three social media platforms (Iskiev, 2023; Ruby, 2023).

Social media often serves as a platform or channel for communication, aiding in forming relationships between people from diverse backgrounds (Kapoor et al., 2018). People mostly rely on social media to share their opinion, exchange their views, and share news/information (Vrontis et al., 2021). Because of its capacity to facilitate interaction with others, social media has a large impact on people's lives. While social media has improved people's lives in certain ways it also has its disadvantages, as some individuals engage in undesirable social media behavior such as committing crimes, spreading false information, and fabricating news. Social media serves various purposes, one of those being for users to voice their thoughts and opinions. Social media users actively participate/engage in conversations that are of public interest and express their opinions (Barisione et.al., 2019; Yang & Su, 2020).

Many law enforcement agencies understand the importance of social media and its use for various purposes. Law enforcement use of social media can include gathering intelligence, investigating leads, identifying suspects, engaging with the public, etc. Almost all law enforcement agencies in the U.S. have social media accounts across the various available platforms. These pages are used to post useful information as well as to make important announcements. Many social media users follow these pages to stay informed and actively participate by responding to the posts made by law enforcement.

Although law enforcement uses social media in many ways, there is not much research related to the social media users' sentiments and responses towards law enforcement agencies or understanding the social media user behavior. This study attempts to bridge this gap by analyzing public response, behavior, and sentiment toward law enforcement. This study is guided by the question "What is the behavior and sentiment of social media users towards law enforcement?".

THEORETICAL FRAMEWORK

Over the last decade, social media channels have become a popular source of communication among members of communities across the globe. Law enforcement agencies worldwide are increasingly leveraging the power of social media to communicate directly and in a timely manner with the communities their serve, whether seeking support in crime solving, crisis mediation, crime prevention, or the overall increase in community engagement. Akar and Mardikyan (2014) conducted a study on the proliferation of technology and the increasing use of the internet defending that those are some of the factors that have contributed to the expansion of social media use by citizens. Law enforcement is using social media to go beyond simple communication, they seek to build relationships. Crump (2012) examined social media and public engagement as used to increase public trust and confidence in the ability of the police to reduce/resolve crime, highlighting the importance of the engagement of social media users and the discussion around local policing.

Akkaya et al. (2019) focused on the use of social media as a strategy in the investigation of a 2016 shooting in Munich. The authors argue that the use of social media, specifically Twitter, played a crucial role in crisis mitigation and public perceptions and the level of interaction online thereafter. The authors demonstrated a successful case of law enforcement using social media in an emergency situation with a documented growth in the degree of community engagement and followers with a positive message and trust in the agency.

Previous studies have investigated police adoption of social media to evaluate citizens' engagement, information sharing, crime prevention, etc. Fernandez, Dickinson and Alani (2017) investigated how social media is being used by law enforcement to communicate with the community about crimes, missing persons, and citizen engagement. Their work concludes that there are effective strategies and specific topics that are more likely to drive a higher level of interaction and increase the probability of attracting citizens' attention to postings. Fernandez et al. (2015) defend that social media is now commonly used to help communicate policing messages to the general public, helping communicate important and timely messages to a wider demographic, enabling greater engagement.

These works focus on improving the understanding of the use of social media by law enforcement agencies with relevant results. There are still gaps in knowledge on how users' responses and behaviors are related to the users' engagement in social media and the success of law enforcement in the goal of serving and protecting, as well as designing policies that are transparent and aligned with the communities' needs and trust.

METHODOLOGY

Data Collection

In this chapter, we conduct a study to analyze public reactions toward law enforcement agencies on social media, specifically focusing on data collected related to the Dallas Police Department (DPD) on Twitter. Established in 1881, DPD is the primary law enforcement agency serving the city of Dallas, Texas (Dallas Police Department, 2023). It is one of the largest law enforcement agencies in the United States and is divided into seven operations divisions based on the geographical subdivisions of Dallas City (List of largest local police departments in the United States, 2023; Dallas Police Department, 2023).

Twitter is one of the most widely used social media platforms. Twitter is a real time network and functions as a communication medium and facilitates connections between friends, family, coworkers, etc. by sharing information via "tweets" (Waters & Jamal, 2011). On Twitter, users can post tweets consisting of text, photos, videos, or links, with a limit of 280 characters. Users can also reply, comment, retweet, or quote other users' tweets to express their opinions or share information. Twitter was chosen as the platform for data collection for several reasons. First, Twitter provides multiple Application Programming Interfaces (APIs) that facilitate the extraction of different data, such as the tweet content, user IDs, user geographical location details, etc. Second, Twitter is one of the widely used social media platforms (Akar & Mardikyan, 2014). Finally, DPD actively uses Twitter to share information and communicate with the public.

Figure 1. Research design
Source: The authors (2023)

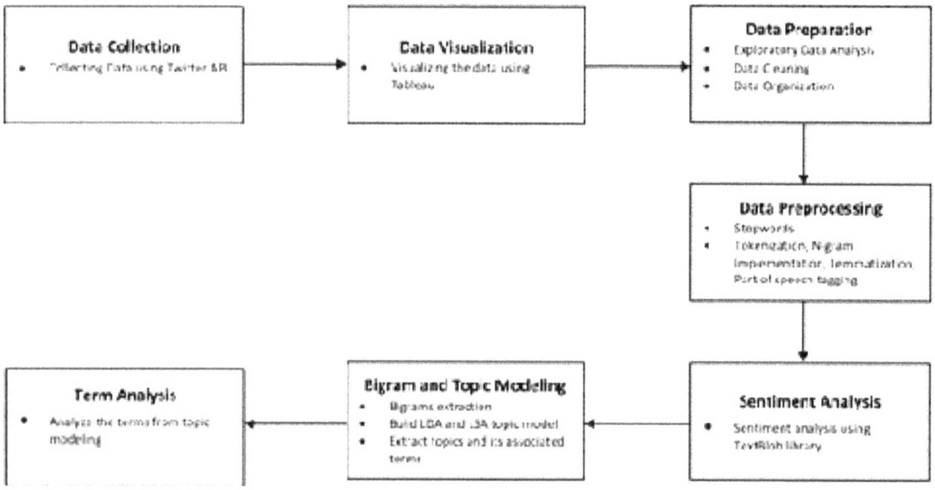

The official Twitter page of the DPD (@DallasPD) was created in 2009 and has amassed approximately 370,000 followers. For this chapter, we collected data from the inception of DPD's Twitter account until June 20th, 2023. We used the Twitter API to extract all tweets that mentioned the DPD username. In total, we retrieved 310,767 tweets from Twitter for analysis. To collect the data, we developed a Python code that utilized the Twitter API. The extracted data included information such as tweet ID, tweet content, date and time of creation, number of retweets, mentions, comments, and other relevant details. This comprehensive dataset provided the foundation for our study on public sentiment and reactions towards DPD on social media.

Research Design

To gain a deeper understanding of the collected data, we performed data visualization using Tableau software. The extracted dataset was imported into Tableau, allowing us to create visualizations that provided valuable insights into the tweet trends related to the Dallas Police Department. Tableau is a powerful data visualization tool that enables users to visually explore and analyze data in an intuitive and interactive manner. By utilizing Tableau, we were able to generate visual representations of the data, making it easier to identify patterns, trends, and correlations within the tweets associated with the Dallas Police Department.

Python programming language was utilized to perform various tasks including exploratory data analysis (EDA), data preprocessing, sentiment analysis, bigram analysis, and topic modeling. Python is a versatile programming language that prioritizes code readability. It follows an object-oriented approach, where objects store both data (fields) and code (procedures/methods). Python is an open-source language that is freely available. The Anaconda software was employed for writing and running Python programs.

Exploratory data analysis (EDA) is a data analysis approach that utilizes different techniques to gain insights into a dataset, identify significant variables, and detect outliers and anomalies. In this study, EDA was conducted to comprehend the dataset, identify potential null values in the columns, and eliminate irrelevant text. Moreover, EDA was employed to analyze the dataset and summarize its key characteristics using visual methods. Subsequently, the data was cleaned to eliminate unnecessary text, symbols, and links. Additionally, the data was organized to facilitate further analysis.

Once the data preparation phase was completed, the data underwent preprocessing before conducting sentiment analysis and topic modeling. Multiple methodologies were employed for data preprocessing:

1. Defining and implementing stop words: Stop words are commonly used English words that carry little semantic meaning in a sentence. In this step, stop words were defined and then implemented using Python. Words such as "me," "we," and "will" were removed from the analyzed data/text after implementing the stop words. The Natural Language Toolkit (NLTK) Python library was utilized to define and implement the stop words.
2. Tokenization: Tokenization is a technique used to split words within sentences into individual units called "tokens." Each token represents a word. During this process, tokens are converted to lowercase, and any letter accents and punctuation marks are removed. Additionally, shorter tokens are disregarded. Tokenization can be classified into word tokenization, character tokenization, and subword (n-grams) tokenization. In this research, both word and subword tokenization were employed.
3. N-gram implementation: This method involves extracting sequences of "n" words that frequently occur in the corpus. While tokenization focuses on individual words, N-gram implementation considers sequences of words. In this research, specifically bigrams (two words in sequence) were extracted and utilized. Gensim's phrases model was employed to construct and implement the bigrams.
4. Lemmatization: Lemmatization aims to remove inflectional endings from tokens and return the base or dictionary form of the word. It helps to reduce words to their canonical or normalized form. For instance, lemmatizing the word "using" would transform it into "use," which represents the base form of the word.
5. Part of speech tagging: During this step, each token/word is labeled with a part of speech tag, indicating whether it is a noun, adjective, adverb, etc. In this research, after performing part of speech tagging, only tokens/words with specific parts of speech tags such as noun, adjective, verb, and adverb were retained, while other tags were discarded.

After preprocessing the data, a word dictionary and a corpus were constructed based on the preprocessed data. The word dictionary contained all the unique words found in the preprocessed data, while the corpus provided information about word frequencies.

Subsequently, sentiment analysis was performed on the data, specifically focusing on the tweet content. Sentiment analysis involves computationally studying people's emotions towards a particular entity, in this case, the tweet data. The Python library "TextBlob" was utilized to process the data and conduct sentiment analysis. TextBlob employs the Natural Language Toolkit (NLTK) to analyze text and assign sentiment to it. Sentiment in TextBlob is defined by the semantic orientation and intensity of each word within a sentence. The analysis conducted by TextBlob returns two values: polarity and subjectivity. The polarity value indicates the sentiment of the text, ranging from -1 (negative sentiment) to 1 (positive sentiment), with 0 representing neutral sentiment. Additionally, TextBlob provides the subjectivity of the text, which lies between 0 and 1. Subjectivity quantifies the degree of opinion present in the text, with higher values indicating a greater presence of subjective content rather than purely factual information.

Bigrams were extracted and analyzed following the sentiment analysis. Bigrams refer to two frequently occurring words in the corpus. Extracting bigrams helps in understanding which words occur together frequently along with their frequency. Bigrams aid in identifying the relationships among the words. Further, topic modeling techniques were employed to create two topic models. Topic modeling is a statistical method used to identify abstract "topics" that appear in a collection of documents or text. It is a text-mining tool that aims to uncover underlying semantic structures within a body of text. Topics generated by topic modeling techniques are clusters of related words. This process captures the statistical patterns of words in each text, allowing the identification and determination of the frequency of relevant topics. A text can contain one or more topics, and each topic can include multiple terms associated with it. The following topic modeling techniques were utilized in this research:

1. Latent Dirichlet Allocation (LDA): LDA assumes that documents are produced from a mixture of topics, and these topics generate words based on their probability distribution. Using a dataset of documents, LDA retroactively infers the topics that would likely generate those documents. In this research, an LDA model was constructed using the "Mallet" package, which is a Java-based tool for statistical natural language processing, document classification, clustering, topic modeling, and other machine learning applications for text.
2. Latent Semantic Analysis (LSA): LSA aims to reduce dimensions for classification purposes. It assumes that words with similar meanings tend to occur in similar pieces of text (the distributional hypothesis). LSA involves constructing a matrix that contains word counts per document from a large text corpus. The matrix is then subjected to singular value decomposition (SVD), a mathematical technique that reduces the number of rows while preserving the similarity structure among columns. Documents are compared by calculating the cosine of the angle between two vectors formed by any two columns, representing their similarity. Values close to 1 indicate highly similar documents, while values close to 0 represent dissimilar documents. In this research, an LSA model was developed using the "Gensim" library and the "LsiModel" function.

RESULTS

Data Visualization

The dataset comprised a total of 310,767 tweets that mentioned "@DallasPD". In Tableau, a bar chart (Figure 2) was created to analyze the distribution of tweets mentioning "@DallasPD" per year. From the chart, it is evident that the year 2016 witnessed the highest number of tweets mentioning "@DallasPD ", totaling 81,083 tweets. Following 2016, the second-highest count of tweets occurred in 2020, with a total of 43,880 tweets mentioning "@DallasPD".

To investigate the reason behind the highest number of tweets in 2016, all the tweets generated in 2016 were filtered out. Subsequently, a bar plot (Figure 3) was created to visualize the monthly distribution of tweets for the year 2016. The analysis revealed that July 2016 had the most significant number of tweets, totaling 62,348 mentions of "@DallasPD". This observation provides valuable insight into the specific month that contributed heavily to the overall high tweet count in the year 2016.

To further investigate the reason behind the highest number of tweets in July 2016, the tweets generated specifically during that month were filtered and daily distribution of tweets (Figure 4) was plotted

Figure 2. Bar plot that displays the number of tweets per year

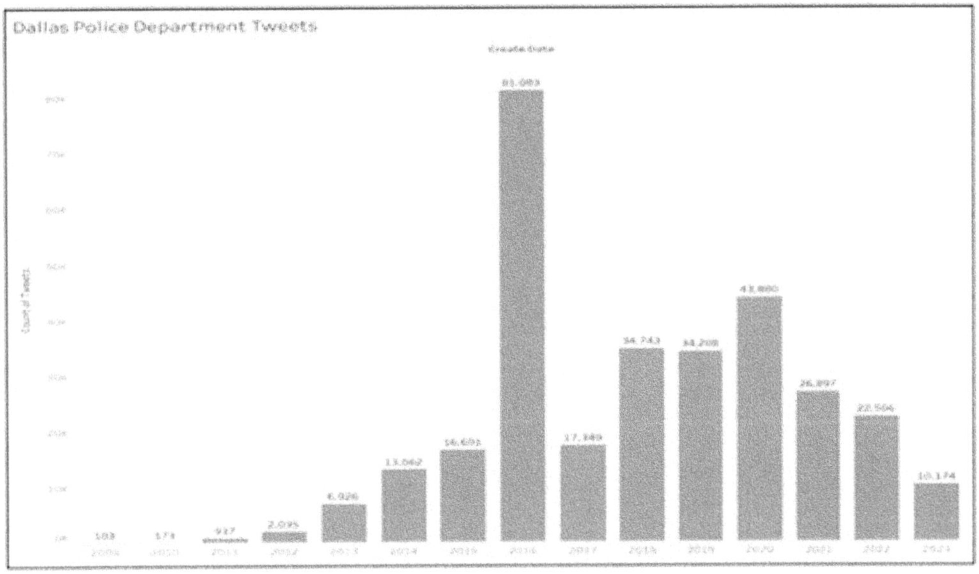

for July 2016. From the chart, it was discovered that the 8th of July had the highest tweet count, with 43,360 mentions of "@DallasPD".

To better understand the significance of this particular date, a carefully analyze of the content of the tweets from July 8th was performed, which evidenced that the reason for the surge in tweets on that day was directly related to a tragic event that occurred on July 7th, 2016. On that evening, five Dallas police officers were fatally shot during a protest against the police killings of two black men, Alton Sterling

Figure 3. Bar plot that displays monthly distribution of tweets in the year 2016

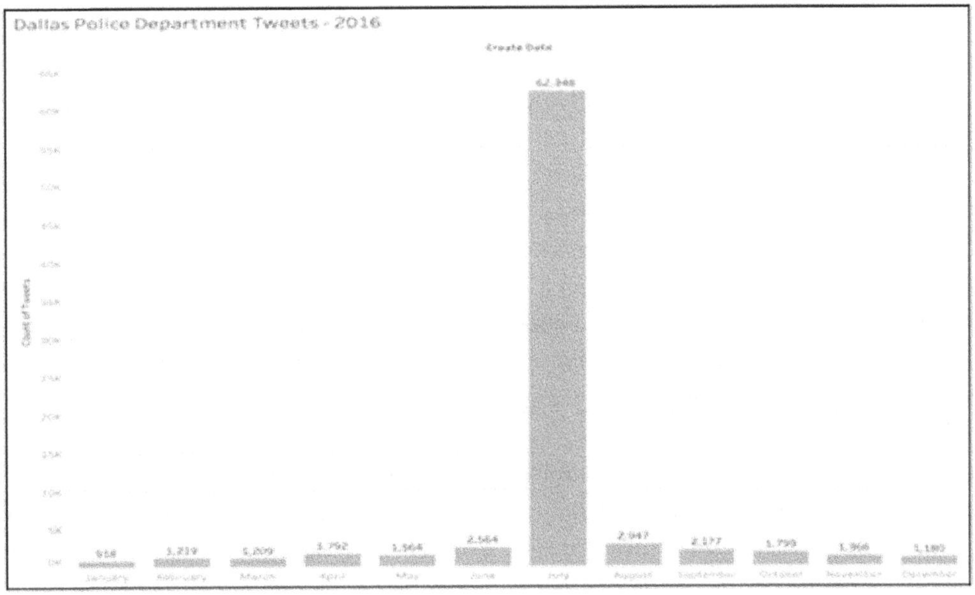

Figure 4. Bar plot that displays the daily distribution of tweets in July 2016

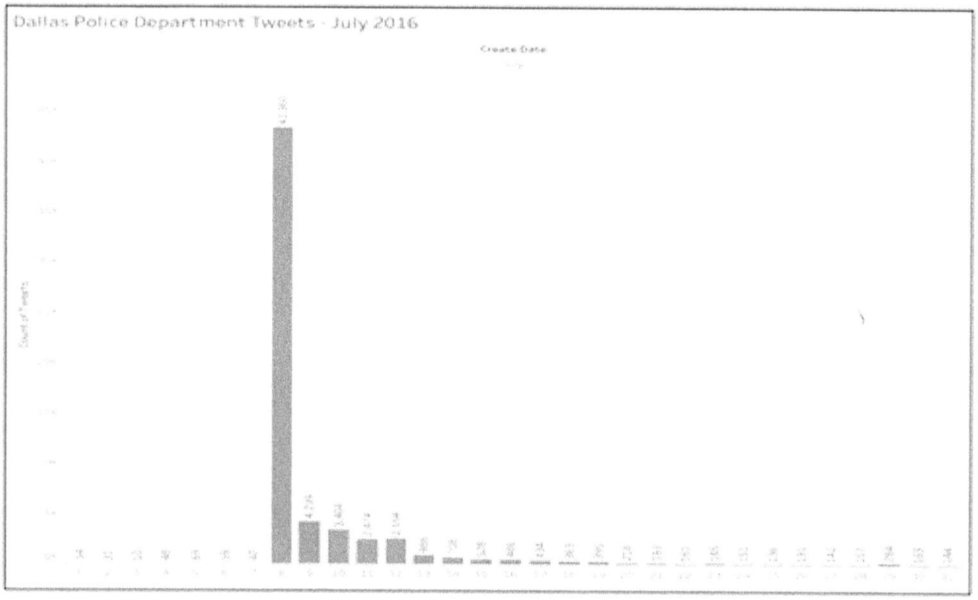

and Philando Castile. The perpetrator of the shooting was identified as Micah Xavier Johnson, and the motive behind his actions was anger over the police shootings of black men.

The shooting incident and its aftermath garnered widespread attention and sparked a significant outpouring of public response and discussions on social media, particularly on Twitter. This explains the exceptionally high number of tweets mentioning "@DallasPD" on July 8th, 2016, as people were sharing their thoughts, reactions, and emotions regarding the tragic event and its impact on the Dallas community and beyond.

Sentiment Analysis

Following the completion of the data visualization and data cleaning and preprocessing a sentiment analysis was performed on all the retrieved tweets. The sentiment analysis provided two key scores for each tweet: 1) the subjectivity score, which indicates whether the tweet is based on personal opinion or factual information, and 2) the polarity score, which indicates the sentiment expressed in the tweet.

The results of the sentiment analysis showed that 56.93% (176,908 tweets) of the tweets related to the Dallas Police Department were subjective in nature, meaning they were based on personal opinions rather than objective facts. In contrast, 43.07% (133,859 tweets) of the tweets were objective and fact-based.

Further analyzing the sentiment of the tweets, the sentiment analysis revealed that 47% (146,047 tweets) of the tweets were neutral, expressing neither positive nor negative sentiment. Positive tweets accounted for 32.69% (101,577 tweets), and negative tweets constituted 20.32% (63,143 tweets) of the total tweets.

To provide a visual representation of the subjectivity and polarity scores, we created a pie chart (Figure 5). The chart illustrates the distribution of subjective and objective tweets, as well as the proportion of neutral, positive, and negative sentiments expressed in the tweets related to the Dallas Police Department.

Figure 5. Subjectivity and polarity scores pie chart

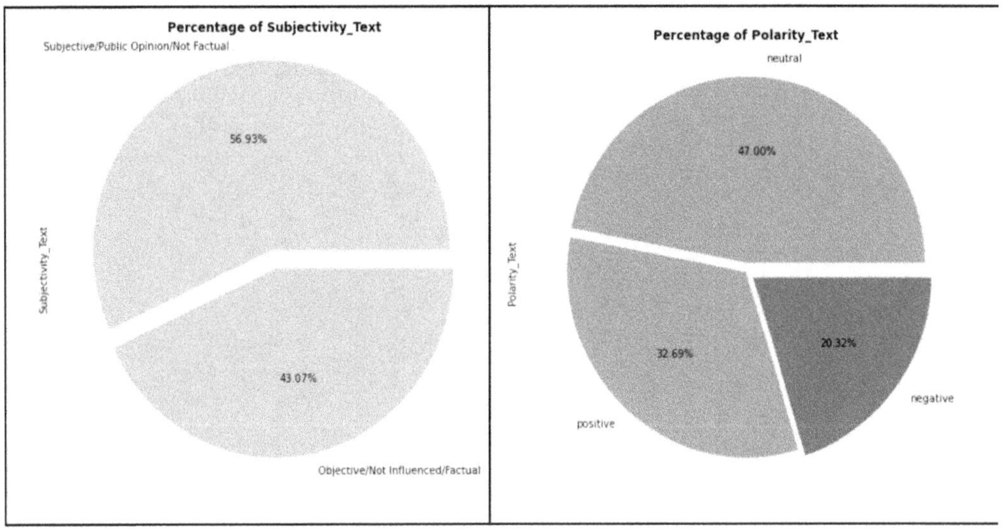

Bigram Analysis

Pursuing a deeper insight into the relationships among words, a bigram analysis was performed. This analysis allowed us to identify commonly occurring word pairs within the dataset. We extracted the top 30 frequently occurring bigrams and visualized them as a network diagram (Figure 6). From Figure 6, it became evident that the handle of the Dallas Police Department, "@DallasPD," was one of the most frequently mentioned words, and it was commonly associated with terms like "@chiefhalldpd" and "@ dpdchiefgarcia." This indicates that in many tweets, users referred to "@DallasPD" together with the Twitter handles of Chief Hall and Chief Garcia, suggesting a close association between them. Furthermore, it is noteworthy that "@DallasPD" was frequently mentioned alongside "fortworthpd," indicating that there were interactions or discussions between the Dallas Police Department and the Fort Worth County Police Department on Twitter. Overall, the bigram analysis provided valuable insights into the co-occurrence patterns of words in the dataset, shedding light on specific associations and mentions within the tweets related to the Dallas Police Department.

Topic Modeling Analysis

Latent Dirichlet Allocation (LDA)

The dataset underwent topic extraction using the Gensim library, resulting in a total of 75 topics. Each topic was associated with 10 specific terms, allowing for interpretation based on these terms. For instance, topic 2 included words such as "time," "long," "response," "difficult," "move," "quick," and "wait." From these terms, we can infer that the Dallas Police Department (DPD) might take a considerable amount of time to respond, and it could be challenging to move quickly in certain situations.

Figure 6. Bigram network diagram

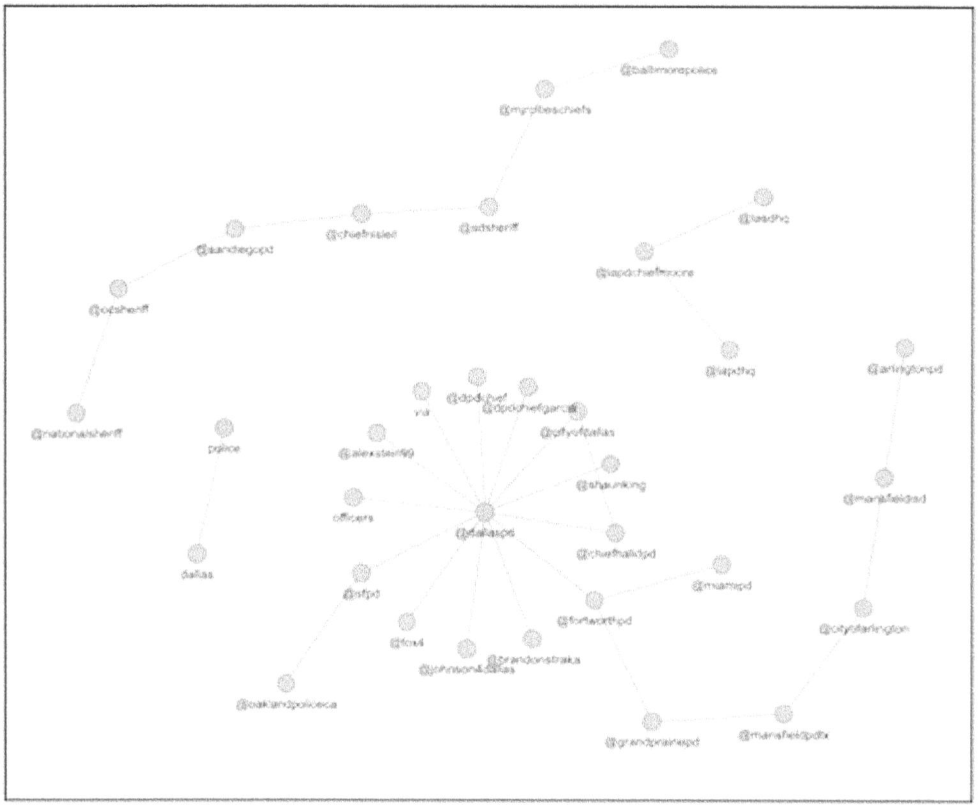

Table 1 presents the first 10 topics extracted from the Latent Dirichlet Allocation (LDA) analysis, offering insights into the recurring themes and subjects found within the dataset. The interpretation of each topic can provide valuable information about the prevalent discussions and concerns surrounding the Dallas Police Department on Twitter.

Latent Semantic Analysis (LSA)

A total of 75 topics were extracted for the Dallas Police Department (DPD) using latent semantic analysis. Similar to LDA, each topic in LSA was represented by 10 associated terms, enabling interpretation based on these terms. For instance, consider topic 3, which included words such as "make," "man," "see," "murder," "suspect," "black," and so on. From these terms, it can be inferred that this topic revolves around a potential scenario where a black man is suspected in a murder.

Table 2 presents the first 10 topics extracted using LSA, offering insights into the recurring themes and subjects found within the dataset related to the DPD. By analyzing the associated terms for each topic, we can gain a deeper understanding of the prevalent discussions and topics of interest concerning the Dallas Police Department on Twitter.

Table 1. LDA topics

Topic	Term 1	Term 2	Term 3	Term 4	Term 5	Term 6	Term 7	Term 8	Term 9	Term 10
Topic 1	thing	wrong	agree	talk	completely	folk	realize	totally	party	understand
Topic 2	time	long	response	week	difficult	spend	move	quick	wait	reporter
Topic 3	live	watch	conference	video	update	deep	press	start	begin	retweet
Topic 4	dog	throw	water	head	leave	cool	animal	poor	horse	eat
Topic 5	cop	bad	kill	blame	reason	killer	hell	coffee	prison	horrible
Topic 6	public	safety	face	cover	late	place	hand	covid	important	news
Topic 7	drug	deal	witness	case	trial	dealer	testify	cash	sell	gang
Topic 8	gun	carry	open	weapon	legal	state	control	rifle	illegal	firearm
Topic 9	pay	money	judge	attention	sign	fraud	give	attorney	tax	dollar
Topic 10	hour	wait	drive	sound	leave	back	set	buy	weed	dude

DISCUSSION

The analysis of both user sentiments and the content of tweets provides valuable insights into user perceptions and behaviors towards law enforcement agencies. Figures 2 and 3 clearly indicate a significant increase in tweets mentioning "@DallasPD" in July 2016. Further investigation revealed that this surge was due to a tragic shooting event involving police officers. This finding suggests that users tend to tweet more about a law enforcement agency when there is a notable incident involving that agency. The sentiment analysis revealed most tweets expressed personal opinions rather than being fact-based. Moreover, most users displayed a neutral sentiment towards law enforcement agencies in their tweets.

Figure 6, the network diagram of bigrams, highlighted a frequent association of "@DallasPD" with the chief of the law enforcement agency. This suggests that users often mentioned the chief in their tweets to capture their attention. Additionally, the network diagram indicated that many tweets linked "@DallasPD" with "@fortworthpd," possibly to bring incidents or relevant information related to Fort

Table 2. LSA topics

Topic	Term 1	Term 2	Term 3	Term 4	Term 5	Term 6	Term 7	Term 8	Term 9	Term 10
Topic 1	know	see	need	take	family	thank	help	man	make	shoot
Topic 2	see	take	need	make	help	man	know	suspect	black	say
Topic 3	make	take	man	see	good	murder	know	suspect	thank	black
Topic 4	need	take	make	help	good	know	suspect	shoot	find	thank
Topic 5	shoot	man	suspect	make	say	family	officer	take	black	need
Topic 6	good	make	work	great	job	shoot	see	cop	thank	take
Topic 7	kill	suspect	would	help	cop	man	need	people	shoot	find
Topic 8	help	kill	suspect	shoot	need	would	man	find	call	murder
Topic 9	would	kill	good	make	know	man	think	see	suspect	take
Topic 10	good	great	work	safe	kill	keep	time	would	thank	suspect

Worth Police Department to the attention of Dallas Police Department, or vice versa. Topic modeling through both LDA and LSA enabled the identification of various topics and their associated terms. For instance, one topic from LDA implied that the Dallas Police Department might experience challenges in responding quickly, while another topic from LSA suggested a scenario involving a suspected black man in a murder. In conclusion, the comprehensive analysis of user sentiments, tweet content, bigrams, and topics provides a nuanced understanding of user perceptions, behaviors, and interactions related to the Dallas Police Department on Twitter. Such insights are valuable for law enforcement agencies to gauge public sentiment and engage with the community effectively.

LIMITATION AND FUTURE RESEARCH

This study's findings may not be representative of all social media users' behavior and attitudes, as it focused on a specific law enforcement agency and utilized data from Twitter only. To gain a more comprehensive understanding of user behavior, future research could expand the scope to include multiple law enforcement agencies, and perhaps multiples social media platforms. This broader approach would allow for a more generalized analysis of user behavior across different law enforcement organizations, and the possibility of a meaningful comparative study between agencies and communities responses, engagement, and sentiments.

Moreover, exploring data from various social media platforms such as Facebook, LinkedIn, and others would be beneficial for future research. Analyzing user behavior across different social media platforms could reveal differences in how individuals engage and express their attitudes towards law enforcement agencies. Additionally, comparing user behavior among various social media platforms could provide valuable insights into the nuances of each platform's impact on public perception and interactions with law enforcement. In conclusion, future studies that encompass a wider range of law enforcement agencies and incorporate data from diverse social media platforms will contribute to a more comprehensive understanding of user behavior and attitudes towards law enforcement on social media.

CONCLUSION

This study provides valuable insights into user behavior and sentiments toward law enforcement agencies on social media. By analyzing the tweeting patterns of users, it becomes evident that social media users tend to mention law enforcement agencies primarily in response to relevant events or incidents. Moreover, the study highlights that users' tweets are driven by their personal opinions, with a majority expressing a neutral sentiment towards law enforcement agencies. The utilization of bigram and topic modeling techniques allows for a deeper understanding of the content and themes prevalent in users' tweets. By acknowledging the public's expression of opinions through social media, law enforcement agencies can gain insight into their constituents' needs and concerns. This knowledge can be instrumental in improving the agency's services and public relations. (Fernandez, et al., 2017).

Law enforcement agencies can leverage the findings from this study to enhance their presence and image on social media platforms. By actively analyzing tweets and their content, agencies can proactively address concerns and engage with the public in a more informed manner. Understanding user sentiments and behaviors will enable law enforcement agencies to adapt their communication strategies and effectively respond to emerging issues or events. In conclusion, this study emphasizes the significance of considering social media as a platform for public expression and opinion. By leveraging the insights gained, law enforcement agencies can work towards improving their interactions with the public and, consequently, their overall image and service provision. Therefore, by leveraging social media, law enforcement can enhance their crime-solving efforts and strengthen their connection with the communities they serve. This research work aims to explore the advantages of social media utilization in law enforcement and help communities to stay better informed and enhance trust in law enforcement agencies.

REFERENCES

Abi-Jaoude, E., Naylor, K. T., & Pignatiello, A. (2020). Smartphones, social media use and youth mental health. [CMAJ]. *Canadian Medical Association Journal, 192*(6), E136–E141. doi:10.1503/cmaj.190434 PMID:32041697

Akar, E., & Mardikyan, S. (2014). Analyzing factors affecting users' behavior intention to use social media: Twitter case. *International Journal of Business and Social Science*, *5*(11), 85–95.

Akkaya, C., Fedorowicz, J., & Krcmar, H. (2019). Successful practices for using social media by police departments: a case study of the Munich police. In Proceedings of the 27th *European Conference on Information Systems* (ECIS). IEEE.

Barisione, M., Michailidou, A., & Airoldi, M. (2019). Understanding a digital movement of opinion: The case of #RefugeesWelcome. *Information Communication and Society*, *22*(8), 1145–1164. doi:10.1080/1369118X.2017.1410204

Crump, J. (2012). What are the police doing on Twitter? Social media, the police and the public. *Policy and Internet*, *3*(4), 1–27. doi:10.2202/1944-2866.1130

Dallas Police Department. (2023, July 7). Wikipedia. https://en.wikipedia.org/wiki/Dallas_Police_Department

Fernandez, M., Dickinson, T., & Alani, H. (2017). An Analysis of UK Policing Engagement via Social Media. In G. Ciampaglia, A. Mashhadi, & T. Yasseri (Eds.), *Social Informatics. SocInfo* (Vol. 10539, pp. 298–304). Springer. doi:10.1007/978-3-319-67217-5_18

Iskiev, M. (2023, April 10). *The Fastest Growing Social Media Platforms of 2023. New Data.* HubSpot. https://blog.hubspot.com/marketing/fastest-growing-social-media-platforms#article

Kapoor, K. K., Tamilmani, K., Rana, N. P., Patil, P., Dwivedi, Y. K., & Nerur, S. (2018). Advances in social media research: Past, present and future. *Information Systems Frontiers*, *20*(3), 531–558. doi:10.1007/s10796-017-9810-y

Ortiz-Ospina, E. (2019). *The rise of social media.* Our World in Data. https://ourworldindata.org/rise-of-social-media

Ruby, D. (2023, June 7). *Social Media Users In The World — (2023 Demographics).* Demands Age. https://www.demandsage.com/social-media-users/

Social Media Fact Sheet. (2021). *Pew Research Center: Internet, Science & Tech*. Pew Research. https://www.pewresearch.org/internet/fact-sheet/social-media/

Vrontis, D., Makrides, A., Christofi, M., & Thrassou, A. (2021). Social media influencer marketing: A systematic review, integrative framework and future research agenda. *International Journal of Consumer Studies*, *45*(4), 617–644. doi:10.1111/ijcs.12647

Waters, R. D., & Jamal, J. Y. (2011). Tweet, tweet, tweet: A content analysis of nonprofit organizations' twitter updates. *Public Relations Review*, *37*(3), 321–324. doi:10.1016/j.pubrev.2011.03.002

Yang, Y., & Su, Y. (2020). Public voice via social media: Role in cooperative governance during public health emergency. *International Journal of Environmental Research and Public Health*, *17*(18), 6840–6858. doi:10.3390/ijerph17186840 PMID:32962172

ENDNOTES

1. This work was presented at the 18th International Conference of Knowledge Management, ICKM, 2023.

2. College of Information, LIS – University of North Texas (UNT) Denton – United States. ORCID: https://orcid.org/0000-0002-2042-5415. e-mail: tereza.merlo@unt.edu
3. College of Information, LIS – University of North Texas (UNT) Denton – United States. ORCID: https://orcid.org/0000-0002-7707-1304. e-mail: nayanapampapuramadali@my.unt.edu
4. Texas Department of Public Safety (DPS) Austin – United States. ORCID: https://orcid.org/0009-0007-4281-7755. e-mail: jasonmerlo@hotmail.com

Chapter 2
Locating Appropriate Executive Sponsorship and the Information Governance Cadillac as Catalysts for a Successful IG Program

Kris Swen Helge
Rutgers University, USA

ABSTRACT

There are many important facets to consider when establishing an information governance (IG) program. Many of these facets include ensuring you have executive sponsorship to support your new IG program, locating a large need in the organization to justify your IG program creation (AKA the grand Cadillac, discussed later in this chapter), securing adequate funding and staff, creating an IG program charter and strategic plan, recruiting organization-wide support through tiered steering committees, procuring efficient technologies, obtaining appropriate IG related education and training, and considering current industry-wide IG trends. However, the two most important aspects one must have in place to initially begin the building and sustainment of an IG program are high level executive sponsorship and a shiny Cadillac or large need in the organization that an IG program can help meet. The first and foremost important facet is the executive sponsor.

APPROPRIATE EXECUTIVE SPONSOR FOR AN INFORMATION GOVERNANCE PROGRAM

There are many important facets to consider when establishing an Information Governance (IG) Program. Many of these facets include ensuring you have executive sponsorship to support your new IG Program, locating a large need in the organization to justify your IG Program creation (AKA the grand Cadillac discussed later in this chapter), securing adequate funding and staff, creating an IG Program charter

DOI: 10.4018/979-8-3693-0472-3.ch002

and strategic plan, recruiting organization-wide support through tiered steering committees, procuring efficient technologies, obtaining appropriate IG related education and training, and considering current industry-wide IG trends. However, the two most important aspects one must have in place to initially begin the building and sustainment of an IG program are high level executive sponsorship and a shiny Cadillac or large need in the organization that an IG Program can help meet (Smallwood, 2014). The first and foremost important facet is the executive sponsor. If an IG lead (the individual responsible for setting up and IG program) or an IG group does not have a CIO, CEO, Legal Counsel, or some other high-level executive sponsor to clear logistical barriers, help force culture change in an organization, and ensure monetary, strategic priority, and personnel precedence; then the likelihood of success is almost nil. Therefore, before any staff, money, time, goodwill, or any other resource is given to build an IG program, a high-level executive such as a General Counsel, a CIO, CEO, CTO… must first commit to the creation of and long-term support and maintenance of an IG Program. It is the IG Lead's responsibility to locate and gain commitment from an executive sponsor (Goodman, Phillips, & Stamper, 2022).

To have executive support, the IG Lead must first locate the correct executive to serve as the IG sponsor. Having conversations with the CIOs, CEOs, CTOs, General Counsel… is the first step to determine which of these individuals is the correct person to serve as a sponsor. It is always advantageous and sometimes serendipitous if one of these executives already understands the value and benefits of an IG program. These benefits consist of a reduction of legal risk, a reduction in costs, and an optimization of information and data storage, use, and implementation (Smallwood, 2014). If one attempting to commence an IG program is aware that a specific executive is cognizant of the IG program benefits and is already supportive of such an implementation, then that is the executive the IG lead needs to commence conversations with to gain high-level executive support (Saldanha, 2019). If the IG Lead is not initially able to identify such and IG executive sponsor, then the IG Lead needs to quickly locate one.

BRING A CONCRETE EXAMPLE OF AN IG BENEFIT

So, who is the best executive sponsor? The IG lead is the person who is ultimately responsible for the creation and continued operation of and IG program. This person might serve as a Certified Information Governance Officer or a Director or Deputy Director of Information Governance (Smallwood, 2014). It is the responsibility of the IG lead to locate and receive an official commitment from an executive that they will serve as an IG executive sponsor. If the IG lead is uncertain who the best executive is to sponsor the IG program, conversations with executives are imperative. Before meeting with executives, the IG lead should first gather and concisely prepare written and oral examples that convey the value of IG programs. This value must concisely convey that IG reduces legal risk, cost, and increases value for an organization. This value can be in optimizing current products or services, discovering new products or services that manifest success for an organization, or that prevent is decrease the odds of litigation, or costs for an organization (Laney, 2018).

Gathering and organizing specific examples of IG value creation one can share with potential IG sponsors is helpful. For example, an IG Lead might locate a case study that displays how an organization without an IG program has lost millions of dollars as a result. A good example might be when a company lost millions due to not being able to logistically track where their inventory was complete or incomplete. Had this organization had an effective IG program, they could have tracked at which distributor locations their inventory was being altered and causing completeness or incompleteness. Because they had no process in place to discover logistically where the inventory was overstocked or understocked, they might have lost millions. Taking these concrete examples to executives will help them understand real world, not hypothetical examples, of what could happen to their organization if an IG program is not commenced (Smallwood, 2014).

Utilizing an example from another organization to depict how an IG program can add value to your company and avoid legal risk and reduce costs is beneficial. However, using an analogous hypothetical example about how it could benefit your own company is even more powerful. Your potential executive sponsor is more likely to entertain the creation of an IG program if the pitch mentions how your organization can specifically benefit. For example, if your organization has trouble locating information, perhaps training materials, meeting minutes, contracts, Human Resource materials, financial documents, or other vital records for an organization; the time is ripe to pitch the idea for an IG program. Part of an IG program involves Knowledge Management (KM), which when properly implemented can save members of an organization 20% of work time per day when trying to locate information. An effective KM program will help organization employees locate information in seconds or minutes, rather than hours or days (Milton, & Lambe, 2020). Using one of these concrete examples mentioned above, can serve as your Cadillac or your huge need the organization currently requires. This second most important factor, the Cadillac that you utilize to drive home your IG Program kickoff, or your enormous organizational need is discussed in the latter part of this chapter.

USE A REAL WORLD EXAMPLE OF HOW THIS LACK OF IG COULD AFFECT YOUR COMPANY

An analogous example of a Cadillac or vast need in your current organization could show how departments spend 20% of their work time trying to find needed information. This 20% effort may be due to everyone in their department storing information if differing places, e.g., shared files, flash drives, on personal devices, on their desktop… If there is not clearly identified standard of where to store information, how to share it, when to delete it…, then knowledge workers will spend at least 20% of their workday looking for information. You can take these facts and convey how an IG program can implement a knowledge management sub-program that concisely defines where to store information, how to share information, how to locate information, and when to delete information (Blumauer & Nagy, 2020).

A chart can be created to depict where to store information as hypothetically indicated in Table 1. below.

By using such a table, the IG program lead can convey to their potential executive sponsor that a KM sub-program could direct knowledge workers where to store and retrieve vital information. This table depicts, for example, one can store, share, and retrieve knowledge articles in an Information Technology Service Management Knowledge Base (Service Now, 2023). Additionally, one can store and share official organizational records (e.g., contracts, HR documents, memorandums of understanding…) in an Enterprise Content Management tool such as Laserfiche. Table 1. also depicts where not to share and store information (N).

The Importance of Retention and Records Management

Along with properly organizing information, one must also stress the importance of getting rid of redundant, outdated, and trivial (ROT) information. 65-70% of information most organizations manage

Table 1. Organizational storage matrix

	OneDrive	ITSM	Canvas	MS TEAMS	AWS	Official Organizational Digital Storage (e.g., Laserfiche)
Working Files	Y	N	Y	Y	N	N
Pedagogy	Y	N	Y	N	N	N
Structured Data Files	N	N	N	N	Y	N
Official Organization Records	N	N	N	N	N	Y
Knowledge Articles	N	Y	N	N	N	N

is ROT. All organizations can locate state defined retention schedules that statutorily determine when they may delete, destroy, or archive information (Colorado State Archives, 2023). By adhering to these statutorily defined records retention schedules, organizations that have never gotten rid of information, or that do not have a standardized process of doing so can literally get rid of approximately 60-70% of the information they currently manage. By ridding their organization of this excess rot, this improves the knowledge management effort by not storing all this ROT in the defined repositories mentioned in Table 1above. This therefore save knowledge workers time in locating and sharing information, because these workers can spend less time sifting through ROT.

If a records management program is not already established, it is a good idea to request an official records manger position for the organization during those initial conversations with high level executives. Really, an organization needs at least 4 or 5 individuals to effectively operate a records management program. These positions consist of an official records manager, 1 or two individuals to manage the digitization and retention of official records. Also, 1 or 2 individuals to manage the physical records and special collections of an organization.

Along with requesting appropriate staff, be certain to convey to executives how a records management program can reduce ROT, which ultimately save money on storge space, reduces legal liability, and improves the optimization of information. The reduction of legal liability is huge. By adhering to a legally defensible records retention schedule prescribed by statute, when a lawsuit occurs, eDiscovery cost will be cheaper. The reduction in cost is realized when an organization only must sift through 7 years, 4 years… depending on the retention schedule of information compared to 40 -50 years of retained information. Also, because an organization is relying upon state statutorily defined retention schedules, the only information they must provide is the length in time provided via statute. Such reliance upon legal defensible destruction of information can greatly dec reduce legal liability (Franks, 2018).

By preparing examples of how a knowledge management subprogram, a records retention and records management program, or some other aspect of a broader Information Governance Program can decrease costs and legal risk while optimizing information value, an IG lead can be well prepared to show a potential IG executive sponsor the benefits an IG Program can offer. Any of the above-mentioned needs that exist in an organization can serve as that Cadillac or avenue to help commence an effective IG Program. After conveying this benefit, a savvy IG Lead can explain to a potential executive sponsor that through their willingness to serve as a sponsor the successes of an IG Program will lead to goodwill and great political capital for the IG executive sponsor. Such goodwill enables more leverage for the executive sponsor with shareholders, board members, the community, and other key stakeholders.

So, Who Is the Best Sponsor?

After meeting with several high level executives such as the Chief Executive Officer, Chief Privacy Officer, Legal Counsel, the Chancellor…, and explaining to them the potential benefits of an IG Program, one of these individuals may become apparent as a natural fit for an executive sponsor. For example, one may have dealt with a specific project or program that revealed the importance of retention programs. Perhaps they endured a lawsuit and had to produce years of email, chat messages because they did not have a legally defensible records or e-communications program. Or maybe they simply cannot locate needed documents in an efficient manner. Maybe stuff is stored everywhere, in shared drives, flash drives, a disorganized SharePoint site… Due to poor organization, perhaps it takes the executive and their organizational peer 20 plus minutes to locate needed documents, or maybe the disorganization broaches potential privacy issues (Hill, 20203). These inefficiencies can lead to an opportunity to find a willing executive sponsor.

Once you do locate a willing executive sponsor, create a memorandum of understanding or some other type of document that memorialized the executive sponsor's willingness to help fund an IG Program, remove unnecessary boundaries, help assist in any needed staff or vendor augmentation, and support any technological needs. Such an agreement should be high-level, concise and serve as a reminder to the executive sponsor, the IG Lead, and to others in the organization that this agreement creates a high priority initiative to commit to crating and sustaining an IG Program. The agreement should be concise, respectful, direct, and non-invasive (Eisen, 2020).

Locating the Cadillac

Along with locating and memorializing an executive sponsor for the IG Program, its is also beneficial to identify a Cadillac in which to role out the first portion of your IG Program. The Cadillac is an analogy for a hefty need the organization is experiencing with which an IG Program or a sub-program (Knowledge Management, records retention…) can meet. I will convey two case studies that display the importance of locating the Cadillac one needs to help initiate an IG Program. One example is the Colorado Judicial Branch which is operating with a case management system (CMS) that was 25 years old. This CMS is the technological tool that attorneys and pro se clients use to file petitions, case responses, and other court filings. Judges and Justices utilize the CMS to view case files, upload their written holdings, and view other pertinent information. Other departments such as Probation, Court Services, local law enforcement, and other department utilize this CMS to share evidence, court filings, and other documentation.

Issues With the Legacy System

Because the CMS is so old, users of the system are not able to upload, share, and retrieve information on an as needed basis. Modern legal databases such as Westlaw (2023), LexisNexis (2023), and HeinOnline (2023) offer intuitive, rich, and flexible search options that allow a panoply of users to efficiently locate needed information. This is the type of access that legal professionals expect. Unfortunately, because the current CMS is a legacy system and built in-house, it does not offer efficient search features such as search for cases by region, District, court level, type of law… Instead, most rely on case numbers or key word searches to locate needed information. Also, because of not having search features legal professionals are not used to, many store information in shared drives, personal devices, or other digital repositories to which only they had access. This creates inefficient sharing and potential risks. The common complaints among many legal professionals consist of I cannot find what I am looking for, the current CMS does not offer intuitive search filters, why can we not search for information like we do in Westlaw, LexisNexis, HeinOnline…, and the technology is too old and is not compatible with other systems.

Introducing the Cadillac Option Plus IG to Judicial

Although the limitations of the current CMS cause frustration and inefficiencies for current legal professionals, these hindrances offer an opportunity for an IG Lead to introduce a needed solution, the Cadillac, and couple that needed solution with an IG Program. The IG Lead has been able to explain to the Chief Justice of the Colorado Supreme Court (currently the IG executive sponsor) that a solution is available. A new CMS could be implemented that would meet the needs of legal professionals if an IG Program could be employed concurrently to ensure all to the needed search features, information storage, sharing, retention processes could be implemented too.

Utilize the Cadillac to Implement an IG Program

The IG Lead effectively explained to the Chief Justice that to implement a new CMS, an IG Program needed to commence that would provide the foundation for a new CMS that would offer all users of the system a cutting edge, efficient tools to store, share, retire when appropriate… necessary legal documents. The IG system would also be as non-invasive as possible, which is a hallmark of successful data governance and IG governance programs (Seiner, 2014). Currently we are laying this groundwork, and the initial IG Program Staff is ensuring Judicial maintains a memorialized and standardized records retention program and data classification scheme. We are also utilizing vendors and internal staff to locate all data and systems across the Colorado state court system. This data will be classified, retention will be applied where necessary, and data and system maps will be created. A file analysis tool will be implemented to create these processes so that automated classification and updating of system maps can be perpetually maintained. Part of this process also requires vendors to help the IG internal staff interview personnel across the state to learn what processes they utilize to interact with the current CMS. The personnel will be queried about what processes work, which did not, what could be improved… Ultimately a set of standardized processes will be created, memorialized, and implemented so that the new CMS will operate similarly to a Westlaw or LexisNexis database, which is what most legal professionals use and prefer.

In summation, the need to replace a 20 year old CSM enabled the commencement and formation of an IG Program. This IG Program will grow and evolve at Judicial. As the program evolves new staff can be added, accessibility issue can be addressed, and data governance can progress into more predictive and prescriptive analytics. The point of emphasis is every organization needs a Cadillac to drive the commencement of their IG Program. Without one the creation of such a program can spin its wheels in perpetuity (Saldanha, 2019).

Perpetual Creation With No Progress

Another case example demonstrates how the attempted creation of an IG Program without a Cadillac can result in unending set-up, no traction, no progress, and an ultimate failure. The Cadillac provides the vital foundation for any program, whether it is a full-blown IG Program or a subset of an IG Program that focuses on privacy matter, records management, legal and compliance, or some other subset (Goodman, Phillips, & Stamper, 2022). At one other organization, I was asked to create an IG Program. I subsequently navigated the process of locating and obtaining executive sponsorship. After obtaining this sponsorship, the sponsor directed me to go forth an create IG. However, there was no organizational need that high level executives could agree upon to fully give me a Cadillac with which to roll out the program.

There were a lot of potential car parts to build the Cadillac with such as some departments conveying a need to digitize paper and needed help to store them somewhere. Another potential part was a need to reduce printing costs, move to a born-digital model, and implement a scanning model. Other potential parts consisted of the need to locate information stored in an unorganized manner in SharePoint or MS TEAMS, and the need for a completely digital workflow in an enterprise content management system from beginning to end. So, a plethora of car parts existed that could have formed a Cadillac, but the executive sponsor was unable to assist the IG Lead remove barriers and obtain enough buy-in from other high level executives to help build the Cadillac for the IG Lead.

I tried to use the need to organize disorganized SharePoint sites and MS TEAMs sites to display how this could save knowledge workers time in saving, later locating, sharing, and deleting information. By organizing the SharePoint sites and the MS TEAMS site, ultimately, a well-developed knowledge graph could have been implemented to save knowledge workers time and money (Blumauer & Nagy, 2020). I with a team, created recommended file storage models, naming conventions, and tips and tricks for organizing SharePoint and MS TEAMS. However, most did not use these simple tools. They conveyed they did not have time to learn the recommend file structures, naming conventions…; they needed to use their own file structures and naming conventions; and that they just did not have time.

I with my team, also tried to commence an IG Program by working with departments who needed to shift from a paper to digital model. We offered logistical solutions about where to go and how to digitize paper or create digital-born solutions. We offered various places to save digitized information – enterprise content management systems such as Laserfiche, MS TEAMS, SharePoint, ITSM knowledge bases, Learning Management Solutions… However, again individuals told us they did not have time, the technologies were too difficult to use, they did not have a license, they did not like the naming conventions and file structures, and every other excuse you can imagine. So instead of turning information chaos and uncertainty into greatness, we continued in inefficiencies (Collins & Hansen, 2011).

Even though thousands of excuses could have been offered as to why knowledge workers did not want to follow a new IG Program creation, the real reason the IG Program did not take off was there was no mandate. The executive sponsor had been found and agreed to serve as so, but the executive sponsor did not help the IG Lead locate a Cadillac to role out the IG Program. Whereas, at Judicial (the above mentioned successful scenario), the IG Lead and executive Sponsor located a mandatory Cadillac. The old case management system had to be replaced, there was no choice of those who use it. They could either help build a new CMS or just not use on at all. Had they not participated in the creation of or use of the new CMS they would have been out of a job. Whereas, in the failure scenario, people were able to get around participating in the creation of the new IG Program and adhering to the recommendation, because they were just recommendations. In essence, the Cadillac must have teeth, it must have some force to get people inside the car. Once inside, knowledge workers see the benefits, cost reduction, risk reductions, optimization of information.

CONCLUSION

In summation, this chapter conveyed the juxtaposition of how having an executive sponsor and a Cadillac can appropriately catalyze the creation or an IG Program, and how not clearly locating and defining an executive sponsor and a Cadillac can result in perpetual aims and misses when trying to commence an IG Program. It is absolutely vital for an IG Lead to locate and gain commitment from an executive sponsor such as a CIO, CEO, Chancellor, CPO, or other. It is also important that an IG Lead locate a Cadillac, a huge void or need the organization has information-wise. This void could be an inability of knowledge workers to locate information in SharePoint, MS TEAMS, OneDrive; or it might be an inability to properly store information in a Knowledge Base. By locating an executive sponsor and an IG Cadillac, unnecessary barriers can be removed, necessary funding and staffing can be obtained, and the opportunity to implement a full or partial IG Program can manifest.

REFERENCES

Blumauer, A., & Nagy, H. (2020 Blumauer, A., & Nagy, H. (2020). *The knowledge graph cookbook: Recipes that work*. Monochrom.

Collins, J., & Hansen, M. T. (2011). *Great by choice: Uncertainty, chaos, and luck—why some thrive despite them all*. Harper Business.

Colorado State Archives. (2023). *Records Management*. Colorado State Archives. https://archives.colorado.gov/records-management

Eisen, L. S. (2020). *A guide to drafting respectful policies and directives* (3rd ed.). Pixley Press.

Franks, P. C. (2018). *Records and Information Management*. ALA Neal-Schuman.

Goodman, D., Phillips, J., & Stamper, M. (2022). *Data privacy program guide: How to build a privacy program that inspires trust*. CISO DRG Publishing.

Hill, K. (2023). *Your face belongs to us: A secretive startup's quest to end privacy as we know it*. Random House.

Laney, D. B. (2018). *Infonomics: How to monetize, manage, and measure information as an asset for competitive advantage* (3rd ed.). Bibliomotion, Inc.

Milton, N., & Lambe, P. (2020). *The knowledge manager's handbook: A step by step guide to embedding effective knowledge management in your organization* (2nd ed.). Kogan Page Limited.

Saldanha, T. (2019). *Why digital transformations fail: The surprising disciplines of how to take off and stay ahead*. Barrett-Koehler Publishers, Inc.

Seiner, R. (2014). *Non-invasive data governance: The path of least resistance and greatest success*. Technics Publications.

Service Now. (2023). *IT Service Management*. Service Now. https://www.servicenow.com/products/itsm.html on November 1, 2023.

Smallwood, R. F. (2014). *Information governance: Concepts, strategies, and best practices*. Wiley.

Westlaw. (2023). *Legal research tools*. Reuters. https://legal.thomsonreuters.com/en/westlaw.

Chapter 3
Role of Information Security and Protection in the Modern Era

Ahmad Tasnim Siddiqui
https://orcid.org/0000-0002-1884-9331
Sandip University, Nashik, India

Gulshaira Banu Jahangeer
https://orcid.org/0000-0003-4877-8738
Taif University, Saudi Arabia

Amjath Fareeth Basha
Taif University, Saudi Arabia

ABSTRACT

The purpose of information security is to protect data by mitigating the risks associated with it. It refers to preventing unauthorized access to disclosure, destruction, disruption, modification of information and the information that they process, store, and transmit. Every information, especially sensitive or confidential, must be protected. It is essential to consider technology, policies, procedures, and people when implementing an effective information security system. In addition, emerging threats and vulnerabilities need to be monitored, assessed, and adapted continuously. Cybercrime, theft, and espionage are some of the threats we face trying to protect our valuable information assets. The goal of information security is to safeguard valuable information assets against a variety of threats. No matter how information is stored, whether electronically or on paper, it must be protected to ensure privacy, integrity, and availability. This chapter talks about the role of information security in modern days.

INTRODUCTION

Protecting sensitive information held by an organization by maintaining its confidentiality, integrity, and availability (CIA) against attacks and threats is a big challenge in the current digital age. Apart from CIA triad, information security can also help in disaster recovery, authentication, encryption, and risk management etc. According to US law, information security is defined as "protecting infor-

DOI: 10.4018/979-8-3693-0472-3.ch003

mation and information systems from unauthorized access, use, disclosure, disruption, modification, or destruction". It is widely accepted in the information security community that no system can be completely secure from all adversaries (Singla & Bertino, 2019). In order to protect their information, organizations around the world invest heavily in technological countermeasures. In spite of this, organizations rarely protect their information assets since they rely primarily on technical solutions that cannot meet their contextual requirements (Khando et al.., 2021). Consequently, organizations continuously struggle to protect their information assets, which forces them to invest a lot of money in technological measures. Information security, however, is a multidisciplinary field and human interaction plays a massive role in it. It is not enough to merely concentrate only on the technical aspects. In most security incidents, both intentional and unintentional misbehavior is the result of human errors.

Any hacker is interested in IT professionals' credentials, including their user names and passwords, as they may have access to sensitive network areas. Hackers could use the credentials of IT professionals to roam freely, download data from the network, or just monitor information of interest, including root access and network description. Hackers began to target the weakest element of the security infrastructure because security systems improved to counter known attack signatures. It has become increasingly clear that humans are the primary conduits for IT attacks. Phishing attacks were reported to have been successful in 84% of companies, and almost 91% were exposed to these attacks (Torten et al., 2018).

ENISA Threat Landscape (ETL) is the annual report on the state of cybersecurity threats released by ENISA, European Union Agency for Cybersecurity (ENISA, 2022). In this report, the report identifies prime threats, major trends concerning threats, threat actors, and attack techniques, as well as mitigation measures that should be implemented. ENISA organized threats into dissimilar groups, based on frequency and impact determine how prominent all of these threats still are:

- Ransomware: 60% of the organizations that have been attacked may have paid a ransom
- Malware: The year 2021 saw 66 leaks of zero-day vulnerabilities
- Social engineering: There are many different types of phishing, including whaling, spear-phishing, vishing, and smishing, but phishing has remained a popular technique for decades
- Threats against data: A proportional increase in the amount of data generated
- Threats against availability: There has never been a more significant Denial-of-Service (DDoS) attack perpetrated in Europe than in July 2022
- Internet: Internet traffic has been rerouted, infrastructure has been destroyed and outages have occurred
- Disinformation or misinformation: Deepfakes, disinformation-as-a-service, and AI-enabled disinformation are on the rise
- Supply chain targeting: In 2021, 17 percent of invasions are caused by third parties, compared to less than one percent in 2020

Organizational data is protected against multiple attacks by Information Security platforms, which are capable of identifying outliers and threats. Information security emphasizes confidentiality, integrity, and availability of data in order to protect them from both active and passive attacks (Alqahtani, 2017).

History of Information Security

Since the 1960s, information security has evolved from being a fun practical joke between colleagues to a serious issue - and the reasons are not hard to find. Even though there are a number of fire safety and security measures that can be applied to physical security, it is imperative to use effective antivirus software in order to prevent cyber-attacks. During the 1960s, organizations started to protect their data and computers. During those eras when the internet and networks were not present, so security focused more on physical measures and preventing access to those who knew how to work computers. To combat this situation, devices were equipped with multiple layers of security protection and passwords. To ensure the safety of the stored data, fire safety measures were also implemented. An early research project on ARPANET (The Advanced Research Projects Agency Network) sparked the beginning of cybersecurity during the 1970s. The ARPANET's network could be moved, leaving a little trail behind it, thanks to a computer program developed by researcher Bob Thomas. He gave the program the name "CREEPER" in reference to the printed message that was left behind while it traveled over the network: "I'M THE CREEPER: CATCH ME IF YOU CAN" (Murphey, 2019).

In the following decades, there was increase in networking, computer viruses, and a barrage of innovative hacking methods that overwhelmed information security systems.

With the increase in users over the Internet, cloud and other social media platforms, the number of adversaries attempting to find new ways to break into these systems has increased dramatically. The participation of state actors in the cybersecurity arms race has also increased the frequency of new attacks and malware (Singla & Bertino, 2019).

Governments started to crack down on hacking in the early 2000s, and those found guilty faced far harsher penalties, such as lengthy prison terms and enormous fines. Compared to the 1980s, when hackers received considerably lighter sentences (ranging from harsh warnings to probation), this was a far cry from those circumstances. As technology continued to advance, hacking became increasingly complex, and a number of significant data breaches have now defined this time period. Fortunately, there are several organizations that provide answers to these possible farces, so everything is not lost. The pitch of information security is continuously growing, and numerous organizations are creating a wide range of basic attack mitigation solutions that make use of techniques like web application firewalls (WAF), denial-of-service (DoS) prevention, and network behavior analysis (NBA).

Effective information security necessitates a complete approach that considers every aspects of the information situation, including technology, policies and procedures, as well as people. It also necessitates ongoing monitoring, valuation, and adaptation to address emerging threats and vulnerabilities.

METHODOLOGY

The chapter examines Information security and protection in current Internet era. It reviews the safety, privacy, and protection of information. Scinapse and Google search engines are used to search most of the literatures. Scientific databases such as IEEExplore, Medline, Google scholar, Springer, Scopus, and others are accessed using a set of keywords as search terms. Research articles published between 2015 and 2023 in reputed research journals are carefully scrutinized and synthesized for the review. Apart from research papers, white papers, articles from magazines, governmental online reports have been surveyed carefully. This chapter is based on the literature review of research papers, online texts, white papers, articles, and various reports. Chapter organization contains various sections. The first section contains an Introduction about the chapter and topic, the second section explains about the Methodology used, the third section exhibits Literature review, the fourth section discusses the elements of information security, the fifth section discusses about the role of information security, and finally, the sixth and the last section concludes.

LITERATURE REVIEW

Since the introduction of information and communication technologies within organizations, security has become a key concern. The term confidentiality refers to the privacy of individuals, integrity to maintaining the integrity, correctness, and reliability of data, and availability to access data 24/7 (Alqahtani, 2017). In response to the growing demand for information systems, many authors have stressed the importance of identifying and eliminating weaknesses (De Lange et al., 2016).

Samonasa et. al. (2020) argues in their article that there are countless examples of unclear information security policies in academic and practitioner literature. Security vulnerabilities identified in Intel processor-based operating systems were highlighted in a 2018 news report. As a result of a design flaw, attackers could access sensitive data stored in computer memory or control low-level program functionality of Intel-based operating systems, according to US-CERT (US Computer Emergency Response Team, 2018).

Barlette et al. (2020), in their researches examine managers' adaptation strategies in light of employee Bring Your Own Device (BYOD) usage. A coping model of user adaptation (CMUA) is operationalized and enriched by the authors. As a result of this study, authors gain a greater understanding of the decisional processes involved in coping strategies adoption. As a function of whether the CMUA constructs are implemented before or after, their impact varies. By using BYOD effectively and maintaining a satisfactory level of corporate information security, this study helps managers maximize BYOD-related benefits.

A real-world issue is addressed by Samonasa et. al. (2020), specifically the misinterpretation of a security policy, which can cause non-malicious compliance violations. According to them, security management practice and literature can benefit from studying stakeholder perceptions regarding a security policy and their convergence and divergence.

Chen et al. (2021), examined that conflicts related to information security have a negative effect on employee performance in terms of information security. The likelihood of employees adopting BYOD practices decreases as their information security fatigue increases. Through the full mediation of information security fatigue, information security-related conflict can indirectly affect employee BYOD adoption.

An IS threat can be either internal or external, and can involve events that are unpredicted or undesirable with harmful consequences for an organization. Employees working within an organization create internal threats, mainly because they have unauthorized access to company information. External threats originate from outside units of organization (Jouini et al., 2014).

In order to create a secure environment for information assets, AlHogail (2015), proposed a framework that addresses a wide range of human behavior issues. This study provides a comprehensive overview of the issues using the STOPE (Strategy; Technology; Organization; People; and Environment) scope as a guide. Using the human factor diamond, we have translated these issues into tasks based on preparedness, responsibility, management, and society and regulation. Cultivating an information security culture was guided by change management principles. By referring to the framework dimensions, you can identify which issues need to be considered in order to cultivate a culture and increase the knowledge, values, and behavior of employees. As well, an organization's information security culture can be assessed using this framework. This assessment allows for the identification of vulnerabilities and weaknesses and the implementation of corrective actions based on them (AlHogail, 2015).

According to Levin (2018), compliance to security policies is too often associated with very long texts that aren't always read by everyone, which explains the incomprehensibility of security policies. To ensure compliance with Intel's security specifications, software engineers would have to read 4,844 pages of documentation in the case of vulnerabilities in Intel-powered computers (Levin, 2018).

Deogirikar & Vidhate (2017) address a variety of IoT attacks that operate on the perception, network, and application layers of an IoT system architecture. They looked at several attacks at various layers, including software, network, physical, and encryption attacks.

One of the most significant turning points in the history of information security occurred a few years later, in 1988, with the creation of the Morris Worm. The use of networks started to grow quickly, and an increasing number of governments, universities, and military institutions connected to them. This implied that the necessary security precautions would also need to progressively grow more stringent, which gave rise to the Morris Worm. As the public gained access to the internet, an increasing number of people started posting personal information online. As a result, organized crime groups began to use the internet to steal data from individuals and governments after realizing that this could be a possible source of income (Murphey, 2019).

For information security decision makers, Diesch et al. (2020), proposes a comprehensive model of management success factors (MSFs) in their research. To identify factors that influence managers' decisions regarding information security, they conducted a literature review utilizing an open-axial-selective approach. According to this research, the following security indicators have a direct influence on an organization's information security status: physical security, vulnerability, access control, infrastructure, and awareness. In order to generate countermeasures that influence the key security indicators, "Security management" needs to take into consideration "Risks", "Organizational factors" and available "Resources". Compliance & Policy is used for the enforcement of countermeasures and compliance with laws.

Alkhudhayr et al.., (2019) examined a few scenarios pertaining to cyber security threats in order to demonstrate how these threats may impact cyberspace. They looked at a variety of scenarios, including digital media, cyberterrorism, home automation, and cyberbullying. Cyberbullying is regarded as a widespread cyber security issue that has the potential to directly harm the target of the bullying. Due to their extensive development, both cyber security and information technology security necessitate ongoing assessment and innovation. The reputation of an organization will be damaged and intellectual property will be jeopardized as a result of a cyberattack. Social engineering is the method of choice for cyber attackers because multi-layer firewall system security is difficult for them to overcome.

In order to enhance ISA in the healthcare industry, Ghazvini and Shukur (2018) created the serious but enjoying game known as InfoSecure. The game covers a number of subjects, including password protection, malicious codes, web usage, and phishing. The game was enjoyable to play and the staff found it to be interactive. According to the evaluation, after participating in the game, employees' ISA levels have comparatively increased. Employees enjoyed playing the game, which further demonstrated their willingness to take part in ISA training (Ghazvini and Shukur, 2018).

Scholl (2019) examined the scientific literature from prestigious academic Information Security journals to investigate how to raise information security awareness to the people living in urban and regional planning. As a means of gaining a deeper comprehension of how to encourage sustainable ISA through innovative means, he introduced Serious Games. Additionally, suggestions for integrating awareness into contemporary urban and regional planning through the application of the Fun Theory and its practice were also explored; however, his work was also incomplete, as it focused only on the use of serious games, which is only one of the strategies used in the development of ISA programs.

Singla & Bertino, (2019), discusses about Deep Learning approach to address the issues of information security. Deep learning (DL) is a promising approach that addresses the flaws of traditional methods. DL is a branch of machine learning (ML) that tries to learn various characteristics from data and uses them for decision making on similar unseen data. Based on biological neural networks (NNs), it is loosely based on human brain neural networks (NNs). Because of the increased amount of data available and its various algorithmic innovations, as well as significant improvements in computing capabilities enabled by GPUs, which have made fast training and deployment of DL models possible, DL techniques have gained interest in the last five years. Previously, deep learning was extremely successful at tasks like image classification, object detection, and text and voice recognition. Recently, methods for using DL for various information security tasks such as malware analysis, intrusion detection, botnet detection, and software analysis have been proposed.

Requirements of Information Security Policy (ISP)

ISPs must be written in a way that addresses all possible human errors, because such errors will negatively affect the organization if not handled carefully. It is important that an organization closely monitors and addresses any variances in its IS assets following the design and development of an ISP. The ISP explains how passwords can be changed, how users can manage their passwords, and how to use the best practices related to password management, including changing passwords regularly, selecting strong passwords, and preventing other users from sharing passwords. Various ISP documents define IT departments' general responsibilities; however, the IT department's responsibilities with regard to email use must be clarified in order to assist users with fishing issues.

Emails automatically forwarded from work mail servers to external accounts may expose sensitive information to security risks. It is important to choose a good password, lock workstations, open attachments, forward emails, check work emails via free networks, install unauthorized software, access dubious websites, use the Internet inappropriately, consider the consequences of Social Networking Sites, use of mobile networks to transfer sensitive information, insert USB devices, dispose of sensitive documents and leave sensitive material unsecure (Alqahtani, 2017).

Srinivas et al. (2019), in an analysis of various attacks as well as the security requirements and solutions involved was presented by the authors in this study. As a result of the discussion, a cyber security incident management framework (CIMF) was developed. A coordinated national cyber incident response should be enabled by CIMF to ensure that each organization can participate fully and effectively. A number of standardization challenges associated with cyber security are then discussed by authors. There are a number of elements that make up a cyber security standard, including tools, security concepts, policies, security protection, risk management, training, and so on. Authors also discussed on National strategy to secure information, cyberspace and many governmental policies. As a final recommendation, they provided some cyber defense as well as security recommendations.

More than any other component of system security, information protection calls for particular behavioral and procedural actions. Data files must be appropriately created, labeled, stored, and backed up in order to maintain information security. Considering how many files each employee uses, it is obvious that these tasks represent a substantial undertaking. By correctly identifying sensitive information stored in the system and carrying out an accurate risk assessment, policymakers can have a positive impact on this effort. Additionally, they ought to support the security manager's organizational efforts as they carry out and keep an eye on security regulations. The power and resources required to properly train employees and then enforce information security policies at all organizational levels must be granted to the security manager.

Risk and information system security are closely intertwined. Risk is an occurrence that could make achieving company goals more difficult. According to ISO (International Organization for Standardization), risk refers to the possibility that an asset or set of assets could be exploited by certain threats. The business value of the loss or damage and the estimated frequency of threat have an impact on the relative severity of the risk (Shouran et al.., 2019).

Szczepaniuk et al. (2020) argues that Information security threats are increasing, and a change in the legal system imposes an obligation on public administration entities to implement and improve their Information Security Management Systems (ISMS). During the development and implementation of ISMS, the authors recommend taking into account the theoretical considerations presented in their research.

Information retention and disposal are a last point of concern for decision-makers. Since the lifespan of all information is limited, policymakers should ensure that procedures are in place to guarantee that information that is no longer needed is disposed of appropriately (NCES).

ELEMENTS OF INFORMATION SECURITY

Information security encompasses various elements to safeguard data from unauthorized access, alteration, or destruction. Security policies and awareness training play vital roles, fostering a culture of compliance. The fundamental concepts of information security are the Confidentiality, Integrity, and Availability, known as CIA triad. The information security specialist can use this tool to help them consider the best ways to safeguard organizational data.

Confidentiality: The goal of confidentiality measures is to stop information from being disclosed without authorization. The confidentiality principle is to protect the privacy of personal information and guarantee that only those individuals have visibility and access to it who require it to carry out their job duties.

Integrity: Consistency involves safeguarding data from illegal alterations, omissions, revisions, and other changes. It ensures that information is accurate and trustworthy and is not accidentally or deliberately altered.

Availability: Availability refers to the safeguarding of a system's capacity to provide data and software systems that are completely accessible to users at a predetermined time or when needed. Availability refers to the ability of an organization's data, applications, and technological infrastructure to be accessed when needed for customer or corporate processes.

Figure 1. Elements of Information Security

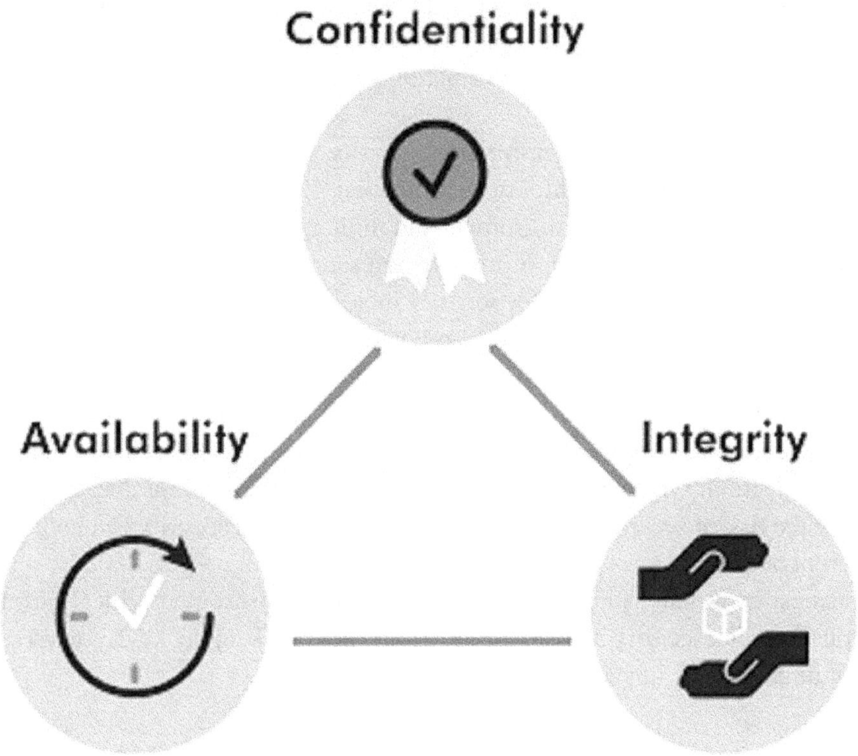

ROLE OF INFORMATION SECURITY

Over time, information security has taken on a different function. Today, information security specialists are integral to the success of business operations as a whole, having been incorporated into companies at the executive level. When information security emerged as a field of study, its main goals were to safeguard IT setups and implement security measures. As time passes on, it became clear that knowing the demands of an organization's business leaders is a prerequisite for successfully securing an IT environment. These days, information security executives' link cyber security to the operations of the company to make sure it keeps up its capacity to service clients.

Information security is required to ensure the confidentiality, integrity, and availability of information, whether it is stored digitally or in other forms such as paper documents. In the increasingly interconnected world of today, it is imperative that every firm comprehends how ISA content is created and maintained. It can be said that, despite ISA being a relatively young area of study, a sizable number of empirical studies have examined the creation of ISA material during the previous ten years (Khando et al.., 2021).

Inadequate information security may lead to disruptions in socially significant activities, inability to do business in an appropriate and efficient manner, and loss of personal integrity protection. Physical assets might be impacted by information system deficiencies as well. Critical infrastructure damage can have lethal repercussions. Serious crises impacting the financial systems, the public health system, national security, or any combination of these may result from incidents that cause these systems and assets to become inoperable or destroyed. Additionally, it can cause people's trust in underlying actors and services to decline. Credibility crises can result from significant and persistent disruptions, and they can also extend to other players, services, and other industries (Advenica). In short, neglecting information security may cause high consequences that are not affordable.

Here are some of the main reasons why information security is important:

- Protecting sensitive information: Information security helps to keep sensitive information safe from unauthorized access, disclosure, or modification. Personal information, financial data, and trade secrets, as well as sensitive government and military information, are all included.
- Risk reduction: The implementation of information security measures can help organizations reduce risks from cyber threats and other security incidents. This includes reducing the possibility of data breaches, denial-of-service attacks, and other malicious activity.
- Regulation compliance: The protection of sensitive data is governed by many regulations in different industries and jurisdictions. It is possible to reduce the risk of legal liability by implementing information security measures. Security measures assist in ensuring regulatory compliance.
- Reputation protection: Organizations can lose business and reputation due to security breaches. By reducing the risk of security incidents, effective information security can help protect an organization's reputation.
- Ensure business continuity: Information security helps to ensure that critical business functions can continue even if a security incident occurs. This includes keeping key systems and data accessible and minimizing the impact of any disruptions.

INFORMATION SECURITY STANDARDS

Several major reasons exist why organizations should comply with information standards: Regulatory compliance, preventing cyberattacks, increasing risk awareness, and enhancing reputation. International Organization for Standardization (ISO), provided some recommendations that are useful for both cyber security and cyber defense. There are two standards ISO 27001 and ISO 27102, the most common information security standards for companies to strive to meet. Technology, manufacturing, management, and more are all covered by this independent, international organization. Over 45 standards are part of the ISO 27000 Series, which covers a wide range of information security topics. ISO 27001 and ISO 27002 are two of the key standards (What are information security standards? 2023).

Typically, an Information Security Management System, or ISMS, is a governance framework that contains a structured suite of activities to manage the risks associated with information security. ISO 27001 outlines the requirements for how companies should implement ISMSs. A successful ISMS includes controlling and addressing information security risks specific to your organization, as well as monitoring and measuring the efficacy and performance of those controls (What are information security standards? 2023).

An organization may implement security controls outlined in ISO 27002, which complement those outlined in ISO 27001, to ensure information security. In addition to providing best practices in selecting, implementing, and managing information security controls, ISO 27002 also accounts for the organization 's risk environment when selecting, implementing, and managing controls (What are information security standards? 2023).

CONCLUSION

In this study, professionals and users across the globe were analyzed about the relationship between awareness programs and desktop security behaviors. Information security is crucial for safeguarding sensitive data and protecting individuals, organizations, and nations from cyber threats. It ensures the confidentiality, integrity, and availability of information, preventing unauthorized access, data breaches, and cyberattacks. Effective information security measures instill trust among users, clients, and partners, bolstering business continuity and reputation. With the increasing digitalization of society, the importance of robust information security practices is paramount to safeguard personal privacy, financial assets, and critical infrastructure, contributing to the overall stability and resilience of interconnected systems in the modern world. Robust security measures, including encryption, access controls, and regular audits, are essential to counter evolving cyber threats and maintain trust in the digital landscape. Prioritizing information security is imperative for fostering a secure and resilient environment in the interconnected world of today. Methods and techniques like Deep Learning may help to secure the sensitive information. But most importantly we need to be extra aware towards the security and protection of our valuable data. Regular audits and incident response plans are essential elements to detect, respond to, and recover from security incidents.

REFERENCES

Advenica. (n.d.). *Why is information security so important? Cybersecurity solutions that protects what matters most.* Advenica. https://advenica.com/en/why-is-information-security-so-important,

AlHogail, A. (2015). Design and validation of information security culture framework. *Computers in Human Behavior, 49*, 567–575. doi:10.1016/j.chb.2015.03.054

Alkhudhayr, F., Alfarraj, S., Aljameeli, B., & Elkhdiri, S. (2019). Information Security: A review of information security issues and techniques. *2019 2nd International Conference on Computer Applications & Information Security.* IEEE. 10.1109/CAIS.2019.8769504

Alqahtani, F. H. (2017). *Developing an Information Security Policy: A Case Study Approach.* 4th Information Systems International Conference 2017, Bali, Indonesia. 10.1016/j.procs.2017.12.206

Barlette, Y., Jaouen, A., & Baillette, P. (2020). Bring Your Own Device (BYOD) as reversed IT adoption: Insights into managers' coping strategies. *International Journal of Information Management.* doi:10.1016/j.ijinfomgt.2020.102212 PMID:32934432

Chen, H., Li, Y., Chen, L., & Yin, J. (2021). Understanding employees' adoption of the Bring-Your-Own-Device (BYOD): The roles of information security-related conflict and fatigue. *Journal of Enterprise Information Management, 34*(3), 770–792. doi:10.1108/JEIM-10-2019-0318

De Lange, J., Von-Solms, R., & Gerber, M. (2016). Information security management in local government. In: Cunningham P, Cunningham M, editors. 2016 IST-Africa Week Conference, Durban, South Africa. doi:10.1109/ISTAFRICA.2016.7530584

Deogirikar, J., & Vidhate, A. (2017). *Security attacks in IoT: A survey, in International Conference on I-SMAC (IoT in Social, Mobile, Analytics and Cloud) (I-SMAC)*. IEEE.

Diesch, R., Pfaff, M., & Krcmar, H. (2020). A comprehensive model of information security factors for decision-makers. *Computers & Security*, *92*, 101747. doi:10.1016/j.cose.2020.101747

ENISA. (2022). *Threat Landscape*. ENSIA. https://www.enisa.europa.eu/topics/cyber-threats/threats-and-trends

Ghazvini, A., & Shukur, Z. (2018). A Serious Game for Healthcare Industry: Information Security Awareness Training Program for Hospital University Kebangsaan Malaysia. *International Journal of Advanced Computer Science and Applications*, *9*(9), 236–245. doi:10.14569/IJACSA.2018.090932

Jouini, M., Rabai, L. B. A., & Aissa, A. B. (2014). Classification of security threats in information systems. *Procedia Computer Science*, *32*, 489–496. doi:10.1016/j.procs.2014.05.452

Khando K., Gao S., Islam S. M., & Salman A. (2021). *Enhancing employees information security awareness in private and public organizations: A systematic literature review*.

Levin, A. (2018). *How a security policy could cause the next killer hack*. INC. https://www.inc.com/adam-levin/how-a-security-policy-could-cause-next-killer-hack.html.

Murphey, D. (2019). *A history of information security. IFSEC Insider, Security and Fire News and Resources*. IFSEC Global. https://www.ifsecglobal.com/cyber-security/a-history-of-information-security/

NCES. (n.d.). *Chapter 6 - Protecting Your System: Information Security. Information security, from safeguarding your technology, NCES publication 98-297 (National center for education statistics)*. National Center for Education Statistics (NCES). https://nces.ed.gov/pubs98/safetech/chapter6.asp

Samonasa, S., Dhillon, G., & Almusharraf, A. (2020). Stakeholder perceptions of information security policy: Analyzing personal constructs. *International Journal of Information Management*, *50*, 144–154. https://www.sciencedirect.com/science/article/abs/pii/S0268401218303451?via%3Dihub. doi:10.1016/j.ijinfomgt.2019.04.011

Scholl, M. C. (2019). Raising Information Security Awareness in the Field of Urban and Regional Planning. Int. [IJEPR]. *International Journal of E-Planning Research*, *8*(3), 62–86. doi:10.4018/IJEPR.2019070104

Shouran, Z., Priyambodo, T. K., & Ashari, A. (2019). *Information System Security: Human Aspects*. Research Gate. https://www.researchgate.net/publication/331859493_Information_System_Security_Human_Aspects

Singla, A., & Bertino, E. (2019). How Deep Learning Is Making Information Security More Intelligent. *IEEE Security and Privacy*, *17*(3), 56–65. doi:10.1109/MSEC.2019.2902347

Srinivas, J., Das, A. K., & Kumar, N. (2019). Government regulations in cyber security: Framework, standards and recommendations. *Future Generation Computer Systems*, *92*, 178–188. doi:10.1016/j.future.2018.09.063

Szczepaniuk, E. K., Szczepaniuk, H., Rokicki, T., & Klepacki, B. (2020). Information security assessment in public administration. *Computers & Security*, *90*, 101709. doi:10.1016/j.cose.2019.101709

Torten, R., Reaiche, C., & Boyle, S. (2018). (2018). The impact of security awareness on information technology professional's behavior. *Computers & Security*, *79*, 68–79. doi:10.1016/j.cose.2018.08.007

US-CERT. (2018). *Vulnerability Note VU#631579: Hardware debug exception documentation may result in unexpected behavior*. Vulnerability Notes Database. https://www.kb.cert.org/vuls/id/631579

What are information security standards? (2023). RiskXchange. https://riskxchange.co/1006780/information-security-standards/

KEY TERMS AND DEFINITIONS

Information Security Policies: Generally, an Information Security Policy is a set of rules, policies, and procedures designed to safeguard data and ensure it is protected within an organization.

Information Security Standards: Information security standards define how to control, identify, manage, and monitor the various aspects of security. It also provides the blueprint of the entire process to achieve the security standards.

Information Security: It is a set of processes and tools designed to prevent sensitive business or personnel data from being modified, disrupted, destroyed, or accessed. Information Security is often abbreviated to InfoSec.

Chapter 4
Building Culture for Sustaining Information Governance

Jennie Lee Khun
https://orcid.org/0000-0001-6076-1782
Purdue Global University, USA

ABSTRACT

The chapter explains what information governance is and why it is important. The problem is identified that organizations know information governance is important but many fail to implement governance or do so poorly. The author questions why companies fail to recognize the benefit of a cultural approach to addressing this critical gap. The chapter introduces the concept that information governance is integral for every organization. The chapter provides insight into hiring, training, professional development, emotional intelligence, and soft skills to build a thriving organization. The chapter explores the need for a positive and dedicated approach to leadership. The chapter explores communication, operational efficiencies, board governance approaches, and examines compliance. Lastly, the chapter explores risk and why organizations must implement a risk management strategy. A conclusion summarizes the need for information governance to build a successful culture that adopts an information governance strategy to be successful.

INTRODUCTION

What is governance; why is it important? Governance is a set of rules regarding how decisions are made that help an individual to continuously act in the best interests of the company. Governance, when done well, can improve the performance of the company by enabling the organization to become stable, productive, and take advantage of opportunities. It can reduce risk, facilitate quicker approaches to company growth, and protect the organization from dangers. Selecting an appropriate governance framework can strengthen the organization from the business process perspective and should be selected based off the industry, specific needs, and nature of the information technology operations being performed. Information governance is an indispensable part of the responsibilities for every organization conducting business in today's competitive and security-centric setting. The question remains: "Why do so many

DOI: 10.4018/979-8-3693-0472-3.ch004

organizations struggle to implement an effective governance program, if they even have a program at all?" In the technology industry, the benefits of culture, emotional intelligence, and soft skills are often overlooked because the focus is on analytical skillsets. These same skills are equally important when it comes to sustaining a governance program. The program is only successful when the program incorporates both analytical and soft skills. The analytical side of the program must focus on data or information. Information and data governance are terms that are often used interchangeably but have subtle nuances. Information governance is the management of data resources or assets through the lifecycle by exploring data through acquisition, creation, transportation, storage, use, curation, and the deletion of data utilized by the organization. Data management follows a hierarchal higher-order construct and progresses from low-level operations towards more managerial functions; this is seen through overarching concepts like information governance (Vojvodic & Hitz, 2022). It would be advantageous to thoroughly explore how the industry can realize the benefits of a thriving culture to supplement the adoption of a viable information governance program. Organizations must actively take part in purposefully building the environment appropriate for their business; this includes cultivating customs and values as part of a cultural development strategy. Effective governance provides value to traditional information management by expanding its span vertically—through alignment with business stakeholders, and horizontally—through cross-functional handling of data issues (Vojvodic & Hitz, 2022). Information technology is essential for organizations' support, viability, and expansion; despite the increasing significance, its usage for benefits and control in the business world remains a problem for corporate management and stakeholders (Singh & Alhulail, 2023). The main purpose of an effective governance program includes accuracy, integrity, safety, compliance, availability, and value addition obligatory for a healthy corporate environment to succeed in this fast-paced global economy.

Strategy and policy are just words on paper. The documents mean nothing if employees do not understand the significance, importance, or the intended outcomes of these items. Both are ineffective if corporate culture does not support the meaning of the initiative. The question to ask is how organizations can help employees understand the necessity and the value of addition of policies that can sometimes make their work more difficult. We must help employees understand why it is important to them, but we must also help them to care about it. If the individual is not directly involved with the strategy and policy setting, it removes them from the sense of ownership that allows an individual to feel naturally integrated into a process. Obviously, not all employees can be involved in the policy setting activities, which simply would not work.

The best way to help employees feel connected is to ensure the adoption of change is integrated into the culture. It can be exponentially more difficult to create a cultural shift rather than just starting fresh with a new group of people. Unfortunately, for many organizations the ability to start anew is simply not an option. One simply cannot replace everyone in the organization and expect things to run smoothly. The question of how to create a valuable cultural shift must be addressed. This is the only way to help the workforce build governance into the core of the organization. Employees should have a strong sense of purpose, have socially accepted normal behaviors and values, and a healthy dose of motivation to ensure the business plans are engrained into the regular everyday work environment using instinctive behaviors. Instinctive behaviors are those habits that employees perform naturally on a consistent and repetitive basis, often without much thought or effort. These are the behaviors that one just automatically does. There has been an abundance of research exploring governance, but gaps exist in how to deploy data or information governance and what strategic actions to take as the volume of data increases considerably over time (Zhang et al., 2022). Information governance is crucial in minimizing risks, ensuring the proper

Figure 1.
Fewings, N. (Photographer)
https://unsplash.com/photos/EkyuhD7uwSM

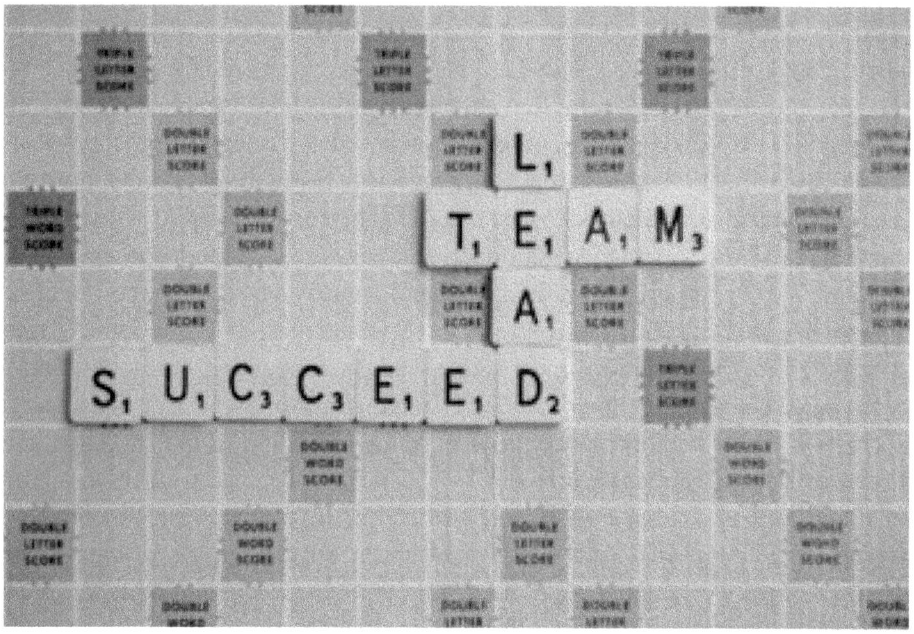

protection, managing archiving and disposal of data, and generating useful analytics that drive a company towards achievable objectives. Organizations must examine the corporate leadership, communications, training, business operations, and management to have a cohesive strategy that allows the direct shaping of a team's culture, thereby promoting information governance as a personal responsibility. The next step is to examine how governance and culture are indeterminably linked.

Leadership

Leadership sets the tone for the rest of the organization. There is a plethora of leadership quotes that many have heard throughout their career. They appear on training materials, are quoted by management, and can be seen hanging on inspirational posters in offices across many companies. "A leader takes people where they want to go. A great leader takes people where they don't necessarily want to go, but ought to be," coined by Rosalynn Carter, former first lady of the United States. (Fallon, 2023.) "The greatest leader is not necessarily the one who does the greatest things. He is the one that gets the people to do the greatest thing spoken by President Ronald Reagan." (Fallon, 2023.) The list of inspirational sayings spoken by leaders across genres goes on. Leadership is not just inspirational quotes, a title, or a term to be used lightly to persuade opinion. A great leader is the difference necessary for positively accepting change, fostering innovation, and encouraging a team to do great work. It is as simple and as complex as that. Leadership's role is to progress, expand, and reconfigure employees' capabilities to provide direction, inspiration, and/or influence organizational members, (Nisar et al., 2021). This is certainly true for supporting the key ingredients for a strong cohesive culture. The organization must determine how its leadership affects culture and subsequently the governance of information.

The influx of various titles and roles has created a challenging environment for leadership to effectively control. There is a variety of ownership-related activities to data that is often unclear. Who is responsible for the data, who can make decisions regarding the data, where and how does the data get stored, how can the data be used, when should the data be removed, and many others. If roles and responsibilities are not well defined, the organization will find itself in a power struggle that it cannot control. Responsibility for information may cross multiple roles such as chief information or data officer, analysts, chief privacy officer, security, records management, general counsel, and information technology staff, along with many others. How do these individuals know what to do and what they have authority to support or change? These significant changes to the corporate structure in the technology era have altered the way many companies are doing business; and not necessarily for the better if they do not build a culture that supports information governance. Information governance provides a framework for individuals to follow as organizations seek to ingest, utilize, control, secure, and archive data throughout the organizational environment. The deluge of data has provided an opportunity to maximize value while reducing the risk of maintaining the data, but only when the company has thoroughly defined the activities for everyone involved in the information lifecycle. The additional roles we have introduced necessitate and justify the need for a formal information governance framework to ensure that the data and information strategy is cohesive. Leadership that fails to define a clear strategy and build a positive culture will ultimately risk collapsing the organization through missed opportunity.

A Leader's Influence

People inherently learn from example and experience. As children and even adults, we learn to emulate the behaviors of those individuals we personally deem as successful. We want to be like those people, so we perform in a similar manner hoping for the same outcomes. Leadership has an obligation to inspire others, to lead by example, and promote behaviors for others to emulate. The most profound power a leader possesses is their ability to influence either positively or negatively, intentionally, or unintentionally. Idealized influence allows leaders to successfully persuade and motivate employees to implement change and innovation aimed at achieving continuous development; intellectual stimulation enhances employees' ability to be revolutionary; inspirational leaders create confidence and hope among employees; and directly arouse greater warmth and efforts of employees (Gui et al., 2022). A great leader recognizes that their behaviors and mannerisms are always being watched. Employees consciously and unconsciously look to leadership for guidance on how to act, behave, and exist within the organizational environment. It is widely acknowledged in management literature that leadership is a relational and inspirational style for creating positive impact on followers' attitudes, behaviors, and individual developments (Gui et al., 2022). Leaders effectively help make informed decisions, promote problem solving, and rally employees around the mission and vision of the organization. It can be concluded that leadership plays an integral part in the employees' adoption and support of a change, including that of an information governance program.

Leaders, Boards, and senior management are responsible for creating appropriate governance frameworks, policies, and processes for information management activities. Additionally, to mitigate risks, the groups are responsible for ensuring the frameworks are followed. The expansion of data and the changes to the way businesses operate cause a challenge for governance to keep pace with new developments. It can be incredibly challenging to fully comprehend the strengths, weaknesses, and risks from all the information management activities throughout an organization. A sound information-governance framework

Figure 2.
Fewings, N. (Photographer)
https://unsplash.com/photos/b8AYYOCUSkQ

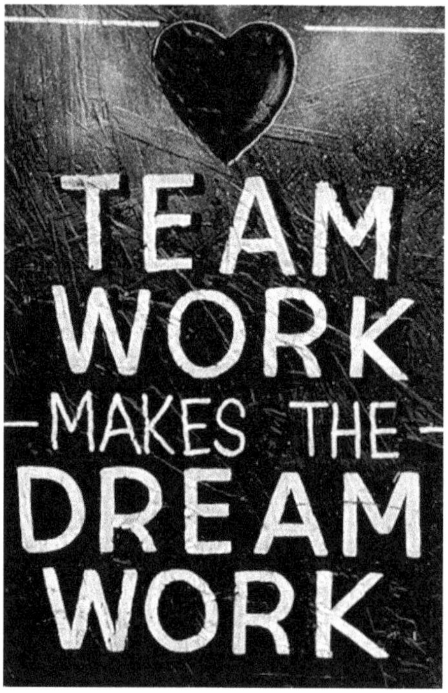

is the foundation that facilitates organizations to govern and manage the information they hold. Leadership sets the stage for the acceptance of the framework. The key to directing and managing information and data throughout the organization is to use a top-down approach. The presence of ethical leadership, starting from the Board of Directors, sets the "tone at the top" necessary for developing and sustaining an ethical corporate culture (Di Miceli da Silveira, 2022). For an information governance framework to be realized and rooted in an organizations culture, there must be strong leadership that champions governance in all facets. Leadership must have careful consideration of the organization's objectives, strategy, and present circumstances, compared against security priorities, legal, and compliance obligations. To enhance Board performance, it is vital that Board members have a variety of complementary skills and expertise, including cybersecurity skills, to contribute to the organization's strategy regarding threats; and legal expertise regarding information activities including privacy, records administration, and information management. It is equally important for leadership to determine who will be responsible for driving and implementing the governance strategy. It is vital to align data-driven decision-making with classic models of governance focused on people and accountability (Kurzhals et al., 2020). This responsibility will adapt to specific organizational needs, and depends on the strategic priorities, size of the organization, resources, constraints, and the current importance of information management.

Communication

Communication has and will continue to be a primary function of doing business in a global marketplace. Communication is of critical importance in establishing organizational cultures as well as organizational identification (Walker, 2021). Communication is a technique that implies the causation and receiving of messages through both verbal and non-verbal approaches, as well as written and visual (Huy, 2021). Organizations rely heavily on email and messaging platforms to conduct daily operations. It is imperative to maintain control over the information exchanged both internally and externally. The misuse of technology can expose an organization to risks. Data breaches are a serious concern for organizations of all sizes and across different industries with associated costs that include technical repair, determining how the breach occurred, offering free credit services to victims, litigation expenses, and various regulatory fees (D'Arcy et al., 2020). The risks associated with communication platforms include breaches or unintentional sharing of private information, issues with record retention, and ensuring business decisions are based off data in a controlled environment, such as the source of record. As part of a collective approach the organization must govern how users utilize the Internet, applications, and email, by ensuring appropriate policies support the information governance objectives. Additionally, leadership must continually communicate the importance of the adopted safeguards to develop a security conscious culture.

Training

The culture of an organization defines the standards to which the employees adhere. When budgets get tough and need to be cut, the first thing to be removed or reduced is the training budget. This is a blatant blunder that discredits the management of the organization. This misstep has long lasting detrimental effects that can be difficult to recover from. Training has countless benefits, including attributes needed for building a positive culture. Why wouldn't you want the best for your employees and the business? One of the best ways to show the highest levels of commitment to employees is to support their ability to acquire new skills. These newly learned skills help the employee stay up to date on his or her abilities, remain relevant in the industry, promote a sense of support, and ultimately benefits the company by employing individuals that are more knowledgeable. Organizations affect culture in a variety of ways, including company values and beliefs that create "unwritten rules." One way to garner a positive culture is to support training initiatives across the various departments, as each provides value in distinct ways. Commitment to growth and innovation are at the center of a developmental culture; encouraging staff to take risks and achieve innovation that aligns to the strategy and objectives of the company (Shahriari & Allameh, 2020). If the organization can promote a consistent approach to training, learning, and developing that is influenced directly by the culture, then both the business and the employees will see numerous remarkable benefits.

Training is an undervalued asset when it comes to instilling the principles for understanding the importance of information governance. Unintentional threats occur when unintended risks to the data and systems cause severe disruptions due to the lack of knowledge or expertise from personnel (Machado de Sousa & Shahzad, 2022). Emphasizing the importance of people being conscious of security risks and working to protect information is essential (Machado de Sousa & Shahzad, 2022). The fundamentals of information governance include strategic planning, policy adoption, social approaches, laws and regulations, risk management, and how to optimize value. It is crucial for employees to develop a culture with a critical understanding of what information governance is and is not, as well as how it is different from other forms of management. Users must learn how to effectively classify data for protection, how to protect various data types, prevent data loss, conduct records management, and successfully leverage the data throughout the lifecycle.

Training Affects Culture

If culture is so critical to organizational success in the market, why do organizations fail to grasp the magnitude of repercussions a negative culture can have on the company? Get a successful culture right, and that positive culture can transform performance and sustain the company for many years. Get culture wrong, however, and the company will be fighting against the adverse effects for years to come. The specific ways a company chooses to complete regular activities are considered part of the culture; this includes training. Training drastically affects how the culture is created and maintained within the organization. It is only when employees are properly trained that they can feel empowered, encouraged, and confident in the skills and knowledge they each possess in support of the company objectives. For training to be beneficial it must meet the real needs of the enterprise and the employees, consider the current situation and prospects of the company, the projection of its requirements for managing future technologies, and necessary changes to worker characteristics (Gil et al., 2021). As the team is encouraged and supported by leadership, the members seek to improve themselves, the infusion of gaining new knowledge becomes contagious throughout the culture. The advantage of a positive culture is the growth among staff. Training needs to happen naturally and be ongoing to achieve a greatly motivated and productive team. Employees must want to improve their own skills; it cannot be forced. When learning is practiced, the staff become more productive and develops a positive attitude towards their work, because they know they are equipped for the challenges, they understand their duties, feel a sense of purpose, and may feel motivated to take on additional work responsibilities. As a direct result, morale and job satisfaction levels are likely to improve; meaning staff are happier, healthier, and more content in their work. As employees become accountable for their responsibilities, they more thoroughly understand the importance of their role and how they add value. This understanding is necessary to align to the mission of the company. Offering employees training gives them a reason to stay with the company and, more importantly, they'll stay because they honestly want to be there. A sense of belonging and connection to the mission cannot be overstated.

Hiring

Culture plays a considerable role in the hiring process and how the organization selects candidates. The culture persuades the hiring process and management on what characteristics to look for during the interview process. The selection and decision-making hiring methods are focused on selecting the best candidates who match the corporate culture, ethics, and political atmosphere (Swamy et al., 2023). Culture affects whether employees solicit referrals on the organization's behalf, the employer's reputation, and impacts associated hiring costs. Additionally, culture influences who applies to the open positions, if a candidate accepts the job offering, how long the individual stays with the company, and how employees talk about their employer. The wrong hire can cost the company through decreases in morale, extra effort and time, and unnecessary expense due to turnover costs. Additionally, an individual who is not a great fit can be disruptive to a cohesive team culture by causing animosity, feelings of discontent, and they even drive away committed employees, if left unchanged. Culture determines the entire work experience for the employee. This is true of the experience and feelings toward the employer long after the individual has left the organization. It is vital to create the right impression.

Additionally, once a selection has been made, a company's culture plays an even greater part in shaping the employees, how they integrate into the environment, what is socially acceptable, and how

Figure 3.
Fewings, N. (Photographer)
https://unsplash.com/photos/GpplHQ-fyvA

they spend their time at work. An attractive culture is a motivating factor for many candidates and can be the greatest justification for accepting an offer of employment and ultimately maintaining that employment. Applicants are sometimes willing to accept a lower salary or lesser benefits if the culture is a better fit with their personality. Ultimately, they want to feel as if they belong and fit in with the other team members. Employees that enjoy their work and have a clear understanding of expectations reduce the turnover rate. Reducing turnover saves an organization the expense and effort associated with the recruitment of new employees, wasted time, and prevents lowering team morale, because it provides the team with stability.

Training for Information Governance

Training is a way of helping new employees understand how the business operates and sets clear expectations of the employer. Additionally, training gives all team members a baseline understanding so that everyone is on the same page moving forward. As part of a comprehensive training strategy, the organization must help employees understand their personal decision rights and develop an accountability framework for information governance. This process is aimed to ensure the individual applies suitable and repetitive behaviors in the valuation, creation, storage, use, and archiving and deletion of information. This training also supports the business by ensuring that both legal and compliance-driven activities are embedded into the culture. Information governance training should include components such as the ability to conduct classification, use definitions, access management, records or retention management, safe document handling practices, information lifecycle, disposal, cybersecurity, and data governance practices. It is not enough to conduct training one time; training refreshers, additional supplemental content, and tracked annual training must be part of the program. This reminds employees that governance is important to the business and, subsequently, should be important to them as well.

Business Operations and Management

Business operations and management allows the organization to explore the value versus the risks in the data the company maintains. The gap between having the data and using the data lies in data governance (Burton, 2021). Business operations must safely determine how to best leverage the information to provide a strategic advantage in a competitive market. Additionally, the organization must be able to navigate complex laws and regulations concerning the data. To further complicate the issue, there is additional intricacy when handling data that crosses countries. The benefit of a culture that supports information governance is one that recognizes the process necessary to turn data into business information. This valuable information reduces risk, improves productivity and profitability, increases agility with better decision-making opportunities, provides better service to customers, streamlines efficiencies, reduces waste, and ensures consistency in the environment.

Ethical leaders are the optimal role models for employees by creating, inspiring, and maintaining a culture supported by the foundational aspects of trust and respect. Ethical theories on leadership approach the topic from two main concepts, the first includes the actions and behavior of leaders; and the second describes the character of leaders. Leadership behaviors and character are inherently intertwined. Ask someone to describe what they consider to be advantageous qualities of a good leader and the responses often include honesty, fairness, integrity, accountability, empathy, effective communication, and possesses strong morals and values. People fundamentally want to work for someone they consider having characteristics that align with their beliefs.

Roles and Responsibilities

Understanding who does what in the information governance lifecycle is a critical component to the policy implementation and processes that support a sustainable governance program. Once the organization has determined the need for governance, the next step is to determine how governance will be managed. For many organizations, this includes the creation of a committee that will continually support the governance program. The framework must define the information governance program's key positions, create an accountability structure, and define which individuals and departments will have autonomy as part of the initial implementation. Second, the group will support the ongoing maintenance of the governance program. For example, it is important to reflect and determine who might have the ultimate responsibility for the oversight of bodies of information. The organization must determine what the risks or consequences of mismanagement in this area are and how they can be mitigated. The creation of an information governance committee or team proves to be a valuable addition to the organization.

Although not all organizations implement the dedicated team approach, the value of the team is amplified when the team's roles and responsibilities are clearly outlined. The committee or team is responsible for the direction and operational business management of information governance projects within the organization. The team reviews information governance compliance-related issues and confirms the alignment of those activities with the related policies and procedures. The group also performs the policy-related concepts associated with the monitoring and enforcement of records management, as well as retention and disposal. Additionally, the team ensures the execution of information security policies and the overall management processes associated with security breach incidents. Organizations use information technology governance to help manage data breach and cybersecurity risks by fully defining the authority, structures, and processes that ensure strategic information technology decision-making delivers value, accountability, and integrity (Lankton et al., 2021). The group takes overall ownership of the information governance framework by acting as the primary supporting champion for information governance. Additionally, the committee will provide timely advice and reports to the Board or Chief Executive Officer (CEO) with respect to information incidents and risks, provide annual reports on the work being accomplished by the committee, understand how the strategic goals of the committee may be influenced by new risks, and how these risks may be managed appropriately based on the risk appetite of the company. The team provides a focus for the management of information governance at the Board level and owns the management of information governance and risk assessment processes within the committee. This includes the establishment of guidance and advice on the effectiveness of information risk management across the committee. It is evident that the importance of this committee cannot be understated.

Information governance-committee roles and responsibilities help to ensure that the organization's authoritative decisions related to information and data are made quickly, systematically, and effectively. The group must be multi-disciplinary in nature, including executives and other influential members, to be well received by the organization. Each delegate on the team will be required to adopt an important strategic role for information governance, and serves as the primary champion for governance on their respective team by utilizing their influential leadership to support the importance of this program. The committee must have the ability to delegate power, offer autonomy, provide guidance, define the roles and authority of those individuals on the committee, determine a frequency for meetings, and develop metrics to ensure progress is being made toward the company's objectives. Researchers have found that organizations respond to data breaches by establishing Board-level technology committees, and as technology committees become more established, the likelihood of a data breach decreases (Higgs et al., 2016). Technology committees of any kind must have roles and processes that review new product selection and technology strategies to ensure management goals and stakeholder expectations are appropriately aligned. Technology committees must have roles to support value delivery, resource management, risk management, and performance measurement to create operational efficiencies. The committee can help the organization members be more knowledgeable about risk mitigation and should thoroughly understand the significance and impact of their involvement in this critical oversight role.

Operational Efficiencies

Operational efficiency is an endless journey. Simply put, operational efficiency is the organization's capacity to decrease wasted effort, time, and materials, while still delivering superior quality service. For an organization to achieve operational efficiency, it is critical to not only recognize, but also resolve problems that prevent the company from achieving their objectives. The only way the company can achieve operational efficiencies for success is to create a shift in mindset. It can be intimidating for supervisors to try to identify areas where the agency is underperforming. The most fundamental aspect to remember is that every obstacle or challenge is an opportunity for growth and continuous progress. Investments to improve efficiency should not be viewed as a waste of time, effort, or resources, because these investments pay off in the long-term. Unfortunately, improvements will not happen instantly, it takes input from all departments and a steadfast commitment from employees. During the process, the organization must be responsive and open to input from both employees and external sources to continue advancing the efficiencies of the organization. This mindset of continual improvement of efficiencies fosters the maturity of employees and the agency.

Once the organization has established a culture committed to operational efficiencies and continuous improvement it must then seek to examine information and/or data processes. Data is an invaluable asset in today's digital information age. Effective data management is essential for achieving operational efficiencies, reducing costs, and improving overall performance. Data provides information to enhance transparency that allows the organization to better investigate and apply appropriate decision-making for future planning and resource deployment. Data assets improve productivity by serving as a tool used for decision-making; with data assets in hand, firms then can shift from a traditional experience-based management approach to a data-based approach, which is data-driven decision-making (Hu et al., 2022). A significant aspect of information or data management is information security to protect sensitive information from unauthorized access, use, disclosure, disruption, modification, or destruction.

Compliance

Compliance is simply concerned with following established rules and regulations. Compliance activities with accompanying regulations are created after corporate wrongdoings have been exposed or uncovered. These actions include fraud, management cover-ups, failures, and security breaches that are the direct result of ethical issues, poor management, and a toxic culture. Regulations are rules or laws created by government or authorities to control behaviors or the way business activities are conducted in a consistent and ethical manner (Mahanti, 2022). Non-compliance associated expenditures are those penalty fees that are a direct result of a failure to comply with rules, guidelines, regulations, procedures, policies, contract agreements, and other legal obligations that aim to ensure consistent ethical behaviors. Compliance requires good quality data and governance strategies to be in place. Early drivers of data governance originated as mandates in the compliance, legal, risk, and audit departments within organizations, and are one of the biggest business drivers of data governance today (Mahanti, 2022). Societies' reliance on data, analytics, and data-driven decisions is unlike anything seen before.

Organizations are under increasing amounts of inspection and scrutiny. There are countless government-imposed regulations, industry required standards, and company procedures that must be met. Data-imposed regulations are becoming much more frequent, and companies must ask for permission to collect data while, at the same time, providing transparency on what they do with the data (Vojvodic & Hitz, 2022). Companies recognize that non-compliance carries substantial penalties and leads to lost business opportunities and reputation, financial penalties, and even prison sentences. Organizations must conform to a range of guidelines, regulations, and industry standards, such as General Data Protection Regulation (GDPR), Health Insurance Portability and Accountability Act (HIPAA), and Payment Card Industry Data Security Standard (PCI DSS), which make it challenging to achieve and maintain compliance without a coordinated governance approach. A strong governance program empowers employees of the organization to observe and comply with all relevant laws, regulations, and industry standards for data management and information security. This commitment to governance and compliance embedded within the culture can significantly reduce the risk of regulatory fines and penalties while also protecting the organization's reputation within the industry. Compliance costs are significant in regulated industries and mainly justified and considered as a necessary cost of staying in business.

The model of utilizing what is considered an active compliance culture has developed from the understanding that the process of compliance means the organization is already striving to achieve industry best practices. The difference is the organization's commitment to continuous improvement and transparency that allows the organization to identify areas for improvement. The processes of automation and standardization inherent in an information governance program drives down operational costs, reduces the likelihood of non-compliance penalty fees, and allows the organization to identify areas of compliance where gains in performance can create a stronger marketplace performance opportunity. If an organization creates a culture of compliance, the culture can be utilized to drive the organization towards a competitive advantage by automatically adhering to industry-established best practices and procedures related to the governance of data. This model helps to minimize risks automatically.

Ethics and Compliance

Ethics and compliance concepts are two distinct subjects; however, the two topics are closely aligned. Both possess the ability to influence human decision-making processes. It is not possible to simply tell the organization to be ethical or to be compliant; ultimately the people who are making the daily decisions within the organization will determine whether that is the case. It is not enough to just assume that employees will make the best choices or make a choice that aligns to the organization's goals. Each person within the organization has their own sets of morals and values that have been developed and shaped since childhood. The leadership within the company must actively cultivate and foster those values that it wishes to have embodied in the culture of the organization.

Societies' reliance and use of the Internet facilitate transparency and citizen involvement and, as a result, the risks of unethical behavior being exposed are greater than ever. Although several ethical approaches emphasize the varying nuances in their definitions of ethical behavior in relation to compliance, ethics is often seen as a self-regulatory approach of adhering to moral practices beyond compliance (De Klerk, 2021). The combined term "ethics and compliance" is routinely used to refer to the aggregation of ethics and compliance functions and programs as a conceptual and structural collective (De Klerk, 2021). The interconnected relationship that exists between both ethics and compliance is complicated and risky in practice. Research confirms that compliant behavior can be enhanced significantly by higher ethical aspirations, and devotion to an ethical culture should come first in any ethics and compliance program to be effective (De Klerk, 2021). A strong ethics program that aims to reinforce ethical concepts can help to produce substantially better organizational outcomes by reducing tension, misconduct, and retaliation. Compliance-based programs motivate with the intent to inhibit, detect, and penalize legal violations. Ethics-based efforts combine integrity with a guided approach for adhering to the law, with values for an organizational culture that supports self-governing behavior. In the compliance-based approach, the key objective is to stop misconduct from happening, and in the ethics approach, it is to enable responsibility to make better decisions.

Risk

The goal of governance is not just the strategic vantage point, but also the overall reduction of risk. It is important to clarify the severity of impact that risks present to the business. Inherent and residual risks exist within all environments. Inherent risks are those risks that exist without any type of mitigation efforts, and residual risks exist within the environment after the mitigation efforts have been applied. Risks introduce complications, uncertainties, and penalties into the organization that make it more difficult to achieve objectives. The organizational settings surrounding risk matter, and the people's perception of risk is shaped by their inherent trust in the organization's ability to implement actions in decision making or their personal feelings of fairness in relation to the abilities needed to achieve organizational goals (Pettersen Gould, 2021). Pettersen Gould (2021) goes on to suggest these inherent perceptions of risk can lead to unrelenting ripple effects throughout the ranks, through which risks are amplified, shaping social perceptions and risk behavior. Risks can ultimately put a company out of business if left unmitigated.

Change adoption is complex and introduces risks to the organization. This is partly due to the underlying cultural effects, but also new processes that change the status quo. As employees learn new processes and technology, the change introduces new risks. It is imperative that the culture fosters a general understanding and has conviction to ensure employees fully understand what is being asked of them. Leaders must serve as role models by emulating behaviors they want others to develop by behaving differently and setting an example for others to follow. The organization must consciously develop talents and skills that support the new ways of performing work by reinforcing structures, processes, and systems that aim to wholly support the change. The change management process defines the need for the change being introduced, implements new procedures and policies for employees to follow, and allows the organization to monitor results that ensure the company is garnering the value it expects. The largest and most detrimental risk of any newly introduced change is that a new system or process will not work as intended and could potentially leave the company worse off. Negative impacts might include decreased morale, wasted money and resources, frustrations, and losing ground to competitors. As a result, risks related to changes must be thoroughly examined. Culture plays a significant part in the successful adoption of changes and, subsequently, a reduction in negatively perceived risks.

Culture change is the first step in helping to mitigate risks introduced through normal behaviors. The tone at the top matters. Leaders must set a message that resonates with the team. Good governance requires accountability, someone who will be the decision maker by identifying roles, responsibilities, accountabilities, and ensuring they are defined correctly. Simple and sustained communication that is collaborative, open feedback, and continuous development sounds easy enough to accomplish, but is often a source of failure. Leaders at the top mistakenly assume that just because they put information out to the masses that the communication has its desired effect. This is not always the case. Information can get lost in translation as it is passed through the ranks, the culture may not be the way the leadership team perceives it to be, the tone may come across as disingenuous, out of touch, or autocratic, which pushes the employee further from the goal of cultural acceptance. The best way to garner support is to be transparent by allowing those performing the work to help facilitate the decision-making. This decision-making provides a sense of ownership. When employees have a sense of ownership, they take on more accountability pertaining to the outcomes of those changes. As a result, employees are more committed to the successful adoption of changes and, by effect, they reduce risk, because they have a better understanding of the processes.

Information Governance Risk Management

One of the simplest things to remember is that risk is an undefined event. Risk is simply something that could happen at any time in the future; risk is not something that has already taken place. A corporate culture that does not fully understand or appreciate risk management activities, or does not devote the necessary resources to it, is unlikely to be successful. Information governance risk is an inherent risk in all organizational activities regardless of industry because all businesses handle data in some way. Information governance risk management strategies are the ongoing process of identifying information or data risks and developing the necessary plans to thoroughly address those risks to an acceptable level. Risk indicators to be monitored include identifying potential risks that could damage the organization or the company reputation; awareness of plausible weaknesses in the company's tools; and maintaining risk monitoring activities and awareness between risk assessments. Information governance risk management strategies are proactive. It is not enough to manage the information; risk management strategies must also look toward what additional information could be valuable in the future, and how the information may be used in new ways. The best information governance strategy plans include: a plan for what data is necessary and who has access to it; privacy is built into the plan; the plan assigns responsibility, and the culture has a clear understanding that effective information governance is imperative for informing risk approaches and providing assurance that risk management is effective. Effective risk management means that the company will experience fewer unwarranted shocks and surprises, better planning and utilization of resources, the ability to avoid distractions, and it will have a better reaction to crises that do arise. The biggest benefit of effective information governance is to help identify and evaluate risks. The more reliable the information one has at their fingertips, the better the risks will be defined.

Frameworks

One-way organizations can utilize tools to strengthen their information governance program is by using frameworks. Frameworks provide industry recognized structure and support through repeatable actions. There are many models or frameworks to explore but choosing the right framework for the business is critical. Additionally, the framework must have executive sponsorship and support to be implemented effectively. The support from leadership is instrumental to ensure that the program has access to the support, resources, commitment, and funding needed for successful adoption. The right level of sponsorship is vital for creating an environment where the sponsor can align the governance model to the organizational objectives. The sponsor will also be critical in helping address the communication messages and channels that deliver the meaning and importance of the framework and governance model in a consistent manner. Frameworks such as Control Objectives for Information and Related Technologies (COBIT) and the Information Governance Reference Model (IGRM) aim to remove complexities by bridging the gap often found in business.

Control Objectives for Information and Related Technologies (COBIT)

The COBIT framework was created by the Information Systems Audit and Control Association (COBIT, 2024). ISACA offers effective governance by providing toolkits, case studies, industry news articles, implementation resources, and supplement videos. COBIT helps enterprises identify why and create the outcomes necessary for information governance. The framework identifies business process areas where project plans need to be implemented. To help the organization identify which COBIT objectives need to be integrated the framework allows the organization to select processes based on relevancy to the organizational needs and identifies which stakeholders need to be involved. A timeline is created for implementation and the framework helps to formulate a strategy using templates and customization to include process activities in a phased approach focused on delivery milestone achievements. Finally, metrics and dashboards allow leadership to monitor performance and adjust activities as necessary. The COBIT toolkit provides organizations with substantial material including an executive summary, overview, governance management objectives practices and activities document, an awareness diagnostic, a responsible, accountable, consulted, and informed (RACI) by role matrix, and outline with the reference model of governance and management objectives. COBIT is specifically designed to work with other implementations and direction is provided to help organizations integrate industry standards, guidelines, regulations, and best practices unique to each organizations governance solution (COBIT, 2024).

In one case study example an organization was able to leverage COBIT to implement information security. The study identified an important step for this organization was to obtain an assessment of the current state of IT governance using a nontechnical, business-focused assessment independent of various competing control frameworks. The organization determined the COBIT governance framework would be used with the associated process assessment techniques to create a maturity model as a means of measurement for progress (COBIT, 2024). Because the system started and ended with COBIT, the consultancy successfully employed COBIT as a "container" or "wrapper'' to allow it to integrate and enforce various competing standards within the enterprise (COBIT, 2024). The main advantage of using the COBIT framework in this case study was the ability to implement a business-focused framework and practical tools that more closely align policy to detailed controls. The company was able to provide supported answers more effectively and help the organization understand how to best answer the questions of how and why organizations should protect information within the organization. This allowed the organization to better align the cost of the suggested security controls to the perceived risk at a business process level rather than based on the technical controls themselves.

Information Governance Reference Model

One example of this is the Information Governance Reference Model (IGRM) that aims to balance value, risk, and cost through a unified approach involving security, privacy, risk, information technology, business, legal, and records information management (EDRM, 2023). The IGRM framework enables cross functional executive dialogue that ultimately serves as a catalyst for defining a unified governance approach to information and showcases the dependencies across these groups for legal compliance and defensible disposal (EDRM, 2023). The IGRM framework defines links value and duty to information assets as a responsibility model rather than a document or case lifecycle model to identify the stakeholders and highlights the intersection dependence across these stakeholders (EDRM, 2023). Information governance is often difficult to establish because stakeholders are not in alignment with objectives. Each group is competing for limited resources and prioritizes the needs of their section. Governance provides an opportunity to help the three groups of stakeholders come to a common understanding. Stakeholder groups include business owners who are responsible for operating the business, the information technology department who is responsible for implementation, and the legal and risk management teams who preserve the value of the information to ensure compliance (EDRM, 2023).

Organization information management can only be successful if the primary business owner and stakeholder is also the primary business user of that data. The business owner must create and establish value by also understanding the legal and compliance implications. Information technology teams must then manage the privacy and security of the information. It is only when all three groups are in alignment that the organization can find the value necessary to achieve success. Figure 4 illustrates the importance of information management at all stages of the information lifecycle – from its creation through its ultimate disposition (EDRM, 2023). This diagram helps the organization to outline specific, repeatable, and actionable steps to implement information governance programs.

Figure 4.
EDRM.net

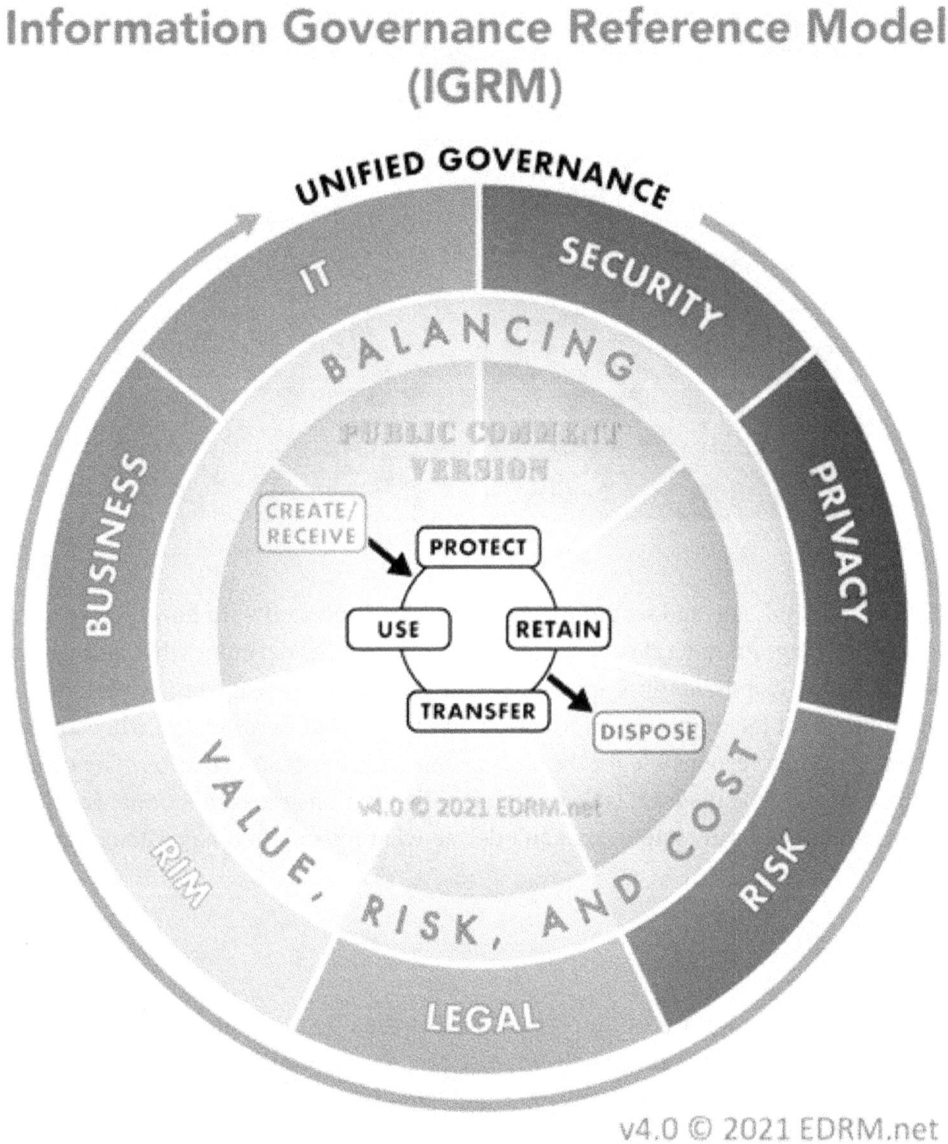

At the core is information, data is the most valuable asset when utilized appropriately by the business. Starting with the business operations, the organization must have an active interest in information or data that is proportional to its value. This means the degree to which the information can assist in increasing profit or the existence of the organization. When the value of data is no longer useful to the operation objectives, the business might lose interest in managing, cleaning, or paying for storage options. One of the things that the IGRM does well is it helps the organization to distinguish value separate from regulatory compliance or IT effectiveness. The diagram defines the individual business group's responsibility and specific value of information; all data doesn't have value and the value of data isn't

Figure 5.
Fewings, N. (Photographer).
https://unsplash.com/photos/GpplHQ-fyvA

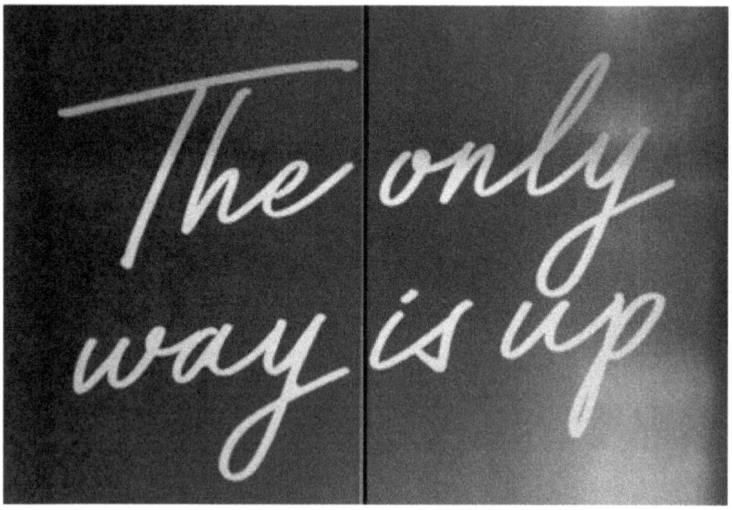

constant (EDRM, 2023). Legal and record management are associated with how the organization plans to manage risk. The diagram reiterates that legal is responsible for defining what and when to collect; and for how long before disposal is appropriate. IT relies solely on legal and records retention to provide specific guidelines about the duties for information including what they are and when and where those obligations end. IT is only responsible for the storing and securing of information. The most significant and noteworthy aspects of the diagram is that without collaboration across functional areas and a unified governance approach, IT doesn't know and can't define what information has value or not.

CONCLUSION

This chapter thoroughly demonstrates that if one ignores the effect of culture on IT governance, then practically everything that is done from a governance perspective could be doomed despite the best efforts. A governance program ultimately adds infinite value to established information management by introducing alignment with business stakeholders, and through cross-functional handling of data issues necessary to be successful. No two information governance programs will be the same, and they should not be. Each company has a unique culture and, as such, the customs and traditions are varied across each individual organization. Implementing a governance framework will be unique to the organization, but any information governance program should aim to support the achievement of the company objectives by using an industry supported framework adoption. The corporate culture is largely influential in supportive enterprise IT governance and is as substantial and an important a stream of work as is the real implementation effort needed to complete projects. In conclusion, creating a stronger culture that supports the adoption and embracement of an information governance framework is essential to the sustainment of the organization. It is not enough to just create a program, policies, or a framework to be successful. Information governance activities that organizations engage in are used to increase the worth of the information while minimizing risks and costs of retaining that information. The organizational leadership must actively and continually promote the importance of information governance for the foundational principles to persist within the culture. Culture is everything when ensuring compliance, and best practices are not only developed, but those habits are utilized daily. As new and changing privacy laws and regulations make achieving compliance difficult, a culturally embedded information governance program has become more imperative than ever before. Organizations must focus resources on managing their information to the best of their ability. Organizations that establish these principles within their culture effectively reduce their privacy-associated risks, better control costs, increase effectiveness, improve data-driven decision-making for better business outcomes, and foster a successful trusting environment for the company to flourish. Governance starts and ends with the culture.

REFERENCES

Burton, S. (2021). Data governance: The path to a data-driven culture. *Applied Marketing Analytics, 6*(4), 298-308. https://www.ingentaconnect.com/content/ hsp/ama/2021/00000006/0000004/art00002

COBIT: Control objectives for Information Technologies. (n.d.). ISACA. https://www.isaca.org/resources/cobit

D'Arcy, J., Adjerid, I., Angst, C. M., & Glavas, A. (2020). Too good to be true: Firm social performance and the risk of data breach. *Information Systems Research, 31*(4), 1200–1223. doi:10.1287/isre.2020.0939

De Klerk, J. J. (2021). Combining ethics and compliance: A systems psychodynamic inquiry into praxis and outcomes. *Business Ethics, the Environment & Responsibility, 30*(3), 432–446. doi:10.1111/beer.12336

De Klerk, J. J. (2021). Combining ethics and compliance: A systems psychodynamic inquiry into praxis and outcomes. *Business Ethics, the Environment & Responsibility, 30*(3), 432–446. doi:10.1111/beer.12336

Di Miceli da Silveira, A. (2022). Corporate governance and ethical culture: Do boards matter? *Review of Managerial Science, 16*(4), 1085–1116. doi:10.1007/s11846-021-00476-7

Fallon, N. (2023). *35 leadership quotes to Inspire You.* Business News Daily. https://www.businessnewsdaily.com/7481-leadership-quotes.html

Gil, A. J., García-Alcaraz, J. L., & Mataveli, M. (2021). The effect of learning culture on training transfer: Empirical evidence in Spanish teachers. *The International Journal of Human Resource Management, 32*(5), 1038-1061. https://doi.org/. 2018.1505763 doi:10.1080/09585192

Gui, L., Lei, H., & Le, P. B. (2022). Determinants of radical and incremental innovation: The influence of transformational leadership, knowledge sharing and knowledge-centered culture. *European Journal of Innovation Management, 25*(5), 1221–1241. doi:10.1108/EJIM-12-2020-0478

Higgs, J. L., Pinsker, R. E., Smith, T. J., & Young, G. R. (2016). The relationship between board-level technology committees and reported security breaches. *Journal of Information Systems, 30*(3), 79–98. doi:10.2308/isys-51402

Hu, C., Li, Y., & Zheng, X. (2022). Data assets, information uses, and operational efficiency. *Applied Economics, 54*(60), 6887–6900. doi:10.1080/00036846.2022.2084021

Huy, D. T. N. (2021). culture: Communication methods. *Journal of Organizational Culture, Communications and Conflict, 25*(1), 1-2. https://www.proquest.com/ docview/2519897270?accountid=12085&pq-origsite=summon&forcedol=true

Information governance reference model. (2023, March 24). EDRM. https://edrm.net/resources/frameworks-and-standards/information-governance-reference-model/

Kurzhals, C., Graf-Vlachy, L., & König, A. (2020). Strategic leadership and technological innovation: A comprehensive review and research agenda. *Corporate Governance*, *28*(6), 437–464. doi:10.1111/corg.12351

Lankton, N., Price, J. B., & Karim, M. (2021). Cybersecurity breaches and the role of information technology governance in audit committee charters. *Journal of Information Systems*, *35*(1), 101–119. doi:10.2308/isys-18-071

Machado de Sousa, E., & Shahzad, A. (2022). Data loss prevention from a malicious insider. *Journal of Computer Information Systems*, *62*(6), 1101–1111. doi:10.1080/08874417.2021.1980748

Mahanti, R. (2022). Compliance, data, quality, and governance. *EDPACS*, *66*(2), 20–25. doi:10.1080/07366981.2022.2026575

Nisar, Q. A., Nasir, N., Jamshed, S., Naz, S., Ali, M., & Ali, S. (2021). Big data management and environmental performance: Role of big data decision-making capabilities and decision-making quality. *Journal of Enterprise Information Management*, *34*(4), 1061–1096. doi:10.1108/JEIM-04-2020-0137

Pettersen Gould, K. (2021). Organizational risk: "Muddling through" 40 years of research. *Risk Analysis*, *41*(3), 456–465. doi:10.1111/risa.13460 PMID:32088928

Shahriari, M., & Allameh, S. M. (2020). Organizational culture and organizational learning: Does high performance work systems mediate? *Journal of Workplace Learning*, *32*(8), 583–597. doi:10.1108/JWL-03-2020-0047

Singh, H. P., & Alhulail, H. N. (2023). Information technology governance and corporate boards' relationship with companies' performance and earnings management: A longitudinal approach. *Sustainability (Basel)*, *15*(8), 6492. doi:10.3390/su15086492

Swamy, C. J., Kethana, A., & Pradeep, M. P. (2023). A study on recruitment and selection process in the manufacturing industry. *Advances in Management*, *16*(2), 1–9. doi:10.25303/1602aim0109

Vojvodic, M., & Hitz, C. (2022). Relation of data governance, customer-centricity and data processing compliance. *Central European Business Review*, *11*(5), 109–148. doi:10.18267/j.cebr.310

Walker, R. (2021). Communication perspectives on organizational culture and organizational identification. *International Journal of Business Communication*, *58*(2), 147–151. doi:10.1177/2329488420957073

Zhang, Q., Sun, X., & Zhang, M. (2022). Data matters: A strategic action framework for data governance. *Information & Management*, *59*(4), 103642. doi:10.1016/j.im.2022.103642

Chapter 5
Strategic Information Governance Review:
Exploring Data Management for Effective Business Op. Intelligence in a Data-Centric Environment

Tereza Raquel Merlo
https://orcid.org/0000-0002-2042-5415
University of North Texas, USA

ABSTRACT

This book chapter, "Strategic Information Governance: Optimizing Business Operations, Business Intelligence, and Data Management," explores the dynamic intersection of information governance and organizational functionality. Grounded in an exhaustive literature review, it guides businesses in enhancing operations, fortifying business intelligence, and refining data management. From principles to practical applications, the chapter emphasizes the symbiotic relationship between information governance and business operations. It provides actionable insights, empowering businesses to strategically leverage information governance for optimized processes. Addressing the evolving data landscape, it offers proven strategies for aligning governance with efficient data practices, ensuring compliance, security, and accessibility. This chapter is an indispensable resource for decision-makers, providing a comprehensive guide for organizations navigating the complexities of strategic information governance in today's dynamic business environment.

INTRODUCTION

Businesses in all segments of society are relying heavily on data processing capabilities for decision making, product management, and pipeline growth. Unquestionably, data is recognized as a critical asset deployed by business intelligence in order to drive opportunities, leverage data assets, and ensure competitiveness. Computing languages, like Sequential Query Language (SQL), Data Mining and Warehousing, and data visualization tools that rely on a Cloud Computing (CC) based platform are ex-

DOI: 10.4018/979-8-3693-0472-3.ch005

amples of how information technology is moving from an on-premises based platform to a cloud-based platform as a response to the need for flexibility, reliability, and security in a data management strategy. In such a competitive, globalized, and powerfully technological corporate environment, the importance of effective data management and knowledge production are essential for the promotion of innovation, operations improvement, and problem-solving.

The generation and acceleration of data analytics frameworks as guiding principles for managers can enable capabilities and optimize client relations and business transformations. Successful data analytics and management is proven to reduce costs, expand product lines, improve teamwork dynamics, and ultimately increase revenue. These aspects cannot be ignored in a society driven by data, big data, and oriented by business intelligence approaches. It can be argued that data governance is a new term -or revised term- with a perspective and implications for data as an asset.

Davenport and Harris (2007) described how some companies gained a sustainable competitive advantage through analytics, defending that companies gain a new dimension and enhance opportunities through insights that resulted from data analytics and superior data management strategies. Organizational interest in big data and knowledge management has been growing, and significant business and process improvements are linked to the organization's ability to manage intangible and tangible resources, which is reflected in economic gain. The efficient adoption, implementation, and utilization of knowledge assets all impact the speed and quality of decision-making processes and complex data analytics for performance evaluations within a business.

The recognizable increase in the complexity of issues related to big data has been prompting a series of ethical, legal, regulatory, and behavioral challenges regarding big data management and governance (Ballard et al., 2014). For instance, Das (2015) elaborates on the "single point of access to the tacit and explicit knowledge that supports members of the institution or organizations in all access of their learning," (p.26) and drew focus on the following aspects when determining governance ideals: marketing, sales, distribution, support, and finance. All of these must be considered in determining the best strategy for approaching business decisions based on customer lifestyle and customer interaction.

Data governance is a collection of processes, roles, policies, standards, and metrics that ensure the effective and efficient use of information in enabling an organization to achieve its goals. Data governance defines user accessibility (who can take what action, upon what data, in what situations) and problem-solving (using what methodological approach). The increase in recognition of the significance of data governance for businesses and the economy, including advancements in data management (Big Data, Artificial Intelligence (AI), Cloud Computing, Data Analytics and Visualization Tools) have resulted in an exceptional demand for information access and sharing and knowledge production. This phenomenon triggers discussions about the effectiveness of layers of information privacy, information quality, information and data analytics strategies and tools, information access and sharing, and knowledge production, all of which ultimately define innovation and competitiveness in organizations and society in general.

In light of the aforementioned challenges there are limitless possibilities within the realm of data management that surpass data governance roadmaps and involve complex solutions in business intelligence strategies. Hence, in today's data-centric knowledge economy businesses need frameworks and governance roadmaps to effectively leverage data to guide their biggest decisions. This article is organized as follows: First, an introduction to the current discourse on data, data management, data governance and the motivation for this paper is presented; In the next section, first the key elements of the different perspectives on the business data governance roadmap are laid out. Then, a general criterion for a conceptual Data Governance Roadmap for Business Intelligence: The Assess, Track, Design, Implement

(ATDI) framework is presented, preceding the conclusions where the authors argue the importance of proper data governance processes, impacts on Key Performance Indicators, and the overall business performance, suggesting that further research should be conducted in the form of an exploratory study to test and validate the proposed roadmap, and continue the dialogue surrounding data governance and business intelligence.

This study aims to contribute to the discussion about data governance and the relevance of operative data governance strategies that are believed to strongly impact business operations and organizational capabilities. Thus, presenting the ATDI conceptual framework, the authors hope to inspire empirical studies to test the theory in the field and expand studies and research in the area and better discuss results and practical implications. It explores the integration of information governance as a strategic approach to enhance business operations, leverage business intelligence, and optimize data management. It delves into the synergies between these aspects, emphasizing the crucial role of strategic information governance in achieving efficiency and effectiveness across diverse business functions. The study seeks to provide insights into methodologies, tools, and best practices for organizations aiming to align their information governance strategies with broader business goals, matching strategy and structure in data and information governance and operations.

THEORETICAL BACKGROUND

Information Governance Fundamentals in the Business Context

Gartner (2009) defines information governance as a subset of corporate governance, claiming that "information governance should not be thought of as part of "IT governance." Why? Because such a view reinforces the notion that information is the responsibility of IT. It isn't. [...] Information governance is NOT the province of IT, or at least not the province of IT alone." (p. 3). The author defends that the objective of information governance is to improve and accelerate decision making and organizational processes; therefore, eliminating or reducing costs and maximizing organizational performance.

Practitioners and scientists in the field have defined information governance "as a collection of capabilities or practices for the creation, capture, valuation, storage, usage, control, access, archival, and deletion of information over its life cycle. (Luftman, Ben-Zvi, 2011; Peterson, 2004; Tallon, 2010). Exponential data growth, most notably in recent years when the pace of data growth has begun to outpace the rate of decline in hardware costs causing total storage spending to climb, has transformed information governance and its related practices into a top issue for senior business and IS management.

Data Governance and Management Framework in Business

Data is unquestionably the main force driving successful business nowadays and the advances in technological apparatuses have dramatically affected the way in which data is generated, retrieved, processed, and used in organizations and beyond. In organizations of different segments, the challenge becomes how to successfully -and timely- adopt organizational systems, operations, technologies, and policies that will embrace data management and processing strategies that will drive innovation, superior customer relationship management, and profitability. The consolidation of a dynamic and constantly evolving work environment that heavily relies on complex datasets and artificial intelligence imposes a new critical way of doing business and strategically use business intelligence approaches for competitiveness. The intricated process of access large amounts of data and analyze business requirements accordingly is no longer an alternative for organizations, but a decisive factor in its survival, valuable decision-making, and overall profitable organizational performance.

Panian (2010) argues that "data governance is evolving as a practice today; its roots should be reviewed in the broader context of corporate and information technology (IT) governance." (p. 939). The author emphasizes that data is the most important asset in organization. According to Panian (2010): "data governance has emerged as an important discipline in its own right. The goals of data governance are to: • Ensure data meets the needs of the business. • Protect, manage and develop data as a valued enterprise asset. • Lower the costs of managing data." (p. 939). Panian and Spremic (2007) acknowledge the recent survey conducted by The Data Warehousing Institute (TDWI) highlighting the increasing number of organizations investing in formal data governance initiatives. According to this study: "Eight percent of the 750 responding organizations have deployed a data governance initiative; 17 percent are designing or implementing one; and 33 percent are considering it (p.940-941). Results of this survey indicate that data governance is an emerging practice area with a great potential for expansion in business.

The literature review focusing on data governance reveals a clear distinction between data, information, and knowledge. Although the three terms are often used interchangeably, the hierarchical and cyclic process in which each aspect is unique within the information systems process determines the level of effectiveness of each in the generation and consumption of knowledge in organizations. The seminal work of Ackoff (1989), articulating the data-information-knowledge-wisdom (DIKW) hierarchy and the theory presented by Nelson and Staggers (2014) hierarchy seeks to bring about a consensus on the definition of the terms and a better understanding of knowledge hierarchy and the transformation process. The author defines information in terms of data, knowledge in terms of information, and wisdom in terms of knowledge, with little reference to the context surrounding wisdom. In the data to wisdom progression model illustrated in **figure 1:** The data to wisdom progression model, below provides a visual framework which projects the richness and complexity of the interactions across and within the data to wisdom continuum, thereby appreciating the importance of context to the application and production of knowledge and the ultimate achievement of wisdom by individuals in organizations.

Data is defined as "a representation of an object" (Miller et al. (2001); as "unprocessed raw representations of reality" (Faucher, et al., 2008) as comprising "facts, observations or perceptions, representing raw numbers or assertions and may therefore be devoid of context, meaning or intent" (Becerra-Fernandez and Sabherwal, 2015, p. 17). In reference to the analyses of prevailing definitions of data, the authors argue that the multifaceted nature of data leads to different perspectives about its management, and governance defines its application. More importantly, for data to be meaningful context is important- it is intrinsic. Information refers to the organized data that is presented in a contextual and meaningful manner, once evolved to a level of comprehension, and understanding that applies concepts and deeper level of insight and interpretation becomes knowledge. In the higher level of intellect and maturity in data processing, wisdom is found, applied in the ability to process, and discern complex scenarios.

Describing Data Governance and Management, and the DAMA International Guide to Data Management -DAMA-DMBOOK

DAMA International (DAMA), in its Guide to the Data Management Body of Knowledge (DAMA-DMBOK) presents Data Management as the overreaching term that describes the processes used in "the

Figure 1. The data to wisdom progression model
Source: Merlo and Makani, 2020. Adapted from: Using Operative Data Governance Roadmaps for Business Process Management Success: The Role of Leadership and the Impact of Information Technology Adoption.

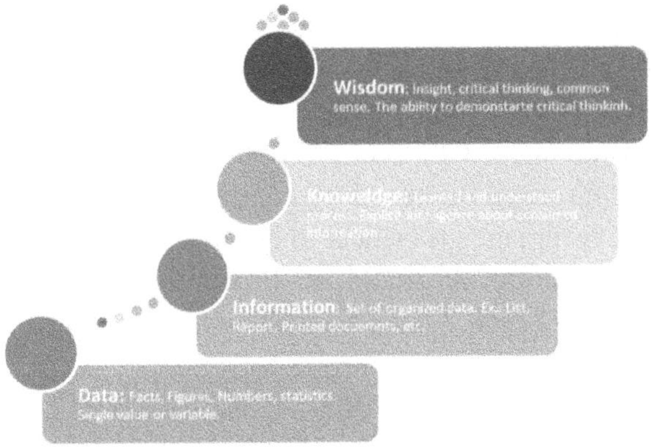

development, execution, and supervision of plans, policies, programs, and practices that deliver, control, protect, and enhance the value of data and information assets throughout their lifecycles" (DAMA, 2017, p.17). Notably, data management processes overlap and interact within 11 data management knowledge areas, the core of which being data governance described as the DAMA-DMBOK2 Guide Knowledge Area Wheel:

- Data architecture
- Data Modeling Design
- Data Storage & Operations
- Data Security
- Data Integration &Interoperability
- Documents & Content
- Reference & Master data
- Data Warehousing & Business Intelligence
- Meta-Data
- Data Quality (DAMA, 2017)

Data governance broadly refers to the policies and procedures that determine how and by whom data can be accessed and used. This concept has grown more important as more and more data is created and exists digitally, and there is a greater public understanding that much of this data is not under the control of [the individuals] who generate it. (Kariotis et al., 2020). Smith (2020) notes that the most adopted definition of data governance defines data governance as "the practice of organizing and implementing policies, procedures, and standards for the effective use of an organization's structured/unstructured information assets" (p. 1) In this study we define data governance as the process of managing the availability and usability of data, while ensuring that its integrity is maintained and kept safe. In this way, we recognize Data Governance "as the coordinating knowledge area" (DAMA, 2017). Data governance is underscored by the organizational policies and standards that are put in place and is "needed to solve data inconsistencies experienced in most organizations. That is where information accessible by various departments in an organization is not the same" (Rouse, 2020, p. 1).

Nevertheless, data governance "guides all other data management functions" through the exercise of authority and control over the management of data (DAMA, 2017). The data governance framework revolves around the practice of data management and authority over it, wrought to increase the value of data and minimize its risks and costs. Abraham, Schneider, and Vom Brocke (2019) proclaim that: "The growing data volumes from diverse sources cause data inconsistencies that need to be identified and addressed before decisions are made based on incorrect data. Companies introduce more self-service reporting and analytics, which create the need for a common understanding of data across the organization." (p.1). Effective data governance is critical to ensure secure capture, storage, and availability of high-quality data, enabling successful integrated data-driven decision making with measurable outcomes. Consequently, effective data governance involves a concerted, ongoing effort that is executed by people enabled by processes and supported by technologies.

However, despite the growing importance of data governance, the current view on this topic is fragmented. Publications address data governance with a focus on specific decision domains such as data quality, data security, and data life. For instance, Abraham et al. (2019) approach data governance as a mix of various mechanisms to help plan and control data management activities. Those data management mechanisms "comprise formal structures connecting business, IT, and data management functions, formal processes and procedures for decision-making and monitoring, and practices supporting the active participation of and collaboration among stakeholders." (p. 12). The authors base their approach on information technology governance theories, defending the three aspects of data governance structural mechanisms: (a) structural, (b) procedural, and (c) relational, describing the roles and responsibilities of each one.

Structural governance encompasses the allocation of decision-making authority. Abraham et al. (2019) describes it as the body that comprises "the executive sponsor, data governance leader, data owner, data steward, data governance council, data governance office, data producer, and the data consumer" (p. 12). The procedural mechanism aims "to ensure that data is recorded accurately, held securely, used effectively, and shared appropriately." (Borgman et al, 2016, p. 4903). Abraham et al. (2019) affirms that: "They comprise (i) the data strategy, (ii) policies, (iii) standards, (iv) processes, (v) procedures, (vi) contractual agreements, (vii) performance measurement, (viii) compliance monitoring, and (ix) issue management." (p. 12). The relational governance framework relates to data strategy, policies, procedures, processes, and standards; performance measurements tools, compliance monitoring, and issue management (Abraham et al., 2019, p. 429).

It is important to note, therefore, that data governance is multi-layered that includes Executive & Board Leadership, Data Governance Committee, data Stewards, Data Architects & Programmers, DBAs & Systems Administrators, data Access control system, and EDW. Those layers will enable a superior flow of data and information, allowing an easier processing by data analysts, and finally the end users that are engaged in what is seemingly hierarchical data access and control but could organically and efficiently complement each other in the process of giving data a meaning and purpose whilst creating a roadmap.

Effective data governance is often characterized by various challenges, such as demonstrating the value achieved by implementing a governance program, evidencing the correlation between data consistency and effectiveness and its challenges translating to reporting (Rouse, 2020). Additionally, multiple data users represent risks of data misuse. Complete data governance is built upon three main bases: policies, processes, and organizational technologies. These three instruments are combined to symbolize knowledge management programs. Data governance efforts are, therefore, important in improving integrity issues that often corrupt business intelligence in an organization, making it challenging to report information correctly. The data governance function facilitates the enterprise reporting, enabling organizations to make appropriate and consistent policies and accurately manage data, which will result in solid data management systems that are reliable for daily business processes and operations, impacting organizational processes and capabilities (Mikalef, Krogstie, van de Wetering, Pappas, Giannakos, 2018).

An ill-intended random user could access and utilize data in a mischievous manner by running afoul of data privacy and the large and complex dataset, which often causes data governance to periodically assess performance, needs, pitfalls, and challenges. The mixed nature of various forms of data necessities is based on a range of data platforms' needs that are often expensive and complex in nature, causing issues with user-interface interaction and business performance, particularly when businesses need to expand data storage capability, for example.

Kariotis et al. (2020) discuss the shifting trends of data governance "from institutional to individual" through the examination of "four case-studies on health data platforms" (Kariotis et al., 2020, p. 1), arguing that data governance broadly refers to the policies and procedures that encompass the understanding of how and by whom data can be accessed and used. This concept has grown more important as more and more data is created and exists/persists digitally, as there is a greater public understanding that "much of these data are not under the control of [the individuals] who generate it" (Kariotis et al., 2020, p. 3).

The authors continue by asserting that one of the most important tools being used to tackle the data governance issue is "the implementation of patient [or personalized knowledge or information] portals" (Kariotis et al., 2020, p. 6). The impact of the increased use of personalized knowledge portals on the healthcare field is that more data is being generated and added and that patients will have the increased ability to actively participate in the conversation about their use of data and clinicians and healthcare providers will have a larger data set to work with, leading to the need for more policies and procedures because "health services and health regulators [will need to] manage this [avalanche of] crowdsourced data and knowledge" (Kariotis et al., 2020, p. 4). This represents a new dynamic within the field that never had to be dealt with in such a large-scale way in the pre-digital era.

Moreover, Tripathi (2017) advocates that data value is strictly dependable on its reliability. The author highlights data value to research activities, arguing that data are valuable resources when properly stored, accessible, used, and built for the future in academic work, research, and for scientific purposes. Regarding business use of data, the author defends that knowledge management is a critical process in organizations and that the need to effectively manage data, metadata, and perform auditing are a guarantee of success in achieving goals. It is important to understand that there are layers of knowledge and data management in organizations that are simultaneously linked to the level of sensitivity of data content in the organization. This phenomenon of layering data will result in the need to create different knowledge portals to manage what Tripathi (2017) classifies as sensitive and non-sensitive information. The use of a knowledge portal in data management "entails all activities and processes which are undertaken or done to ensure that research data is properly documented, organized, stored, archived and curated so that it is available for access, use and reuse whenever the need arises after the research has been done and reported"(Tripathi, 2017, p.2).

Tripathi (2017) argues that organizations should adopt a universal structure to manage data, where data governance comes in as "the exercise of decision-making and authority for data-related matters including internal standards, metadata, and formulation of policies, guidelines for all the stakeholders to follow for describing organizing, preserving, accessing and reusing the research data" (Tripathi, 2017, p.2). The proper data governance process will allow organizations to access and update information, create privacy policies, and the recognition for information owners/updaters that will ensure data security and integrity. With the growing amount of information, it is essential to have a repository where knowledge can be managed easily and with friendly access. Methodically, adoption and use of data governance includes the evaluation and proper use of an information repository and user-centered analysis, and therefore, a superior assessment of how data can help organizations to improve performance and outcomes.

Another relevant aspect of data governance and sharing is approached by Milne & Brayne (2020) who, in a similar approach to Tripathi (2017), stress that data can be trusted as the tool that governs it. Data trusts have "structure, governance, and operating practices [that] make sharing of data possible in a fair, safe, and equitable way" (Milne & Brayne 2020, p. 2). Ideally, this trust would be co-designed by multiple sources and would consider the preferences of patients and stakeholders, as well as families and the wider public (Milne & Brayne 2020). The largest hurdle (and most important tool for any instance of data governance) is trust, "If the users/participants do not trust the governance of their data, the system fails." (Milne & Brayne 2020, p. 2).

Attard and Brennan (2018) discuss the challenges in value-driven data governance, defining data governance as "the exercise of authority and control which includes the planning, monitoring and enforcement over the management of data assets" (p. 2). Data governance helps businesses set policies and procedures for data assets, which are required to ensure security, accountability, and efficiency. In the article, the authors present the case of MyVolts to highlight some of the challenges of value driven data governance. The first challenge mentioned is the quantification of the value of data as it is being acquired. This is a challenge "because without measuring the value of the data the company risks losing money and/or effort that goes into the data acquisition process." (Attard &Brennan, 2018, p. 4).

An additional challenge is to determine what makes data valuable, which is relative and dependent on different contexts of use, where data is valuable now, and might not be relevant for the next user or next problem. As the authors mention in the article, the "data need to be reliable, timely, relevant, accurate, with good potential for impact once it's used and preferably unique to the company." (Attard & Brennan, 2018, p. 4). Furthermore, to optimize data governance in businesses, as the authors suggest, "data storage should have different areas where data that is more valuable can be stored in more reliable and secure storage while less valuable data can be stored using cheaper options, and sensitive data can be restricted to be used by employees with a higher user grade." (Attard &Brennan, 2018, p. 8). Prioritizing data assets depending on how valuable they are to the business leads to higher impact and profits.

Characteristically, "data are managed in the context of how they serve a particular application, rather than how they serve the strategic interests of the overall organization." (Panian, 2010, p.939), resulting in business and technological data governance policies and practices that are designed around information systems and multiples applications disregarding the core of the data, the business goals and strategies, and the desired outcomes with data use, retrieval, and sharing. This phenomenon of data technology prompts individual data-centered use and therefore issues with organizational processes to manage data in the context of corporate-centered.

Data management must contemplate a few critical aspects: line of business, customers' needs and demands, business strategic planning and goals, information technology resources available, organizational culture, and leadership. Those factors will determine the level of engagement and commitment with efficient data governance policies and practices that will be aligned with the core of the business in a way that will leverage resources. Artificial intelligence tools will enable business intelligence approaches and the maximization of data consumption by individuals in organization, driving performance and prompting: "Growing revenue by increasing cross-sell/up-sell rates and improving retention among existing customers with a deep understanding of their existing customers. • Lowering costs by increasing operational efficiency with business process automation and eliminating redundancy. • Ensuring compliance with external regulations and internal governance policies by streamlining the collection of reporting data and increasing auditability" (Panian, 2010, p. 939).

Lazaroiu et al (2018) stresses that the General Data Protection Regulations, GDPR, lays the ground for organizations aiming at documenting processes to improve compliance, train employees, conduct data audit, change data management policies, work with vendors, and IT budget towards allocating resources and implement solutions -hardware and software, and humans- to reallocate and move data from the premise to the cloud, as an example of a digital data management initiative that attends to the customer most recent demands for high quality and faster access to data of quality that will lead to better decisions in business units. The authors defend that: "more reliable data, makes the organization's data rapidly actionable and valuable, will provide better customer knowledge and marketing, and will accelerate the development of new products and services." (p. 137).

IT governance is a pivotal aspect of the data governance-and quality- process and serves in the overall organization. Therefore, its practice is normally designed around organizational applications not its data (Panian, 2010) resulting in many companies to neglect solid data governance structure that will contemplate data format, availability, accessibility, security, businesses drivers, etc. The study of Reim, Åström, and Eriksson (2020) argue that AI and its intelligent systems introduces potential in business processes and operations, and decision-making in organizations through the application of machine learning that define new business models.

IMPORTANCE OF AN EFFECTIVE BUSINESS DATA GOVERNANCE ROADMAP

Data governance initiatives, like most business activities, are underscored by the three pillars of people, process, and technology. In the discussion below, we highlight each of these pillars as we explore the business data governance road map. "Organizational interest in big data is spurred by opportunities to use these new data sources to make faster and better decisions through sophisticated analytics." (Abraham et al., 2019, p. 23). According to Janssen, Brous, Estevez, Barbosa & Janowski (2020) data governance involves "organizations and their personnel defining, applying and monitoring the patterns of rules and authorities for directing the proper functioning of, and ensuring the accountability for, the entire lifecycle of data and algorithms within and across organizations." (p. 2). In other words, data governance provides organizations the ability "to guarantee the delivery of trustworthy decisions" by having "control over the quality of their data and over compliance with relevant legal and ethical requirements" (Janssen et al., 2020, p.1).

Whenever an organization properly uses data governance, it will improve their decision-making because it controls data and ensures that the decisions are legal and ethical. For data governance to assist organizations in decision making, "data governance should focus not just on data, but on the systems through which data is collected, managed and used" (Janssen et al., 2020, p.1). If data governance focused only on data and disregarded the data collection system, the usability, and management of data it would create an unbalance in the decision-making process due to inevitable issues in accessing and controlling data when there is not structured information about it. Consequently, it is important to keep the focus on data and the information structure around it. "A mistake in data governance can lead to serious chaos".

(Janssen et. al., 2020, p.1). The authors defend that "such mistakes can result in systemic bias, unlawful decisions, large financial exposures, political crises, lives lost or any combination thereof" **(p.2).** Data governance needs to be handled by experts with a lot of attention to avoid risks in the domain. Data governance encounters challenges when "...the data flow and logic may not follow the structure of an organization. [...] that conflict will create data silos, duplications, unclear responsibilities, and missing control of data over its entire life cycle" (Janssen, Brous, Estevez, Barbosa & Janowski, 2020, p.3).

Brous' (2016) study supports the idea that data governance must rely on solid research work defending that data has to be organized for it to be stored properly. If the data is not stored properly, then it becomes impossible to find. The decision-making process must be identified for each organization, and data governance must be institutionalized through a formal organizational structure that fits with a specific organization. Thus, organizations must have solid search criteria and proper tools to find data; be in a portal of some sort that takes them directly to the data they need, or a search bar that allows for them to search keywords to find what they are looking for (intranet environment). In addition, the author establishes that data must have value to the business if it is going to make an impact. "Information should be helpful to its intended users or should support the usefulness of other disseminated information." (Brous, 2016, p.8). The article mentions that governmental organizations have challenges to face as they want to achieve data governance in theory, they "often have difficulty justifying the effort unless it has a practical, concrete impact on business." (Brous 2016, p. 9).

Earley (2016) explains the importance of data governance by saying, "it has become more essential than ever; organizations need to be ready to handle it in a meaningful way by prioritizing what is most important to the organization and measuring the impact of governance decisions." (p.25). While Earley's work does not explicitly define knowledge portal, it is implied that knowledge portals are within the process of data governance. Earley's study presents a few models used to organize data governance for best practice, and each has their strengths (security or efficiency). "Governance is about developing and enforcing policies, providing answers to business questions" (Earley, 2016, p. 3).

Panian (2010) defends that the goals of data governance are to: "Ensure data meets the needs of the business; Protect and manage data as valued enterprise asset; and Lower the costs of managing data" (p. 939). The author continues by highlighting that implementing those concepts compels motivation, including a) revenue growth; b) operational efficiency; and c) compliance with regulations (internal-external) – auditability, as examples.

Proposing a Conceptual Framework for Data Governance Roadmap in Business: The ATDI

In the concepts and complexities presented in the theories above, the definition of data provided by many scholars underscore data as devoid of context or meaning, but this does not preclude it from being easily captured, stored, and shared using information technologies systems. The remarkable progress in information systems has facilitated the capture, accumulation, and manipulation of data at an ever-increasing rate, leading to the discovery of new knowledge.

Extant literature suggests that data driven decision-making is not an easy process due to the highly unstructured nature of the data circulating daily in organizations, which may require various mechanisms to capture the value of diverse sets of both structured and unstructured data (Shamim, et al., 2020). Business Intelligence (BI) focuses on providing decision makers with valuable information and knowledge by utilizing a variety of sources of data, and structured and unstructured information via the discovery of the relationships that may exist between these sources of data (Becerra-Fernandez & Sabherwal, 2015). BI can be considered a component of knowledge management (KM). It is more specifically about extracting knowledge from data and makes sense in such a way that it is strategically and structured for business operations. KM includes the process necessary to capture, codify, integrate, transfer and make sense of all types of knowledge across the organization to achieve a competitive advantage. KM in BI means making superior decisions, and the decision-making process begins with the understanding of how to build capabilities in KM, business intelligence and data analytics and how to protect an organization's intellectual property and business goals. In the study investigating the evolution of business intelligence and analytics in organizations, Chen, Chiang, and Storey (2012) highlight the importance and impact of big data and data processing.

Business Intelligence tools are applied in organizations mostly aiming at "...identifying tools for data analysis...for improvement of business decisions using facts and information from supporting systems." (Olszak, 2016, p. 106). As Olszak, (2016) observed, a business intelligence model that is widely used is "Gartner's Maturity Model for Business Intelligence and Performance Management"; which has five levels of maturity employed to assess and/or measure the influence of faster access to better and broader data/information on business decisions or on business results (people, processes, metrics, and technology), the five levels are: unaware, tactical, focused, strategic, and pervasive. (Olszak, 2016, p. 113-114).

The critical purpose of these business intelligence models and processes is to help the organization manage their information more effectively, and to better make use of the knowledge and information they already have, while creating an environment for the creation of new knowledge. This implies the importance of building robust and effective knowledge management systems (KMS). As Hassan (2020) explains, "The primary function of KMS can make share the knowledge with others, and at the same time, it can give an advantage to the organization." (p.2). The author defends that KMS can improve communication between the seller and customers. Serumaga-Zake (2017) defends that if users do not like the process they have been given, it will not be used as effectively as it was intended and therefore not provide the results expected, and potentially could be damaging to the organization, stating that: "User satisfaction mediates the relationship between perceived net benefits and system quality and service quality and moderates the effect of system quality on perceived net benefits by enhancing it, whereas it moderates the effect of service quality on perceived net benefits by reversing it." (Serumaga-Zake, 2017, p. 7).

Business intelligence models are well aligned with knowledge management goals in helping organizations to better utilize the knowledge, information, and data they already have, as well as providing better systems for gaining new knowledge/information and using it effectively in organizations. As organizations better utilize knowledge and information, they improve their capabilities in providing better systems for gaining new knowledge/information and using knowledge resources effectively. The two concepts of BI and KM work well together because they have the same purpose in allowing data management, information flow, and knowledge production. Lack of knowledge management practices in organizations impacts the possibility of business intelligence processes and models that will enable productivity, innovation, and competitiveness. Gartner's Maturity Model for Business Intelligence and Performance Management highlights that business intelligence has the KM in its core.

Pondering the organizational value, strategic and financial impact of data governance to BI and its correlation to KM, Figure 4 below illustrates the business data governance roadmap, the ATDI (Assess, Track, Design, Implement) created with the intent to bring an innovative approach to simple data governance and information flow processes in organizations of multiple segments.

Figure 2. The ATDI roadmap process: Four critical steps in data governance project implementation
Source: Merlo and Makani, 2020. Using Operative Data Governance Roadmaps for Business Process Management Success: The Role of Leadership and the Impact of Information Technology Adoption.

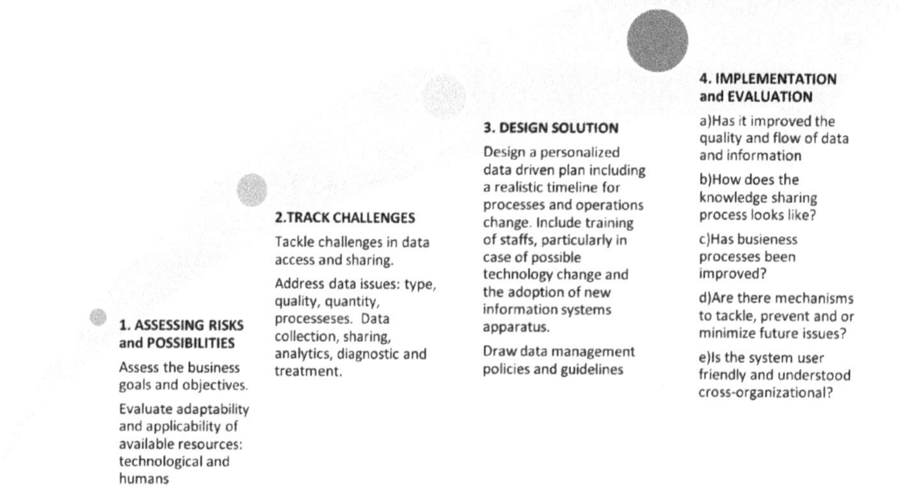

This Roadmap concept is based on the premise that many corporate challenges include high cost, fast evolving technology with new marketing ideas, and responsiveness of customers are priorities. It intends to highlight the importance of effective data flow process, the roles and responsibilities of leaders and the organization in enforcing that proper data governance being applied through the organization in many levels, and that the best business decisions and practice of proper governance are aligned with the business goals.

Collaborating with the importance of roadmaps as ATDI, described above and illustrated below in **Fig. 2**. Panian (2010) discusses the four components of data governance which should ensure accessibility, availability, high quality of data, consistency, auditability, and security, based on the key components of: Standards, Policies and Processes, Organization, and Technology. Those are, according to the author, the building blocks of an effective governance framework.

The ATDI Roadmap Methodology

The four sequential steps presented in the roadmap above and described below, defined as **ATDI**, are considered universal and relatively inclusive of the main aspects in any data flow process in organizations of different segments and sizes. They represent a relatively simple approach embodied in data flow and governance processes that should help stakeholders to better understand and visualize the hierarchic process of assessing data and information needs to implement critical and operational solutions to businesses. The ATDI will, in 4 steps, allow users to:

1. **ASSESS:** ASSESSING RISKS and POSSIBILITIES
   a) Assess the business goals and objectives.
   b) Evaluate adaptability and applicability of available resources: technological and humans.
2. **TRACK:** TRACK CHALLENGES
   a) Tackle challenges in data access and sharing.
   b) Address data issues: type, quality, quantity, processes. Data collection, sharing, analytics, diagnostic and treatment.
3. **DESIGN:** DESIGN SOLUTION
   a) Design a personalized data driven plan including a realistic timeline for processes and operations change. Include training of staff, particularly in case of possible technology change and the adoption of new information systems apparatus.
   b) Draw data management policies and guidelines.
4. **IMPLEMENT:** IMPLEMENTATION and EVALUATION
   a) Has it improved the quality and flow of data and information
   b) What does the knowledge sharing process look like?
   c) Have business processes been improved?
   d) Are there mechanisms to tackle, prevent, and/or minimize future issues?
   e) Is the system user friendly and understood across the organization?

The *ATDI Roadmap* will allow organizations to, through effective and systematic data governance roadmapping, moderate the flow of data and information and leverage knowledge resources in a manner that information systems are the core of the business unit, and knowledge sharing, and contribution is part of the users' behaviors for the consolidation of a culture of learning and innovation. We posit that through the moderation of knowledge resources and effective assessment of data and information processes, there will be a culture of transparency and, therefore, less ambiguity. The more users are encouraged to follow a structured and clear data and information management process, the less inclined they will be to engage in deviant behaviors such as information withholding, misinformation, incomplete information, lack of motivation in sharing information, issues with accessing and trusting data, and challenges processing data and representing it. These factors affect the first step, Assess, in the business roadmap.

Ravindan and Iyer (2014), argue that to leverage knowledge resources, "many organizations deploy knowledge management systems (KMS), which contain at their core a knowledge repository." (p. 271). The successful application of a knowledge repository relies on knowledge workers that will validate the knowledge as an object and apply it explicitly. In discussing ambiguity and KMS, Ravidan and Iyer point out that tolerance to ambiguity is a key influencer in the process of knowledge sharing, playing a role between incentive and knowledge gaps. Based on that concept, it is assumed that the subjectivity involved in assessing data needs must be minimized by a pragmatic assessment of the business needs, first and foremost, then the close evaluation of individual gaps, training capacity, job performance, maturity in understanding and using the KMS available in the company as well as other relevant information systems that might interfere with outcomes. While some employees might feel unmotivated, others could feel disengaged from the process, and therefore misuse, sub-use, or alteration of data and information would result in an ultimate failure in overall process improvement.

The second step in the **ATDI** roadmap, Track, will rely heavily on the successful first step, where qualified system users are core participants in the process improvement. Tracking progress such as mistakes and successes, will be determinant in the Design (step 3) and Implementation (step 4) of solutions and the consolidation of decision-making processes that will lead to solid and measurable Key Performance Indicators (**KPIs**).

The Track step involves complex mechanisms of data analytics, investigation, diagnostics, troubleshooting, and data visualization tools applications. Throughout this process, users will be able to transform tacit knowledge into explicit knowledge, and by relying on a culture of learning and sharing (eliminating or minimizing the deviant behaviors related to information withholding and a lack of incentive and motivation), engage in a culture that favors the business over individuals' feelings and insecurities by enabling significant and transformative knowledge sharing practices. Some of those practices will be conducted via brainstorming, encouraged through formal training, and enabled through internal information technology systems for searching, sharing, and accessing both sensitive and non-sensitive information. For a successful system, users must believe that the system is useful, reliable, and that it improves job performance and adds value to their business roles. This step in the ATDI roadmap will ensure information and data quality, performance improvement, superior implementation and use of information systems and KMS solutions, and the continuous self-awareness and positive attitude about data use and visualization, and most importantly to management, reporting and accountability.

Step 3 of **ATDI**, Design, considers all the data and information gathered from the previous steps and advances to "take action" on designing policies that will address the issues identified: resources (humans and technological), and the processes. Will there be the need for training to improve job performance? Will there be the need to implement any additional information system(s)? If so, why? How? What is the issue to be resolved? In this phase the policies and procedures are designed and all aspects of the business - individuals in all levels of the chain of command- should be "heard", and expectations and division' needs should be aligned with the business purpose and goals. This phase will provide the base for the final phase in the **ATDI** roadmap process, which is the Implementation. The implementation process must consider the minimization or elimination of the knowledge gap, issues with reliability, efficacy, and the elimination of ambiguity. This phase will address the five main questions listed above, while focusing on business performance improvement, the successful achievement and evaluation of variables in KPIs, the overall business intelligence process, and ultimately, profitability, considering all resources and challenges. According to Alhassan, Sammon and Daly (2016): "It can be argued that data governance, from both the academic and practitioner points of view, should be a universal approach to data accountability, fitting all data aspects and needs of an organisation (p. 55).

The research work of Egan (2011) corroborates with the principles presented in the ATDI roadmap discussed above through the investigation of a financial enterprise and its challenges with data governance program, leading the author to conclude that data quality is the driving force behind effective decision-making, and that only consistent data governance program can secure defined processes for successful organizational data management.

CONCLUSION AND FUTURE WORK

This chapter aimed to demonstrate that there are several factors influencing an organization's ability to effectively manage data, use information systems to create meaningful and valuable data, and enable a cultural environment of data reliability and productivity, which depend heavily on the business' commitment to learning and innovation, and the ability to create processes and roadmaps aiming at improving operations, accomplishing organizational goals, and facilitating the identification and achievement of solid KPIs by individuals in all levels of the organizational structure. It resulted from a real project implemented by the author in a high-tech organization, from the 100 fortune companies, within the business intelligence division with the goal of improving processes and productivity through effective data and information governance initiative.

Through policies and governance process structures that encourage the use of data analytics and visualization tools to facilitate organizational learning, organizations have taken a critical step towards promoting access and sharing of knowledge. Leaders can both play a decisive or disruptive role in enabling or discouraging data access and knowledge sharing, potentially optimizing or paralyzing business intelligence processes and impacting innovation and competitiveness. Data is the vital aspect of organizations, it represents customers, employees, suppliers, and the processes and strategies that will lead to outcomes. It is rooted in the information technology capabilities and the culture of information sharing and consumption. Data governance will define and be defined by the organizational policies, information systems availability, auditability, data security. data culture, so data needs are met and protected, and costs are lower as data is valued, successfully managed, and strategically designed (Panian, 2010).

The factors investigated for data management and data governance, particularly, are strongly correlated with business process success in terms of data quality, security, retrieval, storage, and many technological apparatuses. The concept of a business roadmap framework presented in this study: the **ATDI** (Assessing Risks and Possibilities, Track Challenges, Design Solutions, and Implementation and Evaluation), is believed to serve as a tool in designing roadmaps for systematic data access and business processes improvement, and, unquestionably, improving profitability for a few critical reasons: **1.** The optimization in the use of data resources: individuals and productivity, **2.** The improvement of technological use, and **3**. The enablement of an environment of sharing, brainstorming, and innovation; while minimizing data loss, inaccuracy, and financial loss.

Therefore, creating an infrastructure of information technology that is not strategically aligned with a clear Data Envelopment Analysis (DEA) will tragically affect employees' understanding about the data process, individuals' responsibilities in the data governance process, the broad access to enterprise data strategy(ies), the potential of technological infrastructure, and the interoperability of information systems. It is not enough to have access to information systems and data but possess advance skills and resources, so access understand the system, access, process, and consume the data generated and provided to and by one's organizations. Data representation and visualization facilitates comprehending and communicating data, information, and knowledge; and therefore, emphasizing the infrastructure, intelligence, and analytics tools that will allow humans skills and knowledge to be largely applied in benefit of organizational competencies and performance.

Those conclusions lead to the claim that the effective use and management of data analytics and visualization tools and the consolidation of systematic data governance practices are promising indicators of a strong and committed leadership that should focus on best practices for managing knowledge in organizations, resulting in business process improvement. This combination will be reflected in a higher level of the proper use of Knowledge Management Systems (KMS), superior user satisfaction, innovation, and sophisticated job performance though effective methods of performance evaluation (KPIs, Data Envelopment Analysis).

This conceptual research work presents a data governance roadmap framework, the **ATDI**, that should be validated and tested in future work; therefore, contributing to the expansion in studies and knowledge in the field of data governance and management in business processes improvement. As organizations navigate the complexities of the digital era, strategic information governance emerges as a linchpin for success. This chapter provides valuable insights into optimizing business operations, leveraging business intelligence, and achieving excellence in data management. By embracing a strategic approach to information governance, businesses can not only survive but thrive in an era defined by data-driven decision-making.

Aligning Information Governance with Business Intelligence allows the discovery and application of strategies for aligning information governance practices with business initiatives to extract maximum value from data assets. The intersection of business operations and data and information governance potentially enhances day-to-day business operations through the most strategic use and generation of data quality and consistency in driving insightful business intelligence. Information governance practices streamlines and integrates business operations, fostering efficiency and minimizing risks while promoting a level of business intelligence that enables better decision-making. It is worthy to highlight that the successful management of information governance projects must be aligned with the organizational information technology program, so information infrastructure and data and information strategies are in sync and backup each other Patel, 2002; Sambamurthy and Zmud, 1999).

REFERENCES

Abraham, R., Schneider, J., & Vom Brocke, J. (2019). Data Governance: a conceptual framework, structures review, and research agenda. *International Journal of Information Management*. https://www.researchgate.net/publication/334653735

Ackoff, R. L. (1989). From data to wisdom. *Journal of Applied Systems Analysis, 16*(1), 3–9.

Alhassan, I., Sammon, D., & Daly, M. (2016) Data governance activities: an analysis of the literature. *Journal of Decision Systems, 25*. doi:10.1080/12460125.2016.1187397

Attard, J., & Brennan, R. (2018). Challenges in Value-Driven Data Governance. 1-11. http://doras.dcu.ie/22980/1/ODBASE challenges paper.pdf

Baker-Brunnbauer, J. (2020). Management perspective of ethics in artificial intelligence. *AI and Ethics, 1*(2), 173–181. doi:10.1007/s43681-020-00022-3

Becerra-Fernandez, I., & Sabherwal, Rajiv. (2015). *Knowledge management: Systems and processes* (Second ed.). New York: Routledge.

Borgman, H., Heier, H., Bahli, B., & Boekamp, T. (2016). Dotting the I and Crossing (out) the T in IT Governance: New Challenges for Information Governance. *49th Hawaii International Conference on System Sciences*, (pp. 4901-4909). Koloa, Hawaii, USA. 10.1109/HICSS.2016.608

Brous, P., Janssen, M., & Vilminko-Heikkinen, R. (2016, September). Coordinating decision-making in data management activities: a systematic review of data governance principles. In *International Conference on Electronic Government* (pp. 115-125). Springer, Cham. 10.1007/978-3-319-44421-5_9

Chen, H., Chiang, R. H. L., & Storey, V. C. (2012). Business Intelligence and Analytics: From Big Data to Big Impact. *Management Information Systems Quarterly, 36*(4), 1165–1188. doi:10.2307/41703503

Cheong, L. K., & Chang, V. (2007, January). *(PDF) The need for data governance: A case study.* ResearchGate.https://www.researchgate.net/publication/228966685_The_need_for_data_governance_A_case_study

DAMA International. (2017). *DAMA-DMBOK: Data management body of knowledge* (2nd ed.). Technics Publications.

Davenport, T., & Harris, J. (2007). *Competing on analytics.* Harvard Business School.

Davenport, T. H., & Prusak, L. (1998). *Working Knowledge: How Organizations Manage What They Know.* Harvard Business School Press.

De-Graft, J. D. (2019). *Developing an Integrated Framework for Knowledge Management Practices in Organisations.*

Earley, S. (n.d.). *Data governance and digital transformation: Using the customer journey to define a framework.* Doc Server. http://docserver.ingentaconnect.com.libproxy.library.unt.edu/deliver/connect/hsp/20547544/v2n1/s4.pdf?expires=1604953417&id=0000&titleid=72010542&checksum=75FC143F4E424A51DDFC9FFD348F78E6

Egan, P. (2011). Effecting Data Quality Through Data Governance: a Case Study in the Financial Services Industry. *Regis University Student Publications (comprehensive collection).* 465. https://epublications.regis.edu/theses/465

Faucher, J. B. P., Everett, A. M., & Lawson, R. (2008). Reconstituting knowledge management. *Journal of Knowledge Management, 12*(3), 3–16. doi:10.1108/13673270810875822

Gartner. (2009), *Toolkit: Information Governance Project.* Gartner. www.gartner. com/id1/4933912

Janssen, M., Brous, P., Estevez, E., Barbosa, L. S., & Janowski, T. (2020). Data governance: Organizing data for trustworthy Artificial Intelligence. *Government Information Quarterly, 37*(3), N.PAG. https://doi.org/ doi:10.1016/j.giq.2020.101493

Kariotis, T., Ball, M. P., Tzovaras, B. G., Dennis, S., Sahama, T., Johnston, C., & Borda, A. (2020). Emerging health data platforms: From individual control to collective data governance. Data &amp. *Data & Policy, 2,* 1–13. doi:10.1017/dap.2020.14

Lăzăroiu, G., Kovacova, M., Kliestikova, J., Kubala, P., Valaskova, K., & Dengov, V. V. (2018). Data governance and automated individual decision-making in the digital privacy General Data Protection Regulation. *Administratie si Management Public, 31,* 132–142.

Luftman, J. N., & Ben-Zvi, T. (2011). Key issues for IT executives 2011: Cautious optimism in uncertain economic times. *MIS Quarterly Executive, 10*(4), 203–212.

Mansor, N. A. (2020). Knowledge Management System Implementation: Expert System. *International Journal of Information & Knowledge Management, 10*(1), 43–50.

Mikalef, P., Krogstie, J., van de Wetering, R., Pappas, I. O., & Giannakos, M. N. (2018). Information Governance in the Big Data Era: Aligning Organizational Capabilities. *Proceedings of the 51st Hawaii International Conference on System Sciences*. Big Island, Hawaii, USA 10.24251/HICSS.2018.615

Miller, B., Malloy, M. A., Masek, E., & Wild, C. (2001). Towards a framework for managing theinformation environment. *Information, Knowledge, Systems Management*, *2*(4), 359–384.

Milne, R., & Brayne, C. (2020). We need to think about data governance for dementia research in a digital era. *Alzheimer's Research & Therapy*, *12*(1), 1–3. https://doi-org.libproxy.library.unt.edu/10.1186/s13195-020-0584-y. doi:10.1186/s13195-020-0584-y PMID:32005135

Nelson, R., & Staggers, N. (2014). Theoretical Foundations of Health Informatics. In R. Nelson & N. Staggers (Eds.), *Health Informatics: An Interprofessional Approach* (pp. 18–39). Elsevier/Mosby.

Olszak, C. M. (2016). Toward Better Understanding and Use of Business Intelligence in Organizations. *Information Systems Management*, *33*(2), 105–123. https://doi-org.libproxy.library.unt.edu/10.1080/10580530.2016.1155946Serumaga-. doi:10.1080/10580530.2016.1155946

Panian, Z. (2010). Some practical experiences in data governance. *World Academy of Science, Engineering and Technology*, *62*(1), 939–946.

Patel, N. V. (2002). Emergent forms of IT governance to support global e-business models. *Journal of Information Technology Theory and Application*, *4*(2), 33–48. https://www.proquest.com/scholarly-journals/emergent-forms-governance-support-global-e/docview/200053438/se-2

Peterson, R. (2004, Fall). Crafting information technology governance. *Information Systems Management*, *21*(4), 7–22. doi:10.1201/1078/44705.21.4.20040901/84183.2

Reim, W., Åström, J., & Eriksson, O. (2020). Implementation of Artificial Intelligence (AI): A Roadmap for Business Model Innovation. *AI*, *1*(2), 180–191. MDPI AG. doi:10.3390/ai1020011

Sambamurthy, V., & Zmud, R. W. (1999). Arrangements for Information Technology Governance: A Theory of Multiple Contingencies. *Management Information Systems Quarterly*, *23*(2), 261–290. doi:10.2307/249754

Shamim, S., Zeng, J., Khan, Z., & Zia, N. U. (2020). Big data analytics capability and decision making performance in emerging market firms: The role of contractual and relational governance mechanisms. *Technological Forecasting and Social Change*, *161*, 120315. doi:10.1016/j.techfore.2020.120315

Tallon, P. P. (2010). Understanding the dynamics of information management costs. *Communications of the ACM*, *53*(5), 121–125. doi:10.1145/1735223.1735253

Tripathi, M., Shukla, A., & Sonkar, S. K. (2017). Research data management practices in university libraries: A study. *DESIDOC Journal of Library and Information Technology*, *37*(6), 417. doi:10.14429/djlit.37.11336

Weber, K., Otto, B., & Österle, H. (2009). One Size Does Not Fit All---A Contingency Approach to Data Governance. *ACM Journal of Data and Information Quality*, *1*(1), 1–27. doi:10.1145/1515693.1515696

Wende, K. (2007). A Model for Data Governance – Organising Accountabilities for Data Quality Management. *ACIS 2007 Proceedings*. AISEL. https://aisel.aisnet.org/acis2007/80

Zake, P. A. E. (2017). The role of user satisfaction in implementing a Business Intelligence System. *South African Journal of Information Management*, *19*(1), 1–8. https://doi-org.libproxy.library.unt.edu/10.4102/sajim.v19i1.736

Zeggelink, E. (1994). Dynamics of structure: An individual oriented approach. *Social Networks*, *16*(4), 295–333. doi:10.1016/0378-8733(94)90014-0

Chapter 6

Decentralized Data and Privacy:
Exploring the Conflict Between Distributed Ledger Technology and the Right to Be Forgotten Under GDP

Akash Bag
https://orcid.org/0000-0001-8820-171X
Amity University, India

Paridhi Sharma
O.P. Jindal Global University, India

Pranjal Khare
O.P. Jindal Global University, India

Souvik Roy
Adamas University, India

ABSTRACT

Our personal information, or "digital footprint," is gathered and used in today's digital age. Digital footprints are kept, unlike snow footprints. There is a large market for this data, which businesses utilize to analyze consumer preferences. Businesses collecting a lot of data in one place pose a privacy risk. Thus, people are worried. Businesses prefer not to utilize intermediaries to manage client data to save money. Therefore, new technology is needed to make online interactions safer and more efficient. We're considering "distributed ledger technology." This technology is interesting because it securely collects, stores, and processes data without central authority. It has data immutability, transparency, and safety. A problem exists. The European GDPR (general data protection regulation) may conflict with this technology. This chapter will examine this tension, focusing on the right to be forgotten, which permits people to delete their data. It will examine how this new technology and existing privacy policies can function together or need tweaking.

DOI: 10.4018/979-8-3693-0472-3.ch006

INTRODUCTION

In today's digital society, it is hard to forget. The Internet is a public memory for society where anyone can access all the information we humans produce. Enough amounts of data are generated through new digital solutions and services, combined with the expanding use of computers and new technologies. Collecting and processing this enormous amount of information has become a central part of companies' business, as they build large parts of their business on knowing as much as possible about the individual to adapt and provide their services (Al-Abdullah et al., 2020). The fact that people increasingly leave behind digital footprints is not without consequences.

On the one hand, it is easy to imagine a scenario where information about where you are, what you like, and who you spend time with can be used if it falls into the wrong hands. In part, humans risk losing control over our information and the ability to influence others' image of ourselves. Therefore, the developed technical solutions must meet the needs set from a data protection perspective. The legislator must know how the increased digitization and its challenges must be met through data protection to protect the individual and his right to privacy. At the same time, the legislation mustn't become rigid and undynamic. It leaves room for continued technological development (Chase, 2019).

An example of technology that is currently developing at a rapid pace is distributed ledger technology (DLT). The technology can be briefly summarized as a digital system for recording transactions and data transfers without relying on a central actor. The technology is better known under the name blockchain technology or smart contracts and is used to secure and increase control over information by providing various new solutions for identification, data transfer, increased traceability, and a reduced risk of manipulation (Burman, 2020). At the same time, one of the characteristics of the technology is immutability, which means that it is very difficult to delete data from a DLT, and any updates are permanently recorded for posterity (Berberich & Steiner, 2016). Thus, despite the technology's many potential positive effects, there are great concerns about the data protection challenges that the system can create. DLT is primarily associated with blockchain technology virtual currencies and information storage on distributed databases (Berberich & Steiner, 2016). However, the potential for DLT extends far beyond just information storage. In the public sector, utilities are expected to use the technology to calibrate electricity supply, and in healthcare, the technology is expected to improve medical treatment. Technology offers online platforms the infrastructure for specific events; for example, DLT is the building block of the next generation internet, Web 3.0.7. At the same time, banking is undergoing major changes in the financial sector, where technology is used to streamline transactions and make payments increasingly "*intelligent*." This development shows how urgent it is to clarify the DLT and individual data protection issue (Voss, 2016).

This chapter aims to highlight the difficulties that DLT causes for the individual's right to the protection of personal data to investigate the possibilities of ensuring effective data protection without limiting technological innovation and highlighting the potential solutions. Against the background of this purpose and the conflict mentioned above between DLT and GDPR, I intend to investigate the relationship between DLT and GDPR in this chapter. This will be achieved by answering the following question: *How does the use of DLT relate to the right to be forgotten?* To guide the chapter's investigation of the above question, three main aspects of the relationship between GDPR and DLT will be investigated: 1) what are the difficulties associated with deleting data on a DLT, and 2) whether it is possible to apply the GDPR to DLT and 3) whether it is possible to design secure personal data processing on DLT despite the limited possibilities to delete data.

METHODOLOGY

The chapter will be based on a legal analytical method. Unlike the legal dogmatic method, characterized by its attempt to determine the applicable Law, the legal analytical method aims to analyze it and determine the applicable Law (Smits, 2015). This way, the legal analytical method can be considered freer than the legal dogmatic one. Furthermore, the legal dogmatic method is characterized by an attempt to systematize and interpret the generally accepted legal sources, while the legal analytical method opens up the possibility that all forms of material can be used for the analysis. Because the legal analytical method opens up the possibility of analyzing current Law, discussions can conducted regarding what problems GDPR poses to new technological innovations (Smits, 2015). This chapter concerns an area where the regulatory basis consists primarily of EU law; therefore, an EU legal method is also used. The EU legal method is based on the methodology and interpretation methods used by the Court of Justice of the European Union (EUD), where practice from the EUD is the primary interpretive basis for understanding the GDPR's articles. The main legal sources used in the EU -the field of Law differs from the traditional legal method. The sources of Law in the field of EU law can be divided into "*binding*" and "*non-binding*" sources of Law. The binding legal sources consist of, i.e. general legal principles, primary Law, the charter of rights, binding secondary Law, and international agreements.

The non-binding legal sources consist of i.e. non-binding secondary Law, preparatory works, draft rulings, the EU legal doctrine, and economic theories. From the investigation in this chapter, DLT appears to be within a legal gray zone concerning the GDPR (Erdos, 2021). In practice, there may be a lack of specific guidance from both the binding and the non-binding legal sources. As GDPR is a relatively new regulation, there is a lack of interpretations from the EUD that explicitly mention the problems DLT entails for the regulation. Because of this, the basis for interpretation must be expanded. In these cases, guidance from the Article 29 Working Party (Article 29 WP) will play an important role in this chapter in trying to interpret and investigate the applicable Law (Veale & Edwards, 2018). Article 29 WP has today been replaced by the European Data Protection Board (EDPB). These guidelines constitute an extended basis for interpreting the regulation's provisions but are not legally binding. The interpretation material will also largely consist of doctrine and articles. The investigation will, therefore, include articles and discussions written by practicing lawyers and other experts in the field (Veale & Edwards, 2018). About which problems the regulations aim to solve. In addition, it can be mentioned that since much of the existing legal doctrine in the field consists of non-binding legal sources, conclusions and interpretations must be drawn with great caution and careful source criticism. New technologies being developed, such as DLT, have great potential and are often the subject of heavy speculation and investment, while the technology's potential has resulted in few finished products (Voss, 2016).

It is, therefore, not uncommon for articles to have underlying financial motives. Thus, greater criticism must be directed at the content of the sources further away from the primary legal sources the investigation is. The legal informatics method will also be in the chapter's method repository. Since the chapter touches on an area where information and communication technology (IT) and Law meet, the legal informatics method will also be in its methodological arsenal. The legal informatics method is characterized by an attempt to study the approaches used to integrate legal aspects within technically oriented work so that the technology fulfills the legal requirements set. In simpler words, the method can be summarized as an investigation into the interaction between IT technology and the Law, the impact of technology on the Law, and how different legal norms govern the use of technology.

DISTRIBUTED LEDGER TECHNOLOGY

The Emergence of DLT

In November 2008, the article "*Bitcoin: A Peer-to-Peer Electronic Cash System*" was published by the pseudonym Satoshi Nakamoto. In the article, Nakamoto describes a software program where users can quickly, securely, and reliably transfer "*money*" in the form of "*Bitcoin*" between each other online without having to rely on an actor acting as an intermediary, such as a bank, to carry out the transactions. The software protocol behind the technology was named blockchain technology and refers to a particular way of organizing and storing information and transactions through a cryptographically secured chain of data blocks (Cadogan, 2023). Over the years, blockchain technology developed, and new technological solutions inspired by blockchain technology's method of organizing and transferring data were invented, e.g., the so-called smart contracts. This is where the concept of DLT originates. DLT is an umbrella term encompassing all technologies based on identical or similar software protocols, e.g., blockchain technology or smart contracts (Marshall et al., 2023). What distinguishes a DLT-type software protocol from other software protocols is that a DLT has the technical infrastructure to enable simultaneous access, approval, and updating of data records through a network spread over multiple locations and devices (Natarajan et al., 2017).

The following sections will outline which parts make up the main features of DLT. The technology the chapter concerns is complicated to understand. Since a DLT is only a collective term for several similar technologies, a DLT can have different technical designs depending on the purpose of the DLT. For example, the technical structure of a DLT aimed at transferring capital will differ from that of a DLT aimed at conducting data storage, similar to that of a cloud service (Natarajan et al., 2017). However, certain characteristics are common to all types of DLT built on blockchain technology. In light of the above, the purpose of the chapter is not to give the reader a basic and exhaustive understanding of how the technology works or its technical structure. Instead, it is only necessary for the reader to get an overview of the central characteristics of DLT to facilitate the understanding of the legal analysis of the following technology.

How DLT Works

DLT can be summarized as software that provides new approaches to recording and sharing data across several so-called ledgers (data warehouses). Each data warehouse stores identical records collectively stored, processed, maintained, and controlled by a distributed network of nodes, where nodes can be equated with a computer server (Natarajan et al., 2017). The technology can be described as a database, where data, instead of being stored on a computer server that a central actor maintains, is stored on all nodes maintaining the network. By handing over control of the database to the nodes, a DLT does not need to rely on a central actor to carry out data storage, transmission, or processing. In the past, for example, two parties intending to send capital to each other needed to rely on a central actor or intermediary, such as a bank, to carry out the transfer (Soltani et al., 2022). Through DLT, the need for a central actor to act as an intermediary disappears because the nodes, running a special software protocol, verify the transfer to ensure that capital is taken from the right bank account and transferred to the right bank account. The same example can be drawn to other reversal areas than the transfer of capital, for example, the storage of data or communication (Natarajan et al., 2017). A DLT can thus have many different technical designs depending on the purpose of the database. Based on blockchain technology, the type of DLT the paper examines can be summarized as a distributed database where the software protocol underlying the database is built through blockchain technology.

Blockchain technology is a special type of DLT. A blockchain is a data store, i.e., a digital ledger, transaction record, or database, consisting of cryptographically linked blocks in chronological order. In other words, it is a common record that contains every transfer and transaction of data ever performed on the network (Marshall et al., 2023). The blocks in a blockchain consist of data. This data can consist of everything from financial transaction history to various documents with text or digital Art. However, the amount of data stored on an individual block is not unlimited. This means that new blocks must be constantly created. These blocks are linked, creating a digital ledger or transaction record of every data transfer. The blocks are cryptographically locked into a chronological chain of transaction blocks to create a common transaction record that all users agree on (Cadogan, 2023). The structure of a blockchain can be compared to a train. Assume that a block is a train car. Each train carriage has a limited number of seats. When the train car is filled with passengers, which in this example will represent the data, a new train car must be connected to accommodate everyone. The more passengers who use the train, the more train cars have to be connected. To ensure that all railcars attached to the originating train are bound for the same terminal station, the railway staff, representing the nodes, must have a process to verify that the correct railcar (block) is attached to the train (blockchain).

For the nodes to verify that the correct block is connected to the blockchain, the software protocol has a consensus mechanism to ensure that the nodes agree to the new block being added to the transaction register. The most used consensus mechanisms are Proof-of-Work and Proof-of-Stake (Bains, 2022). Proof-of-work is a process in which a computer or other device called miners, who are in charge of the blockchain's software protocol, must perform a certain amount of work in the form of solving complicated mathematical calculations to validate transactions and create new blocks for the blockchain (Li & Kassem, 2021). Proof-of-stake refers to a process where the software protocol randomly selects miners within the blockchain network to validate transactions and create new blocks. Regardless of the consensus mechanism that the blockchain uses, the consensus protocol enables a majority decision to be made among all nodes maintaining the blockchain, whether a block should be added to the chain or not. In this way, only one blockchain is ever generated and objectively verified through the consensus protocol.

The blockchain network is maintained and updated by nodes that run a software protocol, a so-called consensus protocol, which aims to ensure that all nodes follow the same rules. The nodes consist of a computer or other device that runs a software protocol and can be equated with a computer server. All nodes in a network are usually equal parties to each other, where no node has more authority or power than any other node (Finck, 2017). New nodes can join the network by joining other nodes that make up the network. Additionally, nodes can leave and rejoin the network if they accept the blockchain created while the node is disconnected. In this way, the network of interconnected nodes becomes a decentralized network without any hierarchy, where nodes send data and forward data to all other nodes connected. It should further be pointed out that there are huge variations in blockchains and their internal governance structures. Here, blockchains can be divided into different groups, where the two main groups are public and private (Finck, 2017). Public blockchains are public, so anyone can participate and maintain a node by downloading and running the right software protocol (Finck, 2017). An example of a public blockchain is the cryptocurrency Bitcoin. In principle, the only thing needed to use the blockchain and participate as a node in the network is a computer and an Internet connection.

The Special Characteristics of The Technology

In light of the above, it can be stated that the design of DLTs built on blockchain technology varies. However, certain characteristics are unique to this type of DLT. Unlike traditional databases such as cloud services, the first characteristic is decentralized technology. Record keeping has been a centralized process that requires a credible record keeper (Natarajan et al., 2017). What characterizes and distinguishes a DLT from these traditional databases is that several or all network participants have simultaneous control over the database (Natarajan et al., 2017). The consensus mechanism can also be considered a feature that distinguishes DLT. Through the consensus mechanism, the technology becomes more secure than similar technical solutions as the mechanism validates all new data inputs added to the blockchain. This means there is always only one version of the DLT's ledger. Each addition to the system by a network participant is spread to all nodes, and each network participant owns a complete and updated copy of the network's so-called digital ledger or transaction register (Natarajan et al., 2017).

The Disadvantages and Risks Of DLT

Despite the many areas that DLT is expected to revolutionize, it is important - to gain a nuanced insight into the legal problems that the technology can bring - to also pay attention to the criticisms raised in the discussion about DLT. As with other technological innovations, the Law is not always fully adapted to deal with the new problems that the innovation may bring. Professional lawyers must interpret and apply laws not adapted to digital information management (Ng, 2017). This problem becomes particularly apparent regarding new technologies that work in a completely new way. An argument often used against distributed database technology is how the technology is inherently incompatible with European data protection legislation (Chase, 2019). The technology's design and characteristics – decentralization, transparency, immutability – give rise to complicated legal issues that risk stopping its establishment as it may conflict with the EU's digital single market goals (Chase, 2019). In addition, it is particularly complicated to regulate public DLT because no single natural or legal person controls the distributed database (Natarajan et al., 2017). It is thus unclear for authorities which governance arrangements apply and where responsibility should be claimed.

On the other hand, the regulation of private DLT is much simpler as there is usually an administrator or owner of the system who can be subject to legal control (Natarajan et al., 2017). Even the decentralized aspect of DLT has received criticism as the absence of a centralized infrastructure poses a risk by not being able to ensure effective governance of the services provided by DLT (Natarajan et al., 2017). Regulators have relied on regulated actors for effective governance arrangements on a central infrastructure (Natarajan et al., 2017). It can thus be questioned whether an administrator of a DLT network has sufficient means to ensure compliance with the rules in a decentralized infrastructure.

LEGAL STARTING POINTS OF THE DATA PROTECTION REGULATION

Introduction

The individual's right to personal data protection is fundamental in the EU. Of Section. 8.1 EU Charter and Art. 16.1 FEUF states that everyone has the right to protect personal data concerning them. The protection of the personal data of natural persons applies regardless of whether the personal data is provided in physical or digital form. The GDPR mainly regulates the handling of personal data. To be able to investigate and answer the chapter's question about the relationship between DLT and the right to be forgotten, you first need to investigate whether the GDPR applies to the technology at all and what conditions the regulation imposes on the processing of personal data.

GDPR's Scope of Application

The Material Scope

GDPR's scope of application is determined in Art. 2 and 3. The regulation's substantive scope is stipulated in Art. 2.1, where it is clear that the GDPR is primarily applicable to the processing of personal data by automatic means and to the processing of personal data that is part of an archive system or intended to be part of an archive system (Lambert, 2017). By automatic means, mainly the processing of personal data with digital technology (Kulhari, 2018b). The processing of personal data with DLT thus falls under this description. However, the material area of application is not without exception. In Art. 2.2 GDPR states four exceptions when the regulation is not applied to processing personal data. These situations are processing of personal data such as:

a) constitutes a step in an activity that is not covered by Union law,
b) Member States carry out when carrying out activities covered by Title V Chapter 2 of the EU Treaty,
c) a natural person performs as part of an activity of a purely private nature, or which is related to their household,
d) competent authorities carry out to prevent, investigate, uncover, or prosecute crimes or enforce criminal penalties, including protecting against and preventing and preventing threats to public safety.

This petition doesn't need to examine all four exceptions. The exception relevant to this chapter is the household exception appearing in Art. 2.2 (c) GDPR. According to Recital 18 of the GDPR, the household exception means that processing personal data for private or household purposes without connection to professional or business activities falls outside the regulation's scope of application. For example, private persons' correspondence and publications of personal data in social media or blogs are exempt (Coyne, 2019). Although private persons' activity, e.g., social media, is exempt, recital 18 of the GDPR shows that the regulation still applies to personal data controllers or personal data assistants who provide such activities. The question thus becomes whether private individuals who place personal data on a DLT or use DLT for private purposes actualize the household exception. Opinions are divided on this issue. According to the French data protection authority CNIL, the household exception may be interpreted to become relevant when private individuals use DLT for private purposes (Todt, 2019). However, a European Parliament's Investigation Service (EPRS) study believes that practice suggests that the household exception should be interpreted restrictively, and that the exception should not be relevant in these cases. In case C-101/01, Bodil Lindqvist, a private person involved in her church, had created a website and published personal information about her colleagues within the pastorate. In the judgment, the Court stated that the household exception is not applicable when personal data is published on the Internet and thus becomes accessible to an indefinite number of people (Chase, 2019).

This interpretation was confirmed in case *C-73/07 Satamedia*, where the Court ruled that the household exception covers only activities that form part of the individual's private or family life.78 Furthermore, the Court ruled that this could not be the case when personal data becomes known to an indefinite number of people (Global Freedom of Expression, 2017). Also, in *case C-345/17 Sergejs Buivids*, the Court submitted that the publication of a video clip on a website meant that the personal data became public to an indefinite number of people. Thus, the processing of personal data could not be considered purely private, and the household exception was not applicable (Global Freedom of Expression, 2017). It therefore appears doubtful whether the household exception could be applied to DLT, as CNIL claims. Private DLTs are mainly used within a commercial or professional context and thus do not meet the requirement of a private nature (Global Freedom of Expression, 2017). There is reason to assume that when private individuals place personal data on public DLTs, the household exception is not applicable when the data becomes public to an indefinite number of people.

Personal Data

According to Art. 4.1 GDPR defines personal data as information about an identified or identifiable natural person. This information may consist of a name, an identification number, location data online identifiers, or one or more factors specific to the natural person's physical, physiological, genetic, psychological, financial, cultural, or social identity. Outside the concept of personal data fall information about, i.e., legal persons and information about deceased persons (recitals 14 & 27 of the GDPR). The concept of personal data has thus been broadly defined in the regulation. For this reason, depending on the purpose of the DLT, data covered by the regulation's definition of personal data may be processed and stored in data blocks on a DLT. As mentioned earlier, anonymity is a characteristic often associated with DLT. According to Recital 26 of the regulation, it appears that anonymous data falls outside the concept of personal data. Anonymous data refers to data that cannot be directly or indirectly attributed to a natural person (recital 26 of GDPR). In the case of DLT, information can be stored either 1) in its original form or 2) as encrypted information, for example, in a hash (Kulhari, 2018b). When the information is stored in its original form, for example, in a text document, it is clear that the GDPR applies if it concerns personal data. However, the assessment becomes more difficult when the personal data is stored in encrypted form or through a hash.

The GDPR sets high requirements for when data can be considered anonymous and falls outside the scope of the regulation (Finck, 2017). When storing encrypted data on a DLT, it is still possible for users to gain access to the encrypted data if they have the right keys or access to supplementary data, such as identifying the user (Finck, 2017). Therefore, encrypted data should not be considered anonymous data; instead, the data should be considered pseudonymized (Kolain & Wirth, 2018). Pseudonymization can be described as a method of anonymizing information to replace the information in question with a pseudonym that cannot be attributed to a specific person without additional tasks (Art. 4.5 GDPR). In case *C-582/14 Patrick Breyer v Bundesrepublik Deutschland*, the Court stated that a person doesn't need to have all the information necessary to identify the person in question for it to be personal data (Zuiderveen Borgesius, 2017). However, this only applies if it would not require unreasonable resources regarding time, costs, and human resources, so that identification was impossible in practice (Zuiderveen

Borgesius, 2017). How this limit relates to DLT is unclear. DLT is a very advanced technology, and anonymity is one of its important features.

Consequently, it can be assumed that relatively much knowledge of technology and resources, in the form of computer power, is required to get hold of the encrypted information. However, in the absence of guidance from practice, one must rely on other sources of Law. Article 29 WP has stated in a guide regarding anonymization techniques that in the case of data stored on a DLT through a hash, a hash function constitutes a form of pseudonymization (Article 29 WP Opinion 05/2014). According to Recital 26 of the regulation, only anonymous data is exempted from the regulation's scope of application. Data that has been pseudonymized and that could be attributed to a natural person through supplementary data is still considered personal data. Consequently, this means that there is reason to assume that both data that has been encrypted or undergone a hash function should not be considered anonymized according to the GDPR and thus may be covered by the concept of personal data.

The Processing of Personal Data

For the regulation to be applicable, it is further required that it concerns the processing of personal data. It is, therefore, important for this investigation to describe in a little more depth what constitutes the processing of personal data. According to Art. 4.2 GDPR processing is defined as an action or combination of actions regarding personal data or sets of personal data, regardless of whether they are performed automatically. Furthermore, the provision gives examples of measures to be considered as processing, such as collection, registration, processing, storage, deletion, etc. In *case C-101/01 Bodil Lindqvist*, the Court stated that "*every measure or series of measures*" taken with personal data must constitute processing within the meaning of the regulation (Garcia, 2005). Furthermore, the Court stated in case *C-131/12 Google Spain* that the activities of search engine providers – which consist of locating and referring to already published information – must be considered to constitute processing within the meaning of the regulation if the information constitutes personal data (Golden Data Law, 2022b). The regulation has thus given the concept of processing a wide scope, and in principle, all measures taken with personal data are covered (Chassang, 2017). Due to this broad definition, it can be assumed that, in principle, all areas of use with DLT are to be considered as processing. In addition, it can be mentioned that the processing concept covers even keeping or storing personal data without taking any other action.

Personal Data Controller and Personal Data Assistant

For the regulation to be applied, it is required that there is a personal data controller or a personal data assistant who processes personal data within the scope of their activities (Chassang, 2017). Who can be considered a personal data controller or assistant is central to determining who is responsible for processing personal data (Chassang, 2017). In traditional databases, it is relatively straightforward to determine who is considered the personal data controller because there is usually a central actor. The problem with decentralized technology like DLT is that not just one central actor usually determines the purposes for processing personal data. It is, therefore, necessary to investigate the concept of personal data controller concerning DLT to clarify whether actors within DLT must apply the regulation's provisions. According to Art. 4.7 GDPR defines a personal data controller as a natural or legal person, public authority, institution, or other body that, alone or together with others, determines the purposes and means for processing personal data. In the next sentence, it appears that if the purpose and means of the processing are determined by Union law or the national Law of the Member States, the person in charge of personal data can be prescribed in Union law or the national Law of the Member States (Art. 4.7 of GDPR). According to Art. 4.8 GDPR defines a personal data processor as a natural or legal person, public authority, institution, or other body that processes personal data on behalf of the data controller. The personal data controller or assistant must not be established within the Union (Art. 3 of GDPR). It should be noted in this context that according to Art. 26 GDPR, two or more actors can be jointly responsible for personal data, thereby determining the purposes and means for processing personal data.

To ensure the regulation's effectiveness and provide complete protection for the individuals affected, the EU Court of Justice has stipulated that the concept of personal data controller must be given a broad interpretation (Golden Data Law, 2022b). For example, the Court determined in case *C-210/16 Wirtschaftsakademie Schleswig-Holstein* that a company that created a Facebook page was, together with Facebook, the personal data controller for the processing of personal data about visitors to the Facebook page (Golden Data Law, 2022a). There is also no restriction on the design of the personal data controller's organization. This means that an individual, company, or other body can be considered responsible for personal data. In *case C-25/17 Jehovah's Witnesses*, the Court determined that even a group of individuals in a religious community can be considered responsible for personal data (Rothkegel & Strassemeyer, 2019).

Regarding DLT, there are divided opinions in the literature about who can be considered a personal data controller. Some argue that the nodes should be data controllers (Berberich & Steiner, 2016). The nodes independently maintain the DLT network and process data stored on the network and can thus be considered data controllers (Al-Abdullah et al., 2020). In private DLTs, there is also usually a company or authority that controls the entire network, so the nodes that make up the network would likely be considered personal data controllers (Finck, 2018). However, such an interpretation is not unproblematic and raises the question of whether each node should be considered a personal data controller or whether the nodes together can be jointly responsible.

The conclusion of the question depends on how one interprets the role of the nodes in the network. Farkas et al. state that the nodes that process and store data on a DLT do not have the opportunity to exercise any control over the consensus mechanism or the means for processing the personal data (Al-Abdullah et al., 2020). This means that the nodes cannot be considered jointly responsible for personal data according to Art. 26 GDPR because the nodes do not jointly determine the purposes and means of the processing. In addition, it appears from recital 79 of the GDPR that to be jointly responsible for personal data, it is required that one has determined each other's responsibilities, which is not possible in public DLT, where nodes can connect, join and leave the network at any time. However, CNIL believes it is possible to consider the nodes jointly responsible for personal data according to Art. 26 GDPR (European Parliament. Directorate General for Parliamentary Research Services., 2019). According to the CNIL, a group of individuals or nodes that jointly create a DLT with a common purpose should be considered joint personal data controllers unless it has been made clear who should be the personal data controller (Veale & Edwards, 2018).

Regardless of whether one considers that the nodes are to be considered as joint personal data controllers or not, there is reason to assume that each node that maintains the network should be able to be considered a personal data controller, at least in public DLT (Burman, 2020). This means that individuals who have had their rights violated according to the GDPR can assert claims against each node that makes up the network. Such an interpretation of the personal data controller concept would entail several problems because individual nodes cannot change data in the network and thus will have difficulty complying with the requirements that the regulation places on personal data controllers. Another interpretation of the doctrine is that the actors can influence the data on a DLT, who should be seen as personal data controllers. According to the CNIL, the actors within a DLT can be considered personal data controllers in two situations.

The first situation refers to situations when natural persons use DLT to process personal data in their professional activities, and the second situation concerns cases when legal persons process personal data on a DLT (Vavra, 2018). A broker registering an agreement to purchase real estate on a DLT can be considered a personal data controller. A third option is not to consider the nodes but private users of a DLT as data controllers. Such an interpretation is based on the fact that the users of a DLT send their data to fulfill a purpose, for example, to buy cryptocurrencies, who decide on the purposes of the personal data. However, criticism has been leveled against such a view. According to the CNIL, private actors should not be considered personal data controllers. According to the CNIL, users of a DLT can only be considered personal data controllers if 1) the user is a natural person and when the processing of personal data relates to a professional or commercial activity or 2) the user is a legal entity that processes personal data in a DLT (Kulhari, 2018b).

Legal Processing of Personal Data

General About the Principles for Processing Personal Data

For actors to be allowed to process personal data with DLT at all, it is required that the processing of personal data is permitted according to the regulation. To answer the question of whether the processing of personal data is permitted, Art. 5 GDPR some principles that must be taken into account in all personal data processing. The principles of legality, correctness, and transparency are stipulated in Art. 5.1(a) GDPR. The principles of legality can be said to reference the legal grounds applicable when one may process personal data in Art. 6.1 GDPR (Andrus, 2016). The principle of correctness means that personal data must be processed so that the data subject can reasonably expect that the personal data will be processed. The wording of the principle indicates that a balance of interests must be made in each case to determine whether the processing of personal data would be unreasonable. The openness principle means that all information and communication that occurs in connection with the processing of personal data must be easily accessible and simple for the data subject to understand (Savin, 2017). The transparency principle is particularly important because individuals must exercise the rights the GDPR grants them. The purpose principle appears in Art. 5.1(b) GDPR means that personal data must only be collected for an explicit and justified purpose. The principle of data minimization is stipulated in Art. 5.1(c) GDPR entails an obligation to limit the amount of personal data processed to only what is necessary to achieve the purposes (Savin, 2017). The principle of correctness is stipulated in Art. 5.1(d) means that the data must be correct and that personal data controllers must delete or correct incorrect data (Burman, 2020). According to Art. 5.1(e) the principle of storage minimization appears, meaning that personal data should not be stored longer than necessary (recital 39 of GDPR). The principles of integrity and confidentiality are stipulated in Art. 5.1(f) GDPR means that personal data must be processed to protect against unauthorized processing, loss, destruction, or damage.

Along with art. 5, GDPR establishes art. 6 GDPR the legal basis for when personal data processing may take place. According to Art. 6.1 it appears that the processing of personal data is only legal if:

a) The data subject has given his consent to his data being processed for one or more specific purposes,
b) The processing is necessary to fulfill an agreement to which the data subject is a party or to take measures at the request of the data subject before entering into such an agreement,
c) The processing is necessary to fulfill a legal obligation incumbent on the personal data controller,
d) The processing is necessary to protect interests that are of fundamental importance to the data subject or another natural person,
e) The processing is necessary to perform a task of public interest or as part of the personal data controller's exercise of authority,
f) The processing is necessary for purposes related to the legitimate interests of the controller or a third party unless the interests or fundamental rights and freedoms of the data subject outweigh and require personal data protection, especially when the data subject is a child.

The articles are cumulative, meaning that all the principles in Art. 5 GDPR must be followed and that any legal bases stated in Art. 6 must be applicable for the processing of personal data to be permitted. All principles stipulated in Art. 5.1 The GDPR is central to the regulation and sets requirements for personal data controllers regarding how personal data processing may occur. Therefore, this investigation needs to investigate the principles in Art. 5.1 GDPR relates to DLT to answer whether various actors can legally process personal data through a DLT. However, using DLT does not cause any particular conflicts with all the principles. It is, therefore, not necessary to investigate all the principles in Art. 5.1 GDPR but only those where the use of DLT can generate special problems, for example, the principle of data minimization, the principle of storage minimization, and the purpose principle (European Parliament. Directorate General for Parliamentary Research Services., 2019).

The Principles of Data and Storage Minimization

A principle that is of particular relevance to the chapter's investigation is the principle of task minimization. Of species. 5.1(c) GDPR, it appears that the processing of personal data must be adequate, relevant, and not too extensive concerning the purposes for which it is processed. The literature often refers to two DLT features that seem particularly problematic concerning the principle of task minimization. First, as mentioned earlier, DLT is immutable because one cannot modify or delete data posted on a DLT. Secondly, a complete copy of the database is stored in each node, which, in theory, means that the personal data can be replicated an infinite number of times (Finck, 2017). Thus, at first glance, DLT appears to be incompatible with the principle of data minimization. The principle of data minimization can be interpreted as an obligation for personal data controllers to limit the processing of personal data to only what is necessary (recital 38 of GDPR). In case *C-136/17 GC et al.*, the Court stated that information initially relevant to the purposes becomes irrelevant over time (Globocnik, 2020). Furthermore, Recital 39 of the regulation shows that personal data should only be processed if the purposes of the processing cannot be achieved by other means. The compatibility between DLT and the principle of data minimization is thus affected by how one interprets the purposes of the use. Closely related to the principle of task minimization is the principle of storage minimization. In Art. 5.1(e) GDPR, the principle of storage minimization means that personal data may not be stored longer than is necessary for processing. Even this principle seems to conflict with DLT as it is practically impossible to modify or delete personal data processed through DLT.

The Purpose Principle

The purpose principle is of particular importance for the processing of personal data because the principle constitutes protection against personal data controllers using the data subject's data in an inappropriate or otherwise objectionable way.140 Regarding the relationship between the purpose principle and DLT, the study from EPRS shows that the big question is whether only the original processing through DLT is covered by the purpose principle or whether subsequent processing also falls within the purposes of the processing (Erdos, 2021). The purpose principle appears in Art. 5.1(b) GDPR stipulated that personal data must be collected for specific, explicitly stated, and justified purposes and that personal data must not be processed in a way incompatible with these purposes. Furthermore, it appears that certain treatments taking place according to Art. 89.1 GDPR, e.g., scientific or statistical purposes, shall not be incompatible with the original purposes.

The first requirement for the purpose principle to be considered achieved is that it is a special purpose. This means that statements of purpose that are too general cannot be accepted (Chhetri et al., 2022). The second requisite is that personal data must only be collected for explicitly stated purposes. There is no requirement that the purpose be expressed in writing, but the purpose must be formulated, communicated, or expressed in an understandable form (Golden Data Law, 2022b). The third requirement is that there must be a justified purpose for the processing. This requisite can be considered connected to the legal grounds stipulated in Art. 6.1 GDPR (Radsch, 2023b). Personal data controllers who use DLT must convey to the data subject that they are using DLT and the consequences the technology will have on how their data will be processed. Regarding whether subsequent processing can be considered compatible with the purpose principle, EPRS said it is necessary to analyze each case to determine whether subsequent processing can be compatible with the purpose principle. In addition, it can be mentioned that according to EPRS, there is nothing to indicate that the processing of personal data through DLT should automatically be considered incompatible with the purpose principle (Soltani et al., 2022).

THE RIGHT TO BE FORGOTTEN

Introduction

The GDPR gives individuals various rights regarding how, when, and by whom their data can be processed. The previous section determined that the regulation applies to processing personal data with DLT. The following section will build on these conclusions and explore the possibility for individuals to invoke their data protection rights when data controllers use DLT. One of the data protection rights that the GDPR grants individuals is the right to erasure, also known as the right to be forgotten, which appears in Art. 17 GDPR. Briefly, the right to be forgotten can be summarized as a right for the data subject to turn to the personal data controller who processes the personal data and asks them to delete the data. However, one of the important features of DLT is that the data processed through the software protocol is immutable. A conflict arises here because it is clear that individuals have the right to request that data be deleted according to the regulation, but from a technical perspective, it is unclear whether actors who use DLT have the opportunity to fulfill these requirements. To investigate these issues more closely, one must understand what the right to be forgotten means.

General About the Right to Be Forgotten

The right to be forgotten is established in Art. 17 GDPR and means that the data subject shall have the right to have their data deleted by the data controller without undue delay. Furthermore, it appears in Art. 17 GDPR that the person in charge of personal data shall be obliged to delete personal data without undue delay on one of the six grounds stipulated in Art. 17.1(a) – (f) GDPR are fulfilled. The first ground, which appears from Art. 17.1(a), applies to situations where personal data is no longer necessary for the purposes for which it was collected or otherwise processed. The second ground is expressed in Art. 17.1(b) refers to cases where the data subject revokes the consent on which the processing is based and if there is no other legal basis for the processing. This point means that it is sufficient for the data subject to withdraw his consent to exercise his right to erasure (Savin, 2017). The third basis is stipulated in Art. 17.1(c) and concerns situations when the data subject objects to the processing through Art. 21.1, and there is no justifiable reason for the processing that weighs more heavily or that the data subject objects to the processing following Art. 21.2. Of species. 17.1(d), it appears that personal data controllers are obligated to delete personal data if it has been processed illegally. The fifth ground concerns cases where the personal data must be deleted to fulfill a legal obligation in Union law or in the national Law of the Member States to which the personal data controller is subject, see Art. 17.1(e). The last ground appears from Art. 17.1(f) and concerns situations when the personal data has been collected in connection with the offer of information society services in cases where the data subject was a child when the consent was given.

The right to be forgotten is similar to Art. 5 GDPR principles, especially with data minimization. However, the principle of data minimization presupposes that the personal data controller independently limits the number of personal data to what is relevant for the processing. The right to be forgotten differs from this principle by allowing the data subject to delete personal data that directly or indirectly concerns the data subject upon request. The obligation for the personal data controller to delete the personal data requires that the data subject requests this (Radsch, 2023a). From Art. 17.2, it appears that a personal data controller who has made the personal data public must provide information. The notification obligation means that the personal data controller who has published the personal data must - if there is an obligation to delete the data - taking into account the available technology and the cost, take reasonable steps to notify other personal data controllers who process the personal data that they must delete any links to, or copies or reproductions of the data in question. The notification obligation means that the personal data controller must inform the other personal data controllers who process the personal data that the data subject has requested that the personal data in question be deleted (recital 66 of GDPR).

A Right with Reservation

Many have emphasized the difficulty of applying the right to erasure to DLT in the doctrine. Kulms is quoted in the Singapore Journal of Legal Studies: "*[DLT] appears to contradict the regulatory underpinnings of EU's GDPR as storing data is vital for the existence of a distributed ledger*" (Kulms, 2020) While Christian Wirth, who is Senior Blockchain Architect at IBM mentions that a main challenge for DLT developers is to comply with the requirement for erasure in Art. 17 (Kolain & Wirth, 2018). To this, it can be mentioned that the right to be forgotten is not without exceptions. In practice, the right to erasure means a right for the data subject to have a review if there are grounds for erasing his desired personal data (Chhetri et al., 2022). When the data subject makes an erasure request, the personal data controller must assess whether there are grounds for erasing the data (Chhetri et al., 2022). Thus, the personal data controller's assessment determines whether personal data should be deleted (Chhetri et al., 2022). At the same time, it should be mentioned that the right to be forgotten is not an absolute right but must be understood based on its function in society and weighed against other fundamental rights. According to Art. 17.3 GDPR, what is mentioned in Art. 17.1 and Art. 17.2 does not apply if the processing of personal data is necessary for exercising freedom of expression and information, compliance with legal obligations, public health, archival purposes, or legal claims. The obligation for the personal data controller to delete personal data also does not include personal data that cannot identify the data subject without additional information, see Art. 11.2 GDPR. It should also be pointed out that according to Art. 23.1 GDPR allows Member States to introduce additional exceptions within Union law or their national legal system. A balance must, therefore, be made between the data subject's request for erasure and the stated interests. This balance of interests is central to assessing whether the exception rules in Art should cover personal data processed on DLT. 17.3 GDPR or if the data subject's request for erasure is to be granted.

The Balancing of Interests

Google Spain

An attention-grabbing case from the European Court of Justice where the balancing of interests in the right to be forgotten was discussed is case C-131/12 Google Spain. The decision is from 2014 and has long been considered the leading decision from the EUD regarding the right to be forgotten (Kranenborg, 2020). The background to the case was as follows. An advertisement regarding selling properties at executive auction, which had been foreclosed from the Spanish citizen MG, was published in the daily newspaper La Vanguardia. When Internet users searched MG's name on the Google search engine, links to the ad appeared. MG. Requested in the Spanish National Court i.a. complaint that Google would be required to delete or change links to two websites that appeared when searching for his name on Google's search engine (Golden Data Law, 2022b). The Spanish Court upheld the claimant's complaint against Google and, citing the right to the protection of personal data, held that Google had an obligation to remove the data from its website. Google appealed this decision to the Spanish Audiencia Nacional, which turned to the EUD with questions regarding the interpretation of the data protection directive (Golden Data Law, 2022b).

The case drew attention for several reasons. The information MG claimed violated his right to privacy was not incorrect but merely old and no longer current when the ad was published. 15 years earlier. Furthermore, MG's claim was directed against the newspaper that had published the ads and against Google, whose search engines in 2014 were the public's main tool for searching and accessing information. The case thus pitted three different interests against each other: the public's interest in freedom of information, a company's financial interests, and the individual's interest in a right to the protection of personal data. The case can thus be said to attempt to investigate the role of the Internet as a public memory. In his proposed ruling, Advocate General Jääskinen argued that a right to be forgotten should not be derived from the Data Protection Directive. Jääskinen argued that the freedom of expression and information must be weighed against the data subject's right to privacy protection (Lynskey, 2015). Furthermore, search engine providers exercise their freedom of business and expression when they make available tools for searching information on the Internet (Lynskey, 2015). Jääskinen argued that introducing a forgotten right would restrict central rights such as freedom of expression and information (Lynskey, 2015). The Advocate General's argument can be summarized as that a requirement to delete information that has been legally published would constitute an all too severe restriction on the public's freedom of expression and information. In addition, it would likely lead to automatically removing links to all disputed content, burdening search engine providers and curtailing their freedom of expression and business (Lynskey, 2015).

However, the Court did not follow the Advocate General's suggestion. Instead, the Court found that concerning Art. 7 and 8 of the EU Charter on Fundamental Rights, individuals may request that information not be made available to the general public (Golden Data Law, 2022b). The Court stated that, as a general rule, the individual's right to personal data protection outweighs the economic interests of the search engine provider and the public's interest in finding information (Golden Data Law, 2022b). However, this is not the case if the intervention in the fundamental rights of the person concerned under Art. 7 and 8 are for special reasons motivated by the public's interest in freedom of information (Golden Data Law, 2022b). Concerning the information in the current case, the Court stated that concerning the nature of the information, it was published for approx. Fifteen years ago, there were no particular reasons why the public was interested in accessing the data, and thus, MG had a right to demand that the data be deleted from Google's search engine (Golden Data Law, 2022b).

GC etc.

In case C-136/17 GC et al. EUD investigated how the right to erasure should be applied to sensitive personal and criminal data. The case concerned four individuals, GC, AF, BH, and ED, who independently requested that Google remove certain links to websites that appeared after searching for their names in Google's search engine (Zelger, 2023). Like the Google Spain case, the information was not published on websites by Google but by third parties. GC requested that Google delete a link to a satirical photo montage that insinuated that she and the mayor of the municipality where she was head of the mayor's office had an intimate relationship (Zelger, 2023). AF requested that links to an article that mentioned that AF had previously been an information officer for the Church of Scientology would be deleted (Zelger, 2023). BH requested that links to articles about a criminal investigation in which BH and several politicians and business people would be deleted (Zelger, 2023). It should be mentioned that the preliminary investigation did not lead to prosecution, which did not appear in most articles. Finally, ED requested that the links to two articles, which reported on a criminal trial for sexual abuse of minors in which ED was convicted, be deleted (Zelger, 2023). The EUD thus stated that search engine providers could only refuse requests from individuals to remove data of public interest if it was strictly necessary to include the link for the public to exercise their freedom of information under Art. 11 of the statute (Zelger, 2023). Concerning personal data relating to criminal proceedings made public, the EUD submitted that the right to erasure could also cover this data. For a search engine provider to be considered obliged to delete links to such data upon request, however, it is required that the data relate to an earlier stage of the legal process and that the data, taking into account the later developments in the proceedings, no longer reflect the current situation (Zelger, 2023).

The Balancing of Interests and The Relationship To DLT

From the aforementioned legal cases, it can be stated that the Court's balancing of interests aims at the public's interest in freedom of expression and information and the companies' financial interest against the data subject's interest in protecting his data. In the case of DLT, however, it is not particularly likely that the public's freedom of information would be actualized in the balance of interests, as the purposes of processing data on a DLT usually differ from the purpose of a search engine provider's purpose. Instead, interests – for example, the companies' financial interests or technological innovation – will be set against the data subject's right to personal data protection. The main rule is that the data subject's right to request that the data be deleted outweighs the companies' financial and public interest in accessing the data unless there are special reasons. Admittedly, the courts in the referred cases found that the category of information, for example, if the information is more sensitive or relates to an individual's public service, can affect the balancing of interests. As far as financial interests are concerned, these should consider the individual's interest in protecting personal data for the companies' financial interests to weigh more heavily (Andrus, 2016). It is, therefore, possible to question the suitability of using DLT to process personal data because the data subject's interest in the right to be forgotten will probably outweigh the personal data controller's interest in using DLT. Since a data controller can misuse sensitive and non-sensitive personal data, processing personal data on DLT should be done carefully.

Territorial scope of the right to be forgotten - Google v CNIL

Another issue of interest to this investigation is the territorial scope of the right to be forgotten. As mentioned earlier, a DLT network consists of nodes located anywhere on Earth. This raises the question of whether a personal data controller, if the data subject's request for deletion is granted, is obliged to delete the data globally or only from the part of the network within the EU. The issue has been examined by the EUD in case *C-507/17 Google v. CNIL*, where the Court had to examine whether the right to be forgotten means that data must be removed from the entire Internet, i.e., without any geographical limitation. The Court began by stating that the purpose of the GDPR is to ensure a high level of protection for personal data throughout the EU (Samonte, 2020). The Court determined that the right to be forgotten means the data must be removed from all links corresponding to the Member States' country domains (Samonte, 2020). Thus, a request for removal means information from a person registered in Sweden that the information should not only be removed from Swedish ".se" domains but also all other country domains belonging to the member states, e.g., "*.dk*," "*.de*," "*.es*," etc. Furthermore, the EUD stated that the right to be forgotten cannot entail an obligation to remove links from all versions provided outside the EU but an obligation to take measures that can prevent internet users from gaining access to the data from any of the Member States (Samonte, 2020). It should be pointed out that although the EUD stated that the right to be forgotten does not entail an obligation to delete links from all search engine versions, there is also no prohibition against this (Samonte, 2020).

THE DIFFICULTY OF DELETING ON DLT

Introduction

Several authors have pointed out the difficulty of applying the right to be forgotten to DLT. As mentioned earlier, the DLT networks are designed to make it difficult, if not impossible, for actors to make unilateral modifications to the data stored on a DLT. The consequence of a lack of possibility for unilateral modifications is that deleting information from a DLT is extremely difficult. The difficulty of deleting data from a DLT is mainly due to technical factors but also the management structure of the DLT networks. This means that even if technical solutions were to succeed in solving the problem of erasing data from a DLT, the network's governance structure may make it difficult to get all nodes to implement the changes on their copy of the database (Voss, 2016). To truly understand the relationship between DLT and the right to be forgotten, one must first understand the difficulties associated with the erasure of DLT. Against this background, the following part will investigate the difficulties associated with erasure on DLT.

Technical Difficulties

According to Berberich et al., using DLT poses two main challenges concerning the GDPR. Firstly, the technology's decentralized nature entails difficulty identifying personal data controllers. The second and main problem with DLT is that it is, in principle, impossible to implement a request for deletion from a data subject (Berberich & Steiner, 2016). The difficulties with deletion on DLT can be attributed to the underlying design of the technology. A DLT is made up of different blocks that are linked together in a chain-like structure. For a data controller to be able to fulfill a data subject's request for erasure, it would be necessary to destroy each block in the chain until reaching the block of data that one wants to be deleted to recreate the chain again, block by block (Berberich & Steiner, 2016). In addition to this strenuous process, the technology is based on a consensus mechanism, which requires that most connected nodes approve the deletion and the retroactive building up of the blockchain again (Berberich & Steiner, 2016). A hard fork is where most nodes vote to modify the blockchain. According to Finck, it should be emphasized that hard forks cannot be considered meaningful GDPR compliance tools even though they can be used to modify data stored on a DLT (Finck, 2017). Finck states that, in practice, a hard fork is only useful for the latest block in a blockchain because it would be prohibitively expensive, resource-intensive, and time-consuming to invalidate all previous transactions and process all blocks again (Finck, 2017).

The consequences of this technical design are that an attempt by a data controller to modify data stored in a DLT would distort the entire structure of the DLT. It should be stated that the purpose of this design was to create trust and guarantee data integrity for a network that a central actor does not control (Vavra, 2018). A data controller fulfilling a request for deletion from a data subject of data stored on a DLT would thus do so at the expense of the DLT's underlying purpose. This would likely result in damaging user confidence in the DLT.

Structural Difficulties

General

As mentioned at the outset earlier, it is not only technical difficulties but also the basic structure of DLT that can constitute an obstacle to the data subject's right to exercise his right to be forgotten. The basic structure of DLT consists of nodes, where each node stores a copy of all transactions and transfers of data that took place on the network—concerning the right to be forgotten in Art. 17 GDPR, this raises two interesting questions: 1) whether deletion must take place on all nodes that store a copy of DLT, 2) if it is the case that deletion must take place from all nodes, how is this affected by the territorial extent of the right to be forgotten?

Problematization One: The Extent of the Erasure

To answer the first question, one must understand the scope of the erasure obligation. Here, guidance can be obtained from practice. In Google Spain, the ECJ held that the data subject had the right to request the deletion of certain links on the Google search engine that appeared when an internet user searched for the data subject's name. At the same time, the information published on the website was considered worthy of protection from a freedom of expression perspective (Golden Data Law, 2022b). The fact that the EUD distinguished between Google and the news website and did not consider that the deletion covered all data raises the question of whether a request for deletion covers the personal data stored on all nodes or whether one should distinguish between the nodes. According to Kranenborg, the EUD distinguished between Google's obligations as a search engine provider and the obligations of the website that originally published the information. Since the data subject directed his action primarily against Google and not against the website that had originally published the data, the EUD did not discuss the issue of the website's deletion obligations (Kranenborg, 2020). In my opinion, upon carefully reviewing the EUD's ruling, one can find another reason why the EUD distinguished between Google and the news website. In its ruling, the EUD stated that the fact that Google's search engine makes it significantly easier for every internet user to access the relevant data - and plays a decisive role in the dissemination of this data - means that the publication of the data on a search engine constitutes a more extensive intervention in the registrant's right to privacy (Golden Data Law, 2022b). In my opinion, there is reason to assume that processing personal data on a DLT, like a search engine, constitutes a more intrusive intervention in the individual's privacy than publishing the data on a normal website.

The Administrative Court's statement can mean that a search result that does not appear in a search in Google's search engine should not be considered a serious restriction on the public's freedom of information because the information remains with the source. It is reasonable to assume that widely disseminated information is at greater risk of being misused. Distinguishing a search engine that aims to increase access and thus the spread of information for economic purposes from a news website that aims to publish information from journalistic experiences can thus be assumed to be reasonable. When it comes to DLT - especially public DLT - it can be stated that the data, similar to the data on a search engine, is subject to wide dissemination. This is because anyone can read the information on the network, and a copy of the entire network is saved on each node. The fact that the nodes continuously replicate the personal data means significant interference with the data subject's right to integrity and privacy. Furthermore, it can be assumed that regarding the use of DLT, there will be no underlying journalistic interest in the vast majority of cases. This suggests that the deletion obligation means the data must be deleted from all nodes in the DLT network. Article 29 WP has stated in guidance regarding cloud services that store data on different computer servers must ensure that the requested data is deleted from all servers for the deletion obligation according to Art. 17 GDPR must be considered fulfilled. According to EPRS, Article 29 WP's statement can be applied analogously to DLT (Veale & Edwards, 2018). This also supports the interpretation that the erasure obligation covers all nodes in the DLT network.

Problematization Two: Territorial Limitation of Erasure

If one starts from the conclusion that deletion must occur from all nodes, the question of the territorial limitation of the deletion is raised. DLT is cross-border, as the nodes can be located anywhere worldwide. In *Google v CNIL*, the Court stated that the right to be forgotten was limited to the EU and that search engine providers were not obliged to delete the data from all versions established outside the EU's territorial area (Samonte, 2020). At the same time, the EUD stated that personal data controllers are obligated to take measures that prevent internet users from gaining access to the data within the EU.200 Unlike a website that can bind itself territorially through its country domains and block access to the website through so-called geo-blocking, DLT does not bind terrorists similarly (Chase, 2019). A data controller who processes personal data through DLT must be able to ensure that nodes located outside the EU safeguard the data subject's rights to the same extent as nodes located within the EU. In light of this, it can be stated that personal data deletion must occur from all nodes regardless of where the nodes are located in the world.

The Notification Obligation

One of the technical difficulties in applying the right to be forgotten to DLT is that it is practically impossible for a single actor to delete information in the blockchain. Theoretically, however, there is an opportunity for the nodes to delete data stored on a DLT, for example, through a hard fork. Implementing such a request would require a majority of nodes to approve a request to destroy the blockchain and later verify the new chain again, block by block (Berberich & Steiner, 2016). According to Art. 17.2 GDPR, a personal data controller obliged to delete personal data must notify other personal data controllers who process the personal data. Earlier, it was established that it is possible to consider the nodes as personal data controllers. The notification obligation means that the personal data controller who has received a deletion request must if the personal data has been made public, notify other personal data controllers who process the personal data that they must delete any links to or copies or reproductions of this data (art. 17.2 GDPR). For DLT, the single node that receives a deletion request must be able to notify other nodes about this, which is difficult to implement in a decentralized environment. For example, the DLT Ethereum is maintained by a network of approx. 300,000 nodes (Maeng et al., 2020). For this to happen, it is required that there are mechanisms that ensure that all nodes are notified of a deletion request. According to Finck, there are two main problems with the notification obligation within DLT. First, all nodes must be notified of a deletion request, and most nodes must vote to approve the deletion. Secondly, it can be assumed that all nodes will not be within the same jurisdiction, which could lead to nodes and an entire DLT being forced to shut down for non-compliance with the GDPR, which Finck considers disproportionate (Finck, 2017).

It should be pointed out that the notification obligation does not mean that the personal data controller who receives the deletion request must ensure that all other personal data controllers also delete the data, but only that one "takes reasonable measures" to notify other personal data controllers who process the data. According to Recital 66 of the GDPR, the personal data controller has to take reasonable action by "*taking into account the available technology and the aids available to the personal data controller*" (recital 66 of the GDPR & art. 17.2 GDPR). It can thus be questioned whether DLTs are exempt from the notification obligation due to a lack of technical ability. There are no clear answers to this question, neither in the literature nor in practice (Bracy, 2018). In light of the above arguments, it can be assumed that for an effective application of the notification obligation to DLT, mechanisms must enable communication between the nodes.

RECONCILING DLT AND THE RIGHT TO BE FORGOTTEN

Introduction

While there are several difficulties with deleting content on a DLT, the right to be forgotten does not necessarily conflict with DLT. What is to be considered a fulfillment of the erasure obligation will have its starting point in what constitutes erasure. It would be difficult to assess whether deletion of personal data from a DLT is possible if there is no precise guidance on how the term "*deletion*" should be interpreted. The extent to which it is possible to combine technology with the right to be forgotten thus depends largely on how one interprets the concept of erasure. Consequently, it is important for the chapter's question to discuss the scope of the concept of "*deletion*." After dealing with the meaning of the concept of erasure, the following discussion will try to find solutions that can bring together a right to be forgotten using DLT. To this end, various alternatives and proposed solutions in the literature will be discussed.

The Meaning of the Term Erasure

To accurately account for the technology's ability to comply with the regulation's requirements for erasure, it is first necessary to clarify the meaning of the concept of erasure. The obligation to delete personal data is a responsibility that the GDPR imposes on personal data controllers to implement when a data subject invokes the right to be forgotten. Neither the article text of Art. 17 nor the reasons for the GDPR provide any further explanation of the meaning of the concept of erasure (Radsch, 2023a). What counts as the fulfillment of the erasure obligation will thus depend on the interpretations the EUD and the member states' respective supervisory authorities would make (Tatar et al., 2020). Due to the lack of a clear definition of the concept of deletion, these bodies can interpret the meaning of the term deletion in a way that considers the immutability of DLT. By this, I mean that DLT only needs to come into conflict with the right to be forgotten if the meaning of the concept of erasure is something that is not possible to achieve with the technology. The extent to which it is possible to combine technology with the right to be forgotten depends largely on how one interprets the concept of erasure (Vavra, 2018).

The Oxford Learners Dictionary defines the concept of erasure as *"the act of removing writing, drawing, recorded material or data, or the act of removing or destroying all signs of something."* From the above quote, it can be stated that the generally known meaning of the term erasure is to be compared with obliteration/destruction. Such an interpretation was also applied by the EUD in case C-434/16 Nowak, where the Court stated that an individual had, under certain circumstances, the right to have his answers to the tests and the examiner's notes erased (Chase, 2019). Kukhari also states that erasure should be interpreted so that the relevant personal data is destroyed or erased and cannot be recreated (Kulhari, 2018a). Consequently, such an interpretation of the concept of erasure entails several problems for using DLT because the destruction or erasure of data on a DLT is very difficult to implement, if not impossible. However, it should be mentioned that it is unclear whether the concept of erasure should be given the same interpretation concerning the right to be forgotten. In Nowak, the Court failed to clarify whether the term erasure can mean something other than obliteration. In addition, there is a debate in the literature about what constitutes erasure in terms of its meaning, according to Art. 17 GDPR (Hristov & Dimitrov, 2018). In light of the above, there is reason to investigate the meaning of the concept of erasure within the framework of Art. 17 can be interpreted differently than destruction or erasure of the data.

Some argue that the meaning of the term erasure is used in Art. 17 GDPR covers more than the mere erasure of personal data. For example, in Google Spain, the EUD considered that it was enough that the data would no longer be available in a search in Google's search engine for the data subject's right to be forgotten to be considered fulfilled. However, the personal data published in an article remained publicly available to the newspaper supplier. Only the fact that the links to the article were removed from the search engine was considered deletion. Kranenborg points out that the right to be forgotten, as expressed in Google Spain, does not mean that the information concerning the person is "*forgotten*" but only removed from the Internet's "*active memory*" (Kranenborg, 2020). Such an interpretation of the meaning of erasure would mean that the data can remain on a DLT as long as you make it impossible for the public to find the data by searching the data subject's name on the network. According to a study issued by EPRS, there is reason to assume that the meaning of the concept of erasure is within the framework of Art. 17 GDPR can be interpreted in other ways as pure data erasure.218 The study refers to how some member states' data protection authorities have argued for the interpretation that the requirement for erasure can be considered fulfilled if the data is "*put beyond use*"(Berberich & Steiner, 2016). For example, the Austrian Data Protection Authority (DSB) has argued that erasure does not necessarily require pure destruction of the data, but other technical solutions, such as anonymization, can be used to achieve erasure in Art. 17 GDPR's meaning (Golden Data Law, 2019). Article 29 WP has also stated in a guide regarding cloud services that personal data can no longer be deleted or completely anonymized. There is, therefore, reason to assume that data that has been anonymized can be equated with having been deleted.

According to Kulhari, data destroyed through de-identification should be considered to constitute deletion (Kulhari, 2018b). De-identifying personal data means that you destroy all identification possibilities so that the data that continues to be processed can no longer, directly or indirectly, be linked to a natural person. Kulhari's interpretation - that de-identified data should be considered deleted - is largely based on the same reasoning as the interpretation that anonymous data should be equated with deletion. In addition, it should be pointed out that the GDPR places a high demand on what can be considered anonymous data. Article 29 WP has stated in a guide regarding anonymization methods that de-identified and anonymous personal data may still pose a risk to individuals if there are still opportunities to identify the data subject by obtaining additional data from other sources (Article 29 WP Opinion

05/2014). This statement can reference personal data controllers to ensure that the data is anonymized and not pseudonymized, as the GDPR does not cover only anonymized data.

The CNIL has stated that DLT can approach a GDPR-compliant application for the right to be forgotten (Finck, 2017). However, the extent to which this is possible will depend on how the courts interpret the meaning of the term erasure. Against the background of the above, there is, in my opinion, much to suggest that the concept of erasure can include measures other than mere erasure or destruction of data. For example, measures such as anonymization would confer on the data subject the same effects as mere destruction of the data would have done, provided that it is total anonymization and not pseudonymization. That practice would recognize such an interpretation is strengthened by the fact that the GDPR's scope of application does not cover anonymous data, see recital 26 of the GDPR. However, Article 29 WP has stated that technological advances and the constant, abundant access to information in modern society have made it difficult to achieve pure anonymity regarding personal data (Article 29 WP, Opinion 03/2013). According to Article 29 WP, data controllers who decide to anonymize data should regularly and continuously review the risk that data can be identified with new technological innovations (Article 29 WP, Opinion 03/2013).

Implementation of Deletion Mechanisms on a DLT

General

Earlier, it has been stated what difficulties there are concerning erasure on a DLT. A simple application of the right to be forgotten to DLT can thus be excluded. At the same time, it has been stated later in the chapter that the meaning of the concept of erasure is not yet fully clarified, and there are strong arguments that erasure may involve other measures than pure erasure or destruction of personal data. With an increased awareness of the difficulties with Art. 17 GDPR and DLT, several technical options have been considered in the literature and in practice that aim to introduce a GDPR-compatible right to be forgotten on DLT. Thus, evaluating some of these proposed solutions is interesting for the chapter's presentation. Before an account of these proposed solutions begins, it may be worth recalling what was mentioned at the beginning of this chapter. New technologies like DLT are often subject to heavy speculation and investment. At the same time, there are few ready-made products, which means that promises about technical solutions to problems can be difficult to implement in practice.

Built-In Data Protection and Data Protection as Standard

In Blockchain and Privacy Protection in the Case of The European General Data Protection Regulation (GDPR), a study investigated the relationship between GDPR and DLT through the Delphi method (Zichichi et al., 2022). The study found that actors who use DLT should consider an impact assessment on how the technology can protect individuals' right to privacy and protection of personal data. Furthermore, the study found that by using built-in data protection and data protection as a standard, actors can implement a GDPR-compliant use of DLT (Cadogan, 2023). Built-in data protection and data protection as standard is expressed in Art. 25 GDPR. According to Art. 25 GDPR, the personal data controller must implement appropriate technical and organizational measures to ensure the regulation's requirements are met and the data subject's rights are protected. Examples of such measures include that data processing is minimized, personal data is pseudonymized, transparency regarding the processing, and the person responsible for personal data has the opportunity to create and improve security devices (recital 78 of GDPR). According to Finck, art. 25 of The GDPR mentions encryption as an appropriate technical and organizational measure to fulfill the regulation's requirements because there are possibilities to achieve a partially GDPR-compliant DLT (Finck, 2017).

In my opinion, however, it is questionable how data protection by design and data protection by default will help the difficulties of reconciling a right to be forgotten with the GDPR. Admittedly, data protection by design and data protection by default can ease the tensions between DLT and GDPR, as Finck points out. To achieve total compliance with the GDPR when using DLT, however, it is required that there are mechanisms that recognize the registrant's ability to delete data.

Storage of Personal Data Outside the DLT

A proposed solution that directly addresses the problem of erasure and is often advocated in the literature is to store personal data outside the chain (eng: off-chain). For example, Finck and Tatar et al. stated that storing personal data off-chain can achieve GDPR-compliant compliance with the right to be forgotten (Finck, 2017; Tatar et al., 2020). Storing personal data off-chain means that the personal data is disconnected from all other data and stored separately in a storage space outside the DLT network. At the same time, a digital signature, a so-called hash, is created on the blockchain that links the DLT network and the separate storage space (Tatar et al., 2020). This arrangement enables the deletion of personal data on the DLT because you can delete personal data without breaking the chain structure (Tatar et al., 2020). Furthermore, it is not required that most nodes approve a modification of the data because it is not stored on the DLT network. The hash value, i.e., the digital signature, which is stored on the chain, also does not need to be deleted because when the personal data is deleted, the hash linked to the deleted personal data becomes meaningless (Tatar et al., 2020).

Storing personal data outside DLT thus appears as a good solution to the difficulties associated with the right to be forgotten and DLT. At the same time, the storage of personal data outside the DLT is not completely problem-free. A problem that arises concerns the ownership of personal data. According to Tatar et al., storing personal data outside the DLT implies relying on third parties for storage in a separate storage space (Tatar et al., 2020). By moving the personal data outside the DLT to a third party, one also transfers control over the data. Thus, the third party that stores and exercises control over the data may be considered a personal data controller within the meaning of the GDPR. Another problem with storing the spending outside of DLT is that you miss out on the benefits of the technology. For example, the technology's transparency is lost as it becomes more difficult for actors to see who stores or has access to the information because this is not shown on the DLT. In the article The GDPR-Blockchain Paradox: Exempting Permissioned Blockchains from the GDPR, Mirchandani states that although the storage of personal data outside the DLT can ensure regulatory compliance for actors who use DLT, the solution ignores the most important advantage of the technology, the immutability of the technology (Mirchandani, 2019). Mirchandani believes that storing personal data outside the DLT would only lead to increased complexity but with the same functions as an editable database. There would thus be no point in using DLT as the technology would only make the system more complex and inefficient than a normal database (Mirchandani, 2019). In light of the above, it can be stated that storing personal data outside the DLT would enable a GDPR-compliant application of the technology. At the same time, the solution would mean that the use of the technology becomes more difficult to justify. That would mean missing out on the technology's benefits, namely the technology's inherent security of data control, immutability, and transparency.

Other Proposals

The two above-proposed solutions are the most common, but not the only ones, in the debate regarding the relationship between DLT and Art. 17 GDPR. According to CNIL, personal data stored on DLT should be registered as a hash or a ciphertext assigned by a "*state-of-the-art*" algorithm (Bracy, 2018). CNIL believes that by registering personal data on a DLT in a hash or ciphertext, one can make the personal data practically impossible for actors without the right keys to gain access and thus approach the effects of erasure. Mirchandani also argues that personal data stored on a DLT through a hash should be considered to meet the regulation's requirements for erasure (Mirchandani, 2019). It should be noted that a hash constitutes pseudonymized data. The regulation would thus still apply to the data. Another suggestion is the use of so-called zero-knowledge proofs. In short, zero-knowledge proofs make it possible to hide information by only answering a privacy-related question without publicizing the answer's actual content (De Filippi, 2016). For example, the technology enables only a yes or no answer to be obtained to questions if the individual is 18 or if the individual is a woman.

Another proposal that occurs is the use of so-called stealth addresses. In short, the technology enables us to anonymize or pseudonymize the stored data. As stated earlier, data in a DLT is stored in different blocks. The owner or whoever disposes of the data is assigned a public digital signature in the form of a hash. This means that all actors who use the technology and all nodes can see and verify who owns the data. Using so-called stealth addresses, the digital signature is anonymized and remains private between the two actors who send and receive data (Li & Kassem, 2021).

CONCLUSION

The above account has demonstrated that there is a lack of clear guidance regarding the application of GDPR to DLT. Tensions arise when GDPR is applied to new technological innovations such as DLT (Kulhari, 2018a). There is a conflict between the basic features of DLT and the general structure and design of the GDPR. To understand this conflict between these, it can be helpful to see the problem from a broader perspective by evaluating two partly conflicting normative goals of EU law. The GDPR was designed based on the idea that the data collection, storage, and processing methods of personal data should be carried out by centralized models that could clearly demand responsibility from the controlling actor (Finck, 2017). DLT was designed with the idea that decentralized models could be introduced for data management. According to Finck, the GDPR was already partially outdated when it was introduced compared to next-generation technological development (Finck, 2017). That is something I agree with. Admittedly, it can be argued that GDPR enables decentralized models for data management by allowing several actors to be jointly responsible for personal data. However, such an argument would imply a system with thousands, if not hundreds of thousands, of DLT controllers, which would, in my view, undermine the fundamental purpose of the GDPR. It is not unusual for legislation not to develop at the same speed as technology. In today's digital society, however, this gap is getting bigger as the pace of innovation increases ever greater. For example, against the background of the chapter's presentation, one sees how central aspects of the GDPR, such as deleting personal data, cannot be applied to new technologies without difficulty. This leads to trade-offs having to be made between the individual's fundamental right to personal data protection and one of the EU's goals, the promotion of innovation.

The European Commission has stated that the GDPR is technologically neutral and that continued innovation will thrive under the regulation (Mirchandani, 2019). However, according to Mirchandani, the GDPR's design constitutes an obstacle to technological innovation. Mirchandani argues that the language of the GDPR is too ambiguous for developers of DLT to take a chance on starting to store personal data in blockchains because they risk huge fines if the technology violates the GDPR (Mirchandani, 2019). Instead, Mirchandani argues that DLT should be exempted from the GDPR's scope to not obstruct technological innovation. However, such a solution to the balance between the fundamental rights of individuals and technological innovation is hardly desirable. The immutable nature of DLT poses a major threat to individuals' ability to protect their data effectively. In the article The Interplay between Decentralization and Privacy: The Case of Blockchain Technologies, De Filippi warns that decentralized networks such as DLT do not necessarily promote the privacy of individuals (De Filippi, 2016). Instead, the immutable nature of the technology, together with the fact that each node stores its copy of the DLT in public, implies greater transparency and greater dissemination of personal data. This can be much more vulnerable to individuals than actors such as authorities or companies that monitor their centralized counterparts (De Filippi, 2016).

It should be pointed out that De Filippi, in the same article, opens up the possibility that decentralized networks such as DLT can, with the right technical design and if individuals trust the governing actor in a centralized network, be considered the more advantageous platform concerning the promotion of individuals' integrity and the right to protection of personal data (De Filippi, 2016). Finck also believes that DLT, with the right technical design - for example, by being designed according to built-in data protection and data protection as standard or by storing personal data outside the DLT or by anonymizing personal data on the DLT - can fulfill the same function as GDPR, namely to give individuals more control over their data. However, this does not mean that technological innovation should always weigh more heavily than the fundamental rights of individuals. EDPS has stated that although advanced technology increases the risks of reduced privacy and poorer data protection, technological innovations can also bring solutions for better control and transparency for the individuals whose data is processed (European Data Protection Supervisor, 2023). The technology underlying DLT is still relatively new, and the development of the technology is ongoing. In my opinion, the legislator should focus on how to design the GDPR so that it does not hinder technological innovation while ensuring the fundamental rights of individuals. For example, this could be achieved by 1) changing the text of the article in the GDPR to offer individuals the opportunity to consent to their data being processed on DLT or 2) clarifying the meaning of the term erasure to make it easier for actors who want to develop DLT products. However, how the legislature and the courts will ultimately address the conflict between GDPR and DLT will only be revealed with time.

REFERENCES

Al-Abdullah, M., Alsmadi, I., AlAbdullah, R., & Farkas, B. (2020). Designing privacy-friendly data repositories: A framework for a blockchain that follows the GDPR. *Digital Policy Regulation and Governance*, *22*(5/6), 389–411. doi:10.1108/DPRG-04-2020-0050

Andrus, M. T. (2016). The Right to be Forgotten in America: Have Search Engines Inadvertently Become Consumer Reporting Agencies? *Business Law Today*, 1–4. https://www.jstor.org/stable/businesslawtoday.2016.05.06

Bains, P. (2022, January 26). *Blockchain Consensus Mechanisms: A Primer for Supervisors*. IMF. https://www.imf.org/en/Publications/fintech-notes/Issues/2022/01/25/Blockchain-Consensus-Mechanisms-511769

Berberich, M., & Steiner, M. (2016). Practitioner's Corner • Blockchain Technology and the GDPR – How to Reconcile Privacy and Distributed Ledgers? *European Data Protection Law Review*, *2*(3), 422–426. doi:10.21552/EDPL/2016/3/21

Bracy, J. (2018). *CNIL publishes blockchain guidance for GDPR compliance*. IAPP. https://iapp.org/news/a/cnil-publishes-blockchain-guidance-for-gdpr-compliance/

Burman, A. (2020). *The Growth of Privacy Regulation and the Bill* (Will India's Proposed Data Protection Law Protect Privacy and Promote Growth? pp. 3–8). Carnegie Endowment for International Peace. https://www.jstor.org/stable/resrep24293.4

Cadogan, M. S. (2023). *Blockchain and Distributed Ledger Technology: Definition and Scope* (Enforcing Smart Legal Contracts, pp. 2–2). Centre for International Governance Innovation. https://www.jstor.org/stable/resrep47331.7

Chase, P. H. (2019). *Perspectives on the General Data Protection Regulation Of the European Union*. German Marshall Fund of the United States. https://www.jstor.org/stable/resrep21227

Chassang, G. (2017). The impact of the EU general data protection regulation on scientific research. *Ecancermedicalscience*, *11*, 709. doi:10.3332/ecancer.2017.709 PMID:28144283

Chhetri, T. R., Kurteva, A., DeLong, R. J., Hilscher, R., Korte, K., & Fensel, A. (2022). Data Protection by Design Tool for Automated GDPR Compliance Verification Based on Semantically Modeled Informed Consent. *Sensors (Basel)*, *22*(7), 2763. doi:10.3390/s22072763 PMID:35408377

Coyne, H. (2019). The Untold Story of Edward Snowden's Impact on the GDPR. *The Cyber Defense Review*, *4*(2), 65–80. https://www.jstor.org/stable/26843893

De Filippi, P. (2016). *The Interplay between Decentralization and Privacy: The Case of Blockchain Technologies* (SSRN Scholarly Paper 2852689). https://papers.ssrn.com/abstract=2852689

Erdos, D. (2021). The 'right to be forgotten' beyond the EU: An analysis of wider G20 regulatory action and potential next steps. *Journal of Medicine and Law*, *13*(1), 1–35. doi:10.1080/17577632.2021.1884947

European Data Protection Supervisor. (2023, November 16). *Shaping a Safer Digital Future: A New Strategy for a New Decade*. EDPS. https://edps.europa.eu/press-publications/publications/strategy/shaping-safer-digital-future

European Parliament. Directorate General for Parliamentary Research Services. (2019). *Blockchain and the general data protection regulation: Can distributed ledgers be squared with European data protection law?* Publications Office. https://data.europa.eu/doi/10.2861/535

Finck, M. (2017). *Blockchains and Data Protection in the European Union* (SSRN Scholarly Paper 3080322). doi:10.2139/ssrn.3080322

Finck, M. (2018). *Blockchain Regulation and Governance in Europe*. Cambridge University Press. doi:10.1017/9781108609708

Garcia, F. (2005). Bodil Lindqvist: A Swedish Churchgoer's Violation of the European Union's Data Protection Directive Should Be a Warning to U.S. Legislators. *Fordham Intellectual Property, Media and Entertainment Law Journal, 15*(4), 1204. https://ir.lawnet.fordham.edu/iplj/vol15/iss4/10

Global Freedom of Expression. (2017, June 27). *Satakunnan Markkinapörssi Oy and Satamedia Oy v. Finland*. Global Freedom of Expression. https://globalfreedomofexpression.columbia.edu/cases/case-satakunnan-markkinaporssi-oy-satamedia-oy-v-finland/

Globocnik, J. (2020). The Right to Be Forgotten is Taking Shape: CJEU Judgments in GC and Others (C-136/17) and Google v CNIL (C-507/17). *GRUR International, 69*. doi:10.1093/grurint/ikaa002

Golden Data Law. (2019, February 5). Austrian Data Protection Authority: The erasure of personal data is also possible through. *Golden Data*. https://medium.com/golden-data/austrian-data-protection-authority-the-erasure-of-personal-data-is-also-possible-through-4e61b882e4ad

Golden Data Law. (2022a, October 23). Facebook Fan Pages: Liability of co-controllers. *Golden Data*. https://medium.com/golden-data/facebook-fan-pages-liability-of-co-controllers-2a23e7ecd3a9

Golden Data Law. (2022b, October 23). Google Spain v. AEPD: Remembering the "Right to be Forgotten." *Golden Data*. https://medium.com/golden-data/google-v-spain-the-right-to-be-forgotten-aaee50dae43c

Hristov, P., & Dimitrov, W. (2018, October 29). *The blockchain as a backbone of GDPR compliant frameworks*.

KolainM.WirthC. (2018, May 9). *Privacy by BlockChain Design: A Blockchain-enabled GDPR-compliant Approach for Handling Personal Data*. doi:10.18420/blockchain2018_03

Kranenborg, H. (2020). Article 17 Right to erasure ('right to be forgotten'). In C. Kuner, L. A. Bygrave, C. Docksey, & L. Drechsler (Eds.), The EU General Data Protection Regulation (GDPR): A Commentary (p. 0). Oxford University Press. doi:10.1093/oso/9780198826491.003.0049

Kulhari, S. (2018a). *Building-Blocks of a Data Protection Revolution: The Uneasy Case for Blockchain Technology to Secure Privacy and Identity* (1st ed.). Nomos Verlagsgesellschaft mbH. https://www.jstor.org/stable/j.ctv941qz6

Kulhari, S. (2018b). Data Protection, Privacy and Identity: A Complex Triad. In *Building-Blocks of a Data Protection Revolution* (1st ed., pp. 23–37). Nomos Verlagsgesellschaft mbH. https://www.jstor.org/stable/j.ctv941qz6.7

Kulms, R. (2020). Blockchains: Private Lawmatters. *Singapore Journal of Legal Studies*, 63–89. https://www.jstor.org/stable/27032601

Lambert, P. (2017). *Understanding the New European Data Protection Rules*. CRC Press.

Li, J., & Kassem, M. (2021). Applications of distributed ledger technology (DLT) and Blockchain-enabled smart contracts in construction. *Automation in Construction, 132*, 103955. doi:10.1016/j.autcon.2021.103955

Lynskey, O. (2015). Control over Personal Data in a Digital Age: Google Spain v AEPD and Mano Costeja Gonzalez. *The Modern Law Review, 78*(3), 522–534. https://www.jstor.org/stable/43829127. doi:10.1111/1468-2230.12126

Maeng, S. H., Essaid, M., & Ju, H. T. (2020). Analysis of Ethereum Network Properties and Behavior of Influential Nodes. *2020 21st Asia-Pacific Network Operations and Management Symposium (APNOMS)*, 203–207. 10.23919/APNOMS50412.2020.9236965

Marshall, W., McAllister, C., & Vestergaard, C. (2023). *Distributed Ledger Technology—A Possible Solution?* Stimson Center. https://www.jstor.org/stable/resrep52690.6

Mirchandani, A. (2019). The GDPR-Blockchain Paradox: Exempting Permissioned Blockchains from the GDPR. *Fordham Intellectual Property, Media and Entertainment Law Journal, 29*(4), 1201. https://ir.lawnet.fordham.edu/iplj/vol29/iss4/5

Natarajan, H., Krause, S., & Gradstein, H. L. (2017). *Distributed Ledger Technology (DLT) and blockchain: Fintech note no. 1*. https://www.semanticscholar.org/paper/Distributed-Ledger-Technology-(DLT)-and-blockchain-Natarajan-Krause/0188b89179645d52e4a96f8d1054124672e2d59e

Ng, T. S. (2017). Blockchain and Beyond: Smart Contracts. *Business Law Today*, 1–2. https://www.jstor.org/stable/27031184

Radsch, C. C. (2023a). *How the Right to Be Forgotten and the GDPR Automate Abuse of Privacy Protections* (Weaponizing Privacy and Copyright Law for Censorship, pp. 14–15). Centre for International Governance Innovation. https://www.jstor.org/stable/resrep49654.13

Radsch, C. C. (2023b). *The Right to Be Forgotten and the GDPR* (Weaponizing Privacy and Copyright Law for Censorship, pp. 6–7). Centre for International Governance Innovation. https://www.jstor.org/stable/resrep49654.9

Rothkegel, T., & Strassemeyer, L. (2019). Joint Control in European Data Protection Law – How to make Sense of the CJEU's Holy Trinity—A case study on the recent CJEU rulings (Facebook Fanpages; Jehovah's Witnesses; Fashion ID). *Computer Law Review International, 20*(6), 161–171. doi:10.9785/cri-2019-200602

SamonteM. (2020). Google v. CNIL: The Territorial Scope of the Right to Be Forgotten Under EU Law. *European Papers - A Journal on Law and Integration, 2019 4*(3), 839–851. doi:10.15166/2499-8249/332

Savin, A. (2017). *EU Internet Law*. Edward Elgar Publishing. doi:10.4337/9781784717971

Smits, J. M. (2015). *What is Legal Doctrine? On the Aims and Methods of Legal-Dogmatic Research* (SSRN Scholarly Paper 2644088). doi:10.2139/ssrn.2644088

Soltani, R., Zaman, M., Joshi, R., & Sampalli, S. (2022). Distributed Ledger Technologies and Their Applications: A Review. *Applied Sciences (Basel, Switzerland), 12*(15), 15. Advance online publication. doi:10.3390/app12157898

Tatar, U., Gokce, Y., & Nussbaum, B. (2020). Law versus technology: Blockchain, GDPR, and tough tradeoffs. *Computer Law & Security Report, 38*, 105454. doi:10.1016/j.clsr.2020.105454

Todt, K. E. (2019). Data Privacy and Protection: What Businesses Should Do. *The Cyber Defense Review, 4*(2), 39–46. https://www.jstor.org/stable/26843891

Vavra, A. N. (2018). The Right to Be Forgotten: An Archival Perspective. *The American Archivist, 81*(1), 100–111. https://www.jstor.org/stable/48618003. doi:10.17723/0360-9081-81.1.100

Veale, M., & Edwards, L. (2018). Clarity, surprises, and further questions in the Article 29 Working Party draft guidance on automated decision-making and profiling. *Computer Law & Security Report, 34*(2), 398–404. doi:10.1016/j.clsr.2017.12.002

Voss, W. G. (2016). European Union Data Privacy Law Reform: General Data Protection Regulation, Privacy Shield, and the Right to Delisting. *Business Lawyer, 72*(1), 221–234. https://www.jstor.org/stable/26419118

Zelger, B. (2023). Case Note: Strengthening the Role of Google? Recent Developments in the Right to Be Forgotten Case Law of the CJEU (TU and RE v. Google LLC, C-460/20). *Global Privacy Law Review, 4*(2). https://kluwerlawonline.com/api/Product/CitationPDFURL?file=Journals\GPLR\GPLR2023010.pdf

Zichichi, M., Ferretti, S., D'Angelo, G., & Rodríguez-Doncel, V. (2022). Data governance through a multi-DLT architecture in view of the GDPR. *Cluster Computing, 25*(6), 4515–4542. doi:10.1007/s10586-022-03691-3

Zuiderveen Borgesius, F. (2017). *Breyer Case of the Court of Justice of the European Union: IP Addresses and the Personal Data Definition (Case Note)* (SSRN Scholarly Paper 2933781). https://papers.ssrn.com/abstract=2933781 doi:10.21552/edpl/2017/1/21

ADDITIONAL READING

Alafaa, P. U. (2022). *Data Privacy and Data Protection: The Right of User's and the Responsibility of Companies in the Digital World.* (SSRN Scholarly Paper 4005750). doi:10.2139/ssrn.4005750

Chico, V. (2018). The impact of the General Data Protection Regulation on health research. *British Medical Bulletin, 128*(1), 109–118. doi:10.1093/bmb/ldy038 PMID:30445448

Ducato, R. (2020). Data protection, scientific research, and the role of information. *Computer Law & Security Report, 37*, 105412. doi:10.1016/j.clsr.2020.105412

Gruschka, N., Mavroeidis, V., Vishi, K., & Jensen, M. (2018). *Privacy Issues and Data Protection in Big Data: A Case Study Analysis under GDPR*. 5027–5033. doi:10.1109/BigData.2018.8622621

Hoel, T., & Chen, W. (2018). Privacy and data protection in learning analytics should be motivated by an educational maxim—Towards a proposal. *Research and Practice in Technology Enhanced Learning, 13*(1), 20. doi:10.1186/s41039-018-0086-8 PMID:30595748

Hussein, R., Wurhofer, D., Strumegger, E.-M., Stainer-Hochgatterer, A., Kulnik, S. T., Crutzen, R., & Niebauer, J. (2022). General Data Protection Regulation (GDPR) Toolkit for Digital Health. *Studies in Health Technology and Informatics*, *290*, 222–226. doi:10.3233/SHTI220066 PMID:35673005

Mondschein, C. F., & Monda, C. (2019). The EU's General Data Protection Regulation (GDPR) in a Research Context. In P. Kubben, M. Dumontier, & A. Dekker (Eds.), *Fundamentals of Clinical Data Science*. Springer. https://www.ncbi.nlm.nih.gov/books/NBK543521/ doi:10.1007/978-3-319-99713-1_5

Quinn, P. (2021). Research under the GDPR – a level playing field for public and private sector research? *Life Sciences, Society and Policy*, *17*(1), 4. doi:10.1186/s40504-021-00111-z PMID:33648586

KEY TERMS AND DEFINITIONS

Consensus Mechanisms: Protocols governing the agreement among nodes in a blockchain network regarding the validity of transactions and the addition of new blocks. Common mechanisms include Proof-of-Work and Proof-of-Stake, influencing the security and efficiency of blockchain systems.

Digital Footprints: Traces of individuals' online activities, encompassing information about their location, preferences, and social interactions. The increasing prevalence of digital footprints poses potential risks, as unauthorized access may compromise individuals' control over their personal information.

Digital Privacy Concerns: Apprehensions arise from the extensive collection and utilization of personal data in the digital sphere. The chapter delves into the intricate balance between technological innovation, particularly DLT, and the imperative to ensure effective data protection without unduly restricting advancements.

Distributed Ledger Technology (DLT): A: digital system facilitating secure and decentralized recording of transactions and data transfers, exemplified by blockchain technology. DLT, such as blockchain, ensures simultaneous access, approval, and updating of data records across a network, challenging traditional centralization in data management.

GDPR (General Data Protection Regulation): A comprehensive EU regulation aimed at safeguarding individuals' privacy by regulating the processing of personal data. The study investigates challenges and possibilities in applying GDPR principles to the evolving landscape of DLT.

Legal Analytical Method: A methodological approach in legal research characterized by analyzing and interpreting applicable law rather than merely determining it. This method provides flexibility in exploring the implications of legal frameworks on emerging technologies like DLT.

Right to Be Forgotten: A legal concept, particularly within the General Data Protection Regulation (GDPR), allowing individuals to request the removal of personal information from digital platforms. Examining the compatibility of DLT with the right to be forgotten raises complex issues due to the technology's immutability.

Chapter 7

Navigating the Digital Dilemma:
The Right to Be Forgotten, Privacy, and Freedom of Speech in the Age of GDPR

Akash Bag
https://orcid.org/0000-0001-8820-171X
Adamas University, India

Upasana Khattri
O.P. Jindal Global University, India

Aditya Agrawal
O.P. Jindal Global University, India

Souvik Roy
Adamas University, India

ABSTRACT

The 2014 Google Spain lawsuit was a major European Court ruling. It indicated that online name searches yield personal information. Google and other search engine operators must remove or prevent search results that breach privacy rights. The "right to forget" lets users remove their personal information from search engine results. Your internet privacy isn't completely protected. Technology changes quickly, making it hard for laws to stay up. The right to be forgotten is criticized for its deceptive nomenclature and inconsistent application. European websites may remove information, but non-European sites (like the US) may not. This right may also limit free speech. The chapter discusses the "right to be forgotten" from the new GDPR perspective. They are testing whether this right gives internet users more control over their data. It conflicts with privacy and free speech. It's considerably difficult since private firms, whose major objective is to make money, have a say, raising problems about our rights.

DOI: 10.4018/979-8-3693-0472-3.ch007

INTRODUCTION

The legislation faces difficulties due to the quick development of artificial intelligence and technology, especially when resolving the intricate problems related to internet privacy. Laws now in place frequently fail to keep up with the times, particularly in the internet age, where privacy breaches are increasingly common because information can be accessed quickly and easily. In May 2014, the Court of Justice of the European Union rendered a landmark decision in the *Google Spain* and *Google Inc. v. Agencia Española de Protección de Datos and Mario González* case, marking a significant advancement in protecting personal data (*Google Spain SL v. Agencia Española de Protección de Datos*, 2014). The "*right to be forgotten*," which permits people to ask for the removal of information about them if it is freely accessible and causes them damage, was established by this important ruling. Though the idea is not wholly novel, this ruling made it a legally recognized right (Gruschka et al., 2018).

The extant Directive on protecting personal data, created before the development of contemporary search engines, has unclear language that makes it difficult to apply and interpret. Furthermore, it gives EU members the freedom to enact their laws, which could result in differing degrees of protection for people in various nations (Erdos, 2021). The General Data Protection Regulation (GDPR) was suggested by the European Commission in 2012 as a solution to these problems, and it replaced the previous Regulation in 2018. The GDPR prioritizes privacy over freedom of speech and gives citizens the right to be "*forgotten*" online. It is applicable throughout the European Union. It is unclear, nevertheless, to what degree this right can be used to erase all publicly available data, just the personal data that third parties or both processes. Even after the GDPR went into effect, there are still restrictions on cross-border data transfers. Global websites like google.com are not covered under the "*right to be forgotten*," which only applies to European web browsers (Kulhari, 2018). This has produced a global conversation about internet privacy. Proponents contend this strikes a compromise between individual privacy and public access to information, while detractors—particularly in the USA, where free speech is highly valued—see it as a danger. The effect this privilege has on jurisprudence will become clear in the upcoming years (Jones, 2013).

These hypotheses are as follows:

H_1- The right to be forgotten or deleted does not mean that the new GDPR ensures the complete deletion of data from the Internet. Although the GDPR is a welcome attempt to protect individuals from invasions of privacy, on the other hand, it represents a form of censorship.

H_2- The collision between the EU and the USA regulations occurs due to the significantly different importance of the two regulations on the right to privacy. The right to private life is weighted in the EU system, while freedom of speech occupies a more important place in the US system.

METHODOLOGY

The work mainly uses the method of analysis and synthesis, the inductive and deductive methods, the description method, the comparative method, and the compilation method. The analysis method breaks down the concept of the right to be forgotten into simpler components. Within this framework, the chapter (in addition to the concept of the right to be forgotten) analyzes other concepts closely related to the right to be forgotten. It concerns the right to erasure and process personal data (Smits, 2015). The inductive method is used in places where jurisprudence is analyzed. In these places, by inferring from the specific, it is generally possible to determine whether and why the positive legal Regulation is appropriate, and based on the deductive method, the chapter concludes general definitions of some special characteristics of certain issues, which are poorly regulated in some places. The description method is used in several places, but mainly when stating general concepts and facts of some cases from judicial practice (Smits, 2015). Finally, using the compilation method, the chapter summarizes the findings and points out the similarities and differences between the Regulations in the EU and the USA regarding the right to privacy and, thus, the right to be forgotten.

The chapter begins with a brief review of the origin of the right to be forgotten as regulated in the GDPR, which came into force on 25/05/2018. Then, in part 3, which represents the core of this chapter, the GDPR is discussed, and within it, the Regulation of the right to be forgotten, which Article 17 GDPR governs. Part 4 draws attention to the problems that arise concerning the exercise of the right to be forgotten. Next, the chapter compares the Regulation in the EU with the Regulation in the USA (part 5), which is also briefly addressed by exercising the right to be forgotten in the territory of the United Kingdom after Brexit (part 6). In conclusion, the chapter summarizes the most important findings of this assignment and, on this basis, confirms the two theses highlighted in the introductory part.

ORIGIN AND DEVELOPMENT OF THE RIGHT TO BE FORGOTTEN IN THE EU

General

The ideological basis of the right to be forgotten comes from French law, which, in the framework of the "*droit à l'oubli*," allows a convict who has already served his sentence and has gone through the resocialization process to prohibit the publication of information about his prison sentence after that. The purpose of resocialization was certainly one of the main reasons why the right to be forgotten began to develop and gradually recognized in the EU (C. C. Radsch, 2023). In the sixties of the 20th century, information technology began to develop at an extraordinary speed. The need to protect the private lives of individuals quickly became apparent, and thus, the need to strengthen the protection of their data (Andrus, 2016a). The legal history of the right to be forgotten dates back to 2010, when a Spanish citizen and the Spanish National Data Protection Agency (AEPD) sued a Spanish newspaper and the Google Group. The plaintiff claimed that Google violated his right to privacy because Google's search results included information related to a past auction of his property, which was later foreclosed on. The plaintiff requested that the information about it be removed from the newspaper and the results of the Google search engine. In 2014, in judgment *C-131/12 (Google Spain case)*, the CJEU ruled in favor of a Spanish citizen, thereby confirming the existence of the right of data subjects to request the removal of links from internet search engine companies containing personal data of the individuals to whom the data refer (*Google Spain SL v. Agencia Española de Protección de Datos*, 2014). The SEU decided that data removal can be requested under certain conditions, especially when the data is inaccurate, inadequate, irrelevant, or excessive for data processing. The CJEU also emphasized in its judgment that the mentioned right of an individual is not absolute and that it must be weighed, taking into account other fundamental rights, such as freedom of speech (Jones, 2013).

The right to be forgotten is, therefore, a fairly new concept, which, in the digital age, within the framework of the right to privacy, recognizes the right of individuals to control how their data appears and is stored online (Vavra, 2018). Some critics have described the right as "*the greatest threat to free-*

dom of speech on the Internet.", which can be easily abused and thus "*used as a form of censorship.* (Al-Abdullah et al., 2020)" However, this is not the purpose of the law; rather, its purpose is to find a balance between the individual's right to privacy and the public's right to information (Jones, 2013). It does not seem fair, not even meaningful, for the perpetrator of someone the actions of a person who has already served his sentence (whereby the purpose of punishment and resocialization has already been achieved) to continue de facto to punish by continuing to maintain online links to his data in online search engines. Above all, the reasonableness and fairness of maintaining links and displaying personal data in search results should be questioned in cases where the information does not particularly benefit the public and even harms the individuals affected by this information (Jones, 2013). In the past, the right to be forgotten was occasionally mentioned in the legal systems of European countries, but different countries knew it under different names. For the EU legal order to exist (and implement) the right to be forgotten in the form we know today, many heated discussions were necessary, which led to reflections on the right of individuals to privacy even outside of Europe (Erdos, 2021). Unlike the EU legal system, in the US legal system, individuals do not recognize the right to be forgotten (as it exists in the EU). The First Amendment to the US Constitution is an obstacle to it (Bressler et al., 2020).

EU Legal Framework

General

The founding agreements of the European Union (EU), initially intended to be an economic union, did not mention fundamental rights. The Court of Justice of the European Union (CJEU) gradually closed this gap through case law (Cuyvers, 2017). It was first attacked for believing that member states alone were responsible for safeguarding fundamental rights. Since EU law now supersedes national laws, the CJEU has been able to define fundamental rights as universal principles that guarantee uniform protection throughout member states (Cuyvers, 2017). The 1992 Maastricht Treaty established the recognition of fundamental rights under the European Convention for the Protection of Human Rights and Fundamental Freedoms (ECHR). The EU introduced the EU Fundamental Rights Act to strengthen this protection, which eventually created the European Union's Charter of Fundamental Rights in 2000. The 2009 Lisbon Treaty, initially a political agreement, vowed that EU institutions and member states would uphold and execute the Charter. The EU's core rights and principles—derived from the Treaty on European Union (TEU), common constitutional traditions, and the European Convention on Human Rights—are consolidated into the Charter. It is significant because it establishes the right to personal data protection, which becomes a basic right under EU law (Dehousse & Verhoeven, 2014). Individuals can now seek to remove personal data from the public domain, giving them control over the data they acquire, store, move, and publish. The right to protect personal data is not unqualified despite possible conflicts with business interests. Public interest concerns, such as the availability of information about prominent people, may justify limitations. The Data Protection Directive was the first piece of EU legislation governing personal data protection (European Data Protection Supervisor, 2023). In 2015, the CJEU interpreted the Directive and upheld the right to be forgotten in the Google Spain case.

Personal Data Protection Directive

To protect fundamental rights, particularly the right to privacy, within the framework of the freedoms of the internal market, the European Parliament and Council established the Data Protection Directive (DPD) in 1995. A uniform degree of data protection was required due to increased cross-border data transfers inside the European market. Protecting personal data is a top priority for the European Union (EU), which considers it a fundamental human right (Fromholz, 2000). The DPD supports this position. The DPD is unique, nevertheless, in that it provides less latitude than other European directives. Data controllers are required under the DPD to specify the methods and objectives of data processing, which regulates the gathering and use of personal data. It emphasizes that data gathering must be clear, legal, and equitable and defines personal data as information about an identifiable individual. Furthermore, data processing needs to be fair, lawful, and appropriate for the goals for which it is used. The DPD has included the "*right to rectification*," which allows people to ask for the removal or correction of erroneous or incomplete data. The "*right to be forgotten*" in the well-known Google Spain case was established based on this principle. The DPD was implemented inconsistently among member states due to its old-fashioned design, which predated many current internet services (Fromholz, 2000). These differences led to difficulties, legal ambiguities, and administrative expenses. The European Commission recognized that the DPD needed an update and suggested a change in 2012 to solve these issues and comply with the changing digital context.27

General Data Protection Regulation

In 2012, the EC proposed a comprehensive reform of the DPD, the purpose of which was to strengthen online privacy protection. To make the reform as meaningful and effective as possible, the GDPR was adopted (Voss, 2014). The act was adopted in the form of a Regulation because the Regulation is a legally binding act that must be fully applied in all EU member states. In this way, the European legislator avoided the legal uncertainty and inconsistency when member states each regulated how to protect and exercise the right to privacy. In addition, the act in the form of a regulation will contribute to the uniform implementation of the GDPR, as it will, therefore, have to be applied in its entirety and without modification by every EU member state (Voss, 2014). Unlike a directive, a regulation is automatically applicable, immediately becomes part of the national legal system, and replaces conflicting provisions of national laws. This means that EU legislation applies to personal data if they are processed in one of the member states, regardless of which member state they are collected in (Chase, 2019a).

One of the goals of the GDPR is to give individuals control over their data. Rapid technological development and globalization have brought new challenges for protecting personal data, which is why the volume of personal data collection and exchange has increased significantly. In doing so, technology enables private companies and public authorities to use personal data to achieve their goals on a scale that has never been seen before (Victor, 2013). As technology develops, it makes sense to follow it with the aim of the highest protection of the rights it regulates as legislation. The right to be forgotten is governed by Article 17 of the GDPR, which states that "*the individual to whom personal data refer (individual) has the right to obtain that the controller deletes personal data concerning him without undue delay, and the controller should delete delays; when the personal data are no longer necessary for the purposes for which they were collected or otherwise processed when the individual to whom the personal data relates revokes the consent based on which the processing takes place, and when there is no other legal basis for the processing; when the individual objects to the processing, and there are no overriding legal reasons for their processing; when personal data has been processed illegally; when personal data must be deleted to comply with a legal obligation under Union law or the law of a Member State applicable to the controller; or when personal data was collected in connection with the offer information society service*" (John, 2018) When the controller publishes personal data and it is personal data obliged to be deleted, taking into account the available technology and implementation costs, takes reasonable measures, including technical ones, to inform controllers processing personal data that the data subject requests them to delete any links to this personal data or copies thereof (Cuyvers, 2017). After May 25, 2018, when the GDPR came into force in the EU, the right to be forgotten enabled the data subject to request that the data controller delete his data and stop their further dissemination. According to the GDPR, it is the data controller who must prove that the retention of an individual's data is necessary, and therefore, it is not the individual to whom the data refers who should prove that the retention of his data is unnecessary (Victor, 2013). Until the adoption of the GDPR, the default was to carefully find a balance between the right to privacy on the one hand and the public's right to be informed on the other. Instead, the GDPR puts the right to privacy in the foreground, granting freedom of speech and the public's right to information the status of an exception, which has sparked much debate both in and outside the EU (Chase, 2019a).

International Legal Framework

In particular, Article 8 of the European Convention on Human Rights (ECHR) addresses the right to respect for private life as a basic human right recognized by international law (Connelly, 1986). In contrast to privacy, this article highlights the wider range of rights that protect people's independence, dignity, and ability to form personal and interpersonal relationships (Connelly, 1986). Everyone has the right to respect their home, communications, and private and family life, as stated in Article 8. Unless such interference is mandated by law and considered necessary in a democratic society for reasons such as national security, public safety, economic well-being, disorder or crime prevention, health, morality, or protecting the rights and freedoms of others, the right protects people from unjustified interference by public authorities (von Grafenstein, 2018). It's important to remember that, despite its importance, the right to privacy can be curtailed in some situations to protect lawful public interests, including public order, national security, preventing crime, or defending other human rights (von Grafenstein, 2018). The chapter emphasizes how crucial it is to balance freedom of speech and the right to protect one's personal information. This complex strategy seeks to balance people's right to privacy and group interests for the greater good.

GENERAL REGULATION ON THE PROTECTION OF PERSONAL DATA

Territorial Scope

General

The GDPR regulates its territorial validity mainly in Article 3, which stipulates that, regardless of whether the processing of personal data takes place inside the EU or outside it, the GDPR applies to the processing of personal data within the scope of the activities of the controller's or processor's headquarters in the EU. However, where the controller or processor of personal data is not established in the EU, the GDPR applies to the processing of personal data of data subjects located in the EU, where the processing activities are related either to the provision of goods or services to such individuals in the EU, not depending on whether payment of the data subject is required, or by monitoring their behavior to the extent that this takes place in the EU. In addition, "*the regulation also applies to the processing of personal data by a controller not based in the EU, but in the place where the law of the Member State is used based on public international law*" (Kindt, 2016) Based on this, it can be concluded that, for example, Google cannot challenge the application of EU privacy law, even though it is based in the US. Of course, due to the increasing number of cross-border activities, it is becoming increasingly difficult to distinguish between territorial and extraterritorial effects and extraterritorial effects are still often considered a kind of intrusion into state sovereignty (Kindt, 2016).

Before And After GDPR

Before the Google Spain decision, the CJEU had not ruled on the territorial scope of the DPD for a data controller established in a third country. In the Google Spain case, however, this issue was faced for the first time, and the application of Article 4(1)(a) DPD came into question. Here, some questions arose about interpreting the article, as it was unclear to what extent and where personal data was processed (Chase, 2019b). The presumption of "*establishment*" in the sense of Article 4(1)(a) of the DPD could, for example, exclude the use of the "*equipment*" condition of Article 4(1)(c) of the DPD. The CJEU emphasized two conditions arising from Article 4(1)(a) DPD (Andrus, 2016a). To use it, it is not enough merely to be established in the territory of a member state; in addition, the controller must carry out the data processing within the scope of the activities of the establishment. Here, it seems important to emphasize that according to Article 4(1)(a) DPD, it is not necessary that the established entity itself carries out the data processing, but it is only important that the processing is carried out within the scope of its activity (Globocnik, 2020). The situation in which EU data protection legislation does not apply to a global data processing activity has practically been reduced to cases in which a data processor from a third country has no establishment in the EU territory.

Meanwhile, it is noticeable that Article 3(2) GDPR slightly expands the scope of application of the article compared to the previously valid Article 4 DPD, equivalent to Article 3 GDPR. Thus, the reference to the "*territory of the Member State*" of the GDPR has been replaced by the "*territory of the European Union*" (Ghibellini, 2017). At first glance, this text seems to strengthen legal certainty, but it should be noted that Article 3(2) of GDPR applies only to the processing of personal data of individuals by a controller or processor that is not established in the EU (Ghibellini, 2017). Otherwise, Article 3(2) does not apply, and if the data was not processed within the scope of the headquarters' activities, the application of Article 3(1) GDPR is also excluded (Chase, 2019a). There are doubts about the effectiveness of the new Article 3(2) GDPR, especially paragraph (b), because in some cases, even the entire territorial application of the GDPR could depend on the will of the data controller, how he will know and act concerning the processing of personal data. Last, but not least, it is not even clear what constitutes the "*online*" behavior of subjects and when it is considered that this behavior has occurred "within the territory of the EU" (Chase, 2019a).

Scope Ratione Materiae

The content scope of the GDPR is determined by its Article 2, which states that the GDPR "*applies to the processing of personal data in whole or in part by automated means and for processing other than by automated means for personal data that are part of a collection or are intended to form part of a collection*"(Voss, 2016a). It further stipulates that it is not used to process personal data during activities that do not fall within the scope of EU law, particularly concerning national security. The question arises whether the GDPR applies to the processing of data by public authorities. A natural person does not use it during a completely personal or domestic activity, and used by competent authorities to prevent, investigate, detect, or prosecute criminal acts or enforce criminal sanctions is also excluded, including protection against threats to public safety and their prevention (Voss, 2014). A similar scope of use was also determined by the DPD in Article 3, according to which the DPD was used "*for the processing of personal data in whole or in part by automatic means and for processing other than by automatic means for personal data that form part of a collection or are intended to be compiled part of the collection*"(Fromholz, 2000). However, it was not used for the processing of personal data during an activity that does not fall within the scope of EU legislation, and in any case in processing procedures related to public security, defense, national security, and in the activities of the state in the field of criminal law, nor did a natural person use it during a completely personal or domestic activity(Cuyvers, 2017).

The CJEU ruled in the consolidated cases of *Österreichischer Rundfunk* (*Mediengruppe Österreich GmbH v. Austria*, 2022) regarding the substantive scope of the DPD and decided that "*...the application of Directive 95/46 cannot depend on the question of whether the actual situations in the proceedings in the main case are sufficiently related to the exercise of the fundamental freedoms guaranteed by the Treaty .../..., since, based on a different interpretation, the limits of the scope of the said directive would become particularly uncertain and random, which would be contrary to its essential objective, which is to approximate the laws and other regulations of the Member States to remove obstacles to the functioning of the internal market, which originate from differences between national legislations*". The Treaty also protects personal data protection on the Functioning of the European Union (hereafter: TFEU). Article 16 (former Article 286 of the PES) stipulates that everyone has the right to protection of personal data relating to him (Albors-Llorens, 2012). In the second paragraph of Article 16 of the TFEU, it states that The European Parliament and the Council, following the regular legislative procedure, determine the rules relating to the protection of individuals in the processing of personal data by the institutions, bodies, offices, and agencies of the Union and the Member States in the performance of activities falling within the scope of application of Union law, and rules relating to the free flow of this data. Here, compliance with these rules depends on the supervision of independent bodies(Trybus & Rubini, 2012).

The article emphasizes the significance of safeguarding personal data as an integral aspect of the fundamental right to privacy within the framework of EU law. Article 8 of the Charter explicitly outlines that individuals possess the right to protect their data, subject to fair processing for specific purposes and based on either consent or other lawful grounds defined by legislation (Trybus & Rubini, 2012). Furthermore, individuals retain the right to access and rectify data collected about them, overseen by an independent authority, ensuring adherence to these regulations. Importantly, the "*right to be forgotten*" concept is discussed, presenting it as a mechanism crucial for preserving individual privacy (Trybus & Rubini, 2012). This right enables individuals to request the deletion or concealment of outdated information, facilitating a fresh start within the 28 EU member states regardless of their status. Article 17 of the GDPR delineates the conditions and procedures for exercising this right, including the responsibility of data controllers to remove links to third-party websites (Trybus & Rubini, 2012). However, the right to erasure is not absolute, as certain exceptions exist to accommodate historical, statistical, public health, and scientific research purposes. The article highlights a lack of precision from the European Commission regarding the specific circumstances under which data subject to deletion is deemed unnecessary or lacks a legal basis for preservation, leaving this determination to the discretion of the data controller.

Of course, such a decision is not easy. How should the competent authority decide, for example, when there is a photo of two people dancing in a drunken state on a table in one of the bars? After a few months, one of the people in the photo realizes that doing so harms her reputation, especially in applying for the prestigious job she wants. Meanwhile, the other person in the photo may even be proud of doing so and wants the photo to stay online so everyone can see what a fun person she is. Whose wish to respect in such a case? Should the competent authority decide whether the photo should be removed from the web? And what should be the decision when several people can be clearly distinguished in the photo, while some insist on removing the photo from the Internet, while others are against it? The decision is not easy even when one person writing a blog also includes in one of his longer posts the thoughts of his partner, which he published on his website. What should be the decision if one of the partners wants to remove his record and the other does not? Because it can also affect all previous posts. In this case, should the entire post be removed, or just the part that includes the partner's thoughts that they want removed?

The Role of Time In Personal Data Protection Law

In the digital environment, time and space are the main factors concerning the increased accessibility of personal data and their use. It is about the fact that time and space are closely related and have a completely different role in the digital environment than they did in the analog one. If personal information were accessible online for a second, it would not reach the public. The same applies to personal data not uploaded to any website. On the other hand, the World Wide Web allows unlimited information to be permanently accessible to everyone. The main question is: What role does 'time' play in balancing different interests regarding removing personal data accessible on the World Wide Web?

In personal data protection law and the right to be forgotten, time can play two roles. Due to the passage of time, requests to remove personal data from the Internet are often granted because the older the information, the less important it is to preserve it (Garcia, 2005). As mentioned, personal data should be kept for as long as necessary according to the purpose for which it was obtained and processed. After this time, there is no longer a legal basis on which this data can be stored, and the data controllers are obliged to delete it if the data subject so requests. The question arises as to what happens to the data of a deceased person (Erdos, 2021). When a person dies, they no longer have legal capacity, but this does not mean their data must be deleted in all legal systems. In most legal systems, the personal data of the deceased no longer constitutes personal data *stricto sensu*. The right to forget the personal data of the deceased can be exercised only by the relatives of the deceased, but in this case, it is not about protecting personal data but the memory of the deceased (Burman, 2020). With time, some data become merely historical data, gradually losing their nature and thus the basis for asserting the right to be forgotten. But there are also cases in which time plays no role, as the right to be forgotten can never be successfully exercised. Such cases are, of course, personal data of persons performing public functions. In such cases, the person to whom the data refers is considered more like an institution and not an independent person performing their function, and the public interest prevails.

Exceptions

The right to be forgotten, a key aspect of data protection under Article 17(3) of the GDPR, has exceptions that should be narrowly interpreted (IT Governance Publishing, 2017). The data controller is not obligated to delete information if the data subject's request falls under specific legal conditions. These exceptions include situations where erasure is not required:

a) To uphold the right to freedom of expression and information;
b) To fulfill a legal processing obligation based on Union law, Member State law, or for public interest tasks assigned to the controller;
c) For reasons of public interest in public health;
d) For archiving purposes in the public interest, scientific or historical research, or statistical purposes;
e) For asserting, implementing, or defending legal claims.

The European Commission (EC) does not provide specific guidelines for individual cases, leaving the judgment on erasure requests and potential impacts on freedom of speech to be determined in each instance. Although other sources of EU law regulate freedom of speech, they lack the specificity needed by data controllers handling numerous requests annually. European citizens' right to freedom of expression, encompassing speech and information, is broad, with the freedom to express opinions and access information without undue interference (Voss, 2016a). However, this right is not absolute, excluding activities such as defamation or speech threatening national security. The EC provides limited guidance on handling data requests concerning public health policy interests, as outlined in Article 17(3)(c) of the GDPR. Additionally, there is ambiguity on how data controllers should assess the necessity of data processing for historical, statistical, or scientific purposes (Voss, 2014).

Possible Negative Consequences of The Right To Be Forgotten

Censorship?

In the wake of the Google Spain case, where data controllers began removing links to content, instances of such link removals gained public attention, particularly through media outlets like the BBC and The Guardian. Critics denounced this as the "*purification of the Internet*" and a form of press censorship. Notably, the Wikimedia Foundation, overseeing Wikipedia, protested these link removals (European Parliament, 2021). They decided to publish notices for all link removal requests they received, shedding light on attempts to erase certain data. Amidst the debate, concerns were raised by some theorists who feared that an expansive implementation of the right to be forgotten might lead to internet censorship. This right allows individuals to request search engines or websites to remove their data, potentially altering historical records. The clash arises as proponents argue for privacy rights, asserting that the General Data Protection Regulation (GDPR) will fortify existing privacy rights (Reventlow, 2020). However, critics argue that the right to be forgotten restricts the free flow of information, limiting individual choices and depriving the public of essential information for forming opinions. The discussion extends to balancing the right to be forgotten and the right to freedom of speech, both integral components of the GDPR (Reventlow, 2020). Article 80(2) of the GDPR places the responsibility on each Member State to define the freedom of speech exception more precisely. While member states are tasked with ensuring freedom of speech, it's crucial to recognize it as a fundamental right for all EU citizens. The GDPR aims to strike a balance, acknowledging the importance of protecting freedom of speech even within the framework of the right to be forgotten.

Impact on the Journalism Profession

This chapter delves into the concerns surrounding the "*right to be forgotten*" and its potential impact on journalism. Journalists fear complying with this right may hinder their research, leading to gaps in stories being erased from search engine results (Reventlow, 2020). Despite an exception for "*journalistic purposes or artistic/literary expression,*" uncertainty persists regarding its interpretation and effectiveness in safeguarding journalists and online information. The CJEU's judgment in the Google Spain case, related to the Data Protection Directive (DPD), introduced the right to be forgotten. While the DPD lacked explicit provisions for data deletion requests, the CJEU's decision didn't compel search engines to erase posts (C. Radsch, 2023). An initial concern was that removing a link on one website might not truly result in forgetting the information, as it remained accessible elsewhere. However, the GDPR empowered data subjects to demand information deletion from websites and separate links on search engines. Despite journalist apprehensions, the GDPR incorporates safeguards to balance privacy rights with journalistic expression. It urges Member States to legislate exceptions, particularly for audiovisual content, news archives, and printed media (Reventlow, 2020). Defining "*journalistic*" activities broadly includes profit and non-profit endeavors, not limited to traditional media houses. However, ambiguity persists regarding who qualifies as a journalist deserving legal protection. While traditional media is covered, it remains unclear if the exemption extends to bloggers and online commentators, raising concerns about potential broad interpretations by the courts.

An (over)broad interpretation of this right would be to the detriment of another, namely the right to be forgotten. In addition, it is not negligible to mention that the right to be forgotten may differ from Member State to Member State, leading to arbitrary decisions and results depending on the country where personal data was disclosed. There may also be a situation where the right to be forgotten will be easier and faster to exercise in one of the member states than in another, resulting from incomplete harmonization of legislation at the EU level. This problem will be even more noticeable when deciding whether the right to be forgotten should be extended outside the EU. In this case (in the absence of international agreements), there could be noticeable differences in the conditions that must be met for the successful exercise of the right, as it is inevitable that there will be different standards that will have to be met to grant the request after removing certain information from the web (Kohl & Rowland, 2017). The GDPR expressly recognizes the right to be forgotten, which individuals can exercise when they want search engines and other data controllers to remove their data from the web. Although it was emphasized in the Google Spain case that such an obligation only applies to web browsers, based on Article 17 of the GDPR, it can be concluded that an individual can also request the deletion of personal data from the originating website.

Article 17 of the GDPR can be understood to exercise the right when certain conditions are met. It can also refer to other data controllers in addition to web browsers (IT Governance Publishing, 2017). However, this raises the challenge of identifying a certain natural or legal person as the operator of certain contents. This will be especially problematic in cases where users can (re) create content themselves, for example, on social networks or blogs. It is an important issue, as non-compliance with GDPR provisions is followed by high administrative fines (Čtvrtník, 2023). These vary in the amount of up to 10 million euros or up to 2 percent of the total global annual turnover in the previous fiscal year (depending on which amount is higher), or they can be up to 20 million euros or up to 4 percent of the total global annual turnover in the previous fiscal year (again - depending on which amount is higher). The GDPR has two main goals: to give individuals greater control over their data and provide legal certainty while reducing business administrative burdens. The GDPR's goal is to set data protection rules applicable throughout the EU, as using different standards for citizens from those used by non-EU citizens is contradictory to the free use of the Internet.

PROBLEMS OF ENFORCING THE RIGHT TO BE FORGOTTEN

General

Creating new rights is a complex process that, without exception, is met with many criticisms and concerns. This is also the case with the right to be forgotten. Even before the adoption of the GDPR, this had its foundations in European legislation on data protection and ECtHR jurisprudence. However, the exercise of the right often encounters obstacles, as it is opposed (in some legal systems more strongly, in others less so) by the right to freedom of speech and the public interest, which has made the exercise of the right to be forgotten and rights with a similar effect difficult. There are numerous cases in which it has been explained that exercising such a right could be "*inappropriate and in some cases absurd*" due to public interest and concerns about freedom of expression. The right should be exercised based on the ultima ratio, i.e., as a kind of "*emergency exit*," only in cases where other legal remedies prove inadequate or have already been exhausted.

Again, it's worth noting that when a search result is removed on a European domain only, the content will still be easily accessible via the US .com domain. In addition, the content remains on the original page. Even if the information were removed because it would refer to a specific person, who would be marked with a first and last name, this can be easily bypassed, or the information about the individual can still be found by searching with other relevant keywords (Beaney, 1966). Therefore, removing information only in cases where it contains an individual's name does not seem effective and creates the impression that it does not fully consider the individual's well-being. Surely, a more appropriate approach would be to provide a right allowing an individual to request the source site to remove the content. Thus, the burden would shift from browsers to the original content holders, and the solution would be welcome mainly because the damage caused to an individual by the preservation of information is often disproportionate to the relative public interest (Lin, 2002). National data protection authorities could carry out such control, and the courts would represent an appeals mechanism. Although the mentioned approach seems difficult to implement, it is not unfeasible.

Ambiguities of the Provision

The right to be forgotten is criticized for its vagueness and censorship potential. However, one must remember that technology is changing quickly, and thus, privacy is being threatened more quickly. The right to be forgotten is thus intended to eliminate some of the problems related to the protection of privacy that arise with technological innovations, with the help of which both private and public entities gain ever-increasing access to diverse information. The scale of technological changes in recent years has been extraordinary, resulting in individuals putting information online without considering the possible consequences. Individuals have reduced control over the information relating to them. When clicking "*I accept cookies*" or "*I accept the business conditions,*" most of us do not even read what these "*conditions*" cover and how websites and companies will store our data and processes in the future. The way data is recorded and collected is not as limited as when data was entered into records in physical form. Today, governments and economic entities can store data indefinitely, regardless of the amount of data.

Some, therefore, believe that the right to be forgotten should not be understood as something revolutionary and completely unexpected. It should be considered that the DPD from 1995 could not foresee all the progress that has taken place. At the time of DPD's creation, it was impossible to imagine what a web browser like Google, which today has a dominant position in the search engine industry, would eventually be capable of. A broad-based right to be forgotten makes sense, mainly because it can be assumed that the development of technology will continue. Since this development is unpredictable, the right created in this way will make it easier to fill the gap that will always exist to a certain extent between the existing legal framework and the need to protect privacy rights. When the right to be forgotten was created, there were many criticisms that "*we Europeans have a long tradition of creating abstract rights to privacy in theory, which we cannot fully implement in practice.*"

As mentioned, the right to delete information imposes the responsibility on the administrator to remove the content from its interface and thereby limit the accessibility of such content. Some describe the operation of web search engines as a "*master switch*" that directs the user to certain content on the web. Withdrawal of information or removing a link to information is not yet a true right to be forgotten, as the content is not deleted from the original website. However, such a right, which obliges the browser operator to remove it from its interface, is a step towards the right to be forgotten and at least helps limit the accessibility of content with which the individual no longer wishes to be associated. There are some warnings in the literature that the term "*right to be forgotten*" is misleading (Trybus & Rubini, 2012). It should not be expected that information, once made available on the World Wide Web, will be completely deleted from various information systems, nor can it be completely forgotten. Information is more difficult to access by exercising this right, but it does not disappear. At the time when information was freely available, anyone could save it. The World Wide Web allows anyone worldwide to access information, including detailed personal information of people worldwide, at the touch of a button. For this reason, some theorists believe that the ruling in the Google Spain case is not fully enforceable. The point is that the concept of justice is somewhat problematic. If it is too expansive and puts all the responsibility on web browser operators, its implementation quickly becomes impossible. Because without independent control and clear guidelines for implementation, the law is incomplete and, therefore, ineffective.

One of the first questions that arise in connection with the exercise of the right to be forgotten is thus the following: If Ms. A removes her inappropriate photo from an online social network with a simple click of the mouse, would this mean that, say, her supervisor and everyone else, who managed to see this photo, forgot about it only because it is now no longer available? The answer to this question is negative because the photo is "*stored*" in their long-term memory, which can recall the information many years after the brain has received it, perhaps even for a lifetime. From this point of view, the '*right to be forgotten*' has an ex-post effect; therefore, it can only prevent further damage and not repair the damage already caused when the content was first made available online. In addition, more problems arise about exercising the right to be forgotten. The right is ineffective if it cannot be forcibly enforced because people cannot be forced to forget something, so it is also not possible to sue someone for not forgetting something.

For this reason, it is also not possible to formulate a legal provision that would command 'forgetting,' as defined by the 'right to be forgotten,' which, as said, makes the right ineffective. The word 'oblivion' as part of the name of the right is meant metaphorically. Legal provisions, however, are not the place for metaphors. Also, the right cannot have a retroactive effect, and thus, the damage that has already occurred cannot be completely repaired with this right. Furthermore, the exercise of the right to be forgotten could be hindered by the connotation of 'forgetting,' together with some of the arguments that formed the basis for the creation of Article 17 of the GDPR. These arguments presented the right to be forgotten to give individuals a fresh start in removing old information that is no longer relevant and can damage the individual's image.

Thus, people who, for example, have been charged with criminal charges in the past, or people who published inappropriate photos from parties online during their studies, should be allowed to remove the photos or other content from the Internet, as it is something, which happened in the individual's past and is no longer relevant for today. Based on such an argument, it would be possible to conclude that an individual's request to remove recently uploaded content to the web would not be granted. However, justice should prove effective in all cases, not just some (Antani, 2015). The purpose of the right is to prevent the personal data of an individual who wants to be removed from being accessible to the public, as they do not show his true image and can, therefore, harm him in any way in the future (Politou et al., 2018). This does not only include outdated and irrelevant data; this may also include data that has recently been made available online. Article 17 of the GDPR should, therefore, be understood as the right of an individual who no longer consents to the publication of certain personal data to remove it from the Internet, even if he changed his mind about the publication immediately after uploading it. In mind, it is necessary to hold that the individual's right to personal identity includes the individual's right to project his image to the public as he wishes. Some, therefore, believe that, because of all the above, it would be more appropriate to call the '*right to be forgotten*' the '*right to erasure*' (Politou et al., 2018).

Concrete Impact on the Individual

Internet archives, through cached copies and search engines, distort the presentation of an individual, etc., and default forgetting changed to default recall. Looking at personal data differently than in the analog world is necessary. During the rapid growth of information technology, personal data has become a valuable currency that affects the most diverse areas of human life. Certain online services, such as social networks and various search engines, can function based on data collection. On the other hand, inappropriate content that portrays the user in a bad light can have long-term consequences for him, especially in terms of loss of social status and possible future employment. The nature of online communication limits individual control over the flow of information. Before the development of modern technology, information could fade away in archives, giving individuals more opportunities to prevent the spread of past mistakes. When the fact contained in the physical archive of information was unpleasant enough, the individual could move elsewhere, and the information did not accompany him. So, he could afford a 'new start.' Having the possibility of a second chance is an important value. In the online environment, talking about the gradual development of an individual's personality is impossible, as there is room for mistakes and corrections. Anyone who does not know the individual whose information they are reading can easily judge them. In the online environment, everything happens instantly, and the damage caused can be irreversible; however, maintaining such information only expands and thus increases. Social networking sites allow individuals to learn much about someone before meeting them. The right enables an individual to manage and build his online identity.

COMPARISON WITH THE REGULATION IN THE USA

General About the Right to Privacy And its Origin in the Framework of the US Legal System

As already noted, the World Wide Web enables the exchange of information, including the personal data of individuals, regardless of national borders. Therefore, since information travels not only outside the borders of countries but also outside the borders of continents, the harmonization of EU and US legislation would be very welcome so that the same situation would not be treated differently, especially regarding something as important as individual privacy. However, the US and the EU have a slightly different view of privacy. Unlike the EU legal system, the US legal system has, from the beginning existence, recognized a higher level of protection for freedom of speech and the press than the individual's right to privacy (White, 1951). Freedom of speech in the USA connects the foundations of democracy on which it is founded. In fear of possible later regulations that would prevent or limit people and organizations from expressing their ideas and thus threaten freedom of speech or censorship, the framers of the American Constitution protected freedom of speech with the First Amendment (Lin, 2002).

US privacy legislation consists of ad hoc regulations. Still, a specific regulation does not comprehensively regulate the right to privacy. At the same time, the EU has a comprehensive framework (the already mentioned DPD or GDPR from the beginning of its validity) that regulates citizens' right to privacy (Lin, 2002). In 1890, American jurists Samuel Warren and Louis Brandeis published one of the most influential essays on the right to privacy in American legal history in the Harvard Law Review. It is the first contribution in the USA that revolutionary advocates the right to privacy called the "*right to be let alone*." The article examined whether the land owner's right to privacy existed in the legislation in force and the scope of this right (White, 1951). The authors reminded us that the right to privacy is just as much an individual's right as a property right. Property rights have always been protected by law. A person's house, for example, is treated as a castle - a protected fortress into which others may not even look if the owner of the "*castle*" does not allow them to do so. Therefore, if the law does not restrict property rights due to the sheer curiosity of people, there is no reason why this should be the case regarding the right to privacy (Gladstone, 2000).

Their idea of privacy was partially introduced into US legislation only in the 1960s, but not to the same extent as Warren and Brandeis advocated in their paper (Volini, 2023). In general, this right does not provide the same level of protection as the right to privacy in the legal system of The EU, where the right to privacy is seen as a type of right that cannot be overlooked. In the US legal system, removing information from the Internet or the right to be forgotten is impossible. Opponents of recognizing a right to privacy in the United States often cite the First Amendment as their main argument, arguing that such a right could amount to censorship of the World Wide Web. Therefore, the right to be forgotten, as recognized in the EU by the decision in the Google Spain case, is considered unconstitutional in the United States, as it conflicts with the First Amendment. In the USA, only monetary compensation is provided for violations of the right to privacy, and in addition, this compensation is intended for the individual whose right to privacy was violated without his knowledge or consent (Sullivan, 2010).

US jurisprudence suggests that US law is generally very favorable to data disclosure, especially when the disclosed data has some value to the addressees. Here, the concept of "*value for addressees*" is subject to different interpretations, making it even more difficult for individuals to request the removal of personal data from the web successfully. While freedom of speech is protected by the First Amendment to the US Constitution, a citizen's right to privacy does not receive such protection. Thus, in 1975, in the case of *Cox Broadcasting Corporation v. Cohn*7, the US Supreme Court rejected a claim for damages against a newspaper that published the name of a rape victim, considering that it was a name that the public should know (*Cox Broadcasting Corp. V. Cohn*, 1975). In later decisions, the US Supreme Court further established the position that a newspaper may publish information it obtains legally, even if it is sensitive information, such as the name of a rape victim or the name of a minor accused of murder (Pfenninger, 2021).

The First Amendment

Freedom of Speech

Although the US Supreme Court has repeatedly emphasized that the provision of the First Amendment refers to lawfully obtained information, the same court has also found that illegally obtained information can be published as long as the publisher or the website administrator was not the one who illegally obtained the information (White, 1951). Such a point of view is quite problematic, as it encourages the illegal acquisition of personal data and its sale to someone who later publishes it. Moreover, US law even protects users and providers of interactive computing services who publish information provided by others from liability if that information is harmful (Greenawalt, 1992). The importance given to freedom of speech by the US Constitution's First Amendment is a source of pride for many of its citizens. Judge Posner found that "*...the constitution is a charter of negatively rather than positively shaped freedoms*." According to him, the drafters of the US Constitution were not motivated by the fear that it would provide citizens with too few rights but rather by the fear that it would allow them too many. In addition, he emphasized that the legislator usually writes explicitly when he wants to create a positive obligation (Sullivan, 2010).

However, certain disclosures of information are less protected than others. Mainly, it's about arguing, obscenity, and defamation. In these cases, despite the First Amendment, the court repeatedly rules in favor of the right to privacy rather than the right of the public to access information and stimulate curiosity. However, this is not true. The further development of US legislation and case law shows how the trend will develop. The tradition of free speech in the United States presents an almost insurmountable obstacle to the right to privacy. It is difficult to imagine that shortly the USA would introduce the right to be forgotten in its legislation, as it is enforced in the EU, because the provision of the First Amendment will always protect Google or any other company that publishes certain information (Greenawalt, 1992). In 2003, for example, the US Supreme Court ruled in a case involving the online search engine Search King. These charged users search and query fees on websites that appeared high on the list in search results. Search engine King sued Google for allegedly "*deliberately and maliciously*" lowering certain rankings, thereby devaluing its business (Hartman, 1954). The case concerned primarily the connection between Internet search engines and Internet advertising and their joint connection with the First Amendment. In a narrower sense, the court considered whether a page's ranking in search results is protected within the framework of freedom of speech. If the rankings were subjective, they "*relate to matters of public interest*" and represent constitutionally protected freedom of speech (Sullivan, 2010).

Defamation

US law provides for tortious liability in the event of defamation, but this is significantly limited due to the First Amendment and, thus, freedom of speech. In this context, theoretically, some right to be forgotten could exist, but the injured party's claim would be limited only to the person who published the data and whose act could be considered a criminal act, a third party (such as Google, which only enabled the connection to this data) would not be responsible (Zipursky, 2016). It is defamation when personal information harms an individual's reputation, leading to isolation and discouraging others from associating with him. Therefore, it is not defamation if the information does not harm the individual's reputation. In addition, the information must be communicated to the public and untrue, which means that true information or opinion based on verifiable facts cannot be the basis of tort liability in the US legal system (Zipursky, 2016).

The fact that the information must be disclosed to the public to file a compensation claim successfully means that a third party or the public must see this information and, above all, understand its purpose is to defame a certain person. Suppose no one reads or hears the statement of the person who made the information available to the public. In that case, no damage has been done to the individual's reputation and, therefore, no cause of action (White, 1951). In addition, it does not matter how many people this information reaches to cause damage. Namely, the occurrence of damage doesn't need to be related to the fact that a wide circle of people becomes familiar with the information; it can be enough for damage to occur if only one person becomes familiar with the information, and that person is the employer of the individual who is slandered by the information in question, which could in itself cause significant damage to the individual (Beaney, 1966).

Just as the First Amendment, because of its goal of protecting free speech, cannot require that certain personal information be deleted from websites or that links to the websites in question be removed, it also does not protect individuals from defamation. Defamation lawsuits have dropped significantly since the US Supreme Court's decision in *New York Times Co. v. Sullivan*. In this case, the court decided that the plaintiff must prove that the defamation against him was an intentional act, i.e., that the defendant knew that the published information was incorrect or that he did not know this due to his recklessness and not because he wanted to spread false information about a specific person (*New York Times Co. V. Sullivan*, 1964). With this position, the court clearly showed that freedom of speech takes precedence over the right to privacy or an individual's reputation, thus demotivating potential applicants for compensation claims, as it is clear that it is extremely difficult to prove a journalist's bad faith (White, 1951).

Such a condition for filing a compensation claim represents an important difference from the right to be forgotten as we know it in the EU legal system. Although both legal systems (both the EU and the US) protect an individual's reputation at some level, this protection is more prominent in the EU (Voss, 2016b). In the EU, according to the new law (since the decision in the Google Spain case), an individual can request the removal of links to data, even if true (especially and all the falser), if this data has become outdated or irrelevant. The right to be forgotten, as it is currently known, therefore imposes an obligation on a third party - the so-called j. to the operator of the search engine (and not to the person who published the information) since theoretically he is the one who controls whether and to which information the public can access.

Weighing the Rights

EU jurisprudence (more specifically, the Google Spain case) has developed a test whose essence is weighing between different rights that must be taken into account when deciding on a case, namely between the individual's right to privacy concerning the public's right to access personal data, which the individual wants to remove them from the web (Keller & Walther, 2018). This idea of weighing the right of the individual against the right of the public has also been used in US jurisprudence, in the case of the United States and *Landmark Communications, Inc. v. Virginia*, in which a newspaper published an article (containing otherwise true information) about an investigation of a state judge by the Virginia Judicial Investigation and Review Commission (*Landmark Communications, Inc. V. Commonwealth*, 1978). The court refused to punish the newspaper in the said case, as some judicial positions in the US are elected, and therefore, it was in the public's interest to know whether elected judges are corrupt. The criteria for assessing whether there is a public interest in knowing certain personal data were set in the Google Spain case and would also be useful in deciding cases in the USA (Madden, 2014).

In the United States, it is not difficult to find a theorist who argues that a regulation under which the public does not have free access to information is more problematic than a regulation that permits the storage of certain information about individuals. Some refer to the latter option (or the right to be forgotten) as "*shooting SLA*" (Andrus, 2016b). Still, others wonder how the right to be forgotten can come to full expression in a world where information often published by others finds its way onto various online platforms such as Facebook, Twitter, and others. Attempting to take it down could quickly become a game of abuse where the information would appear on every new site, even if others took it down (Newman, 2015). A slightly greater willingness to remove content from the web at an individual's request can be detected in only rare types of cases, such as a situation in which an individual requests the removal of a link to sex tapes that the individual's partner uploaded to the web out of revenge; otherwise, the request is rejected in most other cases (Newman, 2015).

When assessing whether a request to delete content from the web is granted, it is usually also considered whether the applicant is a public or private person. This factor is worth considering because individuals who are not public figures have a reasonable expectation of greater protection of their privacy from public intrusion than individuals who are public figures (Zichichi et al., 2022). In addition, when assessing responsibility, it is also important to determine whether the web search engine is the site of the information or whether the information originates from a third site and the search engine "*merely*" enables a link to this site. Last but not least, whether the information is obtained legally or illegally and whether there is a possibility that the applicant will suffer unfair prejudice as a result of the published information if it is not removed from the website in the future. To illustrate the harmfulness of data that appears online, the example of data on the arrest of a person suspected (although never legally convicted) of child pornography can serve (Voss, 2016b). The appearance of the suspect's name in the search results would undoubtedly (unjustifiably if it was a false accusation) destroy the future of the individual who requested the removal of that information. Such information can ruin everything for a person, from a date to an interview for a job or other opportunities in life. In many cases, prejudices can be created completely unfairly, from which the general public does not particularly benefit (Zichichi et al., 2022).

Reducing Differences Between EU and US Legal Systems

EU legislation, in addition to allowing a request for removal in case of inaccurate, excessive, or irrelevant personal data, as already mentioned, also allows such a request in some other cases. US law is much more restrictive (Antani, 2015). However, in some cases, removing personal data from the Internet is permissible in the United States, which proves that in some cases, it already is the right to be forgotten. Unlike Europe, the right to be forgotten in the USA is largely undeveloped, mainly because of the First Amendment. Nevertheless, it is worth noting that some US states have taken some (albeit modest) measures to reduce the differences between protecting the right to privacy in the EU and the US (Antani, 2015). One such country is, for example, California, where a law was passed in September 2013 that recognizes a limited version of the right to be forgotten, as it is known in EU law under Article 17 of the GDPR. The abovementioned law entered into force on January 1, 2015, and its main purpose is to enable minors to request the deletion of posts they have published on social media websites, such as Facebook. However, with some exceptions, this (narrow) right to erasure only covers the deletion of content that young people have uploaded online, but not content about the individual to whom the data relates, which was not uploaded online by the individual himself. But does not instruct web search engines to remove links (John, 2018).

The same applies when a minor is the perpetrator of a crime. Crimes committed by a minor are treated differently than crimes committed by an adult. This is also taken into account by the legislation when deleting data uploaded online. The stamp of an individual's (adolescent's) criminal history can be a great burden and an obstacle to a normal life later, in adulthood. Suppose information about crimes committed by young people is not (any longer) available online. In that case, an individual's future employer never needs to know about the young person's troubled past because sometimes the past is just that - the past. Similarly, a young person (later on as an adult) could have problems with, for example, a property owner about renting an apartment because they might not want to rent to them if they knew they had a criminal conviction. With this aim in mind, the legislature in California passed a law based on which the records of juvenile crimes are sealed (Antani, 2015).

The California mentioned above law thus illustrates that the right to be forgotten is not necessarily an unwanted right in the United States. Thus, it would be possible to extend the content of this law to other situations as well - so that all individuals (and not only minors) could request the permanent removal of content from the web that they publish and share themselves (Pfenninger, 2021). In doing so, the test used by the court in the Google Spain case should also be considered, weighing the individual's right to privacy and the public's interest in accessing information. Namely, people often share or publish things they did not intend to or change their minds and no longer want the published content displayed. In an age in which data can be published in such an easy and quick way for an indefinite period and are accessible practically everywhere in the world, there should be some guarantee that a person can, so to speak, "*return to the previous state*" if he so wishes and if it is information that concerns him in any way (Fabbrini & Celeste, 2020).

EXERCISE OF THE RIGHT TO BE FORGOTTEN IN THE UK CONCERNING BREXIT

General Information About the Right to Privacy in the UK

The concept of the right to privacy was created in the United Kingdom (hereinafter: UK) in the late nineteenth and early twentieth centuries. Rapid social and technological changes in recent decades have undoubtedly brought new challenges to privacy protection. Thanks to digitization, we can instantly obtain information from any part of the world. Not only can information be accessed remotely, but technological advances have also made it easier to create information and share it with the world, seeing the abandonment of traditional forms of information control. Digitization has provided "*the architecture of perfect memory*." For this reason, effective legal rules that protect individual privacy in the digital environment are all the more necessary. Without adequate privacy controls, there is a risk that an individual's personal information that ends up online now could be stored indefinitely and could be accessed by anyone at any time in the future (Aidinlis, 2020).

Concerns About the Right to Be Forgotten

In theory, many concerns exist about the negative impact of the right to be forgotten. It is often cited as the biggest threat to freedom of speech on the Internet because not only does the right to be forgotten allow an individual to request the deletion of information they have published about themselves, but it also allows them to request the deletion of information that has been published about them (Pamment, 2020). Second. In this way, the Internet loses one of its main characteristics: openness. Additionally, it's worth noting that Google search results, in some ways, represent one of our most important (some would even say primary) records of the history of the human race (Pamment, 2020). For this reason, the right to be forgotten should not be welcomed because we cannot just recreate history whenever we feel like it. However, these concerns are not to be taken lightly. It should be borne in mind that the right to privacy guaranteed by Article 8 of the ECHR and the freedom of expression under Article 10 of the ECHR are equivalent to fundamental rights and deserve the same degree of respect (Kulhari, 2018). The right to be forgotten, which enables a request to remove information (albeit "*only*" when there is no reason to justify the preservation of information), means a conceptual distinction between rights that does not take into account the fact that freedom of expression is also a legitimate reason for the preservation of certain information. Although, at first glance, the judgment in the Google Spain case appears to favor the right to privacy, it nevertheless emphasizes the balance between privacy and freedom of expression (Cadogan, 2023).

Shortly after the CJEU issued its decision in the Google Spain case, which practically established the right to be forgotten in the EU legal space, the British House of Lords recommended in July 2014 to the British government not to include the right to be forgotten in its legal system (Čtvrtník, 2023). The degree to which modern technology has helped limit the privacy of data subjects is extremely high. Once information is legally in the public domain, it is almost impossible to demand its removal, and very little can be done to prevent its dissemination. For this reason, the British government also refused to support the right to be forgotten, as recognized by the EU legal order, because the UK believes in the freedom of information and transfer of information, but at the same time, the full implementation of the right to be forgotten seems unfeasible in practice (Townend, 2017). The fundamentally different nature of modern media compared to the old ones is worth noting. Establishing the right to be forgotten may be well-intentioned, but theorists are skeptical about its effectiveness. Modern web search engines do make it difficult to forget content once it's posted online, but the information was also preserved in the distribution of earlier analog media, albeit somehow limited to a certain time frame before the information was effectively lost in the archives. However, the information was not deleted (Chase, 2019a). The rest are accessible but subject to effort by the person seeking the information. The online disclosure of information fundamentally differs from the disclosure in analog media because, in the digital age, even the most trivial information is easily and immediately accessible. The distinguishing feature of modern media is their ability to provide the already-mentioned architecture of perfect memory (Townend, 2017).

Several requests were made to Google shortly after the SEU decision, such as a request by a former politician running for re-election to remove a link to an article about his misconduct in office, but requests a man convicted of possessing child pornography to remove links to the page detailing his conviction; or requests from a doctor who has requested the removal of data related to negative evaluations of his work by his patients; etc. (Aidinlis, 2020). British newspapers and online news providers, therefore, began to publish lists of stories collected by Google in the act, based on which theorists in the UK based an opposing opinion on the effect of the right to be forgotten, namely for the reason that it is important that those with an interest in the right to be forgotten can check which articles were affected by the decision in the Google Spain case (*Google Spain SL v. Agencia Española de Protección de Datos*, 2014). It is also important to preserve the integrity of the archive of online newspapers. Although links to pages affected by the disclosure may disappear from Google searches, this information still exists on the originating site.

The Right to be Forgotten in the Future

She also warned that maintaining the right to be forgotten is the price for doing business with the EU within the larger trade pact. The fact is that, with Brexit, the UK can limit its trading opportunities with the EU in many areas. If it does not comply with EU law, it will not be able to trade with the EU. So, the right to be forgotten, like all other UK legislation derived from EU law, could remain effective if the UK decides it is a necessary part of a larger data protection agreement with the EU that will form part of new bilateral trade negotiations (Allegri, 2022). Estimating how much UK legislation is passed is difficult because of EU requirements. Agreements between the UK and the EU on the UK's exit from the EU are likely to address important issues. One of the most important questions is whether the decisions of the EU will still bind the UK, and in connection with this, the fate of the right to be forgotten in the UK will probably be part of the negotiations. If the UK (continues) to respect the right to be forgotten, it will have to be included in their legislation. In this case, the right to be recognized by the individual will have to be acquired appropriately, and it will have to be concrete, i.e., benefitting the individual (Fabbrini & Celeste, 2020). What is certain is that the UK has many laws derived from EU law, and there are significant questions about how this will be dealt with and how the UK will deal with new EU legislation, which may also need to be followed to continue trading with the EU in some areas, for example, in consumer sales of goods, services, and digital content. The answer to these questions will partly depend on which path the UK will take in the negotiations regarding the exit from the EU.

CONCLUSION

In the introductory part of the chapter, two hypotheses were set. The findings and interpretation of only these are presented below. The first thesis read: "*The right to be forgotten or deleted does not mean that the new GDPR guarantees the complete deletion of data from the Internet. Although the GDPR is a welcome attempt to protect the individual from invasions of privacy, on the other hand, it represents a form of censorship*" (Finck, 2018). The right to be forgotten has divided theorists into two poles. Some approve of it as a tool that will make it easier for individuals to guarantee their right to privacy, while others see it as a threat to freedom of speech on the Internet. The CJEU decided that under certain conditions, individuals can request the removal of personal data and their further dissemination from data managers, especially when the data is inaccurate, inadequate, irrelevant, or excessive for data processing. The judgment as to whether the deletion request fulfills one of these conditions or threatens freedom of speech is left to data controllers. If data controllers decide an individual's request to delete data relating to them is justified, they must remove the link to this data following the GDPR (Mirchandani, 2019). However, this does not mean the source page will also be removed; it will be harder to get to the content. This confirms the first part of the thesis that the right to be forgotten does not guarantee the complete deletion of data from the Internet.

The right to be forgotten represents a means that allows individuals a fresh start in removing old information that is no longer relevant and can harm their public image. The purpose of the right is to prevent the personal data of an individual who wants to be removed from being accessible to the public, as they do not show his true image and can, therefore, harm him in any way in the future. It should be borne in mind that the individual's right to personal identity includes the individual's right to project his image to the public as he wishes. Not only does the right to be forgotten allow an individual to request the deletion of information they have posted about themselves, but it also allows them to request the deletion of information posted about them by others (Zichichi et al., 2022). In this way, the Internet loses one of its main characteristics - openness. There are criticisms regarding the collision between the right to be forgotten and the right to freedom of speech. The latter should in no way be subject to the right to be forgotten since it is precisely free access to information that enables and encourages public discussion and the exchange of information about the society in which we live. On the other hand, the right to be forgotten inhibits the free flow of information and thus deprives individuals of the ability to decide what to say and even think, depriving potential recipients of the information necessary to form their opinions and ideas (Mirchandani, 2019).

The second thesis comes from comparative law's perspective: "*The collision between the EU and the USA regulations occurs because of the significantly different importance that the two regulations attribute to the right to privacy. Namely, the right to private life is weighed in the EU system, while freedom of speech occupies a more important place in the US system.*" The US and the EU have fundamentally different views on privacy (Al-Abdullah et al., 2020). In contrast to the EU legal system, which treats the right to privacy as a fundamental right, the US legal system has, from the very beginning, recognized a higher level of protection for freedom of speech than the right to privacy. Freedom of speech in the USA is linked to the foundations of democracy, which is why the First Amendment to the US Constitution protects this right. Unlike the EU, therefore, the right to be forgotten is largely undeveloped in the US, mainly because of the First Amendment. According to the GDPR, it is the data controller who must prove that the retention of an individual's data is necessary, and therefore, it is not the individual to whom the data relates who must prove that the retention of his data is unnecessary. The Supreme Court in the USA decided that the plaintiff must prove that the defamation against him was an intentional act, i.e., that the defendant knew that the published information was false or that he did not know this due to his recklessness and not because he wanted to spread false information about a specific person. With this position, the court clearly showed that freedom of speech precedes the right to privacy in the United States. The tradition of free speech in the United States presents an almost insurmountable obstacle to the right to privacy. It is difficult to imagine that shortly, the USA will introduce the right to be forgotten in its legislation, as is enforced in the EU.

REFERENCES

Aidinlis, S. (2020). *The Right to Be Forgotten as a Fundamental Right in the UK After Brexit* (SSRN Scholarly Paper 3554625). https://papers.ssrn.com/abstract=3554625

Al-Abdullah, M., Alsmadi, I., AlAbdullah, R., & Farkas, B. (2020). Designing privacy-friendly data repositories: A framework for a blockchain that follows the GDPR. *Digital Policy Regulation and Governance*, *22*(5/6), 389–411. doi:10.1108/DPRG-04-2020-0050

Albors-Llorens, A. (2012). Remedies Against the Eu Institutions After Lisbon: An Era of Opportunity? *The Cambridge Law Journal*, *71*(3), 507–536. https://www.jstor.org/stable/41819928. doi:10.1017/S0008197312000803

Allegri, M. R. (2022). The Right to be Forgotten in the Digital Age. In F. Comunello, F. Martire, & L. Sabetta (Eds.), *What People Leave Behind: Marks, Traces, Footprints and their Relevance to Knowledge Society* (pp. 237–251). Springer International Publishing. doi:10.1007/978-3-031-11756-5_15

Andrus, M. T. (2016a). The Right to be Forgotten in America: Have Search Engines Inadvertently Become Consumer Reporting Agencies? *Business Law Today*, 1–4. https://www.jstor.org/stable/businesslawtoday.2016.05.06

Andrus, M. T. (2016b). The Right to be Forgotten in America: Have Search Engines Inadvertently Become Consumer Reporting Agencies? *Business Law Today*, 1–4. https://www.jstor.org/stable/businesslawtoday.2016.05.06

Antani, R. (2015). The Resistance of Memory: Could the European Union's Right to Be Forgotten Exist in the United. *Berkeley Technology Law Journal*, *30*(4), 1173–1210. https://www.jstor.org/stable/26377751

Beaney, W. M. (1966). The Right to Privacy and American Law. *Law and Contemporary Problems*, *31*(2), 253–271. doi:10.2307/1190670

Bressler, M., Bogard, C., & Von Bergen, C. (2020). *The Right to be Forgotten in the United States—Part 2*.

Burman, A. (2020). *The Growth of Privacy Regulation and the Bill* (Will India's Proposed Data Protection Law Protect Privacy and Promote Growth? pp. 3–8). Carnegie Endowment for International Peace. https://www.jstor.org/stable/resrep24293.4

Cadogan, M. S. (2023). *Blockchain and Distributed Ledger Technology: Definition and Scope* (Enforcing Smart Legal Contracts, pp. 2–2). Centre for International Governance Innovation. https://www.jstor.org/stable/resrep47331.7

Chase, P. H. (2019a). *Perspectives on the General Data Protection Regulation Of the European Union*. German Marshall Fund of the United States. https://www.jstor.org/stable/resrep21227

Chase, P. H. (2019b). *Perspectives on the General Data Protection Regulation Of the European Union*. German Marshall Fund of the United States. https://www.jstor.org/stable/resrep21227

Connelly, A. M. (1986). Problems of Interpretation of Article 8 of the European Convention on Human Rights. *The International and Comparative Law Quarterly*, *35*(3), 567–593. https://www.jstor.org/stable/759770. doi:10.1093/iclqaj/35.3.567

Cox Broadcasting Corp. V. Cohn, 420 U.S. 469 (Supreme (court of final appeal) March 3, 1975). https://globalfreedomofexpression.columbia.edu/cases/cox-broadcasting-corp-v-cohn/

Čtvrtník, M. (2023). The Right to (Not) Be Forgotten, Right to Know, and Model of Four Categories of the Right to Be Forgottenright to be forgotten. In M. Čtvrtník (Ed.), *Archives and Records: Privacy, Personality Rights, and Access* (pp. 111–137). Springer International Publishing. doi:10.1007/978-3-031-18667-7_5

Cuyvers, A. (2017). The Legal Framework of the EU. In A. Cuyvers, E. Ugirashebuja, J. E. Ruhangisa, & T. Ottervanger (Eds.), *East African Community Law* (pp. 119–138). Brill. https://www.jstor.org/stable/10.1163/j.ctt1w76vj2.10 doi:10.1163/9789004322073_007

Dehousse, F., & Verhoeven, D. (2014). *The Legal Framework* (The Nuclear Safety Framework in the European Union After Fukushima, pp. 11–21). Egmont Institute. https://www.jstor.org/stable/resrep06690.6

Erdos, D. (2021). The 'right to be forgotten' beyond the EU: An analysis of wider G20 regulatory action and potential next steps. *Journal of Medicine and Law*, *13*(1), 1–35. doi:10.1080/17577632.2021.1884947

European Data Protection Supervisor. (2023, November 16). *Shaping a Safer Digital Future: A New Strategy for a New Decade*. EDPS. https://edps.europa.eu/press-publications/publications/strategy/shaping-safer-digital-future

European Parliament. (2021, September 23). *Parliamentary question | No right of reply and consent on Wikipedia | E-004362/2021*. European Parliament. https://www.europarl.europa.eu/doceo/document/E-9-2021-004362_EN.html

Fabbrini, F., & Celeste, E. (2020). The Right to Be Forgotten in the Digital Age: The Challenges of Data Protection Beyond Borders. *German Law Journal*, *21*(S1), 55–65. doi:10.1017/glj.2020.14

Finck, M. (2018). *Blockchain Regulation and Governance in Europe*. Cambridge University Press., doi:10.1017/9781108609708

Fromholz, J. M. (2000). The European Union Data Privacy Directive. *Berkeley Technology Law Journal*, *15*(1), 461–484. https://www.jstor.org/stable/24115723

Garcia, F. (2005). Bodil Lindqvist: A Swedish Churchgoer's Violation of the European Union's Data Protection Directive Should Be a Warning to U.S. Legislators. *Fordham Intellectual Property, Media and Entertainment Law Journal, 15*(4), 1204. https://ir.lawnet.fordham.edu/iplj/vol15/iss4/10

Ghibellini, N. (2017). Some Aspects of the EU's New Framework for Personal Data Privacy Protection. *Business Lawyer, 73*(1), 207–214. https://www.jstor.org/stable/26419199

Gladstone, J. (2000). The U.s. Privacy Balance and the European Privacy Directive: Reflections on the United States Privacy Policy. *Willamette Journal of International Law and Dispute Resolution, 7*(1), 10–32. https://www.jstor.org/stable/26210974

Globocnik, J. (2020). The Right to Be Forgotten is Taking Shape: CJEU Judgments in GC and Others (C-136/17) and Google v CNIL (C-507/17). *GRUR International, 69*. doi:10.1093/grurint/ikaa002

Google Spain SL v. Agencia Española de Protección de Datos, Case C-131/12 (Court of Justice of the European Union (CJEU) May 13, 2014). https://globalfreedomofexpression.columbia.edu/cases/google-spain-sl-v-agencia-espanola-de-proteccion-de-datos-aepd/

Greenawalt, K. (1992). Free Speech in the United States and Canada. *Law and Contemporary Problems, 55*(1), 5–33. doi:10.2307/1191755

Gruschka, N., Mavroeidis, V., Vishi, K., & Jensen, M. (2018). *Privacy Issues and Data Protection in Big Data: A Case Study Analysis under GDPR*. 5027–5033. doi:10.1109/BigData.2018.8622621

Hartman, P. (1954). Freedom of Religion and Speech and the United States Supreme Court. *The Modern Law Review, 17*(3), 220–228. https://www.jstor.org/stable/1090673. doi:10.1111/j.1468-2230.1954.tb02151.x

IT Governance Publishing. (2017). *EU General Data Protection Regulation (GDPR): An Implementation and Compliance Guide*. IT Governance Publishing.

John, B. (2018). Are you ready for General Data Protection Regulation? *BMJ (Clinical Research Ed.), 360*, k941. https://www.jstor.org/stable/26959124. doi:10.1136/bmj.k941 PMID:29500167

Jones, M. L. (2013). *Speaking of Forgetting: Analysis of Possible Non-EU Responses to the Right to Be Forgotten and Speech Exception* (SSRN Scholarly Paper 2238602). doi:10.2139/ssrn.2238602

Keller, H., & Walther, R. (2018). Balancing Test: United Nations Human Rights Bodies. *Max Planck Encyclopedia of International Procedural Law (MPEiPro)*. https://opil.ouplaw.com/view/10.1093/law-mpeipro/e3422.013.3422/law-mpeipro-e3422?rskey=9sW2rG&result=1&prd=MPIL

Kindt, E. J. (2016). Why research may no longer be the same: About the territorial scope of the New Data Protection Regulation. *Computer Law & Security Report, 32*(5), 729–748. doi:10.1016/j.clsr.2016.07.007

Kohl, U., & Rowland, D. (2017). Censorship & Cyberborders through EU Data Protection Law. In *The Net and the Nation State*. Multidisciplinary Perspectives on Internet Governance., doi:10.1017/9781316534168.008

Kulhari, S. (2018). Data Protection, Privacy and Identity: A Complex Triad. In *Building-Blocks of a Data Protection Revolution* (1st ed., pp. 23–37). Nomos Verlagsgesellschaft mbH. https://www.jstor.org/stable/j.ctv941qz6.7

Landmark Communications, Inc. V. Commonwealth, 217 Va. 699 (Supreme Court of Virginia. May 1, 1978). https://uk.practicallaw.thomsonreuters.com/Document/I3e1a87e2042811da83e7e9deff98dc6f/View/FullText.html?originationContext=docHeader&contextData=(sc.PracticalLaw)&transitionType=Document&needToInjectTerms=False&firstPage=true

Lin, E. (2002). Prioritizing Privacy: A Constitutional Response to the Internet. *Berkeley Technology Law Journal*, *17*(3), 1085–1154. https://www.jstor.org/stable/24116979

Madden, M. (2014, November 12). Public Perceptions of Privacy and Security in the Post-Snowden Era. *Pew Research Center: Internet, Science & Tech*. https://www.pewresearch.org/internet/2014/11/12/public-privacy-perceptions/

Mediengruppe Österreich GmbH v. Austria, 37713/18 (European Court of Human Rights (ECtHR) April 5, 2022). https://globalfreedomofexpression.columbia.edu/cases/mediengruppe-osterreich-gmbh-v-austria/

Mirchandani, A. (2019). The GDPR-Blockchain Paradox: Exempting Permissioned Blockchains from the GDPR. *Fordham Intellectual Property, Media and Entertainment Law Journal, 29*(4), 1201. https://ir.lawnet.fordham.edu/iplj/vol29/iss4/5

New York Times Co. V. Sullivan, 376 U.S. 254 (Supreme (court of final appeal) March 9, 1964). https://globalfreedomofexpression.columbia.edu/cases/new-york-times-co-v-sullivan/

Newman, A. L. (2015). What the "right to be forgotten" means for privacy in a digital age. *Science*, *347*(6221), 507–508. https://www.jstor.org/stable/24745781. doi:10.1126/science.aaa4603 PMID:25635090

Pamment, J. (2020). *Current EU Policy on Disinformation* (The EU's Role in Fighting Disinformation: pp. 5–10). Carnegie Endowment for International Peace. https://www.jstor.org/stable/resrep25788.7

Pfenninger, R. (2021). The Right to be Forgotten has Not Found its Home in United States Law: A Comparison of Law between the European Union and the United States. *Willamette Journal of International Law and Dispute Resolution, 28*(2), 291–314. https://www.jstor.org/stable/27137185

Politou, E., Michota, A., Alepis, E., Pocs, M., & Patsakis, C. (2018). Backups and the right to be forgotten in the GDPR: An uneasy relationship. *Computer Law & Security Report*, *34*(6), 1247–1257. doi:10.1016/j.clsr.2018.08.006

Radsch, C. (2023). *Weaponizing Privacy and Copyright Law for Censorship* (SSRN Scholarly Paper 4464300). doi:10.2139/ssrn.4464300

Radsch, C. C. (2023). *The Right to Be Forgotten and the GDPR* (Weaponizing Privacy and Copyright Law for Censorship, pp. 6–7). Centre for International Governance Innovation. https://www.jstor.org/stable/resrep49654.9

Reventlow, N. J. (2020). Can the GDPR and Freedom of Expression Coexist? *Can the GDPR and Freedom of Expression Coexist*, *114*, 31–34. doi:10.1017/aju.2019.77

Smits, J. M. (2015). *What is Legal Doctrine? On the Aims and Methods of Legal-Dogmatic Research* (SSRN Scholarly Paper 2644088). doi:10.2139/ssrn.2644088

Sullivan, K. M. (2010). Two Concepts of Freedom of Speech. *Harvard Law Review*, *124*(1), 143–177. https://www.jstor.org/stable/20788316

Townend, J. (2017). Data Protection and the 'Right to be Forgotten' in Practice: A UK Perspective. *International Journal of Legal Information*, *45*(1), 28–33. doi:10.1017/jli.2017.2

Trybus, M., & Rubini, L. (2012). *The Treaty of Lisbon and the Future of European Law and Policy*. Edward Elgar Publishing. doi:10.4337/9780857932563

Vavra, A. N. (2018). The Right to Be Forgotten: An Archival Perspective. *The American Archivist*, *81*(1), 100–111. https://www.jstor.org/stable/48618003. doi:10.17723/0360-9081-81.1.100

Victor, J. M. (2013). The EU General Data Protection Regulation: Toward a Property Regime for Protecting Data Privacy. *The Yale Law Journal*, *123*(2), 513–528. https://www.jstor.org/stable/23744289

Volini, A. (2023). *The Right to Data Privacy: Revisiting Warren & Brandeis* (SSRN Scholarly Paper 4421290). doi:10.2139/ssrn.4421290

von Grafenstein, M. (2018). The function of the principle of purpose limitation in light of Article 8 ECFR and further fundamental rights. In *The Principle of Purpose Limitation in Data Protection Laws* (1st ed., pp. 109–596). Nomos Verlagsgesellschaft mbH. https://www.jstor.org/stable/j.ctv941v5w.5

Voss, W. G. (2014). European Union Data Privacy Law Developments. *Business Lawyer*, *70*(1), 253–260. https://www.jstor.org/stable/43665699

Voss, W. G. (2016a). European Union Data Privacy Law Reform: General Data Protection Regulation, Privacy Shield, and the Right to Delisting. *Business Lawyer*, *72*(1), 221–234. https://www.jstor.org/stable/26419118

Zichichi, M., Ferretti, S., D'Angelo, G., & Rodríguez-Doncel, V. (2022). Data governance through a multi-DLT architecture in view of the GDPR. *Cluster Computing*, *25*(6), 4515–4542. doi:10.1007/s10586-022-03691-3

Zipursky, B. (2016). The Monsanto Lecture: Online Defamation, Legal Concepts, and The Good Samaritan. *Valparaiso U. L. Rev.*, *51*, 1. https://ir.lawnet.fordham.edu/faculty_scholarship/851

ADDITIONAL READING

Bentotahewa, V., Hewage, C., & Williams, J. (2022). The Normative Power of the GDPR: A Case Study of Data Protection Laws of South Asian Countries. *SN Computer Science*, *3*(3), 183. doi:10.1007/s42979-022-01079-z

Connolly, J. (2021). The right to erasure: Comparative perspectives on an emerging privacy right. *Alternative Law Journal*, *46*(1), 58–63. doi:10.1177/1037969X20959839

Erdos, D. (2021). Special, Personal and Broad Expression: Exploring Freedom of Expression Norms under the General Data Protection Regulation. *Yearbook of European Law*, *40*, 398–430. doi:10.1093/yel/yeab004

Eskens, S. (2020). The personal information sphere: An integral approach to privacy and related information and communication rights. *Journal of the Association for Information Science and Technology*, *71*(9), 1116–1128. doi:10.1002/asi.24354 PMID:32984437

Georgiou, A. (2020). *Balancing the Freedom of Expression and the Right to Privacy in the GDPR era*. IHU. https://repository.ihu.edu.gr//xmlui/handle/11544/29637

Pollicino, O. (2021). *Data Protection and Freedom of Expression Beyond EU borders: EU Judicial Perspectives* (SSRN Scholarly Paper 3824154). doi:10.2139/ssrn.3824154

KEY TERMS AND DEFINITIONS

Censorship: Critics argue that the right to be forgotten, despite its intent to protect privacy, can be perceived as censorship. This term refers to the concern that the regulation may limit the availability of information and impede freedom of speech, especially in regions where the latter is highly valued, such as the United States.

Cross-Border Data Transfers: Even after the implementation of the GDPR, restrictions persist on cross-border data transfers. Notably, global websites like google.com, which are not exclusively European, are not covered under the right to be forgotten. This raises concerns and triggers a global conversation about internet privacy, with potential implications for free speech and individual rights.

Erasure of Information: This term denotes the right of individuals, as established by the GDPR, to request the removal or deletion of their personal information from online platforms and search engine results. The right to be forgotten empowers individuals to control how their data appears and is stored online.

GDPR (General Data Protection Regulation): The GDPR is a comprehensive European Union regulation established in 2018 to address challenges in protecting personal data in the digital age. It prioritizes privacy over freedom of speech, giving individuals the right to be forgotten and control their online data.

Personal Data: Refers to information that relates to an identifiable individual. The GDPR emphasizes the protection of personal data as a fundamental human right, allowing individuals to request the removal or correction of their data through the right to be forgotten.

Privacy: The GDPR underscores the right to privacy as a fundamental right within the European Union. It aims to balance individual privacy with public access to information, particularly in the context of online data processing and search engine results.

Restriction Of Access to Information: The GDPR's emphasis on the right to be forgotten includes restricting access to personal information that is freely accessible and causes harm. This regulation aims to balance protecting individual privacy and maintaining public access to information.

Chapter 8
Study of Literature on Quality Management in Manufacturing and Healthcare for Information Governance

Balaji Gopalan
https://orcid.org/0000-0002-1082-5597
CMS Business School, Bangalore, India

ABSTRACT

The chapter aims to comprehend the best practices of quality management in manufacturing and healthcare services and its relevance to information governance. Quality management principles of quality gurus have contributed significantly to the manufacturing and services sector. Its implementations in manufacturing and health care services provide numerous learning opportunities. Delivery of care processes integrates quality of health and life, lean management, quality assurance, quality implementation, quality control, affordability, and satisfaction with services. These best practices in quality management are relevant across various disciplines of research including information management, psychology, business research, service quality and technology management. The study has explored the challenges of quality management in health care services and manufacturing and integrates studies that may contribute to the subject of quality management and its relevance for information governance.

INTRODUCTION

How do companies manage to manufacture quality products without compromising on performance attributes and what is the cost associated with making quality products? The resounding success of a few manufacturing companies was a perfect cause for industries to take notice and learn about incorporating quality management into their processes and practices. Quality is one of the most important reasons why firms have become profitable and sustainable. For the health care industry, value systems are the core to implementing quality management systems. Quality is also considered the best performance measure

DOI: 10.4018/979-8-3693-0472-3.ch008

across all industries. Total quality management in all their procedures, processes and techniques have transformed many industries. In manufacturing, *six sigma* quality management implementation has facilitated almost zero-defect products and in the services sector service quality has become a standard. The services industry is also setting an example in implementing quality management systems based on the quality principles of gurus such as Deming, Juran, Shewhart, Feigenbaum, Ishikawa and Crosby. The services sector has faced numerous challenges in quality management implementations because customer needs are both tangible and intangible. Research published on industries and quality management based on Toyota Production Systems' applicability to the health care sector has identified many quality objectives and quality parameters. Lean manufacturing management is identified as the core to the production management techniques of the Toyota Production System (Collins et al. 2015). In services or manufacturing, the focus is on eliminating events such as "Jidoka" or "Andon" alerts that disrupt production or services. Lean management principles in manufacturing focuses on eliminating the wastage of material, labor, energy and other resources and improving manufacturing processes, reducing delays and optimizing logistics and supply chain management in the transportation of goods.

Studies on the implementation of the Toyota production system (TPS) for quality management in the health care services have discussed the need for an integrated approach to the quality management of services with a focus on employee involvement in the work design and the setting of performance goals. TPS has become a standard in process innovation for the elimination of defects and the reduction of waste in industries and the services sector and to focus on quality, productivity, dependability, optimization of costs, market share, customer services and safety. TPS depends on organizational knowledge creation, high degree of specification of work processes, employee participation in ideas, innovation and continuous improvement.

The structure and control systems and a decentralized work culture encouraging participative design are also integrated into the TPS philosophy. It emphasized a cordial management-employees work environment facilitating a healthy work culture, customer focus and continuous improvement. It also requires leadership traits in individuals who are operation-oriented team leaders and also employee empowerment in reducing "Jidoka" or "Andon" alerts and focus on problem solving and improvement of services. How can we recognize continuous quality improvement and what are the policy implications and practicalities in quality health care and quality assurance? (Esain et al. 2011; Rubenstein et al. 2013; Claus 1991).

The research published on quality management in the context of manufacturing, service science and healthcare is dispersed taking into consideration articles published from the years 1990 to 2024. Articles published in quality engineering journals refer to Quality Management and Juran's trilogy and legacy (Bisgaard 2008; Kolesar 2008). A systematic review of literature on quality control, total quality management (TQM), service quality and service science published in a journal on quality services and service sciences has covered 30 years of TQM literature (Chen et al. 2022).

Research published on lean six sigma have focused on deployment in manufacturing SMEs, six sigma and competitive advantage with reference to TQM and excellence, six sigma implementations in the pharma sector, six sigma in healthcare, professional safety and health facilities management (Alexander et al. 2022; Collins et al., 2015; Esain et al., 2012; Halpren-Ruder 2020; de Mast 2006; González-Cebrián et al. 2022; Heuvel 2005; Kaplan et al. 2009; ReVelle 2004; Losko and Smeak 2009; Kim et al., 2016). Other articles have focused on achieving peak performance (Brown 1997), Automotive Quality and Training Excellence in manufacturing, Toyota Production Systems, Six Sigma Implementation and Quality Improvement (Cole and Flynn 2009; Entelechy Inc 2009; Collins et al., 2015). Research papers have also focused on seven research subareas in the discipline of quality management, namely, (1) methodologies, (2) projects, (3) business excellence, (4) six sigma training, (5) six sigma processes, (6) engineering management and (7) lean and healthcare management (Niñerola et al., 2021).

Research Methodology and Systematic Literature Review

Edwards Deming, Walter Shewhart, Armand Feigenbaum, Joseph Juran, Philip Crosby and Kaoru Ishikawa are a few of the management gurus who focused on quality management and defined various quality measures relevant to the industry. They conceptualized methods of quality management with philosophies and tools that were later applied and implemented in industries. Statistics has been widely applied in industrial management. The quality management philosophy of Edward Deming and Walter Shewhart focused on improving processes using quality control charts. Philip Crosby discussed a quality management philosophy of attaining zero defects in manufacturing. Joseph Juran emphasized a philosophy of *quality planning, quality assurance and control* and *quality implementation* in manufacturing. These quality gurus contributed significantly to industry best practices and industry standards. This philosophy is seen in many companies who have made affordable world class quality products.

Several journals have published research papers on total quality management from the years 1990 to 2022. These focused on manufacturing, service industries and health care. These articles ranged from the implementation of TQM in automotive quality, Toyota production systems, six sigma implementation, health-care quality improvement, e-health and telehealth, technological and managerial innovation in healthcare, data management and quality research and quality assurance in healthcare. Dahlgaard et al. (1997) discussed about TQM and how historically it has evolved in various stages: quality inspection, quality control, quality assurance that resulted in the emergence of the field of TQM.

EBSCO and Emerald Insight academic database were used to retrieve research on quality management across manufacturing and services industries such as the healthcare sectors. Around 640 research papers were retrieved from Emerald Insight for the years between 1990 to 2024 that focused on manufacturing or healthcare. A search on articles from the year 1990 to 2024 archived on quality management in manufacturing and healthcare by EBSCOHost retrieved 364 research papers. A working list of 35 relevant research papers was created for this study.

The "quality" key term associated with manufacturing and healthcare are in reference to Quality Management and Juran's Legacy, Achieving Peak Performance, Juran's Trilogy, Total Quality Management and Healthcare, Automotive Quality, Toyota Production Systems, Six Sigma Implementation and Quality Improvement. The focus of this paper is also unique in terms of how it attempts to integrate these numerous studies and compare quality management principles and their implementations across manufacturing and healthcare with an emphasis on (1) Opportunities for quality improvement and response mechanism protocols for healthcare (2) quality management across manufacturing and healthcare and the relevance of SERVQUAL, (3) data management and relevance of natural language processing, augmented intelligence and machine learning in healthcare quality management,

(4) core missions and audit standards for quality management, (5) accreditation of healthcare organizations, (6) projects and goals for continuous improvement, (7) Toyota production systems and its relevance to healthcare, (8) TQM for healthcare management, and (9) case studies in quality management implementations across manufacturing and healthcare.

Quality Management Across Manufacturing and Healthcare

An integrated approach to quality management in health care services takes into consideration knowledge management and the use of SERVQUAL (Parasuraman et al. 1988), a tool used in measuring:

a) Customer expectations, service perceptions and values
b) Facility, processes and resource management
c) Cross-functional teams
d) Quality and knowledge management
e) Internal quality and service capabilities
f) Subject matter experts and knowledge sharing protocols.
g) Decision making and accountability.
h) Leadership, scientific methodology and best practices of governance in service quality
i) Requirement for team quality in hospitals
j) Audit and Total Quality Management (TQM) implementation.

The value system is the core to the health care sector, and it is defined by the medical condition, accurate care intervention and diagnosis. It depends on timeliness, knowledge management, technologies and knowledge sharing protocols and processes in treatments.

The value systems in health care (Collins et al. 2015; Vanteddu and McAllister 2014) arc also going through changes due to:

a) Demand for acute care services and specialized services.
b) Aging and uninsured populations
c) Privatization and specialty hospitals
d) Demand for quality services and patient safety.
e) New technologies and scientific improvements
f) Challenges with financial management
g) Labor constraints
h) Stringent accreditation rules

Quality function deployment (QFD) requires implementing and integrating care procedures for the treatment of patients and is a part of the philosophy of continuous quality improvement programs. This requires adherence to technical guidelines, organizational design, team building, control systems and new cultural norms. The QFD customization in an integrated service delivery system for health care services require necessary performance measurement of the effectiveness of quality assurance (Collins et al. 2015, Vanteddu and McAllister 2014; Thor et al. 2008) that focuses on patient safety standards, patient care, timeliness of treatment, personalized and successful treatment and affordability. The implementation of a quality management system in health care also requires optimization of costs associated with medicines, technologies, treatments, labor and regular employment training for improving morale, employee motivation and safety.

In this regard, E-health is adding value to health care services in terms of utilizing technology for telehealth, telemedicine, digitization and patient monitoring. A virtual visit can significantly optimize the costs, clinical efficiency, patient monitoring, service conveniences and enhance information management (Halpren-Ruder 2020). This would in time facilitate improved value systems, quality and economics.

In the management of information systems, studies on data management in industrial companies have focused on standardized performance metrics, responsibilities, problems, data storage and decision making (Martin and Tomáš 2023).

New technology paradigms such as the Internet of Things (IOT), machine learning (ML) and augmented intelligence (AI) are also adding value to health care services.

These include:

a) The role of natural language processing (NLP), machine learning (ML) and augmented intelligence (AI) in facilitating accurate diagnosis, measures of medication and treatment outcomes in health care.
b) The role of technology in advancing an environment of care (EOC) for patients and creating a greater value system.
c) Creating new diagnostic tools, archiving and information management, machine learning for imaging labs, diagnostics and genome sequencing.

Guidelines on review of health services medical records recommend evaluation and archiving of data for records. In the US alone, in the year 2017, 880 million outpatient visits were recorded. The cost of reviewing the records for evaluation was estimated at $293 million even if 5% of the records were evaluated. With an average of 36 million admissions to US hospitals and 10 health care provider visits per hospitalized patient, 5% review of records evaluated was estimated to cost $122 million. Studies have estimated that 50% of a clinician's time is spent on processing information, 30% on preparation of records and the remaining time on other professional responsibilities. Information management systems and natural language processing used for E-health or telehealth services can save more than 300 hours annually in the time spent on information processing and patient record management (Halpren-Ruder 2020). Information management for health care requires structured and documented acquisition of knowledge and may facilitate patient autonomy towards treatments. Healthcare specialists have identified that (1) Information management of patient data can help improve diagnosis and treatment for populations, (2) Individualized treatments can be provided based on diagnosis along with measures of medication and treatment, (3) Consultation with patients on new sciences such as NLP, ML or AI and its benefits for treatment can be more valuable.

Implementation of a Total Quality Management system for health care services firms requires:

1. Technical details that focus on protocol, procedures, timeliness and outcomes.
2. Clear communication between the management, employee and stakeholders.
3. Simplified processes in material and resource management.
4. Scientific method supervised by an instructor or trainer.

In an audit by the Joint Commission on the Accreditation of Healthcare organizations (JCAHO) has identified six patientcare and safety categories (Collins et al. 2015).

They are:

1. Accurate patient identification and details
2. Ongoing communication between health care practitioners

3. Identifying safe medication
4. Infection risk reduction
5. Matching of ailments with medication
6. Safe health care environment
7. Employing expert care givers in clinics
8. Patient and system tracer methodology
9. Information management of patient experiences
10. Information management of processes
11. Consultation, treatment and patient education
12. Working on accreditation standards
13. Quality first and safest care philosophy

The philosophy of JCAHO tries to get a complete comprehension of how individual processes and organizational systems add value to the effectiveness in the health care services. The TPS can provide a way to facilitate an integration of different departments necessary for effective functioning of hospitals. This may produce timely information flow, accurate treatment, optimization of costs and effective co-ordination between healthcare practitioners and staff.

The TPS focuses on:

a) Details of content, sequence of protocols, timeliness and results
b) Clear communication between suppliers, manufacturers, distributors and customers
c) Simplified processes in production and services
d) Use of scientific methodologies

The equivalent in the enhancement of patient care requires:

a) Patient treatments adhering to documented and accurate practices.
b) Direct interactions between patients and nurses
c) No compromise on patient safety
d) Precise communication during patient treatment
e) Treatments based on best practice.
f) Internal auditing for quality improvements
g) Regulatory compliance for patient safety

Leadership in a health care organization with governance that directs control to various departments towards quality improvements and quality management in patient care is the most optimized model of organizational design. Value systems in health care benefit from an integrated approach involving timeliness, detailed processes, technology and expert knowledge towards patient care and their safety. An IDEA methodology (Collins et al. 2015) is also useful in (1) improving treatment processes and protocols, (2) reducing process and implementation constraints, (3) exploring alternatives, (4) activating improvements, (5) trust and commitment in administration.

The IDEA method and the Toyota Principles of Quality Management are applicable to the healthcare sector and are described in Table 1.

Table 1. IDEA and Toyota principles of quality management in manufacturing and health care (Collins et al. 2015; Bisgaard 2008)

Opportunities for Quality Improvement	Response mechanism protocols for patient care
Cause and effect analysis of critical process steps in a production line or health care service	● Analyze processes and level them for a balanced workload.● Fix quality at every level of health care.● Standardization of protocols, practices and audits.● Visualize the entire process and sequence them.● Implement technologies that are thoroughly tested
Explore alternatives to reduce audit-risk management	● Creating a safe environment, mentoring leaders, quality work culture and shared values● Creating partnerships and learning organizations
Activating quality improvement processes	● Implementation of decisions● Cause and effect analysis of audit-risk processes

There are many challenges such as assigning functional teams to audit risk processes in health care services. These are described in Table 2.

The responsibilities of implementing TPS in terms of a quality management system adhering to the regulations of accreditation of health care organizations requires to take into consideration:

1. Training of functional teams for enhanced decision making.
2. Customer and employee rapport.
3. Maintaining zero defects in processes and results that are associated with audit-risk.
4. Minimizing waste and standardizing processes.
5. Creating champions and process coaches in quality management.

Table 2. Quality management systems of TPS and audit standards for health care services (Collins et al. 2015; Losko and Smeak 2019)

Functional teams	Core Mission	Audit process
Ethical responsibilities	Patient empowerment	Complete knowledge of processes
Provision and delivery of care	Effective co-ordination of care, treatment, medications and services	Regular training on patient care
Medication management	Documentation of patient treatments and detailed information of medications	Criteria for medication selection, listings and procurement
Measuring performance of organizations	Using department data for measuring the performance of processes	Quality improvements in processes and reducing audit-risk
Leadership	Adherence to laws and regulations	Patient safety as a priority ensured by the leadership
Environment of care (EOC) philosophy	Reducing risk for patients	Integrated risk management system facilitated by a secure and safe environment and preventing risks from hazardous material, wastes, fires and medical equipment
Human resource management	Constitute employees from various areas of specialization	Qualifications and responsibilities are matched
Information management	Business process management of daily tasks and routines	Privacy management and secure information systems management
Infection control - surveillance and prevention	Hospital protocols to prevent infections	Measures to prevent infections

Table 3. Projects and goals were identified for continuous improvement projects with respect to TPS and health care services (Collins et al. 2015; Rubenstein et al. 2013)

Goals	Implications for Health Care operations	Philosophy of TPS
Identification and documentation of patient information	Improve the diagnosis for treatment and reduce errors	Individualized treatment plan for every patient and documentation of standardized protocols of control
Effective communication between practitioners	Prevention of errors. Accuracy, completeness and timely communication	Clear communication between stakeholders. Identifying processes relevant to the work
Safe medication	Patient treatment plans are manageable, appropriate and standardized	To control variation in processes
Reduce risk of infections	Standardized protocols for maintaining hygiene and reducing risk of infections	Environment of care and safety
Knowledge of medication and reconciliations	Measures for medication and environment of care for patient safety	Delivery plan and protocols for safe medication
Prevent patient falls	Reducing the risk of patient falls and resulting injuries	Evaluation of safety hazards and prevention of patient falls

6. Controlling 'Jidoka' across processes and quality management.
7. Reducing audit risk at every step of critical management processes.
8. Committed leadership, governance and administrative oversight in quality management.
9. Projects that focus on audit-risks, patient safety and customer care.

In terms of identifying implementation goals of the Toyota production systems in healthcare Table 3 describes in detail the methodology that may be applicable.

Case Studies on Quality Management in Manufacturing and Healthcare

Most Japanese manufacturing firms owe their phenomenal success to Deming's teachings. Deming's philosophy for manufacturing transformed management thought processes. This led to many manufacturing industries building world class products and services. Quality management makes it possible for firms to optimize the costs of production and make great quality products and services, making firms more profitable. Crosby also spells this on how manufacturing can profit from comprehending the costs of quality that if usually neglected may result in lost labor and machine utilization, scrap, breakdowns and lost sales (Russell and Taylor, 2011). He realized that knowledgeable firms were aware of this, and others made no sense of it. Deming's quality principle was a philosophy called the plan, do, check and act methodology popularly referred to as the PDCA and was also closely associated with the Shewart cycle (Rienzo 1993). In healthcare services, the quality function deployment (QFD) and the PDCA methodology when working together were found to improve patient's comfort (Collins et al. 2015; Vanteddu and McAllister 2014).

An automobile manufacturer incorporating the PDCA philosophy into their production line may also enhance quality improvements to their product. In manufacturing, if the inspection process identifies a lot of defects in the first batch of production, it may correct the equipment and production processes and perform a cause-and-effect analysis for quality improvements. The use of control charts and lean six sigma methodology may also benefit the manufacture of great quality products. Hence, Deming's philosophy focuses on a 14-point strategy for quality and recommends an audit of the management and production line processes (Russell and Taylor, 2011; Rienzo 1993; Ghobadian and Speller 1994; de Mast 2006).

Manufacturing requires optimization based on systems science and every sub system in manufacturing requires co-ordination between units. The work in many manufacturing firms requires profound knowledge systems within a theory of optimization (Rienzo 1993). For many firms, strong values and ethical principles in conducting business, quality management in manufacturing with a focus on "zero-defects" are the reasons for excellence. For example, excellence in quality management at Ford Motors, Caterpillar, Ritz-Carlton, Hershey's, Kraft Foods, UPS, Motorola required years of consistency whether it was about cost and lead time optimization, improvement in business processes, and near zero-defect production (Russell and Taylor, 2011). The Hershey chocolate company's adherence to Statistical Process Control (SPC) and control charts to control variation in processes has led to greater quality performance in all systems and sub systems and attainment of its quality through an excellence program. The investments in quality management for manufacturing is to reduce the defects that may otherwise increase costs of production.

In manufacturing and assembly, the use of inferior material may also lead to wasteful expenditure resulting in the stoppage of production. Manufacturing may have to control extreme variations in quality during production. This is the reason why employee training programs in Six Sigma and Statistical Process Control become necessary. Six sigma implementation involves mapping and analyzing business processes and applying statistical quality control techniques to study variations and then control the variations that may affect the efficiency or productivity in manufacturing. This led to the reduction of waste and cost control.

Deming conceptualized the use of the plan, do, check and act methodology of quality improvement for manufacturing or service operations management. Deming's 14 points applicable to both manufacturing and health care quality are explained in table 4.

Improvements in the diagnosis for treatment and reduction of errors facilitate direct variation control. Accuracy, completeness and timely communication can enhance the quality of patient treatments. This along with measures of medication can then be manageable, appropriate and standardized. Further, maintenance of hygiene, an environment of care and standardization of protocols reduce the risk of infections adding to the quality management of services.

Case Study: Motorola's Six Sigma Quality

Motorola emerged as a small manufacturer of car radios in the 1920s (hence the name Motorola). It grew to a $30 billion company with more than 68,000 employees operating in 73 countries and having 320 facilities. Its portfolio included the manufacture of semiconductors, cellphones, wireless communication systems, computers, integrated circuits and paging systems. It was an engineering company focused on the manufacturing of products and creating markets. In the 1980s it pioneered the six-sigma quality program and later became the winner of the Malcolm Baldridge National Quality Award (Russell and Taylor 2011). This changed the approach to quality management that previously depended on measuring quality levels in manufacturing as a percentage or parts per hundred. The six-sigma methodology at Motorola evolved into a complete quality management system (QMS) that became a standard. It was also implemented at Kraft Foods, Intel, Microsoft, NASA, UPS, GE, Boeing, Ford, Xerox and the Bank of America to name a few.

Table 4. Deming's 14-point philosophy comparing manufacturing and health care services (Russell and Taylor 2011; Slack et al. 2010; Rienzo 1993)

Sl No	Manufacturing	Health Care Quality
1	Create product or service quality improvement for manufacturing and services	Focus on service quality improvement
2	Adopt a philosophy of good quality management of products and services	Philosophy of quality management in facilities, processes and resource management
3	Implement statistical quality control for manufacturing and eliminate inspection	Statistical quality control of processes and services
4	Select a few suppliers or vendors based on quality rather than competitive prices.	Quality and knowledge information systems of suppliers and vendors
5	Optimize productivity and costs.	Improve timeliness, decision making for diagnosis, accuracy of treatments and optimize costs
6	Institute worker training on quality management and statistical quality-control.	Patient treatment plans are manageable, appropriate and standardized
7	Motivating supervisors on leadership and improving performance.	Subject matter experts and service quality management. Leadership, scientific methodology and best practices of governance for continuous improvement in service quality
8	Employee involvement in quality management without hesitation.	Internal quality, subject matter experts and service capabilities in improving quality management.
9	Inter-functional teams' management and communication.	Cross-functional teams to improve organizational productivity, team quality and quality of services
10	Quality management for production and improving employee performance.	Audit of service quality and implementation of TQM
11	Quality first and then manufacturing targets.	Improve the diagnosis for treatment, accuracy, completeness, timely communication and treatment
12	Enhancing worker motivation, creativity, and self-esteem of employees	Requirement for team quality based on motivation, creativity and dignity in hospitals
13	Implement quality management across the organization.	Mobilizing subject matter experts, service quality, knowledge management, Internal quality and service capabilities. Decision making and accountability
14	Invite top management towards a commitment to implement quality management based on the previous 13 points.	Total Quality Management (TQM) implementation based on the above 13 points

Case Study: E-Health and Healthcare Management

At the National Health Care Services (NHS) UK, Statistical Process Control (SPC) is used for monitoring waiting times, for example, doctor appointments, days for diagnosis or treatment medication time. In today's era of information and communication technologies the emergence of E-health and healthcare devices is transforming the medical profession. E-health unifies telemedicine, telehealth, digital health and remote monitoring of patients (Halpren-Ruder 2020). The cost savings and convenience from the use of information and communication technologies is realized in the clinical efficiency, enhanced patient engagement and improved decision making that depend on thousands or millions of clinical records. This has resulted in significant improvements in quality and cost. Healthcare services enhanced by technologies are benefiting from improved productivity, cost and time savings leading to improved services. Augmented intelligence (AI) and natural language processing (NLP) have begun to support the medical profession in terms of processing archived interactions between clinicians and patients improving desired metrics and treatments.

Innovations such as information and communication technologies, 3D printing and designing, diagnostics and sciences are enhancing the clinician's role in physical examinations, lab imaging and improved treatments for the patients. This has resulted in cost and time savings for clinics, diagnostic centers and hospitals. According to research, in the year 2017, it was discovered that in the US alone there were 880 million hospital outpatient visits and if 5% of diagnostic reports were evaluated for a patient, it would have costed $50/hr per patient for a clinician spending 8 minutes per patient diagnosis. This resulted in $293 million in costs.

The use of NLP for patient clinician interactions can facilitate conversations and dictations to be parsed, recorded and stored for enhanced decision making and quality management. This curation of records may also enhance treatments and standardize treatments for populations. This information processing supported by a technology or innovation may even save a few hours a day for 365 days yielding in hundreds of hours saved annually for the clinician. The entry of digital health devices from FitBit, Apple and Nike are making available monitoring devices, minimally invasive glucometers and pulmonary pressure and sleep monitoring devices for patients who require real time diagnostics and monitoring of vital signs thus adding value towards treatments and improving work life balance for clinicians.

Case Study: The Geneva Construction Insurance Company

Founded in 1922, the Geneva Construction Insurance Company provided insurance for contractors and construction companies in the building industry, initially in German speaking Europe and later USA, in North America. By the year 2000 it was the leading providers of insurance for complex, high-risk construction projects, involving contractual and legal obligations, hazards and uncertainty requiring 'customized' insurance. The insurance coverage required particular professional knowledge and skills from experts including construction underwriters, accountants, engineers, lawyers and risk consultants. The implementation of TQM was initiated after learning about six sigma. Six sigma implementation involves studying business processes and requires the use of statistical quality control techniques to study variations and control them to improve the efficiency or productivity of a business (Slack et al., 2010).

The objective of implementing six sigma was to:

- Optimize costs and improve customer service.
- Reduce process variation and mitigate risks.
- Focus on risk assessment and support Sarbanes Oxley regulations.
- Maintain a process library.
- Identify exceptions in processes.
- Engage senior management and establish process ownership.
- Performing a cause-and-effect analysis and eliminate variances in processes.

After consultation with experts, it was recommended that the management implement a six-sigma pilot program called the Geneva Construction and Risk (GCR) assessment pilot program.

This included:

- A tailored approach to six sigma implementations for specific processes.
- Hiring consultants and external partners to evaluate the processes.
- Establishing tools and techniques to transition from 2 sigma to 4 sigma.
- Quantifying the financial benefits of implementing six sigma.
- Utilizing team-based problem solving and the use of simple statistical techniques

The various steps involved in the pilot program were:

- Prioritizing tasks, confirming budgets and resources for facilitating a six-sigma improvement program
- Identifying external consultants experienced in implementing six sigma methodologies.
- Consensus on deciding where to start the six-sigma implementation.
- Identifying the investments required and quantifying the benefits.
- Customizing the six-sigma implementation to reduce the risks.
- Identifying potential pilot areas for assessing feasibility for implementation
- Formulate a six-sigma pilot plan.
- Conduct and audit the pilot program.

Case Study: North Shore University Hospital, New York

The hospital successfully implemented the six-sigma methodology to reduce the delays in bed assignment time for incoming patients who had arrived for operations. The flawed bed tracking and monitoring system resulted in delays due to communication issues. The define, measure, analyze, improve and control (DMAIC) method was used to map the processes involved in the discharge-admission process at the hospital. An upper limit of 150 minutes was maintained to restrict the response time during requests from registered nurses and maintain bed assignments in a timely manner. A study on 195 patients arriving for medical care indicated that there was a defect rate of 130 that translated to a score of 1 sigma. After an analysis using the DMAIC methodology and a statistical analysis of the process it was found that the constraints were caused due to both communication and technical failure.

The team was trained and appraised on the issues faced and information and communication technologies facilitated timely communication and alerts. This improved the processes that resulted in the hospital attaining a 90-minute turnaround time for tracking the admission-discharge time of patients and reach a 2.3 sigma process control, a significant improvement in its efficiency and customer satisfaction. (Russell and Taylor 2011)

Other Case Studies on Quality Management

At Kawasaki motors, it is generally felt that if the whole system in manufacturing vehicles is optimized and standardized, there will not be any variation. At Mars chocolates, in the production of M & M candies, SPC is applied across production to ensure consistency in quality standards of taste, weight, shape, and color, and packaging (Russell and Taylor, 2011). Because production can differ due to human and machine errors, machine maintenance or equipment setup, processes can be statistically controlled.

In the healthcare industry, literature have discussed the necessity for a Human Resources Management (HRM) evaluation of measures and criteria specified by the Deming Prize, Malcolm Baldridge National

Quality Award, European Quality Award, and George M Low Quality Award. For example, Sears's business focuses on the employee-customer-profit chain model with an emphasis on human resources.

Federal Express uses the strategic philosophy of "People, Service, Profit" with a belief that its employees are the most important resource. Motorola as a company annually trains its employees for 160 hours to manage technological changes and challenges in its business. Employee surveys at these companies are also completed to assess employee satisfaction to improve the quality of services, team building and a healthy work environment acknowledging the fact that there is a direct link between employee satisfaction and customer satisfaction.

Six Sigma quality management philosophy has focused on application of various quality management methodologies into a complete quality management system for processes and transactions internally resulting in improved production, quality control and the creation of markets. GE, Ford, Boeing, Xerox, Kraft Foods, Intel, Microsoft, Sony, UPS are a few businesses who have focused on Quality Six Sigma implementations. It has resulted in the reduction of waste, optimization of costs, improved quality management, customer satisfaction and profitability of businesses. The focus is on the quality of products and services, processes, knowledge management, conceptualization and value systems.

In the USA, Medtronic Inc., a business that is into the production of cardiovascular and neurological healthcare recognizes its employees with awards for their participation in product and service quality improvement. The pharmaceutical industry has demonstrated that quality implementations and quality improvement programs have resulted in improved knowledge management, medical innovations, optimization of costs and profitability (Russell and Taylor 2011; Kim et al. 2016). Pfizer is an example of a pharmaceutical company that has managed its supply chain of inventory successfully with a low inventory turnover that is measured as a ratio of the average aggregate value of the inventory it holds, and the cost of goods sold. Kellogg's model of supply chain management is focused on weekly production, inventory and distribution decisions. Kellogg's supply chain management depends on the customer demand, and it maintains safety stocks for weeks t and t+1 and for advertisement campaigns, it holds safety stocks for a four-week horizon with optimized production and savings in the millions of dollars.

Another example of quality and its role in product design is how Kawasaki has utilized its research and development unit of experts in dynamics and motorbike production to manufacture world class products. The R and D unit became a school or training institute because Kawasaki learned and initiated a philosophy that believed that knowledge does not grow out of experience alone.

Theories and scientific methodologies have resulted in concepts and product design and these experiences have been archived as learnings of excellence. Kawasaki identified that standardization of established and validated results in product design is possible only if there is a theoretical and scientific base.

In the automotive industry, Kawasaki's manufacturing processes and supply chain management and work culture adheres strictly with Deming's philosophy (Gopalan and Iyer 2017). Kawasaki's implementation of Deming's philosophy involves:

1. A focus on competitiveness, leadership, product quality and employment.
2. Implementation of quality control before manufacturing, processes and economies of scale.
3. Optimization of costs of production and integrating suppliers based on loyalty and trust.
4. A quality management training institute for employees and a focus on business excellence.
5. Cross-functional departments and an environment of care.
6. Kawasaki encourages a quality first and zero defects philosophy for productivity.
7. A factory floor that rotates management responsibilities.

8. Awarding employees for excellence in workmanship and quality.
9. Advanced education, training and research facilitating worker loyalty and self-improvement.

Successful Six Sigma Implementations

- At Volvo's North American Truck Division, the implementation of the six-sigma methodology for its truck modification resulted in saving millions of dollars and improved forecasting projects and reduced fuel tank replacement down time.
- At the North Carolina Baptist Hospital, six sigma teams facilitated speedy treatment of heart attack patients by expediting the time taken to move patients from the emergency room to the cardiac catheter lab by an average of 41 minutes.
- Dental insurance companies were able to reduce pending claims by 50% in six sigma projects that focused on processing time and premium reductions.
- Infrastructure projects such as the construction of the channel tunnel rail link in the UK were able to save hundreds of hours on the job.
- Ford Motor Company was able to save $100,000 annually when it solved the problem of body side molding for its vehicles and eliminated wasteful processes. (Russell and Taylor 2011)

QUALITY AND PERFORMANCE MANAGEMENT

The quality control process implemented by many world class organizations depends on training its work force for quality design and performance. For example, at Kawasaki every employee attends compulsory training workshops at least once in 6 months. Training improves learning of production techniques and institutionalizes changes. In manufacturing, incorporating statistical process control by training employees is a Deming philosophy recommended to appreciate quality management (Rienzo 1993). Similarly, the philosophy of Ishikawa recommends training employees in manufacturing and services to learn production processes with the use of flow charts, quality circles, control charts, audits and statistics (Ghobadian and Speller 1994; Russell and Taylor 2011). In manufacturing, quality management training reduces perceived ambiguity and arbitrariness resulting in consistent production management techniques across the organization and improved performance management. This aims at imparting quality techniques to employees that Kawasaki conducts regularly.

Deming encouraged that people perform better in establishments when they feel secure and eliminate fear. The extensive training that employees receive on quality management works in the favor of leadership within their establishment when optimizing system performance for delivering product and service quality (Rienzo 1993; Claus 1991). Workers are no longer focused on production targets. Instead, they have worked towards institutionalizing methods for quality management.

Deming insisted that quality and productivity in manufacturing and services improve from replacing production targets with taking initiatives that encourages workmanship and stabilizing the system performance with teamwork and quality management (Rienzo 1993; Ghobadian and Speller 1994; Russell and Taylor 2011). Windsor Export Supply, a division of Ford Motor Company faced problems with freight auditing and was able to apply Deming's philosophy to correct disruptions in processing invoices and issuing payments on time (Rienzo 1993).

Figure 1.
(Juran Trilogy - Approaches to Quality in a Service Industry)

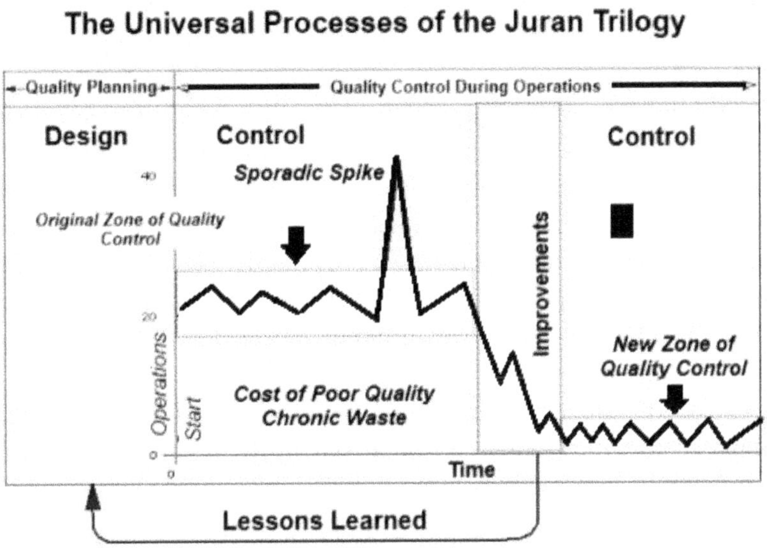

Joseph M Juran's philosophy on quality management is similar to Deming's 14-points. Juran's trilogy of quality planning, quality control and quality improvement tackle firm problems of quality management and are identified with top management constraints rather than the processes or business operations (Kolesar 2008). Juran's pareto analysis identified that quality problems in manufacturing are associated with a few causes. He utilized a pareto chart to explain and measure the cause of poor quality of services at a hospital to be attributed to staff communication and no other day to day routines associated with hygienic cleaning, laundry, patient or family interactions (Russell and Taylor 2011). Taguchi has insisted that the inadequacies in product and service design quality add expenses in terms of product failure (Russell and Taylor 2011, Ghobadian and Speller 1994). He insisted that product designs are considered to be robust if it is durable and handles weather, operational conditions and are easily maintainable. The losses for manufacturing may require optimizing costs and consistency in product performance for implementing quality management. Figure 1 describes the Juran trilogy of Quality planning, Assurance and Control applicable in manufacturing and healthcare services.

Feigenbaum discussed the cost of quality and quality system economics in terms of quality assurance. ISO 9000 standards were established that insisted on measuring quality in the context of manufacturing and services. The investments associated with implementing quality in production depend on (1) quality planning, (2) product-design, (3) processes, (4) training and (5) information. The Design for Six Sigma (DFSS) focuses on the Taguchi method to reduce the variability in design. Juran defines quality as "fitness for use" or robustness of design. Some literature phrase products or service quality as "fitness for purpose" (Ghobadian and Speller 1994). According to Juran, manufacturing firms who prioritize quality management need to have a focus on market growth, product design, production and quality control and also appraisals from customers.

Cross-functional departments in manufacturing and services firms benefit from total quality management (Claus 1991). Leadership and governance in quality management may benefit from the quality management philosophies of Juran, Deming, Taguchi, Ishikawa and Kaizen. To bring in superior quality processes any establishment has to invest in quality planning. Juran organizes his quality program into three facets. The quality planning phase includes the process of preparing to meet quality needs, the quality process of meeting quality needs during deployment and the process of reaching unprecedented performance.

Juran's application to quality bases its concept that quality once instituted needs continuous upgrades so that quality systems are still in place. Quality dynamics require support at all management levels. No establishment is complete without some quality update happening regularly. Quality needs to be underway across the entire establishment (Ghobadian and Speller 1994). Health care services cannot be defined on a basis quantitatively as they are intangible, inseparable to performance parameters, variable from time to time and are generally perishable in nature in the sense that service definitions keep changing from time to time depending upon people's way of living prevalent at that time. These peculiar health care service characteristics pose a great challenge to firms providing these services. The attributes that are closely associated to health care services need identification with some sort of quality definition and the necessity of quality incorporation in the service provision. Not only was this service intangible, but it also became very difficult to measure quality service. This led to arguments about improving service quality and implementing quality across all deliveries.

Juran's trilogy of quality management unified the quality management concepts and brought them together as a system (Bisgaard 2008) known as the Juran's Trilogy. Juran's excellent definition defined quality as 'fitness for use' of a product or service, a definition based on meeting customer needs. This adherence is also rephrased as "fitness for purpose" (Ghobadian and Speller 1994). The design of a technique, product, or service applies to features, while freedom from deficiencies applies to the delivery (Juran and Godfrey 2005). For example, any health care services program admitting patients would require a diagnosis of tests for assessment before entering the program for treatment. If a diagnosis is not identifiable or defined, then the quality health care program loses its value.

Juran's trilogy of quality planning, quality improvement and quality control has become a standard in health care services. Any health care service needs to discover and correct its problems and defects through a structured documentation system. E-health along with new sciences such as NLP, ML and AI may significantly reduce workloads with documentation and evaluations. The role of wearable health devices is also increasing in self-monitoring and patient health care. Quality and standards have to be established in E-health. Organizations such as the American Heart Association, the American Medical Association, The Healthcare Information and Management Systems Society, and the DHX group have got together Xcertia to facilitate the improvement, quality, safety, and value addition of mobile health apps. There has also been an increasing use of wearable healthcare devices that facilitate minimally invasive glucometers and insulin delivery pumps, pulmonary pressure monitoring, posture and vital signs monitoring and sleep metrics. Quality control in health care services should be able to evaluate its performance, audit and make improvements in the diagnosis, accuracy and measures of medication, treatments and effectiveness.

Considering services value added (constant 2005 US$) across India as a measure of value-added products and services, the economy of India from the 1960s to the 21st century has benefited significantly from the growth rate of industries, entrepreneurship, advanced technologies and the use of information and communication technologies.

A time series statistic and a multivariate study of the growth of the telecommunications industry across India in the past forty years (Gopalan 2017) has identified that in today's internet economy, the access to services – value added (constant 2005 US$) in terms of economic and social services value added is associated with mobile cellular subscriptions and energy production needs (kWh). Also, the access to the value-added services for the labor force (total) across India depends on the purchasing power parity conversion factor, GDP (LCU per international US$) or affordability of services and facilitation of the same from the government and industry.

USE OF SIX SIGMA TOOLS IN QUALITY HEALTH CARE SERVICES

Health care services have extensively used quality in improving professional healthcare. Six Sigma may involve Deming's PDCA methodology and Juran's philosophy of quality control and planning along with Kaizen's quality improvement philosophy by studying the processes in production and services (Russell and Taylor 2011). Studies in healthcare that implemented Six Sigma (QI) into the ISO 9001:2000 system demonstrated saving 1.2 million Euros annually and significantly improving quality (Heuvel et al. 2005). The use of *six sigma*, a superior measure in quality planning for healthcare requires a focus on (1) patient care, (2) accuracy of diagnosis, (3) evidence-based treatments, (4) measures of medication, (5) reduction of errors and (6) optimization of costs. This requires structured improvement such as the use of the Define, Measure, Analyze, Improve and Control or DMAIC methodology for quality management.

Process capability and control is also relevant to the Six Sigma philosophy and so is process design. Structured training, leadership and governance of quality management in manufacturing are equally relevant to implementing Six Sigma programs. A health care system similar to the one illustrated in Figure 1 explaining the Juran trilogy of quality planning, quality control, and quality improvements should be able to take care of quality issues in diagnosis and treatment of patients and fitting it into a quality measure making way for consistent improvement. In this regard, Six Sigma implementations need to consider adhering to healthcare service needs by ensuring better information flow and timely facilitation of services. Health care services may also use the SERVQUAL model to measure service quality by assessing customer expectations with service quality. This takes into consideration patient expectations, service perceptions and values. It can be used to evaluate facilities, processes and resource management.

Cross functional teams, scientific methodology, quality and knowledge management are core to the learnings in quality management. Subject matter experts and knowledge sharing protocols are mobilized to measure service quality and facilitate decision making. Leadership and governance are equally relevant for implementing service quality, team quality and TQM across the organization. Service sectors have used the SERVQUAL measure to quantify service and on the contrary, health care services have utilized simple quality management techniques due to the nature of the service without strict adherence to quality management practices. Six sigma programs for quality implementation in health care services hopes to provide total quality healthcare for people and communities. Other tools associated with lean six sigma implementations are listed in Table 5.

CONCLUSION

In manufacturing industries, a noteworthy quality system standard is the QS 9000 suitable for supplier part manufacturing conceptualized by integrating the quality systems at Chrysler, General Motors and Ford (Brown 1997). It incorporates the elements of ISO 9000. The manual documents and explains the

Table 5. Research papers that have cited continuous improvement techniques related to lean six sigma management (Source: Henrique and Filho 2020)

Lean Six Sigma Methodology	Times Cited	Percentage
Value Stream Mapping	45	24.5%
Work Standardization	24	13.0%
Visual Management	19	10.3%
Cause and Effect Diagram	13	7.1%
Kaizen Event	11	6.0%
Process Mapping	7	3.8%
5S	5	2.7%
Kanban	5	2.7%
Control Chart	5	2.7%
Audit Checklist	4	2.2%
Pareto Analysis	3	1.6%
Flowcharts	3	1.6%
Simulations	3	1.6%
Poka-Yoke	1	0.5%

advanced quality planning and control, measurement systems, statistical process control, failure mode and effects analysis and production quality standards. ISO implementations require an implementation team, project management and supervision, structured documentations, audits, information management and maintenance. Businesses and services are now integrating customers into learning systems, adding to the quality management of production and services. Statistics demonstrates that in manufacturing and services, the customer participation in *value co-creation* in learning systems for quality management is significant taking into consideration *information management, new services and products, IT value added to new businesses, values added from access to basic services, government investments in telecommunications and IT infrastructure*. This is very relevant in the world of Internet of Things (IOT), Natural Language Processing (NLP), Machine Learning (ML) and Augmented Intelligence (AI) that are adding value to the manufacturing and service industries. The discussion in this article goes to show that for successful quality management implementations for manufacturing and services, active participation across the organization is required and are relevant for information governance.

REFERENCES

Alexander, P., Antony, J., & Cudney, E. (2022). A novel and practical conceptual framework to support Lean Six Sigma deployment in manufacturing SMEs. *Total Quality Management & Business Excellence*, *33*(11/12), 1233–1263. doi:10.1080/14783363.2021.1945434

Bisgaard, S. (2008). Quality Management and Juran's Legacy. *Quality Engineering*, *20*(4), 390–401. doi:10.1080/08982110802317398

Brown, J. (1997). Achieving peak to peak performance using QS 9000. (cover story). [serial on the Internet]. *IIE Solutions*, *29*(1), 34. Retrieved May 22, 2017, from

Business901 (2011). Does the Juran Trilogy = PDCA? *Viewed on 1.05.17* https://business901.com/blog1/does-the-juran-trilogy-pdca/

Chen, C.-K., Reyes, L., Dahlgaard, J., & Dahlgaard-Park, S. M. (2022). From quality control to TQM, service quality and service sciences: A 30-year review of TQM literature. *International Journal of Quality and Service Sciences*, *14*(2), 217–237. doi:10.1108/IJQSS-09-2021-0128

Claus, L. M. (1991). Total quality management: A healthcare application. *Total Quality Management*, *2*(2), 131–148. doi:10.1080/09544129100000015

Cole, R. E., & Flynn, M. S. (2009). Automotive Quality Reputation: Hard to Achieve, Hard to Lose, Still Harder to Win Back. *California Management Review*, *52*(1), 67–93. doi:10.1525/cmr.2009.52.1.67

Collins, K. F., Muthusamy, S. K., & Carr, A. (2015). Toyota production system for healthcare organizations: Prospects and implementation challenges. *Total Quality Management & Business Excellence*, *26*(7/8), 905–918. doi:10.1080/14783363.2014.909624

de Mast, J. (2006). Six Sigma and Competitive Advantage. *Total Quality Management & Business Excellence*, *17*(4), 455–464. doi:10.1080/14783360500528221

Entelechy Inc. (2009). A Case Study in Training Excellence and Business Results. *Coaching on the Manufacturing Floor Kawasaki Motors Manufacturing Corp., USA*, Viewed May 1, 2017 https://www.unlockit.com/wp-content/uploads/CS-HPMKMM20090213.pdf

Esain, A. E., Williams, S. J., Gakhal, S., Caley, L. M., & Cooke, M. W. (2012). Healthcare quality improvement - policy implications and practicalities. *International Journal of Health Care Quality Assurance*, *25*(7), 565–581. doi:10.1108/09526861211261172 PMID:23276053

Ghobadian, A. and Speller, S. (1994). Gurus of quality: A framework for comparison. *Total Quality Management, Vol 5, 3, p. 53*, Business Source Premier, EBSCO*host*, Viewed on 21 April 2017.

González-Cebrián, A., Hermenegildo, M., Climente, M., & Ferrer, A. (2022). Multivariate Six Sigma: A case study in an outpatient pharmaceutical care unit. *Quality Engineering*, *34*(2), 277–289. doi:10.1080/08982112.2022.2042018

Gopalan, B. (2017). *Value Co-creation - Internet for Development and Telecommunications*. LAP LAMBERT Academic Publishing.

Gopalan, B., & Iyer, R. (2017). Comprehending and Implementing Best Practices of Quality Management Across Industries. *International Journal of Research in Commerce, IT & Management*, Vol. 7, No 7, ISSN 2231-5756.

Hallowell, D. (1994). Tree Diagrams for Six Sigma: Plain and Simple? Viewed on May 1, 2017 https://www.isixsigma.com/wp-con- tent/uploads/images/stories/migrated/graphics/205i.gif

Halpren-Ruder, D. (2020). E-Health and Healthcare Quality management: Disruptive Opportunities. *Rhode Island Medical Journal*, *103*(1), 12–15. PMID:32013296

Henrique, D. B., & Godinho Filho, M. (2020). A systematic literature review of empirical research in Lean and Six Sigma in healthcare. *Total Quality Management & Business Excellence*, *31*(3/4), 429–449. doi:10.1080/14783363.2018.1429259

Heuvel, J. V. D., Does, R. J. M. M., & Verver, J. P. S. (2005). Does RJMM, Verver JPS. Six Sigma in Healthcare: Lessons Learned from a Hospital. *International Journal of Six Sigma and Competitive Advantage*, *1*(4), 380–388. doi:10.1504/IJSSCA.2005.008504

Juran, J. M., & Godfrey, B. A. (Eds.). (2005). *Juran's Quality Control Handbook* (5th ed.). McGraw Hill.

Kaplan, S., Bisgaard, S., Truesdell, D., & Zetterholm, S. (2009). Design for Six Sigma in Healthcare: Developing an Employee Influenza Vaccination Process. *Journal for Healthcare Quality*, *31*(3), 36–43. doi:10.1111/j.1945-1474.2009.00029.x PMID:19522346

Kim, R. H., Gaukler, G. M., & Lee, C. W. (2016). Improving healthcare quality: A technological and managerial innovation perspective. *Technological Forecasting and Social Change*, *113*, 373–378. doi:10.1016/j.techfore.2016.09.012

Kolesar, P. J. (2008). Juran's Lectures to Japanese Executives in 1954: A Perspective and Contemporary Lessons. *The Quality Management Journal*, *15*(3), 7–16. doi:10.1080/10686967.2008.11918191

Losko, J., & Smeak, R. (2019). Handling indoor air quality concerns: A layered approach to ensuring patient and staff safety. *Health Facilities Management*, *32*(6), 48–51.

Martin, W., & Tomáš, P. (2023). Data Management in Industrial Companies: The Case of Austria. *International Journal for Quality Research. 17(3) 847–866. ISSN 1800-6450.*

Niñerola, A., Sánchez-Rebull, M.-V., & Hernández-Lara, A.-B. (2021). Mapping the field: Relational study on Six Sigma. *Total Quality Management & Business Excellence*, *32*(11/12), 1182–1200. doi:10.1080/14783363.2019.1685864

Parasuraman, A., Zeithaml, V. A., & Berry, L. L. (1988). SERVQUAL: A Multiple-Item Scale for Measuring Consumer Perceptions of Service Quality. *Journal of Retailing*, *64*(1), 5–6.

Rajagopalan, R., Francis, M., & Suárez, W. (2004). Developing Novel Catalysts with Six Sigma. Research Technology Management, 47(1), 13–16. https://doi.org/, R., Francis, M., & Suárez, W. (2004). Developing Novel Catalysts with Six Sigma. Research Technology Management, 47(1), 13–16. https://doi.org/ doi:10.1080/08956308.2004.11671602Rajagopalan

ReVelle, J. B. (2004). Six Sigma. *Professional Safety*, *49*(10), 38–46.

Rienzo, T. F. (1993). Planning Deming management for service organizations. *Business Horizons*, *36*(3), 19–29. doi:10.1016/S0007-6813(05)80145-4

Rubenstein, L., Khodyakov, D., Hempel, S., Danz, M., Salem-Schatz, S., Foy, R., O'Neill, S., Dalal, S., & Shekelle, P. (2013). How can we recognize continuous quality improvement? *International Journal for Quality in Health Care : Journal of the International Society for Quality in Health Care*, *26*(1), 6–15. doi:10.1093/intqhc/mzt085 PMID:24311732

Russell, R.S. and Taylor, B.W. (2011). Operations Management. Creating Value Along the Supply Chain. *John Wiley and Sons. ISBN-13 9780470525906*

Slack, N., Chambers, S., & Johnston, R. (2010). *Operations management* (6th ed.). Prentice Hall.

Stankalla, R., Koval, O., & Chromjakova, F. (2018). A review of critical success factors for the successful implementation of Lean Six Sigma and Six Sigma in manufacturing small and medium sized enterprises. *Quality Engineering*, *30*(3), 453–468. doi:10.1080/08982112.2018.1448933

Thor, J., Herrlin, B., Wittlöv, K., Øvretveit, J., & Brommels, M. (2010). Evolution and outcomes of a quality improvement program. *International Journal of Health Care Quality Assurance*, *23*(3), 312–327. doi:10.1108/09526861011029370 PMID:20535903

Vanteddu, G., & McAllister, C. D. (2014). An integrated approach for prioritized process improvement. *International Journal of Health Care Quality Assurance*, *27*(6), 493–495. doi:10.1108/IJHC-QA-05-2013-0051 PMID:25115052

KEY TERMS AND DEFINITIONS

Andon: A light above a workstation that indicates its state, whether working, waiting for work, broken down, etc.

Cause–Effect Diagrams: A technique for searching out the root cause of problems, it is also known as an Ishikawa diagram.

Control Charts: The charts used within statistical process control to record process performance.

Customization: The variation in product or service design to suit the specific need of customers.

DMAIC Cycle: Abbreviation for Define, Measure, Analyze, Improve and Control to study processes.

ISO 9000: A set of worldwide standards that established the requirements for companies' quality management systems.

Kaizen: Japanese term for continuous improvement.

Six Sigma: An approach to improvement and quality management that originated in the Motorola Company.

Statistical process control (SPC): A technique that monitors processes and attempts to distinguish between normal or natural variation in process performance and unusual or 'assignable' causes of variation.

Taguchi Method: A design technique that uses design combinations to test the robustness of a design.

Lean: An approach to operations management that emphasizes the continual elimination of waste of all types, often used interchangeably with just-in-time (JIT).

Pareto Law: Often used in inventory management (20 per cent of products produce 80 per cent of sales value) and improvement activities (20 per cent of types of problems produce 80 per cent of disruption).

PDCA Cycle: Stands for Plan, Do, Check, Act cycle, perhaps the best known of all improvement cycle models.

Poka-Yoke: Japanese term for fail-safe.

Process Mapping: Describing activities within the process. 'process blueprinting' or 'process analysis').

Quality Function Deployment (QFD): Ensuring that the eventual design of a product or service actually meets the needs of its customers (sometimes called 'house of quality').

Total Quality Management (TQM): A holistic approach to the management of quality

Zero Defect: The idea that quality management should strive for perfection as its ultimate objective.

Chapter 9
Privacy of Information and Data: Policies, Threats, and Solutions

Ali Kavak
https://orcid.org/0000-0001-5329-2420
Kırıkkale University, Turkey

ABSTRACT

Information and data privacy is a critical issue in modern society to protect the privacy of individuals and institutions, ensure their security, and prevent the misuse of their information. Rapidly developing technology has posed new challenges in ensuring information and data privacy. Technological developments such as big data, artificial intelligence, cloud computing and the internet of things require innovative solutions to protect information and data privacy. Today, with the acceleration of the digitizing world, individuals' and institutions' concerns about information and data privacy are increasing. By addressing information and data privacy through policies, threats and solutions, this study aims to examine new protection-oriented frameworks, policies, and best practices. Aiming to examine coping strategies with technological developments by emphasizing the importance of information and data privacy, this study is original in terms of presenting innovative policies and practices, guiding readers, and providing solutions to current challenges in this field.

INTRODUCTION

Privacy of information and data is a critical issue in modern society for protecting the confidentiality of individuals and institutions, ensuring security, and safeguarding information from misuse. In the rapidly evolving technological age, concerns in this area are increasing.

Ensuring privacy of information and data stands out for a number of important reasons. First, privacy protects individuals by securing their personal information from potential harm. Second, privacy of information and data protects individuals and institutions by preventing misuses such as fraud and identity theft. Third, it plays a major role in ensuring corporate data security and competitive advantage. Finally, it is necessary for legal compliance.

DOI: 10.4018/979-8-3693-0472-3.ch009

The main purpose of information and data privacy is to prevent unauthorized access and misuse of information. For this purpose, privacy policies and practices aim to safeguard sensitive information and increase transparency and accountability.

Rapidly advancing technology has posed new challenges for ensuring privacy of information and data. Technological developments such as big data, artificial intelligence, cloud computing and the Internet of Things require innovative solutions to protect information and data privacy. Today, with the acceleration of the digitalization of the world, concerns of individuals and institutions about privacy of information and data are increasing.

This book chapter aims to examine threats and existing solutions for privacy of information and data, and guide policy makers, practitioners and stakeholders. The chapter will first discuss the importance of privacy of information and data, then address the threats posed by technological developments. Finally, solution proposals such as policies, regulations and best practices will be presented.

This study aims to raise awareness about the difficulties encountered in the field of privacy of information and data and ensure that relevant stakeholders are informed on this issue. With a solution-oriented approach, it aims to contribute to taking steps for the future.

Increasing concerns about privacy breaches, identity theft, and unauthorized access emphasize the need to find robust solutions. In an environment where technological advancements surpass regulatory frameworks, the aim is to identify gaps and potential vulnerabilities that could jeopardize the confidentiality of work-related information and data. Finding solutions to these issues is of vital importance to create a secure digital environment and enhance trust among individuals, organizations, and stakeholders.

The fundamental question guiding this study is: How can we effectively respond to the evolving challenges related to information and data privacy in the face of rapid technological developments?

This study extensively examines the existing literature on information and data privacy, evaluates case studies, regulatory frameworks, and technological trends. By delving into the details of information and data privacy, this study not only sheds light on the current challenges but also aims to provide practical solutions and policy recommendations. The ultimate goal is to provide policymakers, implementers, and stakeholders with the necessary information and tools to navigate the evolving landscape of information and data privacy.

THE CONCEPT AND IMPORTANCE OF INFORMATION AND DATA PRIVACY

Data consists of raw, unprocessed facts. It is made up of certain symbols such as numbers, texts, images. Data that does not make sense on its own becomes meaningful information when processed and interpreted (Chopra & Chaudhary, 2020). Data are information assets that are vital for institutions. But at the same time, they are targets open to unauthorized access and misuse. Therefore, data security is one of the most basic elements in information systems (Kim & Solomon, 2018).

Information, on the other hand, is the meaningful state of data resulting from the processing of data. Information consists of the relevant group of data that enables decision making. In other words, information elucidates the data. Information plays a critical role for people to make decisions, solve problems and achieve their goals (Zins, 2007). However, misuse of information also poses significant risks. Therefore, the security and privacy of information is very important.

Information has some basic features: Confidentiality, integrity and availability. Confidentiality means that only authorized persons can access it. Integrity refers to the accuracy and completeness of informa-

Figure 1. Fundamental elements of data and information security
(McCumber,1991; Solomon & Chapple, 2004)

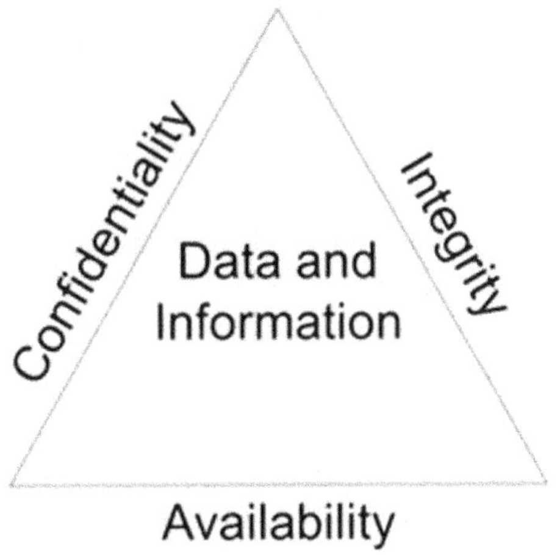

(McCumber,1991; Solomon & Chapple, 2004)

tion. Availability means that information is accessible when needed (Chopra & Chaudhary, 2020). McCumber (1991; 2004) and Solomon & Chapple (2004) focused on these three elements of information in the information security models they developed (See Figure 1). They emphasized that ensuring these components of information would be possible with effective information security practices, otherwise irreparable material and moral losses may occur. It has been especially noted that confidentiality has critical importance among these elements. Confidentiality refers to preventing unauthorized individuals from accessing sensitive and private information belonging to individuals or institutions. Security vulnerabilities in information systems can jeopardize their confidentiality by causing information to be disclosed. These vulnerabilities can seriously violate the confidentiality of information by enabling attackers to gain unauthorized access, damage sensitive data, or use it for malicious purposes. For example, stealing passwords from databases to access a lot of confidential data can be shown as an example of this.

Information and data privacy generally refers to the protection of sensitive and confidential information owned by individuals and institutions against unauthorized access, use, disclosure or modification (Westin, 1967). The controllability of individuals' personal data and privacy under their own control, transparent and auditable access to this data, and protection against risks of unauthorized access, alteration, publication, deletion or loss are key aspects of privacy (Klosek, 2000). Information privacy is a broader concept that includes privacy of personal information. The right to protection of personal data is considered a fundamental human right in democratic and liberal societies (Warren & Brandeis, 1989). Personal information includes any information that reveals or risks revealing an individual's identity. Examples include personal health information, financial records, communication data, location data, online behavioral data (Solove, 2008).

With the proliferation of information technologies and increased internet usage, information privacy has become increasingly important. While digitization has provided conveniences, it has also created new risks regarding the storage, processing and transfer of large amounts of personal data (Watson, 1989). Cyber-attacks, data breaches, misuse of personal information pose serious threats to individuals' privacy rights (Wong, 2013). For instance, the use of data shared on social media platforms for advertising purposes has faced intense criticism (Arrigo et al., 2021). Similarly, cases of financial data theft such as credit card fraud can occur on online shopping sites (Akhilomen, 2013).

Therefore, taking effective measures to protect individuals' information privacy and data is of great importance, otherwise serious victimization can occur. Identity theft, financial losses, blackmail, harassment, discrimination, slander, cyberbullying are some of these risks (McCallister et al., 2010). When personal data falls into the hands of unauthorized third parties, it can have irreparable consequences for individuals. Hence, information privacy and data protection must be treated as fundamental human rights.

In today's digital world where technology advancement facilitates access to and sharing of personal information, protecting data privacy is a critical issue (Monaca, 2010). This has led to a complex and challenging landscape for both consumers and organizations, highlighting the need to further investigate and understand the factors influencing information privacy decisions (Pelteret & Ophoff, 2016). However, the commercial use of online information has also provided significant benefits and privacy concerns may have adverse impacts (Lenard, & Rubin 2009). Nevertheless, debates regarding privacy issues that need to be addressed in current systems continue. Information security is also extremely critical for enterprises.

Company databases contain valuable and sensitive information such as trade secrets, customer data, financial records, patented content and market research findings. Such confidential corporate data become the target of hackers, rival companies, organizations conducting economic espionage activities or other unauthorized individuals or groups (Ording et al., 2022). Data security breaches can impose considerable costs on companies. Financial losses, reputational damage, stock price drops, diminished competitiveness, loss of customer trust are some examples of these costs (Lenard & Rubin, 2010). Research in literature shows companies suffering millions of dollars in damages as a result of data breaches. For instance, Yahoo announced in 2013 that 3 billion user accounts were stolen in a data breach incident (Rushe, 2017). In 2014, eBay suffered a breach resulting in over 150 million users' data being stolen (Mishkin & Kuchler, 2014). Sony PlayStation Network suffered a major data breach in 2011, with user information compromised (Olaniran et al., 2014). The Heartland Payment Systems data breach in 2008 led to over 100 million credit card details being stolen, costing the company $147.6 million in losses (Twentyman, 2015). The 2014 Home Depot breach exposed over 50 million customers data and cost the company $43 million. Target lost 40 million payment cards in a 2013 breach which led to $252 million in costs for the company (Kuchler, 2014). Uber suffered a 2016 breach with 57 million users' data stolen and paid hackers $100,000 to keep the incident secret (Bond & Yuk, 2018; Hook & Kuchler, 2017). These example cases clearly demonstrate the mission critical importance of information security for companies and institutions, otherwise irreparable financial and reputational damages can occur. In the face of these threats, it is inevitable for businesses and governments to take effective measures. Along with technical precautions like strong encryption, intrusion prevention systems, data backup, risk analysis, employee training; legal regulations regarding data security are also gaining importance.

In recent years, major legal regulations have been introduced to ensure information and data privacy. The European Union's General Data Protection Regulation (GDPR), which went into effect in 2016, is considered as the most comprehensive legal text globally regarding information privacy (Tankard, 2016). Meanwhile, many states in the United States, notably California, have enacted laws to protect their citizens' personal data. These laws have imposed various restrictions on companies' data processing activities (Harding et al., 2019). Similarly, other developed countries like Australia, Canada, Japan have introduced regulations to safeguard personal data privacy. As information security increasingly becomes a global issue, international cooperation is also improving among countries. These developments can be considered as important steps taken to ensure information and data privacy. However, rapid technological innovations necessitate keeping the issue constantly on the agenda.

Despite legal steps taken to ensure information and data privacy, the pace of technological advancements brings along new threats and challenges. Innovations like artificial intelligence and machine learning contain both opportunities and unknown risks. Cutting-edge technologies such as Internet of Things, social networks, cloud computing and data analytics have enabled collection of massive amounts of data, but their effective use relies heavily on data security and privacy (Bertino, 2016). The rapid growth of big data applications has necessitated the introduction of new security technologies. In the context of Internet of Things, security and privacy are especially critical and addressing these concerns requires new approaches (Basahel, 2020). Challenges related to security and privacy in Internet of Things and cloud computing environments are profound, requiring efficient solutions to tackle these issues (Thushari, 2022). Therefore, continuous research, development and investment in effective and updated information security measures are vital, otherwise individual privacy violations and institutional data losses will be inevitable.

FACTORS AFFECTING INFORMATION AND DATA PRIVACY

Information and data privacy is an important issue for individuals, institutions and societies today. Protecting the privacy of information and data plays a critical role in ensuring personal privacy and security, safeguarding trade secrets, and complying with legal regulations. There are many factors affecting information and data privacy. However, the most fundamental elements are: Technological developments, human errors, legal regulations, institutional policies, social engineering, and firewalls and encryption. These elements interact continuously, and a dynamic balance must be established between them to ensure information privacy.

Technological Factors

Technological factors cover rapid change and innovation in information and communication technologies. Developments regarding the spread of the internet, mobile technologies, cloud computing, artificial intelligence, big data analytics significantly increase both individuals' and institutions' access to and ability to process information (Unwin & Unwin, 2017). However, in addition to all these positive developments, rapid technological change also poses new risks regarding information security and privacy. First, personal data has become much more shareable and accessible by much wider audiences. Platforms like social media lead to easy dissemination of personal information (Trautman, 2021).

While rapid developments in information and communication technologies facilitate organizations' operations, they also increase information security risks (Whitman & Mattord, 2018). In particular, recent technological innovations like cloud computing, mobile devices, and the Internet of Things pose new threats to corporate data and information security. Cloud-based services enable organizations to store and process their data on central servers. However, this leads to replication of data at different points and a larger attack surface. Therefore, data security is critical for cloud-based systems (Praveena & Smys, 2017).

Widespread use of mobile devices also introduces the Bring-Your-Own-Device (BYOD) [1]threat to corporate networks (Yeboah-Boateng & Boaten, 2016). These devices which are included in the network in an uncontrolled manner create new vulnerabilities for data leakage (Hayes et al., 2020). These uncontrolled devices within an organization pose potential weak spots in terms of cyber security, paving the way for unauthorized access to sensitive information. When mobile devices connect to the corporate network without advanced security measures, the probability of malicious actors accessing internal organizational data through these devices increases. This can lead to new and potentially vulnerable points for data leakage and security breaches (Aldawood & Skinner, 2019; Hayes & Cappa, 2018; Salahdine & Kaabouch, 2019). Hence, mobile device management and security has become vital.

In recent years, there has been a remarkable global increase in cybercrimes and information theft cases. International research points to the continuation of this trend. For instance, striking increases are observed in financial information crimes like credit card fraud and identity theft. According to 2020 data, globally financial cybercrimes causing over $6 trillion in damages annually surged by about 600% during the pandemic (Khiralla, 2020).

Similarly, ransomware displays extremely rapid growth. It is stated that in 2020 one ransomware attack occurred every 11 seconds globally, with this frequency decreasing even more in 2021 (Lallie et al., 2021; Neprash et al., 2022; Yilmaz et al., 2023). Technology-driven increases are seen in cyberbullying and harassment cases. Internet and social media platforms have become mediums where cyberbullies can easily target their victims. Research shows that about one third of children and youth fall victim to cyberbullying. Women and LGBTQ+ individuals are at higher risk. Cyberbullies frequently resort to systematic psychological violence methods like harassment, threat, slander, humiliation (Aboujaoude et al., 2015). 2019 Bedfordshire University research revealed that cyberbullying has become more prevalent than traditional physical bullying. Cyberbullying involves systematic psychological harassment methods like mocking, provocation, insult, threat and violence (Kintonova et al., 2021). This landscape highlights the negative aspects of technological advancement, in addition to its positive aspects. Social risks like cyberbullying can become widespread at the same pace as technological development. Hence, strengthening policies regarding cyber security and human rights is vital, in addition to technology policies.

Additionally, innovations like Internet of Things, smart cities, intelligent transportation systems lead to very different and new data sources compared to the physical world. Highly detailed data about human behaviors and activities can be gathered via sensors, cameras, tracking devices and interconnected devices (Abbas et al., 2018; Alavi et al., 2018; Fantin Irudaya Raj & Appadurai, 2022; Mehmood et al., 2017; Moazzami et al., 2021; Örselli, & Akbay, 2019; Verma et al., 2020). However, all these innovations also contain serious vulnerabilities regarding privacy and information security. For instance, high resolution visual, audio and location data gathered via cameras and sensors in smart cities can violate citizens' privacy if misused (Ahmad et al., 2022).

Similarly, artificial intelligence and big data analytics applications have the capability to infer highly sensitive and private information about individuals based on their online behaviors (Curzon et al., 2021). For example, extremely private matters like political disposition, health status, sexual orientation can be predicted through these methods. However, this also poses the risk of serious privacy violations. Artificial intelligence systems perceive privacy as a fundamental threat and can lead to disclosure of personal data under uncontrolled conditions (Mühlhoff, 2023). This disturbing landscape demonstrates the urgent need for legal and ethical regulations in the artificial intelligence field. As a principle, individuals' right to privacy should be valued above the interests of artificial intelligence systems, otherwise individual freedoms will face serious threats. Hence, ensuring privacy is essential in artificial intelligence policies and practices. Considering all these risks, the need for legal and ethical regulations to minimize the adverse effects of advancing technologies on information privacy and individual freedoms is evident. Otherwise, personal privacy will be under major threat and totalitarian digital surveillance societies will emerge.

Human Factors

One of the most important factors affecting information and data security is the human element. Humans play a critical role in both the production and use of information, while also constituting the weakest links in terms of data security. While being central in the production and use of information, humans are also the main perpetrators in information security breaches and threats (Whitman & Mattord, 2019).

A large part of the risks against information systems originates from humans. While some of these are unintentional, some are with the deliberate intent to cause harm. Password sharing, unauthorized access, data theft falls into this category (Cebula & Young, 2010). However, the main threat stems from people's general lack of knowledge and awareness about information security. Being unprepared against security threats and vulnerable to social engineering are in this context. Therefore, regular training and awareness activities are vitally important. In addition to technical security measures, the human equation must be monitored (Whitman & Mattord, 2019). Otherwise, it will continue to pose the biggest risk factor.

Human-induced threats to information security can be divided into two groups: unintentional threats and intentional threats. Unintentional threats cover mistakes by employees and users stemming from deficiencies in information security training and low levels of awareness. On the other hand, internal and external threats deliberately violating information security policies and procedures are considered intentional threats (Whitman & Mattord, 2019). Employees engaging in violations like password sharing and unauthorized access or providing leeway to computer hackers fall into this category. In addition, employees deliberately stealing, altering, deleting or destroying corporate data are also included in the category of intentional security breaches (Cebula & Young, 2010). People must be trained to prevent them from unintentionally or deliberately harming information systems. Unless education, policy and technology are properly leveraged, the human element will continue its existence as the weakest link in information security management.

Studies in the field of information security demonstrate that the human factor plays a critical role in information and data privacy. Employees' attitudes and behaviors can positively or negatively affect institutional information security policies and procedures (Kavak & Odabaş, 2023). According to Lim et al. (2009) information security culture refers to the whole of behavioral patterns contributing to the protection of information within an institution. However, it is known that employees often disregard institutional information security interests (Andersson et al., 2014). Some recommendations are presented to improve information security culture (Anderson, 2008; Schlienger & Teufel, 2003):

- Measuring information security awareness and analyzing existing policies
- Designing awareness programs with clear targets
- Building a security culture based on training, communication and management participation
- Training employees and including all stakeholders
- Evaluating the effectiveness of implementations

In conclusion, information security culture is significantly affected by employees' attitudes and behaviors. Therefore, comprehensive approaches that take human factors into account are necessary. Human induced errors and threats constitute vulnerabilities that cannot be ignored. Hence, continuous training and awareness raising activities regarding information security are extremely critical. At the same time, risks stemming from the human factor must be effectively managed through technical and physical security precautions.

Legal and Regulatory Factors

Today, legal regulations aimed at protecting information and data privacy are vitally important for institutions. These regulations address issues like protection of personal data and legal liabilities that may arise as a result of data breaches. These factors constitute the fundamental elements that determine and implement an institution's privacy strategies.

Legal regulations in the field of information and data privacy play a critical role in shaping institutions' privacy strategies. In particular, laws regarding protection of personal data and legal responsibilities that may arise as a result of data breaches encourage institutions to invest in information security. In recent years, with developments in information and communication technologies, concerns about misuse of personal data and privacy violations have increased. In particular, the data usage policies of large data gathering companies like social media platforms have frequently been subject to criticism. These concerns have led to development of regulations aimed at protection of personal data globally.

The General Data Protection Regulation (GDPR) enacted by the European Union in 2016 is considered to be the most comprehensive regulation adopted so far regarding protection of personal data. GDPR emphasizes that personal data must be processed in a lawful, fair and transparent manner; while data subjects are granted various rights, responsibilities of institutions and organizations processing data are set out in detail (Díaz, 2016; Hoofnagle et al., 2019; Krzysztofek, 2018). Similarly, many countries like USA, United Kingdom, Japan, Brazil, South Korea and Turkey have also adopted laws on protection of personal data.

There is no comprehensive federal legislation in the United States regarding privacy and protection of personal data. Instead, regulations on protection of personal data are handled through a sectoral approach, unlike the European Union. Federal and state level laws providing protection of personal data in the United States are implemented together with administrative regulations and sectoral self-regulatory mechanisms. There are privacy and data protection guarantee applicable in certain sectors like healthcare, education, finance, communications, and regarding collection of data from children in online settings. Although seemingly fragmented and weak at first glance, regulations in the United States also have some advantages compared to European standards. In short, regarding personal data protection in the US, flexible solutions specific to certain contexts are adopted instead of a standardized approach (Boyne, 2018).

The UK-GDPR, known as the application of the EU's General Data Protection Regulation (GDPR) in the United Kingdom, stands out as a notable regulation regarding personal data protection in the UK and is referred to as the Data Protection Act 2018. This law controls how personal information can be used by organizations, businesses or the government. Anyone responsible for using personal data must adhere to strict rules called the "data protection principles". According to these principles, information must (Phillips, 2021; Spencer & Patel, 2019):

- Be used fairly, lawfully and transparently.
- Be used for specific, explicit and legitimate purposes.
- Be adequate, relevant and limited to what is necessary.
- Be accurate and kept up to date where necessary.

- Be kept for no longer than is necessary.
- Be protected with appropriate security measures against unlawful or unauthorized processing, access, loss, destruction or damage.

In 2016, the Personal Data Protection Law (KVKK) also came into force in Turkey. With the KVKK, the basic principles and conditions to be followed in the processing of personal data are set out, while concrete obligations are imposed on data controllers and processors (Yücedağ, 2019). As of 2022, in addition to KVKK, sub-regulations such as legislation on processing personal health data and data with special qualities have also been announced (Atalay, 2019; Yüksel, 2019).

At the international level, it is stated that the most comprehensive and guiding framework on protection of personal data is constituted by the privacy principles and data protection guidelines formed by the Organization for Economic Cooperation and Development (OECD) (Phillips, 2018). Adopted in 2013, the OECD Privacy Framework presents international standards regarding protection of personal data, including cross-border flow of data (Borgesius et al., 2015).

Although important steps have been taken in recent years both domestically and internationally to protect individuals against misuse of personal data, differences stemming from countries' distinct legal and administrative structures make complete harmonization and standardization difficult globally. For instance, unlike the European Union, there are no comprehensive federal regulations in the United States regarding protection of personal data, with a more sectoral approach followed instead (Boyne, 2018). Some countries and industry associations have also developed voluntary data protection standards and certification programs. Standards like ISO 27701 help increase institutions' reputation and reliability regarding privacy (Kim & Solomon, 2018).

In conclusion, adopting a strategy aligned with legal and regulatory factors to ensure information and data privacy is an important necessity for institutions. This not only fulfils legal responsibilities, but also provides competitive advantage by increasing customer trust.

Social Engineering

Social engineering techniques enable attacks that attempt to access information and data by deceiving individuals or personnel. This poses a serious threat in terms of privacy. In parallel with advancements in information technologies, cyber security threats are also diversifying and increasing. In recent years, social engineering attacks in particular pose a significant threat to information and data privacy. Social engineering is a sophisticated type of attack that aims to access sensitive information by deceiving people (Hatfield, 2019).

Social engineers try to bypass security protocols and access data by manipulating their targets. Passwords and access credentials are obtained using attack types like phishing, baiting, pretexting. Even seemingly harmless phone calls or emails may hide social engineering tactics behind them. Attackers make good use of human nature and take advantage of psychological and emotional weaknesses (Tetri & Vuorinen, 2013).

Social engineering activities can utilize various psychological methods by understanding human behavior and decision-making processes. These effects on cognitive processes can occur without the consent of the persons and create ethically controversial situations. Exploitation of individuals' natural risk-taking tendencies, emotional states or personality traits can lead to unfair consequences. Therefore, public awareness must be raised about the purposes of social engineering and the techniques used. Moreover, it is an ethical necessity that psychological methods are not used without the consent of targeted individuals (Hatfield, 2019).

Various technical and behavioral measures are suggested in literature to prevent social engineering. However, the human factor always remains decisive. Hence, raising awareness and informing personnel through cyber security training is of critical importance. In conclusion, since social engineering methods pose a serious threat to data privacy, organizations must develop comprehensive defense mechanisms against this threat.

THREATS AND RISKS

Threats and Risks With the proliferation of information and communication technologies, security of corporate information assets faces serious risks. Failure to ensure confidentiality of critical information and data can lead to irreparable consequences, both materially and morally. Therefore, it is of great importance to comprehensively analyze information security threats and risks and develop effective defense mechanisms.

While a threat refers to any event or condition that could adversely affect an organization's operations and information assets, an attack involves intentional or unintentional actions that could harm information or supporting systems (ISO, 2018). Information security threat sources are categorized in various ways. An important categorization method is based on the origin of the threat, which is divided into two main categories: internal threat sources and external threat sources. At the same time, threat sources can also be categorized according to hardware, software, network, data, communication, social, economic, human and physical threat layers.

According to Nayak and Rao (2014), threat sources are considered in two main groups: internal threats and external threats. Internal threats stem from lack of information and resources within the organization and are often human-induced threats. In particular, intentional or unintentional actions of employees constitute the main cause of internal threats. This source plays an important role in the emergence of internal threats by affecting technological and physical security layers. Major human-induced internal threats include fraud, misuse of information, and destruction of information. Underlying causes of various internally sourced threats include non-compliance of human resources with information security policies, unawareness, malicious behavior, and unauthorized access to information. Many internally sourced threats arise due to the following reasons:

- Weak information security policies: It is important that security policies have strong qualities. Information security policies need to fully coincide with the operations and functions of the organization. Discrepancy of security policies with the organization's operations can lead to serious risks. Weak practices like information sharing with unauthorized persons and deficiencies in authentication and authorization can negatively affect information security. Security policies must be reviewed, appropriate measures taken, and personnel trained.
- Weak information security management: Poorly planned and implemented security policies can lead to risks like weak administrator and user passwords. Management deficiencies like lack of access restrictions, no oversight over external devices and integration of untrusted software can leave doors open to threats. Continuous monitoring and an effective management approach are important to reduce security vulnerabilities.

- Lack of information security skills among users: Ineffective communication of information security policies to users can lead to deficiencies like ignorance on encryption and passwords, unauthorized information sharing. Information security awareness training and activities play an important role in increasing users' resilience against social engineering attacks. Focusing on continuous education and awareness programs is essential to improve users' information security skills.

External threats originate from the environment and context that the organization operates in. Hardware threats, software threats, network and communication threats, legal threats, socio-economic threats stemming from the country's circumstances and human related threats arising from computer hacking are considered as main external threat sources.

Whitman & Mattord (2018) state that they evaluate information security threat sources under twelve categories stemming from underlying reasons. These categories are listed as follows:

- Intellectual property compromises: Deficiencies in protecting intellectual property rights can lead to attacks by information thieves. Threats like unauthorized use, copyright violations, patent misuse must be watched out for.
- Deviations in service quality: Disruptions stemming from service providers can lead to adverse events within the organization. Factors causing deviations in service quality may include internet service outages and problems with energy sources.
- Espionage and unauthorized transactions: A common attack category violating confidentiality of information. Unauthorized access, espionage and trespassing constitute important threats regarding information security.
- Natural disasters: Natural threats like fire, flood and earthquake can adversely affect information systems. Emergency plans and response strategies make organizations prepare against natural disasters.
- Human error and failure: Includes threats caused by user mistakes or ignorance. Incorrect training, inexperience and non-compliance with information security policies can lead to negative actions.
- Information extortion: Includes actions to steal information assets. Use of malicious software like ransomware has increased information extortion threats.
- Sabotage and vandalism: Includes threats that intentionally sabotage information systems. Actions like website attacks can damage an organization's reputation and standing.
- Software attacks: Includes threats carried out using malicious software. Software like viruses, worms and Trojan horses can severely damage information systems.
- Hardware failures and flaws: Includes threats where technical flaws in hardware can lead to unexpected outcomes. Technical defects can adversely affect the smooth functioning of information systems.
- Software failures and flaws: Includes threats where bugs in software can cause loss of availability. Lack of adequate security audits can jeopardize information systems.
- Technological obsolescence: Includes the threat of outdated infrastructure damaging information systems. Infrastructure not updated to current technology can increase security vulnerabilities.
- Theft: Includes information about theft actions. Electronic theft can be difficult to detect due to its ability to cover up traces.

Information security threats refer to any risk element directed at corporate information assets. If realized, these threats have the potential to lead to consequences that are difficult to compensate. Effective risk management, on the other hand, requires taking proactive measures against possible threats (Whitman & Mattord, 2019). Some basic steps are suggested in the literature regarding threats and risks (Jones & Ashenden, 2005):

- Identifying critical information assets and infrastructures,
- Analyzing possible threat scenarios for the confidentiality of this information asset,
- Assessing the losses and damages that may arise as a result of threats,
- Developing effective defense mechanisms and contingency plans,
- Continuous monitoring and management of threats and risks.

As can be seen, in order to effectively combat information security threats, it is critically important to first conduct a comprehensive risk analysis and take proactive measures. Otherwise, realized threats can lead to consequences that are very difficult to compensate. Therefore, a threat-oriented approach and constant preparedness are vital.

Attacks on information systems consist of deliberate actions to access, destroy or steal data. For a successful attack, it is first necessary to overcome existing security controls (Slade, 2006). Today, the scope and complexity of cyber-attacks is increasing rapidly. Emerging technologies provide new opportunities for attackers while exposing organizations to more threats. Effective security management requires adopting a multi-layered defense approach against all possible attack types (Maiwald, 2004). Some key practices that stand out in this context are:

- Cyber intelligence and threat analysis
- Vulnerability scanning and penetration testing
- Encryption, strong authentication systems
- Access control and logs
- Data backup and disaster recovery plans
- Emergency response teams and procedures

Defense against attacks necessitates a proactive and preventive approach. It is vital for organizations to adopt a dynamic security strategy by combining their current state analysis with threat projections.

Whitman (2003) stated that with the introduction of new technologies to the market, some changes have occurred in information security threats. These changes will lead to radical changes in the information security perspectives of institutions and concerns about the confidentiality of information will increase in the future. In particular, developments in network technologies enable information to spread very quickly, while at the same time bringing along information security threats such as cyber-attacks. Next generation viruses, ransomware, targeted attacks can overwhelm traditional security measures. Storing information in the cloud, widespread use of mobile devices, the internet of things are technologies that, along with the conveniences they provide, pose additional risks regarding the confidentiality of information. For example, attacks targeting cloud systems can jeopardize huge amounts of personal data.

In conclusion, in the face of rapid technological developments, information security threats are also constantly diversifying and evolving. This situation will lead institutions to protect their information assets more effectively and, in the future, ensuring the confidentiality of information will be much more important.

METHODS TO ENSURE INFORMATION AND DATA PRIVACY

In today's digital age, information and data have become one of the most valuable assets of institutions. However, these data are also vulnerable to various internal and external threats. The increase in data breaches has led to the need for more comprehensive information security measures. Many technical and administrative measures have been developed to ensure the confidentiality of information and data.

Technical Measures

The technical measures taken to ensure information security play a very important role in preventing unauthorized access to data. Encryption of data is one of the most common of these measures. With data encryption, data can only be read and made understandable by people with the appropriate key (Gai et al., 2016). Thus, the data is protected against theft or unauthorized access during transmission and storage.

Network and system security measures are also important in ensuring the confidentiality of data. Strong encryption methods, firewalls, protection systems against malicious software, authentication systems that control access to data are among these measures (Vacca, 2013). Security vulnerabilities of information systems should be scanned regularly, and detected vulnerabilities should be fixed immediately.

The network security strategy focuses on three key security actions: Protection, attack detection, and attack prevention. Protection includes security policies and tools designed to prevent attacks on the network. Attack detection or sensing refers to resources that allow predefined analysis of threat risks that could harm network traffic and identification of threats without damaging information systems. Response involves actions to develop countermeasures against identified threats in the shortest time and the ability to solve problems (Ghorbani et al., 2009).

Data represents an important information asset. The number of organizations that collect personal data and use it for various purposes, from scientific research such as medical data to demographic trend analysis and marketing purposes, is increasing. Organizations also provide access to the data they own and can even provide such data to third parties. Thus, the increasing number of data sets poses serious threats to the privacy of individuals and organizations. Since privacy is an important issue, various research studies have been conducted to develop data management techniques that protect privacy. These research studies focus on three techniques that protect the privacy of data (Bertino & Sandhu, 2005).

The first is an approach related to protecting privacy arising from the disclosure of data to third parties. A commonly used method to address this situation is data anonymization. However, the k-anonymity model is proposed, considering that this method may not be adequate in some cases (Wohlgemuth et al., 2011).

The second technique is specifically concerned with protecting privacy in the context of data mining. Data mining techniques can be so effective that they allow information to be retrieved even from scrubbed databases. Therefore, various approaches based on modifying or corrupting the data are used. However, there is a problem that these modifications can reduce the quality of the database and diminish the usefulness of the data (Kreso et al., 2021).

The last technique focuses on database techniques specifically designed to support privacy policies that can be expressed using the P3P standard. This approach includes relational database systems called Hippocratic databases. This system performs privacy checks during query processing and ensures that the query accesses only areas authorized for specific purposes. Thus, an approach focused on protecting privacy in the database has been adopted (Ashley, 2004).

Policy and Procedure Implementations

While technical measures are indispensable elements of information security, they remain inadequate without supporting policies and procedures. Creating, documenting, implementing and auditing comprehensive information security policies is vital to ensuring data confidentiality.

Data security policies should include data classification, access and sharing rules, acceptable use, sanctions for breach incidents. These policies should clearly define employees' roles and responsibilities regarding data security. These policies are key documents that document an organization's information security objectives and explain how management will meet those objectives. The main purpose of these policies is to reduce the risk of attack and ensure security. Clear and understandable policies can provide guidance to managers, facilitating decision making (Kim & Solomon, 2018).

The importance of privacy policies requires great emphasis regarding data confidentiality. Privacy policies are critical for organizations to ensure information security and minimize such adverse effects. By preventing unauthorized access, preventing data loss, and securing information, these policies protect information assets. Data privacy policies provide guidance to employees on information security and help sustain the integrity and reliability of the organization. Therefore, information security specialists play an important role in protecting the information assets and reputation of organizations (Alhassan & Adjei-Quaye, 2017).

The General Data Protection Regulation, which regulates the processing of personal data in the European Union, has had a major impact on privacy policies. This regulation requires companies and organizations to explain more transparently how they process, store and share personal data. Here are some key points regarding the impact of GDPR on privacy policies:

- Consent and transparency: GDPR requires clear and understandable consent from individuals. Privacy policies must transparently explain this consent process and how personal data will be used.
- Individual rights: GDPR grants various rights to individuals. These rights include the right to access personal data, request rectification, right to erasure and data portability. Information about these rights must be included in privacy policies.
- Data security and notifications: GDPR requires preventing breaches of personal data and rapid notification if such breaches occur. Privacy policies should detail data security measures and procedures to follow in case of a breach.
- Children's data: It includes special regulations regarding the processing of children's personal data. Privacy policies should include special measures when determining processes regarding children's data.
- Data processing purposes and retention periods: Privacy policies should explain the purposes for which personal data will be processed and how long it will be retained. This is a requirement to increase transparency and reliability.

The impact of GDPR on privacy policies has led companies and organizations to approach personal data more carefully and responsibly. It has also strengthened privacy by enabling individuals to have more control over their data. This regulation aims to increase data protection standards and build trust in the digital world. In the future, with the widespread adoption of similar regulations, privacy policies are expected to strengthen even more.

To be practical and enforceable, information security policies need to be detailed with standards, guidelines and procedures (Landoll, 2017). Procedures explain how policies are implemented step-by-step and contain specific instructions on issues such as password management. These procedures increase the practical applicability of policies. Information security procedures provide detailed guidance on how policies will be implemented. Emergency response procedures for data leaks should be addressed in this context. In addition, procedures such as reporting information security breaches to senior management within a certain period of time should be implemented (Peltier, 2016).

In conclusion, technical and administrative measures should be considered together, continuously reviewed and updated to effectively protect the confidentiality of information and data. Managing the issue with a holistic approach is vital to prevent potential data losses and reputation damage. As data-driven business models become widespread today, data security has become a strategic issue providing competitive advantage.

BEST PRACTICE STANDARDS TO ENSURE INFORMATION AND DATA PRIVACY

Information security standards are guiding documents that form the basis for protecting the confidentiality, integrity and availability of sensitive data and information owned by organizations. These standards identify the technical and administrative controls in all processes where information is produced, processed, stored and transmitted.

The main purpose of information security standards is to protect corporate data and information assets against threats such as cyber-attacks, data theft, unauthorized access at the highest level. These standards contain best practices recommended by experts and provide guidance to organizations. The effective implementation of security controls included in the standards significantly enhances the defense capabilities of organizations in the face of increasing cyber threats. Information security standards are regularly updated to evolve in response to new technology trends and threats.

There are important international standards for information security management. The most widely accepted information security management frameworks and standards are:

- ISO/IEC 27000 Family of Information Security Standards
- NIST Special Publications 800 Series
- Control Objectives for Information and Related Technologies (COBIT)
- Information Technology Assurance Framework (ITAF)
- Information Technology Infrastructure Library (ITIL)
- Standard of Good Practice for Information Security (SOGP)
- IEEE 802 Standards

Organizations benefit from these standards and frameworks according to their service levels. For example, they can use the ISO/IEC 27000 series information security standards for a detailed corporate information security definition, ITIL for best practices that can be used for information technology processes and workflow integration, COBIT for audit and control models, and NIST for computer security.

ISO/IEC 27000 Family of Information Security Standards

The ISO/IEC 27000 series is a set of standards that define international information security standards. These standards are used to create and certify Information Security Management Systems (ISMS). Developed by the International Organization for Standardization (ISO) and the International Electrotechnical Commission (IEC), this family of standards provides guidance on information security management, risk management and implementation of controls (Blokdyk, 2020).

It provides a framework for securing information assets such as financial information, intellectual property, personnel and customer information, or information entrusted to them by third parties. They contain globally accepted best practices to protect and ensure information security of information assets. By following the guidelines in these standards, organizations can reduce information security risks, increase customer and stakeholder confidence, and comply with legal and regulatory requirements.

NIST Special Publications 800 Series

The National Institute of Standards and Technology (NIST) offers a series of security standards and guidance documents designed to help organizations effectively manage cyber security risks. The NIST SP 800 series standards are among the internationally recognized publications covering activities such as cyber security practices, information security management, risk assessment, risk handling and identification of control measures. These standards have been created to identify, disseminate and guide best practices, methods and security controls for organizations (NIST, 2022):

The purpose of this series is to identify and disseminate best practices, methods and controls in the field of information security and cybersecurity and to provide guidance to organizations. In particular, these documents, known as the NIST Special Publications 800 series, provide a set of standards and guidance for the security activities of information systems. These comprehensive resources are an important reference for organizations looking to improve security practices, conduct risk assessments, and identify appropriate control measures. (Calder, 2018)

Control Objectives for Information and Related Technologies (COBIT)

COBIT, developed by Information Systems Audit and Control Association (ISACA), is a framework and set of standards designed for information technology governance. The most current version of COBIT, first released in 1996, was published in 2019. These documents provide a variety of control objectives and best practices to help organizations effectively govern information and related technologies. COBIT provides a variety of control objectives for supporting business objectives, managing risks, using resources efficiently, monitoring and evaluating information and technology related activities. This framework includes best practices and standards in areas such as IT governance, information security, risk management and business continuity (ISACA, 2019).

Information Technology Assurance Framework (ITAF)

ITAF is a framework that contains a set of standards for information security auditing and security. ITAF, developed by ISACA, is a set of guidance and standards used to support IT auditing. This framework provides auditors and security professionals with planning, implementation and reporting processes through technical guidelines and guides. ITAF standards are organized into three main categories, from general standards to performance standards and reporting standards (ISACA, 2022).

ITAF standards identify the steps, best practices and control objectives that guide information security audit processes. These standards guide audit professionals to effectively perform information security control and offer suggestions to mitigate risks. This framework helps organizations adopt a standard approach to IT security. By contributing to the organization and standard compliance of information security audit processes, ITAF supports organizations in effectively protecting their information assets.

Information Technology Infrastructure Library (ITIL)

ITIL consists of best practices and guidelines used as a framework for IT service management. ITIL provides guidance for businesses to manage IT services in a customer-focused, process-oriented and best-practice manner. Its key objectives include improving service quality, reducing costs, managing risks and ensuring customer satisfaction. The ITIL library explains IT service management processes and best practices through various publications. This framework helps businesses improve their processes and increase service quality, enabling them to manage IT services more effectively and efficiently (Gallacher & Morris, 2012).

Standard of Good Practice for Information Security (SOGP)

The SoGP (Standard of Good Practice for Information Security) standard was first published in 1996 by the Information Security Forum (ISF). This standard represents a detailed documentation of best practices for information security and is updated every two years upon publication. The SoGP Good Practice Standard is a standard that provides a broad perspective in the field of information security and addresses six key security categories. With subcategories such as computer installations, critical business applications, security management, networks, system development and end-user environment, the scope of this standard includes effective security practices across a wide range. Starting from IT professionals to people responsible for business processes, each category aims to enable organizations to effectively manage security-related management decisions and improve their practices by targeting a wide range of users (Whitman & Mattord, 2019).

IEEE 802 Standards

The IEEE 802 standards are a set of standards used to determine the technical specifications related to computer networks. These standards, developed by the Institute of Electrical and Electronics Engineers (IEEE), have been established to ensure compatible and efficient operation of various network technologies such as wireless networks, Ethernet and local area network (LAN) technologies. By creating a common language that enables communication between different devices on computer networks, these standards contribute to the development and industry-wide adoption of networking technologies. IEEE

802 standards play an important role in ensuring compatibility and interaction on computer networks (Guo & Congdon, 2021).

CYBER SECURITY THEORIES, MODELS, AND EDUCATION CAMPAIGNS

The rapid developments in information and communication technologies bring various security threats. The increase in cybercyber-attacks and data breaches poses a threat to organizations and individuals. The increase in cyber security threats and attacks highlights the importance of strengthening and modeling the theoretical foundations in this field. Therefore, theoretical studies in the field of cyber security are of great importance.

Cyber Security Theoretical Models

Cyber security is addressed with various theoretical models in conjunction with the widespread use of information technologies today. These models provide various perspectives to understand, manage, and improve the concept of cyber security. Some prominent theoretical models in the relevant literature are: McCumber's Cyber Security Cube Model (Easttom & Butler, 2019), Solms and Solms' Cyber Security Governance, Risk Management, and Compliance (GRC) Model (2008), and the Comprehensive Cyber Risk Management Framework developed by the National Institute of Standards and Technology (NIST) of the United States (Giuca et al., 2021).

McCumber's Cyber Security Cube Model, proposed in 1991, addresses cyber security in three fundamental dimensions: confidentiality, integrity, and availability. This model emphasizes considering these three fundamental elements when formulating information security strategies. Confidentiality refers to the protection of information against unauthorized access, while integrity focuses on the accuracy and reliability of information. Availability refers to the usability of information at the desired time and place (Easttom & Butler, 2019).

Solms and Solms' Cyber Security Governance, Risk Management, and Compliance (GRC) Model (2008) addresses cyber security strategies within the framework of corporate governance, risk analysis, and compliance with legal regulations. The model brings together these three main components to ensure effective cyber security management at the corporate level. Corporate governance includes determining and implementing cyber security policies, while risk analysis evaluates potential threats and vulnerabilities faced by the organization. Compliance with legal regulations focuses on aligning cyber security strategies with relevant legal regulations.

The Comprehensive Cyber Risk Management Framework created by the National Institute of Standards and Technology (NIST) of the United States comprehensively addresses the cyber risk management process. This framework provides a step-by-step process for identifying, assessing, and addressing cyber risks. Risk management helps organizations effectively manage risks when determining cyber security strategies (Giuca et al., 2021).

These theoretical models contribute to the process of policymaking, threat assessment, and solution development related to information and data confidentiality from different perspectives, by addressing the concept of cyber security. McCumber's model helps determine the fundamental elements of security policies by focusing on the confidentiality, integrity, and availability of information. Solms and Solms' GRC Model provides a comprehensive security approach by emphasizing the combination of corporate governance, risk analysis, and legal compliance. NIST's Cyber Risk Management Framework offers organizations practical solutions by including steps to effectively identify, assess, and address cyber risks. As a result, a strong defense mechanism against cyber threats can be established, and organizations can protect their information assets more effectively.

Strategic Approaches and Cyber Security Solutions with Theories

The increasing complexity and number of cyber-attacks necessitate the development of strategic approaches that leverage next-generation technologies and theories (Ramakrishnan, 2023). Traditional security methods are insufficient in addressing these threats, which include vulnerabilities on the Internet of Things (IoT), exploitation of artificial intelligence (AI) and machine learning (ML), risks posed by quantum computing, supply chain attacks, cloud security challenges, and social engineering and phishing attacks (Ramakrishnan, 2023; Aslan et al., 2023). To address these challenges, innovative solutions such as machine learning, deep learning, cloud platforms, big data, and blockchain are being explored (Aslan, 2023). Machine learning, in particular, is being increasingly applied in cyber security to detect malware, intrusion, spam, DNS attacks, fraud, hidden channels, and advanced persistent threats (Virmani et al., 2020). However, the application of these technologies must also consider evasion techniques used by attackers (Aslan, 2023). The Internet of Things (IoT) is a key area of concern, with critical infrastructures being particularly vulnerable to cyber threats (Djenna et al., 2021).

Social network analysis methods enable the examination of behavioral patterns of cyber threat actors and the mapping of risks. Critical points can be identified with the core-periphery theory, target groups can be determined with the homophily theory, and interaction networks can be analyzed with the web requirement model. In this way, early warning systems for threats can be developed through social media (Laranjo et al., 2015). Additionally, the effectiveness of awareness campaigns can be increased. They are also effective in predicting key players in terrorist networks (Choudhary & Singh, 2015) and improving information security awareness among employees in organizations.

Risk assessment of security vulnerabilities in IoT systems can be done using Markov chain modeling (Casola et al., 2019). Unknown attacks can be detected using artificial neural networks. Security policies suitable for IoT devices can be developed based on data collected using machine learning algorithms (Zolanvari et al., 2019).

Support vector machines, decision trees, and deep neural networks can be used for real-time threat analysis in cyber-attack detection (Wang et al., 2022). This allows for real-time intervention in cyber events. Additionally, maintenance processes can be automated using machine learning and deep learning methods (Luo et al., 2018).

Based on these strategic approaches and theories, data-driven cybersecurity solutions can be developed in the fields of social networks, IoT systems, and machine learning. This will provide protection in areas where traditional methods are insufficient. As advancements in these areas continue in the future, the effectiveness of cybersecurity can be increased.

Cybersecurity Education and Awareness Campaigns

Cybersecurity threats and risks are diversifying and increasing day by day. The methods used by cyber attackers are evolving, and the sectors they target are expanding. Especially young people and children become vulnerable to these threats due to inexperience and lack of awareness.

Therefore, in the fight against cybersecurity threats, education and awareness of the human element are as vital as technical measures. It is of great importance to raise awareness among young generations and children from an early age about information security, protection of personal data, cyberbullying and cybercrimes, privacy settings, and cyber hygiene (Yasin et al., 2018). Otherwise, victimization resulting from ignorance and carelessness can occur.

Therefore, information security and cybersecurity education from an early age are of vital importance. Cybersecurity courses should be added to the curricula of educational institutions, and students should be equipped with basic knowledge and skills. In this way, young people will become aware of cyber threats and be able to adopt secure behavior patterns.

Civil society organizations such as the National Cyber Security Alliance (NCSA) and the International Cyber Security Alliance (ICSA) organize various information and education activities to increase cybersecurity awareness (Robinson et al., 2019). These organizations contribute significantly to raising awareness in the community about digital security by sharing information on cybersecurity topics through various platforms such as public events, online resources, webinars, and awareness campaigns.

In addition, many countries aim to increase digital literacy and create a conscious society against cyber threats by organizing cybersecurity campaigns targeting vulnerable groups such as young people and children. These campaigns support a wide range of methods such as interactive educational materials, games, and workshops that aim to raise awareness among young generations about internet security. As a result, a large part of the community has the necessary knowledge to protect themselves against cyber dangers.

These civil society organizations and national campaigns aim to increase resistance against cyber threats by directing individuals, institutions, and communities towards secure digital practices through education and awareness activities in the field of cybersecurity. These efforts are an important step towards creating a stronger, more conscious, and prepared society in terms of cybersecurity.

The celebration of October as "National Cybersecurity Awareness Month" in the United States is an important initiative to spread cybersecurity awareness to the masses and focus on awareness activities (DHS, 2022). The events, panels, competitions, and other awareness activities organized during this month aim to draw attention to cybersecurity issues and raise awareness in society about these threats. The importance of such campaigns lies in their potential to reach a wide audience and increase cybersecurity awareness.

Social media and digital platforms play a critical role in enhancing the effectiveness of cybersecurity campaigns (Mathur, 2019). Information activities conducted through popular social networks such as Facebook, Twitter, and Instagram attract the attention of the younger generation and raise their awareness about cyber threats (Huang & Chang, 2012). Interactive campaigns organized on these platforms capture the attention of young people and contribute to their awareness on topics such as cyberbullying, personal data breaches, and phishing.

These campaigns on social media include various content such as educational videos, interactive games, question-answer activities, and information sharing. As a result, young people are motivated and educated to develop a more conscious and cautious attitude towards cyber dangers (Arora et al., 2019).

There are many examples in the literature that demonstrate the effectiveness of similar social media-based cybersecurity campaigns. For example, the "CyberAware" campaign is a hashtag used in the United States to increase cybersecurity awareness. This campaign aims to reach a wide audience through informative materials and activities shared on various social media platforms.

Expanding and strengthening such campaigns will contribute to reaching all segments of society with cybersecurity education and awareness. Furthermore, conducting more scientific studies that evaluate the effects of these campaigns and focus on best practices in this field plays an important role in developing cybersecurity education strategies.

THE FUTURE OF INFORMATION AND DATA PRIVACY

Rapid developments in information and communication technologies bring data-driven business models and digital transformation. However, this transformation also poses serious risks and uncertainties regarding basic information security principles such as the confidentiality, integrity and availability of information.

With the widespread use of new generation technologies such as artificial intelligence, internet of things, cloud computing, augmented reality, traditional security approaches may become inadequate (Gandhi et al., 2021). While these technologies provide new targets and attack methods for attackers, they pose new threats to the defense side. In particular, the use of artificial intelligence and machine learning algorithms for both attack and defense has revealed a new threat dimension. It is observed that cyber-attacks supported by artificial intelligence are much faster and more effective than traditional attacks, and that detecting and preventing attacks becomes even more difficult (Rath et al., 2022).

While new generation technologies provide new opportunities for cybercriminals, they mean new and complex threats for the defense side. Therefore, there is a need for risk-focused and adaptable security architectures that go beyond traditional security approaches. Otherwise, unforeseeable new threats that will emerge in the future can have devastating consequences. It is stated that cyber-attacks based on artificial intelligence are much faster and more effective than traditional attacks, and that detecting and preventing attacks becomes even more difficult (Pandey et al., 2022). The use of artificial intelligence by both attackers and defenders can lead to an "arms race".

The rapid proliferation of networked devices brings about the widespread use of internet of things technology. However, this shows that security in this area is not yet mature enough. In recent years, a significant increase has been observed in IoT (Internet of Things) based DDoS (Denial of Service) attacks (Al-Hadhrami & Hussain, 2021). This indicates that IoT technology may pose a major threat to information security in the future.

Day by day, IoT-connected devices, diversifying from smart watches to refrigerators and even cars, are becoming more complex and richer in features. However, with these developments, the security of these devices is becoming increasingly important. It may be difficult to detect whether an IoT device has been compromised, which can jeopardize information security. Being aware of IoT security threats is important to prevent potential losses that cybercriminals can inflict by using smart devices (Shafiq et al., 2022). Therefore, IoT manufacturers should focus on providing customers with a secure experience by integrating preventive measures such as firewalls, VPNs and encryption methods into their products. Users should be careful when connecting their devices to the Internet and to other network services and should take extra security precautions. This can prevent unauthorized access by hackers. Also, if a user suspects that their device or service is under attack, they can immediately disconnect the device's Internet connection and change passwords to regain control (Shafiq et al., 2022). In this context, the future of information and data privacy will be shaped by focusing on IoT security, raising user awareness and manufacturers taking proactive measures.

The widespread use of cloud computing also leads to the accumulation of data with cloud providers, increasing concerns about loss of privacy and sovereignty. In the cloud computing environment, since the data may be located in different parts of the world, this situation becomes especially serious. Data security and privacy protection is the focus of users' concerns about cloud technology (Sun et al., 2014).

Concerns about data security and privacy in cloud computing affect the cloud architecture at both the hardware and software levels. Although this has been extensively researched by academics and industries, data security and privacy protection are becoming increasingly critical for governments, industries and the business world in terms of the future development of cloud computing technology (Pandith, 2015).

On the other hand, it is predicted that a decentralized, transparent and immutable data structure will be possible with blockchain and distributed ledger technology. By providing a structure where blocks are connected to each other and secured by cryptographic methods, blockchain provides significant advantages in terms of data security and integrity. These technologies have potential applications in many areas, from financial transactions to healthcare, supply chain management to voting systems. With their decentralized structures, they allow secure storage and sharing of data without depending on a single authority (Antal et al., 2021). However, blockchain and distributed ledger technologies also have their own risks and limitations. There are a number of issues to be addressed regarding scalability, energy consumption, legal regulations and total cost for their widespread adoption. In addition, new security threats and challenges that may arise with the increased use of these technologies should also be considered (Deshpande et al., 2017).

All these developments indicate that information security and therefore information and data privacy will gain much more strategic importance in the future. It is imperative to adopt an information security approach based not only on reactive but also on proactive risk management in the face of advancing technology. New technologies such as artificial intelligence pose both threats and opportunities and have the potential to improve security when used properly.

Experts working in the field of information security will have to acquire new skills and competencies in the face of constantly evolving threats. It is of great importance that security architectures and controls have the flexibility to keep up with this change. Institutions should closely monitor technology, anticipate potential risks, and direct their security strategies and investments accordingly. Otherwise, being caught unprepared in the face of emerging new threats can have devastating consequences that are very difficult to compensate.

RESULT

This study revealed the process and importance of protecting information and data privacy from past to present. The theoretical foundations, legislation, standards, threats, risks and methods used in the field were examined in detail. Accordingly, uncertain factors regarding in which direction the process may take shape in the future were also discussed. As a result of an in-depth analysis of the study, the following important inferences can be made:

Theoretical Implications

- The roots of the issue of information and data privacy date back to a long time ago, and the protection of individual privacy is considered a fundamental human right.

- The profound transformation in technology and data-driven business models has increased information security risks and threats. Traditional approaches may be insufficient.
- The need for and importance of competencies in the field of information security are predicted to increase in the future.
- Information and data privacy are gaining strategic importance with technological and societal transformations.
- Rapid advancements in technology are challenging traditional security approaches by creating new risks and uncertainties.
- Areas such as the Internet of Things, artificial intelligence, and cloud computing have not yet reached sufficient maturity.
- New technologies can be considered both threats and opportunities.
- The increase in cybersecurity threats has increased the importance of theoretical modeling and studies in this field.
- Different theoretical models contribute to policy development and solution generation by approaching cybersecurity from different perspectives.
- Models assist in determining the fundamental elements of information security strategies, risk management processes, etc.
- The understanding and development of the concept of cybersecurity requires theoretical studies.
- The increase in cyber threats highlights the importance of education and awareness activities.

Practical Implications

- International standards and regulations have increased awareness and corporate compliance, but different country demands can make full compliance difficult.
- Organizations should consider data security as a strategic issue and develop proactive measures against constantly evolving threats.
- Organizations should invest early in risky areas, keep up with innovations, and lead security-focused transformations.
- Compliance with standards should be mandatory, and legal regulations should be brought in line with international norms.
- Information security education and awareness should be increased, and competency development in the field should be supported.
- Cybersecurity education should be included in school curricula to raise awareness levels.
- Education and information activities of NGOs and national campaigns should be supported.
- Digital channels, including social media, should be effectively utilized to reach the masses.
- Campaigns should be made interactive with various content and made interesting.
- This way, cybersecurity awareness can be increased both among individuals and society as a whole.
- Effective policies and models can be developed by researching best practices.

Solution Suggestions

In conclusion, when the developments in the field of information security are examined, it is seen that the issue is as old as human history, but it has become much more critical, especially with digitization.

Given that almost every individual and institution produce data today, and that the value of this data is increasing day by day; it is clear that ensuring data security is of vital importance.

However, it is observed that the standards, regulations and practices on the subject cannot keep up with rapid technological developments, remain insufficient against new data-based business models. On the other hand, there are also uncertainties that new generation technologies such as artificial intelligence, internet of things, cloud computing, which are developing at a dizzying pace, will bring.

Therefore, information and data security are likely to be one of the top agenda items for institutions and states in the coming period. Developing flexible and proactive strategies against constantly evolving threats, transitioning to risk-focused approaches, human resource planning based on merit and competency, closing the gap between technology and law will be vital during this period. Otherwise, it seems unlikely that any institution or state that fails to adequately ensure data security will survive in the future.

In this context, the following solution suggestions can be developed:

- Implementation of comprehensive legal regulations for the protection of personal data: As mentioned in the study, the GDPR regulation of the European Union can be taken as an example.
- Preparation of a National Cyber Security Strategy: There is a need for an action plan that will ensure inter-agency coordination and draw a common roadmap.
- Dissemination of education and awareness-raising activities to increase awareness of cybersecurity.
- Conducting research and developing predictions on the potential risks brought by new technologies such as artificial intelligence, cloud computing, and the Internet of Things.
- Joint collaboration between defense industry, universities, and technology companies, with a focus on R&D.
- Organizing media campaigns, competitions, and drills to increase social awareness.
- Establishment of a national incident response team and preparation of emergency protocols and infrastructure.

REFERENCES

Abbas, K., Tawalbeh, L. A. A., Rafiq, A., Muthanna, A., Elgendy, I. A., & Abd El-Latif, A. A. (2021). Convergence of blockchain and IoT for secure transportation systems in smart cities. *Security and Communication Networks*, *2021*, 1–13. doi:10.1155/2021/5597679

Aboujaoude, E., Savage, M. W., Starcevic, V., & Salame, W. O. (2015). Cyberbullying: Review of an old problem gone viral. *The Journal of Adolescent Health*, *57*(1), 10–18. doi:10.1016/j.jadohealth.2015.04.011 PMID:26095405

Ahmad, K., Maabreh, M., Ghaly, M., Khan, K., Qadir, J., & Al-Fuqaha, A. (2022). Developing future human-centered smart cities: Critical analysis of smart city security, data management, and ethical challenges. *Computer Science Review*, *43*, 100452. doi:10.1016/j.cosrev.2021.100452

Akhilomen, J. (2013). Data mining application for cyber credit-card fraud detection system. In P. Perner (Ed.), *Advances in data mining: Applications and theoretical aspects* (pp. 218–228). Springer. doi:10.1007/978-3-642-39736-3_17

Al-Hadhrami, Y., & Hussain, F. K. (2021). DDoS attacks in IoT networks: A comprehensive systematic literature review. *World Wide Web (Bussum)*, *24*(3), 971–1001. doi:10.1007/s11280-020-00855-2

Alavi, A. H., Jiao, P., Buttlar, W. G., & Lajnef, N. (2018). Internet of Things-enabled smart cities: State-of-the-art and future trends. *Measurement*, *129*, 589–606. doi:10.1016/j.measurement.2018.07.067

Aldawood, H., & Skinner, G. (2019). Challenges of implementing training and awareness programs targeting cyber security social engineering. In 2019 cybersecurity and cyberforensics conference (CCC) (pp. 111-117). IEEE. doi:10.1109/CCC.2019.00004

Alhassan, M. M., & Adjei-Quaye, A. (2017). Information security in an organization. [IJC]. *International Journal of Computer*, *24*(1), 100–116. https://ijcjournal.org/

Anderson, R. J. (2008). *Security engineering: a guide to building dependable distributed systems.* John Wiley & Sons. https://books.google.com.tr/

Andersson, D., Reimers, K., & Barreto, C. (2014). Post-secondary education network security: results of addressing the end user challenge. In *INTED2014 Proceedings* (pp. 6018–6027). IATED. https://library.iated.org/view/ANDERSSON2014POS

Antal, C., Cioara, T., Anghel, I., Antal, M., & Salomie, I. (2021). Distributed ledger technology review and decentralized applications development guidelines. *Future Internet*, *13*(3), 62. doi:10.3390/fi13030062

Arora, A., Bansal, S., Kandpal, C., Aswani, R., & Dwivedi, Y. (2019). Measuring social media influencer index-insights from Facebook, Twitter and Instagram. *Journal of Retailing and Consumer Services*, *49*, 86–101. doi:10.1016/j.jretconser.2019.03.012

Arrigo, E., Liberati, C., & Mariani, P. (2021). Social media data and users' preferences: A statistical analysis to support marketing communication. *Big Data Research*, *24*, 100189. doi:10.1016/j.bdr.2021.100189

Ashley, P. (2004, November 26). Enforcement of a P3P Privacy Policy. In Cowan University (ed) *2nd Australian Information Security Management Conference* (pp. 11-26). We-B Centre. https://dl.acm.org/doi/abs/10.1145/644527.644538

Aslan, Ö., Aktuğ, S. S., Ozkan-Okay, M., Yilmaz, A. A., & Akin, E. (2023). A comprehensive review of cyber security vulnerabilities, threats, attacks, and solutions. *Electronics (Basel)*, *12*(6), 1333. doi:10.3390/electronics12061333

Atalay, A. Ö. (2019). Evaluation of molecular genetic examinations in criminal procedure law in terms of protection of sensitive personal data. *Journal of Penal Law and Criminology*, *7*(2), 127–184. doi:10.26650/JPLC2019-0018

Basahel, A. M., & Yamin, M. (2020). Cyber Security and Privacy in Internet of Things. *International Journal of Human Potentials Management*, *2*(1), 43–53. https://nla.gov.au/

Bertino, E. (2016, December). Data privacy for IoT systems: Concepts, approaches, and research directions. In *2016 IEEE International Conference on Big Data (Big Data)* (pp. 3645-3647). IEEE. 10.1109/BigData.2016.7841030

Blokdyk, G. (2020). *ISO IEC 27000 A Complete Guide* (2021 Edition). 5STARCooks.

Bond, S., & Yuk, P. K. (2018). Uber to pay record $148m to settle 2016 data breach claims. *Financial Times*. https://www.ft.com/content/7fa7100c-c1a7-11e8

Borgesius, F. Z., Gray, J., & Van Eechoud, M. (2015). Open data, privacy, and fair information principles: Towards a balancing framework. *Berkeley Technology Law Journal*, *30*(3), 2073–2131. https://www.jstor.org/stable/26377585

Boyne, S. M. (2018). Data protection in the United States. *The American Journal of Comparative Law*, *66*(1, suppl_1), 299–343. doi:10.1093/ajcl/avy016

Calder, A. (2018). *NIST Cybersecurity Framework: A pocket guide*. IT Governance Publishing Ltd. doi:10.2307/j.ctv4cbhfx

Casola, V., De Benedictis, A., Rak, M., & Villano, U. (2019). Toward the automation of threat modeling and risk assessment in IoT systems. *Internet of Things : Engineering Cyber Physical Human Systems*, *7*, 100056. doi:10.1016/j.iot.2019.100056

Cebula, J. J., & Young, L. R. (2010). *A taxonomy of operational cyber security risks (Final rept.)*. Software Engineering Institute, Carnegie Mellon University. https://apps.dtic.mil/sti/citations/ADA537111

Chopra, A., & Chaudhary, M. (2020). *Implementing an information security management system: security management based on ISO 27001 guidelines*. Apress L.P. https://link.springer.com/book/10.1007/978-1-4842-5413-4

Choudhary, P., & Singh, U. (2015). A Survey on Social Network Analysis for Counter- Terrorism. *International Journal of Computer Applications*, *112*, 24–29.

Curzon, J., Kosa, T. A., Akalu, R., & El-Khatib, K. (2021). Privacy and artificial intelligence. *IEEE Transactions on Artificial Intelligence*, *2*(2), 96–108. doi:10.1109/TAI.2021.3088084

Deshpande, A., Stewart, K., Lepetit, L., & Gunashekar, S. (2017). Distributed Ledger Technologies/ Blockchain: Challenges, opportunities and the prospects for standards. *Overview report The British Standards Institution (BSI)*, *40*, 40. https://www.bsigroup.com/

Díaz, E. (2016). The new European Union General Regulation on Data Protection and the legal consequences for institutions. *Church. Communication and Culture*, *1*(1), 206–239. doi:10.1080/23753234.2016.1240912

Djenna, A., Harous, S., & Saidouni, D. E. (2021). Internet of things meet internet of threats: New concern cyber security issues of critical cyber infrastructure. *Applied Sciences (Basel, Switzerland)*, *11*(10), 4580. doi:10.3390/app11104580

Easttom, C., & Butler, W. (2019, January). A modified McCumber cube as a basis for a taxonomy of cyber attacks. In *2019 IEEE 9th Annual Computing and Communication Workshop and Conference (CCWC)* (pp. 0943-0949). IEEE. 10.1109/CCWC.2019.8666559

Fantin Irudaya Raj, E., & Appadurai, M. (2022). Internet of things-based smart transportation system for smart cities. In S. Mukherjee, N. B. Muppalaneni, S. Bhattacharya, & A. K. Pradhan (Eds.), *Intelligent Systems for Social Good: Theory and Practice* (pp. 39–50). Springer Nature Singapore. https://link.springer.com/chapter/10.1007/978-981-19-0770-8_4 doi:10.1007/978-981-19-0770-8_4

Gai, K., Qiu, M., Zhao, H., & Xiong, J. (2016, June). Privacy-aware adaptive data encryption strategy of big data in cloud computing. In *2016 IEEE 3rd International Conference on Cyber Security and Cloud Computing (CSCloud)* (pp. 273-278). IEEE. 10.1109/CSCloud.2016.52

Gallacher, L., & Morris, H. (2012). *ITIL foundation exam study guide*. John Wiley & Sons.

Gandhi, V., Ramkumar, K. R., Kaur, A., Kaushal, P., Chahal, J. K., & Singh, J. (2021, October). Security and privacy in IoT, Cloud and Augmented Reality. In *2021 6th International Conference on Signal Processing, Computing and Control (ISPCC)* (pp. 131-135). IEEE. 10.1109/ISPCC53510.2021.9609520

Ghorbani, A. A., Lu, W., & Tavallaee, M. (2009). *Network intrusion detection and prevention: concepts and techniques* (*Vol. 47*). Springer Science & Business Media. https://books.google.com.tr/

Giuca, O., Popescu, T. M., Popescu, A. M., Prostean, G., & Popescu, D. E. (2021). A survey of cybersecurity risk management frameworks. In *Soft Computing Applications: Proceedings of the 8th International Workshop Soft Computing Applications (SOFA 2018), Vol. I 8* (pp. 240-272). Springer International Publishing. https://link.springer.com/chapter/10.1007/978-3-030-51992-6_20

Guo, L., & Congdon, P. (2021). *IEEE 802 Nendica Report: Intelligent Lossless Data Center Networks*. IEEE SA Industry Connections. https://ieeexplore.ieee.org/iel7/9457236/9457237/09457238.pdf

Harding, E. L., Vanto, J. J., Clark, R., Hannah Ji, L., & Ainsworth, S. C. (2019). Understanding the scope and impact of the California consumer privacy act of 2018. *Journal of Data Protection & Privacy*, 2(3), 234–253. https://www.ingentaconnect.com/content/hsp/jdpp/2019/00000002/00000003/art00007

Hatfield, J. M. (2019). Virtuous human hacking: The ethics of social engineering in penetration-testing. *Computers & Security*, *83*, 354–366. doi:10.1016/j.cose.2019.02.012

Hayes, D., Cappa, F., & Le-Khac, N. A. (2020). An effective approach to mobile device management: Security and privacy issues associated with mobile applications. *Digital Business*, *1*(1), 100001. doi:10.1016/j.digbus.2020.100001

Hayes, D. R., & Cappa, F. (2018). Open-source intelligence for risk assessment. *Business Horizons*, *61*(5), 689–697. doi:10.1016/j.bushor.2018.02.001

Hoofnagle, C. J., Van Der Sloot, B., & Borgesius, F. Z. (2019). The European Union general data protection regulation: What it is and what it means. *Information & Communications Technology Law*, *28*(1), 65–98. doi:10.1080/13600834.2019.1573501

Hook, L., & Kuchler, H. (2017). Uber hid massive data breach from passengers and regulators. *Financial Times*. https://www.ft.com/content/ed66a21a-cf0e

Huang, S. L., & Chang, C. Y. (2020). Understanding how people select social networking services: Media trait, social influences and situational factors. *Information & Management*, *57*(6), 103323. doi:10.1016/j.im.2020.103323

International Organization for Standardization. (2018). *Information technology - Security techniques - Information security management systems - Overview and vocabulary* (ISO Standard No. 27000:2018). ISO. https://www.iso.org/standard/73906.html adresinden erişildi.

ISACA. (2019). *COBIT 5 Implementation -Supplemental Tools and Materials.* USA: ISACA.

ISACA. (2022). *IT Audit Framework (ITAF),* (4th ed.). ISACA. https://store.isaca.org/s/store#/store/browse/detail/a2S4w000004Ko91EAC adresinden erişildi.

Jones, A., & Ashenden, D. (2005). *Risk management for computer security: Protecting your network and information assets*. Elsevier.

Kavak, A., & Odabaş, H. (2023). The impact of information security management guide utilization on technological and institutional information security measures in university libraries in Türkiye. *Journal of Academic Librarianship*, *49*(6), 102800. doi:10.1016/j.acalib.2023.102800

Khiralla, F. A. M. (2020). Statistics of cybercrime from 2016 to the first half of 2020. *Int. J. Comput. Sci. Netw.*, *9*(5), 252–261. https://www.ijcsn.org/

Kim, D., & Solomon, M. G. (2018). *Fundamentals of ınformation systems security* (3rd ed.). Jones & Bartlett Learning.

Kintonova, A., Vasyaev, A., & Shestak, V. (2021). Cyberbullying and cyber-mobbing in developing countries. *Information and Computer Security*, *29*(3), 435–456. doi:10.1108/ICS-02-2020-0031

Klosek, J. (2000). *Data privacy in the information age*. Quorum Books.

Kreso, I., Kapo, A., & Turulja, L. (2021). Data mining privacy preserving: Research agenda. *Wiley Interdisciplinary Reviews. Data Mining and Knowledge Discovery*, *11*(1), e1392. doi:10.1002/widm.1392

Krzysztofek, M. (2018). *GDPR: General Data Protection Regulation (EU) 2016/679: Post-reform Personal Data Protection in the European Union*. Kluwer Law International BV. https://books.google.com.tr/

Kuchler, H. (2014). Home Depot attack bigger than Target's. *Financial Times.* https://www.ft.com/content/7f9a2b26-3f74-11e4-984b-00144

La Monaca, G., & Schiralli, I. (2010). Data protection, privacy. *La Clinica Terapeutica*, *161*(2), 189–191. https://www.clinicaterapeutica.it/download/404/fascicolo-2/7145/161-02-20_tact_la_monaca.pdf PMID:20499037

Lallie, H. S., Shepherd, L. A., Nurse, J. R., Erola, A., Epiphaniou, G., Maple, C., & Bellekens, X. (2021). Cyber security in the age of COVID-19: A timeline and analysis of cyber-crime and cyber-attacks during the pandemic. *Computers & Security*, *105*, 102248. doi:10.1016/j.cose.2021.102248 PMID:36540648

Landoll, D. J. (2017). *Information Security Policies, Procedures, and Standards: A Practitioner's Reference*. CRC Press. https://books.google.com.tr/

Laranjo, L., Arguel, A., Neves, A. L., Gallagher, A. M., Kaplan, R., Mortimer, N., Mendes, G. A., & Lau, A. Y. (2015). The influence of social networking sites on health behavior change: A systematic review and meta-analysis. *Journal of the American Medical Informatics Association : JAMIA*, *22*(1), 243–256. doi:10.1136/amiajnl-2014-002841 PMID:25005606

Lenard, T. M., & Rubin, P. H. (2010). In defense of data: Information and the costs of privacy. *Policy and Internet*, *2*(1), 149–183. doi:10.2202/1944-2866.1035

Lim, J. S., Chang, S., Maynard, S., & Ahmad, A. (2009). Exploring the relationship between organizational culture and ınformation security culture. In *Proceedings of the 7th Australian Information Security Management Conference* (pp. 88-97). ACM. 10.4225/75/57b4065130def

Luo, B., Wang, H., Liu, H., Li, B., & Peng, F. (2018). Early fault detection of machine tools based on deep learning and dynamic identification. *IEEE Transactions on Industrial Electronics*, *66*(1), 509–518. doi:10.1109/TIE.2018.2807414

Maiwald, E. (2004). *Fundamentals of Network Security*. McGraw Hill Professional.

Mathur, M. (2019). Where is the security blanket? Developing social media marketing capability as a shield from perceived cybersecurity risk. *Journal of Promotion Management*, *25*(2), 200–224. doi:10.1080/10496491.2018.1443310

McCallister, E. (2010). *Guide to protecting the confidentiality of personally identifiable information* (*Vol. 800*, No. 122). Diane Publishing. https://books.google.com.tr/

McCumber, J. (1991). Information systems security: A comprehensive model. *In Proceedings of the 14th National Computer Security Conference* (pp. 328-337). NIST. https://csrc.nist.gov/publications/history/nissc/1991-14th-NCSC-proceedings-vol-1.pdf

McCumber, J. (2004). *Assessing and Managing Security Risk in IT Systems: A Structured Methodology* (1st ed.). Auerbach Publications., doi:10.1201/9780203490426

Mehmood, Y., Ahmad, F., Yaqoob, I., Adnane, A., Imran, M., & Guizani, S. (2017). Internet-of-things-based smart cities: Recent advances and challenges. *IEEE Communications Magazine*, *55*(9), 16–24. doi:10.1109/MCOM.2017.1600514

Mishkin, S., & Kuchler, H. (2014, 21 Mayıs). *Ebay reveals cyber attack on database.* Financial Times. https://www.ft.com/content/41a20592-e0f5-11e3-a934-00144feabdc0

Moazzami, M., Sheini-Shahvand, N., Kabalci, E., Shahinzadeh, H., Kabalci, Y., & Gharehpetian, G. B. (2021, October). Internet of things architecture for intelligent transportation systems in a smart city. In *2021 3rd Global Power, Energy and Communication Conference (GPECOM)* (pp. 285-290). IEEE. 10.1109/GPECOM52585.2021.9587692

Mühlhoff, R. (2023). Predictive privacy: Collective data protection in the context of artificial intelligence and big data. *Big Data & Society*, *10*(1), 1–14. doi:10.1177/20539517231166886

Nayak, U., & Rao, U. H. (2014). *The InfoSec handbook: An introduction to information security*. Apress.

Neprash, H. T., McGlave, C. C., Cross, D. A., Virnig, B. A., Puskarich, M. A., Huling, J. D., Rozenshtein, A. Z., & Nikpay, S. S. (2022, December). Trends in ransomware attacks on US hospitals, clinics, and other health care delivery organizations, 2016-2021. In *JAMA Health Forum* (Vol. 3, No. 12, pp. e224873-e224873). American Medical Association. 10.1001/jamahealthforum.2022.4873

NIST. (2022). *NIST Publications.* National Institute of Standards and Technology. https://www.nist.gov/standardsgov/resources/publications

Olaniran, B. A., Potter, A., Ross, K. A., & Johnson, B. (2014). A gamer's nightmare: An analysis of the Sony PlayStation hacking crisis. *Journal of Risk Analysis and Crisis Response*, *4*(3), 151–159. https://jracr.com/index.php/jracr/article/view/107. doi:10.2991/jrarc.2014.4.3.4

Ording, L. G., Gao, S., & Chen, W. (2022). The influence of inputs in the information security policy development: an institutional perspective. *Transforming Government: People. Transforming Government*, *16*(4), 418–435. doi:10.1108/TG-03-2022-0030

Örselli, E., & Akbay, C. (2019). Technology and the transformation of urban life: Smart cities. *International Academy of Management Journal*, *2*(1), 228–241. doi:10.33712/mana.544549

Pandey, A. B., Tripathi, A., & Vashist, P. C. (2022). A survey of cyber security trends, emerging technologies and threats. *Cyber Security in Intelligent Computing and Communications*, 19-33. https://link.springer.com/chapter/10.1007/978-981-16-8012-0_2

Pandith, M. Y. (2015). Data security and privacy concerns in cloud computing. *Internet of Things and Cloud Computing*, *2*(2), 6–11. doi:10.11648/j.iotcc.20140202.11

Pelteret, M., & Ophoff, J. (2016). A Review of Information Privacy and Its Importance to Consumers and Organizations. *Informing Sci. Int. J. an Emerg. Informing Science*, *19*, 277–301. doi:10.28945/3573

Peltier, T. R. (2016). *Information Security Policies, Procedures, and Standards: guidelines for effective information security management.* CRC press. https://books.google.com.tr/

Phillips, B. (2021). UK further education sector journey to compliance with the general data protection regulation and the data protection act 2018. *Computer Law & Security Report*, *42*, 105586. doi:10.1016/j.clsr.2021.105586

Phillips, M. (2018). International data-sharing norms: From the OECD to the General Data Protection Regulation (GDPR). *Human Genetics*, *137*(8), 575–582. https://link.springer.com/article/10.1007/s00439-018-1919-7. doi:10.1007/s00439-018-1919-7 PMID:30069638

Praveena, A., & Smys, S. (2017, April). Ensuring data security in cloud based social networks. In 2017 international conference of electronics, communication and aerospace technology (ICECA) (Vol. 2, pp. 289-295). IEEE. doi:10.1109/ICECA.2017.8212819

Ramakrishnan, R. (2023). The future of cybersecurity and its potential threats. *International Journal for Research in Applied Science and Engineering Technology, 11*(7), 269-274. (https://doi.org/ doi:10.22214/ijraset.2023.54603

Rath, M., Satpathy, J., & Oreku, G. S. (2021). Artificial intelligence and machine learning applications in cloud computing and Internet of Things. In *Artificial intelligence to solve pervasive internet of things issues* (pp. 103–123). Academic Press. doi:10.1016/B978-0-12-818576-6.00006-X

Robinson, M., Jones, K., Janicke, H., & Maglaras, L. (2019). Developing cyber peacekeeping: Observation, monitoring and reporting. *Government Information Quarterly, 36*(2), 276-293. https://doi.org/ rights and content doi:10.1016/j.giq.2018.12.001Get

Rushe, D. (2017). Yahoo says all of its 3bn accounts were affected by 2013 hacking. *Guardian*. https://www.theguardian.com/technology/2017/oct/03/yahoo-says-all-of-its-3bn-accounts-were-affected-by-2013-hacking

Salahdine, F., & Kaabouch, N. (2019). Social engineering attacks: A survey. *Future Internet*, *11*(4), 1–17. doi:10.3390/fi11040089

Schlienger, T., & Teufel, S. (2003). Information security culture: From analysis to change. *South African Computer Journal = Suid-Afrikaanse Rekenaartydskrif*, *31*, 46–52. https://hdl.handle.net/10520/EJC27949

Shafiq, M., Gu, Z., Cheikhrouhou, O., Alhakami, W., & Hamam, H. (2022). The rise of "Internet of Things": Review and open research issues related to detection and prevention of IoT-based security attacks. *Wireless Communications and Mobile Computing*, *2022*, 1–12. doi:10.1155/2022/8669348

Slade, R. (2006). *Dictionary of information security*. Syngress Publishing.

Solms, S. V., & Solms, R. (2008). *Information security governance*. Springer Science & Business Media.

Solomon, M. G., & Chapple, M. (2004). *Information Security Illuminated*. Jones & Bartlett Publishers.

Solove, D. J. (2010). *Understanding privacy*. Harvard university press. https://books.google.com.tr/

Spencer, A., & Patel, S. (2019). Applying the data protection act 2018 and general data protection regulation principles in healthcare settings. *Nursing Management*, *26*(1), 34–40. Advance online publication. doi:10.7748/nm.2019.e1806 PMID:31468753

Sun, Y., Zhang, J., Xiong, Y., & Zhu, G. (2014). Data security and privacy in Cloud computing. *International Journal of Distributed Sensor Networks*, *10*(7), 190903. doi:10.1155/2014/190903

Tankard, C. (2016). What the GDPR means for businesses. *Network Security*, *2016*(6), 5–8. doi:10.1016/S1353-4858(16)30056-3

Tetri, P., & Vuorinen, J. (2013). Dissecting social engineering. *Behaviour & Information Technology*, *32*(10), 1014–1023. doi:10.1080/0144929X.2013.763860

Thushari, P. D. (2022, November). Current security and privacy issues, and concerns of Internet of Things (IoT) and Cloud Computing: A review. In *2022 International Conference on Computing, Communication, and Intelligent Systems (ICCCIS)* (pp. 13-17). IEEE. 10.1109/ICCCIS56430.2022.10037730

Trautman, L. J. (2021). Rapid Technological Change and US Entrepreneurial Risk in International Markets: Focus on Data Security, Information Privacy, Bribery and Corruption. *Cap. UL Rev.*, *49*, 69-121. https://heinonline.org/

Twentyman, J. (2015). Fear of reputational damage after security leaks may be overhyped. *Financial Times*. https://www.ft.com/content/b6395d84-cc8f-11e4-b5a5-00144feab7de

Unwin, P. T. H., & Unwin, T. (2017). *Reclaiming information and communication technologies for development*. Oxford University Press., https://books.google.com.tr/ doi:10.1093/oso/9780198795292.001.0001

Vacca, J. R. (Ed.). (2013). *Network and system security*. Elsevier., https://books.google.com.tr/

Verma, B., Snodgrass, R., Henry, B., Smith, B., & Daim, T. (2020). Smart cities-an analysis of smart transportation management. In *Managing Innovation in a Global and Digital World: Meeting Societal Challenges and Enhancing Competitiveness* (pp. 367-388). Springer Fachmedien Wiesbaden. https://link.springer.com/chapter/10.1007/978-3-658-27241-8_23

Virmani, C., Choudhary, T., Pillai, A., & Rani, M. (2020). Applications of Machine Learning in Cyber Security. In *Handbook of Research on Machine and Deep Learning Applications for Cyber Security*. IGI Global. https://www.igi-global.com/gateway/chapter/235038

Wang, W., Harrou, F., Bouyeddou, B., Senouci, S. M., & Sun, Y. (2022). A stacked deep learning approach to cyber-attacks detection in industrial systems: Application to power system and gas pipeline systems. *Cluster Computing*, *25*(1), 1–18. https://link.springer.com/article/10.1007/s10586-021-03426-w. doi:10.1007/s10586-021-03426-w PMID:34629940

Warren, S., & Brandeis, L. (1989). The right to privacy. In *Killing the Messenger: 100 Years of Media Criticism* (pp. 1–21). Columbia University Press. doi:10.7312/gold91730-002

Watson, D. S. (1989). Computers, Confidentiality and Privation. *Computers in Human Services*, *5*(1-2), 153–168. doi:10.1300/J407v05n01_12

Westin, A. F. (1967). Special report: Legal safeguards to insure privacy in a computer society. *Communications of the ACM*, *10*(9), 533–537. https://dl.acm.org/doi/pdf/10.1145/363566.363579. doi:10.1145/363566.363579

Whitman, M. E. (2003). Enemy at the gate: Threats to information security. *Communications of the ACM*, *46*(8), 91–95. doi:10.1145/859670.859675

Whitman, M. E., & Mattord, H. J. (2018). *Principles of information security* (8th ed.). Cengage Learning.

Whitman, M. E., & Mattord, H. J. (2019). *Management of Information Security*. Cengage.

Whitmer, M. G. (2007*). IT security awareness and training: Changing the culture of state government*. NASCIO. https://www.nascio.org/wp-content/uploads/2019/11/NASCIO-ITSecurityAwarenessAndTraining.pdf

Wohlgemuth, S., Echizen, I., Sonehara, N., & Müller, G. (2011). On Privacy-compliant Disclosure of Personal Data to Third Parties using Digital Watermarking. *J. Inf. Hiding Multim. Signal Process.*, *2*(3), 270–281. https://bit.nkust.edu.tw/2011/vol2/JIH-MSP-2011-04-007.pdf

Wong, R. (2013). *Data security breaches and privacy in Europe*. Springer. doi:10.1007/978-1-4471-5586-7

Yasin, A., Liu, L., Li, T., Wang, J., & Zowghi, D. (2018). Design and preliminary evaluation of a cyber Security Requirements Education Game (SREG). *Information and Software Technology*, *95*, 179–200. doi:10.1016/j.infsof.2017.12.002

Yeboah-Boateng, E. O., & Boaten, F. E. (2016). Bring-Your-Own-Device (BYOD): an evaluation of associated risks to corporate information security. *arXiv preprint arXiv:1609.01821*. https://doi.org//arXiv.1609.01821 doi:10.48550

Yilmaz, Y., Cetin, O., Grigore, C., Arief, B., & Hernandez-Castro, J. (2023). Personality types and ransomware victimization. *Digital Threats : Research and Practice*, *4*(4), 1–25. doi:10.1145/3568994

Yücedağ, N. (2019). General principles under the personal data protection law. Journal of Personal *Data Protection,1*(1), 47-63. https://dergipark.org.tr/en/pub/kvkd/issue/45759/566993

Yüksel, G. (2019). Legal protection of personal health data. *Journal of Health Academics*, *6*(1), 1–10. https://dergipark.org.tr/en/pub/sagakaderg/issue/43967/542618

Zins, C. (2007). Conceptual approaches for defining data, information, and knowledge. *Journal of the American Society for Information Science and Technology*, *58*(4), 479–493. doi:10.1002/asi.20508

Zolanvari, M., Teixeira, M. A., Gupta, L., Khan, K. M., & Jain, R. (2019). Machine learning-based network vulnerability analysis of industrial Internet of Things. *IEEE Internet of Things Journal*, *6*(4), 6822–6834. doi:10.1109/JIOT.2019.2912022

KEY TERMS AND DEFINITIONS

Artificial Intelligence: Machine learning-based systems capable of performing cognitive functions specific to human intelligence.

Big Data: It is the whole of technologies that require the processing of high-volume, high-velocity and high-variety data sets.

Cloud Computing: It is a distributed computing infrastructure where computing resources are offered as a service via the Internet.

Cybersecurity: The practice of protecting computers, servers, mobile devices, electronic systems, networks, and data from malicious attacks.

Information and Data Privacy: Policies and procedures aimed at preventing unauthorized individuals from accessing, disclosing or modifying information and data.

Information Security: It is the whole of principles, policies and procedures that ensure the protection of information assets in terms of confidentiality, integrity and availability.

Internet of Things: It is the network where physical objects connect to each other and systems over the Internet.

Policy: It is the whole of rules, standards and guiding principles established to ensure information security.

Procedure: Step-by-step instructions prepared to implement policies.

Risk: It is the impact and likelihood of damage that may arise as a result of threats.

Social Engineering: It refers to attempts to gain unauthorized access to information and data by exploiting human psychology.

Threat: Any risk factor directed at information security.

ENDNOTES

1 BYOD is an emerging trend where employees bring and use personal computing devices on the companys network to access applications and sensitive data like emails, calendar and scheduling applications, documents, etc.

Chapter 10
Implementing Information Governance in Academic Libraries:
An Exploration of Opportunities

Amanda Zerangue
https://orcid.org/0009-0009-6563-5713
University of North Texas Libraries, USA

Kristin Clark
Texas Woman's University Libraries, USA

Adrian Shapiro
Texas Woman's University Libraries, USA

ABSTRACT

This chapter focuses on opportunities to implement an information governance framework within an academic library. Due to their mission and breadth of information management activities, academic libraries face numerous challenges in organizing and preserving information and records, and governing data. Implementing information governance strategies, specifically in the areas of records and information management, metadata creation, institutional repositories, digital preservation, and data management will result in well-informed and collaborative policies which protect the library as well as the institution. Developing this skill set within the library requires a culture shift towards transparency, collaboration, and accountability. Additionally, library and information science curricula should reflect the current demands of the academic library landscape and expand course offerings to build information governance competencies.

DOI: 10.4018/979-8-3693-0472-3.ch010

INTRODUCTION

This chapter explores the Information Governance (IG) framework and its potential for implementation in academic libraries. IG refers to the activities and practices developed to control information use (MacLennan, 2014). More specifically, IG consists of the "standards, processes, roles, and metrics that hold organizations and individuals accountable to create, organize, secure, maintain, use, and dispose of information in ways that align with and contribute to the organization's goals" (ARMA, 2014). While not traditionally used in the library setting, IG practices permeate information work, and the rationale for applying these practices in an academic library environment is strong. Academic libraries are libraries attached to a higher education institution with a common mission to support the curriculum and research of the institution. Because of their mission and scope, they face numerous challenges in organizing and preserving information, governing data, and ensuring privacy while meeting accreditation and other higher education data reporting requirements. This chapter aims to highlight the potential role of IG in addressing these challenges while identifying opportunities for academic libraries to enhance their information management practices.

Enhancing information practices within an academic library will be a multidisciplinary initiative requiring the active participation of a broad cross-section of functional groups and stakeholders. Similarly, implementing IG in an academic library would involve multiple departments, including digital services, assessment, archives, and data management. Implementing IG opens the door to increased collaborations with departments external to the library– information technology systems, institutional research/data management, general counsel, and sponsored research. The relevant research illustrates that involving multiple academic departments in IG compliance will result in well-informed policies which protect the library and the institution. The policies may reflect how the institution complies with regulations and laws, meets ethical standards when managing information, addresses confidential information, and organizes assets.

An academic library interested in an IG framework may find this chapter helpful, as literature and case studies on implementing IG specifically in academic libraries are lacking. The following suggestions in this chapter may lead to policies that outline the needs of the larger institution. While each area within the library may benefit from an IG implementation, starting with one department or process may better suit your library. Eventual integration into your library's strategic plan may solidify efforts and build consensus behind this change in operations. This chapter will discuss opportunities for IG implementation within the library areas of records and information management, including metadata creation, records maintenance in repositories, and final preservation; data governance; and the need for additional education and training for library and information science students and those currently employed in academic libraries.

BACKGROUND

An IG framework is the overarching umbrella strategy for organizational information by establishing the processes, capabilities, structures, and infrastructure to enable information to be a useful asset and reduced liability to an organization. Creating such a framework can be a big undertaking for an academic library of any size, but libraries can learn from organizations who have advanced information governance experience and trusted models. The National Archives of Australia (NAA), for instance, is a leader in information governance and has created a framework that guides the creation and management of their organization's information assets (National Archives of Australia, n.d.). In fact, the framework is not only used within the NAA, but it is also the recommended guide for agencies throughout the Australian government who are developing or reviewing their own practices. Essentially, the NAA framework defines the environment in which information assets are created, the principles that affect information creation and management, and outlines general governance as well as the roles, responsibilities, and leadership involved in the implementation of IG practices. The NAA claims that with a sound information governance framework in place, an organization will see benefits in the reduced time and effort spent on locating and accessing records, improved service delivery, and simplified compliance with laws and regulations. The NAA provides an open template and framework outline that can easily be adapted for the academic library setting.

Another leading information governance organization is ARMA International, originally known as the Association of Records Managers and Administrators. According to ARMA International, the records management profession has become vital to information governance making the association a leader in best practices (ARMA,n.d.). The organization outlines the global standard of record keeping and information management through the principles of accountability, transparency, integrity, protection, compliance, availability, retention, and disposition (ARMA, 2017). According to ARMA, these principles, combined with their Information Governance Maturity Model, provide organizations with the proper guidance for building an information governance program. When ARMA's principles of accountability are examined closely, it is evident that library and archives professionals have shared priorities and practices. ARMA's "availability" principle, for example, involves the organization, indexing, and storage of information and the assurance that information can be accurately and efficiently retrieved (Saffady, 2015). Another close tie to library and archives competencies and practices can be seen in ARMA's "Protection" principle, which describes the need to maintain the privacy and confidentiality of certain records and information as well as their eventual disposition.

Library and archives professionals have regular experience with these issues, and they are often handled through standard donor agreements, forms, and contracts that outline the specifics of privacy, confidentiality, and disposition. That said, with the decades long transition to electronic records within academia, establishing a formal IG program is a responsible solution to the needs of a modern academic library, particularly in the areas of records management and the academic library's integration into the records lifecycle and data governance. Records and information management, which incorporates metadata creation, institutional repositories, and digital preservation, as well as data governance are areas within an academic library in which IG may be most relevant and successfully implemented.

RECORDS MANAGEMENT AND INFORMATION GOVERNANCE

Records and information management (RIM), a key area of IG, is defined as the area of management "responsible for the efficient and systematic control of the creation, receipt, maintenance, use, and disposition of records, including the process for capturing and maintaining evidence of and information about business activities and transactions in the form of records" (ISO, 2001). Stated another way, it is the management of the records created, received, and maintained by a business to conduct the business itself. The scholarly literature in this field is typically explored through a corporate or business lens, however, an academic library functions similarly in many aspects and would be a successful candidate for the implementation of an RIM program.

Role of the Academic Library in Records Information Management

While many higher education institutions have implemented RIM programs at a cross-institutional level, for others the responsibility is tenuously embedded within the university archives area of the library. University archives are tasked with collecting and preserving the historical records, collections, data, photographs of the university's origin, development, activities, and community. When records management is integrated into university archives the result is often an allocation of resources to create records retention schedules and disposal of records (Kaczmarek, 2014). While the records retention is an important aspect of RIM, with a current landscape of almost exclusively electronic records, it would be more appropriate to expand the scope to a full RIM program with multiple partners across the university and library. Expansion could encompass electronic university records such as email records traditionally managed by the IT department and student enrollment records managed by the Registrar. Whether it be one aspect of an overarching information governance program, or simply a program centered on the records of the library, a RIM program will ensure that all records are retained for the correct time limits, and managed and preserved in a way that assures accuracy, value, and addresses access control (Kaczmarek, 2014). In collaboration with external partners, an RIM program implementation would allow the library to become a key player in the institution's information governance framework.

Records Lifecycle and RIM

The first question in implementing an RIM program within an academic library will most likely be: What does this mean? RIM focuses on the record lifecycle, and as such, would prioritize the management of a library record from creation to disposition. It is important to understand that records are always information, but information is not always a record. For example, a completed performance report for a library grant report is a record, however the form itself is not, even if it provides valuable information regarding how to complete the performance report. The records lifecycle begins with the creation or receipt of a record. Depending on the type of record, the record is retained for a certain period, and its accuracy is maintained—this is the second stage. The final stage of this basic records lifecycle is the disposition phase, where the record is either destroyed at the end of its retention period or archived within the library for long-term preservation, depending on the record's type and value.

For academic libraries within public institutions in the United States, records management is dictated by state agency laws and rules for public offices and agencies. Approved retention schedules are provided, and a reporting infrastructure is maintained at the state level. Other records created and maintained by academic libraries are retained and disposed of as part of external funder requirements, Human Resources requirements, or even institutional procedures regarding research.

A successful RIM program formalizes the roles, responsibilities, and control over the diverse types of records throughout the records lifecycle via transparent documentation and policies, a clarification of roles, and a designation of control within the different units regarding access and maintenance of records. A collaborative approach, considering the stakeholders and their reporting and retention needs, is vital. Collaborators will identify and inventory records, conduct the necessary legal research, develop retention schedules, determine disposition strategies, and assess impact (Smallwood, 2019).

Implementing RIM at an Academic Library

Implementing formal RIM within an academic library as part of an IG program offers many benefits to the library and other institutional partners. These benefits range from improving the ability and authority to make decisions at the time of need, resulting in increased productivity and compliance. Guidance on implementing RIM in the library focuses on addressing concerns in library culture, capacity and capability, communication, and technology infrastructure (DIR, n.d). The following suggestions may support RIM implementation within an academic library:

- Library Culture: In terms of library culture, RIM must be part of an organizational culture of continuous improvement and engagement.
- Sustainability: Capacity and capability concerns may be assuaged with a review of library roles to identify current employee expertise, areas of record management overlap, and make job description adjustments accordingly.
- Communication: As with any information governance implementation, change management strategies will always be apt, with a focus on continuous and clear communication and assessment.
- Assessment of Needs: An evaluation of the library's technological infrastructure may result in small steps to build scalable technology solutions within limited budgets.

A shared understanding of future challenges and willingness to collaborate with colleagues within the library as well as external partners will provide a clearer path towards the first steps of implementing RIM. After an assessment of needs, many academic libraries may focus on three sub-areas of the records lifecycle-- metadata creation, maintaining public access to records in an archive or institutional repository, and final disposition or preservation.

METADATA CREATION AND ACADEMIC LIBRARIES

Metadata creation is a critical area within an RIM framework for academic libraries, serving as a core activity for academic libraries. Metadata forms the foundation of library information retrieval systems such as catalogs and digital collection systems and its creation and maintenance enables academic libraries to fulfill their mission of connecting users with information they seek. Sharing and harvesting of metadata allows libraries to move beyond their own patrons and share their collections and resources more broadly.

Most simply defined, metadata is "data about data". Metadata can be used to describe a variety of resources in digital collections such as images, text, collections, finding aids, audio, video, datasets and web pages. While metadata finds its roots in the data management and systems design communities, in the library science field, metadata "usually alludes to data that facilitates the description, discovery, and retrieval of networked electronic resources" (Hudgins, Agnew, & Brown, 1999). This descriptive and identifying information, such as the title, creator, date, and subject, enables digital objects to be discoverable in information retrieval systems. Descriptive metadata contextualizes items and makes the materials understandable within the context of the collection, other materials, and historic events. In this regard, metadata can be seen as just as valuable as the digital assets it describes because without one, the other cannot be understood.

When digital resources are appropriately defined, search results are more accurate, and users are better able to make connections and explore collections. In addition to descriptive elements, metadata can also capture administrative, technical, structural, rights, and preservation data important to the understanding and management of the item over time. With the prevalence of metadata harvesting protocols (OAI-PMH) and Linked Data models, metadata can be widely shared between repositories, increasing its impact.

To be effective, metadata must be detailed and consistent across collections. Descriptive elements must encompass what an item is, what it is about, how it came to be, and how it relates to other items. Creating consistent records can be challenging when dealing with different types of resources, systems, and actors who are involved in describing the resources. Certain metadata fields, such as subject and description, can be highly subjective and vary greatly between metadata creators. Syntax variations and misapplication of fields can affect cross-collection searching and inhibit discovery. Green (2022) notes additional challenges to library metadata include "staff shortages or turnover, siloed metadata practices across departments, lack of metadata guidance documentation, lack of staff training or support, inconsistent or outdated metadata practices or migration to a new system." Interoperability also presents its own challenges. Not only does metadata need to be detailed and consistent, but it should also be carefully structured so that it can be shared between systems. Challenges arise when attempting to balance local metadata needs with demands of sharing metadata with communities or large discovery systems like the Digital Public Library of America (DPLA) (Green, 2022).

To create and maintain shareable metadata, libraries should consider building policies and processes that guide how metadata is created, maintained, and managed within an organization. Libraries can identify a governing unit over metadata and a set of policies that outline responsibilities of library units and standards for processes and work product. LeBlanc and Kurth (2007) suggest an operational model for metadata maintenance loosely based on the ISA framework, which involves six generic interrogatives: what, where, who, when, why, and how. From these six questions, an IG framework can be built that documents who oversees metadata and how metadata will be managed within a given library. With focused strategies, IG activities can streamline processes, foster collaboration, and contribute to an overall improvement in the quality of metadata created by an organization.

Standards and Interoperability

Standardization is key to making metadata understandable by both machines and humans. Standardization also promotes interoperability, the exchange and sharing of information between systems and the enabling of cross-domain searching (Ma, 2009). Metadata can be difficult to standardize because the collections and materials being described are unique, and each institution has diverse needs and use cases.

To standardize how items are described and enable interoperability between systems, academic libraries rely on schemas and controlled vocabularies. Schemas are predefined element sets and rules for their usage. Some of the predominant schemas include Dublin Core (DC), Metadata Object Description Schema (MODS), Visual Resources Association's Core Categories (VRA), and Encoded Archival Description (EAD). Controlled vocabularies are another standardization tool as they outline the acceptable values of a field. Widely adopted controlled vocabularies include those developed by the Library of Congress and Getty Museum- Library of Congress Subject Headings (LCSH), Library of Congress Genre/Form, Art & Architecture Thesaurus (AAT) and the Thesaurus for Geographic Names (TGN) (Gentry et al., 2020).

Selecting and adopting an appropriate metadata schema and controlled vocabulary for a given digital collection or repository involves considering several factors, "the type of institution, staff expertise, the purpose and structure of the metadata standard, the materials to be digitized, interoperability, and the objectives of the project" (Foulonneau & Riley, 2008). The digital collection management system itself should also be considered as most systems include a default schema. For example, the default schema for two widely utilized systems, CONTENTdm and DSpace, is Dublin Core.

To ensure that the necessary factors relevant to an institution are considered when adopting schemas and controlled vocabularies, libraries can create policies outlining the decision-making framework required to implement a schema or controlled vocabulary. If digital collections already exist, libraries should document what schemas and controlled vocabularies are in use within their collections and why they are utilized. By doing this, libraries will have a basis of what they have and policies to guide future decision making.

Implementing Standards

In addition to what schemas and controlled vocabularies are in use, libraries need policies to outline how they apply their selected schemas to their collections. Even with the number of schemas developed, there is not a one-size-fits all schema. International schemas do not always lend themselves to local needs and local elements and vocabularies are implemented or elements are mixed-and-matched between schemas in order to fill those gaps (Lopatin, 2010). In a survey of metadata practices in American Research Libraries (ARL) Gentry et al. (2020) found that 53% of libraries use local vocabularies to describe names, geographic locations, material types, genres, or specialized fields of study. Lopatin (2010) found that 81% of academic libraries use local names and labels in their metadata schemas. To capture local implementation practices and standards, libraries should consider developing metadata application profiles (MAPs) to provide guidance to metadata specialists and increase consistency in metadata records.

MAPs document local metadata standards by defining element fields and their use. They provide guidelines for what controlled vocabularies to apply to given fields, appropriate syntax, and examples. Often MAPs include information about a field's obligation, whether it is required, recommended, or optional. In a review of openly available MAPs, Green (2021) found that all reviewed MAPs included a list of elements and the top sections included were vocabulary/standard, definition/description, input guidelines, and obligation. Green (2021) draws from the literature that "a MAP could resolve metadata ambiguity or misapplication issues by providing explicit guidelines and usage examples to distinguish elements, giving metadata specialists more confidence in their work and information seekers greater consistency in their search results."

Quality Control

Metadata creation is not a one and done process. New metadata must go through a quality control check to confirm it aligns with identified standards and legacy metadata must be regularly maintained to remain relevant and usable. Legacy metadata need not conform to a newly implemented MAP but should be reviewed regularly as authority records are updated or information regarding an object change or is discovered. Reparative description projects are another mode that may trigger legacy metadata updates. The Society of American Archivists (SAA) defines reparative description as "remediation of practices or data that exclude, silence, harm, or mischaracterize marginalized people in the data created or used by archivists to identify or characterize archival resources" (n.d.). Reparative projects are gaining prominence in academic libraries and resources such as the Homosaurus and the Archives for Black Lives in

Philadelphia's Anti-Racist Description Resources were created to aid metadata specialists in updating metadata to more inclusive and person-centered language.

When performing quality control of records, the most important aspects libraries consider are accuracy, completeness, and consistency (Gentry et al., 2020). Activities can be performed using automated methods and tools but often involve some element of human intervention. Some metadata elements are easier to perform quality control on than others. Survey respondents of a quality control study noted that free-text elements were more challenging to check because they lack standardized formatting as opposed to other fields such as names or date (Gentry et al., 2020). To evaluate these fields, the most common method used was manual checks by staff.

MAPs are a valuable resource for metadata specialists performing manual checks and clear policies on when, who, and how legacy records are updated can help projects progress efficiently. "The current necessity of manual metadata assessment reinforces the need for streamlined tactics that partner efficient resources with human effectiveness to maximize metadata evaluation impact" (Gentry et al., 2020).

Workflows

Metadata's prominence in academic libraries is due to their involvement in digitization projects and maintenance of institutional repositories (Ma, 2009; Lopatin, 2010). Digitization is an inherently collaborative process as different responsibilities are often associated with different departments. One department, often special collections, has the items to be digitized, another department completes the digitization, while another department may create and manage the metadata. Ma (2009) notes challenges surround "creating the right internal organization for providing metadata services, developing/accommodating workflow for metadata creation, and managing projects that cross so many departments/divisions of the libraries and that involve other units across campus." With many departments involved in this work, it is important to have one governing body charged with making final decisions about metadata- whether that be an individual or a unit. Ma (2009) states that it is "imperative to have a leader who oversees the metadata activities and standards, identifies metadata relationships and processes, and promotes the sharing and reuse of metadata resources." Establishing a governing unit or person and standardized processes for how digitization and metadata projects are initiated and completed can provide clarity over roles and responsibilities and aid in decision making.

Describing digital collections is a crucial and multi-faceted task for academic libraries to undertake. Uncertainty and guesswork in how to create and maintain metadata can lead to undiscoverable collections and frustrated users. Investing time and resources to outline an information governance plan for metadata can have a positive impact on output and collection usability. Academic libraries should consider appointing a governing body or unit overseeing metadata at the institution and charging this leader with developing collaborative policies and processes surrounding how metadata is created and maintained, integrating MAPs and standards within.

INSTITUTIONAL REPOSITORIES AND INFORMATION GOVERNANCE

Another area where academic libraries can achieve IG is within the archival arena. Specifically, by implementing IG framework for maintaining public access to academic library records in an archive or institutional repository. Typically managed by academic libraries, institutional repositories are digital archives that preserve and share the scholarly and creative products of an institution and make them available to researchers worldwide. Theses, dissertations, journal articles, and conference proceedings are among the leading content types found within repositories, but institutions can tailor the content according to their own preferences, unique programs, and collections. Institutions of all sizes use repository platforms to showcase scholarly and creative work and most support a multitude of file types and formats that include everything from PDFs to audio and video files.

Significant amounts of information are stored within institutional repositories and their contents should be governed by policies that assure efficient organization and access while also protecting and ensuring long-term preservation. The good stewardship of information and records is central to library principles, and in turn, libraries create repository policies to ensure oversight. A library's institutional repository policy will typically define the basics: what content is eligible for the repository, who may contribute work, what file types and formats are accepted, withdrawal protocols, etcetera. These foundational elements are necessary to guide library staff and patrons in the use and management of the repository, but it will take a greater leap to manage the potential threats to digital collections. Data breaches, for example, could lead to the unauthorized access and release of copyrighted, embargoed, or restricted research and data. Other threats include phishing attacks, general data corruption, and malware attacks (Aregbesola & Nwaolise, 2023). The creation and implementation of a full-fledged information governance framework that identifies the actors, responsibilities and processes in place to protect digital collections can be one of the most effective defenses against these threats.

DIGITAL PRESERVATION

The third area of an academic library's records lifecycle in which an IG framework could be implemented is within preservation activities. As mentioned previously, academic libraries are investing increased resources into creating digital collections through digitization while born-digital collections continue to grow naturally as information is created in a primarily digital format. Digital collections and records are inherently fragile and come with their own preservation needs and challenges. Digital materials are easily deleted, corrupted, and prone to format obsolescence. "The unifying characteristic of digital materials is their machine-dependency. Information can only be accessed, and functions can only be executed through a computer. As technology becomes more sophisticated this dependence becomes an ever more elaborate chain of inter-dependencies that are hard to track and tricky to maintain." (Digital Preservation Coalition, n.d.).

To protect valuable digital information, academic libraries must commit to digital preservation as heavily as they commit to traditional preservation of paper records. Digital preservation "refers to the series of managed activities necessary to ensure continued access to digital materials for as long as necessary. . . (digital preservation) refers to all of the actions required to maintain access to digital materials beyond the limits of media failure or technological and organizational change" (Digital Preservation Coalition Glossary, n.d.).

Digital preservation requires a different approach from traditional preservation as the goal of digital preservation is to preserve the information in a digital item rather than the item itself. "By definition, digital preservation does not necessarily guarantee 'preservation' of the actual digital artifact or object, but its informational value and how it is rendered and accessed" (Noonan, 2014). Digital preservation activities may include format migration, emulation, storing geographically distributed copies, integrity checking, securing preservation files, and capturing/storing preservation metadata. Not all organizations can employ all of these approaches, and it is not necessary that they do. A digital preservation plan often mixes and matches different activities and tools to create a custom strategy that utilizes an organization's unique expertise, resources, and technological infrastructure. Organizations should use assessments such as the NDSA Levels of Preservation or DPC Rapid Assessment Model (RAM) to decide to what level they would like and are able to preserve their digital collections.

With many different approaches and strategies available to preserve digital information, and many different actors involved in carrying out those activities within an organization, governance is needed to provide clarity and direction. A digital preservation policy should form the basis of that governance, affirming an organization's commitment to preservation and identifying what is being preserved, who is preserving it, and how it is being preserved. Proper governance of a digital preservation program will ensure the long-term accessibility of digital assets and information.

Developing a Digital Preservation Policy

The American Library Association (ALA) defines digital preservation as a combination of "policies, strategies and actions that ensure access to digital content over time" (Association for Library Collections and Technical Services, 2007). Policy is a single piece in the puzzle, but without managed strategies and actions, loss will happen to some degree. "Preservation activities are realized using a combination of three resources: people, hardware, and software. The resources are tied together in processes and workflows. And lastly, policies form a guideline framework for all activities" (Lindar, 2012).

In a 2016 study of digital preservation policies in American Research Libraries (ARL), Dressler recommends libraries create a high-level preservation policy that includes:

1. financial and staff accountability;
2. intellectual property issues;
3. distributed services;
4. metadata standards compliance;
5. re-formatting of object;
6. implementation;
7. storage and media strategy;
8. review and certification;
9. auditing and risk assessment;
10. invested parties involved; and
11. glossary.

While Dressler's recommended policy areas include implementation activities and specific strategies, Noonan argues that policies should not include these detailed sections. "The policy must be developed at a conceptually high level that addresses what the policy entails and why it is important to the institution/organization, not how it is to be accomplished- that is an implementation matter" (Noonan, 2014). A 2021 international review of institutional repository digital preservation policies found that implementation activities were absent in the policies and further research into preservation strategies is needed to help managers and practitioners improve their own programs (Barrueco & Termens, 2021). Regardless of where activities, strategies, and collection decisions are recorded, the most important factor is that they are recorded somewhere. The "who", "how", "where" and "when" of digital preservation processes are just as important as the "what", and "why" that high-level policies may capture.

Preserving digital collections in perpetuity can be a huge undertaking for both individuals and organizations. No one can predict what new types of digital information will be created in the future and how current information will hold up. If managed actions are taken now, libraries will be better able to face the future with greater certainty surrounding the survival of their digital collections. No perfect solution for digital preservation exists, so it is up to libraries to determine what actions they can take and manage those actions appropriately. Without policies, resources, and accountability, digital collections will be lost to time.

DATA GOVERNANCE AND ACADEMIC LIBRARIES

While the phrase information governance is often used interchangeably with data governance, for this chapter's purposes, data governance is viewed as one part of the broader program of information governance. In its broadest sense, data governance is defined as the exercise of authority and control over the management of data. While most of the scholarly literature describes data governance though a corporate lens, the following definition from Ladley (2012) provides more specific examples to describe this somewhat nebulous concept, "Data governance is the organization and implementation of policies, procedures, structure, roles, responsibilities which outline and enforce rules of engagement, decision rights, and accountabilities for the effective management of information assets." Abraham, Schneider, and vom Brock (2019) further expand the definition of data governance as a "cross-functional framework for managing data as a strategic enterprise asset." Taken together, data governance is a collaboratively designed framework which designates authority and control over data management through policies to effectively use data as an asset. Because of this chapter's focus on opportunities for governance in academic libraries, the discussion of data governance is limited to the formal manner in which data created by the library—including data created and/or managed by library employees, library related technology, infrastructure, databases, and researchers — and data created by external partners and archived within the library, is managed and monitored.

Creating the Case for a Data Governance Program Within Your Academic Library

For universities with an existing data governance program, the academic library can situate itself as a valuable contributor and collaborator. If the institution does not have a formal data governance program, the academic library is uniquely positioned to serve as a pilot program for the university. There are multiple data domains within an academic library, and this creates a need for an overarching program to aid assessment and ensure accurate reporting and data sharing. Aside from the prolific growth of data within higher education settings, there are many reasons a data governance framework may become increasingly important within academic libraries. First, the growth of data management services in academic libraries supports a formalized data governance framework. For the past decade, academic libraries have developed data management services such as designing data management plans, facilitating data sharing and preservation, and providing data literacy training and programming. Second, library employees engage in multiple activities that create data, ranging from a traditional reference statistic to data included in reporting to external funders. Third, the digital infrastructure of academic libraries creates an abundance of data, some protected by privacy laws and others ruled by contractual agreements. Similarly, transformative research tools – technologies such as artificial intelligence and machine learning-- result in new types and increasing amounts of data, making the need to establish a baseline framework even more critical.

Strategies for Implementing a Data Governance Framework Within Your Library

The 2023 EDUCAUSE Action Plan: Data Governance lists steps to start a data governance program at an institutional level—steps that can be adapted to support the academic library as an active participant or pilot a data governance program within the library itself. In their Action Plan, Roberts and Reinitz (2023) suggest beginning with a planning activity to get a better understanding of data governance needs. First, identify key stakeholders interested in shaping a data governance plan. Second, from the list of stakeholders, select a sample to determine the current state of data governance, challenges, assets, and why data governance may be important. Third, reflect on your findings and plan for the next steps.

In line with this plan, the first step in implementing a data governance framework or program within an academic library is to understand its needs. The list of relevant stakeholders for an academic library must include at least one top-level library administrator, as well as library employees with current data responsibilities such as assessment, technology, collection management, digital services, and those responsible for external funding. External stakeholders may include the institution's research and data management department and legal counsel. From this list of stakeholders, identify a sample to discuss the current state of data governance at the library. A non-exclusive list of questions may start with the following: What data is needed for external reporting, including grants, accrediting agencies, and institutional partners? What library infrastructure accumulates data (repositories, archives, collections) and how is it stored or reported? How does the library support the collection and creation of data for research? How is it stored, maintained, and checked for accuracy? Does the library engage in data literacy programming? After reflection, develop an action plan.

One preferred approach to developing an action plan comes from Seiner's (2008) Non-Invasive Data Governance. Non-Invasive Data Governance relies upon formalizing existing accountability for the management of data. The approach focuses on what can be done toward improving data governance without major disruptions to current processes. In line with the non-invasive data governance lens, the first action may be to define roles and responsibilities for managing data within the library and assign accountability to the specific groups or data domains. To better support this effort, it is important to formally codify data governance responsibilities in job roles and responsibilities (Robert & Reinitz, 2023). Next steps may include drafting policies that define data governance and data management standards, establishing mechanisms to ensure currency and accuracy, and developing processes to assess impact. Throughout the process, it is essential to communicate the importance and impact of data governance.

Developing a thoughtful data governance framework specific which focuses on library data can serve two important tasks: illustrate an alignment with the institution's strategic plans and goals and showcase the value of the academic libraries' infrastructure, services, and programming. Ideally, a data governance framework will be planned in conjunction with a larger information governance strategy, but piloting a data governance plan alone could be an effective way to build buy-in for a larger strategy while providing clarity, management strategies, and authority to those in responsible for the library's data.

RECOMMENDATIONS: TRAINING AND EDUCATION

IG is necessary for the use, preservation, and protection of information, and experts are needed to administer best practices. It is not unusual for an organization's departments or units to manage information in relatively siloed environments, but information governance requires collaboration. A group of representatives from multiple units, departments, and offices from across an organization must collaborate and adhere to uniform policies and practices and ensure that policies are properly carried out. Librarians and archivists are ideal for these strategic positions because their professions prioritize competencies that support successful and efficient information governance. The American Library Association and the Association of College and Research Libraries' core competencies for library and special collections professionals include the ability to "maintain the systems of cataloging, collection, metadata, indexing, and classification standards and structures, and implement methods used to apply, create, and discover recorded knowledge and information;" all of which are tenets of information governance best practices (ALA, 2023). Other competencies include management of the knowledge and information lifecycle, the application of long-term preservation and curative practices of information collections, identification of the weaknesses and strengths of metadata and indexing systems, and knowledge of which technologies appropriately support the access and delivery of information (ALA, 2023). Similarly, ARMA International states that information governance requires taxonomy, metadata, format standards, classification/sensitivity labels, and protocols (ARMA, n.d.)

Although librarians and archivists should play essential information governance roles within their institutions, they often find themselves at the bottom, or even outside of, their organizations' decision-making hierarchies. Maurel and Zwarich (2021) argue that this is largely due to common organizational power structures that limit librarian participation and can, potentially, lead to information security risks and ineffective information governance. Because information governance frameworks define who within an organization will make information decisions, it is important that library professionals assert themselves and be included in the discussion. Transversal competencies that should be prioritized by library and archives professionals include change management, communication skills, and project management (Maurel & Zwarich, 2021).

Unfortunately, library and information science (LIS) degree programs often lack instruction in these areas as well as general leadership and managerial skills. This gap in training and education can hinder opportunities in the workplace for LIS graduates. LIS students may graduate having received excellent training in the field of library, archival, and information science but many of their degree programs need to adapt to the demands of the real-world workplace and the collaborative environments and positions many graduates will find themselves in. Training in information governance, records and information management, data governance, leadership, administration, and management would instill in new library and archives professional the confidence and knowledge necessary to meet the demands of their workplace. Developing these skill sets takes time and experience, but training should begin in the LIS program or for early-career professionals, rather than solely as a skill set developed as an experienced professional.

CONCLUSION

With the complete transition to electronic records and data, the skyrocketing growth of information and records management needs within an academic institution, and multiple information arenas within the academic library itself, IG implementation is becoming increasingly critical. Though the practice of IG is new to the library field, librarians have been adjacently performing different aspects of IG for decades. Formally implementing an IG framework with the academic library, particularly in the areas of records management, metadata creation, institutional repositories, digital preservation, and data governance will result in collaborative workflows and well-informed policies which direct and protect the library, library employees, and users. An IG framework would provide a holistic, structured, and collaborative approach to manage the work that librarians are already engaged in. Supporting implementation through non-invasive practices, a change management framework, and new library and information science curricula may help the culture shift towards consistent information management, control, and accountability within the academic library.

REFERENCES

Abraham, R., Schneider, J., & vom Brocke, J. (2019). Data governance: A conceptual framework, structured review, and research agenda. *International Journal of Information Management*, *49*, 424–438. doi:10.1016/j.ijinfomgt.2019.07.008

American Library Association. (2023, January 28). *ALA's core competencies for librarianship.* ALA. https://www.ala.org/educationcareers/sites/ala.org.educationcareers/files/content/2022%20ALA%20Core%20Competences%20of%20Librarianship_FINAL.pdf

Aregbesola, A., & Nwaolise, E. (2023). Securing digital collections: Cyber security best practices for academic libraries in developing countries. *Library Philosophy and Practice (e-journal).* Digital Commons. https://digitalcommons.unl.edu/libphilprac/7822

ARMA. (2017). *Generally Accepted Recordkeeping Principles.* ARMA. https://cdn.ymaws.com/www.arma.org/resource/resmgr/docs/Generally_Accepted_Recordkee.pdf

Association for Library Collections and Technical Services. (2007, June 24). *Definitions of Digital Preservation.* ALA. https://www.ala.org/alcts/resources/preserv/defdigpres0408

Barrueco, J. M., & Termens, M. (2021). (2021.) Digital preservation in institutional repositories: A systematic literature review. *Digital Library Perspectives*, *38*(2), 161–174. doi:10.1108/DLP-02-2021-0011

Dressler, V. A. (2017). The state of affairs with digital preservation at ARL member libraries: A survey and analysis of policy. *Digital Library Perspectives*, *33*(2), 137–155. doi:10.1108/DLP-08-2016-0030

Gentry, S., Hale, M. L., Payant, A., Tarver, H., White, R., & Wittmann, R. (2020). *Survey of Benchmarks in Metadata Quality: Initial Findings.ul* https://digital.library.unt.edu/ark:/67531/metadc1637685/m1/1/

Goodsett, M., & Koziura, A. (2016). *Are library science programs preparing new librarians? Creating a sustainable and vibrant library community.* Michael Schwartz Library Publications. doi:10.1080/01930826.2015.1134246

Green, A. (2021). Metadata Application Profiles in U. S. Academic Libraries: A Document Analysis. *Journal of Library Metadata*, *21*(3-4), 3–4, 105–143. doi:10.1080/19386389.2022.2030172

Hudgins, J., Agnew, G., & Brown, E. (1999). *Getting mileage out of metadata: Applications for the library*. American Library Association.

International Standard for Organization. (2016). *Information and documentation-- Records management Part 1: Concepts and principals*. ISO. https://www.iso.org/standard/62542.html

Kaczmarek, J. (2014). Supporting information governance through records and information management. Research bulletin. *ECAR*. https://library.educause.edu/~/media/files/library/2014/4/erb1402-pdf.pdf

Ladley, J. (2012). *Data governance: How to design, deploy and sustain an effective data governance program*. Elsevier. doi:10.1016/B978-0-12-415829-0.00002-2

LeBlanc, J., & Kurth, M. (2008). An operational model for library metadata maintenance. *Library Resources & Technical Services*, *52*(1), 54–59. doi:10.5860/lrts.52n1.54

Lindlar, M. (2014). Time to change: Effects and implications of digital preservation in an organizational context. *IASSIST Quarterly*, *36*(3-4), 8. doi:10.29173/iq471

Lopatin, L. (2010). Metadata practices in academic and non-academic libraries for digital projects: A survey. *Cataloging & Classification Quarterly*, *48*(8), 716–742. doi:10.1080/01639374.2010.509029

Ma, J. (2009). Metadata in ARL Libraries: A Survey of Metadata Practices, *Journal of Library Metadata*, 9:1-2, 1-14, oi:10.1080/19386380903094977

Maurel, D., & Zwarich, N. (2021). Information governance and power relations: Reflections on archival education in Québec. *Education for Information*, *37*(1), 33–51. doi:10.3233/EFI-190360

Noonan, D. (2014) *Digital Preservation Policy Framework: A Case Study*. EDUCAUSE. https://er.educause.edu/articles/2014/7/digital-preservation-policy-framework-a-case-study

OpenDOAR. (n.d.). *OpenDOAR Statistics*. OpenDOAR. https://v2.sherpa.ac.uk/view/repository_visualisations/1.html

Robert, J., & Reinitz, B. (2023). *2023 Horizon action plan: Data governance*. EDUCAUSE. https://library.educause.edu/-/media/files/library/2023/3/2023horizonapdatagovernance.pdf?la=en&hash=FA306932947338DB9353D05A48369FFBB6A9C653

Saffady, W. (2015). Records management or information governance? *Information & Management*, *49*(4), 38–41, 47. https://magazine.arma.org/wp-content/uploads/simple-file-list/2015_04_records_management_or_IG-Saffady.pdf

Seiner, R. S. (2016, April 1). *What is noninvasive data governance?* The Data Administrator Newsletter. https://tdan.com/what-is-non-invasive-data-governance/7354

Smallwood, R. (2019). *Information governance: Concepts, strategies, and best practices*. John Wiley & Sions, Inc. doi:10.1002/9781119491422.ch9

Texas Department of Information Resources. (n.d.). *Governing data, records, and information together*. DIR. https://dir.texas.gov/sites/default/files/2023-10/DMO%20RMO%20Guidance.pdf

Chapter 11
Spatial Data Infrastructure for Information Governance:
The Case Study From Pakistan

Munir Ahmad
https://orcid.org/0000-0003-4836-6151
Survey of Pakistan, Pakistan

Asmat Ali
https://orcid.org/0000-0002-8804-2285
Survey of Pakistan, Pakistan

Froilan Delute Mobo
https://orcid.org/0000-0002-4531-8106
Philippine Merchant Marine Academy, Philippines

Hammad Hussain
https://orcid.org/0009-0009-0552-2549
COMSATS University Islamabad, Wah, Pakistan

ABSTRACT

By examining the case study of spatial data infrastructure (SDI) implementation in Pakistan and its relationship with information governance, this chapter contributed to a deeper understanding of how effective spatial data management can support information governance objectives. A feasibility study is ongoing to establish NSDI in Pakistan. Moreover, a provincial-level SDI under PULSE is also planned. However, challenges such as the absence of uniform standards, a poor technology setup, and a shortage of qualified manpower are associated with NSDI implementation in Pakistan. By enhancing data quality and consistency and facilitating data sharing & collaboration, NSDI Pakistan would strengthen information governance in Pakistan by supporting decisions as well as policymaking. The findings and recommendations will help policymakers and practitioners in Pakistan, as well as researchers interested in the fields of spatial data infrastructure and information governance, advance their understanding and implementation of these critical concepts.

DOI: 10.4018/979-8-3693-0472-3.ch011

INTRODUCTION

Information is an embodiment form of knowledge. It serves as a conduit that molds the mental status and physical reactions of its recipients (Farradane, 1979). This notion exceeds simple communication and encompasses many factors including data, text documents objects, or events (Buckland, 1991). By acknowledging information as a multidimensional concept encompassing different formats and mediums, a better understanding of its role in constructing intellectual and physical realities can be materialized.

As far as governance is concerned, information becomes an anchor for all governments being one of the major tools through which governments can play numerous roles (C. C. Hood, 1983; C. Hood & Margetts, 2007). Therefore, the appropriate management of such information is crucial for governments in order to perform their numerous roles and functions. In the digital era when information becomes extremely important, the term “information governance” takes center stage. Information governance, coined by (C. Hood & Margetts, 2007) is a tight and intentional method of governing governmental information as well as addressing its rising importance in contemporary environments. This wide and readily evolving concept of information governance encompasses a range of rules to practices, as well as technological implications required for the lifecycle management of data and content (Kooper et al., 2011).

In recent years, policies that are used for different government procedures mostly depend on spatial data to fetch insights. Every day, lots of bytes of spatial data are generated through the public sector, private, and academic spheres. Second, social media can also be an important source of implicit and explicit geographical information. However, there is a significant challenge to effectively governing this large reservoir of geographical data.

Spatial Data Infrastructure (SDI) is a critical data framework implemented globally to facilitate e-governance and g-governance in diverse government sectors. Emerging technologies have revolutionized the implementation of SDI (Ahmad, 2023; Ahmad et al., 2023; Ahmad & Ali, 2023b) and the remarkable capabilities of SDI make it a valuable solution for tackling the numerous challenges related to information governance. In Pakistan SDI implementation at the national level is under process (Ahmad et al., 2022; Ahmad & Ali, 2023a), thus, it is useful to test the applicability of SDI in the context of information governance. Against this backdrop, the main objectives of this study are as under.

i. Explore the implementation of SDI in Pakistan
ii. Investigate the impact of SDI on Information Governance in Pakistan

To achieve the above-stated objectives, this chapter is structured in the following manner. First, in Section 2, the conceptual framework of SDI and information governance is presented to lay a solid foundation for understanding these concepts. Next, in Section 3, a case study of SDI implementation in Pakistan is showcased by shedding light on its current status and challenges. In Section 4, the crucial role of SDI in information governance in Pakistan is explored. Finally, a summary of our key findings and recommendations for policymakers and stakeholders is endorsed in the last section.

LITERATURE REVIEW

This section provides an overview of the key concepts involved in the chapter such as spatial data infrastructure and information governance.

Spatial Data Infrastructure

The Spatial Data Infrastructure is a framework that includes institutional arrangements, policies, and technologies that are intended to improve the accessibility and availability of spatial data and information (Diaz et al., 2012). It can be intellectualized as a collective initiative focused on promoting simpler access, greater dissemination, and more efficient utilization of spatial data to benefit society in the larger interest (Cetl et al., 2009).

Moreover, SDI fosters interoperability between regions as well as between provinces, states, and countries by acting as an information highway linking socioeconomic, environmental, and institutional databases (Coleman & Nebert, 1998). According to (McLaughlin & Nichols, 1994), this interconnection is essential for building a national spatial data infrastructure, which guarantees more efficient access to information goods and services for organizations, governmental bodies, and the general public.

As SDI has evolved, it has gone from being a second-generation service-oriented system to a third-generation user-centric system, with a focus on geospatial data exchange and access as essential parts of its information architecture (Granell et al., 2011). This trend is consistent with promoting and coordinating the flow of spatial data across stakeholders in the spatial data community, which supports decision-making processes across different governmental jurisdictions (Rajabifard et al., 2002, 2006).

According to (Nedović-Budić et al., 2011), SDIs are essential for tackling issues including data policy, technological standards, and integration. Through the improvement of spatial data's affordability, accessibility, and interoperability, SDI plays a major role in breaking down barriers within the spatial data industry. Thus, the sharing of spatial data continues to be the fundamental narrative anchor for spatial data infrastructures (Crompvoets et al., 2018; Masser, 2019).

Benefits of SDI

SDI can provide access to accurate and updated spatial data, thus improving significant decision-making processes. In many fields such as education, public health, disaster management, agriculture, and land management, SDI can help decision-makers make well-informed assessments (Manfré et al., 2012). SDI can benefit decision-makers by enabling them to see linkages and patterns that they might have overlooked in the absence of SDI (Boerboom, 2010). For example, when there is a calamity like an earthquake, SDI can inform the policymakers accurately and quickly on the affected areas. With this information, they can then make good decisions that will lead to the success of their response and recovery efforts (Manfré et al., 2012).

Organizations can also achieve substantial savings by adopting SDI. This is because it eliminates duplication of activities and resources associated with data collection, maintenance, and dissemination which reduces costs significantly (Bishop et al., 2000). Cost savings are obtained through web-based portals and services that share spatial datasets thereby reducing expenses incurred in expensive data acquisition and maintenance while eliminating those related to managing multiple data sources (Borzacchiello & Craglia, 2013). These cost savings can release resources for other activities, such as data analysis and decision-making, offering additional benefits to organizations utilizing SDI.

SDI can also play a role in increasing efficiency through consolidating data management and sharing processes thereby lowering administrative load and promoting faster and improved processing of data (Borzacchiello & Craglia, 2013). By employing standardized data models and metadata, SDI can automate tasks such as data discovery, validation, and integration leading to significant savings in time

Figure 1. Components of SDI

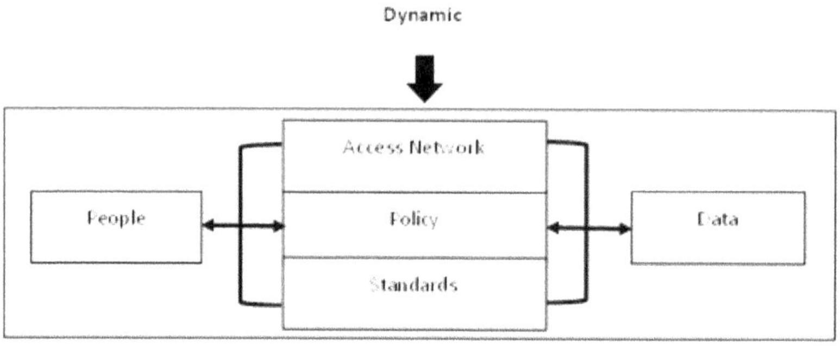

and energy spent on spatial data management (Crompvoets et al., 2011). This makes organizations more efficient in their operations while enabling them to respond promptly to the changes that are taking place in the market.

Additionally, SDI may enhance the cooperation of various entities such as public-private sector corporations, government agencies, or the general public. Apart from fostering public engagement and interaction processes, SDI can promote accountability and transparency through a common platform for information sharing and collaboration (Bishop et al., 2000; Crompvoets et al., 2011). For example, with participatory mapping techniques and crowdsourcing, SDIs can offer citizens the opportunity to be actively involved in the collection and analysis of geographic information necessary for the policy-making process or decision support system.

SDI Component

The design of SDI is a combination of several components, which work together to enable sharing and management of spatial data. These components share similar characteristics and have been defined differently by scholars and organizations due to their goals, concepts, and priorities. In the study by (Rajabifard et al., 2002), five components of SDI are proposed: policy, access network, standards, people, and data, as illustrated in Figure 1 (Rajabifard et al., 2002).

Figure 1 shows that the two segments such as geographic information and individuals are influenced by a range of dynamic technological factors of SDI like standards or access networks. It follows from this dynamic model that an all-round approach to SDI should involve issues like interoperability standards and networks as it goes beyond mere involvement of spatial data and people (Rajabifard et al., 2002). To give an in-depth analysis of SDI components the GSDI Cookbook (GSDI, 2004), highlighted metadata catalogues web applications giving a further explanation of the aspects of SDI as shown in Figure 2 (GSDI, 2004).

With the evolution of the SDI framework, new elements have become significant. Capacity building, spatial data sharing, partnerships, and governance have been identified as crucial factors influencing the effectiveness and success of SDIs (Mohammadi, 2008).

Figure 2. Elements of SDI

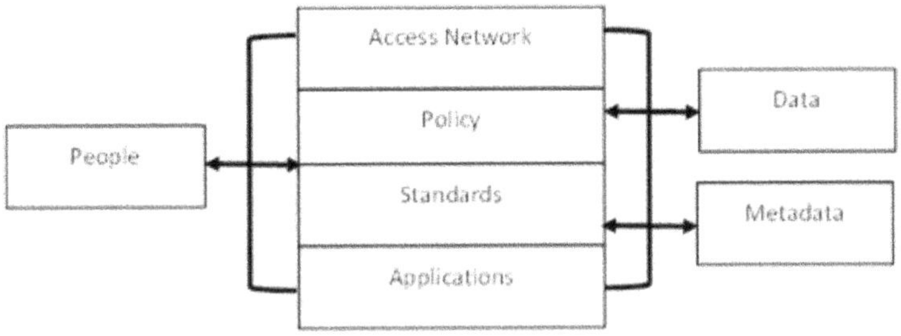

Information Governance

The concept of "information governance" substitutes the skillset and procedures guiding all phases through which information as well as other resources pass—its generation, acquisition, appraisal, usage, management etc., including accessibility preservation, or even disposability (Mikalef, Krogstie, et al., 2018; Tallon et al., 2013). It goes beyond this conceptualization by incorporating structural practices of decision-maker positions, procedural practices concerning task decisions, and relational ones in reference to individual participation and growth (Weber et al., 2009).

What information governance does in its practical sense is that it ensures that data and information are managed appropriately, privately, and securely (Rees et al., 2023). It is a modern strategy designed to streamline the utilization of information not only within organizations but also outside them, based on established IT governance principles (Kooper et al., 2011). This strategy is necessary for achieving all five values including business, establishing compliance, risk management, and security (Hulme, 2012). The rise of the significance of information governance as an integral element that participates in planning big data projects is reflected by the prioritization of senior IT and business management (Mikalef, Pappas, et al., 2018).

Importantly, information governance is central to the digital transformation of public sector institutions as a link between old systems and modern technological platforms (Brown & Toze, 2017). The concept of information governance is built on the premise that recognizing information as a critical public administration resource affects policy, services, and accountability throughout its lifecycle. Its value lies in providing ways to use information efficiently within multiple public policies, coping with challenges, and solving inherent contradictions of informationally. In governments of digital metamorphoses, information governance becomes a leader in preserving information as an instrument for diplomacy decision-making, public service, and accountability (Brown & Toze, 2017).

In a similar vein, the concept of data governance that is guided by information governance systems facilitates to reduction of the complexity of data management in controlling decision-making and responsibilities for all processes regarding data (Castro et al., 2021). Tallon et al. (2013), emphasized that information governance practices can open value and opportunities for organizations, considering their rising data volume industry wide. Moreover, data governance technology is highlighted as it plays a part in the development of information systems and ongoing improvement within the field of data engineering

(Wang et al., 2020). Therefore, the complementarity of information governance and data governance is established as a whole that defines what good practice in terms of effective management should look like.

METHODOLOGY

This chapter deploys the case study approach as a tool to investigate and analyze the complex system of NSDI in Pakistan. The methodology of a case study allows researchers to explore into details of critical phenomena in a given scene. It involves examining individual cases to gain insight into a specific situation (Tasci et al., 2020). The application of case study methodology is a vital tool for unveiling complex phenomena, which manifests the fact that. Using the case study methodology this chapter explores the implementation of SDI in Pakistan at the national level and investigates the impact of SDI on Information Governance in Pakistan.

SDI IMPLEMENTATION IN PAKISTAN

This section explores the current status of the implementation of the National Spatial Data Infrastructure in Pakistan. Various activities are in process that are described in the subsequent paragraphs.

A feasibility study is currently being carried out for the purpose of setting up a National Spatial Data Infrastructure in Pakistan. The main objective of this feasibility study is to analyze and record the available financial, legal, technical as well as human resources required for the project. Furthermore, the feasibility study addresses issues related to governance structure, management frameworks; financial model, business model, and NSDI secretariat design. The feasibility study has been informed by research conducted through workshops, surveys, and meetings which provide data for numerous analyses. For instance, a workshop held at COMSATS University Islamabad discussed various dimensions of the Pakistan National Spatial Data Infrastructure.

It is predicted that the benefits of using National Spatial Data Infrastructure will be greater than just upgrading cadastral systems. This is especially important in the aspect of effective agricultural policy-making as underlined by Ali and Imran (2021). In particular, the PULSE (Punjab Urban Land Systems Enhancement) Project launched by PLRA Punjab Pakistan seeks to strengthen and control land management in the Province of Punjab. One of the key elements in this project is to develop a provincial SDI with land administration and management as its focal point.

There are no successful SDIs without the active participation of stakeholders. To facilitate cooperation between various stakeholders in guiding the implementation of Pakistan's NSDI, a coordination committee has been formed by the Survey of Pakistan which is currently mandated to create and develop the country's NSDI. The possible major stakeholders of Pakistan NSDI are listed below.

Survey of Pakistan (SoP) is the national mapping authority of Pakistan. SoP is responsible for topographic surveys and the production of topographical maps. At the same time, SoP has the responsibility for setting up and sustaining the geodetic network. SoP also produces tourist maps, guide Maps, district maps, forest maps, atlases, and several others of national importance. With its spatial data of these maps, SoP can support NSDI.

The National Disaster Management Authority (NDMA) is a federal organization that was put in place to address natural and human-induced disasters. Thus, mitigation, response, and readiness are the primary concepts of NDMA. It is therefore crucial to converge different sectors in order to come up with ways of reducing the impacts that follow disasters and fostering community-based resiliency. NMDA can help in data-sharing activities under NSDI through spatial data indicating areas prone to natural and man-made disasters as well as assessment of the vulnerability of different regions.

The Space & Upper Atmosphere Research Commission (SUPARCO) is an autonomous agency of the government that is engaged in space research and exploration. The Agency SUPARCO can supply satellite images for different applications in the context of NSDI.

Pakistan Meteorological Department (PMD) is a national-level body to give public warnings and weather forecasts. PMD focuses on improving the country's early warning and response capacities for several hazards. PMD can help NSDI geoportal by provisioning timely and historical weather data from various regions as well as providing information on climate trends with long-term descriptions of variations.

Pakistan Bureau of Statistics (PBS) is a federal institution that gathers, assembles, and distributes accurate and timely statistical data to assist in the development of evidence-based policies and decision-making throughout the nation's numerous sectors. Spatial data related to population distribution, education, health, and other social indicators can be fueled by PBS.

Provincial Revenue Departments are responsible for land administration and record keeping. These departments can play a vital role in integrating land-related data into the SDI framework. For example, the Punjab Land Record Authority (PLRA) contributes to the PULSE project in Punjab.

SDI Components and Implementation Challenges in Pakistan

For analysis in this chapter, the five Components of SDI are adopted from (Rajabifard et al., 2002).

Policy

It is essential to establish trust and cooperation among agencies for successful data sharing. An important aspect of instilling this trust is the establishment and implementation of clear data governance policies. These policies would be used as a guide, informing the processes, requirements, and responsibilities of handling data exchange.

The Surveying and Mapping Act of 2014 entrusts the Survey of Pakistan with the responsibility to establish and oversee the National Spatial Data Infrastructure (NSDI) within the specific context of Pakistan. But to avoid the duplicate collection of similar data by several agencies, which leads to information silos and inconsistencies; there should be statutory provisions and a stringent set of data governance policies in place (Ali et al., 2021). Furthermore, fostering public awareness regarding the accessibility and potential applications of NSDI data is vital for enhancing the pools.

However, special legislative frameworks should be developed to increase support, enhance information transfer, and create trust among stakeholders. Such a framework would not only strengthen the base for data governance but also act as a bridge to promote cooperation among different entities.

Access Network

For effortless storage, management, and distribution of spatial data, an IT infrastructure that is both robust and well-built is essential. These include online portals and spatial data repositories. This large infrastructure would act as a basis of current data ecologies and is critical for the improvement of many processes involving information.

In the Pakistani context, a significant gap exists as there is currently no national-level geoportal to effectively disseminate spatial data. Many organizations do not offer spatial data through their websites, and for those that do, the data is often presented in a PDF format. Unfortunately, the provision of vector-based online data dissemination is rare in Pakistan. Moreover, some organizations lack the necessary technical infrastructure for data sharing. These insufficient technological capabilities lead to low stakeholder participation and hinder Pakistan's national spatial data infrastructure implementation efforts (Ali & Imran, 2020).

This deficiency in accessible and interactive spatial data hampers the potential for effective decision-making, planning, and collaboration across various sectors. To address this gap, there is a pressing need for the establishment of a comprehensive national geoportal. This platform would make it easy for users to obtain geographical data in a variety of forms, with a focus on using vector-based data to improve usability and analysis. In addition to bridging the current information gap, putting such a system into place will greatly advance the nation's geospatial capabilities and encourage data-driven decision-making.

Standards

The establishment and enforcement of data standards for formats, metadata, and quality control are imperative for achieving seamless integration within any data-driven ecosystem. These standards serve as a foundation that ensures consistency, interoperability, and reliability across diverse datasets.

In the Pakistani context, the absence of agreed-upon standards poses a significant challenge (Ali & Imran, 2020). Currently, each organization generates spatial data following its own locally established standards and procedures. This divergence results in inconsistencies across data sources and formats, creating hurdles for effective data integration and sharing. The lack of standardized practices not only complicates collaborative efforts but also impedes the seamless exchange of information, emphasizing the critical need for a unified and widely accepted set of standards within the spatial data landscape.

People

Users with insufficient technological skills may find it difficult to access and use complicated geospatial data. The complexities of managing such data could put up obstacles that prevent geographical information from being used effectively. Furthermore, the implementation efforts of Pakistan's national spatial data infrastructure face a significant hurdle in the form of low stakeholder participation due to a shortage of skilled human resources (Ali & Imran, 2020). Additionally, the shortage of skilled human resources may hinder the effective planning, implementation, and maintenance of the spatial data infrastructure.

Data

Documenting current data is an essential first step in starting to construct a Spatial Data Infrastructure. The production of spatial data encompasses a wide range of categories, including topography, cadaster, soil, geology, hydrology, orthoimagery, and crops, and is actively undertaken by both public and private institutions. Producing this kind of spatial data is typically a mandatory task given to public sector organizations (Ali & Imran, 2020).

The problem, though, is that these directives differ from one organization to the next. As a result, there are notable differences between the kinds of data generated and the formats in which they are preserved. Some public sector entities may be accountable for specific sorts of data, while others focus on various domains. Moreover, the data may exist in multiple formats, including both analog and digital versions.

IMPACT OF SDI ON INFORMATION GOVERNANCE IN PAKISTAN

This section explores the impact of National Spatial Data Infrastructure on information governance in Pakistan.

Enhancing Data Quality and Consistency

Spatial information quality and information governance are two concepts that together ensure the accuracy of geospatial data, as poor-quality spatial data results in poor analysis, flawed decisions, and even legal responsibilities.

SDI programs promote the development of sophisticated technologies such as remote sensing and LiDAR, which afford greater accuracy and timeliness as compared to traditional approaches. This emphasis on data quality directly strengthens information governance by fostering transparency, informing effective policy, and empowering citizen engagement. In addition, standardized data formats and validation tools contribute significantly to minimizing inconsistencies that ensure trustworthy information from various sources. Therefore, SDI has the capability to enhance data efficiency effectiveness, and quality in processes such as collection and sharing of information (Tu et al., 2009).

In the context of Pakistan, SDI implementation would improve data quality and consistency to contribute to achieving Pakistan's national development goals and addressing critical challenges in areas like disaster management and resource allocation. By prioritizing spatial data quality through NSDI initiatives, Pakistan can build a robust foundation for effective information governance and sustainable development.

Facilitating Data Sharing and Collaboration

Effective information governance is based on the unrelenting pillars of data interoperability and common standards which have a spiral effect that allows collaboration among different individuals in an organization to make informed decisions. Without the enduring pillar of data interoperability and a set of uniform standards, information governance may collapse accompanied by fragments remnants that may be misleading or unreachable.

Reliance on SDI is particularly important for local governments to participate where it elicits collaboration and trust among the government agencies, increases sharing of geographic information as well as upscaling through cooperation (Harvey, 2003). SDI can provide significant facilitation and coordination of spatial data exchange among stakeholders, with both product- and process-based approaches contributing to their evolution and uptake (Rajabifard et al., 2002). SDI portals and discovery tools allow authorized users to obtain the data in an easy manner, thus fostering collaboration and knowledge sharing while keeping confidentiality. Therefore, the implementation of NSDI would help to encourage data sharing and stakeholder collaboration in Pakistan. NSDI implementation in Pakistan will also enhance data interoperability and common standards.

Through the capabilities that Spatial Data Infrastructures have, e-government can benefit significantly as they will be able to share data more effectively and efficiently; both of which are crucial for resource management administrators (Crompvoets et al., 2011). As such, NSDI implementation would facilitate information governance in the backdrop of E-Government practices within Pakistan. Access to timely, accurate spatial information available through SDI platforms ensures that better preparedness measures are taken in response and recovery from disasters.

Strengthening Decision-making and Policy Formulation

The provision of accurate and easily accessible spatial data enables policymakers to make decisions based on concrete facts, as well as perform comprehensive analysis. Enhancing the resolution of spatial data issues through SDI and web-based systems contributes to better decisions in addition to increased response efficiency (Mansourian et al., 2006).

The participation of governments and the private sector is increasingly important in building spatial data infrastructures, contributing significantly to improved decision-making across many different levels within national settings (Rajabifard et al., 2006). For example, in the Arctic, Spatial Data Infrastructures can assist in determining climate change vulnerability. Such infrastructures can be used to support the interactive dialogue between scientists, stakeholders, and decision-makers as shown by (Bernard & Ostländer, 2008).

National Spatial Data Infrastructure implementation can particularly support evidence-based decision-making and policy development in Pakistan to mitigate governance challenges, as well as encourage sustainable development. Integration of land data from SDI appears to have the capacity to improve land management, minimize land disputes, and facilitate better planning for sustainable use of these resources. In addition, the inclusion of environmental information such as air pollution and forest cover in SDI can allow for efficient monitoring of the environment and to manage resources.

CONCLUSION

The implementation of the National Spatial Data Infrastructure in Pakistan is presented with a case study about progress made and challenges faced for implementing an all-inclusive geospatially inclined framework. The ongoing feasibility study and economic benefits are highlighted. Various projects such as the Punjab Urban Land Systems Enhancement (PULSE) Project indicate a strong commitment to leveraging spatial data for informed decision-making and sustainable development.

However, there are several challenges associated with NSDI in Pakistan. Some of these serious challenges include the absence of uniform standards, a poor technology setup, and a shortage of qualified manpower. Data sharing and aggregation are additionally impeded by the lack of a national geoportal as well as diverse spatial data formats.

Policy Implications

There is an absolute requirement for a specific legislative framework that not only strengthens many organizations like the Survey of Pakistan but also puts forward the implementation and data governance policies transparently. Legal regulation would help to avoid redundancy in data gathering while advocating for collaboration and providing the groundwork needed for a trustworthy stakeholder relationship.

Standards need to be set and implemented for data exchange in the spatial data landscape. It is important to strive towards an understanding and implementation of recommended standard data formats, metadata standards, and quality control measures that are generally accepted to promote consistency between diverse datasets.

REFERENCES

Ahmad, M. (2023). Leveraging Blockchain for Spatial Data Infrastructure: Challenges and Opportunities. *Supporting Technologies and the Impact of Blockchain on Organizations and Society*, (pp. 177–194). IEEE.

Ahmad, M., & Ali, A. (2023a). A Review of Governance Frameworks for National Spatial Data Infrastructure. In A. Correia & P. B. Agua (Eds.), *Innovation, Strategy, and Transformation Frameworks for the Modern Enterprise* (pp. 186–207). IGI Global. doi:10.4018/979-8-3693-0458-7.ch008

Ahmad, M., & Ali, A. (2023b). Integrated Geospatial Information Management in the World of Metaverse. In P. Lekhi & G. Kaur (Eds.), *Concepts, Technologies, Challenges, and the Future of Web 3* (pp. 248–270). IGI Global. doi:10.4018/978-1-6684-9919-1.ch013

Ahmad, M., Ali, A., & Khiyal, M. S. H. (2023). Fog Computing for Spatial Data Infrastructure: Challenges and Opportunities. In Multi-Disciplinary Applications of Fog Computing: Responsiveness in Real-Time (pp. 152–178). IGI Global. doi:10.4018/978-1-6684-4466-5.ch008

Ahmad, M., Khayal, M. S. H., & Tahir, A. (2022). Analysis of Factors Affecting Adoption of Volunteered Geographic Information in the Context of National Spatial Data Infrastructure. *ISPRS International Journal of Geo-Information*, *11*(2), 120. doi:10.3390/ijgi11020120

Ali, A., & Imran, M. (2020). The Evolution of National Spatial Data Infrastructure in Pakistan-Implementation Challenges and the Way Forward. *International Journal of Spatial Data Infrastructures Research*, *15*(0).

Ali, A., Imran, M., Jabeen, M., Ali, Z., & Mahmood, S. A. (2021). Factors influencing integrated information management: Spatial data infrastructure in Pakistan. *Information Development*. doi:10.1177/02666669211048483

Bernard, L., & Ostländer, N. (2008). Assessing climate change vulnerability in the arctic using geographic information services in spatial data infrastructures. *Climatic Change*, *87*(1–2), 263–281. doi:10.1007/s10584-007-9346-0

Bishop, I. D., Escobar, F. J., Karuppannan, S., Williamson, I. P., Yates, P. M., Suwarnarat, K., & Yaqub, H. W. (2000). Spatial data infrastructures for cities in developing countries. Lessons from the Bangkok experience. *Cities (London, England)*, *17*(2), 85–96. doi:10.1016/S0264-2751(00)00004-4

Boerboom, I. (2010). Integrating spatial planning and decision support system infrastructure and spatial data infrastructure. *GSDI 12 World Conference Singapore*. http://www.gsdi.org/gsdiconf/gsdi12/papers/82.pdf

Borzacchiello, M. T., & Craglia, M. (2013). Estimating benefits of spatial data infrastructures: A case study on e-Cadastres. *Computers, Environment and Urban Systems*, *41*, 276–288. doi:10.1016/j.compenvurbsys.2012.05.004

Brown, D. C. G., & Toze, S. (2017). Information governance in digitized public administration. *Canadian Public Administration*, *60*(4), 581–604. doi:10.1111/capa.12227

Buckland, M. K. (1991). Information as thing. *Journal of the American Society for Information Science*, *42*(5), 351–360. doi:10.1002/(SICI)1097-4571(199106)42:5<351::AID-ASI5>3.0.CO;2-3

Castro, A., Villagrá, V. A., García, P., Rivera, D., & Toledo, D. (2021). An ontological-based model to data governance for big data. *IEEE Access : Practical Innovations, Open Solutions*, *9*, 109943–109959. Advance online publication. doi:10.1109/ACCESS.2021.3101938

Cetl, V., Ivić, S. M., & Tomić, H. (2009). Improvement of national spatial data infrastructure as a public project of permanent character. *Kartografija i Geoinformacije, 8*(11).

Coleman, D. J., & Nebert, D. D. (1998). Building a North American Spatial Data Infrastructure. *Cartography and Geographic Information Systems*, *25*(3), 151–160. doi:10.1559/152304098782383098

Crompvoets, J., Vancauwenberghe, G., Bouckaert, G., & Vandenbroucke, D. (2011). Practices to develop spatial data infrastructures: Exploring the contribution to e-government. In *Practical Studies in E-Government*. Best Practices from Around the World. doi:10.1007/978-1-4419-7533-1_13

Crompvoets, J., Vancauwenberghe, G., Ho, S., Masser, I., & Timo De Vries, W. (2018). Governance of national spatial data infrastructures in Europe. *International Journal of Spatial Data Infrastructures Research*, *13*, 253–285.

Diaz, L., Remke, A., Kauppinen, T., Degbelo, A., Foerster, T., Stasch, C., Rieke, M., Schaeffer, B., Baranski, B., Bröring, A., & Wytzisk, A. (2012). Future SDI - Impulses from Geoinformatics research and IT trends. *International Journal of Spatial Data Infrastructures Research*, *7*. Advance online publication. doi:10.2902/1725-0463.2012.07.art18

Farradane, J. (1979). The nature of information. *Journal of Information Science*, *1*(1), 13–17. doi:10.1177/016555157900100103

Granell, C., Schade, S., & Hobona, G. (2011). Linked Data: Connecting Spatial Data Infrastructures and Volunteered Geographic Information. In Geospatial Web Services: Advances in Information Interoperability.

GSDI. (2004). Developing Spatial Data Infrastructures: The SDI Cookbook. In GSDI/Nebert.

Harvey, F. (2003). Developing geographic information infrastructures for local government: The role of trust. *The Canadian Geographer. Geographe Canadien*, *47*(1), 28–36. doi:10.1111/1541-0064.02e10

Hood, C., & Margetts, H. (2007). *The tools of government in the digital age*. Bloomsbury Publishing. doi:10.1007/978-1-137-06154-6

Hood, C. C. (1983). *The tools of government*. No Title. doi:10.1007/978-1-349-17169-9

Hulme, T. (2012). Information governance: Sharing the IBM approach. *Business Information Review, 29*(2), 99–104. doi:10.1177/0266382112449221

Kooper, M. N., Maes, R., & Lindgreen, E. E. O. R. (2011). On the governance of information: Introducing a new concept of governance to support the management of information. *International Journal of Information Management, 31*(3), 195–200. doi:10.1016/j.ijinfomgt.2010.05.009

Manfré, L., Hirata, E., Silva, J. B., Shinohara, E. J., Giannotti, M., Larocca, A. P. C., & Quintanilha, J. (2012). An Analysis of Geospatial Technologies for Risk and Natural Disaster Management. *ISPRS International Journal of Geo-Information, 1*(2), 166–185. doi:10.3390/ijgi1020166

Mansourian, A., Rajabifard, A., Valadan Zoej, M. J., & Williamson, I. (2006). Using SDI and web-based system to facilitate disaster management. *Computers & Geosciences, 32*(3), 303–315. Advance online publication. doi:10.1016/j.cageo.2005.06.017

Masser, I. (2019). Geographic Information Systems to Spatial Data Infrastructure. In Geographic Information Systems to Spatial Data Infrastructure. Taylor & Francis. doi:10.1201/9780429505904

McLaughlin, J., & Nichols, S. (1994). Developing a national spatial data infrastructure. *Journal of Surveying Engineering, 120*(2), 62–76. doi:10.1061/(ASCE)0733-9453(1994)120:2(62)

Mikalef, P., Krogstie, J., van de Wetering, R., Pappas, I. O., & Giannakos, M. N. (2018). Information governance in the big data era: Aligning organizational capabilities. *Proceedings of the Annual Hawaii International Conference on System Sciences, 2018-January*. IEEE. 10.24251/HICSS.2018.615

Mikalef, P., Pappas, I. O., Krogstie, J., & Giannakos, M. (2018). Big data analytics capabilities: A systematic literature review and research agenda. *Information Systems and e-Business Management, 16*(3), 547–578. doi:10.1007/s10257-017-0362-y

Mohammadi, H. (2008). *The Integration of multi-source spatial datasets in the context of SDI initiatives.* [PhD thesis. Department of Geomatics. The University of Melbourne].

Nedović-Budić, Z., Crompvoets, J., & Georgiadou, Y. (2011). Spatial data infrastructures in context: North and South. In *Spatial Data Infrastructures in Context*. North and South. doi:10.1201/b10857

Rajabifard, A., Binns, A., Masser, I., & Williamson, I. (2006). The role of sub-national government and the private sector in future spatial data infrastructures. *International Journal of Geographical Information Science, 20*(7), 727–741. doi:10.1080/13658810500432224

Rajabifard, A., Feeney, M. E. F., & Williamson, I. P. (2002). Future directions for SDI development. *International Journal of Applied Earth Observation and Geoinformation, 4*(1), 11–22. doi:10.1016/S0303-2434(02)00002-8

Rees, N., Holding, K., & Sujan, M. (2023). Information governance as a socio-technical process in the development of trustworthy healthcare AI. *Frontiers of Computer Science, 5*, 1134818. doi:10.3389/fcomp.2023.1134818

Tallon, P. P., Ramirez, R. V., & Short, J. E. (2013). The information artifact in IT governance: Toward a theory of information governance. *Journal of Management Information Systems, 30*(3), 141–178. Advance online publication. doi:10.2753/MIS0742-1222300306

Tasci, A. D. A., Wei, W., & Milman, A. (2020). Uses and misuses of the case study method. *Annals of Tourism Research*, *82*, 102815. Advance online publication. doi:10.1016/j.annals.2019.102815

Tu, Y., Li, Q., & Mao, X. (2009). Research on the conceptual model of spatial data infrastructure for natural disaster management. *Sixth International Symposium on Digital Earth: Models, Algorithms, and Virtual Reality, 7840*. SPIE. 10.1117/12.871969

Wang, H., Meng, H., Zhang, L., Chen, Z., & Wang, S. (2020). Data System Configuration and Organizing and Management Technologies of Information System. *Journal of Physics: Conference Series*, *1575*(1), 012057. doi:10.1088/1742-6596/1575/1/012057

Weber, K., Otto, B., & Österle, H. (2009). Ones size does not fit all -A contingency approach to data governance. *ACM Journal of Data and Information Quality*, *1*(1), 1–27. Advance online publication. doi:10.1145/1515693.1515696

Chapter 12
Navigating the Legal Landscape of Information Governance

Hemendra Singh
O.P. Jindal Global University, India

ABSTRACT

There has been a massive increase in information volume in the modern business environment. This means that it has become very important to understand the complex relationship between information governance and the legal framework. This chapter aims to explore the various dimensions that define this intersection. It provides a comprehensive examination of general data protection regulation as a global legal framework for information governance. It also examines sector specific regulations, legal implications of information management and real-world cases to see how organizations can proactively address the legal dimensions of information governance. By exploring different dimensions of this intersection, this chapter serves as a strategic guide for organizations that want to strengthen their information governance frameworks.

INTRODUCTION

Ensuring proper governance of information has become vital for an organization's success within an evolving commercial landscape. The abundance and intricacy of information have been continuously rising each day and corporations must manoeuvre an intricate legal structure influencing how they address and protect sensitive material. This chapter offers an exhaustive review of the delicate connection between information governance and the legal framework. This shall act as a useful manual for companies searching to develop their information governance structure in accordance with legal standards.

The development of information governance within legal frameworks has been a constantly changing process, shaped by technological advancements and regulatory initiatives. It has come a long way from its origins in paper-based records management to the present era of digitalization. Initially, laws and regulations provided fundamental guidance for record-keeping practices, but the rise of computers and the internet demanded more comprehensive frameworks to manage electronic data and privacy concerns. The creation of extensive data protection laws signifies a growing recognition of the importance

DOI: 10.4018/979-8-3693-0472-3.ch012

of safeguarding personal data in the digital age. As technology continues to evolve, legal frameworks for information governance will need to adapt to address emerging challenges and ensure compliance with evolving regulatory standards (Smallwood, 2019).

It is imperative for businesses globally to comprehend the legal framework not solely for regulatory necessities but as a strategic importance (Tanaka, 2019). One of the most substantial legislations regarding this is the General Data Protection Regulation (GDPR). It has substantially transformed the approach to information protection across the world. The initial segment of this chapter delves into the subtleties of GDPR including its principles, results and its profound effect on information governance practices. By having a clear comprehension of GDPR, organizations can guarantee consistency with the legal framework and practice responsible and moral information administration practices.

The next part of the chapter delves deeper and centres around how information governance connects to regulations particular to certain fields. Industries for example healthcare, financial services, technology, and communications work inside unique legal structures, each with their own set of obstacles and demands to comply with. By understanding these industry-specific regulations, companies can customize their information governance approaches to synchronize with sector benchmarks, decrease hazards, and guarantee a strong legal position.

Third portion of the chapter delves deeply into the intricate legal issues regarding information maintenance and storage, concentrating on e-discovery and legal holds. Since electronic information can considerably affect legal matters, it is extremely important for companies to understand the lawful consequences of managing information. This segment provides useful understandings to assist companies in navigating e-discovery procedures and legal holds, guaranteeing they satisfy their lawful duties.

To strengthen theoretical concepts with practical real-world situations, the final section of the chapter draws inspiration from genuine legal disputes. By studying high-profile cases such as Zubulake, Equifax, and Anthem Inc, we investigate the difficulties companies face in their information governance endeavours. These case studies function as warning signs and useful sources of insights gathered, assisting organizations in building sturdy information governance structures that can withstand legal examination.

Essentially, this chapter is a guide for organizations that want to stay ahead and take care of the legal aspects of managing their information. It looks at GDPR, specific rules for different sectors, the legal aspect of handling information, and examples from the real world. This will help businesses to not just meet but even stay ready for the changing legal requirements of our digital world. Existing literature often provides general overviews of information governance principles but lacks an in-depth exploration of specific legal issues that organizations face. This chapter aims to fill these gaps by providing a comprehensive analysis of the legal framework surrounding information governance.

LEGAL FRAMEWORK OF INFORMATION GOVERNANCE

The General Data Protection Regulation constitutes a pivotal framework devised to protect personal privacy in today's persistently transforming digital sphere. This regulation was presented by the European Union in 2018 and signifies a fundamental shift in how individual's information is dealt with. The GDPR responds to the complications posed by emerging technologies and strives to confirm that individuals' information is safeguarded.

Key Principles of GDPR

The GDPR outlines a series of guiding principles that form the ethical basis for handling people's information. These standards are Lawfulness, Fairness, and Transparency - promoting transparent and legal practices regarding information (Dumas, 2019). Limiting Purpose and Data Minimization encourage companies to only gather necessary details for specific reasons, aligning with minimizing unnecessary stockpiling of information. The GDPR also gives people control over their own information through rights like access, correction, and removal, empowering individuals in the age of big data collecting vast amounts of information.

The GDPR establishes concepts such as Data Protection by Design and by Default, assigning organizations accountability to integrate privacy safeguards into their procedures (Bygrave, 2017). Furthermore, it advocates for a risk-based method and employing Information Protection Impact Evaluations (DPIAs) to examine and reduce possible dangers linked to handling information.

GDPR has had widespread effects, as its extraterritorial application makes it relevant for organizations everywhere. The onestop-shop mechanism streamlines international data sharing, exemplifying the global coordination required. GDPR signifies more than rules; it demands a change in mindset, challenging businesses to reconsider how they manage information. It stresses compliance, for sure, but also ethical practices, openness, and collective accountability for protecting the digital world.

GDPR Compliance Requirements for Information Governance

For any information handling activities falling under the General Data Protection Regulation, establishing a valid legal ground is paramount. There are a few potential lawful bases recognized: contract necessitation, compliance with legal duties, essential interest safeguarding, consent provision, public task fulfilment, or legitimate interests of either the information controller or third parties. Proper identification and recording of the applicable lawful basis justifying each and every instance of personal information processing is indispensable. All processing operations must relate with one of the specified lawful grounds.

The General Data Protection Regulation places importance on Data Limitation and Purpose Specification. It encourages organizations to collect only the information necessary for the intended purpose. This methodology promotes a mindful approach to information collection and discourages indiscriminate accumulation of information. It advocates a culture of data minimalism. Organisations have to follow these principles to remain compliant with the Geneal Data Protection Regulation. Ensuring compliance with GDPR regulations means organizations must comprehend and enable data subject rights. Individuals possess the right to be aware of what personal information is being utilized, the right to correct inaccuracies, the right to deletion under specific situations, and the right to dispute processing activities. Companies ought to establish methods to honor these rights, empowering individuals to govern their personal information.

When it comes to handling information, the General Data Protection Regulation (GDPR) needs businesses to do Data Protection Impact Assessments (DPIAs). These are for activities with high risks. DPIAs let businesses look at how their information processing operations will affect people and their personal information (Joshua, 2018). DPIAs enable businesses to identify areas of vulnerability and implement robust controls to safeguard individuals' personal data. Furthermore, DPIAs serve as a proactive mechanism for mitigating risks, allowing organizations to stay ahead of regulatory requirements and evolving privacy threats. This active way of managing risks fits into GDPR's overall plan for handling potential risks.

Companies handling vast amounts of information fall under new regulations mandating the appointment of Data Protection Officers (DPOs). These assigned people oversee compliance, confirming the company follows the General Data Protection Regulation standards. The DPOs help interaction with overseeing bodies, offer guidance on Data Protection Impact Assessments, and serve as contacts for individuals whose information is being used (Smouter-Umans, 2017).

The General Data Protection Regulation mandates robust security precautions for guarding individual information. Companies must establish ways to confirm the secrecy, integrity, and accessibility of information. In unfortunate circumstances where information is compromised, GDPR necessitates fast notifications of such incidents to both overseeing agencies and impacted persons, cultivating openness and allowing quick steps to alleviate potential damage. Within our modern interconnected world, the GDPR includes rules governing how personal information moves globally. Businesses can share customer information outside the European Union only if appropriate safeguards are in place. This stipulation demonstrates the careful balance strived for between enabling international information sharing and protecting individual privacy.

Following GDPR's stringent stipulations demands a comprehensive and continuous dedication to privacy and information management. Organizations must weave these principles into their information governance structures, cultivating an atmosphere of responsibility and liability. In doing so, they satisfy not just legal duties but also contribute to a digital environment where people can believe that their individual information is treated with the utmost care and regard.

Impact of GDPR on Global Organizations

When the European Union enacted the General Data Protection Regulation in 2018, it had major consequences for how companies manage information on a global scale. This new regulation elevated information privacy standards within the EU and applied to any organization doing business with European citizens, regardless of physical location (Wang, 2020). GDPR triggered a complete change in how information is collected, maintained, and safeguarded everywhere. No longer could information be collected and kept without purpose or oversight. Personally identifiable details now required careful handling and protection under this new legal framework. While challenging for many to implement, GDPR helped strengthen privacy as a basic right for internet users in Europe and beyond.

GDPR had a major effect because of how far its power extends. Even if a company operates from outside the European Union, it must still follow GDPR's rules for handling personal information from any EU customer. This global impact made businesses everywhere reconsider how carefully they manage people's private information. Now all organizations, no matter where located, needed strong plans to protect client details per GDPR's rigorous requirements.

The General Data Protection Regulation has become a driving factor in promoting standardized information protection practices globally. Organizations operating across multiple regions must take a uniform stance on handling personal information (Anand, 2023). This helps them efficiently meet all legal requirements regardless of location. The push for consistent approaches stems not just from regulations but also from an expanding understanding of how crucial it is to respect privacy internationally. No matter where customers reside, protecting their personal information deserves equal care and attention.

The General Data Protection Regulations focus on strengthening an individual's control over their information has deeply influenced how global companies engage with people around the world. The principles of the GDPR, like the ability to view, change, and remove personal information, have established a gold standard for customer-oriented information management. This movement providing more openness and empowering each person has become a leading idea for organizations navigating the intricate landscape of worldwide information governance.

The arrival of the GDPR's principle of responsibility has inspired companies globally to embrace a culture of accountability. The regulation requires that organizations must show compliance rather than simply state it. Because of this, businesses have built robust governance systems, internal rules, and documentation procedures that advance a proactive and answerable way of handling information.

Organizations around the world must now make Data Protection Impact Assessments a top priority for managing risks proactively, no matter where they are located. By including DPIAs in their information governance plans, companies can find and lessen dangers connected to how they handle information. This allows them to make choices about processing information with full knowledge of potential issues on a global level. Moving information across international borders has become a challenge for global corporations as they strive to balance business needs with Europe's stringent standards for sharing information. This has compelled companies to reevaluate how they handle people's information and put steps in place to protect privacy no matter where a person lives. Juggling the demands of operating worldwide while respecting an individual's right to control their own information is a complex balancing act with no easy answers. Firms must thoughtfully design processes with oversight to ensure respect for all affected.

Large multinational businesses function within intricate systems of sellers and third-party ties. The consequences of the General Data Protection Regulation have spilled over into these systems, compelling companies to confirm that their suppliers and associates follow similar information security protocols. This has induced a chain response of adherence, where the GDPR's principles are implemented at each degree of the worldwide commercial community.

Essentially, GDPR has radically changed how global businesses govern information. From adjusting compliance protocols to fostering an atmosphere of accountability and openness, GDPR has vastly impacted how organizations deal with information internationally. As regulations keep progressing, the lessons extracted from GDPR serve as a roadmap for companies to guarantee that safeguarding information is not simply a legal duty, but also a basic part of moral and conscientious commercial behaviour.

GDPR and CCPA

Comparing the General Data Protection Regulation (GDPR) in the European Union with enactments such as the California Consumer Privacy Act (CCPA) in the United States reveals both shared objectives and notable distinctions. Both frameworks prioritize safeguarding individuals' personal data and promote transparency and accountability in data processing practices. They afford individuals rights over their data and apply extraterritorially, impacting organizations beyond their respective jurisdictions. However, differences emerge in their scope, consent mechanisms, enforcement mechanisms, and specific rights granted to data subjects. While GDPR mandates opt-in consent and imposes significant fines for non-compliance, CCPA focuses on opt-out mechanisms and provides for statutory damages and enforcement actions by the California Attorney General (Voss, 2021). Additionally, GDPR includes provisions such as data portability and the right to object to automated decision-making, which are not explicitly mirrored in CCPA. These distinctions underscore the need for organizations to carefully assess and address the nuanced requirements of each regulatory framework when developing comprehensive data protection and privacy compliance strategies on a global scale.

NAVIGATING REGULATORY COMPLIANCE FOR INFORMATION GOVERNANCE

Navigating today's intricate business environment necessitates that companies adhere to sector-specific rules. However, these guidelines are far from uniform and fluctuate contingent on the nation or area where an organization functions. Formed according to lawful, societal, financial, and cultural settings, these sector-specific guidelines may share comparable aims but have divergent standards, expectations, and oversight approaches. This section will zoom in on sector-specific regulations within the United States and how organizations work to comprehend various necessities.

Healthcare Sector

Healthcare sector is always changing and keeping patient information private is very important. The Health Insurance Portability and Accountability Act (HIPAA) plays a big role in protecting patient privacy and securing their information. However, with how common digital data is today, healthcare groups must also use strong information rules. This helps make sure they follow HIPAA and keep patient information safe and true. Passed in 1996, HIPAA aims to protect the secrecy and safety of patient information. It wants to make sure their information stays private, safe, and can be used when needed. The law includes different rules. The Privacy Rule and Security Rule are especially important for information governance.

Privacy Rule: A set of guidelines known as the Privacy Rule establishes regulations for how Protected Health Information, or PHI, can be used and shared. Healthcare providers and other covered organizations must receive a patient's permission for certain PHI uses and closely follow disclosure directions (Sloan, 2014). These standards aim to balance appropriate information access with safeguarding privacy.

Security Rule: The Security Rule works alongside the Privacy Rule by establishing protections for electronic personal health information (ePHI). Healthcare providers and insurers must implement precautions to prevent unauthorized access, use, and sharing of ePHI without permission.

Information Governance in Healthcare

Guiding information through its entire lifespan requires great care and planning. An organization must thoughtfully handle information from the moment it arrives to its final departure. This comprehensive approach includes establishing policies, outlining processes, and utilizing technologies. In the healthcare field specifically, implementing an effective information governance strategy is crucial. It allows an organization to maintain compliance with HIPAA regulations and ensure patient information remains safe. To accomplish this, systems must be developed to identify and classify sensitive information (Wilkes, 2014). This enables better control and protection of information. Clear guidelines must also be set regarding how long information is kept. The policies should specify the needed time periods while minimizing the risk of unauthorized access.

Maintaining privacy of personal health information through stringent access protocols is essential for adherence to HIPAA regulations. Supplementing security with encryption offers additional safeguarding of information (Hsieh, 2014). Consistently overseeing entry and dealings regarding individual records is likewise indispensable. Logs can furnish a thorough history of who got to what specifics and when, helping with conformity audits and examinations. Human blunders are a noteworthy factor in information breaches. Therefore, broad training programs can guarantee mindfulness of HIPAA necessities and best hones for taking care of sensitive information.

The field of healthcare is constantly changing, bringing new issues and chances for information governance. The growth of telemedicine, more use of health applications, and efforts to allow different computer systems to communicate to each other produce extra difficulties that organizations must sort out while keeping to HIPAA compliance (Frazee, Finley, & Rohack, 2016). The rising use of telemedicine in healthcare demands that practices for information governance be applied to virtual platforms too. This guarantees that patient details are securely transmitted and kept during remote consultations.

Protecting patient privacy while enabling seamless information sharing within the healthcare industry requires prudent reflection on security and privacy precautions. Information governance needs to adapt to back these efforts as adherence to HIPAA rules is maintained. Navigating where HIPAA and information governance intersect is pivotal for healthcare organizations dedicated to safeguarding patient information. By establishing robust policies, harnessing innovative technologies, and nurturing a culture of adherence, healthcare providers can guarantee the privacy, accuracy, and accessibility of patient information in today's increasingly digital world.

It is imperative that healthcare institutions remain cognizant of the ever-changing nature of the industry in order to protect patient privacy. As new developments arise, organizations must carefully monitor emerging patterns to ensure compliant practices under HIPAA rules. This close attention allows institutions to respect patient confidence by securing sensitive information through adaptive information management.

Financial Sector

The world of finance functions within a complex set of rules implemented by governing organizations. These regulations strive for stability, consumer protection, and fair markets. Several agencies oversee the system, such as the Securities and Exchange Commission and the Federal Reserve. On a national and global scale, additional regulators monitor institutions. Their aim is upholding security and safeguarding sensitive client information. A labyrinth of requirements exists to shield information and guard consumers. Overall, this framework works to provide structure, oversight, and recourse within the financial sector.

When the Gramm-Leach-Bliley Act (GLBA) was passed in 1999, it required financial institutions to establish steps protecting customers' private and secure information (Shroff, 2005). Companies must create and enforce information security programs containing policies and procedures shielding non-public personal details. The programs must protect client information confidentiality whether the information is on paper files or digital formats. Institutions adopting a zero-tolerance stance towards information breaches better serve clients through maintaining privacy and building trust.

The Sarbanes Oxley Act, also known as SOX, was passed in 2002 in response to several major corporate accounting scandals. SOX requires all public companies to implement and sustain internal controls over their financial reporting. While the legislation itself does not center around information governance, SOX underscores the significance of information precision, dependability, and protection in financial reporting procedures. By stressing the importance of accurate, reliable, and secure information in a company's financials, SOX highlights how governance impacts reporting even if not directly addressed.

It is extremely important for organizations that handle credit card transactions to follow the Payment Card Industry Data Security Standard (PCI DSS). This standard lays out necessary precautions for securely managing payment card information, focusing on encrypting information, controlling who can access it, and routinely evaluating security measures. Regular security assessments are emphasized to verify that protocols are properly safeguarding customers' sensitive financial details from theft or misuse. Strict compliance is required to maintain trust in electronic commerce and protect consumers

Information Governance in the Financial Sector

Within the financial sector, successful information management extends beyond mere regulatory obedience. It represents a pivotal strategic necessity for mitigating hazards, confirming information precision, and sustaining customers' faith. To process the extensive assortment of information, spanning from consumer particulars to market-sensitive insights, financial establishments require a resilient information categorization framework. Such a framework guarantees that information is treated fittingly depending on its sensitivity, thereby diminishing the prospect of unauthorized admission and potential information security gaps.

Financial institutions have a duty to protect sensitive client information and systems from persistent cyber threats (Arner, Castellano, & Selga, 2023). Conducting thorough security evaluations on a consistent basis, alongside vulnerability testing and innovative security solutions, helps ensure prompt detection and remediation of potential risks that could jeopardize confidential information. Well-defined policies for information preservation are also critical, outlining expectations for maintaining compliance-driven documentation in a controlled manner while appropriately removing outdated files to lessen vulnerabilities. It is important that record-keeping practices balance legal obligations with proactive risk reduction, retaining only what is necessary for oversight according to clear timeframes while minimizing extraneous materials that could enable unauthorized access, should defenses be compromised. Safeguarding client trust requires ongoing diligence across multiple dimensions.

The management of risk associated with third parties is equally crucial as financial institutions regularly depend on outside vendors to provide various services. Conducting thorough due diligence, creating contractual agreements, and continuous monitoring are essential to confirming adherence to information security protocols and preserving customer confidence.

Technology and Communications

Within the technology and communications industry, companies must navigate a complex global regulatory environment addressing critical issues. This framework oversees information privacy, cybersecurity, and ensuring new technologies are handled responsibly. Around the world, regulations seek to establish standards for protecting user information, strengthening security, and guiding development with care. It is an ecosystem requiring attentiveness to diverse international rules.

The California Consumer Privacy Act is the comprehensive state legislation in America that focuses on information privacy. It offers Californians specific rights regarding their personal information. Companies must unveil how they gather information, make provisions to opt out, and securely protect sensitive information (Harris, 2020).

Several nations around the globe, including the United States, rely heavily on the Telecommunications Act to structure the telecom industry. The Act tackles important matters like safeguarding Consumer

Proprietary Network Information (CPNI) and fostering competition within the field. By establishing consistent guidelines, it aims to protect users while also promoting innovation among telecom providers.

Moreover, the Network and Information Systems Directive (NISD) aim to boost cyber protection of essential services and online service providers across the European Union. Under these guidelines, operators of these services and providers must adopt security measures to safeguard network and information systems.

Information Governance in Technology and Communications

The technology and communications field progresses swiftly, necessitating that companies take a proactive, flexible approach to governing information. To accomplish this, organizations in this area must emphasize particular important factors, such as:

1. Information collection should be limited and specifically purposed. This principle involves gathering solely the pertinent information needed for clear and legal objectives. Restricting information collection in this way helps to decrease the risk of approved access being exceeded and stops concerns about private details being mishandled.
2. Cybersecurity safeguards are indispensable as cyber risks multiply. Regular risk evaluations, encryption practices, and response mechanisms are essential to defend information and confirm the correctness of information. Routinely assessing vulnerabilities can help recognize and plug security gaps before exploitation. Encrypting sensitive files and communications makes stolen information unusable. Preparing response plans ahead of time equips organizations to act decisively if incidents occur.
3. Establishing ethical standards is crucial when emerging technologies like artificial intelligence and the internet of things are implemented. Organizations must develop guidelines to ensure technologies are used transparently, fairly, and with accountability.
4. International Information Sharing: Adhering to regulations frequently necessitates traversing the intricacies of sharing information across borders. Companies must implement mechanisms like standardized contractual clauses and binding corporate policies to legitimately allow information to flow globally.

Other Industry-Specific Regulations

Companies function inside an intricate network of rules that oversee numerous aspects of their activities. To practice strong information governance, corporations must adhere to information security regulations like the General Data Protection Regulation and take into account the subtle necessities developing from various industries.

Environmental regulations present companies with complex challenges. The Environmental Protection Agency (EPA) takes the lead in enforcing regulations such as the Clean Air Act, Clean Water Act, and Resource Conservation and Recovery Act in the United States. These laws establish strict standards for air and water quality, waste management, and how businesses handle hazardous materials. Within the European Union, the Emissions Trading System (EU ETS) places limits on pollution emissions for industries that use large amounts of energy. It also encourages lower emissions by allowing companies trade pollution allowances. To guarantee compliance with these rules, businesses need a robust information governance strategy. This strategy must provide transparency and responsibility when handling environmental data.

Energy policy differs around the world and from location to location, with National Energy Policy Act in the United States establishing guidelines for energy generation, transmission, and utilization. These rules incorporate goals for renewable resources, benchmarks for energy efficacy, and eco-friendly techniques. Furthermore, many localities have Renewable Energy Standards (RES) that need a part of overall energy sourcing from sustainable alternatives, necessitating firms adopt methods and solutions synchronized with aims for sustainability. Managing information associated with production, usage, and adherence to such benchmarks involves information governance in the energy industry.

Ensuring safety in manufacturing presents unique challenges that require diligent oversight. Standards established by the Occupational Safety and Health Administration (OSHA) aim to protect American workers through protocols like safety training and documentation. Internationally recognized certifications also factor in to demonstrate quality and environmental stewardship. ISO 9001 certification affirms a focus on quality management while ISO 14001 reflects a dedication to minimizing environmental impact. Effectively handling manufacturing information connected to safety, quality testing, and ecological consequences demands prudent information governance.

At its core, upholding information governance amid diverse industry regulations necessitates a holistic strategy. Companies must devise plans addressing ubiquitous information protection facets as well as catering to specific demands from environmental, energy, and manufacturing rules. This involves proactively overseeing information handling, fostering transparency and correctness, and ethical viewpoints to skilfully navigate the intricate regulatory environment.

LEGAL IMPLICATIONS OF INFORMATION MANAGEMENT AND RETENTION

Today's digital world allows information to flow smoothly within companies. This benefits operations but also creates challenges. As information proliferates, properly managing and keeping it carries legal duties. For organizations where electronic information underpins daily work, information handling affects legal issues profoundly. E-Discovery, a crucial process in lawsuits, necessitates companies skilfully navigating complexities around finding, safeguarding, and supplying electronically stored information. Similarly, legal hold procedures become critical when litigation threatens, requiring companies to freeze applicable information to avoid carelessly destroying it. A methodical approach to securely and transparently discarding information when allowed defines defensible disposal.

Electronic Discovery

In today's legal landscape, the electronic discovery (e-discovery) process is a pivotal yet important piece of legal matters. E-discovery refers to identifying, preserving, gathering, organizing, analysing, reviewing, and providing electronically stored information (ESI) that may be pertinent to legal cases. As companies progressively function within digital environments, comprehending the intricacies of e-discovery is not only a lawful necessity but also a strategic imperative for organizations aiming to safeguard their interests in the multifaceted world of electronic records.

The E-Discovery Process

Identifying and gathering electronically stored information (ESI) for legal reasons involves several important stages. The identification phase requires organizations to carefully find potential sources of applicable information. This includes comprehending where information is located, mapping out information storage areas, and pinpointing individuals who may possess pertinent information. Preservation comes next, where holds are put in place to stop the modification or deletion of possible evidence. This ensures the integrity of the information. The collection phase involves obtaining and assembling information from different sources. This demands meticulous attention to avoid corrupting information and keeping an accurate record of where the information came from.

The next step involves processing the collected information. Organizing and filtering the information ensures only relevant and usable material moves forward. This streamlining is crucial. It reduces the volume legal teams must analyse later on. Carefully processing the information ultimately saves valuable time and resources. The review phase then takes place where legal teams examine the processed information. They scrutinize it for relevance to the case, for privilege issues, and for any potential evidence. Advanced analytics and technology tools are increasingly used during this phase. They help speed up the review process and improve accuracy. Finally, the production phase involves presenting the pertinent electronic information in a format meeting legal guideline (Jaar, 2009). This facilitates open sharing and allows the evidence to be accepted in court.

Legal Challenges in E-Discovery

The process of electronic information discovery poses many challenges for legal teams. This is mainly due to the vast and complex nature of digital data. There is simply too much information to handle, often spread across multiple systems. Advanced tools and methods are needed to effectively find and analyse the information. Additionally, protecting sensitive information is a big concern. E-discovery regularly involves working with private information. Therefore, legal teams must follow privacy laws and take steps to safeguard personally identifying information during the process. While technology can create more efficiency, it also presents problems (Beisner, 2010). Legal teams have to adapt and understand how technologies such as data analytics and artificial intelligence may impact the process.

In today's digital landscape, understanding e-discovery is crucial for companies. To successfully navigate the online legal terrain, businesses require a thorough grasp of the e-discovery process, its challenges, and integrating technology. This ensures a justifiable and streamlined method for discovering electronic evidence. Organizations that truly comprehend e-discovery's nuances are better prepared to safeguard their legal interests and remain compliant in our constantly developing digital environment.

Legal Hold Proceedings

Within our ever-changing information landscape, companies must navigate various rules and lawful duties that demand vigilant oversight of information handling. A crucial part of this is Legal Hold, which is more than just a procedural task, it is a proactive regulatory step organizations must take when litigation seems likely. This part explores the nuanced role of Legal Hold under the expansive regulatory umbrella of information governance. It emphasizes its importance, the difficulties in enforcing it, and how central it is to maintaining legal adherence.

At the core, a Legal Hold is a legal process that demands companies to halt routine destruction of certain documents and electronically stored information (ESI) when litigation can reasonably be anticipated (Winslow & Malone, 2011). This proactive strategy intends to stop the destruction of applicable evidence, which is pivotal in sustaining information integrity and guaranteeing legal defensibility in possible legal actions.

A legal hold serves several important functions. First, it helps maintain evidence in its original form, which is critical for organizations to safeguard information integrity that may relate to legal issues. Secondly, a legal hold is key for fulfilling the compliance obligations established by various governing bodies and industry-specific rules. By temporarily halting regular information deletion processes, companies can satisfy their duty to retain applicable files and adhere to regulatory guidelines.

Adhering to a litigation hold is intertwined with wider information governance routines and acts as a pivotal part of an organization's regulatory adherence initiatives. This also involves coordinating with information security and privacy laws, which emphasize appropriately dealing with personal information. Moreover, implementing a litigation hold supports records management policies by temporarily stopping regular information deletion protocols, letting organizations fulfil their lawful duties to preserve relevant records. In industry-specific settings like healthcare under HIPAA rules, enacting a litigation hold plays a strategic role in confirming adherence.

Legal Hold is a vital process in information governance and plays a core role within the regulatory system. It represents more than just a routine procedural step as it also involves safeguarding evidence, adhering to legal duties, and reducing legal risks. In today's digital world, organizations must thoughtfully incorporate Legal Hold into their information governance practices in order to shield their legal and reputational interests. By properly setting priorities for and carrying out Legal Hold efficiently, companies can place themselves at the cutting edge of legal compliance and conscientious information oversight.

Implementing a litigation hold properly requires following established guidelines. The process must begin quickly once legal action is reasonably foreseen. Waiting to enact it risks important evidence being misplaced, jeopardizing an organization's position in potential suits. Clear, transparent coordination is vital, and all applicable parties like attorneys, tech staff, and record keepers must participate. Thorough paperwork on the litigation hold process, teamwork between lawyers and technologists, and consistent checks are core elements of a well-run implementation.

Defensible Disposal

Properly getting rid of information is an essential process that securely destroys information that is no longer important for business tasks or rules in a step-by-step and documented way. The term "defensible" emphasizes how organizations must be able to clarify and show the lawfulness and good sense of how they threw away records if questioned, investigated legally, or supervised closely.

Complying regulations is one of the main reasons companies choose defensible disposal. Businesses must abide by an intricate set of rules where laws similar to the General Data Protection Regulation (GDPR) and rules for particular industries demand accountable information handling. Thoughtful deletion guarantees accordance with these rules and helps lessen the danger of punishments for poorly managed or unapproved information access. As an organization, it should strive to respect people's privacy and do their part to protect sensitive information. While regulations aim to prevent misuse, defensible disposal helps ensure information removal in a way that respects both the letter and spirit of compliance.

Proper information removal also serves an important purpose in managing threats. Information that has outlived its usefulness, especially details made obsolete or unimportant by time, can pose security concerns. The larger an organization's information stockpile grows, the broader a target it presents to online dangers (Kiker, 2014). Responsible deletion aims to shrink this attack area by discarding information that might attract ill-intentioned individuals. While information must still support essential functions, removing excess helps strengthen an entity's protections.

Ensuring efficient use of resources is an important reason for adopting responsible deletion methods. When companies hold onto and administer excessive amounts of information that are not truly needed, it leads to supplementary costs such as expanded storage, tighter security, and more oversight. Responsible deletion helps organizations make the most of what they have by keeping only what is essential, simplifying processes, and decreasing non-essential spending. While information retention is normal and sometimes required, it is wise to evaluate what information remains important and what can be removed so the organization is not weighed down by surplus information. A balanced strategy allows focusing resources on forward progress rather than maintaining obsolete information.

Safeguarding organizational integrity and mitigating risks necessitates proactive strategies to dispose of information defensibly. As information assumes greater importance in business operations, adopting practices for responsibly disposing of information has become a vital step in managing it prudently and bolstering an organization's resilience overall. While defensible disposal represents best practices, following this approach helps shield the organization through a conscientious handling of its information assets.

NAVIGATING CHALLENGES IN INFORMATION GOVERNANCE

Companies grapple with intricate problems in Information Governance that necessitate profound comprehension of legal repercussions and proactive administration tactics. Three pivotal case studies, particularly Zubulake v. UBS Warburg LLC, the Equifax case, and the Anthem Inc. healthcare records violation, provide understandings into essential facets of information governance. These cases underscore the significance of legal structures, records privacy, and sturdy information administration practices, all of which intersect to generate a thorough Information Governance approach.

Challenges in Information Retention: Zubulake v. UBS Warburg LLC

During a legal battle that changed e-discovery and records management protocols, Laura Zubulake sued her former employer UBS Warburg for gender discrimination. Problems emerged in the litigation regarding how electronic documents were kept and shared. Zubulake's case highlighted the importance of organizations properly saving and providing digital files. UBS failed to preserve certain emails relevant to the allegations. This led to sanctions against the company for their mishandling of evidence materials. The rulings in Zubulake v. UBS established new responsibilities for companies to monitor electronic communication trails (Smallwood, 2019). Courts decided that employers must take active steps to retain workplace correspondences that could connect to potential legal issues.

For this case, the judges centred on uncovering digital evidence and the necessity of protecting electronic documents. The situation underscored the difficulties related to e-discovery by acknowledging how critical electronic records are to modern commercial and legal situations. The court stressed the duty of companies to shield applicable digital proof once litigation becomes reasonably expected. This resulted in the development of the legal hold procedure, which demands businesses to recognize and safeguard possibly pertinent material from being destroyed or lost.

The Zubulake rulings showed the serious repercussions of destroying evidence, with penalties enforced on UBS Warburg due to its inability to keep relevant electronic documents and provide them (Li, 2014). The case impacted how companies manage information, necessitating they actively take steps. Organizations had to put strong systems in place for finding, preserving, and handing over electronic evidence during legal battles.

The court decision underscored the crucial importance for companies to synchronize their technology and information governance policies to adhere to legal duties. They mandated that firms must have systems in place to ensure the suitable maintenance of electronically stored information. The Zubulake case brought attention to companies regarding their legal obligations related to information governance, particularly in the setting of possible litigation. It served as a trigger for enhancing information management and preservation practices.

The Zubulake case had a major effect on information governance, especially within legal circles. Its impact is clear in how e-discovery processes have changed over time and in the rising awareness among companies about the must for strong information governance to fulfil legal duties during lawsuits. Studying what happened in Zubulake gives important understandings into where legal systems intersect with information governance, emphasizing how essential it is to have a proactive and clear-cut strategy for handling electronic records in a legally compliant way.

Challenges in Information Privacy: The Equifax Case

The massive Equifax data breach back in 2017 drives home the vital need for strong information governance policies to safeguard user data and keep the public's trust. In September of that year, Equifax - one of the largest credit bureaus globally - fell prey to a huge cyberattack. The intruders capitalized on a weakness in the company's website, gaining illegal entry to nearly 147 million people's personal details. Individuals lost information containing their names, Social Security numbers, birthdates and, sometimes, even driver license numbers. With just one vulnerable point, so many lives became exposed. As guardians of sensitive financial facts, organizations must stay vigilant.

The Equifax data breach in 2017 teaches us how important it is for companies to carefully protect customer information and keep public trust. In September 2017, Equifax got hacked. Equifax is one of the biggest credit reporting companies in the world. The hackers took advantage of a problem in Equifax's website. This let them access the personal details of almost 147 million people without permission. The stolen information included names, Social Security numbers, birthdays, and sometimes even driver license numbers. Equifax faced investigations from various agencies including the Federal Trade Commission (FTC). Laws about protecting information and customer privacy became very important as Equifax got in big trouble for not guarding sensitive information adequately.

The Equifax data breach brought to light some important issues with how the company handled private information. The attack showed weaknesses in Equifax's technical security systems, highlighting the need for strong protections against unauthorized access (Kenny, 2018). Equifax received criticism for how it dealt with sensitive customer details. This event emphasized the significance of properly managing information through encryption and safely storing it away. Equifax faced resentment for not informing the public about the breach sooner. The delayed reaction destroyed trust and raised legal concerns around promptly reporting obligations.

Equifax's lack of oversight over its information led to serious legal and monetary repercussions. Government agencies, such as the FTC, levied hefty penalties on the company for failing to sufficiently safeguard consumer details. These penalties underscore the legal obligation of companies to establish vigorous information governance systems. Equifax faced numerous class lawsuits from affected persons due to the disclosure of their sensitive information. These legal proceedings exemplified the fiscal consequences of deficient information governance.

The Equifax data breach significantly influenced information management methods across various sectors. It motivated regulators to more closely examine information governance practices. Companies encountered increased demands to adhere to existing data security laws and execute stricter information security steps. The significance of clear communication during and following an information breach became apparent. Equifax's postponed disclosure highlighted the necessity for prompt and honest communication with impacted people and regulatory bodies. The breach prompted organizations to reassess and boost investments in cybersecurity measures. Information management became comparable with proactive cybersecurity strategies to prevent, find, and adequately react to possible dangers.

Healthcare Information Breach - Anthem Inc. (2015)

The year 2015 saw a notable occurrence within the healthcare sector when Anthem Inc., one of the largest health insurance firms in the United States, endured one of the most serious information infringements in its past. This breach served as a huge setback for both the company and the estimated 78.8 million current and former customers and workers impacted (McGee, 2017). Personal records from so many individuals unprotected highlighted vulnerabilities that threatened privacy and stirred concerns. A thorough review aimed to determine what allowed unauthorized access and how best to strengthen safeguards for sensitive information in the future, guiding efforts to regain trust while respecting those affected.

This security incident stemmed from cyber intruders deploying customized, sophisticated malware to access Anthem's records. Stored within this database was a bounty of individualized, delicate information - names, addresses, birthdays, social security numbers, and medical identification figures (Mills & Harclerode, 2017). The techniques utilized signalled how digital lawbreakers continually refine their strategies to infiltrate extensive databases. While the exact causes remain unclear, analysts agree the incident highlighted the evolving threats facing organizations and underscored the importance of vigilant protection measures.

The Anthem data breach quickly got the attention of important agencies like the U.S. health department and state legal offices. It showed them how easy it is for hackers to steal private medical information. This made protecting patients' health records a bigger priority. The attack proved that cybercrimes can seriously hurt people, especially in healthcare. Doctors and nurses need to keep patient details and test results very safe from hackers.

Anthem Inc.'s data breach carried substantial legal and financial consequences. The breach severely impacted Anthem, requiring the largest healthcare settlement at the time with HHS - a $16 million agreement. This underscored how crucial following HIPAA guidelines is for maintaining privacy and security of sensitive patient information. The breach's severity led Anthem into costly negotiations after such sensitive data lacked protection. Taxpayers understood protecting medical files as important, shown through endorsing the government penalty. Overall, companies learned from this that properly safeguarding confidential healthcare records aligned with legal compliance and preventable monetary loss.

This event had a deep influence on those impacted, exposing their private details and putting them in danger of fraud and theft. To help limit the damage, Anthem offered services to watch affected people's credit and identities. However, the situation highlighted how a health records hack can continue affecting people's privacy and money over time. It emphasized the necessity for organizations to have strong protections for sensitive information and stop these types of events from recurring down the road.

FINAL REFLECTIONS AND FUTURE CONSIDERATIONS

By concluding our thorough examination into the complex meeting point of information governance and the legal framework, it is becoming progressively obvious that successful governance of information is not exclusively a specialized or operational test, yet rather a legal necessity. Our journey through this chapter has uncovered the multifaceted nature of this relationship, featuring key contemplations that associations must address to thrive in a time controlled by information.

Throughout our examination, the tremendous importance of the General Data Protection Regulation has become clear as a pivotal influence shaping the global conversation surrounding information privacy and protection. By basing our comprehension in the principles and consequences of GDPR, organizations can construct not only compliant but also ethical and accountable information governance systems. This regulatory foundation delivers a rock-solid base for navigating the intricate legal landscape encompassing information.

When developing their framework concerning information, prioritizing governance strategies is crucial for organizations. These strategies must coordinate with legal standards and proven methods. With the GDPR acting as a major benchmark, companies can successfully handle their information, safeguard sensitive information, and respect individuals' privacy rights. By taking such steps, they can establish trust with stakeholders, encourage innovation, and gain an edge over competition in today's environment driven by information.

The rules that govern different industries emphasize the need for companies to tailor their information governance plans based on the particular challenges faced within each sector. No matter if you work in healthcare, finance, technology, or communications, addressing the specific compliance rules and risks related to that field is paramount. This understanding is critical when devising information governance methods that comply with regulatory expectations while also safeguarding the priorities of those involved. By recognizing industry unique demands, organizations can craft governance strategies balancing regulations and stakeholder interests.

When considering the legal implications of how organizations manage and store information, especially regarding the discovery of electronic information and legal preservation requirements, the importance of proactively governing information strategically becomes clear in limiting potential risks. Companies need to thoughtfully maintain and control information holdings, with a definite grasp of the duties linked to these activities. Possessing this awareness constructs an important safeguard versus possible legal disputes and allows organizations to handle legal processes with assurance.

Through analysing real world examples, the practical implications of breakdowns in information governance are highlighted. The Zubulake, Equifax, and Anthem Inc situations offer useful understandings into the difficulties companies face and the learnings they can gain from others' errors. These examples emphasize the significance of consistent progress in information governance routines to foresee and decrease legal dangers productively.

Ultimately, companies must acknowledge that legal issues are fundamental to their information governance plans. By skilfully combining adherence to regulations, moral practices, and a nuanced grasp of lawful consequences, enterprises can confidently traverse the intricacies of the legal environment. The travel toward successful information governance is continual, necessitating flexibility, watchfulness, and a dedication to upholding the maximum criteria of lawfulness and ethics in managing information.

The intersection of emerging technologies such as AI, blockchain, and IoT presents complex privacy challenges necessitating innovative regulatory frameworks. AI's ability to process vast amounts of personal information raises concerns regarding consent, transparency, and algorithmic bias. Blockchain, touted for its immutability, poses dilemmas in reconciling transparency with privacy, especially in public ledgers. IoT's ubiquity amplifies data collection, necessitating safeguards against unauthorized access and breaches. Regulatory strategies should encompass dynamic mechanisms adaptable to rapid technological advancements, emphasizing accountability, ethical guidelines, and international cooperation to navigate the evolving landscape of digital privacy.

DEFINITIONS

1. Information Governance - A comprehensive approach to managing and protecting organizational information assets while ensuring information integrity, security, and compliance.
2. General Data Protection Regulation - EU regulation which establish guidelines for responsible data management and empower individuals' privacy rights and imposes penalties for non-compliance.
3. E-Discovery: The systematic process of identifying, collecting, and producing electronically stored information (ESI) in response to legal requests or investigations.
4. Legal Hold: A legal directive requiring the preservation of relevant information during legal proceedings also preventing its alteration or deletion to maintain data integrity.
5. Proactive Information Governance: An approach that emphasizes anticipation and preparation for legal and regulatory changes, enabling organizations to stay ahead of compliance requirements
6. Defensible Disposal: A systematic and legally compliant process of permanently removing unnecessary information or records to mitigate legal and compliance risks while promoting efficient data management.
7. Consumer Proprietary Network Information (CPNI) is a sensitive information about a customer's usage, billing, and service details.

REFERENCES

Anand, A. (2023). GDPR and Healthcare: Balancing Data Privacy and access to medical information. *NUJS Journal of Regulatory Studies*, *8*(1), 27–35.

Arner, D. W., Castellano, G. G., & Selga, E. K. (2023). Financial Data Governance. *The Hastings Law Journal*, *74*(2), 235–292.

Beisner, J. H. (2010). Discovering a better way: The need for effective civil litigation reform. *Duke Law Journal*, *60*(3), 547–596. https://www.jstor.org/stable/27896012

Blume, J. (2018). Contextual extraterritoriality analysis of the DPIA and DPO provisions in the GDPR. *Georgetown Journal of International Law*, *49*(4), 1425–1460.

Bygrave, L. A. (2017). Data protection by design and by default: Deciphering the EU's legislative requirements. *Oslo Law Review*, *4*(2), 105–122. doi:10.18261/issn.2387-3299-2017-02-03

Dumas, J. (2019). General Data Protection Regulation (GDPR): Prioritizing resources. *Seattle University Law Review*, *42*(3), 1115–1128.

Frazee, J. J., Finley, M. M., & Rohack, J. J. (2016). mHealth and unregulated data: Is this farewell to patient privacy. *Indiana Health Law Review / [Indiana University School of Law-Indianapolis]*, *13*(2), 384–414. doi:10.18060/3911.0021

Harris, R. (2020). Forging path towards meaningful digital privacy: Data monetization and the CCPA. *Loyola of Los Angeles Law Review*, *54*(1), 197–234.

Hsieh, Roger. (2014). Improving HIPAA enforcement and protecting patient privacy in digital healthcare environment. *Loyola University Chicago Law Journal*, *46*(1), 175-224.

Jaar, D. (2009). E-discovery tips for everyday cases how to put the process in perspective. *Law Practice*, *35*(2), 50–54.

Kenny, C. (2018). The Equifax data breach and the resulting legal recourse. Brooklyn Journal of Corporate. *Financial & Commercial Law*, *13*(1), 215–238.

Kiker, D. R. (2014). Defensible Data Deletion: A Practical Approach to Reducing Cost and Managing Risk Associated with Expanding Enterprise Data. *Richmond Journal of Law and Technology*, *20*(2).

Li, V. (2014). Zubulake 10 Years After: Landmark case created an industry-and still stirs debate. *ABA Journal*, *100*(9), 48–53. https://www.jstor.org/stable/44653176

McGee, M. K. (2017). *New In-Depth Analysis: Anthem Breach*. BankInfoSecurity. https://www.bankinfosecurity.com/new-in-depth-analysis-anthem-breach-a-9627

Mills, J. L., & Harclerode, Kelsey. (2017). Privacy, mass intrusion, and the modern data breach. *Florida Law Review*, *69*(3), 771–830.

Shroff, J. (2005). California: Privacy Statute Meets the GLBA & (and) FCRA. North Carolina Banking Institute, 9, 223-242.

Sloan, P. (2014). The Compliance Case for Information Governance. *Richmond Journal of Law and Technology*, *20*(2).

Smallwood, R. F. (2019). *Information Governance: Concepts, Strategies, and Best Practices* (2nd ed.). Wiley. doi:10.1002/9781119491422

Smouter-Umans, K. L. (2017). Research, GDPR, and the DPO how GDPR changes the game for those conducting research and the data supervisors. International Journal for the Data Protection Officer [iv]. *Privacy Officer and Privacy Counsel*, *1*(1), 26.

Tanaka, H. (2019). Impact of the GDPR on Japanese companies. *Business Law International, 20*(2), 137–146.

TyagiA. (2021). Information Governance Program Implementation and Strategies in Banking Sector. http://dx.doi.org/ doi:10.2139/ssrn.3804620

Voss, W. G. (2021). The CCPA and the GDPR Are Not the Same: Why You Should Understand Both. *CPI Antitrust Chronicle, 1*(1). https://www.competitionpolicyinternational.com/the-ccpa-and-the-gdpr-are-not-the-same-why-you-should-understand-both/

Wang, F. Y. (2020). Cooperative Data Privacy: The Japanese model of data privacy and the EU-Japan GDPR adequacy agreement. *Harvard Journal of Law & Technology, 33*(2), 661–692.

Wilkes, J. J. (2014). The creation of HIPAA culture: Prioritizing privacy paranoia over patient care. *Brigham Young University Law Review, 2014*(5), 1213–1250.

Winslow, T., & Malone, J. (2011). Don't hold back: When and how corporate counsel should implement litigation hold. *Jurimetrics, 51*(3), 245–278.

Chapter 13
Information Governance for Public Authorities:
An Indian Perspective

Kirt Agarwal
Dr. B.R. Ambedkar University, Delhi, India

Sneha Hooda
O.P. Jindal Global University, India

Shashank Maheshwari
O.P. Jindal Global University, India

ABSTRACT

In an era dominated by digital transformation, public authorities globally face a profound challenge in effectively managing and governing the burgeoning volumes of information under their purview. Using specific case study of teacher attendance monitoring system (TAMS) in State of Meghalaya, this chapter seeks to explore the landscape of information governance within the context of public authorities in India. As the country undergoes significant advancements in digital infrastructure and governance, understanding the nuances of information governance becomes imperative for ensuring transparency, accountability, and optimal service delivery. This chapter aims to provide a comprehensive analysis of the current state of information governance in Indian public authorities, identifying key challenges, proposing strategic solutions, and offering insights into the potential impact on public administration and citizen engagement.

INTRODUCTION

Governance refers to the processes adopted to address a common cause and devise mechanisms to regulate it afterward. When public institutions uphold the rights of citizens while addressing their issues, the scheme is called good governance. Among others, the two main components of good governance

DOI: 10.4018/979-8-3693-0472-3.ch013

remain 'transparent and accountable processes and institutions' and 'sustainability' to reach the ultimate development goal (About Good Governance, n.d.). These ensure that fundamental human rights, such as the right to education and privacy, are effectively implemented. Without a good governance setup, society cannot see the progression of human rights.

The institutional bodies of the State can act as torchbearers of the governance model through custom-made strategies and programs. In the digital age, strategy requires technology to discover newer and sustainable solutions for niche problems. Information access, storage, and security are all handled by well-developed information management strategies in most government agencies. Nevertheless, these have frequently developed at the departmental level to address single solutions. Furthermore, government agencies often implement knowledge management initiatives to identify the value of this data. Managing the information explosion in the digital age to foster greater cooperation and direct government access while safeguarding personal information and privacy is challenging. A comprehensive information governance plan is needed for this.

This chapter first introduces the reader to the advantages of digital tools deployment in service delivery by the government, highlighting good governance strategies of the Indian administration. It then utilizes a recent technology adoption move by the education department of East Jaintia Hills in Northeast State of Meghalaya, India to highlight how the good governance aspiration of State entities hinders the privacy rights of its employees. It further explores the possibility of creating a consent-based database of employees with enhanced security features and with option of deleting personal information once the employee leaves. The intermediary apps being used in the process of good governance should also be made accountable in case of data breach.

Methodology

The chapter uses doctrinal methods of analysis. It engages with literature, legal frameworks, and case studies related to information governance in public authorities, both within India and globally. It utilizes case laws that have been decided by the Indian Supreme Court and relevant High Courts, reports of government entities on privacy concerns, House debates on the Digital Personal Data Protection Bill, 2023 (hereinafter referred to as DPDP Act) in India, and the general outline of education and good governance setup. Media reports will be used only to highlight the current debates and suggest a theoretical information governance model by public authorities owing to their particular responsibilities and limited resources.

Expected Outcomes

1. Comprehensive assessment:

Offer an all-encompassing evaluation of the information governance situation in Indian public authorities, stressing advantages, disadvantages, possibilities, and risks.

2. Strategic Recommendations:

Make recommendations that are specifically suited to the Indian environment, taking into account changes for improvement and resolving issues that have been highlighted.

3. Effect on Public Administration:

Examine how better information governance may affect public administration, focusing on how expedited procedures may boost administrative effectiveness and service delivery.

4. Citizen-Centric Governance:

Examine how healthy information governance and citizen-centric government are related, focusing on how transparent and accountable information practices promote public involvement and confidence.

Significance of Study

This research is significant as it addresses a critical gap in the literature concerning information governance in the context of Indian public authorities. The chapter intends to inform policymakers, administrators, and academics by understanding the existing conditions and difficulties. This will facilitate the development of focused measures to strengthen information governance frameworks. Ultimately, the chapter aims to further the current conversation about efficient public administration in the digital era, with consequences for national and international governance methodologies.

GOOD GOVERNANCE

India's continued pursuit of good governance is viewed with scepticism because of its many obstacles and complexities. Still, among the maze of problems, some admirable efforts show promise for improvement. Here, we examine four current strategies from various industries, stressing their advantages and disadvantages to provide a window of opportunity within the system. The following projects undertaken by the Indian administration system underscores the advantage of employing digital tools in service delivery wings of the government. It highlights the keenness within the governance structure to adopt technology due to the ease of reach through mobile communication devices and wider audience. Reaching out to people to make them aware of such adoption moves and launch of newer schemes has become easier and quicker for the administration. The four schemes mentioned below have incorporated digital medium in multiple ways to connect with the stakeholders-

Mission Shakti: Empowering Women Entrepreneurship (2018 - Present)

The Ministry of Rural Development started Mission Shakti to establish a national mission for self-help groups (SHGs) to empower rural women. It aims to concentrate on offering tactics for enhancing convergence at various levels of governance and across Ministries/Departments. In addition to bolstering support for digital infrastructure, it aims to encourage increased involvement and backing from Panchayats and other local level governing entities (Minsitry of Women and Child Development, 2022). Through the program's provision of financial aid, training in skill development, and connections to markets, over 75 lakh women have become entrepreneurs. Its impact is demonstrated by success stories like Poonam Devi of Haryana, who manages a profitable dairy farm, and Anarkali of Bihar, who founded a mushroom cultivation unit. Even though obstacles like getting loans and finding marketing opportunities still exist, Mission Shakti is a big step in the right direction for women's economic empowerment(Limited (UPICON), n.d.).

Digital medium played crucial role in reaching out to these women. The administrative bodies are responsible to carve out niche solutions based on data provided by the registration portal of the scheme.

E-Gram Swaraj Project: Digital Transformation in Panchayats (2014 - Present)

The E-Gram Swaraj project aims to digitalize Gram Panchayats all over India to strengthen grassroots local governance. This program provides panchayats with computers, internet access, and training to facilitate online operations such as payment processing, service provision, and grievance resolution. Promising outcomes from the project have increased public participation in decision-making and transparency (Digitalisation of Panchayats, n.d.). For example, after implementing the program, the village of Kothapalli in Andhra Pradesh saw a notable increase in financial management transparency. Addressing issues with digital literacy and infrastructure deficiencies in rural areas is necessary for a more comprehensive and inclusive effect.

Swachh Bharat Abhiyan: Cleanliness Campaign with a Vision (2014 - Present)

Swachh Bharat Abhiyan, one of the government's most ambitious flagship initiatives, seeks to eliminate open defecation in India by 2024. With the help of digital awareness campaigns, building restrooms, and community involvement, the program has made great strides toward declaring over 6 lakh rural villages ODF (SwachhBharat.). The initiative's capacity to promote constructive change is demonstrated by inspiring tales like those of Binita Kumari of Jharkhand, who encouraged her village to build toilets, and Hargovind Singh of Punjab, who used recycling to turn waste into wealth. However, issues like waste management, sustainability, and behavioural change still exist and call for ongoing work and community involvement.

The digital medium has proved to be a significant contributor in awareness campaigns for the scheme (Gupta & Bakshi, 2023). The data collected by the Swachh Bharat Mission Portal is used to generate health reports of villages and urban locations. It also makes it easier for administrative bodies to list non-performing regions and build strategies to improve social conditions of the concerned area.

National Digital Health Mission (NDHM): Towards a Connected Healthcare System (2020 - Present)

NDHM aims to establish a cohesive national digital health ecosystem for India. With the creation of a digital platform for personal health records, electronic medical records (EMRs), and health ID cards, the initiative hopes to guarantee easy access to healthcare nationwide (National et al. (NHA), n.d.). Although in their early phases, the pilot programs in multiple states have demonstrated the potential to enhance healthcare accessibility and efficacy. Projects like the Arogya Setu app show how useful digital tools can be for providing healthcare (Tabeck & Jain, 2022) (Nagori, 2021).

These are a few illustrations of the many technology-based adoption steps that have been taken by the Indian administration for good governance. Even though each project has its setbacks, they all teach important lessons about how effective technology can be to bring positive changes in society. Core elements to foster change mindset can be a strong political will, community involvement, technological innovation, and data-driven decision-making. These isolated instances of effective governance are catalysts, providing encouragement and hope for developing a more just and productive India. However, for long-term impact and widespread success, it is imperative to ensure transparency, accountability, and inclusivity. Issues with data privacy, cybersecurity, and fair access to technology must be resolved for long-term success.

The Arogya Setu app is one such example that sheds light on the positive as well as negative outcome of employing technology by the administration in collaboration with health ministry, corporate sector and NGOs as a public-private partnership. It was launched amidst the COVID 19 pandemic as a safety measure to keep people aware of the infected population in their vicinity. It works on the principle of contact tracing (India, 2020). Consequently, it required regular input from infected people and the public authorities without addressing the privacy concerns of citizens. This prevented people from regular usage of the app. The disruption in data feed hindered the efficient service delivery from the administration (Narain, 2024). Austria, Germany, and several other European nations had also collaborated with multiple private app developers to evaluate potential technological advancements during this emergency moment (Lanzing, Lievevrouw, & Siffles, 2021). They also met with the same concerns (Renda, 2022) (Raposo, 2022).

It is universally accepted practice that health emergency trumps certain fundamental rights. But the pandemic gave rise to newer set of enquiries such as whether such trumping feature of social responsibility surpasses basic right to privacy which is akin to human right. The social value of privacy has never been higher before but digital age has brought with it such nuanced concerns. The perception of State's interference in managing the health data of population using the 'apps' has instilled fear in people, preventing them from regular usage of such platforms (Narain, 2024). The fear of continued usage of the app for purposes other than contact tracing denotes lack of trust in the State and the accountability of administration (Suraksha & Thacker, 2022). Similar line of fear is observed across tangents wherever public authorities mandates the usage of digital medium. Further sections in the chapter engages with such privacy concerns in case of another mandatory app usage while reflecting on the data protection regime.

IMPORTANCE OF DATA IN DIGITAL AGE

Data has become the lifeblood of societies in the age of interconnection, and responsible data management is a fundamental component of good governance in democracies. Robust democracies are inextricably linked to effective data management and protection principles, facilitating well-informed decision-making and enhancing transparency and accountability. One will not be wrong to conclude that evidence-based policymaking is fuelled by data (OECD & EU, 2017).

Earlier, the governments took policy decisions on gut feelings and anecdotal evidence (Miller, 1989). This practice was largely based on the two-culture theory propounded by Charles Percy Snow in Rede lecture, 1959. As per this concept, world's problems were not solved because the intellectual space of western society had split into two worlds, of science and humanities (Snow, 1961). The decision making for public was not done using any scientific study or through analytical decision-making tools. Even today, with the advent of artificial intelligence the policy making still under utilize the efficient service that technology can offer (Schneier, 2019) (Vydra & Klievink, 2019). Large data sets, such as census records and healthcare metrics, can now offer unmatched insights into the populace's needs and difficulties. When used appropriately, this data can direct the creation of focused policies that deal with urgent problems like healthcare inequities, unemployment, and poverty (Steelman et al., 2014) (Hossin, Du, Mu, & Asante, 2023). Consider developing educational policies or addressing environmental issues without monitoring real-time pollution levels or student performance data analysis. Governments can use data to prioritize policies that improve citizens' lives and go beyond educated guesswork.

Data also promotes accountability and transparency (Wandaogo, 2022). Information asymmetry has historically increased public scepticism and fostered mistrust of the government. These days, government operations and decision-making procedures can be better-understood thanks to open data initiatives, which make anonymized and aggregated data sets publicly accessible. The public can monitor public spending, evaluate the distribution of resources, and hold elected officials responsible for their deeds. Consider examining public health interventions or infrastructure projects without access to budget expenditures or anonymized patient data analysis. Access to open data gives people the ability to actively engage in democratic processes and make sure their elected officials are looking out for their interests.

Data promotes trust and protects citizen privacy. Although there is no denying the advantages of data, improper use or management can have disastrous results. Unauthorized surveillance, biased algorithms, and data breaches can erode public confidence in the government and threaten democratic principles. Sensitive personal data is gathered, stored, and used ethically and responsibly when adequate data protection is in place (Mishra, 2023). Imagine losing money due to stolen personal data or discrimination in employment applications because of biased algorithms. Building trust and ensuring citizens feel comfortable sharing their data for the greater good requires strong enforcement mechanisms and robust data protection laws and regulations.

Navigating the data landscape, however, takes time and effort. A careful approach is needed to balance the advantages of data-driven governance and the requirements for security and privacy. Governments, civil society organizations, and the private sector must work together to strike the correct balance. Governments must invest in a robust cybersecurity infrastructure, pass comprehensive data protection legislation, and encourage citizen data literacy (Asgarkhani, 2005). The need to establish robust cybersecurity policy was concluded in a recent work that studied current cybersecurity provisions in seven nations (Mishra, Alzoubi, Anwar, & Gill, 2022). Transparent user consent procedures and ethical data practices must be prioritized by the private sector, which is responsible for gathering and processing most of the data. Holding governments responsible for their data practices and promoting powerful data protection frameworks are essential for civil society organizations. It aids in establishing good governance strategies and instil a sense of trust within public.

Data Management and Good Governance

The idea of good governance has evolved beyond simple platitudes in the ever-changing field of governance to become an essential tenet for creating compelling, accountable, and transparent systems. Fundamentally, information makes good governance work through carefully gathered, examined, and applied data that empowers citizens, shapes public policy, and yields tangible benefits. This reliance on data, though, has drawbacks as well. Accessible information is a driving force behind progress, but it can also be abused or exploited, making even the best-intentioned governance practices useless. In light of this harsh reality, data security and protecting individual privacy rights become essential components that serve as the cornerstones around which genuine good governance can be constructed (Digital Rights in Perspective: The Evolution of the Debate in the Internet Governance Forum - Meireles - Politics & Policy - Wiley Online Library, n.d.).

Envision a situation where millions of lives are at risk due to a cyberattack on carefully collected data on public health trends (Tracking Healthcare Data Breaches, n.d.). As an alternative, picture a scenario in which citizens' financial data—gathered for welfare programs—is disclosed, throwing vulnerable groups into financial disarray. These are terrifying reminders of the dire repercussions of ignoring data security and privacy, not just hypothetical scenarios. Under such circumstances, sensitive data is compromised, and confidence in the organizations tasked with protecting it is irreversibly damaged. The implications go well beyond short-term injury. Citizens are deterred from participating in governance initiatives by an atmosphere of fear and suspicion fostered by instability. When data privacy is violated, people are reluctant to share information necessary for effective service delivery, policy creation, and public involvement. This lack of information makes it challenging to make wise decisions. It leads to creating policies based on incorrect data, ultimately hindering progress and maintaining social inequality. Moreover, data insecurity can stifle dissent, change public opinion, and threaten democratic processes. When misused, personal data can be utilized for discriminatory actions, targeted surveillance, and the repression of fundamental rights. This potential for abuse directly threatens the foundation of a free and just society and undermines the legitimacy of governance.

Therefore, robust data security and privacy protections are essential for good governance. Necessary first steps include putting money into a robust cybersecurity infrastructure, enforcing strict data protection regulations, and cultivating an environment of openness and accountability (Mishra, Alzoubi, Anwar, & Gill, 2022). This flimsy fortress is further strengthened by giving citizens vital redressal avenues and informed consent mechanisms. The foundations of good governance are trust, inclusivity, and open discourse. However, the citizens' trust can only be fostered if they receive assurances regarding the security and privacy of their information. As the data-driven era progresses, protecting data security and privacy rights becomes morally and strategically essential (Hamelink, 2003) (Li & Liu, 2021). It is the cornerstone around which we can construct a genuinely open, accountable, and efficient system of government—one that empowers people, promotes advancement, and creates a better future for everybody. Following is a case study of a well-intentioned good governance digital initiative undertaken by public authority in State of Meghalaya, India. It highlights how a strategic decision to improve service delivery can come under scrutiny due to lack of well-rounded evaluation of the policy. Especially in light of privacy rights of the stakeholders.

TEACHER ATTENDANCE MANAGEMENT SYSTEM & SERVICE DELIVERY: EAST JAINTIA HILLS, MEGHALAYA (INDIA)

There is a common problem in several areas around India with regards to low attendance of teachers and students in government schools especially in case of primary schools. There are several reports which states that many students drop out of the school at primary level itself due to the lack of teachers and other facilities in the school. This is a gross violation of Right to Education Act 2009 (RTE Act), which states that it is an obligation of government to provide free and compulsory education to children below 14 years of age. Absence of employed teachers remain the major concern of government. This has a direct effect on the educational quality catered to students.

One such glaring example is of district located in East Jaintia Hills, Meghalaya where there were reports of parents pulling their wards out of primary government schools due to the lack of teacher's attendance. Taking all of these into consideration, the district authorities of East Jaintia Hills engaged certain digital experts to make sure that teachers do report to their schools. This digital method was called Teacher Attendance Monitoring System (TAMS), which was launched on 2nd June 2023 by a local Member of Legislative Assembly and a State Minister Kyrmen Shylla. It is part of the web-based application called Teacher Information Management System (TIMS) envisaged to capture all information about various teachers working in the State of Meghalaya, either in government or government-aided schools (Government of Meghalaya Education Department, n.d.). The idea behind this system is to record the attendance of the teachers who are employed in the government schools. For marking their attendance, "the app basically entails taking a selfie for registering attendance. Its unique features are facial recognition, geofencing, and recording the time spent in school" (Karmakar, 2023).

With regards to facial technology, it is to make sure that only the concerned teacher gets marked present and there is no proxy, as there were several complaints that the enrolled teachers were engaged in some other activity during the time of school and they were sending some other individuals on behalf of them, to mark their attendance, in return for certain money from their salary. Therefore, this facial recognition removed this problem of proxy teachers. In respect to geofencing, the system ensures that the teachers are able to mark attendance only at the school premises and nowhere else. This system uses Global Positioning System (GPS) to locate the geographic position of the teacher.

This system has worked very well, and this has resulted in many teachers turning up for classes and there is an increase in the enrolment of the students in the schools as well (Karmakar, 2023). However, the system is not without its own flaws. Concern is with regards to facial recognition and the right to privacy. Under the Digital Personal Data Protection Act, 2023 (DPDP Act) this system finds no support under the law.

TAMS

The question of whether technological advancements can improve educational governance while upholding ethical principles and respecting individual rights is brought up by implementing TAMS in East Jaintia Hills, India. Through time tracking, geo-fencing, and facial recognition, TAMS is trying to increase teacher attendance. This could help allay public concerns about absenteeism and encourage openness. A deeper look, however, uncovers a complicated picture woven with possible advantages, moral conundrums, and significant obstacles to realizing good governance.

Promising Prospects

TAMS proponents contend that real-time teacher presence data improves accountability and transparency, in line with a fundamental tenet of good governance. A higher attendance rate may give students regular access to instruction, enhancing learning outcomes. Furthermore, by helping to identify staffing patterns and optimize resource allocation, the gathered data may also support effective governance (Amirulloh et al., 2020). Again, TAMS may need to improve providing educational services in response to public concerns regarding teacher absenteeism.

Web of Concern

Notwithstanding these possible advantages, TAMS is clouded by severe worries about efficacy, ethics, and privacy. Facial recognition technology raises concerns about data privacy and potential abuse (Sadam, 2023). Biometric data collection and storage can be invasive, bringing the possibility of data breaches, monitoring, and discriminatory practices (Hernandez-de-Menendez, Morales-Menendez, Escobar, & Jorge, 2021). Furthermore, the nuances of teaching responsibilities may not be fully captured by using geo-fencing as the only means of determining presence within the school. One such nuanced responsibility is election duties of government teachers which is an offsite assignment. Absence of a teacher from school premises owing to such duty will not automatically get converted into marked presence, leading to multitude of practical issues such as unwanted leave or reduction from salary. It is also possible for teachers to legitimately need to leave the building for a variety of tasks, which could result in unfair judgments and inaccurate assessments. Furthermore, the system might be abused to impose punitive measures rather than beneficial enhancements, departing from the fair and responsible administration that is the cornerstone of good governance.

Transparency and Consent

The absence of informed consent and transparency raises more ethical questions. It is critical to communicate clearly about data collection, storage, use, and security precautions. Transparent and honest governance principles are jeopardized if teachers are not asked for their informed consent before implementing a system like this.

Beyond Monitoring

Alternative strategies provide more ethical and long-lasting solutions for resolving concerns about teacher attendance than just monitoring. In line with participatory and inclusive governance principles, open communication and cooperation between educators and administrators can foster a trustworthy environment where attendance problems can be constructively resolved. In the long run, it might be more advantageous to look into the underlying causes of absenteeism, such as workload, a lack of support, or infrastructure problems, rather than just keeping an eye on attendance. Providing teachers with professional development opportunities can enhance their motivation, engagement, and skill sets, which may increase attendance and performance through internal variables instead of external monitoring.

Issue of Ethics and Effectiveness

Although TAMS might seem like a quick fix for attendance issues, a more sophisticated strategy is needed, weighing its possible advantages against serious risks and restrictions is necessary. Investigating alternate strategies that emphasize open communication, root cause analysis, and assisting teachers' professional development is required due to concerns about privacy (Hakimi, Eynon, & Murphy, 2021), ethics, and efficacy. In the end, actual good governance in education requires coming up with solutions that are not only practical but also moral, open, and considerate of people's rights, as well as that enhance the learning environment for both educators and students. In light of this, it becomes crucial to understand the privacy concerns erupting out of TAMS in light of Indian DPDP Act.

Scrutinizing the Digital Personal Data Protection Act, 2023

The purpose of the TAMS in East Jaintia Hills is to track teacher attendance using location tracking and facial recognition, two sensitive biometric data sets. Advocates emphasize that it could increase accountability, but serious privacy issues remain. Such data collection and storage violate the spirit of the Indian DPDP Act, which has yet to be implemented, and increases the risk of misuse, data breaches, and potential surveillance. Furthermore, because the system depends on geo-fencing, it cannot account for the subtleties of a teacher's workday, which could result in unfair judgments and erroneous assessments. Concerns are also heightened by the lack of transparency surrounding the use and storage of data. It is possible that educators need to be fully aware of their data rights or the purposes for which the information is gathered, which damages confidence and undermines moral data governance guidelines. The concerns surrounding DPDP Act and TAMS demand both legal examination and ethical analysis. Both initiatives raise concerns concerning necessity, proportionality, and possible discriminatory effects. Are these actions required to meet their objectives as stated? Could less invasive options accomplish the same goals while protecting people's privacy rights?

Addressing performance or attendance issues can be accomplished more by putting money into transparent communication (McMillan, 2024) and building a culture of trust within the organization. Furthermore, rather than depending only on surveillance techniques, addressing the underlying causes of absenteeism, such as workload, a lack of support, or infrastructure problems—may provide a more long-lasting solution.

Despite being praised for creating a legal framework for protecting personal data, the DPDP Act exposes a few issues that require further investigation. Of particular note is that Section 87's government exemption clause gives it the authority to access personal information for "any purpose in the interests of the State". This broad exemption violates people's privacy rights and does not provide enough protection against possible abuse. Furthermore, the lack of a Data Protection Authority (DPA) creates accountability questions and currently obscures enforcement procedures. This is one of the factors that prevents the citizens from putting their complete faith in the governmental measures of service delivery (Narain, 2024).

Moreover, the Act defines "personal data" as any data about an individual who is identifiable by or in relation to such data" (MoL&J, 2023). It is a narrow definition that leaves out important details like financial and political views. This restrictive definition leaves some sensitive data open to misuse and opens up loopholes. Because only the personal data remains protected under the scheme of the legislation. The consent framework also presents some issues. Although opt-in consent is good, the "deemed consent" clause[1], predicated on inactivity, may not ensure that consent was genuinely provided voluntarily and intelligently.

Even though it was intended to be the primary enforcement agency, the act's implementation and accountability procedures could be more precise because of the lack of a working DPA. This raises questions about how well it protects people's rights. Important information such as political opinions and financial information is not included in the act's definition of "personal data". This restrictive classification exposes sensitive data to possible abuse and exploitation. Although granting consent by opting in is a good move, there are questions about ensuring that consent is freely provided and fully informed, given the "deemed consent" clause based on inactivity. People ought to be in complete control of how they use their data. There is still uncertainty surrounding the Act's rules regarding cross-border data transfers, which could impede global corporate operations and give rise to worries about data security in these transfers. Facial recognition technology presents serious privacy risks even though the act does not specifically cover it.

This is especially true given the unclear regulations surrounding its use and the possibility of discriminatory applications. Since the Act only covers "digital personal data" and leaves out non-digital forms, some personal data may not be protected. The Act gives private organizations extensive authority to gather and process data, which raises questions about possible monitoring and improper use of personal data for profit. Concerns regarding accountability and data security procedures are presented by the act's need for more precise enforcement mechanisms for handling data breaches. Due to the Act's technical jargon and complex nature, extensive public awareness campaigns are required to enable people to recognize and effectively exercise their legal rights. It is critical to recognize that India's DPDP Act is a step in the right direction for data protection. However, to ensure that it protects individual rights in the digital age, it is imperative that these essential privacy concerns are addressed and its provisions are strengthened.

Although the Indian government works hard to manage and safeguard data responsibly, there have regrettably been data breaches, which have raised questions about the security and privacy of its citizens. Here is a closer look at a few noteworthy cases to show the difficulties and nuances involved.

GOVERNMENT MAINTAINED DATA: ISSUES OF DATA BREACH

Aadhaar Data Breaches (Livemint, 2023): There have been disputes surrounding data breaches involving the Aadhaar, a 12-digit identity number specific to each citizen. A Tribune journalist bought over a million people's records in 2017 via a government website, revealing flaws in the system (Gopal, 2022). The incident spurred discussions about data security and privacy concerns surrounding Aadhaar, even though the Unique Identification Authority of India (UIDAI) denied a breach had occurred. 2018 saw reports that over 130 million people had their Aadhaar data compromised through state government websites (Gopal, 2022). These incidents demonstrate the importance of solid data protection protocols, such as Aadhaar, for sensitive data.

COVID-19 Test Data Breach (Verizon, 2023): In October 2023, a cybersecurity researcher discovered a large-scale data leak on a hacking forum that purportedly included UID numbers, COVID-19 test results, and the personal information of over 81.5 crore Indian citizens. It has been reported that the data came from a server connected to the government, which raises questions regarding the security of private health data.

EPFO Data Breach: Reports of a data breach that may have affected millions of users at the Employees' Provident Fund Organization (EPFO) surfaced in 2018. The Indian Computer Emergency Response Team (CERT-In) investigated in 2023 and found evidence of unauthorized access to the system despite the EPFO's initial denial of the breach. This incident highlighted the necessity of solid cybersecurity safeguards to secure financial data.

Kudankulam Nuclear Power Plant Breach: Possible data breaches were raised in 2019 after malware was found at the Kudankulam nuclear power plant. Although the incident demonstrated the susceptibility of critical infrastructure to cyberattacks and the significance of solid cybersecurity measures, authorities maintained that the malware did not gain access to critical systems.

Sensitive patient data was exposed by several other data breaches that impacted government organizations, including the Indian Council of Medical Research (ICMR) and the All India Institute of Medical Sciences (AIIMS).

These incidents demonstrate how difficult it is for government agencies to secure data. These cases demonstrate the variety of data breaches that impact the Indian government, including financial information, health records, personal information, and vital infrastructure. Every incident is complex, posing issues with data collection procedures, security flaws, and the efficiency of reaction systems.

The abovementioned instances reinforce the need to have clear, unambiguous and simple data protection rules which can be sustained.

DATA PROTECTION AND GOOD GOVERNANCE

Data is now essential to governance in the digital age because it informs policy decisions, promotes transparency, and encourages citizen participation. This reliance on data, though, has drawbacks as well. Although it has excellent potential for good, misuse can threaten fundamental rights, erode trust, and stifle innovation—all critical components of good governance. This calls for a paradigm change, with data security and protection becoming essential components of all sound governance schemes rather than optional extras.

The fundamental right to privacy is at the heart of data protection. People expect governments to handle their personal information responsibly when they entrust them with it, whether for online interactions, healthcare access, or social security benefits. This trust can be destroyed by data breaches, unapproved surveillance, and biased algorithms, which can lead to disengagement, anxiety, and even opposition to government programs. Imagine an entrepreneur avoiding online government services out of concern for data misuse or a citizen reluctant to engage in a public health program because of privacy concerns. Such situations undermine social cohesion and economic advancement, undermining the fundamental objectives of good governance (Manupatra, n.d.).

Data security is essential for maintaining the integrity and efficacy of good governance schemes, in addition to privacy concerns. Cyberattacks can compromise vital services like healthcare and social welfare, damage infrastructure, and alter data to influence policy decisions. Envision a situation in which cybercrime compromises election results, malware cripples vital infrastructure, or public funds are misappropriated. These violations undermine confidence and cause severe social and economic harm, jeopardizing the pillars of prosperity and stability.

Additionally, security protects public involvement. The vulnerability of online platforms used for public consultations or grievance redressals to cyberattacks silences citizen voices and undermines democratic processes. Consider a situation where individuals are reluctant to disclose corruption because they fear reprisals made possible by data breaches. Such a lack of involvement and trust impairs governments' capacity to deal with pressing problems and impedes the growth of responsible and responsive governance. Data security and protection are not just technical issues; they are essential to establishing good governance practices in the digital age, encouraging innovation, and establishing trust. Governments can harness the power of data to build a more secure, inclusive, and prosperous future for all by prioritizing data protection, investing in strong security measures, and fostering a culture of transparency and accountability.

In the history of India's democracy, the Supreme Court has supported fundamental rights; in the digital age, the right to privacy has become paramount. The Court has made significant legal decisions highlighting the critical role that data security and protection play in maintaining good governance, acknowledging that these concerns are not merely technical but a fundamental component of transparency, citizen empowerment, and trust.

A unanimous ruling in the historic Puttaswamy v. Union of India case in 2017 established the right to privacy as a fundamental freedom protected by Article 21 of the Constitution. This ruling, which acknowledged the innate link between privacy and other fundamental rights like freedom of speech and expression, profoundly impacted the country. The Court made clear how the unrestricted gathering, storing, and use of personal data can result in widespread surveillance, discriminatory practices, and the weakening of the fundamental tenets of a just and free society. This ruling acted as a potent catalyst, driving the necessity of strong data protection laws and a change in the way governments handle data in good governance initiatives.

The decisions made by the Court go beyond a conceptual framework. It has aggressively contested government actions in later rulings that were thought to be intrusive or to lack sufficient protections. In the Aadhaar cases, the Court underlined the necessity for solid data protection measures and expressed concerns about the possibility of misuse of this unique identity system. Similarly, the court ordered the government to create social media platform regulations to safeguard user privacy in the K.S. Puttaswamy (Retd.) v. Union of India (Privacy in Social Media) case. Using these interventions, the Court has served as a driving force behind legislative and policy reforms while emphasizing the value of data protection. Though the Supreme Court's rulings offer a clear path forward, several obstacles remain to overcome (Rai, 2020). There are questions about the adequacy and scope of the draft Personal Data Protection Bill being considered. Robust cybersecurity infrastructure necessitates ongoing funding and capacity expansion. Furthermore, robust institutional mechanisms and public awareness are necessary to close the gap between policy declarations and their successful implementation.

Steps to Ensure Data Security in Good Governance: Recommendations

In the age of digital revolution, data is now essential to governance. Although there is no denying its potential to improve citizen engagement, make policy decisions with more excellent knowledge, and deliver services more effectively, it can damage fundamental rights, undermine trust, and stifle innovation when misused. India understands this and finds itself at a pivotal point where it must weigh the advantages of data-driven governance against the critical necessity of data security and protection. This requires a multifaceted strategy, including robust infrastructure, capacity building, legislative reforms, and an accountable and transparent culture.

Legislation Structure

The Indian government's reliance on data for good governance schemes, while promising, presents a critical challenge in ensuring data protection and security. This necessitates robust legislative measures safeguarding citizen privacy, fostering trust, and upholding fundamental rights. Here, we explore potential remedies through legislative reforms:

Comprehensive Data Protection Law

- **Right to Privacy as Cornerstone:** The law must enshrine the right to privacy as a fundamental right, echoing the Supreme Court's Puttaswamy judgment.

- **Defining Personal Data:** Clearly define personal data, encompassing direct and indirect identifiers, and include provisions for sensitive data categories like health and financial information.
- **Data Minimization:** Mandate data collection only for specific, legitimate purposes, limiting it to what is strictly necessary.
- **Informed Consent:** Implement a robust informed consent framework, ensuring individuals understand how their data will be used and have the right to withdraw consent.
- **Data Subject Rights:** Grant individuals the right to access, rectify, erase, and port their data, empowering them to control its use.
- **Data Protection Authority:** Establish an independent Data Protection Authority with adequate powers to enforce the law, investigate breaches, and impose penalties.

Strengthening Existing Legislation

- **Revise IT Act, 2000:** Update the Information Technology Act to align with evolving data protection principles, especially regarding data breach notifications and penalties.
- **Sector-Specific Regulations:** Enact sector-specific data protection regulations for healthcare, finance, and telecommunications, addressing unique risks and sensitivities.

Ensuring Transparency and Accountability

- **Mandatory Data Protection Impact Assessments (DPIAs):** Require DPIAs for all government initiatives involving data collection, evaluating potential risks and mitigating measures.
- **Public Disclosure of Data Collection Practices:** Mandate transparency about data collection purposes, retention periods, and sharing protocols.
- **Right to Explanation:** Implement a "right to explanation" for automated decisions based on personal data, empowering individuals to understand and challenge them.

Building Robust Security Infrastructure

- **Cybersecurity Standards and Best Practices:** Enact legislation mandating cybersecurity standards and best practices for government entities, including data encryption, access controls, and incident response mechanisms.
- **Investment in Cybersecurity Infrastructure:** Allocate adequate resources for infrastructure upgrades, personnel training, and security awareness campaigns.
- **Data Breach Notification and Response:** Implement a mandatory data breach notification framework with precise reporting requirements and response protocols.

Fostering a Culture of Data Protection

- **Privacy Impact Assessments:** Integrate privacy considerations into policy and program development through mandatory privacy impact assessments.
- **Data Protection Training:** Provide regular training on best practices and legal obligations for government officials and data handlers.

- **Public Awareness Campaigns:** Launch public awareness campaigns to educate citizens about their data rights and responsibilities, encouraging informed participation in data-driven governance.

International Collaboration

- **Engage with international frameworks:** Participate in international data protection frameworks and collaborate with other countries on cross-border data flows and cybercrime prevention.
- **International Data Transfer Agreements:** Implement robust agreements with other countries to ensure adequate data protection standards.

Technological Infrastructure

Data is essential to good governance in the digital age because it allows for transparent policymaking, informed decision-making, and increased citizen involvement. However, there are risks associated with this reliance on data, as its misuse can damage confidence, stifle creativity, and infringe upon fundamental rights. The Indian Supreme Court has underlined the necessity of strong data protection measures and urged the government to implement technological solutions that put security and privacy first. Here, we examine potential technological solutions that could protect Indian good governance schemes' data and promote a more inclusive and safe digital future:

- **Decentralized Identity Management:**

We can investigate decentralized identity solutions like blockchain technology as an alternative to centralized data repositories like Aadhaar. People now have more control over who can access their data and how thanks to the ability to hold and manage their own digital identities. Zero-knowledge proofs enable people to authenticate themselves without disclosing any underlying personal information and can further improve privacy.

- **Secure Multi-Party Computation (MPC)**

Several parties can calculate their data using this cryptographic technique without ever disclosing the data itself. Ensuring data privacy and promoting collaboration and insights are two benefits that make this especially valuable for sensitive data analysis in fields like healthcare, finance, and social welfare.

- **Homomorphic Encryption**

Using this cryptographic technique, multiple parties can perform calculations on their data without ever revealing the data itself. This is especially valuable for sensitive data analysis in healthcare, finance, and social welfare industries because it protects data privacy and fosters collaboration and insights.

- **Differential Privacy**

By adding controlled noise to data sets, this statistical technique preserves the privacy of individual records while enabling accurate analysis. Large-scale data analysis in fields like public health and urban planning benefits significantly from this, as it allows for important insights to be gained without jeopardizing personal privacy.

- **Federated Learning:**

This statistical technique allows accurate analysis without compromising individual records' privacy by introducing controlled noise into data sets. This is very beneficial for large-scale data analysis in areas like public health and urban planning, as it permits significant insights to be obtained without compromising individual privacy.

- **Secure Communication Protocols**

All government platforms and communication channels must use secure protocols like HTTPS and TLS. This ensures secure transmission of sensitive data by encrypting it while it is in transit, shielding it from unwanted interception.

- **Data Minimization and Purpose Limitation**

Governmental organizations should only gather the minimal amount of information required for specified goals that are made explicit and shared with the public. By doing this, the attack surface is decreased, and the likelihood of a data breach is decreased. In order to prevent data from being kept longer than necessary, data retention periods should also be precisely specified and enforced.

- **Data Governance Frameworks**

Robust frameworks for data governance are crucial, providing explicit guidelines for data gathering, storing, accessing, and using. These frameworks should be open, available to the public, and subject to frequent reviews and updates.

- **Public Awareness**

It is essential to educate the public about data security and protection. Accessible resources, awareness campaigns, and educational programs can empower people to know their rights, make wise data-sharing decisions, and report possible violations.

Capacity Building

Data is now the weft and woof of good governance, woven into the colourful tapestry of Indian democracy. However, this dependence has a drawback. Although data facilitates informed policymaking, encourages openness, and stimulates citizen involvement, its susceptibility can shatter the foundations of accountability and trust. India must adopt robust technological solutions that secure data throughout its governance schemes to protect this delicate balance.

- **Encryption: The Sentinel at the Gate**

Similar to a watchful sentinel, data encryption protects against unwanted access. When data is encrypted, both in transit and at rest, using solid algorithms such as AES-256, it becomes unintelligible to anyone lacking the decryption key. This protects private data, including health records and Aadhaar numbers, even in the case of a data breach. Using hardware security modules (HSMs) for crucial management reinforces defences even more and guarantees that the keys remain unbreakable.

- **Privacy-Enhancing Technologies: Weaving a Shield of Anonymity**

Privacy-enhancing technologies (PETs) provide an imperceptible shield that protects personal information while facilitating the use of data for public benefit. Strategies like differential privacy—adding noise to data purposefully—make extracting insightful information possible without jeopardizing specific individuals' privacy. Similarly, collaborative analysis is enabled without centralized data storage through federated learning, where data stays on individual devices and only aggregated results are shared. These technologies create a veil of anonymity to protect citizens while enabling data to be used to inform critical policy choices.

- **Decentralization: Distributing Power, Sharing Trust**

Attackers find centralized data storage to be an alluring target. Decentralization spreads the risk and makes it more difficult for a single breach to compromise the system by distributing data among several nodes. With its distributed consensus methods and unchangeable ledger, blockchain technology presents a viable option for safe data storage, especially for private data like financial transactions or land records. Trust is distributed when power and control are decentralized, reducing the possibility of abuse and promoting a more accountable ecosystem.

- **Zero-Knowledge Proofs: Verifying Identity, not Information**

As digital passports, zero-knowledge proofs enable people to authenticate their identities without disclosing the underlying data. Cryptographic techniques allow people to demonstrate that they meet specific requirements (such as qualifying for a particular welfare program) without disclosing personal information. By doing this, data collection is reduced, and sensitive information is safeguarded, giving citizens more control over their online persona.

- **Homomorphic Encryption: Computing on Encrypted Data**

A revolutionary step forward is provided by homomorphic encryption, which enables computations to be done directly on encrypted data. Envision examining de-identified health data to spot illness trends without unlocking personal data. This technology opens the door to innovative research and policy insights without compromising individual rights by enabling the potential for advanced data analysis while maintaining privacy.

- **Beyond Technology: Building a Culture of Security**

Technology on its own is insufficient. A cultural revolution is necessary for a robust data protection ecosystem. Programs for user education must enable citizens to recognize their data rights and make wise decisions. It is imperative to diligently implement and enforce data governance frameworks, which provide explicit data collection, storage, and utilization guidelines. Security gaps should be proactively identified and fixed through routine audits and vulnerability assessments. Establishing a transparent and accountable culture prioritizing prompt reporting and investigation of data breaches promotes responsible data stewardship and fosters trust.

- **Collaboration for a Collective Future**

In Indian governance, data security is a collaborative effort. Collaborating with global organizations to exchange knowledge, conducting collaborative research on cutting-edge technologies, and coordinating cyber-attack responses are essential. By combining the knowledge of the public and private sectors, public-private partnerships can guarantee that technology solutions are workable and intuitive. Civil society organizations strongly support data protection legislation, holding government agencies responsible for their data practices.

By integrating these technological solutions into the framework of Indian governance, the country can create a digital future in which trust is paramount, transparency flourishes, and data empowers. Although the road ahead will be difficult, India can guarantee that the digital fabric of its governance is dynamic, safe, and open to all, with a solid commitment to data protection.

International Collaboration

The burgeoning reliance on data in Indian good governance schemes presents opportunities and challenges. While it empowers informed decision-making, fosters transparency, and fuels citizen engagement, it raises crucial questions about data privacy and security. To effectively navigate this complex terrain, international collaboration emerges as a potent remedy, offering valuable insights, best practices, and collective action.

- **Shared Challenges, Shared Solutions**

Around the world, discriminatory algorithms, poor cybersecurity, and data breaches are commonplace. By working together, India can benefit from the combined experience of other nations dealing with comparable problems. India can create strong data protection laws by taking inspiration from the California Consumer Privacy Act (CCPA) and the General Data Protection Regulation (GDPR) of the European Union. Furthermore, exchanging best practices for incident response procedures and developing cybersecurity infrastructure can strengthen national defences against cyberattacks.

- **Building a Global Framework**

International collaboration can foster the development of a global framework for data protection and governance. India can actively participate in forums like the Organisation for Economic Co-operation and Development (OECD) and the Asia-Pacific Economic Cooperation (APEC) to advocate for common principles and standards for data collection, storage, and use. Such harmonization can facilitate cross-border data flows while ensuring adequate safeguards for citizen privacy. Furthermore, collaboration with international bodies like the United Nations can create robust international legal instruments to address the challenges of transnational data flows.

- **Knowledge Sharing**

Data governance is a complex and evolving field. India can benefit from collaborating with developed nations to build data protection law enforcement capacity, cybersecurity expertise, and public awareness campaigns. Sharing knowledge through workshops, training programs, and exchange programs can equip Indian policymakers, administrators, and citizens with the necessary skills and understanding to navigate the digital landscape responsibly.

- **Innovation and Technology Transfer**

International collaboration can unlock the potential of cutting-edge technologies for data protection. Sharing expertise in anonymization techniques, privacy-enhancing technologies, and secure data storage solutions can bolster India's data security infrastructure. Collaboration on research and development initiatives can also lead to innovative solutions tailored to India's needs and context.

- **Multi-Stakeholder Engagement**

Ensuring adequate data protection requires the involvement of all stakeholders. International collaboration can facilitate dialogue and knowledge sharing between governments, civil society organizations, the private sector, and academia. By fostering a multi-stakeholder approach, India can create a more inclusive and responsive data governance ecosystem that prioritizes the rights and interests of all citizens.

Addressing Specific Challenges

Collaboration can address specific challenges faced by India, such as:

- **Data Localization:** By working with other developing nations, India can advocate for a balanced approach to data localization that respects data sovereignty while facilitating cross-border data flows for economic growth.
- **Social Media Platforms:** Collaboration with other democracies can lead to developing shared norms and regulations for social media platforms to address issues like content moderation, data privacy, and online disinformation.
- **Cybersecurity:** Partnering with international cybersecurity agencies can enhance India's ability to detect, prevent, and respond to cyber threats.

These are few recommendations that can help improve the digital protection regime in India and bring sense of trust within the citizens towards the State. Accountability plays major role in case of public delivery systems through governmental authorities. The concerns of employees as well as other citizens should be seen from a human rights perspective because right to privacy erupts from the basic right to life which is considered fundamental to human existence.

CONCLUSION

In the digital age, data protection is essential to good governance rather than just a technical problem. The issue of mandatory usage of digital tools intersecting with privacy concern has brought to the centre stage a nuanced understanding of balancing the two equally important demands. Service delivery by public authorities is a function that can be enhanced by using data generated through mandatory app usages. But it needs to be carefully planned through public deliberations and putting an authority in place that can hold public authorities accountable in case of data breach. The lack of trust in the State by citizens is borne out of multiple data breach incidents. Such fear should be addressed by the public authorities which is clearly lacking currently. For an efficient public governance structure, public support is crucial as well.

Therefore, India can harness the power of data for good while safeguarding the security and privacy of its citizens by putting in place a thorough framework for data protection, building vital infrastructure, and encouraging a culture of accountability and transparency. Together, policymakers, technologists, civil society, and the general public must embark on this journey. By cooperating, India can create a data ecosystem that stimulates innovation, gives citizens more power, and fortifies the pillars of a fair and just society.

REFERENCES

About good governance. (n.d.). OHCHR. https://www.ohchr.org/en/good-governance/about-good-governance

Amirulloh, I., Iskandar, I. D., Apriyani, Y., Warnilah, A. I., Purnia, D. S., & Surahman, M. (2020). Teacher Attendance Monitoring System Teaching with QR-Code and Geo Location using Android Platform. *Journal of Physics: Conference Series, 1641*(1), 012030. doi:10.1088/1742-6596/1641/1/012030

Asgarkhani, M. (2005). Digital Government and Its Effectiveness in Public Management Reform. *Public Management Review, 7*(3), 465–487. doi:10.1080/14719030500181227

Digital rights in perspective: The evolution of the debate in the Internet Governance Forum—Meireles—Politics & Policy. (n.d.). Wiley. https://onlinelibrary.wiley.com/doi/10.1111/polp.12571

Digitalisation of Panchayats. (n.d.). PIB. https://pib.gov.in/pib.gov.in/Pressreleaseshare.aspx?PRID=1983086

Gopal, R. V. (2022, December 19). Aadhaar Data Breach — How Sensitive Data Of 1.3 Billion Indians Was Compromised. *Medium.* https://medium.com/@rithikvgopal/aadhaar-data-breach-how-sensitive-data-of-1-3-billion-indians-was-compromised-cb01d0c2d7d3

Gupta, J., & Bakshi, R. (2023). Social Media as a Potent Factor in Promoting Awareness about Swachh Bharat Abhiyaan: A Critical Analysis. *Asian Journal of Education and Social Studies*, *49*(4), 346–358. doi:10.9734/ajess/2023/v49i41213

Hakimi, L., Eynon, R., & Murphy, V. A. (2021). The Ethics of Using Digital Trace Data in Education: A Thematic Review of the Research Landscape. *Review of Educational Research*, *91*(5), 671–717. doi:10.3102/00346543211020116

Hamelink, C. J. (2003). Digital Risks and Security in CyberSpace. In C. J. Hamelink (Ed.), *The Ethics of Cyberspace* (pp. 107–138). SAGE Publications Ltd. doi:10.4135/9781446219911.n5

Hernandez-de-Menendez, M., Morales-Menendez, R., Escobar, C., & Jorge, A. (2021). Biometric applications in education. *International Journal on Interactive Design and Manufacturing*, *15*(2-3), 365–380. doi:10.1007/s12008-021-00760-6

Hossin, M. A., Du, J., Mu, L., & Asante, I. O. (2023). Sage Open). *Big Data-Driven Public Policy Decisions: Transformation Toward Smart Governance.*, *13*(4), 1–19. doi:10.1177/21582440231215123

Karmakar, R. (2023, June 18). Digital eye deters proxy attendance among Meghalaya's teachers. *The Hindu*. https://www.thehindu.com/news/national/meghalayas-new-attendance-app-keeps-proxy-teachers-away/article66980082.ece

Lanzing, M., Lievevrouw, E., & Siffles, L. (2021). It Takes Two to Techno-Tango: An Analysis of a Close Embrace Between Google/Apple and the EU in Fighting the Pandemic Through Contact Tracing Apps. *Science as Culture*, *31*(1), 136–148. doi:10.1080/09505431.2021.1999403

Li, Y., & Liu, Q. (2021). A comprehensive review study of cyber-attacks and cyber security; Emerging trends and recent developments. *Energy Reports*, *7*, 8176–8186. doi:10.1016/j.egyr.2021.08.126

Livemint. (2023, October 31). *Aadhaar data leak: Massive data breach exposes about 81 crore Indians' personal information on dark web*. Live Mint. https://www.livemint.com/news/india/aadhaar-data-leak-massive-data-breach-exposes-815-million-indians-personal-information-on-dark-web-details-here-11698712793223.html

Manupatra. (n.d.). *Right to Privacy in Digital Age*. Manupatra. https://articles.manupatra.com/article-de tails?id=undefined&ifile=undefined

McMillan, C. (2024). *UK experts talk driving a data-sharing culture in the public sector*. Online: Global Government Forum.

Miller, T. I. (1989). Gut-Level Decisionmaking: Implications for Public Policy Analysis. *Journal of Policy Analysis and Management*, *8*(1), 119–125. doi:10.2307/3324431

Mishra, A., Alzoubi, Y. I., Anwar, M. J., & Gill, A. Q. (2022). Attributes impacting cybersecurity policy development: An evidence from seven nations. *Computers & Security*, *120*, 1–23. doi:10.1016/j.cose.2022.102820

Mishra, N. C. (2023, September 27). *Sequestering Digital Autonomy: How New Data Protection Act Affects Digital Accessibility*. LiveLaw. https://www.livelaw.in/articles/data-protection-digital-accessibility-digital-personal-data-protection-act-238792

MoL&J. (2023, August 11). Digital Data Protection Act. *Statute*. New Delhi, Delhi, India: Government of India.

Nagori, V. (2021). "Aarogya Setu": The mobile application that monitors and mitigates the risks of COVID-19 pandemic spread in India. *Journal of Information Technology Teaching Cases*, *11*(2), 66–80. doi:10.1177/2043886920985863

Narain, M. (2024). Practices on Aarogya Setu: Mapping Citizen Interaction with the Contact-Tracing App in the Time of COVID-19. *East Asian Science, Technology and Society*, 1–21. doi:10.1080/18752160.2024.2312342

OECD, & EUJR. (2017). Conference Summary. *Governing Better Through Evidence-Informed Policy Making* (pp. 1-19). Paris: OECD, EUJRC, INGSA, Campbell. Retrieved from https://www.oecd.org/gov/governing-better-through-evidence-informed-policy-making-proceedings.pdf

Privacy in India in the Age of Big Data.pdf. (n.d.). Defindia. https://www.defindia.org/wp-content/uploads/2017/09/Privacy%20in%20India%20in%20the%20Age%20of%20Big%20Data.pdf

Rai, N. (2020). *Right to Privacy and Data Protection in the Digital Age – Preservation, Control and Implementation of Laws in India*. NBU. https://ir.nbu.ac.in/handle/123456789/4009

Raposo, V. L. (2022). 'I'm right behind you': Digital contact tracing under European law. *Maastricht Journal of European and Comparative Law*, *29*(4), 434–450. doi:10.1177/1023263X221116227

Renda, A. (2022). COVID-19 and privacy: A European dilemma. *Digital Policy. Regulation & Governance*, *24*(2), 109–117. doi:10.1108/DPRG-04-2020-0043

Sadam, R. (2023, February 6). Efficiency vs privacy threat — Andhra govt, employees spar over facial recognition attendance app. *The Print*. https://theprint.in/india/governance/efficiency-vs-privacy-threat-andhra-govt-employees-spar-over-facial-recognition-attendance-app/1352076/

Schneier, B. (2019, November 12). *We must bridge the gap between technology and policymaking. Our future depends on it*. W. E. Forum, Producer. https://www.weforum.org/agenda/2019/11/we-must-bridge-the-gap-between-technology-and-policy-our-future-depends-on-it/

Snow, C. P. (1961). *The Two Cultures and The Scientific Revolution* (7th ed.). Cambridge University Press. doi:10.1063/1.3057748

Steelman, Z. R., Hammer, B. I., & Limayem, M. (2014). Data Collection in the Digital Age: Innovative Alternatives to Student Samples. *Management Information Systems Quarterly*, *38*(2), 355–378. https://www.jstor.org/stable/26634930. doi:10.25300/MISQ/2014/38.2.02

Suraksha, P., & Thacker, T. (2022, August 1). Aarogya Setu's Data Sharing Protocol Discontinued, But Privacy Activists Still Raise Concerns Over Security. *Economic Times*. telecom.economictimes.indiatimes.com/: https://telecom.economictimes.indiatimes.com/news/aarogya-setus-data-sharing-protocol-discontinued-but-privacy-activists-still-raise-concerns-over-security/93261919

SwachhBharat- Swachh Bharat Abhiyan a nation-wide campaign in India. (n.d.). SwachhBharat. https://swachhbharat.mygov.in/

Tabeck, P. S., & Jain, V. (2022). Fighting Pandemic: The Mobile Application Way (a Case of the Aarogya Setu App). *Emerging Economies Cases Journal*, *4*(2), 95–102. doi:10.1177/25166042221147097

The Digital Personal Data Protection Bill, 2023. (n.d.). PRS Legislative Research. https://prsindia.org/billtrack/digital-personal-data-protection-bill-2023

Tracking healthcare data breaches. (n.d.). Healthcare Dive. https://www.healthcaredive.com/news/tracking-healthcare-data-breaches-cybersecurity-hacking-hospitals/696184/

Verizon. (2023, January 1). *Analyzing the COVID 19 Data Breach Landscape*. https://www.verizon.com/business/resources/articles/analyzing-covid-19-data-breach-landscape/

Vydra, S., & Klievink, B. (2019). Techno-optimism and policy-pessimism in the public sector big data debate. *Government Information Quarterly*, *36*(4), 1–10. doi:10.1016/j.giq.2019.05.010

Wandaogo, A. (2022). Does digitalization improve government effectiveness? Evidence from developing and developed countries. *Applied Economics*, *54*(33), 3840–3860. doi:10.1080/00036846.2021.2016590

ENDNOTES

1 Section 7: A Data Fiduciary may process personal data of a Data Principal for any of following uses, namely:— (a) for the specified purpose for which the Data Principal has voluntarily provided her personal data to the Data Fiduciary, and in respect of which she has not indicated to the Data Fiduciary that she does not consent to the use of her personal data…

Chapter 14
Tax Authorities Big Data Analytics in Developing Countries:
A Case Study of Indonesia

Susanna Hartanto
https://orcid.org/0000-0002-6936-6049
Widya Mandala Catholic University, Indonesia

ABSTRACT

Nowadays, most tax authorities in the world are utilizing various technologies, including big data analytics to be more efficient and effective in their works. Utilization of big data analytics and business intelligence by tax authorities in developing countries can be used to help identify the non-compliance taxpayers and support other activities in order to explore potential tax revenues. Directorate General of Taxes, Indonesian Tax Autbority, uses combination of compliance risk management application and business intelligence. There are nine types of compliance risk management applications. Currently, seven types of compliance risk management applications have been launched and used by the directorate general of taxes. The last two compliance risk management applications will be released in the near future. The series of nine compliance risk management applications will be supported by four business intelligence. Those compliance risk management and business intelligence applications will lead directorate general of taxes to be data driven organization.

INTRODUCTION

Tax authorities are "flooded with data." Most tax authorities are progressively utilizing various technologies, including big data analytics, to be more efficient and effective in their work. Big data and data analysis are not new, but in recent years, technological advances have made their use possible in companies, public administration, and tax authorities. Big data primarily refers to data sets that are too large or complex to be dealt with by traditional data-processing application software. Big data refers to

DOI: 10.4018/979-8-3693-0472-3.ch014

any large and complex collection of data. Data analytics is the process of extracting meaningful information from data.

Big data analytics is the use of advanced analytic techniques against very large, diverse big data sets that include structured, semi-structured, and unstructured data from different sources and in different sizes, from terabytes to zettabytes. The ultimate goal of big data is to create value, largely in an analytical capacity, including a reduction of costs from the great expansion of processing and storage capacity, the increasing availability of communications networks, the development of effective models to capture, store, and process massive data and advanced cognitive algorithms, the emergence of new data sources, including electronic invoices, and the exchange of tax information between countries.

This book chapter aims to examine the big data analytics that are used by tax authorities nowadays in developing countries, especially one of the emerging developing countries in Southeast Asia, Indonesia. The chapter will first discuss the implementation of big data analytics in other countries and then in Indonesia. This study aims to raise awareness about the implementation of big data analytics and the difficulties or constraints encountered during the process. This study uses the qualitative research method with a case study approach. The qualitative research method is used in investigating, locating, and describing the object under study. This method is best used to study the condition or situation of the research object.

The process of the qualitative research method involves emerging questions and procedures, including observation, interviews, and further follow-up sessions. Qualitative researchers collect data themselves by examining documents, observing behavior, or interviewing participants. Qualitative researchers typically gather multiple forms of data, such as interviews, observations, documents, and audiovisual information, rather than relying on a single data source (Creswell & Creswell, 2018).

In this study, data was collected through interviews, observation, and documentation. It was combined with a literature review to enrich the chapter, especially from the Directorate of General of Taxes regulations, to get further details of the implementation rules and guidelines of big data analytics in the Directorate of General of Tax Regulations system and databases. Work limitation data was collected through interviews, only with the Directorate General of Taxes. It would be great if there were interviews and data gathering from taxpayers' perspectives, but the new system will be implemented in July 2024, so it can only be conducted after July 2024.

The Principles of Tax System

According to Hector De Leon (De Leon, 2022), there are three main principles of a tax system:

1. The principle of adequacy of revenue states that if tax revenue is sufficient, the total must be an adequate source of the state budget.
2. The principle of justice states that the tax burden must be proportional (comparable) to the taxpayer's ability to pay taxes. Justice in tax collection is divided into horizontal justice and vertical justice. A tax collection system is said to be fair horizontally if the tax burden is the same for all taxpayers earning the same income with the same number of dependents, without distinguishing the type of income or source of income.
3. The principle of administrative feasibility states that all tax regulations must be administered cheaply, easily, and effectively. Administration Taxation is the key to the successful implementation of tax policy. As the organizer of tax collection based on law, tax administration must be structured in

such a way that it can become an instrument that works effectively and efficiently. Information completion and accountability are the keys to effective and efficient tax administration. Basics for The implementation of good tax administration consists of four things, namely:

a. The clarity and simplicity of the provisions of the law facilitate administration and provide clarity for mandatory tax.
b. Simplicity will reduce tax smuggling. Simplicity is meant to make the juridical formulation easy to understand.
c. There must be real tax reform considering the ease of achieving efficiency and effectiveness in tax administration.
d. Effective and efficient tax administration needs to be developed by paying attention to the arrangement of collection, processing, and utilization of information about tax subjects and tax objects. An effective information system is the key to its ability to collect taxes fairly. If the tax administration is not supported by the existence of an effective information system, it will cause inequality, namely the existence of tax subjects who should be taxpayers but are not registered with the tax administration, so the implementation of collection taxes becomes unfair.

A country's tax system reflects its evolutionary response to various social, economic, and political influences (Musgrave & Musgrave, 1989). The form of a tax system, therefore, has wide economic, political, and social implications. In the process of determining the tax policy and tax system, each tax authority unit has to weigh tax policies and systems in terms of the following basic criteria, including (Jenkins, Kuo, & Shukla, 2000):

a. Simplicity. A tax system should be transparent so that it is easy to administer and simple for taxpayers to comprehend and comply with. Simplicity must apply to the administration of the law as well as its legal structure. A complex tax system may impose a disproportionately high level of compliance costs on taxpayers as well as a high cost of tax administration on the government. Complexity in tax administration and opaqueness in tax laws help to induce corrupt behavior on the part of both taxpayers and tax officials. In such an environment, much of the efforts of taxpayers and tax officials, which otherwise could have been used constructively for economic development, are channeled into circumventing the system.
b. Low administration and compliance costs. The simpler and more transparent a tax system, the lower its administration and compliance costs. As tax revenue is collected mainly to finance government needs, the high cost of tax collection reduces the net tax revenue available to the government. High compliance costs for taxpayers should reduce the resources available to the private sector for productive activities. Therefore, one of the criteria of a good tax system is low administration and compliance costs. If these costs constitute a major portion of the tax revenue, the tax system needs to be restructured.

The tax system must also cope with the current practical side of tax administration, how tax administration responds to the increasing digitalization of the economy, how digital technology can be used to improve tax administration, and the implications for tax administration in emerging and developing countries. The Forum on Tax Administration stated the evolution of tax administration digitalization into three stages (Asian Development Bank, 2024):

1. Tax Administration 1.0. The characteristics are:
    a. Processes are paper-based and siloed.
    b. There is a tax administration-centered view of how the tax system should operate.
2. Tax Administration 2.0. The characteristics are:
    a. Taxpayers become customers.
    b. An increasingly taxpayer-centric view has been adopted.
    c. New technology tools and significant increases in digital data sources have allowed for the growth of e-administration.
    d. There is an increasing suite of e-services.
    e. There is better joining up within the revenue body and with some other parts of government.
    f. There is better targeting of resources.
3. Tax Administration 3.0. The characteristics are:
    a. Taxpayers' natural systems are at the center.
    b. The tax administration and other parts of government adopt processes to work seamlessly with those systems.
    c. The tax administration simultaneously becomes more resilient and more agile, something that "just happens."

Earlier phases of technology and its adoption for tax administration, which it placed into two broad categories, Tax Administration 1.0 and Tax Administration 2, had reached the limits of their capability while leaving significant challenges, which it termed "structural limitations," still to be addressed. These structural limitations, which still largely exist, are outlined below:

1. Voluntary compliance still applies widely. The paper observed that the notion of "voluntary compliance" was still relevant in many parts of the tax system in a practical sense, with many taxpayers having opportunities to make choices as to the proper reporting and payment of their tax liabilities. These choices do not always lead to the right compliance outcomes in practice, contributing to an economy's tax gap (i.e., the difference between the amounts of tax that should be paid and what is paid). With tax gaps even in advanced economies estimated to be in the range of 5% to 10% each year, this is concerning, given the revenue leakage it represents.
2. The compliance burden. Complying with tax obligations in some areas of an economy's tax system remains burdensome for many taxpayers, given the complexities and efforts associated with understanding the full range of tax obligations and administrative requirements. Such requirements have impacts on small and medium-sized enterprises (SMEs) in particular. Compliance costs, both monetary and opportunities, resulting from this burden are significant, according to the findings of the cited research.
3. Tax verification is often conducted "downstream." Liability for taxes is typically calculated at the end of a tax period and, thereafter, may be subject to a revenue body's post-assessment verification checks (e.g., audits) well after the return filing event (i.e., "downstream"). This downstream feature of tax administration can lead to uncertainty among some taxpayers, with potential implications for cash flow management and revenue bodies' tax debt inventories, and with further compliance costs for taxpayers when dealing with verification inquiries.
4. Taxation is often an isolated part of government administration. Despite efforts made over the many years to develop "whole-of-government" approaches to the delivery of public services, the

variety of systems and approaches that most government agencies still use complicates data sharing or common processes. This can cause tension and related issues with taxpayers as citizens, for example, when they are required to use multiple identity credentials to gain access to online systems and may be subject to multiple reporting requirements.

Taking account of the potential opportunities from increasing digitalization at large, the paper's authors envisaged a series of likely developments, which they presented as constituting a paradigm shift in tax administration, termed "Tax Administration 3.0." As more interconnections become possible between the different systems that taxpayers in businesses use to run their business, called "natural" systems, it will become more possible to move taxation processes (upstream) into these systems, subject to there being appropriate assurance mechanisms in place. Under this approach, it becomes possible in an increasing number of areas to build in tax compliance at the time a taxable event arises. A business' employee payroll system is an often-cited example of such a "natural" system. Taking this thinking to a further level of detail.

Core features of Tax Administration 3.0 are outlined below:

a. Embedded within taxpayers' natural systems. Revenue bodies will increasingly adapt their processes to fit in (i.e., become integrated with) taxpayers' natural systems.
b. Part of a reliant "system of systems." Digital platforms will increasingly become agents of the tax authority, carrying out tax administration processes within their systems.
c. A real-time tax certainty provider. Tax administration processes will increasingly be carried out in real-time or close to real-time. This development will be supported by artificial intelligence and advanced algorithms in the assessment phase.
d. Transparent and trustworthy. All taxpayers will have the ability to check and validate the taxes assessed and paid, as and when required.
e. Better integrated with other parts of government. Taxation will increasingly be "joined up" with other government services and functions, seamlessly supported by one digital identity across services and processes.
f. Presenting a human touch and becoming a high-tech adaptive organization. Tax authorities will increasingly be structured and governed around taxpayers, maximizing human skills with advanced analytics and decision-making support tools to engage with taxpayers as needed.

According to the OECD, the tax authorities engaged in this work identified six core building blocks of future tax administration (OECD, 2021):

a. Digital identity. The secure identification of taxpayers is key to the efficient functioning of modern revenue bodies, allowing the matching of administration processes (communication, tax return filing, incorporation of other data sources, self-service options, etc.) to individual and business taxpayers.
b. Taxpayer touchpoints. Communicating, interacting, and facilitating engagements with taxpayers is central to the smooth running of tax administration. In practice, this is supported through several touchpoints, including face-to-face interactions, phone calls, multifunction websites, e-services, business management systems, etc. Advances in digitalization allow revenue bodies to improve existing taxpayer touchpoints or create new ones.

c. Data management and standards. Tax administration is, at its heart, a data processing operation heavily reliant on the availability and quality of data. With increasing digitalization, revenue bodies have increasingly captured and processed more tax-related data from taxpayers and third parties (e.g., data from e-invoicing and online cash registers, and financial account information). To maximize the value of the data that revenue bodies have at their disposal, they also need to consider how to share it effectively and responsibly with other agencies and ecosystem partners.
d. Tax rule management and application. Currently, tax rule management and applications are undertaken primarily within processes driven or supported by the tax administration. This usually involves several steps, including guidance on tax law compliance and deadlines, the use of forms and e-forms that require taxpayers' input of specific information, and the finalization of relevant processes within the administration. The digital transformation of tax administration will enable a more decentralized and distributed method of rule application, supporting upstream compliance and the provision of tax certainty at an earlier stage.
e. New skill sets. The skill sets within the current system of tax administration (Tax Administration 2.0) have been adapted over the past few years to support more customer-centric e-services and greater use of analytic capability across the organization, including risk assessment and remote verifications. In the aspirational stage of Tax Administration 3.0, these processes will ordinarily be run automatically (and AI-enabled) within the tax administration, including through inputs from other organizations or within taxpayers' natural systems. The skills required will be more focused on supporting the operation and evolution of the tax administration system as a whole.
f. Governance frameworks. How tax administration is governed depends on political, cultural, societal, and technological factors. This is not only relevant to the organization and control of the tax administration itself but also includes cooperation with businesses, other governmental organizations, and non-governmental organizations, including taxpayer representative groups. The nature of the transformation to Tax Administration 3.0 requires the joining-up of systems and processes across the public and private sectors, as well as internationally.

However, no tax policy, whether in developed or developing countries, can be successful without an effective system of tax administration, including how taxes are administered in practice and how taxpayers respond. The tax system must include the legal side of tax administration, including the control of avoidance and the availability of legal mechanisms for the government to investigate taxpayers and enforce tax rules, as well as the resolution of tax disputes. It shows how important it is that the tax system is administered by tax authorities always keeps up with current technologies.

Big Data Usage in Tax Administration

In developed countries, most Western countries, tax authorities have already used big data analytics. Some developed countries are included:

a. United States. Big data is being used by the Internal Revenue Service to prevent tax fraud and to distinguish between legitimate taxpayers and those who attempt to manipulate the system to either reduce their tax obligations or obtain larger refunds. Social media data mining is being used to demonstrate that individuals are leading wealthier lives than their tax returns. Big Data uses data classification and trail-based pattern recognition to distinguish between legitimate taxpayers and fraudsters, which solves this challenge.

b. United Kingdom. One of the first big data analytics used in tax administration to enhance tax management is this one. To detect fraudulent behavior, HM Revenue and Customs (HMRC) uses a computerized data mining system called Connect, which uses social network analysis software to cross-check tax records of individuals and businesses with other databases. It can integrate analytical tools, gather data, and apply predictive analysis to compare data with multivariate statistical models to find a relationship between lifestyle and income.

ADEPT (Analytics for Debt Profiling and Targeting) is another tool available from HMRC. Using a combination of data from internal and external sources, this big data analysis system tracks changes to debt information, the payment amounts made and due, field auditor notes, and taxpayer-returned letters. It establishes a distinct source of information for managing debt.

c. Spain. Big data is also being used by the Spanish Tax Administration Agency (Agencia Estatal de Administracion Tributaria, AEAT) to track down affluent individuals who want to relocate overseas for tax reasons. It can perform some control functions, such as tracking information about restaurant costs or familial ties, to ascertain the whereabouts of huge assets. AEAT can identify fictitious non-residents with pertinent assets by analyzing a large amount of data.

AEAT also applies big data analysis to personal income tax under Tax Control Plan 2021. By applying the knowledge acquired, it aims to lessen the mistakes made by the taxpayer when filing their tax returns. It backs the behavioral insight method, which aims to better understand taxpayer conduct by combining global tactics with nudge approaches to encourage and promote appropriate tax activity.

d. Canada. To stop tax evasion overseas, the Canada Revenue Agency (CRA) used big data analysis. To combat aggressive tax avoidance and foreign tax evasion, CRA keeps up its emphasis on increasing data collection and data utilization to inform its compliance initiatives.
e. Australia. The Australian Tax Office (ATO) used the Automated Network and Grouping Identification Engine (ANGIE) network analytic solution to assist the tax avoidance and tax evasion task force in identifying intricate and multi-layered relationships between taxpayers, particularly multinational corporations, sizable public and private enterprises, and related individuals. It will make it possible to see new connections between taxpayers and identify patterns of interest. The global tax enforcement group, which is made up of revenue officials from the US, UK, Australia, the Netherlands, and Canada, is also anticipated to use the ANGIE graph database to find instances of tax evasion and avoidance.
f. South Korea. To prevent tax evasion via borrowed-name accounts, the National Tax Service (NTS) has developed a large data analytics system based on artificial intelligence. This system can evaluate a variety of data, including tax invoices, cash receipts, and the data of relatives and friends. The current NTS transaction analytic system identifies suspicious activity related to offshore accounts by utilizing comparable keywords to analyze foreign exchange revenues to monitor offshore tax evasion.

In developing countries and most Asian countries, some tax authorities have already used big data analytics, and some other tax authorities are still underway to use big data analytics. Some developing countries are included:

a. India. The taxpayers' data will be collected into segments. Incorporating the address, signature, and tax refund profile into the taxpayer's master profile will result from this progress. Another area that focuses on finding non-compliant individuals is called business intelligence. Collecting pertinent papers and web pages that may be examined is part of the insight project, which will create an integrated information management system. Business intelligence will be used to identify taxpayers who are not in compliance, and it will also categorize taxpayers according to criteria including income, profit, and capital gains.
b. Mexico. To improve its systems for meeting tax responsibilities, SAT (Servicio de Administración Tributaria) uses artificial intelligence, which enables the collection of vast amounts of data from electronic invoices. Before artificial intelligence was used, SAT used large data to handle three primary problems: creating algorithms, transforming data into structured information, and ensuring that the information was available instantly.
c. Costa Rica. Using big data, the Costa Rican Ministry of Finance's predictive model, which was created using data mining techniques, identified instances of payments to third parties being simulated.

Big Data Usage in Indonesia Tax Administration

Indonesia, officially the Republic of Indonesia, is a country in Southeast Asia, between the Indian and Pacific Oceans. The Indonesian Tax Authority is called the Directorate General of Taxes. The development of big data analytics at the Directorate General of Taxes is certainly inseparable from the goal of achieving sustainable compliance. Therefore, the provision of data in the context of tax monitoring is very important for field officers. DGT's goal is to create a data-driven organization, namely an organization that can work, make decisions, and establish a policy using appropriate and adequate data analysis. DGT always tries to increase the value of every data utilization.

According to the Directorate General of Taxes Public Relations during the interview, the Big Data Analytics development journey at the Directorate General of Taxes is following strategic initiatives of the Ministry's Bureaucratic Reform and Institutional Transformation program in Finance. Development of Big Data Analytics in the Ministry of Finance, consisting of central themes (bureaucracy, agile, effective, and efficient public services), sustainable fiscal management theme, management of state spending and management of the Treasury, state assets, as well as accountable and productive financing with controlled risks.

The development of big data analytics has a flow in its management, which starts with the utilization of internal and external data. A data warehouse is a place for data scientists to collect, process, and analyze data. Data scientists themselves are human resources professionals who have an important role in producing the appropriate big data analytics.

The history of data analytics development at the Directorate General of Taxes started formally in 2014 with the development of compliance risk management. Compliance Risk Management is a risk-based compliance improvement effort that gives treatment to taxpayers according to risk obedience. Compliance Risk Management Development is one of the ten transformation themes that aim to increase the tax ratio listed in the Minister of Finance Regulation Number 36/KMK.01/2014. Compliance Risk Management development is preceded by the establishment of an appropriate ad hoc team decree of the Director General of Taxes Number 105/PJ/2014. The team was tasked with developing a compliance risk management risk engine based on recommendations for the development of 16 strategic initiative programs. This team continues in the year next, namely according to Decree of the Director General of

Taxes Number 181/PJ/2015 in 2015, Decree of the Director General of Taxes Number 61/PJ/2016 in 2016, Decree of the Director General of Taxes Number 79/PJ/2017 in 2017, and Decree of the Director General of Taxes Number 105/PJ/2018 in 2018.

Compliance Risk Management Development at the Directorate General of Taxes is also aimed at fulfilling performance indicators based on the Tax Administration Diagnostic Assessment Tool Field Guide (TADAT). TADAT is a guide designed to provide an objective assessment of the health level of the main components in a tax institution. Focused health assessment is conducted in nine Performance Outcome Areas (POA), one of which is POA 2 regarding effective risk management. Based on POA 2, the Directorate General of Taxes can be declared to have implemented effective risk management if overall Directorate General of Taxes risks have been managed effectively.

Regarding the utilization of this data, the Directorate General of Taxes also studies various big data analytics best practices in the field of tax administration. One of them is in the audit case selection area. Several countries have implemented big data analytics in the form of structured income flows in the United States, tax agent risk in Australia, and VAT risk in the Netherlands, Norway, and Ireland. In addition, the application of data analytics related to income tax risk is also carried out in the Netherlands, Norway, Ireland, Sweden, and the United Kingdom.

In another area, namely filing and payment compliance, big data analytics has also been implemented as a support for decision-making regarding the language of communication to taxpayers to support voluntary compliance. Countries that have implemented this include Australia, Canada, Norway, the United Kingdom, and Singapore. In addition, regarding the Taxpayer Service, big data analytics has also been applied in the classification and analysis of input from taxpayers in countries, such as Singapore, the United Kingdom, Canada, Ireland and Norway.

Furthermore, in the debt management area, big data analytics is implemented in the default risk analysis applied in Finland, Ireland, Singapore, and Sweden. Predictions of ability and propensity to pay were applied in Australia and Norway. Finally, regarding the policy area, big data analytics is implemented in the form of a tax gap analysis in Finland, England, and China. In addition, China also applies big data analytics when establishing value-added tax reform policies.

Indonesia itself has developed big data analytics according to predetermined milestones, including the application of prescriptive data analytics through compliance risk mmanagement development, which continues with the launch of various compliance risk management functions. In addition, the application of predictive data analytics was carried out by piloting value-added tax fraud detection in 2018 and continued with the development of Smartweb and Ability to Pay.

Furthermore, diagnostic data analytics was carried out by piloting text analytics in 2019 to produce 99 trigger data and 69 test data. Regarding descriptive data analytics, there was the development of Soneta and DJP Search in 2017, the implementation of the Directorate General of Taxes Foreman (Managerial Dashboard and Online Reporting), and the launch of the taxpayers Middle Dashboard and Self-Service Business Intelligence.

The Directorate General of Taxes also implemented OLTP enablers, namely e-Faktur, Tax Amnesty, and Exchane of Information from 2014 to 2018, eBupot, and Country by Country Report in 2019, as well as OLAP with the launch of Approweb v.3, Derik in 2020, and application integration in 2021. Going forward, the application of predictive and prescriptive data analytics will lead to the acceptance of business intelligence, human resources, organization, and regulatory business intelligence, which are expected to be used in 2023. Trigger data, and test data, and dashboards that are currently being developed will also be implemented in 2023.

Business Intelligence Concept and Best Practice

Business intelligence, abbreviated to BI, is a technique that combines architecture, information technology tools, and databases for collecting, storing, managing data, and knowledge management with data analysis tools to present information that is useful for planners and decision- makers.

This data management policy consists of ten areas, namely: data architecture, data modeling and design, master and reference data, data storage and operations, integration and interoperability, enterprise data warehouse and business intelligence, document and content, metadata, data security, and data quality. These ten areas will then be arranged in more detail into a form of guidance that contains more technical matters. One area of data management is business intelligence development, which is one of the big data analysis applications.

Business intelligence is the process of adding value to data into information and insight that is used in making decisions in an organization. Business intelligence based on the type of data analytics can be divided into descriptive analytics, diagnostic analytics, predictive analytics, and prescriptive analytics.

1. Descriptive Analytics

Descriptive analytics is a form of analysis and reporting on past events. Simple analysis on the dashboard is important for management to observe and understand conditions based on historical data. Descriptive analytics is generally used for management reporting purposes. At the Directorate General of Taxes, examples of this kind of analytics are the "receipt dashboard" and "smartboard."

2. Diagnostic Analytics

Diagnostic analytics is not only used to observe and understand a condition but also to find the cause of a situation based on historical data. For example, analyzing the reasons why sales in one location are higher than in other locations, or the reasons why one product is more popular in one location than in another location.

3. Predictive Analytics

Predictive analytics uses machine learning technology, algorithms, and artificial intelligence. This type of analysis has been carried out by data scientists to analyze and explore historical data. Statistical skills, computer science, and business expertise are very necessary for the development of predictive business intelligence. An example of applying predictive analytics to business intelligence development at the Directorate General of Taxes is "Ability to Pay". This "Ability to Pay" is a business intelligence that predicts the taxpayer's ability to pay.

4. Prescriptive Analytics

Like predictive analytics, prescriptive analytics is the highest-level type of analytics. This type of prescriptive business intelligence development also utilizes data scientists. Data-driven organizations need predictive and prescriptive analytics in their decision-making. Apart from providing predictions

Figure 1. Stages in cross-industry standard process for data mining (CRISP-DM) (Directorate General of Taxes, 2022)

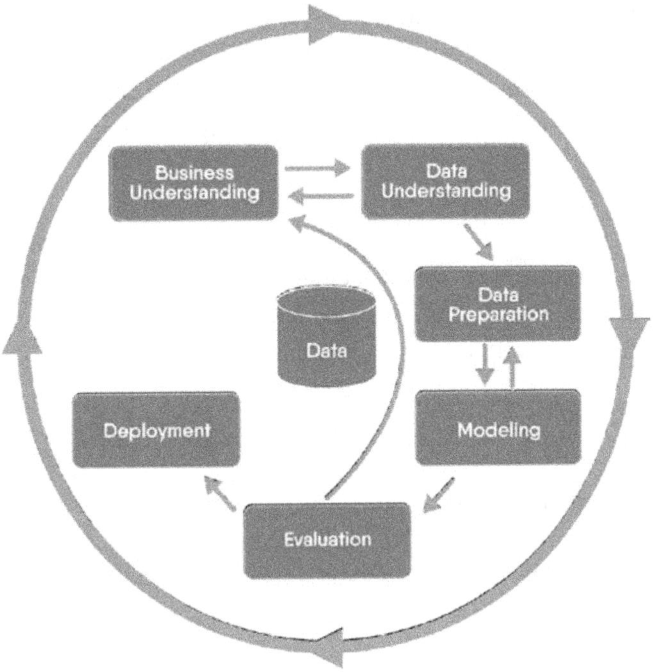

of a condition, these two types of analytics also provide alternative solutions that are useful in decision-making. An example of prescriptive analytics type business intelligence development at the Directorate General of Taxes is the Compliance Risk Management risk engine. Treatment recommendations for taxpayers are offered to users of this Compliance Risk Management risk engine.

Business intelligence development applies the Cross-Industry Standard Process for Data Mining (CRISP-DM) approach, which is one of the data mining process models. This model was developed by a consortium consisting of NCR Systems Engineering Copenhagen, DaimlerChrysler AG, SPSS Inc., and OHRA Verzekeringen en Bank Groep. In CRISP-DM, the data analytics process model developed consists of six stages. The stages in CRISP-DM take place sequentially, with the opportunity to return to the previous stage if the stage being carried out encounters difficulties.

The Cross-Industry Standard Process for Data Mining (CRISP-DM) stages in Figure 1 are Business Understanding, Data Understanding, Data Preparation, Modeling, Evaluation, and Deployment. In detail, the six stages can be described as follows:

1. Business Understanding

This stage defines the problem formulation, research objectives, and discussions related to business processes. At this stage, it is necessary to ascertain the objectives of the work unit or the problems being faced. Data analytics projects also need to be prepared in terms of resources, data, risks, costs, and benefits. Project management is also determined, which includes project objectives and project planning.

2. Data Understanding

This stage focuses on understanding the data and selecting data that supports the research objectives. Activities included in this stage include collecting initial data, understanding the data that has been collected, data exploration, verifying data quality, understanding the condition of anomalous data or outliers, anticipating the relationship between indicators, and performing visualization to understand the data.

3. Data Preparation

This stage includes selecting attributes that can be arranged to become a data set that will be used in modeling. The activities that are part of this stage are selecting data to be used, cleaning data that will not be used, creating new indicators if needed, and data integration.

4. Modeling

At this stage, data mining techniques or methods are applied to obtain modeling that suits the research objectives. Some of activities need to be carried out, namely determining the model that will be used, compiling or sorting data that will be used as a sample, forming a model, evaluating the resulting model to see important indicators, and consulting with the business process owner unit.

5. Evaluation

This stage is carried out to evaluate the modeling that has been created previously to achieve the research objectives. Several activities that need to be carried out include evaluating the overall result and whether the project objectives are met, evaluating technical and practical aspects of the model, such as performance and speed, reviewing the process carried out, and determining whether the resulting model will be continued to the deployment stage or not.

6. Deployment

This stage indicates that the modeling carried out is in accordance with the research objectives and is ready to be used. If the evaluation results show that the model is ready for production, then the steps that need to be prepared include determining a deployment plan, monitoring, and maintenance, as well as preparing final project documents.

The series of processes above is not a process that can only be done once. If the resulting model is already running in a production environment, it must still be evaluated periodically to see if there are any changes to the previous model. Model changes need to be made when the model being used is deemed ineffective based on calculations that can be measured in terms of the objectives of the business process owner unit.

Business intelligence development at the Directorate General of Taxes cannot be separated from data management. Data management policy is a form of data regulation that is prepared by adopting provisions in data management. In this case, the Data Management Body of Knowledge (DMBOK) is a guide used to design data governance at the Directorate General of Taxes.

According to the Directorate General of Taxes Public Relations during the interview, Compliance Risk Management and Business Intelligence aims to ensure that the Directorate General of Taxes can become a data-driven organization. However, to achieve this goal, the Directorate General of Taxes needs to go through several phases, because the management of big data analytics theoretically has four levels.

First, it is descriptive. In this initial phase, the Directorate General of Taxes went through this phase by creating a dashboard containing basic data, such as actual revenue. Second, there is a level that is diagnostic. In this phase, data and information can be processed and tested early, for example, on taxpayer compliance because Indonesia adheres to a self-assessment system. This phase also requires other data to be compared. The data held by the Directorate General of Taxes, such as the annual tax return, certificate of withholding tax, and tax invoice, is based on data obtained from agencies, institutions, associations, and other parties (ILAP). The third and fourth phases will require high-level data analytics.

Compliance Risk Management

According to the Directorate General of Taxes Public Relations, the Directorate General of Taxes has the task of collecting state revenues from the tax sector, to support the state revenue and expenditure budget. To carry out this task, the Directorate General of Taxes is equipped with a system to carry out the process of managing taxpayer compliance risks. The system is compliance risk management. Currently, the administration system continues to be developed to be able to administer taxpayers and data. Apart from that, appropriate strategies are needed to provide more effective and efficient services, supervision, and law enforcement following the level of risk and compliance of the taxpayer concerned. The strategies are the implementation of compliance risk management and business intelligence.

The Directorate General of Taxes launched its newest application, namely the Compliance Risk Management (CRM) Law Enforcement Function and the Compliance Risk Management Assessment Function. This launch was inaugurated directly by the Directorate General of Taxes, Suryo Utomo, at the Directorate General of Taxes Head Office, Jakarta, on April 8, 2022. The Directorate General of Taxes implements compliance risk management to carry out supervision in extensification, supervision, audit, and tax collection activities. The implementation of compliance risk management is one part of sustainable tax reform from the tax amnesty, as well as the transparency of financial information.

According to Circular Letter of Directorate General of Taxes Number 39/PJ/2021 (Implementation of Compliance Risk Management and Business Intelligence, 2021) about implementation of Compliance Risk Management and Business Intelligence, which amended Circular Letter of Directorate General of Taxes Number 24/PJ/2019 (Implementation of Compliance Risk Management in Extensification, Monitoring, Inspection, and Collection Activities in Directorate General of Taxes, 2019), compliance risk management is a taxpayer compliance risk management process that is carried out systematically, measurably, objectively, and repeatedly to form a risk engine to support decision-making at the Directorate General of Taxes more efficiently and effectively. The risk determination engine is used in risk weighting to produce risk levels, which are displayed in the form of a taxpayer compliance risk map.

Currently, The Directorate General of Taxes has implemented compliance risk management following the Circular Letter of Directorate General of Taxes Number 39/PJ/2021 (Implementation of Compliance Risk Management and Business Intelligence, 2021) about the implementation of compliance risk management and business intelligence, concerning the implementation of compliance risk management in extensification, supervision, audit, and collection activities at The Directorate General of Taxes.

However, in line with the need to accelerate the implementation of compliance risk management in all business processes at The Directorate General of Taxes, it is necessary to increase the implementation of compliance risk management in the service function and tax education function, as well as improvements to the monitoring, inspection, and billing functions in the form of implementing compliance risk management transfer pricing with business intelligence support. The implementation of business intelligence is intended to automate and maintain added value to the compliance risk management process. These additions and improvements were made to encourage more effective and efficient service, supervision, and law enforcement.

Apart from supporting the implementation of compliance risk management in developing priority action plans, the implementation of business intelligence can be used at every stage of the implementation and evaluation of monitoring, inspection, and billing activities. Business intelligence produces output that is integrated with all strategic decisions in every business process at the Directorate General of Taxes.

Taxpayer Compliance Risk

In its development, compliance risk management was carried out through stages and international best practices of the OECD compliance risk management model, as well as fulfilling the health assessment parameters of world tax authorities, the Tax Administration Diagnostic Assessment Tools (TADAT). Validation tests have been carried out with the business owner and vertical units to ensure the quality of the compliance risk management machine to meet user needs in the field.

The development of compliance risk management is part of the fundamental reforms carried out as a prerequisite for the implementation of a modern tax administration system. With compliance risk management, the Directorate General of Taxes will have the measurement of setting priorities with regular, measurable, simple, efficient, and productive references.

The compliance risk management product is the result of the collaborative efforts of many parties who worked together in its development, including the relevant technical directorates as business owners, application developers, business processes, and vertical units as users.

Taxpayer compliance risk is any possibility or uncertainty that has an impact on or consequences for taxpayer compliance. A compliance risk map is a matrix or map that depicts a combination of possibility level and impact level and contains the value of the taxpayer's compliance risk based on a combination of elements of possibility level and impact level.

There are six taxpayer compliance risks, as follows:

1. Taxpayer Compliance Risk: The Extensification Function is the level of possibility of non-fulfillment of tax obligations due to non-compliance by taxpayers who have fulfilled subjective and objective requirements but have not registered to be given a taxpayer identification number.
2. Taxpayer Compliance Risk: The Service Function is the level of possible loss of tax revenue due to taxpayer non-compliance in registering, reporting on time, paying, and reporting correctly.
3. Taxpayer Compliance Risk: The Tax Education Function is any possibility or uncertainty that has an impact or consequences on taxpayer compliance regarding the implementation of their tax rights and obligations to increase knowledge and skills and changing taxpayer behavior.
4. Taxpayer Compliance Risk: The Audit and Supervisory Function is any possibility or uncertainty that has an impact or consequences on taxpayer compliance related to loss of tax revenue due to

taxpayer non-compliance in making timely reporting (timely filing), correct payment time (timely payment), and complete and correct reporting (complete and correct reporting).

5. Taxpayer Compliance Risk: The Transfer Pricing Function is any possibility or uncertainty that has an impact or consequences in the form of a loss of tax revenue from taxpayers who have transactions that are influenced by special relationships.
6. Taxpayer Compliance Risk: The Collection Function is any possibility or uncertainty that has an impact or consequences on taxpayer compliance in the form of loss of tax revenue due to non-fulfillment of payment obligations for tax arrears caused, among other things, by the loss of the opportunity to collect tax debts and/or disbursing tax receivables.

A taxpayer compliance risk map can serve some functions, including:

1. Compliance Risk Map: The Extensification Function (CRM Extensification Function): a map that depicts taxpayer compliance risk in registering as a taxpayer, to be given a tax identification number that is prepared based on the level of possible taxpayer non-compliance and the level of taxpayer contribution to revenue.
2. Compliance Risk Map: The Service Function (CRM Service Function): a map that describes the taxpayer's compliance risk in registering, reporting, making payments, and reporting accuracy, which is prepared to determine the treatment given to taxpayers when providing tax services.
3. Compliance Risk Map: The Tax Education Function (CRM Tax Education Function): a map that depicts the compliance risk of taxpayers in carrying out their tax rights and obligations, which is prepared based on the level of possible taxpayer non-compliance and the level of taxpayer contribution to revenue, to increase knowledge and skills and change taxpayer behavior.
4. Compliance Risk Map: The Audit and Monitoring Function (CRM Audit and Monitoring Function): a map that depicts the taxpayer's compliance risk in making reports, payments, and the correctness of reporting, which is prepared based on the level of possible non-compliance of the taxpayer and the level of the contribution to revenue.
5. Compliance Risk Map: The Transfer Pricing Function (CRM Transfer Pricing Function): a map that depicts the level of compliance risk of taxpayers who have transactions that are affected by special relationships or other transfer pricing transactions, which is prepared based on the level of possible taxpayer non-compliance and the level of the taxpayer's contribution to revenue.
6. Compliance Risk Map: The Billing Function (CRM Billing Function): a map that depicts taxpayer compliance risk in paying tax receivables, which is arranged based on the level of collectability of tax receivables, the existence of taxpayers and/or tax insurers, and the ability to pay taxpayers and/or tax insurers.

Compliance risk management implementation in general is the process of using a risk determination engine that produces a taxpayer compliance risk map to be used as a consideration in planning activities and determining priority actions in business processes, as follows:

a. Extensification function. CRM Compliance Risk Map: The Extensification Function is used to plan the database, which will later be used to determine priorities for granting taxpayer identification numbers to taxpayers who have met subjective and objective requirements.

b. Service function. CRM Compliance Risk Map: The Service Function is used to differentiate the type of notification for the compliance risk level of taxpayers who apply for certain services.
c. Tax education function. CRM Compliance Risk Map: The Tax Education Function is used to plan which will later be used to determine taxpayer priorities for tax education.
d. Supervision and inspection functions. CRM Compliance Risk Map: The Monitoring and Inspection Function as well as the CRM Compliance Risk Map Transfer Pricing, Ability to Pay, SmartWeb, and other data are used in preparing a database to determine priorities for exploring the potential of taxpayers who will be supervised and audited.
e. Billing function. CRM Compliance Risk Map: The Billing Function in the form of a Disbursement Priority List and Action Priority List is used to plan tax collection actions with forced letters accompanied by the use of Ability to Pay and SmartWeb.

At the end of 2023, the Compliance Risk Management Law Enforcement and Compliance Risk Management Assessment Functions have already been successfully launched following their predecessors, namely Compliance Risk Management for Monitoring and Inspection Functions, Compliance Risk Management for Billing Functions, Compliance Risk Management for Extensification Functions, Compliance Risk Management for Transfer Pricing, and Compliance Risk Management for Tax Education. The Compliance Risk Management Law Enforcement Function and Compliance Risk Management Assessment Function are indicator tools in determining taxpayer priorities for law enforcement actions and assessment activities.

Compliance Risk Management law enforcement function gives taxpayers priority law enforcement, which refers to tax criminal acts regulated in Article 37 to Article 42 of The Law of General Provisions and Tax Procedures (Directorate General of Taxes, 2007) as amended in Harmonization of Tax Law (UU No. 7 Tahun 2021 about Harmonization of Tax Law, 2021). Meanwhile, the Compliance Risk Management Assessment function provides a taxpayer compliance map based on activities regulated in Article 10 and Article 18 of the Income Tax Law (Directorate General of Taxes, 2008) as amended in Harmonization of Tax Law (UU No. 7 Tahun 2021 about Harmonization of Tax Law, 2021) and Article 16C of the Value Added Tax Law (Directorate General of Taxes, 2000) as amended in Harmonization of Tax Law (UU No. 7 Tahun 2021 about Harmonization of Tax Law, 2021).

The Compliance Risk Management application continues to be developed by the Directorate General of Taxes. Later, there will be nine types of compliance risk management that will support the Directorate General of Taxes's business processes. Currently, seven types of compliance risk management have been launched and used by The Directorate General of Taxes. The last two compliance risk management will be released in the near future. The seven compliance risk management aforementioned are:

1. Law and enforcement Compliance Risk Management
2. Inspection and monitoring Compliance Risk Management
3. Transfer Pricing Compliance Risk Management
4. Assessment Compliance Risk Management
5. Tax Education Compliance Risk Management
6. Extensification Compliance Risk Management
7. Billing Compliance Risk Management

The two new compliance risk management that will be launched are service compliance risk management and objection compliance risk management. The series of nine compliance risk management will be supported by four business intelligence, as mentioned in figure 2.

As part of the Directorate General of Taxes's data analytics, according to the Directorate General of Taxes Public Relations, compliance risk management is also supported by business intelligence, namely Ability to Pay, Madya Taxpayers Dashboard, Smartweb, and Smartboard. All of these products are a form of the Directorate General of Taxes's commitment to becoming a data-driven organization.

By implementing the Compliance Risk Management Law Enforcement and Assessment Function, according to the Directorate General of Taxes Public Relations, it is hoped that law enforcement and assessment activities will become more measurable, systematic, and objective. Compliance Risk Management is also a breakthrough in responding to the challenges of limited human resources and time (early warning based on risk position) so that law enforcement and assessment activities can be carried out more precisely, on target, focused, and optimally.

Compliance Risk Management will notify to taxpayers of tax obligations that have not been fulfilled. The scope of tax obligations that have not been fulfilled by taxpayers is taxpayer non-compliance in terms of timely registration, payment, and reporting. Notification consists of three models: gentle notification (gentle reminder), moderate notification (moderate reminder), and loud notification (harsh reminder).

For taxpayers with a high-risk profile, the information system at the Directorate General of Taxes forwards a list of tax obligations that have not been fulfilled by the taxpayer as intended in a letter to the Account Representative and/or State Tax Bailiff on Aproweb for supervision under the provisions of the laws and regulations. A list of tax obligations that have not been fulfilled by the taxpayer can be printed and submitted directly to the taxpayer or the taxpayer's attorney.

If requests for certain tax services are submitted online via the Directorate General of Taxes page, notifications to inform the taxpayers of tax obligations that have not been fulfilled are displayed on the page when taxpayers access the service menu, along with a list of tax obligations that have not yet been fulfilled by the taxpayers. It is delivered automatically to the taxpayer's email address registered in the information system at the Directorate General of Taxes after the taxpayers apply for tax services.

Implementation of Business Intelligence

The Directorate General of Taxes continues to strive to develop compliance risk management systems in its business processes. Hopefully, the Directorate General of Taxes can provide services, supervision, and law enforcement in accordance with the level of risk and compliance of the taxpayers concerned. Initially, the implementation of compliance risk management was regulated in Directorate General of Taxes Circular No. 24/PJ/2019 (Implementation of Compliance Risk Management in Extensification, Monitoring, Inspection, and Collection Activities in Directorate General of Taxes, 2019). However, in its development, the Directorate General of Taxes added and perfected compliance risk management implementation by utilizing business intelligence. These additions and improvements are regulated in the Circular Letter of the Directorate General of Taxes No. 39/PJ/2021 (Implementation of Compliance Risk Management and Business Intelligence, 2021). Based on this regulation, the implementation of business intelligence is intended to automate and maintain added value to the compliance risk management process.

The use of Approweb, which consists of Ability to Pay and SmartWeb, can be carried out in the implementation of compliance risk management monitoring and inspection functions as well as compli-

Figure 2. Compliance risk management integration and business intelligence
(Directorate General of Taxes, 2022)

ance risk management billing functions. Apart from that, Ability to Pay and SmartWeb can also be used in the monitoring, inspection, and billing activity stages.

Approweb is an application owned by the Directorate General of Taxes to compare internal and external data, which is used as a tool to supervise taxpayers. Ability to Pay is an application created through a data analytics process that is used to provide a description or prediction of the taxpayer's ability to pay. SmartWeb is a graph analytics-based application that is capable of grouping taxpayers by presenting taxpayer relationships in network form, information on high-wealth individual taxpayers and their group companies, information on beneficial owners and ultimate beneficial owners, as well as indications of the risk of non-compliance.

Ability to Pay

In the Compliance Risk Management Billing Function, Ability to Pay provides an overview of the taxpayer's ability to pay to determine the prognosis of disbursement of receivables and collection activity plans. SmartWeb provides a network overview and profile of taxpayers to determine the prognosis of the disbursement of receivables and plan collection activities. Ability to Pay and SmartWeb can be used at every stage of implementation and monitoring or evaluation activities, including inspection, billing, installment requests, and postponement of tax payments.

Ability to Pay is an indicator that provides a predictive picture of a taxpayer's ability to pay and is formed based on historical data. Ability to Pay is displayed in the Approweb application in the Compliance Risk Management module and is divided into three classes, namely:

1. The large class consists of taxpayers registered with the Large Taxpayer Tax Office.
2. The Medium or intermediate class consists of taxpayers registered with the Madya Tax Office and the Directorate General of Taxes Special Regional Office in Jakarta.
3. The Small class consists of taxpayers registered with the Pratama Tax Office.

Ability to Pay uses a measurement scale approach (scoring) based on 4C analysis, namely capacity, capital, character, and condition to provide a qualitative picture of the taxpayer's ability to pay, which consists of:

1. Very low, which indicates the taxpayer's liquidity level is relatively low compared to other taxpayers in its class.
2. Low, which indicates the taxpayer's liquidity level is relatively low compared to other taxpayers in its class.
3. Moderate, which indicates the taxpayer's liquidity level is relatively moderate compared to other taxpayers in its class.
4. High, which indicates the taxpayer's liquidity level is relatively high compared to other taxpayers in its class.
5. Very high, which indicates the taxpayer's liquidity level is relatively high compared to other taxpayers in its class.

The Ability to Pay can be used in implementing Compliance Risk Management Monitoring Functions and inspection functions as well as Compliance Risk Management Billing Function. In addition, the Ability to Pay application can be used for monitoring, inspection, and billing activities. In the Compliance Risk Management monitoring function, Ability to Pay provides an overview of taxpayers' ability to pay to determine the Potential Exploration Priority Target List (Daftar Sasaran Prioritas Penggalian Potensi, DSP3), Supervision Priority List (Daftar Prioritas Pengawasan, DPP) and Audit Priority Target List (Daftar Sasaran Prioritas Pemeriksaan, DSPP).

Meanwhile, in the Compliance Risk Management Collection Function, Ability to Pay provides an overview of taxpayers' ability to pay to determine the prognosis for the disbursement of receivables and plans for collection activities. For collection activities, Ability to Pay can be used as a consideration of the taxpayer's ability to pay in determining the Potential Exploration Priority Target List (Daftar Sasaran Prioritas Penggalian Potensi, DSP3).

Account Representatives can also utilize Ability to Pay to optimize the disbursement of potential revenue from a letter requesting an explanation of data or information (Surat Permintaan Penjelasan atas Data dan atau Keterangan, SP2DK) that has been issued. For inspection activities, Ability to Pay can be used as a reference for the level of collectability in inspection proposals. Then, for collection activities, the Ability to Pay can be used as a consideration in determining the prognosis for the disbursement of tax receivables and planning collection activities. The Ability to Pay indicator can also be used for other activities, such as the research process for requests for installments or postponement of tax payments, as well as the research process for request for reduction and/or elimination of administrative sanctions.

Utilization of Ability to Pay in Tax Audit

The Ability to Pay indicator can be used as a reference for the level of collectability in proposed inspections. The Ability to Pay indicator can provide an understanding of the taxpayer's ability to pay at the stage of preparing the audit plan and carrying out the audit, but the Ability to Pay is not used to change the concept of the findings.

The use of the Ability to Pay in a tax audit can be used as a consideration in determining the prognosis for the disbursement of tax receivables and planning collection activities. Utilization of the ability to pay in other activities, such as:

1. The Ability to Pay indicator can be used to optimize the disclosure of untruthful acts or termination of investigations for the benefit of state revenue in initial evidence examination and investigation activities.
2. Ability to Pay can be used in the process of researching installment requests or postponing tax payments.
3. The Ability to Pay can be used in the process of researching applications for reducing the amount of Income Tax Article 25.
4. Ability to Pay can be used in the process of researching applications for reducing or eliminating administrative sanctions.
5. The Ability to Pay can be used to support other activities at the Directorate General of Taxes in order to explore potential tax revenue.

Smartweb

The Directorate General of Taxes is trying to accelerate the implementation of compliance risk management in all of its business processes. The Directorate General of Taxes uses various methods, one of which is utilizing business intelligence to automate and maintain added value to the compliance risk management process. The implementation of business intelligence in compliance risk management can be seen in the presence of an application called Smartweb. Smartweb is one of the four data analysis-based applications released by the Directorate General of Taxes.

Regulations regarding Smartweb are contained in the Circular Letter of the Directorate General of Taxes No. 39/PJ/2021 concerning the implementation of compliance risk management and business intelligence (Implementation of Compliance Risk Management and Business Intelligence, 2021). According to the Circular Letter of the Directorate General of Taxes No. 39/PJ/2021, Smartweb is a graph analytics–based application that is capable of presenting taxpayer relationships in the form of a network, tax information on high-wealth individuals and their group companies, beneficial owner and ultimate beneficial owner information, as well as an indication of the risk of non-compliance.

Smartweb has the benefit of supporting the implementation of compliance risk management monitoring and inspection functions, as well as compliance risk management billing functions. Not only that, compliance risk management can also be used in the monitoring, inspections, and billing activity stages. Some of Smartweb' benefits in compliance risk management are:

1. Smartweb for monitoring and inspection functions will produce a network picture and profile of taxpayers to determine the Potential Exploration Priority Target List (Daftar Sasaran Prioritas Penggalian Potensi, DSP3).
2. For the billing function, Smartweb will provide benefits by providing a network overview and taxpayer profile, which are used to determine the prognosis for the disbursement of receivables and plan collection activities.
3. For monitoring functions, Smartweb will provide benefits by assisting in determining the Potential Exploration Priority Target List (Daftar Sasaran Prioritas Penggalian Potensi, DSP3). Account representatives can also use Smartweb to identify special relationships between taxpayers in the context of preparing letters requesting explanations of data or information (Surat Permintaan Penjelasan atas Data dan atau Keterangan, SP2DK).
4. For the inspection function, Smartweb can be used as a consideration in determining indications of non-compliance when proposing an inspection. Smartweb can also be used as a consideration for making group taxpayer audit proposals.
5. In billing activities, Smartweb can be used to help identify the taxpayer. Smartweb also has other benefits for billing functions. The Smartweb application can be used to support other Directorate General of Taxes activities to extract potential tax revenue.

Smartweb will be an application that helps the Directorate General of Taxes implementing compliance risk management and business intelligence, which will further advance various Directorate General of Taxes functions as mentioned. Smartweb also really helps the Directorate General of Taxes increase state tax revenue.

Utilization of Smartweb

Smartweb is displayed in the Approweb application in the Taxpayer Account Module. Smartweb displays information in the form of:

a. A beneficial owner, or ultimate beneficial owner, who is an entity or individual who ultimately owns or controls a legal entity, such as a company, trust, or foundation.
b. A taxpayer group is a collection of two or more taxpayers in a business group consisting of parties who have a special relationship in accordance with the provisions of Article 18 paragraph 4 of the Income Tax Law or Article 2 paragraph 2 of the Value Added Tax Law, or parties with no special or associated relationship but are known as a business group.
c. Affiliate transactions are, in this case, transactions between parties who have a special relationship in accordance with the provisions of Article 18 paragraph 4 of the Income Tax Law.
d. An indication of the risk of non-compliance in reporting affiliate transactions.
e. High-wealth individual taxpayers and their families, or group companies.

Utilization of Smartweb in monitoring activities is:

a. Smartweb can be used as material in determining non-compliance taxpayers.
b. An account representative selects taxpayers listed and conducts comprehensive research on data and/or information in the context of preparing letters to taxpayers by utilizing Smartweb to identify special relationships between taxpayers.

Smartweb can also be used for inspection activities. The utilization of Smartweb in inspection activities includes:

a. Smartweb can be used as a consideration in determining indications of non-compliance when proposing an inspection.
b. Smartweb can be used as a consideration for making group taxpayer audit proposals.
c. Smartweb can provide an overview of special relationships and enrich the taxpayer's profile at the stage of preparing the audit plan and carrying out the audit.

The utilization of Smartweb in billing activities can be used to identify taxpayers. Smartweb can be used to support other activities at the Directorate General of Taxes to explore potential tax revenues.

Taxpayer User Interface

According to the Directorate General of Taxes (DGT) public relations, the system will have transition from DGT online to the Coretax Administration System on July 1, 2024. Currently, the Coretax Administration System is still in the process of pilot testing for some taxpayers. Coretax will provide three portals for stakeholders, including a taxpayer portal, an internal portal, and a third-party portal. A third-party portal will include an exchange of information and a tax consultant.

All tax payment and reporting applications will be connected to one Taxpayer Account Management (TAM) and not separated into several applications, which is really difficult to understand for taxpayers. Taxpayer Account Management (TAM) will have three sub-applications: Taxpayer Profiling, Revenue Accounting System (RAS), and Potential Tax Revenue. According to the Directorate General of Taxes during the interview, taxpayer account management has at least four benefits for taxpayers:

1. Integrated. Taxpayer Account Management will give data or information to taxpayers in one application.
2. Reliable. Taxpayer Account Management will provide relevant tax information that can be accessed easily by taxpayers.
3. Comprehensive. Taxpayer Account Management will give tax data or information to taxpayers in one system.
4. Ease of access. Taxpayer Account Management will help taxpayers easily fulfill their tax rights and obligations and access all available tax services.

According to the Directorate General of Taxes Public Relation, overall, there are two scopes of taxpayer account management, taxpayer profile and taxpayer ledger. Taxpayers' profiles will consist of taxpayers' identities, like address, phone number, email address, business classification code, active e-billing code, list of tax cases, list of tax facilities, etc. In taxpayers' ledgers, there are credit and debit positions. The credit positions will show taxpayers 'rights, while the debit position will show taxpayers' obligations.

All of those will be opened to taxpayers, so that it will be more transparent and accountable, and taxpayers can clarify data proactively. This user interface will help taxpayers, and at the same time, it will increase the Directorate General of Taxes' database and tax revenue as it is more user-friendly. As a conclusion, we can conclude that big data analytic implementation in the Directorate General of Taxes' database brings a lot of good changes, especially to taxpayers' user interface and taxpayers' compliance monitoring and tax audit. Compliance Risk Management, Business Intelligence Applications, and Taxpayer Management Accounts will lead the Directorate General of Taxes to be a data-driven organization. The Directorate General of Taxes will still learn best practice of big data analytics from other countries, like audit case selection with big data analytics, like Structure Income Flows in the United States of America, Tax Agent Risk in Australia, and VAT Risk in the Netherlands, Norway, and Ireland.

REFERENCES

Asian Development Bank. (2024). *A Comparative Analysis of Tax Administration in Asia and The Pasific*. Asian Development Bank.

Creswell, J. W., & Creswell, J. D. (2018). *Research Design: Qualitative, Quantitative and Mixed Method Approaches*. Sage Publications Asia-Pacific Pte. Ltd.

De Leon, H. (2022). *The Fundamentals of Taxation*. Rex Book Store.

Directorate General of Taxes. (2000). *Value Added Tax on Goods and Services and Sales Tax on Luxury Goods as Lastly Amended by Law Number 18 of 2000*. Directorate General of Texas.

Directorate General of Taxes. (2007). *General Provisions and Tax Procedures as Lastly Amended by The Law Number 28 of 2007*. Directorate General of Texas.

Directorate General of Taxes. (2008). *Income Tax as Lastly Amended by Law Number 36 of 2008*. Directorate General of Texas.

Directorate General of Taxes. (2022). CRMBI: First Step to Data Driven Organization. Directorate General of Texas.

Implementation of Compliance Risk Management and Business Intelligence. (2021). https://perpajakan.ddtc.co.id/sumber-hukum/peraturan-pusat/surat-edaran-direktur-jenderal-pajak-se-39pj2021

Implementation of Compliance Risk Management in Extensification, Monitoring, Inspection, and Collection Activities in Directorate General of Taxes. (2019). Data Center. Https://Datacenter.Ortax.Org/Ortax/Aturan/Show/16857

Jenkins, G., Kuo, C.-Y., & Shukla, G. (2000). *Tax Analysis and Revenue Forecasting*. Harvard Institute for International Development, Harvard University.

Musgrave, R., & Musgrave, P. (1989). *Public Finance in Theory and Practice*. McGraw- Hill, Inc.

UU No. 7 Tahun 2021 about Harmonization of Tax Law. (2021). *UU No. 7 Tahun 2021 about Harmonization of Tax Law*. 1–224.

OECD. (2021). *Digital Transformation Maturity Model*. OECD.

KEY TERMS AND DEFINITIONS

Ability to Pay: an application created through a data analytics process that is used to provide a description and or predictions of the taxpayer's ability to pay.

Approweb: An application owned by Directorate General of Taxes for the purpose of comparing internal data and external data which is used as a tool to supervise taxpayers.

Big Data Analytics: The process of uncovering trends, patterns and correlations in large amounts of unstructured raw data to help make data-informed decisions. These processes use familiar statistical analysis techniques, like clustering and regression and apply them to more extensive datasets with the help of newer tools.

Business Intelligence: A technique that combines architecture, information technology tools and databases for collecting, storing, managing data and knowledge management with data analysis tools in order to present information that is useful for planners and decision makers.

Compliance Risk Management: A risk-based compliance improvement effort by giving treatment to taxpayers according to risk obedience that is carried out systematically, measurably, objectively, and repeatedly to form a risk engine to support decision-making at the Directorate General of Taxes more efficiently and effectively.

Directorate General of Taxes: Subordinate of Indonesian Ministry of Finance which has the task of administering taxation, formulating and implementing policies and technical standardization in the field of taxation in Indonesia.

Smartweb: A graph analytics – based application that is capable of presenting taxpayer relationship in the form of a network, tax information on high wealth individuals and their group companies, beneficial owner and ultimate beneficial owner information, as well as indication of the risk of noncompliance.

TADAT: Tax Administration Diagnostic Assessment Tool Field Guide - a guide designed to provide objective assessment of the health level of the main components in a tax institution.

Chapter 15
An Overarching Guide to Data Governance

Kritika
https://orcid.org/0000-0002-1186-6032
Independent Researcher, India

ABSTRACT

The advent of advanced technologies like blockchain, cryptocurrency, etc. has posed threats to the humongous data of the organisations at voluminous scale hindering day to day activities of the institution which paves way for governance of data at every level of the organisation defining roles and responsibilities of each and every member. Data governance is one such way of collocating and administering policies, plan of action and calibre for the tacit usage of organisation's structured or unstructured information with the focus on 5 V's—namely, volume, veracity, value, variety, and velocity. The chapter focuses on providing the details of the need of data governance, the tools used, data governance framework, challenges posed to models of data governance and its solution.

Data that sit unused are no different from data that were never collected in the first place. -Doug Fisher

INTRODUCTION

With the augmented magnification of data, a stringent regulatory skeleton with transparent data notions, standardization and processes to expeditiously and precisely capture and storing of data is necessary which can be quickly outpoured, perpetuated, sustained and transported. Data governance(Abraham et. al., 2019) is the hegemony and stewardship of the organizational data of worldly possessions which encompasses the fabrication of plan of action and specifications that ensure that data is precise, thoroughgoing and reliable. Data Governance Institute defines the term as the practice of collocating and administering policies, plan of action and caliber for the tacit usage of organization's structured or unstructured

DOI: 10.4018/979-8-3693-0472-3.ch015

Figure 1. Components of big data

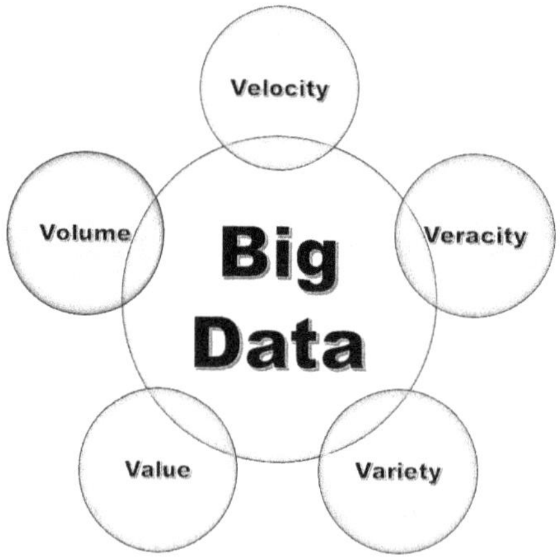

information. The globe today is surrounded by big data which comprises the data of 5V's (Kaur et. al., 2017), namely, volume, veracity, value, variety, and velocity as shown in Figure 1.

The protection of data determines the triumph of an organization's business which makes it assertive to position a data governance framework to fit the organization's demands along with delegation of roles and responsibilities on its operation relevant to critical information. The *why* element(Viljoen, 2021) in the context of securing data demands vital attention in correlation with *should* element to build a safe data driven erudition.

Figure 2 depicts the why aspect the data governance in pursuance of an organization.

Figure 2. The "WHY" aspect

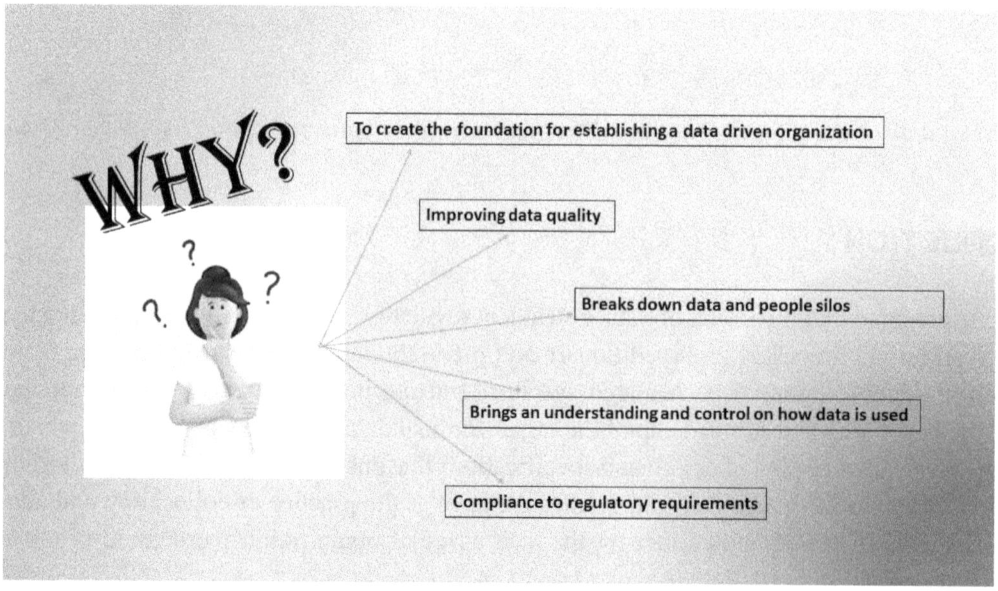

Figure 3. Key components of data governance process

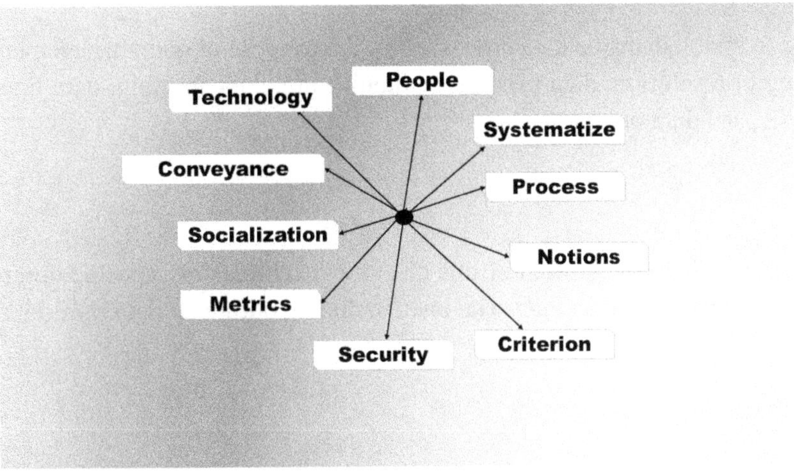

Data governance manifest the subpoena to systematize, intermingle, fortify and accumulate the institutional data. The key goals that thwack the calculated, adroit and serviceable levels include:

- Reducing data security risks
- Subpoena intricate rules for data usage
- Intermingling compliance requisites
- Upgrading internal and external communication
- Rocketing the value of data
- Opening the door for a vigorous foundation for the continued existence of the company through risk management and optimization

The foundation of management of data provides an outlay(Benfeldt et. al., 2020), onus and sound judgement to hold sway over the organization's data. The key components of data governance process hold key as depicted in Figure 3 which are:

1. People

The professionals, stewards of data, and relevant key business and information technology personnel are the mainstays of a data governance program who establishes and develops outlays to ensure that the enterprise requisites are met.

2. Systematize

The manpower involved play a critical role in the evolution and accomplishment of roadmap of an organization's systematize data which is a governing document that provides high-level enterprise requisites for data and ensures that those requisites are met, an indispensable step in the organization's managerial journey of data.

3. Process

A prerequisite to establish prime data processes for the purpose of data management which includes data issue tracking or resolution, data peculiarity monitoring, data splitting, data lineage tracking, repercussion analysis, and data quality testing,

4. Notions

A data notion is a high-level disposal of one or more statements of expected outcomes of data that influence and direct data habits at an industrial level including outbound data sharing, regulatory adherence, etc.

5. Criterion

A criterion provides a scaffolding and adherence to a data notion, e.g., ISO, NIST frameworks that instructs or constrains behavior to ensure adherence to data norms, which are in compliance to data notions. In general, organizations tend to exhibit rules for master and reference data, data interpretation and domain development, metadata management, classification, accessibility.

6. Security

It involves safeguarding electronic data in a database from destructive forces and unwanted actions of authorized and unauthorized users which refers to espionage, cyber-attack, or data breach.

7. Conveyance

Conveyance includes all written, spoken, and electronic interactions with associated targets and audiences who need to gather information regarding the activities. A conveyance plan encompasses non-discriminatory, result oriented, and a gizmo for all communications that identifies how to portray governance and stewardship challenges and success to the various stakeholders and the rest of the organization.

8. Socialization

Socialization of data governance is an important activity which is a plan that aids integrate data governance ventures into an enterprise's notions, internal culture, pecking order, and processes to ensure its uniqueness and adherence to the organization's tailored culture.

9. Metrics

Establishing business metrics and key performance indicators (KPIs) for keeping a check on and evaluating on the whole the impact of the data governance vitality to the program's triumph. The metrics and KPIs must be measurable, tracked over time, and consistently measured the same way every year.

10. Technology

The data governance program demands various technologies to make the procedure look seamless and automated with smaller data governance programs using the available technology within their organization and larger data governance tend to leverage software specific to data governance and the requisites which further amplify the process of gaining hold of the required metadata, its management, automation, decision trees, and collaboration.

Data Intelligence

Data intelligence(Zheng et. al., 2015) is the pedagogical apprehension of data enabled by metadata-driven cognizance into data classes, standard, roots, ownership, metamorphosis and relationships which helps to better understand the constitutionality of data by procuring its meaningful attributes — the who, what, where, when and how. With the ever increasing data in modern era comes great responsibility for upholding the integrity of data which empowers the employees to establish enterprise value, accredit consumer's data and drive outcomes for business venture, immanent trust, establish right set of circumstances to apprehend the data and boost capabilities of business evolution. For example, in order to predetermine the risk associated with particular data for digital transformation initiatives or its reliability, data intelligence helps enable data-driven decision making that can be deemed authentic, accurate and principled.

Why Data Intelligence Matters?

The influx of data flows that led to the era of big data, emerged as a way to help companies understand and unleash data's business value with data-driven decision making(Kayabay et. al., 2022). The challenges associated with the big data or meta data is overcome with the help of sensitive data intelligence, a solution to discover, investigate and safeguard humongous volumes of data by allowing them to classify datasets according to their sensitivity, risk factor and dependency in future.

The organizations should adopt data intelligence due to following reasons:

1. To be in compliance with the global privacy laws

The legality of data becomes more important where there are data privacy laws and regulations like GDPR, CCPA, NIST to mitigate the requirements of data as per the demands.

2. To mitigate privacy and security risks

There may be in addition privacy and security issues with different data types, the danger of which increases with the sensitivity of the data. Sensitive Data Intelligence, assist an organization adopt a security, gives businesses the ability to comprehend their data risk profile, quickly spot new risk areas, and put the required controls in place before their data is compromised in the event of a security incident.

Figure 4. Steps to data intelligence

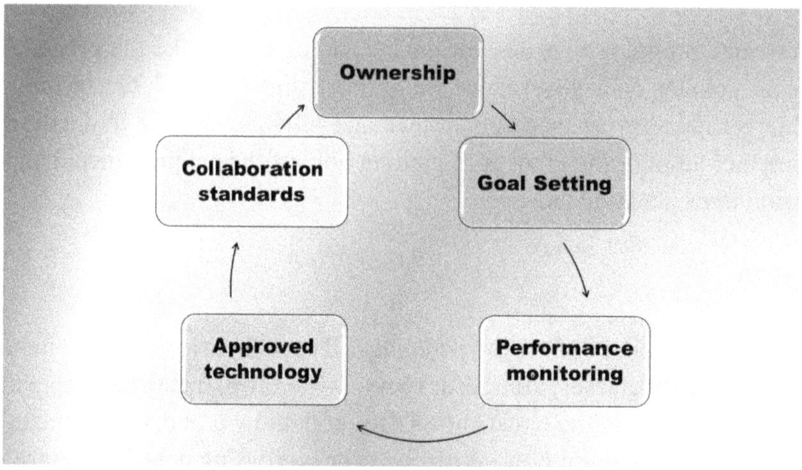

3. For secure cloud data migration projects

In order for companies to migrate locally data to cloud-based data warehouses and information lakes without knowing what and where personally identifiable information is stored within an organization who might migrate their data to the cloud securely and effectively with the aid of sensitive data intelligence to find, examine, and categorize on-premises data.

4. For automated privacy-by-design approach in agile SDLC

For its products and services, Sensitive Data Intelligence incorporates privacy issues at all stages of software/product development. A software development life cycle generally consists of the five processes of planning, growth, assurance, administration, and monitoring, each of these has a role for sensitive data intelligence, enabling companies to integrate dynamic assessment processes into the SDLC that carry out evaluations anytime new confidential data elements are introduced to their products or services. This happens rapidly and continuously.

Abbreviations used:

GDPR- General data protection regulation

CCPA- California Consumer Privacy Act

NIST- National institute of standards and technology

SDLC- Software development lifecycle model

Steps to develop an effective and intelligent data from the sources in order to retain its value in the longer run for successful businesses as mentioned in Figure 4 are as follows:

1. *Identify:* Determines what and how data is preserved and how it moves and alters throughout the enterprise by identifying and examining the working details of any component of an organization's data management systems (data stores, data integration/movement).

2. *Capture:* Create an automatic and enduring technique to collect and organize information from diverse sources so that one may provide an organization with a single, consistent view from which to interpret, integrate, regulate, and deploy data.
3. *Connect:* Add value to physical metadata by tying it to business terminology, rules, and usage to offer different viewpoints and integrated context for stakeholder knowledge, capability, and collaboration independent of role, expertise, or technological prowess.
4. *Analyze:* Easily identify and be conscious of how different data elements, sources and data management infrastructure come together and colligate to satisfy particular business use cases.
5. *Map:* Understand the predetermined flow of data and exploit that flow in support of business operations and strategic transformation to capture lineage, enable analysis of various ramifications and accelerate the integration and deployment of new data sources and data management infrastructure.
6. *Govern:* Apply policy, course of action, pronouncements, excellence and best practices to any/all data (at rest or in motion), regardless of technology, to provide guidance, apprehension and capability around the solitude, security, proper utilization, ownership/responsibilities and risk mitigation of enterprise data.
7. *Unify:* Provision and manage access to a consolidated view into the content, contrivance, and controls of your data assets and infrastructure that must be tailored to the state of affairs and perspective of the consumer's role, ensuring they have visibility into the appropriate data assets, can easily look up and browse on their terms, and collaborate with their partners in the business, breaking down business and technical silos, increasing self-service potential and promoting stakeholder fluency.

LITERATURE REVIEW

(Morabito V, 2015) emphasized the role of information and data governance creating trusted, high-quality information for effective big data analytics by reviewing common definitions of big data governance and its core components, as well as big data maturation models. He highlighted the reviews with common definitions of big data governance and its core components, as well as big data maturation models and argued that analytics alone cannot be the basis for competition, as information needs to be trusted for effective use.

(Al-Ruithe etl. al., 2016) contributes to the research community by presenting a conceptual framework for designing data governance for cloud computing. It highlights the importance of data governance for organizational success and the lack of research and industrial initiatives. Future work will focus on developing a more detailed holistic framework for cloud data governance strategy, including main pillars, processes, and attributes. The proposed framework will be validated with relevant stakeholders through case studies in some countries.

(Akoka et. al., 2019) suggested a multi-criteria hierarchy for assessing big data governance making it possible to evaluate big data governance thoroughly while taking into account a variety of factors based on systems theory's primary aspects. Big data's primary goals are to increase corporate competitiveness and streamline decision-making. The method integrates big data governance's organizational and technical facets, offering a comprehensive view of the tool's efficacy.

(Abraham et. al., 2019) developed a conceptual framework for data governance, identified knowledge gaps, and proposed a research agenda with five promising fields. It provided valuable insights for practitioners, identified major building blocks, and provided a 15-question research agenda. It also provided an overview of antecedents, scoping parameters, and governance mechanisms.

(Gupta et al., 2020) analyzed that data governance is a global issue affecting organizations due to technological and political factors. With the increasing volume and value of data, it presents challenges and risks. Definitions of data governance are customized to each country, and a review of 50 definitions from various industries and institutions is provided. The analysis focuses on specificity, focus, and attitudes towards control, and recommends developing customized definitions aligned with mission and stakeholders. The language of data governance does not significantly differ between nations.

(Graef et. al., 2021) emphasized on the need for mandatory sharing of user information in data-driven markets is urgent. Current legal mechanisms, such as EU competition law and GDPR, are insufficient. To address this issue, a governance structure combining centralization and decentralization is needed. Three feasible options include centralizing investigations and enforcement in a European Data Sharing Agency, establishing a Data Sharing Cooperation Network, or combining both governance structures and tasking national authorities with investigation and decision-making. The mixed option is most efficient as it eliminates the need for duplicate technical infrastructure across NCAs and eliminates the need for new investigation and enforcement powers. The proposed governance structures incorporate data protection and intellectual property protection, providing a concrete approach for future data regulation. This approach is easily adopted by policymakers and can be implemented at the EU level.

(Zorrilla et. al., 2022) work aims to create a reference framework for Data Governance systems for Industry 4.0, supported by 3P technologies such as IoT, Social Technology, Mobile Devices, Big Data, and Cloud/Edge Computing. The framework must meet specific requirements and standards, such as constant updating profiles and roles, automating policies, extending DG at all organizational levels, and integrating Big Data and Cloud Computing technologies with massively distributed and heterogeneous legacy systems. The framework includes an Architecture Building Block (ABB) for instantiating services, processes, and software artifacts, and a maturity model to help organizations identify and assess gaps between their current data governance processes and best practices.

(Bozkurt et. al., 2022) in his paper mentions that despite the data governance significance in managing numerous stakeholders, intricate IT structures, and diverse processes, data governance in the context of smart cities has not received much research. Cities may benefit from and modify the corpus of knowledge now available on data governance to support their digital transformation. The review also provides a baseline for upcoming studies on the creation of a framework for urban data governance.

(Liu et. al., 2023) explores the impact of corporate governance on non-financial firms' financialization. A model was developed to illustrate how governance affects financialization. Results show that enhanced governance can suppress financialization by mitigating moral hazards, reducing entrusted loans, and influencing profit distribution and financialization trends. The study suggests that better governance can influence these factors.

Data Governance Framework

A data governance framework(Al-Badi etl. al., 2018) also known as data management framework is a defined edifice that directs the implementation of data governance in an enterprise and serves as the foundation of a data governance program which provide transparent visualization of how to corroborate the quality, uprightness, solidness, discernibility, accessibility, and usage of data assets.

Figure 5. Working of data governance framework

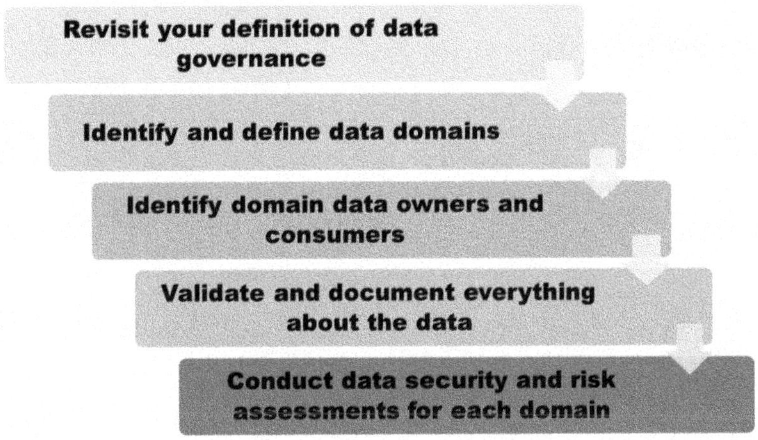

The *three pillars* of any data governance framework that reciprocate the nucleus of governance making the data more traceable and transparent to perform and achieve desired results are:

Governance circumscribing all data assets, from dashboards and codification to data science models is a data asset for data analytics.

A practitioner-led, bottom-up approach, making a small group of individuals (data custodians or engineers) responsible for data governance isn't a viable strategy while the amount of information customers and consumers keeps growing. The way forward is a bottom-up, decentralized data management paradigm that holds each data creator accountable for data governance. The data mesh is an illustration of a decentralized, community-driven strategy. The data mesh architecture suggests a federated computational regulation model in which each organization is a confederation of business domains. Data created by domain owners is totally managed by them. Each domain nevertheless abides by a set of international (or governmental) guidelines for data definitions, standards, workflows, and discovery.

Governance practices embedded within daily workflows, data governance has always been associated with adherence, command, and imperil mitigation to support well thought out business functions for decision making to be precise, apposite, reliable and high facet.

Data governance frameworks as projected by Data Governance Institute (DGI)[1] listed the components' essentiality in any combination of work as mentioned in Figure 5 which may be found below.

Ownership

The responsibility of the individual firms to lay the foundations of the rules, processes, procedures and roles assigned to each and every individual within the framework for data governance, who may establish a Data Governance Office (DGO) in furtherance of this initiative, uphold documentation, convey policies, and keep track of the metrics. The DGO is a team of people or stakeholders, or data stewards assigned throughout to carry tasks.

Figure 6. Steps to create enterprise data governance framework

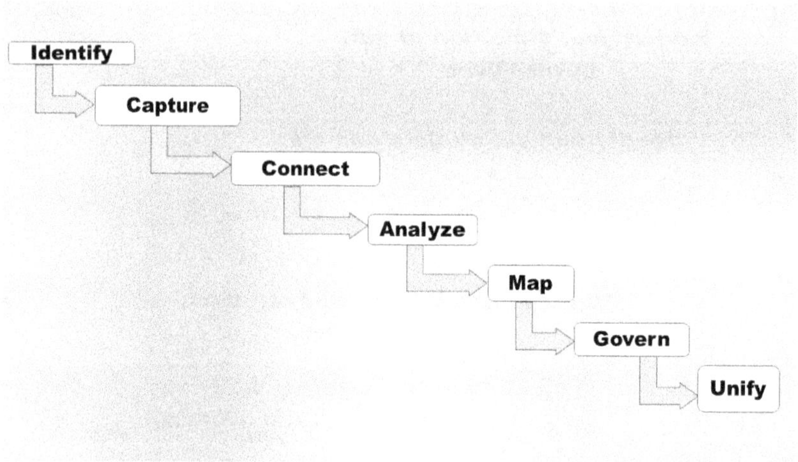

Goal-Setting

The laying down of specified goals and tasks for the success of the initiative taken, recommended by the Data Governance Institute which impacted '4Ps', namely, programs, projects, professional disciplines and people to evaluate cost, profits or non-observance of likelihood of an event.

Performance Monitoring

The evaluation and obedience of all the events performed in order to comply with the structure of data governance so as to carry out the processes to be unremitting, put on record and aimed at various aspects such as earmarking the rights of the decisions taken, commanding substitution, setting things right and delineating idiosyncrasy of data.

Approved Tech

In a data governance framework, stakeholders should approve the technological advancements being used to process, retain, and data usage, along with corroborating controls that are specific to particular event or task.

Collaboration Standards

Data stakeholders are all the employees who establish, use, and modulate data across the organization, inclusion and consultation of whom depends upon the kingpin of the initiative of the data governance during culminating decision making process.

Enterprise data governance framework procedure:

The steps to carry out enterprise data governance[2,3] as mentioned in Figure 6 are as follows:

Step 1. Revisit your definition of data governance

The ever evolving nature of the data governance projects demands revisiting of the earlier defined definition for formulating a framework to meet the structural demands of the new project as with neo project, emerges neo data and access points for systematic review of the process.

Here are few questions that should be kept in mind while revisiting the definition of data governance:

What is the steadfastness behind data governance?

Does it counterbalance all data assets of the organization?

Does the steadfastness enrich organization-wide data apportion and collaboration?

Step 2. Identify and define data domains

The data management framework covers all data assets, which should draw a parallel and bring into line the data domains across the organization such as finance, marketing, sales, etc.

The questions include:

Which are the protruding data domains of an organization?

What data do they engender?

Who is the consumer of the data?

Step 3. Identify domain data owners and consumers

The shared responsibility of managing data and ensuring its security, integrity and privacy and providing access to the right fit by analyzing the questions, namely,

Who is the key holder of the data within each and every domain?

How does the routine flow of work look like?

What current dependencies are there to get legitimate access to the data in a particular domain?

Step 4. Validate and document everything about the data

The stage involves transparency in the flow of data within an organization to standardize definitions, rules, policies, procedures and more in a documented manner including answer to the questions by forming a proper work force such as:

What is the source of data?

How is the flow of the data carried in an organization?

Does it aid in meeting goals and support business outcomes?

Step 5. Conduct data security and risk assessments for each domain

The last but not the least is to set up subpoena to carry out incessant data security and risk assessments for each and every domain to ensure its continuity in the long run.

Challenges to Data Governance

To fully utilize their data and obtain a competitive advantage, organizations must now adopt efficient data governance practices(Ladley, J., 2019). However, implementing data governance can be a challenging(Janssen et. al., 2020) task that frequently comes with a number of obstacles.

Here are some typical data governance issues you might encounter:

1. Defining transparent roles and responsibilities

Making sure that each individual has a clearly defined position and the proper rights is one of the main problems associated with data governance. This procedure can take a while, especially in larger organizations. It entails defining and distributing data governance roles and duties, defining permissions, and upholding a clear awareness of each person's obligations within the data governance framework.

2. Data quality and consistency

A significant challenge to ensure accuracy, completeness and consistency of data is crucial which requires establishing procedures and mechanisms to identify, monitor and resolve data quality issues(Pansara, 2023).

3. Establishing policies and procedures

Proper creation and implementation of data governance procedures and policies to ensure that data is managed and maneuvered appropriately, requiring data classification, security and privacy policies as well as providing guidelines for data usage and access.

4. Scalability

Your data governance structure must be scalable and flexible to accommodate new users, data sources, and use cases as your organization expands. In order to maintain their effectiveness and efficiency, this may entail upgrading rules, processes, and technologies.

5. Limited or misallocated resources

The next data governance difficulty is going to be inadequate resources and improper resource allocation once the C-suite realizes how essential data governance is, how the business influences governance, and how IT is responding and most importantly to find a data steward. The majority of organizations attempt to teach someone with tribal expertise to be a data steward because the lack of skills is a major barrier to attaining ROI in data governance.

6. Poor data quality and lack of trustworthy data

Data quality is a problem for data governance as it undermines confidence, which in turn discourages use and prevents the achievement of strategic goals, data being a barrier to strategic decision-making if teams don't feel confident using it to make important judgements.

7. Lack of data control

A lack of access to those who can extract the most value from the data is caused by concerns about defending your attack surface or safeguarding your trade secrets. Keeping the individuals who will benefit the most from your organization's data from being turned away is one of the objectives of data governance.

8. Cross functional collaboration

Collaboration between many divisions and stakeholders, including IT, business, and data teams, is necessary for effective data governance. It might be difficult to get everyone on the same page and working towards a common goal.

9. Training and education

A need to offer training and instruction in order to guarantee that all data users comprehend and abide by data governance policies and procedures which could entail creating instructional materials, running workshops, or providing continuous support.

10. Siloed data

Different approaches to processing information and technological iterations are largely to blame for the phenomenon of segregated data. When modernizing, one of the things that most businesses ignore is finding out how to move the systems that house their legacy data. The cost of tearing and rebuilding those systems is exorbitant, but they still function well. Additionally, it's less expensive to try to remedy the issue through downstream integration if you don't know what the historical data contains. The data silos happen due to fast pace of data collection, constant turnover of newer technologies, addition of new data sources, evolving infrastructure and corporate culture with internal friction and communication barriers.

Ways to Overcome the Challenges of Data Governance

1. Defining roles and responsibilities transparently with documenting permissions and maintaining a clear understanding of each other's responsibilities in data governance.
2. Data quality and consistency should be maintained by establishing processes and mechanisms to identify, monitor, and resolve data quality issues.
3. Overcoming resistance to change and fostering a culture of acceptance and adaptability, a vitality for change management.
4. Communication and alignment among different stakeholders of varied departments to understand the aim, benefits and prerequisites of the new governance framework.
5. Accommodating and integrating latest technologies in the data governance framework while updating policies, procedures, and tools to ensure they remain relevant and effective.
6. Proper management of data growth and its complexity on expansion of an organization's activity without compromising the quality of data quality, security and compliance.
7. Automation of data with respect of its speed, accuracy, quality, profiling with tracking user behaviour and automating metrics tracking guide.

Figure 7. OpenMetadata sample project

Recommended Tools for Data Governance

1. OpenMetadata

OpenMetadata[4] is a unified platform and one of the fastest growing open-source vibrant project for data discovery, data descent, data idiosyncrasy, compliance, governance, and team collaboration and adopted by a variegated set of companies in various industry verticals, powered by amalgamated metadata based on Open Metadata Standards/APIs, supporting junction to a wide range of data services, and enables end-to-end metadata management.0

The aid provided to different data teams includes:

- Incorporate one point source of truth for all collected metadata.
- Unearth the right forte and limit dependencies.
- Nurture team fraternization with conversations, tasks, announcements, and alerts in real time.
- Establish trustworthiness with data peculiarity tests to ensure completeness and precision.
- Keep an eye on data evolution with full length data lineage.
- Safeguarding access susceptible data by defining roles and policies.
- Boost organizational data discernment to gain climacteric insights to drive innovation.
- Administer data governance to maintain data integrity, safety, and compliance.

Figure 7 showcases the sample project being run on OpenMetadata tool.

Various features provided by the tool as depicted in Figure 8 are:

2. Amundsen[5]

Figure 8. Features of OpenMetaData

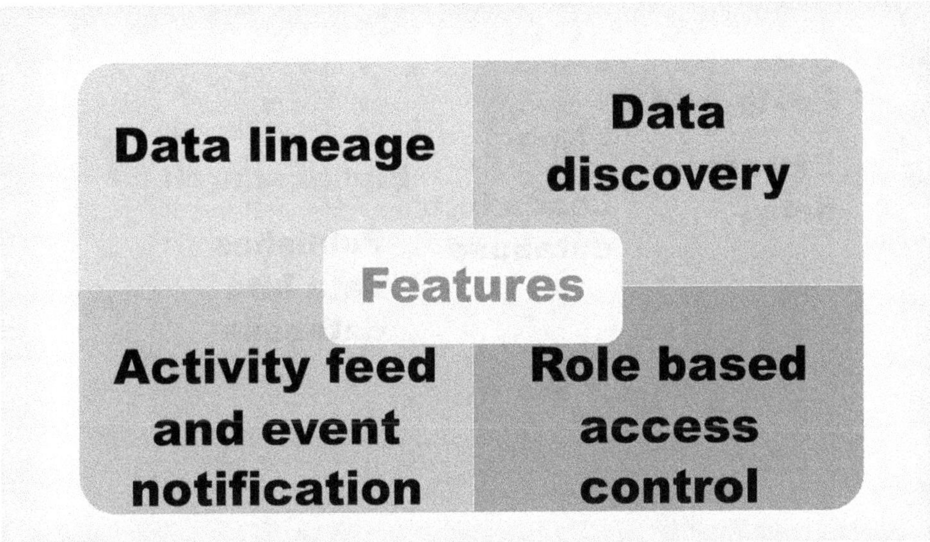

An open-source platform for data discovery and meta data platform. It comprises four major components as depicted in Figure 10, namely,

a. Meta data services

Meta data services imparts a communication pathway with the database that accumulates the data in actuality which can be technical data, business data or lineage data, exposed with the aid of rest api.

b. Search service

It serves the purpose of discovery and searching features of data with the aid of search api for varied types of data. The primary search engine is Elasticsearch but also supports other service engines such as AWS, Apache Solr and many others.

c. Front service

Built on react is responsible for forecasting all the metadata in literate and understandable way. It also provides a communication with BI tools and query interface for data preview feature.

d. Data builder utility

It provides within built extraction and ingestion scripts which can be automated using a scheduler called Airflow DAG which does the following as represented in Figure 9:

Figure 9. Snippet of airflow DAG

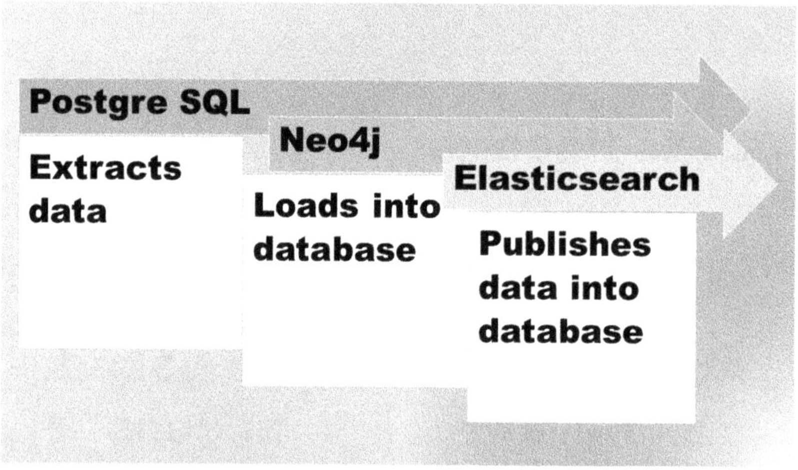

3. IBM Cloud Pak for Data[6]

A flexible set of non-segregated software components for data analysis, organization and managerial setup, availed as self-hosting software or managed using IBM Cloud. The cloud platform available can be chosen from IBM Cloud, Amazon web services or Microsoft Azure.

The provided solution areas are as portrayed in Figure 11.

Data fabric and AI models provides automating integration, metadata management and AI governance with features such as data governance and security, data integration, data observability, and master data management.

Data Insights and Applications aids in delivering decisions from data and AI apps to consumer with features like business analytics and providing business apps understandability.

Figure 10. Architecture of amundsen tool

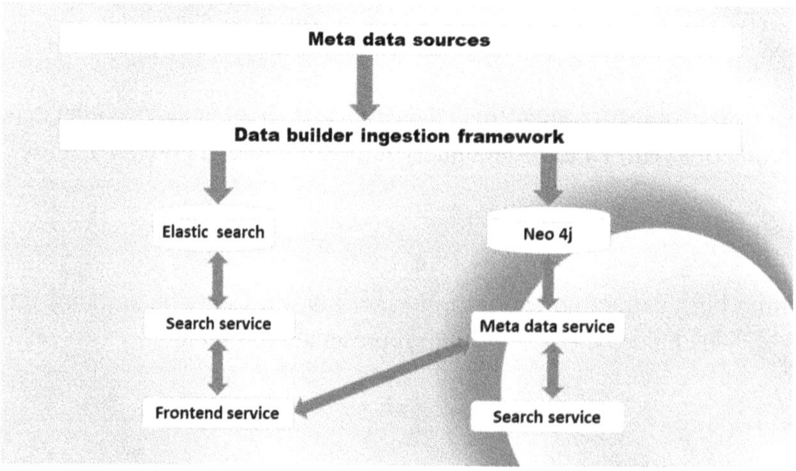

Figure 11. Solution areas provided by IBM Cloud Pak for data

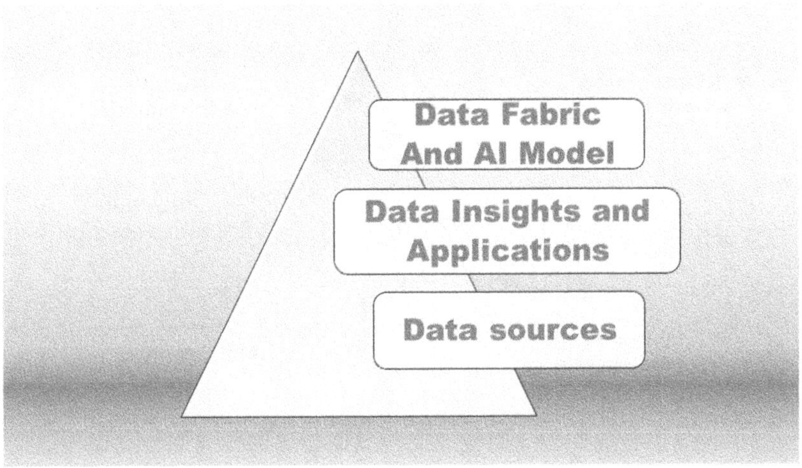

Data Sources aids in storing, managing and unlocking the value of data for various purposes like transactions, warehousing, and strategic partnerships.

The services provided by the AI suite as portrayed in Figure 12 includes the following processes, namely,

Collect features provides connectivity to data from multiple sources from multiple locations via a connection page that lists all the available connections used by multiple services with provision for supporting additional data sources to have simplex access to one's data.

Organize feature provides support with the help of The Watson™ Knowledge Catalog service to organize data through data classification and governance and aids in developing a knowledge architecture that is on-point and ready to keep up with the scale of your data.

Figure 12. Suite of services provided by AI

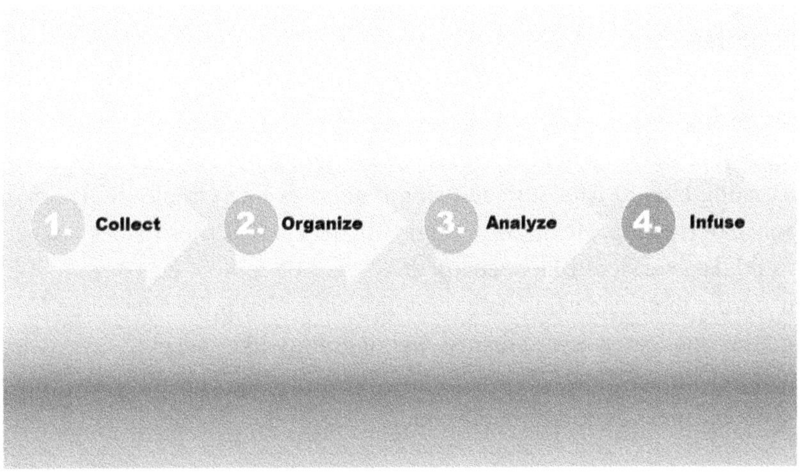

Figure 13. Features of oracle enterprise metadata management

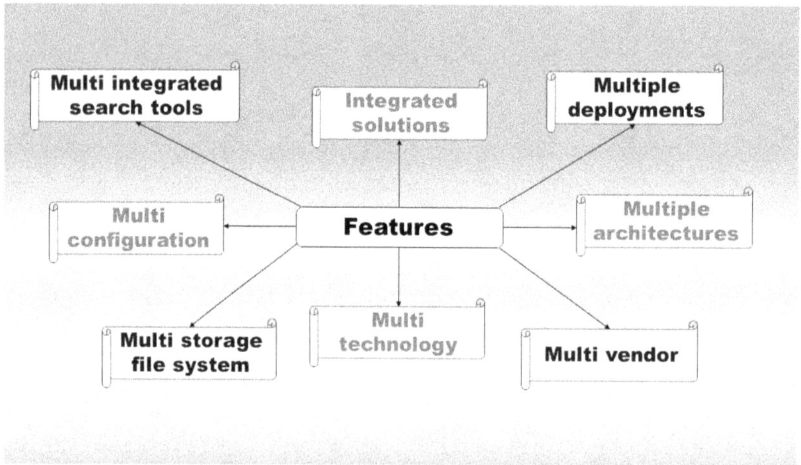

Analyze feature provides numerous analytics services to generate scalable insight on demand, create stunning dashboards to quickly visualize data and SPSS® Modeler to enables to create flows to prepare and blend data, build and manage models, and visualize the results.

Infuse feature aids in building smarter apps with premium Watson services, deploy machine learning models into production at scale with Watson Machine Learning, or infuse your AI with trust and transparency with Watson OpenScale.

4. Oracle Enterprise Metadata Management[7]

The software provides an all-inclusive and well non- segregated set of Metadata Management (MM), Data Cataloging (DC) and Data Governance (DG) solutions supporting on premise, cloud based or hybrid Enterprise Architectures ranging from the classic Data Warehouse to the latest Data Lakes and Data Vaults. The Figure 13 represents the following features of the software for ease of handling tasks.

Characteristics of the Tool

1. Metadata Harvesting

The metadata harvesting aids in data storage using databases like Oracle, SQL Server, IBM, Postgre SQL; Big Data tools like Hadoop, Hcatalog, Google big query; Flat files like csv, xlsx; file systems like linux or windows and data services like open api etc.

It also helps in storing metadata using data modeling tools like power designer, Erwin; management of metadata using atlas, navigator; and semantic web ontology like owl etc.

Other useful features include data integration, business intelligence and providing various business applications like SAP business suite, warehouse etc.

2. Metadata Management

It includes features like model manager, metadata search, metadata browser, metadata reporting capabilities, metadata reporting capabilities, data model visualizer, data flow lineage and impact analyzer and many other things.

3. Data Governance

It includes features like:

- Business Glossary (with customizable workflow automation)
- Semantic Mapper (search driven, auto map, and multi-levels from glossaries to data stores via design models)
- Semantic Lineage Analyzer (term usage, and automatic glossary definition on data pass through)
- Local Documentation (quick in place editing of business names and descriptions while browsing harvested data stores)
- Glossary Linking (quick in place semantic linking while browsing harvested data stores, DI jobs, and BI reports)
- Data Tagging (applying reusable Labels available in search)
- Comments and Reviews (collecting business user feedback and managing reviews)

4. Data Cataloging

It aids in features like:

- File System Crawling (file type auto-detection, partitioning auto-detection)
- Data Profiling (from data sampling to full data profiling with statistical results)
- Semantic Discovery (semantic types, patterns/lists machine learning)
- Relationship Discovery (data driven matching semantic types and metadata driven inferred from usage in DI, BI, SQL, etc.)
- Social Curation (endorsement, warnings, certifications with impact on search)
- Data Modeling
- Data Store Documenter (automatic reverse engineering of naming standards with supervised machine learning)
- Data Store Modeler (with full data model diagram editing)
- Data Store Designer (new data store specifications and design)\

5. Data Mapping

It includes features like:

- Data Mapper (from business user data mapping specifications to design for bulk and feature/SQL with joins/filters/lookups)
- Metadata Applications
- BI Web Portal (Multi-vendor BI Web Portal with bi-directional integration, and glossary generation

6. Active Data Governance

It includes features like:

- Data Modeling Tools (Erwin, ER/Studio, PowerDesigner, etc.)
- Data Integration Scripts (PL/SQL, BTEQ, HiveQL, etc.)
- Data Integration (to self-service / data prep tools)
- Business Intelligence (to self-service like Tableau or design layers like BO Universes.)

7. Administration, Customization and Extensions

It includes features like:

- Custom Attribute Extensions (MyCompanyCertificationLevel, etc.)
- Customizable UI (menus, widget layout, etc.)
- REST API (glossary lookups, linage trace, automatic harvesting, search, browse, update, etc.)

8. Collibra[8]

A tool to operationalize data governance workflows and processes to deliver trustworthy data across the organization by providing a single platform to find, understand and create a shared language around data.
It includes features like:

1. Comprehensive Business Glossary

It helps in defining terminology, rules and regulations concerning the business to make everyone be on the same page.

2. Stewardship Management

It aids in assigning roles and responsibilities allowing data stewards to share, protect and improve data assets.

3. Reference Data Management

Reconciling data between systems for more accurate reporting and analysis by identifying missing records and broken relationships across systems.

4. Centralized policy management

It includes features like creation, review and updating data policies to ensure maintenance and adoption is maintained in business.

5. Intuitive Workflow

Interacting with common workflows and processes to facilitate collaborative approach to governance.

6. Data Dictionary

Documenting metadata with details related to origin, formatting, use, structure and relationship to other data.

Benefits associated with using the tool:

1. Quickly find, understand and govern your data

Utilize a single platform to gain complete visibility into all business-critical data assets, such as KPIs, reports, APIs, models, data products, and technological assets, along with the full business context that goes with them.

2. Drive a common language around data to speed decision making

Create a company dictionary to guarantee that crucial business concepts and KPIs are clear and consistent. Establish a common language for data within your company so that everyone can rely on a single source of information.

3. Leverage automation to keep pace with change

Combine human and machine intelligence to enhance the context surrounding data assets. Automate your processes to keep governance practices current as your company grows.

4. Mobilize your workforce to encourage collaboration

Enable data stewards to join forces with subject matter experts and data owners through automated workflows, role-based dashboards and interactive views. Automate processes with out-of-the-box and customizable workflows for common governance and stewardship processes.

5. Ensure compliance and mitigate risks

Scale compliance procedures more effectively and affordably, enabling your company to put its faith in reliable data sources. Find, classify, and map sensitive information automatically. Recognize the technical and commercial provenance of your data to better understand where it comes from and how it is used.

Data Governance Index

The Data Governance Index (DGI) is a comprehensive framework that provides a systematic approach to measuring the effectiveness of data governance programs. The DGI consists of 12 dimensions, each with multiple indicators, used to assess the overall performance of a data governance program are as follows:

Figure 14. Features of worldwide governance index

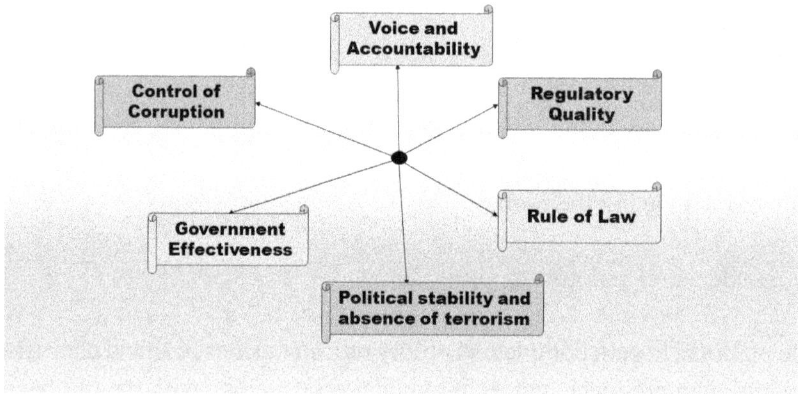

1. Data Strategy and Vision
2. Data Quality and Metrics
3. Data Rights and Obligations
4. Data Security and Privacy
5. Data Access and Use
6. Data Integration and Interoperability
7. Data Stewardship and Ownership
8. Data Governance Processes
9. Data Governance Organization and Resources
10. Data Governance Awareness and Training
11. Data Governance Reporting and Communication
12. Data Governance Review and Improvement

To calculate the overall DGI score, organizations can assign a weight to each dimension based on their specific needs and priorities. The weighted scores for each dimension are then summed to produce the overall DGI score.

The DGI can be used by organizations to benchmark their data governance performance, identify areas for improvement, and track progress over time. By implementing a systematic approach to data governance, organizations can enhance their ability to manage and use data effectively, ultimately leading to improved decision-making, increased innovation, and increased value creation.

Worldwide Data Governance Index

The index is fabricated to aid researchers and analysts assess broad perspectives in perception of governance across countries over time by aggregating data from 30 think tanks, international organizations, non-governmental organization and private firms based on three prime criteria, namely, production by credible organizations, comparable cross country data and regular updating of data.

The aggregate features of WGI over 200 countries as portrayed in Figure 14 are:

1. Voice and Accountability

In addition to freedom of expression, freedom of association, and a free press, voice and accountability encapsulates perceptions of how much a nation's citizens can take part in choosing their administration. The individual variables from each data source that were utilized to create this measure for the Worldwide Governance Indicators are listed such as EIU, FRH, GWP, IPD,PRS etc.

2. Regulatory Quality

The feature aids in capturing perceptions of the ability of the government to hatch and discharge sound policies and regulations to permit and kick upstairs private sector development which includes parameters like unfair competitive practices, burden of government regulations, financial freedom, investment portfolio and many such things.

3. Rule of Law

The feature aids in capturing the perceptions to the extent of which agents have confidence in and abide by the rules of the society and more specifically the quality of contract enforcement, property rights, the police and the courts including parameters like violent crime, organized crime, judicial independence, law and order and such like things.

4. Political stability and absence of terrorism

The feature aids in capturing the perceptions of likelihood of political instability or motivated violence including parameters like orderly transfers, armed conflicts, intensity of violent activities, protests and riots, right to freedom from disappearance etc.

5. Government Effectiveness

The feature captures the perceptions of the quality of public services, civil services and the degree of its independence from the pressure of political men, quality of policy formulation and implementation and the credibility of the government's commitment including parameters like quality of bureaucracy, quality of primary education, infrastructure disruption, police instability and such like things.

6. Control of Corruption

The features aids in capturing to the extent of which public power is exercised for private gain by state of elites and private interests including parameters such as corruption among public officials, irregular payments in tax collection, corruption index, transparency, accountability etc.

REFERENCES

Abraham, R., Schneider, J., & Vom Brocke, J. (2019). Data governance: A conceptual framework, structured review, and research agenda. *International Journal of Information Management*, *49*, 424–438. doi:10.1016/j.ijinfomgt.2019.07.008

Al-Badi, A., Tarhini, A., & Khan, A. I. (2018). Exploring big data governance frameworks. *Procedia Computer Science*, *141*, 271–277. doi:10.1016/j.procs.2018.10.181

Al-Ruithe, M., Benkhelifa, E., & Hameed, K. (2016). A conceptual framework for designing data governance for cloud computing. *Procedia Computer Science*, *94*, 160–167. doi:10.1016/j.procs.2016.08.025

Benfeldt, O., Persson, J. S., & Madsen, S. (2020). Data governance as a collective action problem. *Information Systems Frontiers*, *22*(2), 299–313. doi:10.1007/s10796-019-09923-z

Graef, I., & Prüfer, J. (2021). Governance of data sharing: A law & economics proposal. *Research Policy*, *50*(9), 104330. doi:10.1016/j.respol.2021.104330

Gupta, U. G., & Cannon, S. (2020). A Review of Data Governance Definitions and Emerging Perspectives. *International Journal of Data Analytics (IJDA)*, *1*(2), 30-47.2

Janssen, M., Brous, P., Estevez, E., Barbosa, L. S., & Janowski, T. (2020). Data governance: Organizing data for trustworthy Artificial Intelligence. *Government Information Quarterly*, *37*(3), 101493. doi:10.1016/j.giq.2020.101493

Kaur, N., & Sood, S. K. (2017). Dynamic resource allocation for big data streams based on data characteristics (5 V s). *International Journal of Network Management*, *27*(4), e1978. doi:10.1002/nem.1978

Kayabay, K., Gökalp, M. O., Gökalp, E., Eren, P. E., & Koçyiğit, A. (2022). Data science roadmapping: An architectural framework for facilitating transformation towards a data-driven organization. *Technological Forecasting and Social Change*, *174*, 121264. doi:10.1016/j.techfore.2021.121264

Ladley, J. (2019). *Data governance: How to design, deploy, and sustain an effective data governance program*. Academic Press.

Liu, Z., Tang, H., & Zhang, C. (2023). Corporate governance, moral hazard, and financialization. *International Review of Economics & Finance*, *88*, 318–331. doi:10.1016/j.iref.2023.06.042

Morabito, V., & Morabito, V. (2015). Big data governance. *Big Data and Analytics: Strategic and Organizational Impacts*, 83-104. Akoka, J., & Comyn-Wattiau, I. (2019, July). Evaluation of Big Data Governance-Combining a Multi-Criteria Approach and Systems Theory. In *2019 IEEE World Congress on Services (SERVICES)* (Vol. 2642, pp. 398-399). IEEE.

Bozkurt, Y., Rossmann, A., & Pervez, Z. (2022). A literature review of data governance and its applicability to smart cities. In *Proceedings of the 55th Hawaii International Conference on System Sciences (HICSS 2022),* (pp. 2680-2689). University of Hawai'i at Manoa.

Pansara, R. (2023). Unraveling the Complexities of Data Governance with Strategies, Challenges, and Future Directions. *Transactions on Latest Trends in IoT*, *6*(6), 46–56.

Viljoen, S. (2021). A relational theory of data governance. *The Yale Law Journal, 131*, 573.

Zheng, Z., Wang, P., Liu, J., & Sun, S. (2015). Real-time big data processing framework: Challenges and solutions. *Applied Mathematics & Information Sciences, 9*(6), 3169.

Zorrilla, M., & Yebenes, J. (2022). A reference framework for the implementation of data governance systems for industry 4.0. *Computer Standards & Interfaces, 81*, 103595. doi:10.1016/j.csi.2021.103595

ENDNOTES

1 https://datagovernance.com/the-dgi-data-governance-framework/
2 https://cspring.com/5-steps-for-effective-data-governance/
3 https://blog.quest.com/5-steps-for-creating-a-data-governance-framework/
4 https://open-metadata.org/
5 https://www.amundsen.io/
6 https://www.ibm.com/products/cloud-pak-for-data
7 https://www.oracle.com/middleware/technologies/enterprise-metadata-management.html
8 https://www.collibra.com/us/en

Chapter 16
The Library and Information Science Perspective on Knowledge Management

Muhammad Rosyihan Hendrawan
https://orcid.org/0000-0003-0438-2571
University of Brawijaya, Indonesia

Luh Putu Sri Ariyani
Universitas Pendidikan Ganesha, Indonesia

Aniesa Samira Bafadhal
https://orcid.org/0000-0002-5666-0660
University of Brawijaya, Indonesia

ABSTRACT

Knowledge management (KM) creates value and competitive advantage via innovation. Library and information science (LIS) developed KM using social epistemology and varied scientific methods. LIS continued to study KM to guarantee its understanding and usage in the organization. KM attitudes and actions must also be agreed upon. This chapter discusses the LIS viewpoint on KM and delivers the fundamental point, which implies that LIS may advance knowledge management. Thus, readers should ask questions about LIS and all of the preceding advances, especially KM. The perception of data, information, and knowledge especially has changed significantly. LIS perspective should be dynamic, and librarianship has individuality and dignity with knowledge managing tradition. LIS and Librarianship roles, especially KM, may help drive these new advancements. Instead of only watching or ignoring improvements, active engagement and additional research are expected to raise LIS roles on KM.

INTRODUCTION

In the information age, knowledge stands out in the annals of human civilization. Knowledge as capital has a significant impact on the development of an organization or agency. If knowledge is not immediately and perpetually updated through the learning process, it can become obsolete in today's environment of

DOI: 10.4018/979-8-3693-0472-3.ch016

accelerated change. In this globalization era, science and technology advancement is rapid. The agency's or organization's proficiency in these two areas is one of the organization's most crucial factors. According to Milton and Lambe (2019), knowledge management (KM) is a system that enables organizations to assimilate their employees' knowledge, experience, and creativity for organizational growth. KM systematically administers an organization's intellectual and knowledge assets for competitive advantage.

The first special conference on KM was convened in Boston, United States, in the summer of 1993, the year considered to be the commencement of KM. According to Koenig and Neveroski (2018), KM was coined in the 1980s as a descriptor for Library and Information Science (LIS) at the School of Information Studies at Syracuse University, New York, United States. As we know it today, KM originated in the consulting industry and was popularized by consulting firms. Consulting firms perceive the potential of the Internet's intranets to link geographically dispersed knowledge-based organizations. Consulting firms quickly realized that the expertise acquired through knowledge leverage could be packaged and sold to other businesses. The product requires a name, and KM has been selected. KM is, therefore, extensively taught in the School of Management, Economics, Business Administration, and Library and Information Science.

The topic of KM has been a subject of discussion within the International Federation of Library Associations and Institutions (IFLA) since 2001, as observed from the standpoint of professional library organizations (IFLA, 2023). The KM Section in IFLA was formally established in December 2003 as a constituent unit within Division III, specifically within the Library Services framework. The increasing interest in implementing Knowledge Management (KM) within the library and information services sector necessitates librarians to enhance their comprehension of the several aspects of KM relevant to their responsibilities.

KM is an interdisciplinary academic discipline with roots in many academic disciplines, such as Economics, Management, Business Administration, and LIS (Dalkir, 2017). In simple terms, KM consists of explicit knowledge, which means open and recorded knowledge, and tacit knowledge, namely hidden knowledge or knowledge that is in the minds of each individual, along with processes involving the creation, organization, transfer, and application of knowledge. Consequently, KM can be implemented in numerous domains and organizations. KM is gaining popularity due to the significance of collaboration in a world where competition for excellence intensifies. Only the mastery of knowledge determines an organization's superiority, as demonstrated by the intense competition. KM is unquestionably contingent on how an organization uses and applies knowledge.

BACKGROUND

Knowledge management (KM) entails leveraging the collective knowledge possessed by all personnel to attain the specific objectives of a firm or organization effectively. The aim of KM is not to oversee the entirety of knowledge but rather to focus on the knowledge that is fundamental and significant for the company (Milton & Lambe, 2019). The primary objective is to ensure employees get the requisite knowledge at the appropriate time and location. The adage frequently posited is that possessing the proper knowledge, situated in the appropriate location, and occurring at the appropriate moment is paramount.

KM is a series of systematic approaches to managing, evaluating, and utilizing diverse knowledge assets. These assets may include tacit knowledge carried by each and explicit knowledge in databases, archives, records, documents, rules, etc. In conclusion, KM is a technique and strategy for managing organizational knowledge to generate value and increase competitive advantage through innovation. Today, an organization or institution must constantly develop or innovate and discern the current state of affairs or situations of global change to recognize and adapt to new circumstances. KM remains at the forefront of many disciplines today. Large multinational corporations such as IBM and Price Waterhouse Cooper brought KM specifically to the commercial field by adopting its principles. The writings of Nonaka and Takeuchi in the Harvard Business Review in 1991 established KM as a field of business and management studies. Since 1996, following the first KM conference in 1994, this field of study has evolved into examining information technology (IT), particularly artificial intelligence and databases, management, particularly organizational change, and economics.

Few individuals view KM as a trivial ploy by business people to find new terms, which rapidly translates into new advantages in the IT industry. Librarianship as LIS practices is a source of suspicion. Similarly, when Daniel Bell and his peers introduced the term information society (IS), librarians frequently exhibited skepticism regarding the popularity of KM. Sociology and Computer Science have taken the lead in researching and implementing IS principles, while LIS has merely caught up. When information retrieval (IR) emerged as a new focus of attention with the Cranfield Test, LIS's skepticism was also displayed. If LIS had also focused on evaluating machine-based indexing, information science would not have needed to emerge as a separate discipline (Bawden & Robinson, 2015). We now know that Computer Science, particularly database design and development, and psychoanalysis, particularly information-seeking behavior, pay more attention to IR. Regarding LIS, its position in the study and application of IS principles makes it a follower of the two disciplines above of study.

The LIS skepticism is not without foundation. Since information retrieval (IR), then information society (IS), and finally, KM became prominent, academics and practitioners in the library have founded their ignorance and suspicion on the misconception that LIS is the premise of all the new vocabulary. When IR emerged, librarians believed it was merely a practical application of machine use that was already similar to library affairs, such as classification and cataloging (Hendrawan & Mukhlis, 2021). When IS became prevalent, LIS abandoned the notion that ancient Public Librarianships originated the social information dissemination principle. Then, when KM emerged, librarians believed that their involvement with bibliographical data since the Middle Ages was the foundation for disseminating and applying knowledge.

Upon closer inspection, LIS has every reason to be skeptical, as all terminology derives from the dependence of human civilization on written language, which, of course, began with the invention of mass technology such as books. LIS may concede that they have dealt with vast data, information, and knowledge before other disciplines. Librarians may identify as founding progenitors and claim to be IR, IS, or KM's ancestors.

According to IFLA (2023), the KM division of IFLA endeavors to promote the adoption of KM by conducting initiatives that provide expert guidance for the effective implementation of KM within individual organizations. In this instance, IFLA defines KM as the systematic procedure of generating, retaining, disseminating, employing, and reutilizing organizational knowledge to attain organizational goals and objectives. KM broadens the conventional understanding of "knowledge" by encompassing more than the prevailing notions of memory, storage, and information. KM is commonly understood to encompass various domains, including tacit and explicit knowledge. KM includes a multitude of facets within the realm of organizational management.

The activities of the KM Section in IFLA aim to demonstrate this objective by offering a diverse range of events in partnership with other Sections and Divisions within IFLA, as well as relevant professional organizations (IFLA, 2023). The aims of this section are as follows: firstly, to facilitate the establishment of a KM culture within the library and information environment; secondly, to foster international professional communication and enhance librarians' and their institutions' comprehension of KM; and thirdly, to monitor advancements in KM and advocate for its adoption within the IFLA community.

In response to the need for librarians to enhance their competencies in an evolving work environment, this section aims to acquire theoretical and practical knowledge in KM. The specific areas of focus include 1) facilitating knowledge sharing, 2) enhancing performance metrics, 3) shifting towards a value-oriented approach rather than solely emphasizing service provision, 4) examining the advantages and disadvantages of KM implementation, 5) utilizing interactive communication methods to organize information for knowledge sharing initiatives, 6) leveraging information technology to transform knowledge into actionable data, and 7) ensuring the retention and knowledge preservation. The primary endeavors undertaken encompass the following: 1) The KM Section in IFLA engages in collaborative efforts with other Sections to formulate initiatives and prospects centered around diverse facets of KM. Additionally, it explores shared interests in domains such as education and training, professional growth, LIS theory and methodology, intercultural communication, organizational advancement, information technology, and media. 2) Provide illustrative instances of exemplary methodologies and empirical analyses to facilitate the broader implementation of KM among information professionals throughout global libraries and information centers. This study aims to examine the impact and assistance provided by professional associations in promoting the implementation of KM practices inside libraries and other information settings. 4) The responsibilities of managing the KM Section on the IFLA website involve curating and maintaining a comprehensive collection of KM resources.

Additionally, establishing and overseeing a KM list-serve platform is crucial for facilitating effective communication among members of the KM Section in IFLA. Furthermore, disseminating pertinent information to the KM Section in IFLA members is a key task, which may be achieved by various means, such as newsletters published semi-annually. Nowadays, the focus of LIS and Librarianship attention is required in relation to Jesse Shera's proposition about social epistemology. As delineated earlier, the establishment and sustenance of human relationships cannot be exclusively accomplished or maintained via the examination of categorization systems. In order to effectively contribute to the advancement of KM, the field of LIS and librarianship must allocate enough resources to foster the cultivation and enhancement of interpersonal relationship-building skills.

After conducting a comprehensive analysis of many KM development initiatives, Dalkir (2017) also arrived at a similar result on the significance of human relationships. The concept is a knowledge-friendly culture characterized by freedom and a collective disposition to exchange information among individuals. When considering the preceding paragraph, it becomes evident that the effectiveness of a data representation system is contingent upon the manager's ability to establish and foster an environment characterized by mutual trust and collaboration. A data representation system without measures to develop user confidence might impede the progress of KM or result in wasteful expenditure.

THE LIBRARY AND INFORMATION SCIENCE AND SOCIAL EPISTEMOLOGY

Epistemology is a philosophical concept that pertains to examining knowledge, encompassing its connection to truth, belief, and the societal principles that regulate it. The epistemological crisis discussed relates to a situation wherein society critically examines the legitimacy of knowledge and the associated values. Indeed, an in-depth analysis of this matter is not deemed essential within this context. The mention of MacIntrye (2007) serves as a means to employ a widely utilized framework for analyzing the evolution of a certain tradition.

According to Floridi (2002a & 2002b), an inherent correlation exists between philosophy and Library and Information Science (LIS), unlike social epistemology, which fails to offer a sufficient basis for LIS. Social epistemology and LIS share a common foundation, which is rooted in the scientific exploration of information and is further examined within a developing scientific field known as information science (Bawden & Robinson, 2015; Flynn, 2020). Floridi established the fundamental essence of the philosophy of information, which encompasses the philosophical discipline dedicated to examining the fundamental principles of information, its dynamics, and the associated challenges it presents (Dodig & Hofkirchner, 2011). In the context of this discussion, LIS can be characterized as an applied manifestation of the philosophy of information.

The field of LIS frequently has a strong association with philosophy, mostly due to the depth, breadth, and content of its scholarly investigations. The correlation between these two disciplines appears intuitive and irrefutable, but delving into the fundamental principles underpinning their connection proves to be a multifaceted and contentious endeavor. A notable correlation exists between Librarianship and philosophy since both disciplines share a comparable level of theoretical research. Librarianship and philosophy probably possess distinct yet fundamentally similar subject matter, positioning them as sciences of equal standing (Herold, 2001).

In order to comprehend the correlation between the subject in question and the Library and Information Science field, a more precise and detailed analysis is required. According to Hjorland (2000, 2005), a need exists for LIS to cultivate specialized knowledge that is somewhat independent of empirical science yet avoids being a mere superficial compilation of a singular source. Efforts have been made to address the challenges above by viewing LIS as a component of social epistemology or establishing social epistemology as the theoretical basis for LIS (Floridi, 2002).

Upon examining the scope and topic matter of the research, it has been posited that similar to the library profession and the philosopher profession; there exists a shared belief in a suitable domain of expertise, including all knowledge and civilizations. Librarians possess a comprehensive understanding of information and are adept at promptly and effectively locating and managing it under optimal circumstances. They prioritize the enhancement of its utility while also considering human factors. The Library and Information Science and Philosophy fields encompass a wide range of subjects, a characteristic also applicable to the broader realm of scientific inquiry. Like a scientific endeavor, philosophy encompasses a wide range of distinct scientific subjects.

Shera is a prominent personality in this context (Rawski, 1973). Social epistemology encompasses two distinct areas of scholarly inquiry: the Sociology of Knowledge, which involves the descriptive and empirical examination of the historical factors and circumstances that contribute to the formation of knowledge, and the social epistemology, which entails a critical analysis and understanding of the social aspects of knowledge production, involving multiple actors.

In contrast to the field of Sociology of Knowledge, the discipline of LIS is characterized by its normative nature, necessitating an approach that extends beyond mere description. The library serves as a space that caters to the requirements and principles of communication and education. It provides support and assistance in the advancement of these needs while also evaluating and selecting appropriate content for public consumption. Consequently, activities such as cataloging, for instance, cannot be considered impartial, as they involve an inherent assessment process. The presence of this normative characteristic renders Library and Information Science more predisposed towards the domain of social epistemology.

Shera (1970) posited that he clearly distinguished between the Sociology of Knowledge and the social epistemology upon adopting a sociological perspective. Furthermore, he advocated for the interpretation of librarianship in a manner that prioritized the social epistemology over the Sociology of Knowledge. A strong emphasis on inclusivity characterizes Shera's perspective on social epistemology. The individual believes that the social aspect is fundamentally intertwined with epistemology and perceives this perspective as a comprehensive theory that includes several epistemic concepts. This discipline is currently referred to as social epistemology, which encompasses the thorough study of the various processes through which a collective group endeavors to establish a wise connection with its entire environment, encompassing physical, psychological, and intellectual aspects.

Social epistemology is a branch of epistemology that specifically focuses on the acquisition, dissemination, and evaluation of knowledge within the context of society, country, or culture (Shera, 1965). In her work, Shera highlights a significant connection between social epistemology and Librarianship. Furthermore, she asserts that social epistemology can draw upon the intellectual principles of library science, which has long been pursued. The findings are evident in Shera's scholarly article concerning the presence of a significant and unresolved tension between establishing the principles of Librarianship within the framework of social epistemology and the definition of librarianship as social epistemology (Pendit, 2019).

Librarianship refers to the professional field and practice of managing and providing access to library information resources. This phenomenon originates from the integration of two distinct scientific disciplines. The realm of communication undoubtedly encompasses a crucial component wherein language, or linguistics, has a central role. According to Pendit (2018), Librarianship, in its capacity as knowledge management, is fundamentally grounded in the field of epistemology, which pertains to the understanding of knowledge itself. Specifically, it is closely intertwined with social epistemology, which examines how knowledge is shared within a social context and shapes the conduct of the society in question (Shera, 1961).

As a discipline, LIS encompasses the administration and organization of human knowledge. It is noteworthy for its extensive scope, surpassing other scientific fields in breadth. Furthermore, due to its inherent connection to the philosophy of science, Library Science has the capacity to evolve into the most philosophical discipline compared to other professions (Shera, 1965 & 1973). According to Shera, LIS, in principle, ought to be seen as a discipline encompassing the philosophical aspects of science and functioning as a practical application of social epistemology.

According to Putu (2019), in more accessible terms, social epistemology can be categorized into two distinct approaches. The initial concept can be classified as classical, whereas the subsequent one can be considered revolutionary. However, the latter option appears capable of generating the necessary components in the field of LIS. The topic of discussion pertains to classical social knowledge. Epistemology can be understood as a development stemming from the Cartesianism project, which encompasses the philosophical doctrines of Descartes, particularly the philosophy of mechanism (Liu, 2017). This branch of philosophy investigates truth and the underlying foundations upon which truth is established.

This approach entails the substitution of conventional methodologies, specifically a fixed structure centered around individual intellect and solitary researchers, with a novel and more fluid framework that relies on the dispersion of knowledge, intellect, and interactions about epistemic and doxastic processes, i.e., the logic of thinking, involving multiple actors (Pendit, 2003). This approach entails broadening the research focus to encompass a wider range of phenomena that have previously been given little consideration, such as testimony, trust, and power, thereby establishing scientific connections among them. Nevertheless, the classical framework of social epistemology continues to prioritize the veritistic aspect of knowledge, namely its alignment with truth.

The primary objective remains the pursuit and validation of integrity, with science continuing to serve as the exclusive subject of investigation. Information does not possess inherent existence but refers to meaningful content or data that contributes to a study objective. In contrast, the paradigm-shifting social epistemology capitalized on the emerging framework, particularly its radical iteration, to scrutinize the Cartesian endeavor and contend that science, truth, and their justificatory foundations are products of social creation. The individual in question was more inclined to perceive information as a novel subject of investigation.

However, this perspective was perceived solely as a critique of the scientific discipline. The acquisition of this ancient and revolutionary knowledge holds significant importance. The primary objective of both types of social epistemology is to demonstrate not personal ideas regarding celestial bodies but rather the beliefs one should have and the justifications for these beliefs. Both subjects share a common research focus, which centers around studying social dynamics and epistemic phenomena. Simultaneously, this can be deemed excessive or insufficient in establishing a good basis for the field of LIS. The assertion that LIS is considered excessive stems from its focus on aims. While this field may possess normative qualities, it is important to note that it does not hold epistemic authority and should not be regarded as such.

The term “too little” is employed due to its relevance to the field’s breadth. LIS has a wide range of sources, from children’s literature to ancient astrological maps and from digital records of organizations to audio recordings—the process of capturing and documenting sporting events. According to Floridi (2002), Shera’s methodology fails to account for changes in aim and scope, as Shera’s conceptualization of science in his theoretical study may have been overly general. These disparities elucidate why methodological dispositions could take aback librarians.

Integrating social epistemology with LIS is not seamlessly compatible due to the differing foundational levels at which these disciplines operate. The focus lies not on science per se but rather on the sources of information that facilitate its functioning, even if only indirectly. According to Rubin and Rubin (2020), Library Science refers to the specialized expertise and competencies in identifying, examining, arranging, and utilizing information resources to fulfill library users’ information inquiries and requirements.

Indeed, it is worth noting that any entity has the potential to serve as a repository of knowledge. This is primarily due to the inherent capacity of all entities to provide insights and information about their nature and the entities they are associated with. However, the origin of this phenomenon might be attributed to the field of LIS, which encompasses a wider range of topics compared to the discipline of epistemology. Concluding that the scope of LIS alone includes the domain of knowledge authority is highly deceptive. The field of LIS encompasses a wide range of topics and offers numerous opportunities for exploring various social epistemological perspectives. Nevertheless, it appears that both social epistemology and LIS necessitate a lesser extent of foundational material that is more fundamental and conceptual compared to the field of philosophy of science. Both necessitate a shared philosophy of information.

Social epistemology remains a philosophical domain in which LIS effectively addresses its theoretical requirements. This option is considered to be the most optimal selection. The relationship between LIS and social epistemology can be better comprehended by considering them as two areas of the philosophy of information rather than in a hierarchical manner while examining their origins. The philosophy of information can be more appropriately aligned with LIS rather than social epistemology.

KNOWLEDGE MANAGEMENT: DATA, INFORMATION, KNOWLEDGE, AND CLASSIFICATION INTERCONNECTION

The data, information, and Knowledge axiom, often referred to as DIK, is a conceptual framework that describes the progression from raw data to meaningful information and, ultimately, to knowledge. Conversely, as discussed by Debons (2008), the KID framework represents the reverse progression. The area of Library and Information Science (LIS) and Librarianship, along with several other disciplines, often believes that the DIK axiom is a suitable framework for knowledge management (KM). The underlying premise is that the management of variable D implies the effective management of variables I and K. If proper management is implemented, the use of the system becomes far more straightforward. If this method is implemented, it demonstrates practicality, effectiveness, and efficiency within the framework of the K application. In essence, KM is founded upon the principles and practices of data management. If individuals who work as librarians possess expertise in data management, then it may be inferred that they also have expertise in KM.

An additional argument may be identified in this context. The predominant concern in the field of KM is that it does not relate to the conventional data management methods often used by librarians. Suppose the matter under consideration relates to the management of data. In that case, it is plausible to argue that conventional practices in the field of LIS are likely to be adequate in tackling this particular problem.

The justification for this claim is as follows: the notion of raw data lacks existence when contemplating its interpretation as apart from the entities represented by the variables "I" or "K." The presence of data relies on persons knowing its potential uses, expected utilization, contextual significance, and theoretical underpinnings. An illustrative case may include a number quantity, such as 5,000. This numerical value depends on the association of potential, optimism, contextual factors, and conceptual framework. The notion of money emerges when it is seen as a measurable quantity that enables the facilitation of transactions within a certain context and for a specific objective. The perceived insignificance of the numerical value 5,000 is subject to the context of the currency in question and its intended use.

According to some perspectives, the presence of hope, possibility, context, or similar elements implies the involvement of information. To clarify, when data is generated, before its storage, all prospects, opportunities, contextual information, and conceptual frameworks associated with it are relinquished. How can one disentangle an entity from its aspirations, capabilities, circumstances, and composition? The proposition seems unattainable unless an entity had the characteristic of being devoid of all attributes, hence rendering it non-existent.

The crux of the issue above is that when we refer to "managing data," we are primarily concerned with manipulating and organizing data representations rather than the underlying data itself. To effectively handle data representation, it is essential to consider the expectations, possibilities, context, and constructions associated with the original data. If it has been previously stated that these characteristics pertain to information, it follows that the management of data representation necessitates the use of information. Put otherwise, the variable D does not ascertain the variable I; rather, it is the variable I that determines D.

The concepts of hope, potential, context, and construct are inherently interconnected and do not exist in isolation. Inquiring into the factors influencing expectations about the Euro's exchange rate *vis-à-vis* the Dollar, engaging in foreign exchange trading based on perceived potential, formulating a strategic approach to identify currency buyers and sellers, and ultimately aspiring to achieve financial success like George Soros. In order to achieve a level of success comparable to that of George Soros, one must acquire a comprehensive understanding of foreign exchange with a set of moral and ethical principles, which may not always align with one's own beliefs. Additionally, cultivating resilience and bravery are essential attributes to possess. Put otherwise, my existence has always been contingent upon the existence of the preceding K. The use of KID, rather than DIK, is not applicable in this context.

In light of this novel premise, it is essential to construct KM using the KID concept. The ability to construct a data management system is contingent upon possessing enough intelligence and knowledge. The issue at hand pertains to the inherent impossibility for any individual to have the whole of both I and K. In order to effectively generate a data representation that encompasses the expectations, potential, context, and construct of the data, it is important to possess a comprehensive understanding of these aspects. The acquisition of such information is a prerequisite for successfully executing this task. The feasibility of this task is quite improbable.

This is why knowledge management cannot be founded only on data management via its representation. In order to achieve effective knowledge management, it is important to move beyond mere data representation and the mere dissemination of data properties. What is the specific object or entity that is being subjected to management? The explanation lies in the observation that K is a social phenomenon whereby knowledge is not confined to individual minds as isolated units. The process of thinking, acquiring information, and constructing knowledge is not an individual endeavor. Furthermore, individuals need interpersonal connections grounded in reciprocal will and trust to engage in critical thinking, obtain information, and construct understanding. In the field of knowledge management, there exists a kind of management that involves the implicit handling of human connections. This phenomenon may be seen in the work of Gupta and Govindarajan (2000), who provide a relevant example.

Given the perspective above, practitioners in librarianship have a significant challenge in actively contributing to the advancement of knowledge management (KM) if they persist in maintaining that the central focus of their work is only managing data via its representation. The KID concept within the field of KM necessitates that Librarianship exhibits its "human side." Indeed, the endeavor to revive this idea formally may be traced back to the 1960s, when Shera introduced the concept of social epistemology in the field of LIS and Librarianship (Warner, 2001).

According to Shera's proposition, the field of LIS and Librarianship should shift its focus away from classification and cataloging and instead prioritize developing a profession and scientific discipline centered upon human connections (Pendit, 2019). The proposition in question is often undervalued by library practitioners and academics, who believe that focusing just on classification and cataloging is enough to define the essence of Librarianship. In this particular scenario, there is a complete absence of any presumption that the significance of classification is negligible. The following section underscores the importance of classification as a preliminary focus before delving into the subsequent discussion on the need for supplementary abilities beyond classification proficiency.

Aristotle established a systematic framework for organizing knowledge using hierarchical classification. The notion articulated by this philosopher continues to serve as the guiding principle for librarians, having been refined by notable figures such as Melville Dewey and S. R. Ranganathan. Classification is often regarded as humans' most effective cognitive strategy to organize and manage their thoughts.

Aristotle and other philosophers effectively demonstrated the inherent dominance of humans over their cognitive faculties, enabling civilization's development via rationality.

Based only on this fact, it is unequivocal that the significance of classification within human knowledge, particularly in the field of KM, cannot be refuted. According to Lambe (2014) and Hedden (2022), different forms of hierarchical classification, such as tree, paradigm, and facet classification, have significantly contributed to the organization and management of documents within the framework of advancing human knowledge. These alternative classification methods have played a crucial role, whether used together or individually.

According to Kwasnik (2020), many significant factors contribute to the classification of knowledge and information, as identified by 1). Proficient at synthesizing information concisely and understandably; 2). Present a comprehensive and detailed depiction of a specific body of information and its connection to another existing knowledge; 3). The demonstration of the interconnectedness of knowledge to assist users in developing a more complete and holistic understanding; 4). Demonstrating the disparity or divergence of individual knowledge units, particularly within a hierarchical classification framework; additionally, 5). The benefit of using a systematic approach is its ability to assist in identifying patterns or regularities in assigning criteria to objects of knowledge.

Nevertheless, it is important to acknowledge that the existing classification system has several limitations, including 1). Hierarchical classification is most appropriate for well-established knowledge domains, whereby each entity has distinct bounds and well-defined definitions; 2). Although potentially more adaptable in emerging fields, tree classification is only applicable for delineating unidimensional trajectories of knowledge advancement; 3). Paradigm classification, which is based on the convergence of two qualities of entities, often imposes constraints on the user's viewpoint as well; 4). The aspect classification system developed by S. R. Ranganathan is very successful at accommodating many views. However, its effectiveness relies heavily on a comprehensive understanding of the classified domain and the user's specific requirements using the classification system.

Furthermore, it is crucial to remember that classification system development occurs within distinct socio-political contexts. Therefore, it would be too simplistic to assert that all ideologies are adequately represented in classification systems such as the Dewey Decimal Classification (DDC) (Fox, 2016). The classification system does not provide thorough and equitable representation for all faiths. The classification system inherently marginalizes some perspectives. The aforementioned exclusionary practices give rise to the formation of slum zones or ghettos within the overall classification system. The expeditious advancement of information also imposes constraints on the utilization of classification since classification methods need uniformity and well-defined standards to be used with efficacy and efficiency. The divergence between the classification system and the advancement of knowledge may be exacerbated when practitioners responsible for its application fail to engage actively with the evolving information they are classifying (Hendrawan & Mukhlis, 2021).

At this juncture, it is opportune to revisit the discourse above pertaining to DIK and KID, particularly in the context of KM as a system that encompasses social systems and relies on interpersonal connections and trust. Classification systems play a crucial role in developing data representation management systems. As elucidated in the preceding section, when a manager undertakes processing data representations for storage in a database system, they must possess access to all the pertinent properties of the data, including expectations, potential, context, and construct.

The classification system assumes a significant role in this context since its primary function is to condense information so that those without comprehensive topic expertise can navigate and comprehend it effectively. Upon observation, it becomes evident that in addition to possessing the skill to use a classification system, one must also have other essential information pertaining to the intended users of the data representation being created. The recognition by the system manager of the existence of other individuals who will use the data representation he has developed is a crucial factor in the whole process.

As previously elucidated, human knowledge is not comprised of discrete entities but emerges through interconnectedness fostered by consensus and reliance. The acquisition and use of information within a human organization, as well as its potential success or failure, are contingent upon human organizations' conscious utilization of knowledge. This conscious utilization is predicated upon establishing agreement and mutual trust among the organization's members. Organizational members who may be classified as knowledge users for specific reasons prioritize confidence in the system management as their primary need when using a data representation system for their knowledge. In order for a data representation system to establish itself as an integral component of an institution in the realm of knowledge consumption, it is essential to cultivate a foundation of agreement and trust between the system administrators and the knowledge consumers.

THE ROLE OF TECHNOLOGY IN KNOWLEDGE MANAGEMENT

Upon engaging in a comprehensive analysis of the preceding part, it has come to our attention that knowledge emanates from information, possessing a greater depth and significance than just information alone. Knowledge encompasses various components, such as habit, consciousness, and comprehension, acquired through practice or learning. Knowledge is achieved through the cognitive processes of comparing, discerning implications and establishing correlations and connections. There exist perspectives that incorporate sagacity and conceptual notions within the conceptualization of knowledge. From a practical standpoint, corporations commonly conceptualize knowledge as applying skills and expertise. According to Kotler et al. (2021), technology can facilitate knowledge, enabling individuals to take further actions rather than being an ultimate objective in and of itself.

The fundamental components of KM encompass the processes of information collection and knowledge integration. The initial dimension encompasses endeavors to establish connections among personnel, specifically about acquiring and distributing explicit knowledge facilitated by technology. The linking dimension refers to the process of establishing connections between individuals, particularly those who seek knowledge and those who possess knowledge. This facilitates the transmission of tacit information through the augmentation of human interactions. The outcome, undoubtedly, is that the dissemination of information inside the business becomes more extensive and profound (Hendrawan, 2019).

Prior to this juncture, one can ponder the extent to which a knowledge management (KM) system is seen as "concrete" from the perspective of a Library and Information Science (LIS) and Librarianship. The term "concrete" is often linked to physical entities, particularly machinery, with a specific emphasis on information technology and computers, as seen by a significant portion of the population (Rubin & Rubin, 2020). The term "concrete" does not only refer to physical substances. It is necessary to comprehensively examine the technical facets associated with the specific elements of knowledge management. According to Tan and Lambe (2019) and Botha et al. (2014), the technology aspect of KM, namely Knowledge repositories, generally includes databases, resource directories, learning resource directories, and groupware.

Furthermore, the business model is subject to several factors, including but not limited to IT architecture, IT platform or hardware, communications, interfaces, software, and user support. Expert systems are widely recognized as a fundamental technology in the field of KM, particularly due to their use in four distinct implementation schemes, including 1). Case-based reasoning (CBS) is a knowledge representation approach that relies on experiential knowledge, including examples and corresponding answers; 2). Rule-based reasoning (RBS) is a problem-solving approach that uses a set of rules to represent human knowledge and address complex scenarios; 3). Model-based reasoning (MBR) involves using knowledge representation in the form of characteristics, behavior, inter-relationships, and simulations to facilitate the process of knowledge production; and 4). Constraint-satisfaction reasoning is a hybrid approach that combines rule-based systems (RBS) with model-based reasoning (MBR).

Upon first examination, it becomes apparent that, except for databases, the technologies above are not often recognized within the realm of Librarianship. One factor contributing to this phenomenon is the hesitancy within the field of Librarianship to extend its scope beyond the mere management of data representation. The concepts pertaining to interface and user assistance, as identified by Beckman (1999), are regarded as integral components of the business model for knowledge management. However, these principles are not widely recognized within the field of Librarianship. The integration of expert systems with information retrieval (IR) has been explored in the field of Librarianship but without much enthusiasm.

The hesitancy above does not inherently define the field of Librarianship. The concepts underlying reference services may be regarded as the first mode of interface and user assistance inside a system dedicated to managing information and knowledge. One may argue that the field of LIS and Librarianship has inherent potential. However, it seems to have encountered obstacles in fully realizing this potential because reference services focus mostly on locating materials rather than assisting consumers in problem-solving. The assertion that the accessibility of documents is equivalent to the accessibility of information is an integral aspect of this argument, particularly if the knowledge framework used by the reference officer during interviews adheres to a stringent methodology utilized for document classification or data representation (Rubin & Rubin, 2020).

The recent years have seen a considerable technological influence on knowledge management and information systems in the field of Librarianship. The essence of Librarianship has always been disseminating knowledge, culture, and expertise. The advent of new digital technologies serves to interact with patrons and provide librarians with various services. The integration of knowledge management elements with technology has had a substantial influence on the adoption of digital resources. Three transformative technologies significantly influencing knowledge management are information retrieval, taxonomy, information systems, and graph databases.

Hence, the impact of technology on knowledge management and information systems in the field of librarianship has been substantial. The use of new technology in knowledge management presents advantages and difficulties. An advantage of this technology is its ability to enhance organizational efficiency by offering librarians a wide range of alternatives to improve their operations and procedures. Additionally, it may foster knowledge innovation, enhance knowledge inter-networking, and accelerate knowledge dissemination. Nevertheless, using new information technology might present difficulties, necessitating librarians to be flexible and open to enhancing their skills and capabilities.

The issue of schema rigidity, which pertains to the organization of data representation, has been acknowledged by librarians and database developers. In contemporary database creation, there is a notable emphasis on the flexibility of reinterpreting data representation after its rediscovery during the search process. In contrast, Librarianship places less emphasis on addressing challenges that may arise because of disparities between the reference officers' and service users' reference systems. Despite the increasing use of library databases, librarians remained unconcerned with the interface, seeing it as non-problematic and not warranting attention. In several instances, librarians have preferred using the printed output catalog of a database management system.

There is a prevalent perception that Librarianship demonstrates a lack of criticality toward the technology it ultimately adopts and a reluctance to embrace new technological advancements. Within the KM paradigm, such a disposition will likely give rise to various challenges and complications, particularly considering that KM also encompasses tacit knowledge management. The existing information technology has mostly been designed to accommodate explicit knowledge, as described by Nonaka and Takeuchi (2007), characterized by its logical, sequential, and digital nature. In order to effectively address tacit knowledge, technology developers must not just depend on data representations of information that have been made apparent, such as via the use of documents. To transition from implicit to explicit knowledge without compromising the context and structure of information, it is essential to have a more comprehensive understanding of the functioning of the human brain.

Due to the absence of technological advancements capable of replicating the rapidity and precision shown by the human brain in converting tacit knowledge into explicit form and vice versa, existing technology only manages to extract explicit knowledge data representations. However, this achievement comes at the cost of compromising the adaptability and potential for re-interpretation. Therefore, the presence of human aid is important to address this technology's inherent limits, as opposed to relying only on computer support. The field of Librarianship can provide support and assistance, particularly when it adopts a critical posture toward existing information technology and maintains a persistent commitment to its ongoing exploration. This perspective can be fostered by expanding the scope beyond the simple recall of correctly stored documents and, instead, actively participating in productive problem-solving efforts.

FUTURE RESEARCH AND CONCLUSION

From a philosophical standpoint, it is not widely recognized that people possess an innate ability to engage in knowledge management. The scholars and professionals in the Library and Information Science (LIS), through the use of social epistemology stance and diverse scientific methodologies, ultimately developed the perspective of Knowledge Management (KM). Moreover, the field of LIS and Librarianship will persist in examining KM to ensure its ongoing comprehension and practical use within organizations. Additionally, it is imperative to establish consensus on attitudes and subsequent measures pertaining to the presence of KM.

This chapter encourages the reader to set aside doubts regarding LIS and Librarianship concerning all of the developments listed above, particularly KM, as this point is intended to discuss the LIS perspective on KM. LIS should be a dynamic field, and Librarianship has personality and dignity, which does not require it to be a devotee. There are innovative aspects of LIS that can significantly contribute to the aforementioned new developments, particularly KM. From this perspective, it is clear that there is a need for technological advancements that can effectively handle the essential knowledge required to understand the representation of data contained within the system. This represents a significant change in how data, information, and knowledge are perceived.

The author articulates their hope that the portrayal mentioned in this chapter conveys the main argument, which suggests that the field of Librarianship has the potential to make a substantial contribution to the progress of knowledge management. This objective can be accomplished by modifying the perspective on data, information, and knowledge and avoiding prioritizing classification as its primary focus. A comprehensive examination of the topics covered in this chapter necessitates further investigation through later research endeavors. The author hopes this chapter will incite a more profound discourse on the contribution and significance of LIS and Librarianship in advancing KM. Furthermore, it is anticipated that an inclination towards active participation and further study will elevate the status of LIS and Librarianship, as opposed to only observing or disregarding advancements.

REFERENCES

Bawden, D., & Robinson, L. (2015). *Introduction to Information Science*. Facet Publishing. doi:10.29085/9781783300761

Beckman, T. J. (1999). The Current State of Knowledge Management. *Knowledge Management Handbook, 1*(5), 1.

Botha, A., Kourie, D., & Snyman, R. (2014). *Coping With Continuous Change in The Business Environment: Knowledge Management and Knowledge Management Technology*. Elsevier.

Dalkir, K. (2017). *Knowledge Management in Theory and Practice*. MIT Press.

Debons, A. (2008). *Information Science 101*. Scarecrow Press.

Dodig, C. G., & Hofkirchner, W. (2011). Floridi's "Open Problems in Philosophy of Information," Ten Years Later. *Information (Basel), 2*(2), 327–359. doi:10.3390/info2020327

Floridi, L. (2002a). On Defining Library and Information Science as Applied Philosophy of Information. *Social Epistemology, 16*(1), 37–49. doi:10.1080/02691720210132789

Floridi, L. (2002b). What is the Philosophy of Information? *Metaphilosophy, 33*(1-2), 123–145. doi:10.1111/1467-9973.00221

Flynn, R. (2020). *An introduction to information science*. CRC Press. doi:10.1201/9781003065517

Fox, M. J. (2016). Legal Discourse's Epistemic Interplay with Sex and Gender Classification in the Dewey Decimal Classification System. *library trends, 64*(4), 687-713.

Hedden, H. (2022). *The Accidental Taxonomist* (3rd ed.). Information Today, Inc.

Hendrawan, M. R. (2019). *Manajemen Pengetahuan: Konsep dan Praktik Berpengetahuan pada Organisasi Pembelajar*. UB Press.

Hendrawan, M. R. & Mukhlis. (2021). *Pengantar Pengorganisasian dan Temu Balik Informasi: Pendekatan Konsep dan Praktik*. Malang: UB Press.

Herold, K. R. (2001). Librarianship and the Philosophy of Information. *Library Philosophy and Practice, 3*(2), 1–15.

Hjørland, B. (2000). Library and Information Science: Practice, Theory, and Philosophical Basis. *Information Processing & Management, 36*(3), 501–531. doi:10.1016/S0306-4573(99)00038-2

Hjørland, B. (2005). Empiricism, Rationalism, And Positivism in Library and Information Science. *The Journal of Documentation, 61*(1), 130–155. doi:10.1108/00220410510578050

Ichijo, K., & Nonaka, I. (2007). *Knowledge Creation and Management, New Challenges for Managers*. Oxford University Press.

Koenig, M., & Neveroski, K. (2018). Knowledge Management: Early Development. Encyclopedia of Library and Information Sciences 4th Ed. Flordia: CRC Press.

Kotler, P., Kartajaya, H., & Setiawan, I. (2021). *Marketing 5.0: Technology for Humanity*. Wiley & Sons.

Kwaśnik, B. H. (2020). Changing Perspectives on Classification as a Knowledge-Representation Process. *Knowledge Organization, 46*(8), 656–667. doi:10.5771/0943-7444-2019-8-656

Lambe, P. (2014). *Organising Knowledge: Taxonomies, Knowledge, and Organisational Effectiveness*. Elsevier.

Liu, J. H. (2017). Neo-Confucian Epistemology and Chinese Philosophy: Practical Postulates for Actioning Psychology as a Human Science. *Asian Journal of Social Psychology, 20*(2), 137–149. doi:10.1111/ajsp.12168

McIntyre, L. (2007). Emergence and Reduction in Chemistry: Ontological or Epistemological Concepts? *Synthese, 155*(3), 337–343. doi:10.1007/s11229-006-9111-3

Milton, N., & Lambe, P. (2019). *The Knowledge Manager's Handbook: a Step-by-Step Guide to Embedding Effective Knowledge Management in Your Organization*. Kogan Page Publishers.

Pendit, P. L. (2003). *Penggunaan Teori dalam Penelitian Ilmu Perpustakaan & Informasi*. Jurusan Ilmu Perpustakaan Universitas Indonesia.

Pendit, P. L. (2017). *Pustaka dan Kebangsaan*. Jakarta: Ikatan Sarjana Ilmu Perpustakaan dan Informasi Indonesia Press

Pendit, P. L. (2018). *Pustaka dan Kebangsaan*. Jakarta: Ikatan Sarjana Ilmu Perpustakaan dan Informasi Indonesia Press.

Pendit, P. L. (2019). *Pustaka: Tradisi dan Kesinambungan*. Jakarta: Ikatan Sarjana Ilmu Perpustakaan dan Informasi Indonesia Press.

Rawski, C. H. (Ed.). (1973). *Toward a Theory of Librarianship: Papers in Honor of Jesse Hauk Shera*. Scarecrow Press.

Rubin, R. E., & Rubin, R. G. (2020). *Foundations of Library and Information Science*. American Library Association.

Shera, J. H. (1961). What is librarianship? Louisiana Library Association Bulletin, 24.

Shera, J. H. (1965). *Libraries and the Organization of Knowledge* (D. J. Foskett, Ed.). Archon Books.

Shera, J. H. (1970). *Sociological Foundations of Librarianship.* Asia Publishing House.

Shera, J. H. (1973). *Knowing Books and Men: Knowing Computers Too.* Libraries Unlimited.

Tan, E., & Lambe, P. (2019). *KM Approaches Methods and Tools: A Guidebook.* Straits Knowledge.

The International Federation of Library Associations and Institutions (IFLA). (2023). *The IFLA Knowledge Management Unit.* IFLA.

Warner, J. (2001). W(h)ither information sciences? *The Library Quarterly, 71*(2), 243–255. doi:10.1086/603263

KEY TERMS AND DEFINITIONS

Academic Discipline: This refers to a specialized field of knowledge that is both taught and studied within the context of higher education institutions, such as colleges and universities.

Dewey Decimal Classification: This is a widely used method for organizing general information, which undergoes regular revisions in order to remain up-to-date with the expanding body of knowledge. The method was established by Melvil Dewey in the year 1873 and afterward made available to the public in 1876.

Faceted Classifications: These organize knowledge; they combine generic or subject-specific semantic categories to form the whole classification item. Numerous library categorization systems combine a predefined, enumerative taxonomy of ideas with subordinate aspects that define the subject.

Hierarchical Classification: This is a systematic approach to categorizing entities based on a hierarchical structure, whereby several levels and orders are used for grouping purposes.

Information Retrieval: This refers to the systematic procedure of seeking and acquiring relevant information from a given dataset.

Information Society: This refers to a societal structure in which the use of electronic information technology predominantly enables the processes of producing, distributing, and consuming products and services.

Information-Seeking Behavior: This refers to the actions taken by individuals who have identified a need for information and then rely on official or informal sources or services to fulfill that need. The outcome of this process may either lead to the successful acquisition of relevant information or fail to do so.

Knowledge Production: This encompasses a range of interconnected activities conducted within the context of a higher education institution, research center, or company, with the primary objective of generating new knowledge.

Librarianship: This encompasses the activities of acquiring, classifying, conserving, and distributing information to those with a demonstrated need for it.

Library and Information Science: This is a multidisciplinary academic discipline that focuses on documenting narratives, collective memory, historical records, and knowledge.

Paradigm Classification: This is structured as a two-dimensional method, like a spreadsheet. The concept being referred to is a component of faceted categorization. The concept of paradigm classification pertains to a specific subset of faceted classification, whereby an object may be categorized based on two distinct dimensions.

Tree Classification: This is used to predict the response, specifically in knowledge and information management, which is situated inside the parent node, along with determining the percentage of variables that possess a positive value.

Compilation of References

Abbas, K., Tawalbeh, L. A. A., Rafiq, A., Muthanna, A., Elgendy, I. A., & Abd El-Latif, A. A. (2021). Convergence of blockchain and IoT for secure transportation systems in smart cities. *Security and Communication Networks, 2021*, 1–13. doi:10.1155/2021/5597679

Abi-Jaoude, E., Naylor, K. T., & Pignatiello, A. (2020). Smartphones, social media use and youth mental health. [CMAJ]. *Canadian Medical Association Journal, 192*(6), E136–E141. doi:10.1503/cmaj.190434 PMID:32041697

Aboujaoude, E., Savage, M. W., Starcevic, V., & Salame, W. O. (2015). Cyberbullying: Review of an old problem gone viral. *The Journal of Adolescent Health, 57*(1), 10–18. doi:10.1016/j.jadohealth.2015.04.011 PMID:26095405

About good governance. (n.d.). OHCHR. https://www.ohchr.org/en/good-governance/about-good-governance

Abraham, R., Schneider, J., & Vom Brocke, J. (2019). Data Governance: a conceptual framework, structures review, and research agenda. *International Journal of Information Management*. https://www.researchgate.net/publication/334653735

Abraham, R., Schneider, J., & vom Brocke, J. (2019). Data governance: A conceptual framework, structured review, and research agenda. *International Journal of Information Management, 49*, 424–438. doi:10.1016/j.ijinfomgt.2019.07.008

Ackoff, R. L. (1989). From data to wisdom. *Journal of Applied Systems Analysis, 16*(1), 3–9.

Advenica. (n.d.). *Why is information security so important? Cybersecurity solutions that protects what matters most*. Advenica. https://advenica.com/en/why-is-information-security-so-important,

Ahmad, M. (2023). Leveraging Blockchain for Spatial Data Infrastructure: Challenges and Opportunities. *Supporting Technologies and the Impact of Blockchain on Organizations and Society*, (pp. 177–194). IEEE.

Ahmad, M., Ali, A., & Khiyal, M. S. H. (2023). Fog Computing for Spatial Data Infrastructure: Challenges and Opportunities. In Multi-Disciplinary Applications of Fog Computing: Responsiveness in Real-Time (pp. 152–178). IGI Global. doi:10.4018/978-1-6684-4466-5.ch008

Ahmad, K., Maabreh, M., Ghaly, M., Khan, K., Qadir, J., & Al-Fuqaha, A. (2022). Developing future human-centered smart cities: Critical analysis of smart city security, data management, and ethical challenges. *Computer Science Review, 43*, 100452. doi:10.1016/j.cosrev.2021.100452

Ahmad, M., & Ali, A. (2023a). A Review of Governance Frameworks for National Spatial Data Infrastructure. In A. Correia & P. B. Agua (Eds.), *Innovation, Strategy, and Transformation Frameworks for the Modern Enterprise* (pp. 186–207). IGI Global. doi:10.4018/979-8-3693-0458-7.ch008

Ahmad, M., & Ali, A. (2023b). Integrated Geospatial Information Management in the World of Metaverse. In P. Lekhi & G. Kaur (Eds.), *Concepts, Technologies, Challenges, and the Future of Web 3* (pp. 248–270). IGI Global. doi:10.4018/978-1-6684-9919-1.ch013

Ahmad, M., Khayal, M. S. H., & Tahir, A. (2022). Analysis of Factors Affecting Adoption of Volunteered Geographic Information in the Context of National Spatial Data Infrastructure. *ISPRS International Journal of Geo-Information*, *11*(2), 120. doi:10.3390/ijgi11020120

Aidinlis, S. (2020). *The Right to Be Forgotten as a Fundamental Right in the UK After Brexit* (SSRN Scholarly Paper 3554625). https://papers.ssrn.com/abstract=3554625

Akar, E., & Mardikyan, S. (2014). Analyzing factors affecting users' behavior intention to use social media: Twitter case. *International Journal of Business and Social Science*, *5*(11), 85–95.

Akhilomen, J. (2013). Data mining application for cyber credit-card fraud detection system. In P. Perner (Ed.), *Advances in data mining: Applications and theoretical aspects* (pp. 218–228). Springer. doi:10.1007/978-3-642-39736-3_17

Akkaya, C., Fedorowicz, J., & Krcmar, H. (2019). Successful practices for using social media by police departments: a case study of the Munich police. In Proceedings of the 27th *European Conference on Information Systems* (ECIS). IEEE.

Al-Abdullah, M., Alsmadi, I., AlAbdullah, R., & Farkas, B. (2020). Designing privacy-friendly data repositories: A framework for a blockchain that follows the GDPR. *Digital Policy Regulation and Governance*, *22*(5/6), 389–411. doi:10.1108/DPRG-04-2020-0050

Alavi, A. H., Jiao, P., Buttlar, W. G., & Lajnef, N. (2018). Internet of Things-enabled smart cities: State-of-the-art and future trends. *Measurement*, *129*, 589–606. doi:10.1016/j.measurement.2018.07.067

Al-Badi, A., Tarhini, A., & Khan, A. I. (2018). Exploring big data governance frameworks. *Procedia Computer Science*, *141*, 271–277. doi:10.1016/j.procs.2018.10.181

Albors-Llorens, A. (2012). Remedies Against the Eu Institutions After Lisbon: An Era of Opportunity? *The Cambridge Law Journal*, *71*(3), 507–536. https://www.jstor.org/stable/41819928. doi:10.1017/S0008197312000803

Aldawood, H., & Skinner, G. (2019). Challenges of implementing training and awareness programs targeting cyber security social engineering. In 2019 cybersecurity and cyberforensics conference (CCC) (pp. 111-117). IEEE. doi:10.1109/CCC.2019.00004

Alexander, P., Antony, J., & Cudney, E. (2022). A novel and practical conceptual framework to support Lean Six Sigma deployment in manufacturing SMEs. *Total Quality Management & Business Excellence*, *33*(11/12), 1233–1263. doi:10.1080/14783363.2021.1945434

Al-Hadhrami, Y., & Hussain, F. K. (2021). DDoS attacks in IoT networks: A comprehensive systematic literature review. *World Wide Web (Bussum)*, *24*(3), 971–1001. doi:10.1007/s11280-020-00855-2

Alhassan, I., Sammon, D., & Daly, M. (2016) Data governance activities: an analysis of the literature. *Journal of Decision Systems, 25.* doi:10.1080/12460125.2016.1187397

Alhassan, M. M., & Adjei-Quaye, A. (2017). Information security in an organization. [IJC]. *International Journal of Computer*, *24*(1), 100–116. https://ijcjournal.org/

AlHogail, A. (2015). Design and validation of information security culture framework. *Computers in Human Behavior*, *49*, 567–575. doi:10.1016/j.chb.2015.03.054

Ali, A., & Imran, M. (2020). The Evolution of National Spatial Data Infrastructure in Pakistan-Implementation Challenges and the Way Forward. *International Journal of Spatial Data Infrastructures Research*, *15*(0).

Ali, A., Imran, M., Jabeen, M., Ali, Z., & Mahmood, S. A. (2021). Factors influencing integrated information management: Spatial data infrastructure in Pakistan. *Information Development*. doi:10.1177/02666669211048483

Alkhudhayr, F., Alfarraj, S., Aljameeli, B., & Elkhdiri, S. (2019). Information Security: A review of information security issues and techniques. *2019 2nd International Conference on Computer Applications & Information Security.* IEEE. 10.1109/CAIS.2019.8769504

Allegri, M. R. (2022). The Right to be Forgotten in the Digital Age. In F. Comunello, F. Martire, & L. Sabetta (Eds.), *What People Leave Behind: Marks, Traces, Footprints and their Relevance to Knowledge Society* (pp. 237–251). Springer International Publishing. doi:10.1007/978-3-031-11756-5_15

Alqahtani, F. H. (2017). *Developing an Information Security Policy: A Case Study Approach.* 4th Information Systems International Conference 2017, Bali, Indonesia. 10.1016/j.procs.2017.12.206

Al-Ruithe, M., Benkhelifa, E., & Hameed, K. (2016). A conceptual framework for designing data governance for cloud computing. *Procedia Computer Science, 94*, 160–167. doi:10.1016/j.procs.2016.08.025

American Library Association. (2023, January 28). *ALA's core competencies for librarianship.* ALA. https://www.ala.org/educationcareers/sites/ala.org.educationcareers/files/content/2022%20ALA%20Core%20Competences%20of%20Librarianship_FINAL.pdf

Amirulloh, I., Iskandar, I. D., Apriyani, Y., Warnilah, A. I., Purnia, D. S., & Surahman, M. (2020). Teacher Attendance Monitoring System Teaching with QR-Code and Geo Location using Android Platform. *Journal of Physics: Conference Series, 1641*(1), 012030. doi:10.1088/1742-6596/1641/1/012030

Anand, A. (2023). GDPR and Healthcare: Balancing Data Privacy and access to medical information. *NUJS Journal of Regulatory Studies, 8*(1), 27–35.

Anderson, R. J. (2008). *Security engineering: a guide to building dependable distributed systems.* John Wiley & Sons. https://books.google.com.tr/

Andersson, D., Reimers, K., & Barreto, C. (2014). Post-secondary education network security: results of addressing the end user challenge. In *INTED2014 Proceedings* (pp. 6018–6027). IATED. https://library.iated.org/view/ANDERSSON2014POS

Andrus, M. T. (2016). The Right to be Forgotten in America: Have Search Engines Inadvertently Become Consumer Reporting Agencies? *Business Law Today*, 1–4. https://www.jstor.org/stable/businesslawtoday.2016.05.06

Andrus, M. T. (2016a). The Right to be Forgotten in America: Have Search Engines Inadvertently Become Consumer Reporting Agencies? *Business Law Today*, 1–4. https://www.jstor.org/stable/businesslawtoday.2016.05.06

Andrus, M. T. (2016b). The Right to be Forgotten in America: Have Search Engines Inadvertently Become Consumer Reporting Agencies? *Business Law Today*, 1–4. https://www.jstor.org/stable/businesslawtoday.2016.05.06

Antal, C., Cioara, T., Anghel, I., Antal, M., & Salomie, I. (2021). Distributed ledger technology review and decentralized applications development guidelines. *Future Internet, 13*(3), 62. doi:10.3390/fi13030062

Antani, R. (2015). The Resistance of Memory: Could the European Union's Right to Be Forgotten Exist in the United. *Berkeley Technology Law Journal, 30*(4), 1173–1210. https://www.jstor.org/stable/26377751

Aregbesola, A., & Nwaolise, E. (2023). Securing digital collections: Cyber security best practices for academic libraries in developing countries. *Library Philosophy and Practice (e-journal).* Digital Commons. https://digitalcommons.unl.edu/libphilprac/7822

ARMA. (2017). *Generally Accepted Recordkeeping Principles.* ARMA. https://cdn.ymaws.com/www.arma.org/resource/resmgr/docs/Generally_Accepted_Recordkee.pdf

Arner, D. W., Castellano, G. G., & Selga, E. K. (2023). Financial Data Governance. *The Hastings Law Journal*, *74*(2), 235–292.

Arora, A., Bansal, S., Kandpal, C., Aswani, R., & Dwivedi, Y. (2019). Measuring social media influencer index-insights from Facebook, Twitter and Instagram. *Journal of Retailing and Consumer Services*, *49*, 86–101. doi:10.1016/j.jretconser.2019.03.012

Arrigo, E., Liberati, C., & Mariani, P. (2021). Social media data and users' preferences: A statistical analysis to support marketing communication. *Big Data Research*, *24*, 100189. doi:10.1016/j.bdr.2021.100189

Asgarkhani, M. (2005). Digital Government and Its Effectiveness in Public Management Reform. *Public Management Review*, *7*(3), 465–487. doi:10.1080/14719030500181227

Ashley, P. (2004, November 26). Enforcement of a P3P Privacy Policy. In Cowan University (ed) *2nd Australian Information Security Management Conference* (pp. 11-26). We-B Centre. https://dl.acm.org/doi/abs/10.1145/644527.644538

Asian Development Bank. (2024). *A Comparative Analysis of Tax Administration in Asia and The Pasific*. Asian Development Bank.

Aslan, Ö., Aktuğ, S. S., Ozkan-Okay, M., Yilmaz, A. A., & Akin, E. (2023). A comprehensive review of cyber security vulnerabilities, threats, attacks, and solutions. *Electronics (Basel)*, *12*(6), 1333. doi:10.3390/electronics12061333

Association for Library Collections and Technical Services. (2007, June 24). *Definitions of Digital Preservation*. ALA. https://www.ala.org/alcts/resources/preserv/defdigpres0408

Atalay, A. Ö. (2019). Evaluation of molecular genetic examinations in criminal procedure law in terms of protection of sensitive personal data. *Journal of Penal Law and Criminology*, *7*(2), 127–184. doi:10.26650/JPLC2019-0018

Attard, J., & Brennan, R. (2018). Challenges in Value-Driven Data Governance. 1-11. http://doras.dcu.ie/22980/1/ODBASE challenges paper.pdf

Bains, P. (2022, January 26). *Blockchain Consensus Mechanisms: A Primer for Supervisors*. IMF. https://www.imf.org/en/Publications/fintech-notes/Issues/2022/01/25/Blockchain-Consensus-Mechanisms-511769

Baker-Brunnbauer, J. (2020). Management perspective of ethics in artificial intelligence. *AI and Ethics*, *1*(2), 173–181. doi:10.1007/s43681-020-00022-3

Barisione, M., Michailidou, A., & Airoldi, M. (2019). Understanding a digital movement of opinion: The case of #RefugeesWelcome. *Information Communication and Society*, *22*(8), 1145–1164. doi:10.1080/1369118X.2017.1410204

Barlette, Y., Jaouen, A., & Baillette, P. (2020). Bring Your Own Device (BYOD) as reversed IT adoption: Insights into managers' coping strategies. *International Journal of Information Management*. doi:10.1016/j.ijinfomgt.2020.102212 PMID:32934432

Barrueco, J. M., & Termens, M. (2021). (2021.) Digital preservation in institutional repositories: A systematic literature review. *Digital Library Perspectives*, *38*(2), 161–174. doi:10.1108/DLP-02-2021-0011

Basahel, A. M., & Yamin, M. (2020). Cyber Security and Privacy in Internet of Things. *International Journal of Human Potentials Management*, *2*(1), 43–53. https://nla.gov.au/

Bawden, D., & Robinson, L. (2015). *Introduction to Information Science*. Facet Publishing. doi:10.29085/9781783300761

Beaney, W. M. (1966). The Right to Privacy and American Law. *Law and Contemporary Problems*, *31*(2), 253–271. doi:10.2307/1190670

Becerra-Fernandez, I., & Sabherwal, Rajiv. (2015). *Knowledge management: Systems and processes* (Second ed.). New York: Routledge.

Beckman, T. J. (1999). The Current State of Knowledge Management. *Knowledge Management Handbook, 1*(5), 1.

Beisner, J. H. (2010). Discovering a better way: The need for effective civil litigation reform. *Duke Law Journal, 60*(3), 547–596. https://www.jstor.org/stable/27896012

Benfeldt, O., Persson, J. S., & Madsen, S. (2020). Data governance as a collective action problem. *Information Systems Frontiers, 22*(2), 299–313. doi:10.1007/s10796-019-09923-z

Berberich, M., & Steiner, M. (2016). Practitioner's Corner • Blockchain Technology and the GDPR – How to Reconcile Privacy and Distributed Ledgers? *European Data Protection Law Review, 2*(3), 422–426. doi:10.21552/EDPL/2016/3/21

Bernard, L., & Ostländer, N. (2008). Assessing climate change vulnerability in the arctic using geographic information services in spatial data infrastructures. *Climatic Change, 87*(1–2), 263–281. doi:10.1007/s10584-007-9346-0

Bertino, E. (2016, December). Data privacy for IoT systems: Concepts, approaches, and research directions. In *2016 IEEE International Conference on Big Data (Big Data)* (pp. 3645-3647). IEEE. 10.1109/BigData.2016.7841030

Bisgaard, S. (2008). Quality Management and Juran's Legacy. *Quality Engineering, 20*(4), 390–401. doi:10.1080/08982110802317398

Bishop, I. D., Escobar, F. J., Karuppannan, S., Williamson, I. P., Yates, P. M., Suwarnarat, K., & Yaqub, H. W. (2000). Spatial data infrastructures for cities in developing countries. Lessons from the Bangkok experience. *Cities (London, England), 17*(2), 85–96. doi:10.1016/S0264-2751(00)00004-4

Blokdyk, G. (2020). *ISO IEC 27000 A Complete Guide* (2021 Edition). 5STARCooks.

Blumauer, A., & Nagy, H. (2020 Blumauer, A., & Nagy, H. (2020). *The knowledge graph cookbook: Recipes that work.* Monochrom.

Blume, J. (2018). Contextual extraterritoriality analysis of the DPIA and DPO provisions in the GDPR. *Georgetown Journal of International Law, 49*(4), 1425–1460.

Boerboom, I. (2010). Integrating spatial planning and decision support system infrastructure and spatial data infrastructure. *GSDI 12 World Conference Singapore*. http://www.gsdi.org/gsdiconf/gsdi12/papers/82.pdf

Bond, S., & Yuk, P. K. (2018). Uber to pay record \$148m to settle 2016 data breach claims. *Financial Times*. https://www.ft.com/content/7fa7100c-c1a7-11e8

Borgesius, F. Z., Gray, J., & Van Eechoud, M. (2015). Open data, privacy, and fair information principles: Towards a balancing framework. *Berkeley Technology Law Journal, 30*(3), 2073–2131. https://www.jstor.org/stable/26377585

Borgman, H., Heier, H., Bahli, B., & Boekamp, T. (2016). Dotting the I and Crossing (out) the T in IT Governance: New Challenges for Information Governance. *49th Hawaii International Conference on System Sciences*, (pp. 4901-4909). Koloa, Hawaii, USA. 10.1109/HICSS.2016.608

Borzacchiello, M. T., & Craglia, M. (2013). Estimating benefits of spatial data infrastructures: A case study on e-Cadastres. *Computers, Environment and Urban Systems, 41*, 276–288. doi:10.1016/j.compenvurbsys.2012.05.004

Botha, A., Kourie, D., & Snyman, R. (2014). *Coping With Continuous Change in The Business Environment: Knowledge Management and Knowledge Management Technology*. Elsevier.

Boyne, S. M. (2018). Data protection in the United States. *The American Journal of Comparative Law*, *66*(1, suppl_1), 299–343. doi:10.1093/ajcl/avy016

Bozkurt, Y., Rossmann, A., & Pervez, Z. (2022). A literature review of data governance and its applicability to smart cities. In *Proceedings of the 55th Hawaii International Conference on System Sciences (HICSS 2022),* (pp. 2680-2689). University of Hawai'i at Manoa.

Bracy, J. (2018). *CNIL publishes blockchain guidance for GDPR compliance.* IAPP. https://iapp.org/news/a/cnil-publishes-blockchain-guidance-for-gdpr-compliance/

Bressler, M., Bogard, C., & Von Bergen, C. (2020). *The Right to be Forgotten in the United States—Part 2.*

Brous, P., Janssen, M., & Vilminko-Heikkinen, R. (2016, September). Coordinating decision-making in data management activities: a systematic review of data governance principles. In *International Conference on Electronic Government* (pp. 115-125). Springer, Cham. 10.1007/978-3-319-44421-5_9

Brown, D. C. G., & Toze, S. (2017). Information governance in digitized public administration. *Canadian Public Administration*, *60*(4), 581–604. doi:10.1111/capa.12227

Brown, J. (1997). Achieving peak to peak performance using QS 9000. (cover story). [serial on the Internet]. *IIE Solutions*, *29*(1), 34. Retrieved May 22, 2017, from

Buckland, M. K. (1991). Information as thing. *Journal of the American Society for Information Science*, *42*(5), 351–360. doi:10.1002/(SICI)1097-4571(199106)42:5<351::AID-ASI5>3.0.CO;2-3

Burman, A. (2020). *The Growth of Privacy Regulation and the Bill* (Will India's Proposed Data Protection Law Protect Privacy and Promote Growth? pp. 3–8). Carnegie Endowment for International Peace. https://www.jstor.org/stable/resrep24293.4

Burton, S. (2021). Data governance: The path to a data-driven culture. *Applied Marketing Analytics, 6*(4), 298-308. https://www.ingentaconnect.com/content/ hsp/ama/2021/00000006/0000004/art00002

Business901 (2011). Does the Juran Trilogy = PDCA? *Viewed on 1.05.17* https://business901.com/blog1/does-the-juran-trilogy-pdca/

Bygrave, L. A. (2017). Data protection by design and by default: Deciphering the EU's legislative requirements. *Oslo Law Review*, *4*(2), 105–122. doi:10.18261/issn.2387-3299-2017-02-03

Cadogan, M. S. (2023). *Blockchain and Distributed Ledger Technology: Definition and Scope* (Enforcing Smart Legal Contracts, pp. 2–2). Centre for International Governance Innovation. https://www.jstor.org/stable/resrep47331.7

Calder, A. (2018). *NIST Cybersecurity Framework: A pocket guide.* IT Governance Publishing Ltd. doi:10.2307/j.ctv4cbhfx

Casola, V., De Benedictis, A., Rak, M., & Villano, U. (2019). Toward the automation of threat modeling and risk assessment in IoT systems. *Internet of Things : Engineering Cyber Physical Human Systems*, *7*, 100056. doi:10.1016/j.iot.2019.100056

Castro, A., Villagrá, V. A., García, P., Rivera, D., & Toledo, D. (2021). An ontological-based model to data governance for big data. *IEEE Access : Practical Innovations, Open Solutions*, *9*, 109943–109959. Advance online publication. doi:10.1109/ACCESS.2021.3101938

Cebula, J. J., & Young, L. R. (2010). *A taxonomy of operational cyber security risks (Final rept.).* Software Engineering Institute, Carnegie Mellon University. https://apps.dtic.mil/sti/citations/ADA537111

Cetl, V., Ivić, S. M., & Tomić, H. (2009). Improvement of national spatial data infrastructure as a public project of permanent character. *Kartografija i Geoinformacije, 8*(11).

Chase, P. H. (2019). *Perspectives on the General Data Protection Regulation Of the European Union*. German Marshall Fund of the United States. https://www.jstor.org/stable/resrep21227

Chase, P. H. (2019a). *Perspectives on the General Data Protection Regulation Of the European Union*. German Marshall Fund of the United States. https://www.jstor.org/stable/resrep21227

Chase, P. H. (2019b). *Perspectives on the General Data Protection Regulation Of the European Union*. German Marshall Fund of the United States. https://www.jstor.org/stable/resrep21227

Chassang, G. (2017). The impact of the EU general data protection regulation on scientific research. *Ecancermedicalscience, 11*, 709. doi:10.3332/ecancer.2017.709 PMID:28144283

Chen, C.-K., Reyes, L., Dahlgaard, J., & Dahlgaard-Park, S. M. (2022). From quality control to TQM, service quality and service sciences: A 30-year review of TQM literature. *International Journal of Quality and Service Sciences, 14*(2), 217–237. doi:10.1108/IJQSS-09-2021-0128

Chen, H., Chiang, R. H. L., & Storey, V. C. (2012). Business Intelligence and Analytics: From Big Data to Big Impact. *Management Information Systems Quarterly, 36*(4), 1165–1188. doi:10.2307/41703503

Chen, H., Li, Y., Chen, L., & Yin, J. (2021). Understanding employees' adoption of the Bring-Your-Own-Device (BYOD): The roles of information security-related conflict and fatigue. *Journal of Enterprise Information Management, 34*(3), 770–792. doi:10.1108/JEIM-10-2019-0318

Cheong, L. K., & Chang, V. (2007, January). *(PDF) The need for data governance: A case study*. Research Gate.https://www.researchgate.net/publication/228966685_The_need_for_data_governance_A_case_study

Chhetri, T. R., Kurteva, A., DeLong, R. J., Hilscher, R., Korte, K., & Fensel, A. (2022). Data Protection by Design Tool for Automated GDPR Compliance Verification Based on Semantically Modeled Informed Consent. *Sensors (Basel), 22*(7), 2763. doi:10.3390/s22072763 PMID:35408377

Chopra, A., & Chaudhary, M. (2020). *Implementing an information security management system: security management based on ISO 27001 guidelines*. Apress L.P. https://link.springer.com/book/10.1007/978-1-4842-5413-4

Choudhary, P., & Singh, U. (2015). A Survey on Social Network Analysis for Counter- Terrorism. *International Journal of Computer Applications, 112*, 24–29.

Claus, L. M. (1991). Total quality management: A healthcare application. *Total Quality Management, 2*(2), 131–148. doi:10.1080/09544129100000015

COBIT: Control objectives for Information Technologies. (n.d.). ISACA. https://www.isaca.org/resources/cobit

Coleman, D. J., & Nebert, D. D. (1998). Building a North American Spatial Data Infrastructure. *Cartography and Geographic Information Systems, 25*(3), 151–160. doi:10.1559/152304098782383098

Cole, R. E., & Flynn, M. S. (2009). Automotive Quality Reputation: Hard to Achieve, Hard to Lose, Still Harder to Win Back. *California Management Review, 52*(1), 67–93. doi:10.1525/cmr.2009.52.1.67

Collins, J., & Hansen, M. T. (2011). *Great by choice: Uncertainty, chaos, and luck—why some thrive despite them all*. Harper Business.

Collins, K. F., Muthusamy, S. K., & Carr, A. (2015). Toyota production system for healthcare organizations: Prospects and implementation challenges. *Total Quality Management & Business Excellence*, *26*(7/8), 905–918. doi:10.1080/14783363.2014.909624

Colorado State Archives. (2023). *Records Management*. Colorado State Archives. https://archives.colorado.gov/records-management

Connelly, A. M. (1986). Problems of Interpretation of Article 8 of the European Convention on Human Rights. *The International and Comparative Law Quarterly*, *35*(3), 567–593. https://www.jstor.org/stable/759770. doi:10.1093/iclqaj/35.3.567

Cox Broadcasting Corp. V. Cohn, 420 U.S. 469 (Supreme (court of final appeal) March 3, 1975). https://globalfreedomofexpression.columbia.edu/cases/cox-broadcasting-corp-v-cohn/

Coyne, H. (2019). The Untold Story of Edward Snowden's Impact on the GDPR. *The Cyber Defense Review*, *4*(2), 65–80. https://www.jstor.org/stable/26843893

Creswell, J. W., & Creswell, J. D. (2018). *Research Design: Qualitative, Quantitative and Mixed Method Approaches*. Sage Publications Asia-Pacific Pte. Ltd.

Crompvoets, J., Vancauwenberghe, G., Bouckaert, G., & Vandenbroucke, D. (2011). Practices to develop spatial data infrastructures: Exploring the contribution to e-government. In *Practical Studies in E-Government*. Best Practices from Around the World. doi:10.1007/978-1-4419-7533-1_13

Crompvoets, J., Vancauwenberghe, G., Ho, S., Masser, I., & Timo De Vries, W. (2018). Governance of national spatial data infrastructures in Europe. *International Journal of Spatial Data Infrastructures Research*, *13*, 253–285.

Crump, J. (2012). What are the police doing on Twitter? Social media, the police and the public. *Policy and Internet*, *3*(4), 1–27. doi:10.2202/1944-2866.1130

Čtvrtník, M. (2023). The Right to (Not) Be Forgotten, Right to Know, and Model of Four Categories of the Right to Be Forgottenright to be forgotten. In M. Čtvrtník (Ed.), *Archives and Records: Privacy, Personality Rights, and Access* (pp. 111–137). Springer International Publishing. doi:10.1007/978-3-031-18667-7_5

Curzon, J., Kosa, T. A., Akalu, R., & El-Khatib, K. (2021). Privacy and artificial intelligence. *IEEE Transactions on Artificial Intelligence*, *2*(2), 96–108. doi:10.1109/TAI.2021.3088084

Cuyvers, A. (2017). The Legal Framework of the EU. In A. Cuyvers, E. Ugirashebuja, J. E. Ruhangisa, & T. Ottervanger (Eds.), *East African Community Law* (pp. 119–138). Brill. https://www.jstor.org/stable/10.1163/j.ctt1w76vj2.10 doi:10.1163/9789004322073_007

D'Arcy, J., Adjerid, I., Angst, C. M., & Glavas, A. (2020). Too good to be true: Firm social performance and the risk of data breach. *Information Systems Research*, *31*(4), 1200–1223. doi:10.1287/isre.2020.0939

Dalkir, K. (2017). *Knowledge Management in Theory and Practice*. MIT Press.

Dallas Police Department. (2023, July 7). Wikipedia. https://en.wikipedia.org/wiki/Dallas_Police_Department

DAMA International. (2017). *DAMA-DMBOK: Data management body of knowledge* (2nd ed.). Technics Publications.

Davenport, T. H., & Prusak, L. (1998). *Working Knowledge: How Organizations Manage What They Know*. Harvard Business School Press.

Davenport, T., & Harris, J. (2007). *Competing on analytics*. Harvard Business School.

De Filippi, P. (2016). *The Interplay between Decentralization and Privacy: The Case of Blockchain Technologies* (SSRN Scholarly Paper 2852689). https://papers.ssrn.com/abstract=2852689

De Klerk, J. J. (2021). Combining ethics and compliance: A systems psychodynamic inquiry into praxis and outcomes. *Business Ethics, the Environment & Responsibility, 30*(3), 432–446. doi:10.1111/beer.12336

De Lange, J., Von-Solms, R., & Gerber, M. (2016). Information security management in local government. In: Cunningham P, Cunningham M, editors. 2016 IST-Africa Week Conference, Durban, South Africa. doi:10.1109/ISTAFRICA.2016.7530584

De Leon, H. (2022). *The Fundamentals of Taxation.* Rex Book Store.

de Mast, J. (2006). Six Sigma and Competitive Advantage. *Total Quality Management & Business Excellence, 17*(4), 455–464. doi:10.1080/14783360500528221

Debons, A. (2008). *Information Science 101.* Scarecrow Press.

De-Graft, J. D. (2019). *Developing an Integrated Framework for Knowledge Management Practices in Organisations.*

Dehousse, F., & Verhoeven, D. (2014). *The Legal Framework* (The Nuclear Safety Framework in the European Union After Fukushima, pp. 11–21). Egmont Institute. https://www.jstor.org/stable/resrep06690.6

Deogirikar, J., & Vidhate, A. (2017). *Security attacks in IoT: A survey, in International Conference on I-SMAC (IoT in Social, Mobile, Analytics and Cloud) (I-SMAC).* IEEE.

Deshpande, A., Stewart, K., Lepetit, L., & Gunashekar, S. (2017). Distributed Ledger Technologies/Blockchain: Challenges, opportunities and the prospects for standards. *Overview report The British Standards Institution (BSI), 40*, 40. https://www.bsigroup.com/

Di Miceli da Silveira, A. (2022). Corporate governance and ethical culture: Do boards matter? *Review of Managerial Science, 16*(4), 1085–1116. doi:10.1007/s11846-021-00476-7

Díaz, E. (2016). The new European Union General Regulation on Data Protection and the legal consequences for institutions. *Church. Communication and Culture, 1*(1), 206–239. doi:10.1080/23753234.2016.1240912

Diaz, L., Remke, A., Kauppinen, T., Degbelo, A., Foerster, T., Stasch, C., Rieke, M., Schaeffer, B., Baranski, B., Bröring, A., & Wytzisk, A. (2012). Future SDI - Impulses from Geoinformatics research and IT trends. *International Journal of Spatial Data Infrastructures Research, 7.* Advance online publication. doi:10.2902/1725-0463.2012.07.art18

Diesch, R., Pfaff, M., & Krcmar, H. (2020). A comprehensive model of information security factors for decision-makers. *Computers & Security, 92*, 101747. doi:10.1016/j.cose.2020.101747

Digital rights in perspective: The evolution of the debate in the Internet Governance Forum—Meireles—Politics & Policy. (n.d.). Wiley. https://onlinelibrary.wiley.com/doi/10.1111/polp.12571

Digitalisation of Panchayats. (n.d.). PIB. https://pib.gov.in/pib.gov.in/Pressreleaseshare.aspx?PRID=1983086

Directorate General of Taxes. (2000). *Value Added Tax on Goods and Services and Sales Tax on Luxury Goods as Lastly Amended by Law Number 18 of 2000.* Directorate General of Texas.

Directorate General of Taxes. (2007). *General Provisions and Tax Procedures as Lastly Amended by The Law Number 28 of 2007.* Directorate General of Texas.

Directorate General of Taxes. (2008). *Income Tax as Lastly Amended by Law Number 36 of 2008.* Directorate General of Texas.

Directorate General of Taxes. (2022). CRMBI: First Step to Data Driven Organization. Directorate General of Texas.

Djenna, A., Harous, S., & Saidouni, D. E. (2021). Internet of things meet internet of threats: New concern cyber security issues of critical cyber infrastructure. *Applied Sciences (Basel, Switzerland), 11*(10), 4580. doi:10.3390/app11104580

Dodig, C. G., & Hofkirchner, W. (2011). Floridi's "Open Problems in Philosophy of Information," Ten Years Later. *Information (Basel), 2*(2), 327–359. doi:10.3390/info2020327

Dressler, V. A. (2017). The state of affairs with digital preservation at ARL member libraries: A survey and analysis of policy. *Digital Library Perspectives, 33*(2), 137–155. doi:10.1108/DLP-08-2016-0030

Dumas, J. (2019). General Data Protection Regulation (GDPR): Prioritizing resources. *Seattle University Law Review, 42*(3), 1115–1128.

Earley, S. (n.d.). *Data governance and digital transformation: Using the customer journey to define a framework.* Doc Server. http://docserver.ingentaconnect.com.libproxy.library.unt.edu/deliver/connect/hsp/20547544/v2n1/s4.pdf?expires=1604953417&id=0000&titleid=72010542&checksum=75FC143F4E424A51DDFC9FFD348F78E6

Easttom, C., & Butler, W. (2019, January). A modified McCumber cube as a basis for a taxonomy of cyber attacks. In *2019 IEEE 9th Annual Computing and Communication Workshop and Conference (CCWC)* (pp. 0943-0949). IEEE. 10.1109/CCWC.2019.8666559

Egan, P. (2011). Effecting Data Quality Through Data Governance: a Case Study in the Financial Services Industry. *Regis University Student Publications (comprehensive collection).* 465. https://epublications.regis.edu/theses/465

Eisen, L. S. (2020). *A guide to drafting respectful policies and directives* (3rd ed.). Pixley Press.

ENISA. (2022). *Threat Landscape.* ENSIA. https://www.enisa.europa.eu/topics/cyber-threats/threats-and-trends

Entelechy Inc. (2009). A Case Study in Training Excellence and Business Results. *Coaching on the Manufacturing Floor Kawasaki Motors Manufacturing Corp., USA*, Viewed May 1, 2017 https://www.unlockit.com/wp-content/uploads/CS-HPMKMM20090213.pdf

Erdos, D. (2021). The 'right to be forgotten' beyond the EU: An analysis of wider G20 regulatory action and potential next steps. *Journal of Medicine and Law, 13*(1), 1–35. doi:10.1080/17577632.2021.1884947

Esain, A. E., Williams, S. J., Gakhal, S., Caley, L. M., & Cooke, M. W. (2012). Healthcare quality improvement - policy implications and practicalities. *International Journal of Health Care Quality Assurance, 25*(7), 565–581. doi:10.1108/09526861211261172 PMID:23276053

European Data Protection Supervisor. (2023, November 16). *Shaping a Safer Digital Future: A New Strategy for a New Decade.* EDPS. https://edps.europa.eu/press-publications/publications/strategy/shaping-safer-digital-future

European Parliament. (2021, September 23). *Parliamentary question | No right of reply and consent on Wikipedia | E-004362/2021.* European Parliament. https://www.europarl.europa.eu/doceo/document/E-9-2021-004362_EN.html

European Parliament. Directorate General for Parliamentary Research Services. (2019). *Blockchain and the general data protection regulation: Can distributed ledgers be squared with European data protection law?* Publications Office. https://data.europa.eu/doi/10.2861/535

Fabbrini, F., & Celeste, E. (2020). The Right to Be Forgotten in the Digital Age: The Challenges of Data Protection Beyond Borders. *German Law Journal, 21*(S1), 55–65. doi:10.1017/glj.2020.14

Fallon, N. (2023). *35 leadership quotes to Inspire You.* Business News Daily. https://www.businessnewsdaily.com/7481-leadership-quotes.html

Fantin Irudaya Raj, E., & Appadurai, M. (2022). Internet of things-based smart transportation system for smart cities. In S. Mukherjee, N. B. Muppalaneni, S. Bhattacharya, & A. K. Pradhan (Eds.), *Intelligent Systems for Social Good: Theory and Practice* (pp. 39–50). Springer Nature Singapore. https://link.springer.com/chapter/10.1007/978-981-19-0770-8_4 doi:10.1007/978-981-19-0770-8_4

Farradane, J. (1979). The nature of information. *Journal of Information Science, 1*(1), 13–17. doi:10.1177/016555157900100103

Faucher, J. B. P., Everett, A. M., & Lawson, R. (2008). Reconstituting knowledge management. *Journal of Knowledge Management, 12*(3), 3–16. doi:10.1108/13673270810875822

Fernandez, M., Dickinson, T., & Alani, H. (2017). An Analysis of UK Policing Engagement via Social Media. In G. Ciampaglia, A. Mashhadi, & T. Yasseri (Eds.), *Social Informatics. SocInfo* (Vol. 10539, pp. 298–304). Springer. doi:10.1007/978-3-319-67217-5_18

Finck, M. (2017). *Blockchains and Data Protection in the European Union* (SSRN Scholarly Paper 3080322). doi:10.2139/ssrn.3080322

Finck, M. (2018). *Blockchain Regulation and Governance in Europe*. Cambridge University Press. doi:10.1017/9781108609708

Floridi, L. (2002a). On Defining Library and Information Science as Applied Philosophy of Information. *Social Epistemology, 16*(1), 37–49. doi:10.1080/02691720210132789

Floridi, L. (2002b). What is the Philosophy of Information? *Metaphilosophy, 33*(1-2), 123–145. doi:10.1111/1467-9973.00221

Flynn, R. (2020). *An introduction to information science*. CRC Press. doi:10.1201/9781003065517

Fox, M. J. (2016). Legal Discourse's Epistemic Interplay with Sex and Gender Classification in the Dewey Decimal Classification System. *library trends, 64*(4), 687-713.

Franks, P. C. (2018). *Records and Information Management*. ALA Neal-Schuman.

Frazee, J. J., Finley, M. M., & Rohack, J. J. (2016). mHealth and unregulated data: Is this farewell to patient privacy. *Indiana Health Law Review / [Indiana University School of Law-Indianapolis], 13*(2), 384–414. doi:10.18060/3911.0021

Fromholz, J. M. (2000). The European Union Data Privacy Directive. *Berkeley Technology Law Journal, 15*(1), 461–484. https://www.jstor.org/stable/24115723

Gai, K., Qiu, M., Zhao, H., & Xiong, J. (2016, June). Privacy-aware adaptive data encryption strategy of big data in cloud computing. In *2016 IEEE 3rd International Conference on Cyber Security and Cloud Computing (CSCloud)* (pp. 273-278). IEEE. 10.1109/CSCloud.2016.52

Gallacher, L., & Morris, H. (2012). *ITIL foundation exam study guide*. John Wiley & Sons.

Gandhi, V., Ramkumar, K. R., Kaur, A., Kaushal, P., Chahal, J. K., & Singh, J. (2021, October). Security and privacy in IoT, Cloud and Augmented Reality. In *2021 6th International Conference on Signal Processing, Computing and Control (ISPCC)* (pp. 131-135). IEEE. 10.1109/ISPCC53510.2021.9609520

Garcia, F. (2005). Bodil Lindqvist: A Swedish Churchgoer's Violation of the European Union's Data Protection Directive Should Be a Warning to U.S. Legislators. *Fordham Intellectual Property, Media and Entertainment Law Journal, 15*(4), 1204. https://ir.lawnet.fordham.edu/iplj/vol15/iss4/10

Gartner. (2009), *Toolkit: Information Governance Project*. Gartner. www.gartner. com/id1/4933912

Gentry, S., Hale, M. L., Payant, A., Tarver, H., White, R., & Wittmann, R. (2020). *Survey of Benchmarks in Metadata Quality: Initial Findings.ul* https://digital.library.unt.edu/ark:/67531/metadc1637685/m1/1/

Ghazvini, A., & Shukur, Z. (2018). A Serious Game for Healthcare Industry: Information Security Awareness Training Program for Hospital University Kebangsaan Malaysia. *International Journal of Advanced Computer Science and Applications*, *9*(9), 236–245. doi:10.14569/IJACSA.2018.090932

Ghibellini, N. (2017). Some Aspects of the EU's New Framework for Personal Data Privacy Protection. *Business Lawyer*, *73*(1), 207–214. https://www.jstor.org/stable/26419199

Ghobadian, A. and Speller, S. (1994). Gurus of quality: A framework for comparison. *Total Quality Management, Vol 5, 3, p. 53*, Business Source Premier, EBSCO*host*, Viewed on 21 April 2017.

Ghorbani, A. A., Lu, W., & Tavallaee, M. (2009). *Network intrusion detection and prevention: concepts and techniques* (*Vol. 47*). Springer Science & Business Media. https://books.google.com.tr/

Gil, A. J., García-Alcaraz, J. L., & Mataveli, M. (2021). The effect of learning culture on training transfer: Empirical evidence in Spanish teachers. *The International Journal of Human Resource Management, 32*(5), 1038-1061. https://doi.org/. 2018.1505763 doi:10.1080/09585192

Giuca, O., Popescu, T. M., Popescu, A. M., Prostean, G., & Popescu, D. E. (2021). A survey of cybersecurity risk management frameworks. In *Soft Computing Applications: Proceedings of the 8th International Workshop Soft Computing Applications (SOFA 2018), Vol. I 8* (pp. 240-272). Springer International Publishing. https://link.springer.com/chapter/10.1007/978-3-030-51992-6_20

Gladstone, J. (2000). The U.s. Privacy Balance and the European Privacy Directive: Reflections on the United States Privacy Policy. *Willamette Journal of International Law and Dispute Resolution, 7*(1), 10–32. https://www.jstor.org/stable/26210974

Global Freedom of Expression. (2017, June 27). *Satakunnan Markkinapörssi Oy and Satamedia Oy v. Finland.* Global Freedom of Expression. https://globalfreedomofexpression.columbia.edu/cases/case-satakunnan-markkinaporssi-oy-satamedia-oy-v-finland/

Globocnik, J. (2020). The Right to Be Forgotten is Taking Shape: CJEU Judgments in GC and Others (C-136/17) and Google v CNIL (C-507/17). *GRUR International, 69.* doi:10.1093/grurint/ikaa002

Golden Data Law. (2019, February 5). Austrian Data Protection Authority: The erasure of personal data is also possible through. *Golden Data.* https://medium.com/golden-data/austrian-data-protection-authority-the-erasure-of-personal-data-is-also-possible-through-4e61b882e4ad

Golden Data Law. (2022a, October 23). Facebook Fan Pages: Liability of co-controllers. *Golden Data.* https://medium.com/golden-data/facebook-fan-pages-liability-of-co-controllers-2a23e7ecd3a9

Golden Data Law. (2022b, October 23). Google Spain v. AEPD: Remembering the "Right to be Forgotten." *Golden Data.* https://medium.com/golden-data/google-v-spain-the-right-to-be-forgotten-aaee50dae43c

González-Cebrián, A., Hermenegildo, M., Climente, M., & Ferrer, A. (2022). Multivariate Six Sigma: A case study in an outpatient pharmaceutical care unit. *Quality Engineering, 34*(2), 277–289. doi:10.1080/08982112.2022.2042018

Goodman, D., Phillips, J., & Stamper, M. (2022). *Data privacy program guide: How to build a privacy program that inspires trust.* CISO DRG Publishing.

Goodsett, M., & Koziura, A. (2016). *Are library science programs preparing new librarians? Creating a sustainable and vibrant library community*. Michael Schwartz Library Publications. doi:10.1080/01930826.2015.1134246

Google Spain SL v. Agencia Española de Protección de Datos, Case C-131/12 (Court of Justice of the European Union (CJEU) May 13, 2014). https://globalfreedomofexpression.columbia.edu/cases/google-spain-sl-v-agencia-espanola-de-proteccion-de-datos-aepd/

Gopal, R. V. (2022, December 19). Aadhaar Data Breach — How Sensitive Data Of 1.3 Billion Indians Was Compromised. *Medium.* https://medium.com/@rithikvgopal/aadhaar-data-breach-how-sensitive-data-of-1-3-billion-indians-was-compromised-cb01d0c2d7d3

Gopalan, B., & Iyer, R. (2017). Comprehending and Implementing Best Practices of Quality Management Across Industries. *International Journal of Research in Commerce, IT & Management*, Vol. 7, No 7, ISSN 2231-5756.

Gopalan, B. (2017). *Value Co-creation - Internet for Development and Telecommunications.* LAP LAMBERT Academic Publishing.

Graef, I., & Prüfer, J. (2021). Governance of data sharing: A law & economics proposal. *Research Policy, 50*(9), 104330. doi:10.1016/j.respol.2021.104330

Granell, C., Schade, S., & Hobona, G. (2011). Linked Data: Connecting Spatial Data Infrastructures and Volunteered Geographic Information. In Geospatial Web Services: Advances in Information Interoperability.

Green, A. (2021). Metadata Application Profiles in U. S. Academic Libraries: A Document Analysis. *Journal of Library Metadata, 21*(3-4), 3–4, 105–143. doi:10.1080/19386389.2022.2030172

Greenawalt, K. (1992). Free Speech in the United States and Canada. *Law and Contemporary Problems, 55*(1), 5–33. doi:10.2307/1191755

Gruschka, N., Mavroeidis, V., Vishi, K., & Jensen, M. (2018). *Privacy Issues and Data Protection in Big Data: A Case Study Analysis under GDPR.* 5027–5033. doi:10.1109/BigData.2018.8622621

GSDI. (2004). Developing Spatial Data Infrastructures: The SDI Cookbook. In GSDI/Nebert.

Gui, L., Lei, H., & Le, P. B. (2022). Determinants of radical and incremental innovation: The influence of transformational leadership, knowledge sharing and knowledge-centered culture. *European Journal of Innovation Management, 25*(5), 1221–1241. doi:10.1108/EJIM-12-2020-0478

Guo, L., & Congdon, P. (2021). *IEEE 802 Nendica Report: Intelligent Lossless Data Center Networks.* IEEE SA Industry Connections. https://ieeexplore.ieee.org/iel7/9457236/9457237/09457238.pdf

Gupta, U. G., & Cannon, S. (2020). A Review of Data Governance Definitions and Emerging Perspectives. *International Journal of Data Analytics (IJDA), 1*(2), 30-47.2

Gupta, J., & Bakshi, R. (2023). Social Media as a Potent Factor in Promoting Awareness about Swachh Bharat Abhiyaan: A Critical Analysis. *Asian Journal of Education and Social Studies, 49*(4), 346–358. doi:10.9734/ajess/2023/v49i41213

Hakimi, L., Eynon, R., & Murphy, V. A. (2021). The Ethics of Using Digital Trace Data in Education: A Thematic Review of the Research Landscape. *Review of Educational Research, 91*(5), 671–717. doi:10.3102/00346543211020116

Hallowell, D. (1994). Tree Diagrams for Six Sigma: Plain and Simple? Viewed on May 1, 2017 https://www.isixsigma.com/wp-con- tent/uploads/images/stories/migrated/graphics/205i.gif

Halpren-Ruder, D. (2020). E-Health and Healthcare Quality management: Disruptive Opportunities. *Rhode Island Medical Journal, 103*(1), 12–15. PMID:32013296

Hamelink, C. J. (2003). Digital Risks and Security in CyberSpace. In C. J. Hamelink (Ed.), *The Ethics of Cyberspace* (pp. 107–138). SAGE Publications Ltd. doi:10.4135/9781446219911.n5

Harding, E. L., Vanto, J. J., Clark, R., Hannah Ji, L., & Ainsworth, S. C. (2019). Understanding the scope and impact of the California consumer privacy act of 2018. *Journal of Data Protection & Privacy, 2*(3), 234–253. https://www.ingentaconnect.com/content/hsp/jdpp/2019/00000002/00000003/art00007

Harris, R. (2020). Forging path towards meaningful digital privacy: Data monetization and the CCPA. *Loyola of Los Angeles Law Review, 54*(1), 197–234.

Hartman, P. (1954). Freedom of Religion and Speech and the United States Supreme Court. *The Modern Law Review, 17*(3), 220–228. https://www.jstor.org/stable/1090673. doi:10.1111/j.1468-2230.1954.tb02151.x

Harvey, F. (2003). Developing geographic information infrastructures for local government: The role of trust. *The Canadian Geographer. Geographe Canadien, 47*(1), 28–36. doi:10.1111/1541-0064.02e10

Hatfield, J. M. (2019). Virtuous human hacking: The ethics of social engineering in penetration-testing. *Computers & Security, 83*, 354–366. doi:10.1016/j.cose.2019.02.012

Hayes, D. R., & Cappa, F. (2018). Open-source intelligence for risk assessment. *Business Horizons, 61*(5), 689–697. doi:10.1016/j.bushor.2018.02.001

Hayes, D., Cappa, F., & Le-Khac, N. A. (2020). An effective approach to mobile device management: Security and privacy issues associated with mobile applications. *Digital Business, 1*(1), 100001. doi:10.1016/j.digbus.2020.100001

Hedden, H. (2022). *The Accidental Taxonomist* (3rd ed.). Information Today, Inc.

Hendrawan, M. R. & Mukhlis. (2021). *Pengantar Pengorganisasian dan Temu Balik Informasi: Pendekatan Konsep dan Praktik*. Malang: UB Press.

Hendrawan, M. R. (2019). *Manajemen Pengetahuan: Konsep dan Praktik Berpengetahuan pada Organisasi Pembelajar*. UB Press.

Henrique, D. B., & Godinho Filho, M. (2020). A systematic literature review of empirical research in Lean and Six Sigma in healthcare. *Total Quality Management & Business Excellence, 31*(3/4), 429–449. doi:10.1080/14783363.2018.1429259

Hernandez-de-Menendez, M., Morales-Menendez, R., Escobar, C., & Jorge, A. (2021). Biometric applications in education. *International Journal on Interactive Design and Manufacturing, 15*(2-3), 365–380. doi:10.1007/s12008-021-00760-6

Herold, K. R. (2001). Librarianship and the Philosophy of Information. *Library Philosophy and Practice, 3*(2), 1–15.

Heuvel, J. V. D., Does, R. J. M. M., & Verver, J. P. S. (2005). Does RJMM, Verver JPS. Six Sigma in Healthcare: Lessons Learned from a Hospital. *International Journal of Six Sigma and Competitive Advantage, 1*(4), 380–388. doi:10.1504/IJSSCA.2005.008504

Higgs, J. L., Pinsker, R. E., Smith, T. J., & Young, G. R. (2016). The relationship between board-level technology committees and reported security breaches. *Journal of Information Systems, 30*(3), 79–98. doi:10.2308/isys-51402

Hill, K. (2023). *Your face belongs to us: A secretive startup's quest to end privacy as we know it*. Random House.

Hjørland, B. (2000). Library and Information Science: Practice, Theory, and Philosophical Basis. *Information Processing & Management, 36*(3), 501–531. doi:10.1016/S0306-4573(99)00038-2

Hjørland, B. (2005). Empiricism, Rationalism, And Positivism in Library and Information Science. *The Journal of Documentation, 61*(1), 130–155. doi:10.1108/00220410510578050

Hood, C. C. (1983). *The tools of government*. No Title. doi:10.1007/978-1-349-17169-9

Hood, C., & Margetts, H. (2007). *The tools of government in the digital age*. Bloomsbury Publishing. doi:10.1007/978-1-137-06154-6

Hoofnagle, C. J., Van Der Sloot, B., & Borgesius, F. Z. (2019). The European Union general data protection regulation: What it is and what it means. *Information & Communications Technology Law*, *28*(1), 65–98. doi:10.1080/13600834.2019.1573501

Hook, L., & Kuchler, H. (2017). Uber hid massive data breach from passengers and regulators. *Financial Times*. https://www.ft.com/content/ed66a21a-cf0e

Hossin, M. A., Du, J., Mu, L., & Asante, I. O. (2023). Sage Open). *Big Data-Driven Public Policy Decisions: Transformation Toward Smart Governance.*, *13*(4), 1–19. doi:10.1177/21582440231215123

Hristov, P., & Dimitrov, W. (2018, October 29). *The blockchain as a backbone of GDPR compliant frameworks.*

Hsieh, Roger. (2014). Improving HIPAA enforcement and protecting patient privacy in digital healthcare environment. *Loyola University Chicago Law Journal, 46*(1), 175-224.

Huang, S. L., & Chang, C. Y. (2020). Understanding how people select social networking services: Media trait, social influences and situational factors. *Information & Management*, *57*(6), 103323. doi:10.1016/j.im.2020.103323

Hu, C., Li, Y., & Zheng, X. (2022). Data assets, information uses, and operational efficiency. *Applied Economics*, *54*(60), 6887–6900. doi:10.1080/00036846.2022.2084021

Hudgins, J., Agnew, G., & Brown, E. (1999). *Getting mileage out of metadata: Applications for the library*. American Library Association.

Hulme, T. (2012). Information governance: Sharing the IBM approach. *Business Information Review*, *29*(2), 99–104. doi:10.1177/0266382112449221

Huy, D. T. N. (2021). culture: Communication methods. *Journal of Organizational Culture, Communications and Conflict, 25*(1), 1-2. https://www.proquest.com/ docview/2519897270?accountid=12085&pq-origsite=summon&forcedol=true

Ichijo, K., & Nonaka, I. (2007). *Knowledge Creation and Management, New Challenges for Managers*. Oxford University Press.

Implementation of Compliance Risk Management and Business Intelligence. (2021). https://perpajakan.ddtc.co.id/sumber-hukum/peraturan-pusat/surat-edaran-direktur-jenderal-pajak-se-39pj2021

Implementation of Compliance Risk Management in Extensification, Monitoring, Inspection, and Collection Activities in Directorate General of Taxes. (2019). Data Center. Https://Datacenter.Ortax.Org/Ortax/Aturan/Show/16857

Information governance reference model. (2023, March 24). EDRM. https://edrm.net/resources/frameworks-and-standards/information-governance-reference-model/

International Organization for Standardization. (2018). *Information technology - Security techniques - Information security management systems - Overview and vocabulary* (ISO Standard No. 27000:2018). ISO. https://www.iso.org/standard/73906.html adresinden erişildi.

International Standard for Organization. (2016). *Information and documentation-- Records management Part 1: Concepts and principals*. ISO. https://www.iso.org/standard/62542.html

ISACA. (2019). *COBIT 5 Implementation -Supplemental Tools and Materials*. USA: ISACA.

ISACA. (2022). *IT Audit Framework (ITAF),* (4th ed.). ISACA. https://store.isaca.org/s/store#/store/browse/detail/a2S-4w000004Ko91EAC adresinden erişildi.

Iskiev, M. (2023, April 10). *The Fastest Growing Social Media Platforms of 2023. New Data.* HubSpot. https://blog.hubspot.com/marketing/fastest-growing-social-media-platforms#article

IT Governance Publishing. (2017). *EU General Data Protection Regulation (GDPR): An Implementation and Compliance Guide.* IT Governance Publishing.

Jaar, D. (2009). E-discovery tips for everyday cases how to put the process in perspective. *Law Practice, 35*(2), 50–54.

Janssen, M., Brous, P., Estevez, E., Barbosa, L. S., & Janowski, T. (2020). Data governance: Organizing data for trustworthy Artificial Intelligence. *Government Information Quarterly, 37*(3), N.PAG. https://doi.org/ doi:10.1016/j.giq.2020.101493

Jenkins, G., Kuo, C.-Y., & Shukla, G. (2000). *Tax Analysis and Revenue Forecasting.* Harvard Institute for International Development, Harvard University.

John, B. (2018). Are you ready for General Data Protection Regulation? *BMJ (Clinical Research Ed.), 360,* k941. https://www.jstor.org/stable/26959124. doi:10.1136/bmj.k941 PMID:29500167

Jones, M. L. (2013). *Speaking of Forgetting: Analysis of Possible Non-EU Responses to the Right to Be Forgotten and Speech Exception* (SSRN Scholarly Paper 2238602). doi:10.2139/ssrn.2238602

Jones, A., & Ashenden, D. (2005). *Risk management for computer security: Protecting your network and information assets.* Elsevier.

Jouini, M., Rabai, L. B. A., & Aissa, A. B. (2014). Classification of security threats in information systems. *Procedia Computer Science, 32,* 489–496. doi:10.1016/j.procs.2014.05.452

Juran, J. M., & Godfrey, B. A. (Eds.). (2005). *Juran's Quality Control Handbook* (5th ed.). McGraw Hill.

Kaczmarek, J. (2014). Supporting information governance through records and information management. Research bulletin. *ECAR.* https://library.educause.edu/~/media/files/library/2014/4/erb1402-pdf.pdf

Kaplan, S., Bisgaard, S., Truesdell, D., & Zetterholm, S. (2009). Design for Six Sigma in Healthcare: Developing an Employee Influenza Vaccination Process. *Journal for Healthcare Quality, 31*(3), 36–43. doi:10.1111/j.1945-1474.2009.00029.x PMID:19522346

Kapoor, K. K., Tamilmani, K., Rana, N. P., Patil, P., Dwivedi, Y. K., & Nerur, S. (2018). Advances in social media research: Past, present and future. *Information Systems Frontiers, 20*(3), 531–558. doi:10.1007/s10796-017-9810-y

Kariotis, T., Ball, M. P., Tzovaras, B. G., Dennis, S., Sahama, T., Johnston, C., & Borda, A. (2020). Emerging health data platforms: From individual control to collective data governance. Data &amp. *Data & Policy, 2,* 1–13. doi:10.1017/dap.2020.14

Karmakar, R. (2023, June 18). Digital eye deters proxy attendance among Meghalaya's teachers. *The Hindu.* https://www.thehindu.com/news/national/meghalayas-new-attendance-app-keeps-proxy-teachers-away/article66980082.ece

Kaur, N., & Sood, S. K. (2017). Dynamic resource allocation for big data streams based on data characteristics (5 V s). *International Journal of Network Management, 27*(4), e1978. doi:10.1002/nem.1978

Kavak, A., & Odabaş, H. (2023). The impact of information security management guide utilization on technological and institutional information security measures in university libraries in Türkiye. *Journal of Academic Librarianship, 49*(6), 102800. doi:10.1016/j.acalib.2023.102800

Kayabay, K., Gökalp, M. O., Gökalp, E., Eren, P. E., & Koçyiğit, A. (2022). Data science roadmapping: An architectural framework for facilitating transformation towards a data-driven organization. *Technological Forecasting and Social Change, 174*, 121264. doi:10.1016/j.techfore.2021.121264

Keller, H., & Walther, R. (2018). Balancing Test: United Nations Human Rights Bodies. *Max Planck Encyclopedia of International Procedural Law (MPEiPro)*. https://opil.ouplaw.com/view/10.1093/law-mpeipro/e3422.013.3422/law-mpeipro-e3422?rskey=9sW2rG&result=1&prd=MPIL

Kenny, C. (2018). The Equifax data breach and the resulting legal recourse. Brooklyn Journal of Corporate. *Financial & Commercial Law, 13*(1), 215–238.

Khando K., Gao S., Islam S. M., & Salman A. (2021). *Enhancing employees information security awareness in private and public organizations: A systematic literature review.*

Khiralla, F. A. M. (2020). Statistics of cybercrime from 2016 to the first half of 2020. *Int. J. Comput. Sci. Netw., 9*(5), 252–261. https://www.ijcsn.org/

Kiker, D. R. (2014). Defensible Data Deletion: A Practical Approach to Reducing Cost and Managing Risk Associated with Expanding Enterprise Data. *Richmond Journal of Law and Technology, 20*(2).

Kim, D., & Solomon, M. G. (2018). *Fundamentals of information systems security* (3rd ed.). Jones & Bartlett Learning.

Kim, R. H., Gaukler, G. M., & Lee, C. W. (2016). Improving healthcare quality: A technological and managerial innovation perspective. *Technological Forecasting and Social Change, 113*, 373–378. doi:10.1016/j.techfore.2016.09.012

Kindt, E. J. (2016). Why research may no longer be the same: About the territorial scope of the New Data Protection Regulation. *Computer Law & Security Report, 32*(5), 729–748. doi:10.1016/j.clsr.2016.07.007

Kintonova, A., Vasyaev, A., & Shestak, V. (2021). Cyberbullying and cyber-mobbing in developing countries. *Information and Computer Security, 29*(3), 435–456. doi:10.1108/ICS-02-2020-0031

Klosek, J. (2000). *Data privacy in the information age*. Quorum Books.

Koenig, M., & Neveroski, K. (2018). Knowledge Management: Early Development. Encyclopedia of Library and Information Sciences 4th Ed. Flordia: CRC Press.

Kohl, U., & Rowland, D. (2017). Censorship & Cyberborders through EU Data Protection Law. In *The Net and the Nation State*. Multidisciplinary Perspectives on Internet Governance., doi:10.1017/9781316534168.008

KolainM.WirthC. (2018, May 9). *Privacy by BlockChain Design: A Blockchain-enabled GDPR-compliant Approach for Handling Personal Data*. doi:10.18420/blockchain2018_03

Kolesar, P. J. (2008). Juran's Lectures to Japanese Executives in 1954: A Perspective and Contemporary Lessons. *The Quality Management Journal, 15*(3), 7–16. doi:10.1080/10686967.2008.11918191

Kooper, M. N., Maes, R., & Lindgreen, E. E. O. R. (2011). On the governance of information: Introducing a new concept of governance to support the management of information. *International Journal of Information Management, 31*(3), 195–200. doi:10.1016/j.ijinfomgt.2010.05.009

Kotler, P., Kartajaya, H., & Setiawan, I. (2021). *Marketing 5.0: Technology for Humanity*. Wiley & Sons.

Kranenborg, H. (2020). Article 17 Right to erasure ('right to be forgotten'). In C. Kuner, L. A. Bygrave, C. Docksey, & L. Drechsler (Eds.), The EU General Data Protection Regulation (GDPR): A Commentary (p. 0). Oxford University Press. doi:10.1093/oso/9780198826491.003.0049

Kreso, I., Kapo, A., & Turulja, L. (2021). Data mining privacy preserving: Research agenda. *Wiley Interdisciplinary Reviews. Data Mining and Knowledge Discovery*, *11*(1), e1392. doi:10.1002/widm.1392

Krzysztofek, M. (2018). *GDPR: General Data Protection Regulation (EU) 2016/679: Post-reform Personal Data Protection in the European Union*. Kluwer Law International BV. https://books.google.com.tr/

Kuchler, H. (2014). Home Depot attack bigger than Target's. *Financial Times*. https://www.ft.com/content/7f9a2b26-3f74-11e4-984b-00144

Kulhari, S. (2018). Data Protection, Privacy and Identity: A Complex Triad. In *Building-Blocks of a Data Protection Revolution* (1st ed., pp. 23–37). Nomos Verlagsgesellschaft mbH. https://www.jstor.org/stable/j.ctv941qz6.7

Kulhari, S. (2018a). *Building-Blocks of a Data Protection Revolution: The Uneasy Case for Blockchain Technology to Secure Privacy and Identity* (1st ed.). Nomos Verlagsgesellschaft mbH. https://www.jstor.org/stable/j.ctv941qz6

Kulhari, S. (2018b). Data Protection, Privacy and Identity: A Complex Triad. In *Building-Blocks of a Data Protection Revolution* (1st ed., pp. 23–37). Nomos Verlagsgesellschaft mbH. https://www.jstor.org/stable/j.ctv941qz6.7

Kulms, R. (2020). Blockchains: Private Lawmatters. *Singapore Journal of Legal Studies*, 63–89. https://www.jstor.org/stable/27032601

Kurzhals, C., Graf-Vlachy, L., & König, A. (2020). Strategic leadership and technological innovation: A comprehensive review and research agenda. *Corporate Governance*, *28*(6), 437–464. doi:10.1111/corg.12351

Kwaśnik, B. H. (2020). Changing Perspectives on Classification as a Knowledge-Representation Process. *Knowledge Organization*, *46*(8), 656–667. doi:10.5771/0943-7444-2019-8-656

La Monaca, G., & Schiralli, I. (2010). Data protection, privacy. *La Clinica Terapeutica*, *161*(2), 189–191. https://www.clinicaterapeutica.it/download/404/fascicolo-2/7145/161-02-20_tact_la_monaca.pdf PMID:20499037

Ladley, J. (2012). *Data governance: How to design, deploy and sustain an effective data governance program*. Elsevier. doi:10.1016/B978-0-12-415829-0.00002-2

Ladley, J. (2019). *Data governance: How to design, deploy, and sustain an effective data governance program*. Academic Press.

Lallie, H. S., Shepherd, L. A., Nurse, J. R., Erola, A., Epiphaniou, G., Maple, C., & Bellekens, X. (2021). Cyber security in the age of COVID-19: A timeline and analysis of cyber-crime and cyber-attacks during the pandemic. *Computers & Security*, *105*, 102248. doi:10.1016/j.cose.2021.102248 PMID:36540648

Lambe, P. (2014). *Organising Knowledge: Taxonomies, Knowledge, and Organisational Effectiveness*. Elsevier.

Lambert, P. (2017). *Understanding the New European Data Protection Rules*. CRC Press.

Landmark Communications, Inc. V. Commonwealth, 217 Va. 699 (Supreme Court of Virginia. May 1, 1978). https://uk.practicallaw.thomsonreuters.com/Document/I3e1a87e2042811da83e7e9deff98dc6f/View/FullText.html?originationContext=docHeader&contextData=(sc.PracticalLaw)&transitionType=Document&needToInjectTerms=False&firstPage=true

Landoll, D. J. (2017). *Information Security Policies, Procedures, and Standards: A Practitioner's Reference*. CRC Press. https://books.google.com.tr/

Laney, D. B. (2018). *Infonomics: How to monetize, manage, and measure information as an asset for competitive advantage* (3rd ed.). Bibliomotion, Inc.

Lankton, N., Price, J. B., & Karim, M. (2021). Cybersecurity breaches and the role of information technology governance in audit committee charters. *Journal of Information Systems, 35*(1), 101–119. doi:10.2308/isys-18-071

Lanzing, M., Lievevrouw, E., & Siffles, L. (2021). It Takes Two to Techno-Tango: An Analysis of a Close Embrace Between Google/Apple and the EU in Fighting the Pandemic Through Contact Tracing Apps. *Science as Culture, 31*(1), 136–148. doi:10.1080/09505431.2021.1999403

Laranjo, L., Arguel, A., Neves, A. L., Gallagher, A. M., Kaplan, R., Mortimer, N., Mendes, G. A., & Lau, A. Y. (2015). The influence of social networking sites on health behavior change: A systematic review and meta-analysis. *Journal of the American Medical Informatics Association : JAMIA, 22*(1), 243–256. doi:10.1136/amiajnl-2014-002841 PMID:25005606

Lăzăroiu, G., Kovacova, M., Kliestikova, J., Kubala, P., Valaskova, K., & Dengov, V. V. (2018). Data governance and automated individual decision-making in the digital privacy General Data Protection Regulation. *Administratie si Management Public, 31*, 132–142.

LeBlanc, J., & Kurth, M. (2008). An operational model for library metadata maintenance. *Library Resources & Technical Services, 52*(1), 54–59. doi:10.5860/lrts.52n1.54

Lenard, T. M., & Rubin, P. H. (2010). In defense of data: Information and the costs of privacy. *Policy and Internet, 2*(1), 149–183. doi:10.2202/1944-2866.1035

Levin, A. (2018). *How a security policy could cause the next killer hack.* INC. https://www.inc.com/adam-levin/how-a-security-policy-could-cause-next-killer-hack.html.

Li, J., & Kassem, M. (2021). Applications of distributed ledger technology (DLT) and Blockchain-enabled smart contracts in construction. *Automation in Construction, 132*, 103955. doi:10.1016/j.autcon.2021.103955

Lim, J. S., Chang, S., Maynard, S., & Ahmad, A. (2009). Exploring the relationship between organizational culture and ınformation security culture. In *Proceedings of the 7th Australian Information Security Management Conference* (pp. 88-97). ACM. 10.4225/75/57b4065130def

Lindlar, M. (2014). Time to change: Effects and implications of digital preservation in an organizational context. *IASSIST Quarterly, 36*(3-4), 8. doi:10.29173/iq471

Lin, E. (2002). Prioritizing Privacy: A Constitutional Response to the Internet. *Berkeley Technology Law Journal, 17*(3), 1085–1154. https://www.jstor.org/stable/24116979

Liu, J. H. (2017). Neo-Confucian Epistemology and Chinese Philosophy: Practical Postulates for Actioning Psychology as a Human Science. *Asian Journal of Social Psychology, 20*(2), 137–149. doi:10.1111/ajsp.12168

Liu, Z., Tang, H., & Zhang, C. (2023). Corporate governance, moral hazard, and financialization. *International Review of Economics & Finance, 88*, 318–331. doi:10.1016/j.iref.2023.06.042

Li, V. (2014). Zubulake 10 Years After: Landmark case created an industry-and still stirs debate. *ABA Journal, 100*(9), 48–53. https://www.jstor.org/stable/44653176

Livemint. (2023, October 31). *Aadhaar data leak: Massive data breach exposes about 81 crore Indians' personal information on dark web.* Live Mint. https://www.livemint.com/news/india/aadhaar-data-leak-massive-data-breach-exposes-815-million-indians-personal-information-on-dark-web-details-here-11698712793223.html

Li, Y., & Liu, Q. (2021). A comprehensive review study of cyber-attacks and cyber security; Emerging trends and recent developments. *Energy Reports, 7*, 8176–8186. doi:10.1016/j.egyr.2021.08.126

Lopatin, L. (2010). Metadata practices in academic and non-academic libraries for digital projects: A survey. *Cataloging & Classification Quarterly*, *48*(8), 716–742. doi:10.1080/01639374.2010.509029

Losko, J., & Smeak, R. (2019). Handling indoor air quality concerns: A layered approach to ensuring patient and staff safety. *Health Facilities Management*, *32*(6), 48–51.

Luftman, J. N., & Ben-Zvi, T. (2011). Key issues for IT executives 2011: Cautious optimism in uncertain economic times. *MIS Quarterly Executive*, *10*(4), 203–212.

Luo, B., Wang, H., Liu, H., Li, B., & Peng, F. (2018). Early fault detection of machine tools based on deep learning and dynamic identification. *IEEE Transactions on Industrial Electronics*, *66*(1), 509–518. doi:10.1109/TIE.2018.2807414

Lynskey, O. (2015). Control over Personal Data in a Digital Age: Google Spain v AEPD and Mano Costeja Gonzalez. *The Modern Law Review*, *78*(3), 522–534. https://www.jstor.org/stable/43829127. doi:10.1111/1468-2230.12126

Ma, J. (2009). Metadata in ARL Libraries: A Survey of Metadata Practices, *Journal of Library Metadata*, 9:1-2, 1-14, oi:10.1080/19386380903094977

Machado de Sousa, E., & Shahzad, A. (2022). Data loss prevention from a malicious insider. *Journal of Computer Information Systems*, *62*(6), 1101–1111. doi:10.1080/08874417.2021.1980748

Madden, M. (2014, November 12). Public Perceptions of Privacy and Security in the Post-Snowden Era. *Pew Research Center: Internet, Science & Tech*. https://www.pewresearch.org/internet/2014/11/12/public-privacy-perceptions/

Maeng, S. H., Essaid, M., & Ju, H. T. (2020). Analysis of Ethereum Network Properties and Behavior of Influential Nodes. *2020 21st Asia-Pacific Network Operations and Management Symposium (APNOMS)*, 203–207. 10.23919/APNOMS50412.2020.9236965

Mahanti, R. (2022). Compliance, data, quality, and governance. *EDPACS*, *66*(2), 20–25. doi:10.1080/07366981.2022.2026575

Maiwald, E. (2004). *Fundamentals of Network Security*. McGraw Hill Professional.

Manfré, L., Hirata, E., Silva, J. B., Shinohara, E. J., Giannotti, M., Larocca, A. P. C., & Quintanilha, J. (2012). An Analysis of Geospatial Technologies for Risk and Natural Disaster Management. *ISPRS International Journal of Geo-Information*, *1*(2), 166–185. doi:10.3390/ijgi1020166

Mansor, N. A. (2020). Knowledge Management System Implementation: Expert System. *International Journal of Information & Knowledge Management*, *10*(1), 43–50.

Mansourian, A., Rajabifard, A., Valadan Zoej, M. J., & Williamson, I. (2006). Using SDI and web-based system to facilitate disaster management. *Computers & Geosciences*, *32*(3), 303–315. Advance online publication. doi:10.1016/j.cageo.2005.06.017

Manupatra. (n.d.). *Right to Privacy in Digital Age*. Manupatra. https://articles.manupatra.com/article-details?id=undefined&ifile=undefined

Marshall, W., McAllister, C., & Vestergaard, C. (2023). *Distributed Ledger Technology—A Possible Solution?* Stimson Center. https://www.jstor.org/stable/resrep52690.6

Martin, W., & Tomáš, P. (2023). Data Management in Industrial Companies: The Case of Austria. *International Journal for Quality Research. 17(3) 847–866. ISSN 1800-6450.*

Masser, I. (2019). Geographic Information Systems to Spatial Data Infrastructure. In Geographic Information Systems to Spatial Data Infrastructure. Taylor & Francis. doi:10.1201/9780429505904

Mathur, M. (2019). Where is the security blanket? Developing social media marketing capability as a shield from perceived cybersecurity risk. *Journal of Promotion Management, 25*(2), 200–224. doi:10.1080/10496491.2018.1443310

Maurel, D., & Zwarich, N. (2021). Information governance and power relations: Reflections on archival education in Québec. *Education for Information, 37*(1), 33–51. doi:10.3233/EFI-190360

McCallister, E. (2010). *Guide to protecting the confidentiality of personally identifiable information* (*Vol. 800*, No. 122). Diane Publishing. https://books.google.com.tr/

McCumber, J. (1991). Information systems security: A comprehensive model. *In Proceedings of the 14th National Computer Security Conference* (pp. 328-337). NIST. https://csrc.nist.gov/publications/history/nissc/1991-14th-NCSC-proceedings-vol-1.pdf

McCumber, J. (2004). *Assessing and Managing Security Risk in IT Systems: A Structured Methodology* (1st ed.). Auerbach Publications., doi:10.1201/9780203490426

McGee, M. K. (2017). *New In-Depth Analysis: Anthem Breach.* BankInfoSecurity. https://www.bankinfosecurity.com/new-in-depth-analysis-anthem-breach-a-9627

McIntyre, L. (2007). Emergence and Reduction in Chemistry: Ontological or Epistemological Concepts? *Synthese, 155*(3), 337–343. doi:10.1007/s11229-006-9111-3

McLaughlin, J., & Nichols, S. (1994). Developing a national spatial data infrastructure. *Journal of Surveying Engineering, 120*(2), 62–76. doi:10.1061/(ASCE)0733-9453(1994)120:2(62)

McMillan, C. (2024). *UK experts talk driving a data-sharing culture in the public sector.* Online: Global Government Forum.

Mediengruppe Österreich GmbH v. Austria, 37713/18 (European Court of Human Rights (ECtHR) April 5, 2022). https://globalfreedomofexpression.columbia.edu/cases/mediengruppe-osterreich-gmbh-v-austria/

Mehmood, Y., Ahmad, F., Yaqoob, I., Adnane, A., Imran, M., & Guizani, S. (2017). Internet-of-things-based smart cities: Recent advances and challenges. *IEEE Communications Magazine, 55*(9), 16–24. doi:10.1109/MCOM.2017.1600514

Mikalef, P., Krogstie, J., van de Wetering, R., Pappas, I. O., & Giannakos, M. N. (2018). Information Governance in the Big Data Era: Aligning Organizational Capabilities. *Proceedings of the 51st Hawaii International Conference on System Sciences.* Big Island, Hawaii, USA 10.24251/HICSS.2018.615

Mikalef, P., Pappas, I. O., Krogstie, J., & Giannakos, M. (2018). Big data analytics capabilities: A systematic literature review and research agenda. *Information Systems and e-Business Management, 16*(3), 547–578. doi:10.1007/s10257-017-0362-y

Miller, B., Malloy, M. A., Masek, E., & Wild, C. (2001). Towards a framework for managing theinformation environment. *Information, Knowledge, Systems Management, 2*(4), 359–384.

Miller, T. I. (1989). Gut-Level Decisionmaking: Implications for Public Policy Analysis. *Journal of Policy Analysis and Management, 8*(1), 119–125. doi:10.2307/3324431

Mills, J. L., & Harclerode, Kelsey. (2017). Privacy, mass intrusion, and the modern data breach. *Florida Law Review, 69*(3), 771–830.

Milne, R., & Brayne, C. (2020). We need to think about data governance for dementia research in a digital era. *Alzheimer's Research & Therapy, 12*(1), 1–3. https://doi-org.libproxy.library.unt.edu/10.1186/s13195-020-0584-y. doi:10.1186/s13195-020-0584-y PMID:32005135

Milton, N., & Lambe, P. (2019). *The Knowledge Manager's Handbook: a Step-by-Step Guide to Embedding Effective Knowledge Management in Your Organization*. Kogan Page Publishers.

Milton, N., & Lambe, P. (2020). *The knowledge manager's handbook: A step by step guide to embedding effective knowledge management in your organization* (2nd ed.). Kogan Page Limited.

Mirchandani, A. (2019). The GDPR-Blockchain Paradox: Exempting Permissioned Blockchains from the GDPR. *Fordham Intellectual Property, Media and Entertainment Law Journal, 29*(4), 1201. https://ir.lawnet.fordham.edu/iplj/vol29/iss4/5

Mishkin, S., & Kuchler, H. (2014, 21 Mayıs). *Ebay reveals cyber attack on database.* Financial Times. https://www.ft.com/content/41a20592-e0f5-11e3-a934-00144feabdc0

Mishra, N. C. (2023, September 27). *Sequestering Digital Autonomy: How New Data Protection Act Affects Digital Accessibility*. LiveLaw. https://www.livelaw.in/articles/data-protection-digital-accessibility-digital-personal-data-protection-act-238792

Mishra, A., Alzoubi, Y. I., Anwar, M. J., & Gill, A. Q. (2022). Attributes impacting cybersecurity policy development: An evidence from seven nations. *Computers & Security, 120*, 1–23. doi:10.1016/j.cose.2022.102820

Moazzami, M., Sheini-Shahvand, N., Kabalci, E., Shahinzadeh, H., Kabalci, Y., & Gharehpetian, G. B. (2021, October). Internet of things architecture for intelligent transportation systems in a smart city. In *2021 3rd Global Power, Energy and Communication Conference (GPECOM)* (pp. 285-290). IEEE. 10.1109/GPECOM52585.2021.9587692

Mohammadi, H. (2008). *The Integration of multi-source spatial datasets in the context of SDI initiatives.* [PhD thesis. Department of Geomatics. The University of Melbourne].

MoL&J. (2023, August 11). Digital Data Protection Act. *Statute*. New Delhi, Delhi, India: Government of India.

Morabito, V., & Morabito, V. (2015). Big data governance. *Big Data and Analytics: Strategic and Organizational Impacts*, 83-104. Akoka, J., & Comyn-Wattiau, I. (2019, July). Evaluation of Big Data Governance-Combining a Multi-Criteria Approach and Systems Theory. In *2019 IEEE World Congress on Services (SERVICES)* (Vol. 2642, pp. 398-399). IEEE.

Mühlhoff, R. (2023). Predictive privacy: Collective data protection in the context of artificial intelligence and big data. *Big Data & Society, 10*(1), 1–14. doi:10.1177/20539517231166886

Murphey, D. (2019). *A history of information security. IFSEC Insider, Security and Fire News and Resources.* IFSEC Global. https://www.ifsecglobal.com/cyber-security/a-history-of-information-security/

Musgrave, R., & Musgrave, P. (1989). *Public Finance in Theory and Practice*. McGraw- Hill, Inc.

Nagori, V. (2021). "Aarogya Setu": The mobile application that monitors and mitigates the risks of COVID-19 pandemic spread in India. *Journal of Information Technology Teaching Cases, 11*(2), 66–80. doi:10.1177/2043886920985863

Narain, M. (2024). Practices on Aarogya Setu: Mapping Citizen Interaction with the Contact-Tracing App in the Time of COVID-19. *East Asian Science, Technology and Society*, 1–21. doi:10.1080/18752160.2024.2312342

Natarajan, H., Krause, S., & Gradstein, H. L. (2017). *Distributed Ledger Technology (DLT) and blockchain: Fintech note no. 1*. https://www.semanticscholar.org/paper/Distributed-Ledger-Technology-(DLT)-and-blockchain-Natarajan-Krause/0188b89179645d52e4a96f8d1054124672e2d59e

Nayak, U., & Rao, U. H. (2014). *The InfoSec handbook: An introduction to information security*. Apress.

NCES. (n.d.). *Chapter 6 - Protecting Your System: Information Security. Information security, from safeguarding your technology, NCES publication 98-297 (National center for education statistics).* National Center for Education Statistics (NCES). https://nces.ed.gov/pubs98/safetech/chapter6.asp

Nedović-Budić, Z., Crompvoets, J., & Georgiadou, Y. (2011). Spatial data infrastructures in context: North and South. In *Spatial Data Infrastructures in Context*. North and South. doi:10.1201/b10857

Nelson, R., & Staggers, N. (2014). Theoretical Foundations of Health Informatics. In R. Nelson & N. Staggers (Eds.), *Health Informatics: An Interprofessional Approach* (pp. 18–39). Elsevier/Mosby.

Neprash, H. T., McGlave, C. C., Cross, D. A., Virnig, B. A., Puskarich, M. A., Huling, J. D., Rozenshtein, A. Z., & Nikpay, S. S. (2022, December). Trends in ransomware attacks on US hospitals, clinics, and other health care delivery organizations, 2016-2021. In *JAMA Health Forum* (Vol. 3, No. 12, pp. e224873-e224873). American Medical Association. 10.1001/jamahealthforum.2022.4873

New York Times Co. V. Sullivan, 376 U.S. 254 (Supreme (court of final appeal) March 9, 1964). https://globalfreedomofexpression.columbia.edu/cases/new-york-times-co-v-sullivan/

Newman, A. L. (2015). What the "right to be forgotten" means for privacy in a digital age. *Science*, *347*(6221), 507–508. https://www.jstor.org/stable/24745781. doi:10.1126/science.aaa4603 PMID:25635090

Ng, T. S. (2017). Blockchain and Beyond: Smart Contracts. *Business Law Today*, 1–2. https://www.jstor.org/stable/27031184

Niñerola, A., Sánchez-Rebull, M.-V., & Hernández-Lara, A.-B. (2021). Mapping the field: Relational study on Six Sigma. *Total Quality Management & Business Excellence*, *32*(11/12), 1182–1200. doi:10.1080/14783363.2019.1685864

Nisar, Q. A., Nasir, N., Jamshed, S., Naz, S., Ali, M., & Ali, S. (2021). Big data management and environmental performance: Role of big data decision-making capabilities and decision-making quality. *Journal of Enterprise Information Management*, *34*(4), 1061–1096. doi:10.1108/JEIM-04-2020-0137

NIST. (2022). *NIST Publications*. National Institute of Standards and Technogy. https://www.nist.gov/standardsgov/resources/publications

Noonan, D. (2014) *Digital Preservation Policy Framework: A Case Study*. EDUCAUSE. https://er.educause.edu/articles/2014/7/digital-preservation-policy-framework-a-case-study

OECD, & EUJR. (2017). Conference Summary. *Governing Better Through Evidence-Informed Policy Making* (pp. 1-19). Paris: OECD, EUJRC, INGSA, Campbell. Retrieved from https://www.oecd.org/gov/governing-better-through-evidence-informed-policy-making-proceedings.pdf

OECD. (2021). *Digital Transformation Maturity Model*. OECD.

Olaniran, B. A., Potter, A., Ross, K. A., & Johnson, B. (2014). A gamer's nightmare: An analysis of the Sony PlayStation hacking crisis. *Journal of Risk Analysis and Crisis Response*, *4*(3), 151–159. https://jracr.com/index.php/jracr/article/view/107. doi:10.2991/jrarc.2014.4.3.4

Olszak, C. M. (2016). Toward Better Understanding and Use of Business Intelligence in Organizations. *Information Systems Management*, *33*(2), 105–123. https://doi-org.libproxy.library.unt.edu/10.1080/10580530.2016.1155946Serum aga-. doi:10.1080/10580530.2016.1155946

OpenDOAR. (n.d.). *OpenDOAR Statistics*. OpenDOAR. https://v2.sherpa.ac.uk/view/repository_visualisations/1.html

Ording, L. G., Gao, S., & Chen, W. (2022). The influence of inputs in the information security policy development: an institutional perspective. *Transforming Government: People. Transforming Government*, *16*(4), 418–435. doi:10.1108/TG-03-2022-0030

Örselli, E., & Akbay, C. (2019). Technology and the transformation of urban life: Smart cities. *International Academy of Management Journal*, *2*(1), 228–241. doi:10.33712/mana.544549

Ortiz-Ospina, E. (2019). *The rise of social media.* Our World in Data. https://ourworldindata.org/rise-of-social-media

Pamment, J. (2020). *Current EU Policy on Disinformation* (The EU's Role in Fighting Disinformation: pp. 5–10). Carnegie Endowment for International Peace. https://www.jstor.org/stable/resrep25788.7

Pandey, A. B., Tripathi, A., & Vashist, P. C. (2022). A survey of cyber security trends, emerging technologies and threats. *Cyber Security in Intelligent Computing and Communications*, 19-33. https://link.springer.com/chapter/10.1007/978-981-16-8012-0_2

Pandith, M. Y. (2015). Data security and privacy concerns in cloud computing. *Internet of Things and Cloud Computing, 2*(2), 6–11. doi:10.11648/j.iotcc.20140202.11

Panian, Z. (2010). Some practical experiences in data governance. *World Academy of Science, Engineering and Technology, 62*(1), 939–946.

Pansara, R. (2023). Unraveling the Complexities of Data Governance with Strategies, Challenges, and Future Directions. *Transactions on Latest Trends in IoT, 6*(6), 46–56.

Parasuraman, A., Zeithaml, V. A., & Berry, L. L. (1988). SERVQUAL: A Multiple-Item Scale for Measuring Consumer Perceptions of Service Quality. *Journal of Retailing, 64*(1), 5–6.

Patel, N. V. (2002). Emergent forms of IT governance to support global e-business models. *Journal of Information Technology Theory and Application, 4*(2), 33–48. https://www.proquest.com/scholarly-journals/emergent-forms-governance-support-global-e/docview/200053438/se-2

Pelteret, M., & Ophoff, J. (2016). A Review of Information Privacy and Its Importance to Consumers and Organizations. *Informing Sci. Int. J. an Emerg. Informing Science, 19*, 277–301. doi:10.28945/3573

Peltier, T. R. (2016). *Information Security Policies, Procedures, and Standards: guidelines for effective information security management.* CRC press. https://books.google.com.tr/

Pendit, P. L. (2017). *Pustaka dan Kebangsaan.* Jakarta: Ikatan Sarjana Ilmu Perpustakaan dan Informasi Indonesia Press

Pendit, P. L. (2018). *Pustaka dan Kebangsaan.* Jakarta: Ikatan Sarjana Ilmu Perpustakaan dan Informasi Indonesia Press.

Pendit, P. L. (2019). *Pustaka: Tradisi dan Kesinambungan.* Jakarta: Ikatan Sarjana Ilmu Perpustakaan dan Informasi Indonesia Press.

Pendit, P. L. (2003). *Penggunaan Teori dalam Penelitian Ilmu Perpustakaan & Informasi.* Jurusan Ilmu Perpustakaan Universitas Indonesia.

Peterson, R. (2004, Fall). Crafting information technology governance. *Information Systems Management, 21*(4), 7–22. doi:10.1201/1078/44705.21.4.20040901/84183.2

Pettersen Gould, K. (2021). Organizational risk: "Muddling through" 40 years of research. *Risk Analysis, 41*(3), 456–465. doi:10.1111/risa.13460 PMID:32088928

Pfenninger, R. (2021). The Right to be Forgotten has Not Found its Home in United States Law: A Comparison of Law between the European Union and the United States. *Willamette Journal of International Law and Dispute Resolution, 28*(2), 291–314. https://www.jstor.org/stable/27137185

Phillips, B. (2021). UK further education sector journey to compliance with the general data protection regulation and the data protection act 2018. *Computer Law & Security Report, 42*, 105586. doi:10.1016/j.clsr.2021.105586

Phillips, M. (2018). International data-sharing norms: From the OECD to the General Data Protection Regulation (GDPR). *Human Genetics*, *137*(8), 575–582. https://link.springer.com/article/10.1007/s00439-018-1919-7. doi:10.1007/s00439-018-1919-7 PMID:30069638

Politou, E., Michota, A., Alepis, E., Pocs, M., & Patsakis, C. (2018). Backups and the right to be forgotten in the GDPR: An uneasy relationship. *Computer Law & Security Report*, *34*(6), 1247–1257. doi:10.1016/j.clsr.2018.08.006

Praveena, A., & Smys, S. (2017, April). Ensuring data security in cloud based social networks. In 2017 international conference of electronics, communication and aerospace technology (ICECA) (Vol. 2, pp. 289-295). IEEE. doi:10.1109/ICECA.2017.8212819

Privacy in India in the Age of Big Data.pdf. (n.d.). Defindia. https://www.defindia.org/wp-content/uploads/2017/09/Privacy%20in%20India%20in%20the%20Age%20of%20Big%20Data.pdf

Radsch, C. (2023). *Weaponizing Privacy and Copyright Law for Censorship* (SSRN Scholarly Paper 4464300). doi:10.2139/ssrn.4464300

Radsch, C. C. (2023). *The Right to Be Forgotten and the GDPR* (Weaponizing Privacy and Copyright Law for Censorship, pp. 6–7). Centre for International Governance Innovation. https://www.jstor.org/stable/resrep49654.9

Radsch, C. C. (2023a). *How the Right to Be Forgotten and the GDPR Automate Abuse of Privacy Protections* (Weaponizing Privacy and Copyright Law for Censorship, pp. 14–15). Centre for International Governance Innovation. https://www.jstor.org/stable/resrep49654.13

Radsch, C. C. (2023b). *The Right to Be Forgotten and the GDPR* (Weaponizing Privacy and Copyright Law for Censorship, pp. 6–7). Centre for International Governance Innovation. https://www.jstor.org/stable/resrep49654.9

Rai, N. (2020). *Right to Privacy and Data Protection in the Digital Age – Preservation, Control and Implementation of Laws in India*. NBU. https://ir.nbu.ac.in/handle/123456789/4009

Rajabifard, A., Binns, A., Masser, I., & Williamson, I. (2006). The role of sub-national government and the private sector in future spatial data infrastructures. *International Journal of Geographical Information Science*, *20*(7), 727–741. doi:10.1080/13658810500432224

Rajabifard, A., Feeney, M. E. F., & Williamson, I. P. (2002). Future directions for SDI development. *International Journal of Applied Earth Observation and Geoinformation*, *4*(1), 11–22. doi:10.1016/S0303-2434(02)00002-8

Rajagopalan, R., Francis, M., & Suárez, W. (2004). Developing Novel Catalysts with Six Sigma. Research Technology Management, 47(1), 13–16. https://doi.org/, R., Francis, M., & Suárez, W. (2004). Developing Novel Catalysts with Six Sigma. Research Technology Management, 47(1), 13–16. https://doi.org/ doi:10.1080/08956308.2004.11671602Raja gopalan

Ramakrishnan, R. (2023). The future of cybersecurity and its potential threats. *International Journal for Research in Applied Science and Engineering Technology, 11*(7), 269-274. (https://doi.org/ doi:10.22214/ijraset.2023.54603

Raposo, V. L. (2022). 'I'm right behind you': Digital contact tracing under European law. *Maastricht Journal of European and Comparative Law*, *29*(4), 434–450. doi:10.1177/1023263X221116227

Rath, M., Satpathy, J., & Oreku, G. S. (2021). Artificial intelligence and machine learning applications in cloud computing and Internet of Things. In *Artificial intelligence to solve pervasive internet of things issues* (pp. 103–123). Academic Press. doi:10.1016/B978-0-12-818576-6.00006-X

Rawski, C. H. (Ed.). (1973). *Toward a Theory of Librarianship: Papers in Honor of Jesse Hauk Shera*. Scarecrow Press.

Rees, N., Holding, K., & Sujan, M. (2023). Information governance as a socio-technical process in the development of trustworthy healthcare AI. *Frontiers of Computer Science*, *5*, 1134818. doi:10.3389/fcomp.2023.1134818

Reim, W., Åström, J., & Eriksson, O. (2020). Implementation of Artificial Intelligence (AI): A Roadmap for Business Model Innovation. *AI, 1*(2), 180–191. MDPI AG. doi:10.3390/ai1020011

Renda, A. (2022). COVID-19 and privacy: A European dilemma. *Digital Policy. Regulation & Governance*, *24*(2), 109–117. doi:10.1108/DPRG-04-2020-0043

ReVelle, J. B. (2004). Six Sigma. *Professional Safety*, *49*(10), 38–46.

Reventlow, N. J. (2020). Can the GDPR and Freedom of Expression Coexist? *Can the GDPR and Freedom of Expression Coexist*, *114*, 31–34. doi:10.1017/aju.2019.77

Rienzo, T. F. (1993). Planning Deming management for service organizations. *Business Horizons*, *36*(3), 19–29. doi:10.1016/S0007-6813(05)80145-4

Robert, J., & Reinitz, B. (2023). *2023 Horizon action plan: Data governance.* EDUCAUSE. https://library.educause.edu/-/media/files/library/2023/3/2023horizonapdatagovernance.pdf?la=en&hash=FA306932947338DB9353D05A48369FFBB6A9C653

Robinson, M., Jones, K., Janicke, H., & Maglaras, L. (2019). Developing cyber peacekeeping: Observation, monitoring and reporting. *Government Information Quarterly, 36*(2), 276-293. https://doi.org/ rights and content doi:10.1016/j.giq.2018.12.001Get

Rothkegel, T., & Strassemeyer, L. (2019). Joint Control in European Data Protection Law – How to make Sense of the CJEU's Holy Trinity—A case study on the recent CJEU rulings (Facebook Fanpages; Jehovah's Witnesses; Fashion ID). *Computer Law Review International*, *20*(6), 161–171. doi:10.9785/cri-2019-200602

Rubenstein, L., Khodyakov, D., Hempel, S., Danz, M., Salem-Schatz, S., Foy, R., O'Neill, S., Dalal, S., & Shekelle, P. (2013). How can we recognize continuous quality improvement? *International Journal for Quality in Health Care : Journal of the International Society for Quality in Health Care*, *26*(1), 6–15. doi:10.1093/intqhc/mzt085 PMID:24311732

Rubin, R. E., & Rubin, R. G. (2020). *Foundations of Library and Information Science.* American Library Association.

Ruby, D. (2023, June 7). *Social Media Users In The World — (2023 Demographics).* Demands Age. https://www.demandsage.com/social-media-users/

Rushe, D. (2017). Yahoo says all of its 3bn accounts were affected by 2013 hacking. *Guardian.* https://www.theguardian.com/technology/2017/oct/03/yahoo-says-all-of-its-3bn-accounts-were-affected-by-2013-hacking

Russell, R.S. and Taylor, B.W. (2011). Operations Management. Creating Value Along the Supply Chain. *John Wiley and Sons. ISBN-13 9780470525906*

Sadam, R. (2023, February 6). Efficiency vs privacy threat — Andhra govt, employees spar over facial recognition attendance app. *The Print.* https://theprint.in/india/governance/efficiency-vs-privacy-threat-andhra-govt-employees-spar-over-facial-recognition-attendance-app/1352076/

Saffady, W. (2015). Records management or information governance? *Information & Management*, *49*(4), 38–41, 47. https://magazine.arma.org/wp-content/uploads/simple-file-list/2015_04_records_management_or_IG-Saffady.pdf

Salahdine, F., & Kaabouch, N. (2019). Social engineering attacks: A survey. *Future Internet*, *11*(4), 1–17. doi:10.3390/fi11040089

Saldanha, T. (2019). *Why digital transformations fail: The surprising disciplines of how to take off and stay ahead.* Barrett-Koehler Publishers, Inc.

Sambamurthy, V., & Zmud, R. W. (1999). Arrangements for Information Technology Governance: A Theory of Multiple Contingencies. *Management Information Systems Quarterly, 23*(2), 261–290. doi:10.2307/249754

Samonasa, S., Dhillon, G., & Almusharraf, A. (2020). Stakeholder perceptions of information security policy: Analyzing personal constructs. *International Journal of Information Management, 50,* 144–154. https://www.sciencedirect.com/science/article/abs/pii/S0268401218303451?via%3Dihub. doi:10.1016/j.ijinfomgt.2019.04.011

SamonteM. (2020). Google v. CNIL: The Territorial Scope of the Right to Be Forgotten Under EU Law. *European Papers - A Journal on Law and Integration, 2019 4*(3), 839–851. doi:10.15166/2499-8249/332

Savin, A. (2017). *EU Internet Law.* Edward Elgar Publishing. doi:10.4337/9781784717971

Schlienger, T., & Teufel, S. (2003). Information security culture: From analysis to change. *South African Computer Journal = Suid-Afrikaanse Rekenaartydskrif, 31,* 46–52. https://hdl.handle.net/10520/EJC27949

Schneier, B. (2019, November 12). *We must bridge the gap between technology and policymaking. Our future depends on it.* W. E. Forum, Producer. https://www.weforum.org/agenda/2019/11/we-must-bridge-the-gap-between-technology-and-policy-our-future-depends-on-it/

Scholl, M. C. (2019). Raising Information Security Awareness in the Field of Urban and Regional Planning. Int. [IJEPR]. *International Journal of E-Planning Research, 8*(3), 62–86. doi:10.4018/IJEPR.2019070104

Seiner, R. S. (2016, April 1). *What is noninvasive data governance?* The Data Administrator Newsletter. https://tdan.com/what-is-non-invasive-data-governance/7354

Seiner, R. (2014). *Non-invasive data governance: The path of least resistance and greatest success.* Technics Publications.

Service Now. (2023). *IT Service Management.* Service Now. https://www.servicenow.com/products/itsm.html on November 1, 2023.

Shafiq, M., Gu, Z., Cheikhrouhou, O., Alhakami, W., & Hamam, H. (2022). The rise of "Internet of Things": Review and open research issues related to detection and prevention of IoT-based security attacks. *Wireless Communications and Mobile Computing, 2022,* 1–12. doi:10.1155/2022/8669348

Shahriari, M., & Allameh, S. M. (2020). Organizational culture and organizational learning: Does high performance work systems mediate? *Journal of Workplace Learning, 32*(8), 583–597. doi:10.1108/JWL-03-2020-0047

Shamim, S., Zeng, J., Khan, Z., & Zia, N. U. (2020). Big data analytics capability and decision making performance in emerging market firms: The role of contractual and relational governance mechanisms. *Technological Forecasting and Social Change, 161,* 120315. doi:10.1016/j.techfore.2020.120315

Shera, J. H. (1961). What is librarianship? Louisiana Library Association Bulletin, 24.

Shera, J. H. (1965). *Libraries and the Organization of Knowledge* (D. J. Foskett, Ed.). Archon Books.

Shera, J. H. (1970). *Sociological Foundations of Librarianship.* Asia Publishing House.

Shera, J. H. (1973). *Knowing Books and Men: Knowing Computers Too.* Libraries Unlimited.

Shouran, Z., Priyambodo, T. K., & Ashari, A. (2019). *Information System Security: Human Aspects.* Research Gate. https://www.researchgate.net/publication/331859493_Information_System_Security_Human_Aspects

Shroff, J. (2005). California: Privacy Statute Meets the GLBA & (and) FCRA. North Carolina Banking Institute, 9, 223-242.

Singh, H. P., & Alhulail, H. N. (2023). Information technology governance and corporate boards' relationship with companies' performance and earnings management: A longitudinal approach. *Sustainability (Basel), 15*(8), 6492. doi:10.3390/su15086492

Singla, A., & Bertino, E. (2019). How Deep Learning Is Making Information Security More Intelligent. *IEEE Security and Privacy, 17*(3), 56–65. doi:10.1109/MSEC.2019.2902347

Slack, N., Chambers, S., & Johnston, R. (2010). *Operations management* (6th ed.). Prentice Hall.

Slade, R. (2006). *Dictionary of information security*. Syngress Publishing.

Sloan, P. (2014). The Compliance Case for Information Governance. *Richmond Journal of Law and Technology, 20*(2).

Smallwood, R. (2019). *Information governance: Concepts, strategies, and best practices*. John Wiley & Sions, Inc. doi:10.1002/9781119491422.ch9

Smallwood, R. F. (2014). *Information governance: Concepts, strategies, and best practices*. Wiley.

Smallwood, R. F. (2019). *Information Governance: Concepts, Strategies, and Best Practices* (2nd ed.). Wiley. doi:10.1002/9781119491422

Smits, J. M. (2015). *What is Legal Doctrine? On the Aims and Methods of Legal-Dogmatic Research* (SSRN Scholarly Paper 2644088). doi:10.2139/ssrn.2644088

Smouter-Umans, K. L. (2017). Research, GDPR, and the DPO how GDPR changes the game for those conducting research and the data supervisors. International Journal for the Data Protection Officer [iv]. *Privacy Officer and Privacy Counsel, 1*(1), 26.

Snow, C. P. (1961). *The Two Cultures and The Scientific Revolution* (7th ed.). Cambridge University Press. doi:10.1063/1.3057748

Social Media Fact Sheet. (2021). *Pew Research Center: Internet, Science & Tech*. Pew Research. https://www.pewresearch.org/internet/fact-sheet/social-media/

Solms, S. V., & Solms, R. (2008). *Information security governance*. Springer Science & Business Media.

Solomon, M. G., & Chapple, M. (2004). *Information Security Illuminated*. Jones & Bartlett Publishers.

Solove, D. J. (2010). *Understanding privacy*. Harvard university press. https://books.google.com.tr/

Soltani, R., Zaman, M., Joshi, R., & Sampalli, S. (2022). Distributed Ledger Technologies and Their Applications: A Review. *Applied Sciences (Basel, Switzerland), 12*(15), 15. Advance online publication. doi:10.3390/app12157898

Spencer, A., & Patel, S. (2019). Applying the data protection act 2018 and general data protection regulation principles in healthcare settings. *Nursing Management, 26*(1), 34–40. Advance online publication. doi:10.7748/nm.2019.e1806 PMID:31468753

Srinivas, J., Das, A. K., & Kumar, N. (2019). Government regulations in cyber security: Framework, standards and recommendations. *Future Generation Computer Systems, 92*, 178–188. doi:10.1016/j.future.2018.09.063

Stankalla, R., Koval, O., & Chromjakova, F. (2018). A review of critical success factors for the successful implementation of Lean Six Sigma and Six Sigma in manufacturing small and medium sized enterprises. *Quality Engineering, 30*(3), 453–468. doi:10.1080/08982112.2018.1448933

Steelman, Z. R., Hammer, B. I., & Limayem, M. (2014). Data Collection in the Digital Age: Innovative Alternatives to Student Samples. *Management Information Systems Quarterly, 38*(2), 355–378. https://www.jstor.org/stable/26634930. doi:10.25300/MISQ/2014/38.2.02

Sullivan, K. M. (2010). Two Concepts of Freedom of Speech. *Harvard Law Review, 124*(1), 143–177. https://www.jstor.org/stable/20788316

Sun, Y., Zhang, J., Xiong, Y., & Zhu, G. (2014). Data security and privacy in Cloud computing. *International Journal of Distributed Sensor Networks, 10*(7), 190903. doi:10.1155/2014/190903

Suraksha, P., & Thacker, T. (2022, August 1). Aarogya Setu's Data Sharing Protocol Discontinued, But Privacy Activists Still Raise Concerns Over Security. *Economic Times.* telecom.economictimes.indiatimes.com/: https://telecom.economictimes.indiatimes.com/news/aarogya-setus-data-sharing-protocol-discontinued-but-privacy-activists-still-raise-concerns-over-security/93261919

SwachhBharat- Swachh Bharat Abhiyan a nation-wide campaign in India. (n.d.). SwachhBharat. https://swachhbharat.mygov.in/

Swamy, C. J., Kethana, A., & Pradeep, M. P. (2023). A study on recruitment and selection process in the manufacturing industry. *Advances in Management, 16*(2), 1–9. doi:10.25303/1602aim0109

Szczepaniuk, E. K., Szczepaniuk, H., Rokicki, T., & Klepacki, B. (2020). Information security assessment in public administration. *Computers & Security, 90*, 101709. doi:10.1016/j.cose.2019.101709

Tabeck, P. S., & Jain, V. (2022). Fighting Pandemic: The Mobile Application Way (a Case of the Aarogya Setu App). *Emerging Economies Cases Journal, 4*(2), 95–102. doi:10.1177/25166042221147097

Tallon, P. P. (2010). Understanding the dynamics of information management costs. *Communications of the ACM, 53*(5), 121–125. doi:10.1145/1735223.1735253

Tallon, P. P., Ramirez, R. V., & Short, J. E. (2013). The information artifact in IT governance: Toward a theory of information governance. *Journal of Management Information Systems, 30*(3), 141–178. Advance online publication. doi:10.2753/MIS0742-1222300306

Tanaka, H. (2019). Impact of the GDPR on Japanese companies. *Business Law International, 20*(2), 137–146.

Tan, E., & Lambe, P. (2019). *KM Approaches Methods and Tools: A Guidebook.* Straits Knowledge.

Tankard, C. (2016). What the GDPR means for businesses. *Network Security, 2016*(6), 5–8. doi:10.1016/S1353-4858(16)30056-3

Tasci, A. D. A., Wei, W., & Milman, A. (2020). Uses and misuses of the case study method. *Annals of Tourism Research, 82*, 102815. Advance online publication. doi:10.1016/j.annals.2019.102815

Tatar, U., Gokce, Y., & Nussbaum, B. (2020). Law versus technology: Blockchain, GDPR, and tough tradeoffs. *Computer Law & Security Report, 38*, 105454. doi:10.1016/j.clsr.2020.105454

Tetri, P., & Vuorinen, J. (2013). Dissecting social engineering. *Behaviour & Information Technology, 32*(10), 1014–1023. doi:10.1080/0144929X.2013.763860

Texas Department of Information Resources. (n.d.). *Governing data, records, and information together.* DIR. https://dir.texas.gov/sites/default/files/2023-10/DMO%20RMO%20Guidance.pdf

The Digital Personal Data Protection Bill, 2023. (n.d.). PRS Legislative Research. https://prsindia.org/billtrack/digital-personal-data-protection-bill-2023

The International Federation of Library Associations and Institutions (IFLA). (2023). *The IFLA Knowledge Management Unit.* IFLA.

Thor, J., Herrlin, B., Wittlöv, K., Øvretveit, J., & Brommels, M. (2010). Evolution and outcomes of a quality improvement program. *International Journal of Health Care Quality Assurance, 23*(3), 312–327. doi:10.1108/09526861011029370 PMID:20535903

Thushari, P. D. (2022, November). Current security and privacy issues, and concerns of Internet of Things (IoT) and Cloud Computing: A review. In *2022 International Conference on Computing, Communication, and Intelligent Systems (ICCCIS)* (pp. 13-17). IEEE. 10.1109/ICCCIS56430.2022.10037730

Todt, K. E. (2019). Data Privacy and Protection: What Businesses Should Do. *The Cyber Defense Review, 4*(2), 39–46. https://www.jstor.org/stable/26843891

Torten, R., Reaiche, C., & Boyle, S. (2018). (2018). The impact of security awareness on information technology professional's behavior. *Computers & Security, 79*, 68–79. doi:10.1016/j.cose.2018.08.007

Townend, J. (2017). Data Protection and the 'Right to be Forgotten' in Practice: A UK Perspective. *International Journal of Legal Information, 45*(1), 28–33. doi:10.1017/jli.2017.2

Tracking healthcare data breaches. (n.d.). Healthcare Dive. https://www.healthcaredive.com/news/tracking-healthcare-data-breaches-cybersecurity-hacking-hospitals/696184/

Trautman, L. J. (2021). Rapid Technological Change and US Entrepreneurial Risk in International Markets: Focus on Data Security, Information Privacy, Bribery and Corruption. *Cap. UL Rev., 49*, 69-121. https://heinonline.org/

Tripathi, M., Shukla, A., & Sonkar, S. K. (2017). Research data management practices in university libraries: A study. *DESIDOC Journal of Library and Information Technology, 37*(6), 417. doi:10.14429/djlit.37.11336

Trybus, M., & Rubini, L. (2012). *The Treaty of Lisbon and the Future of European Law and Policy.* Edward Elgar Publishing. doi:10.4337/9780857932563

Tu, Y., Li, Q., & Mao, X. (2009). Research on the conceptual model of spatial data infrastructure for natural disaster management. *Sixth International Symposium on Digital Earth: Models, Algorithms, and Virtual Reality, 7840.* SPIE. 10.1117/12.871969

Twentyman, J. (2015). Fear of reputational damage after security leaks may be overhyped. *Financial Times.* https://www.ft.com/content/b6395d84-cc8f-11e4-b5a5-00144feab7de

TyagiA. (2021). Information Governance Program Implementation and Strategies in Banking Sector. http://dx.doi.org/doi:10.2139/ssrn.3804620

Unwin, P. T. H., & Unwin, T. (2017). *Reclaiming information and communication technologies for development.* Oxford University Press., https://books.google.com.tr/ doi:10.1093/oso/9780198795292.001.0001

US-CERT. (2018). *Vulnerability Note VU#631579: Hardware debug exception documentation may result in unexpected behavior.* Vulnerability Notes Database. https://www.kb.cert.org/vuls/id/631579

UU No. 7 Tahun 2021 about Harmonization of Tax Law. (2021). *UU No. 7 Tahun 2021 about Harmonization of Tax Law.* 1–224.

Vacca, J. R. (Ed.). (2013). *Network and system security.* Elsevier., https://books.google.com.tr/

Vanteddu, G., & McAllister, C. D. (2014). An integrated approach for prioritized process improvement. *International Journal of Health Care Quality Assurance, 27*(6), 493–495. doi:10.1108/IJHCQA-05-2013-0051 PMID:25115052

Vavra, A. N. (2018). The Right to Be Forgotten: An Archival Perspective. *The American Archivist, 81*(1), 100–111. https://www.jstor.org/stable/48618003. doi:10.17723/0360-9081-81.1.100

Veale, M., & Edwards, L. (2018). Clarity, surprises, and further questions in the Article 29 Working Party draft guidance on automated decision-making and profiling. *Computer Law & Security Report, 34*(2), 398–404. doi:10.1016/j.clsr.2017.12.002

Verizon. (2023, January 1). *Analyzing the COVID 19 Data Breach Landscape.* https://www.verizon.com/business/resources/articles/analyzing-covid-19-data-breach-landscape/

Verma, B., Snodgrass, R., Henry, B., Smith, B., & Daim, T. (2020). Smart cities-an analysis of smart transportation management. In *Managing Innovation in a Global and Digital World: Meeting Societal Challenges and Enhancing Competitiveness* (pp. 367-388). Springer Fachmedien Wiesbaden. https://link.springer.com/chapter/10.1007/978-3-658-27241-8_23

Victor, J. M. (2013). The EU General Data Protection Regulation: Toward a Property Regime for Protecting Data Privacy. *The Yale Law Journal, 123*(2), 513–528. https://www.jstor.org/stable/23744289

Viljoen, S. (2021). A relational theory of data governance. *The Yale Law Journal, 131*, 573.

Virmani, C., Choudhary, T., Pillai, A., & Rani, M. (2020). Applications of Machine Learning in Cyber Security. In *Handbook of Research on Machine and Deep Learning Applications for Cyber Security.* IGI Global. https://www.igi-global.com/gateway/chapter/235038

Vojvodic, M., & Hitz, C. (2022). Relation of data governance, customer-centricity and data processing compliance. *Central European Business Review, 11*(5), 109–148. doi:10.18267/j.cebr.310

Volini, A. (2023). *The Right to Data Privacy: Revisiting Warren & Brandeis* (SSRN Scholarly Paper 4421290). doi:10.2139/ssrn.4421290

von Grafenstein, M. (2018). The function of the principle of purpose limitation in light of Article 8 ECFR and further fundamental rights. In *The Principle of Purpose Limitation in Data Protection Laws* (1st ed., pp. 109–596). Nomos Verlagsgesellschaft mbH. https://www.jstor.org/stable/j.ctv941v5w.5

Voss, W. G. (2021). The CCPA and the GDPR Are Not the Same: Why You Should Understand Both. *CPI Antitrust Chronicle, 1*(1). https://www.competitionpolicyinternational.com/the-ccpa-and-the-gdpr-are-not-the-same-why-you-should-understand-both/

Voss, W. G. (2014). European Union Data Privacy Law Developments. *Business Lawyer, 70*(1), 253–260. https://www.jstor.org/stable/43665699

Voss, W. G. (2016). European Union Data Privacy Law Reform: General Data Protection Regulation, Privacy Shield, and the Right to Delisting. *Business Lawyer, 72*(1), 221–234. https://www.jstor.org/stable/26419118

Vrontis, D., Makrides, A., Christofi, M., & Thrassou, A. (2021). Social media influencer marketing: A systematic review, integrative framework and future research agenda. *International Journal of Consumer Studies, 45*(4), 617–644. doi:10.1111/ijcs.12647

Vydra, S., & Klievink, B. (2019). Techno-optimism and policy-pessimism in the public sector big data debate. *Government Information Quarterly, 36*(4), 1–10. doi:10.1016/j.giq.2019.05.010

Walker, R. (2021). Communication perspectives on organizational culture and organizational identification. *International Journal of Business Communication, 58*(2), 147–151. doi:10.1177/2329488420957073

Wandaogo, A. (2022). Does digitalization improve government effectiveness? Evidence from developing and developed countries. *Applied Economics*, *54*(33), 3840–3860. doi:10.1080/00036846.2021.2016590

Wang, F. Y. (2020). Cooperative Data Privacy: The Japanese model of data privacy and the EU-Japan GDPR adequacy agreement. *Harvard Journal of Law & Technology*, *33*(2), 661–692.

Wang, H., Meng, H., Zhang, L., Chen, Z., & Wang, S. (2020). Data System Configuration and Organizing and Management Technologies of Information System. *Journal of Physics: Conference Series*, *1575*(1), 012057. doi:10.1088/1742-6596/1575/1/012057

Wang, W., Harrou, F., Bouyeddou, B., Senouci, S. M., & Sun, Y. (2022). A stacked deep learning approach to cyber-attacks detection in industrial systems: Application to power system and gas pipeline systems. *Cluster Computing*, *25*(1), 1–18. https://link.springer.com/article/10.1007/s10586-021-03426-w. doi:10.1007/s10586-021-03426-w PMID:34629940

Warner, J. (2001). W(h)ither information sciences? *The Library Quarterly*, *71*(2), 243–255. doi:10.1086/603263

Warren, S., & Brandeis, L. (1989). The right to privacy. In *Killing the Messenger: 100 Years of Media Criticism* (pp. 1–21). Columbia University Press. doi:10.7312/gold91730-002

Waters, R. D., & Jamal, J. Y. (2011). Tweet, tweet, tweet: A content analysis of nonprofit organizations' twitter updates. *Public Relations Review*, *37*(3), 321–324. doi:10.1016/j.pubrev.2011.03.002

Watson, D. S. (1989). Computers, Confidentiality and Privation. *Computers in Human Services*, *5*(1-2), 153–168. doi:10.1300/J407v05n01_12

Weber, K., Otto, B., & Österle, H. (2009). One Size Does Not Fit All---A Contingency Approach to Data Governance. *ACM Journal of Data and Information Quality*, *1*(1), 1–27. doi:10.1145/1515693.1515696

Wende, K. (2007). A Model for Data Governance – Organising Accountabilities for Data Quality Management. *ACIS 2007 Proceedings*. AISEL. https://aisel.aisnet.org/acis2007/80

Westin, A. F. (1967). Special report: Legal safeguards to insure privacy in a computer society. *Communications of the ACM*, *10*(9), 533–537. https://dl.acm.org/doi/pdf/10.1145/363566.363579. doi:10.1145/363566.363579

Westlaw. (2023). *Legal research tools*. Reuters. https://legal.thomsonreuters.com/en/westlaw.

What are information security standards ? (2023). RiskXchange. https://riskxchange.co/1006780/information-security-standards/

Whitman, M. E. (2003). Enemy at the gate: Threats to information security. *Communications of the ACM*, *46*(8), 91–95. doi:10.1145/859670.859675

Whitman, M. E., & Mattord, H. J. (2018). *Principles of information security* (8th ed.). Cengage Learning.

Whitman, M. E., & Mattord, H. J. (2019). *Management of Information Security*. Cengage.

Whitmer, M. G. (2007). *IT security awareness and training: Changing the culture of state government.* NASCIO. https://www.nascio.org/wp-content/uploads/2019/11/NASCIO-ITSecurityAwarenessAndTraining.pdf

Wilkes, J. J. (2014). The creation of HIPAA culture: Prioritizing privacy paranoia over patient care. *Brigham Young University Law Review*, *2014*(5), 1213–1250.

Winslow, T., & Malone, J. (2011). Don't hold back: When and how corporate counsel should implement litigation hold. *Jurimetrics*, *51*(3), 245–278.

Wohlgemuth, S., Echizen, I., Sonehara, N., & Müller, G. (2011). On Privacy-compliant Disclosure of Personal Data to Third Parties using Digital Watermarking. *J. Inf. Hiding Multim. Signal Process.*, *2*(3), 270–281. https://bit.nkust.edu.tw/2011/vol2/JIH-MSP-2011-04-007.pdf

Wong, R. (2013). *Data security breaches and privacy in Europe*. Springer. doi:10.1007/978-1-4471-5586-7

Yang, Y., & Su, Y. (2020). Public voice via social media: Role in cooperative governance during public health emergency. *International Journal of Environmental Research and Public Health, 17*(18), 6840–6858. doi:10.3390/ijerph17186840 PMID:32962172

Yasin, A., Liu, L., Li, T., Wang, J., & Zowghi, D. (2018). Design and preliminary evaluation of a cyber Security Requirements Education Game (SREG). *Information and Software Technology, 95*, 179–200. doi:10.1016/j.infsof.2017.12.002

Yeboah-Boateng, E. O., & Boaten, F. E. (2016). Bring-Your-Own-Device (BYOD): an evaluation of associated risks to corporate information security. *arXiv preprint arXiv:1609.01821*. https://doi.org//arXiv.1609.01821 doi:10.48550

Yilmaz, Y., Cetin, O., Grigore, C., Arief, B., & Hernandez-Castro, J. (2023). Personality types and ransomware victimization. *Digital Threats : Research and Practice, 4*(4), 1–25. doi:10.1145/3568994

Yücedağ, N. (2019). General principles under the personal data protection law. Journal of Personal *Data Protection,1*(1), 47-63. https://dergipark.org.tr/en/pub/kvkd/issue/45759/566993

Yüksel, G. (2019). Legal protection of personal health data. *Journal of Health Academics, 6*(1), 1–10. https://dergipark.org.tr/en/pub/sagakaderg/issue/43967/542618

Zake, P. A. E. (2017). The role of user satisfaction in implementing a Business Intelligence System. *South African Journal of Information Management, 19*(1), 1–8. https://doi-org.libproxy.library.unt.edu/10.4102/sajim.v19i1.736

Zeggelink, E. (1994). Dynamics of structure: An individual oriented approach. *Social Networks, 16*(4), 295–333. doi:10.1016/0378-8733(94)90014-0

Zelger, B. (2023). Case Note: Strengthening the Role of Google? Recent Developments in the Right to Be Forgotten Case Law of the CJEU (TU and RE v. Google LLC, C-460/20). *Global Privacy Law Review, 4*(2). https://kluwerlawonline.com/api/Product/CitationPDFURL?file=Journals\GPLR\GPLR2023010.pdf

Zhang, Q., Sun, X., & Zhang, M. (2022). Data matters: A strategic action framework for data governance. *Information & Management, 59*(4), 103642. doi:10.1016/j.im.2022.103642

Zheng, Z., Wang, P., Liu, J., & Sun, S. (2015). Real-time big data processing framework: Challenges and solutions. *Applied Mathematics & Information Sciences, 9*(6), 3169.

Zichichi, M., Ferretti, S., D'Angelo, G., & Rodríguez-Doncel, V. (2022). Data governance through a multi-DLT architecture in view of the GDPR. *Cluster Computing, 25*(6), 4515–4542. doi:10.1007/s10586-022-03691-3

Zins, C. (2007). Conceptual approaches for defining data, information, and knowledge. *Journal of the American Society for Information Science and Technology, 58*(4), 479–493. doi:10.1002/asi.20508

Zipursky, B. (2016). The Monsanto Lecture: Online Defamation, Legal Concepts, and The Good Samaritan. *Valparaiso U. L. Rev., 51*, 1. https://ir.lawnet.fordham.edu/faculty_scholarship/851

Zolanvari, M., Teixeira, M. A., Gupta, L., Khan, K. M., & Jain, R. (2019). Machine learning-based network vulnerability analysis of industrial Internet of Things. *IEEE Internet of Things Journal, 6*(4), 6822–6834. doi:10.1109/JIOT.2019.2912022

Zorrilla, M., & Yebenes, J. (2022). A reference framework for the implementation of data governance systems for industry 4.0. *Computer Standards & Interfaces, 81*, 103595. doi:10.1016/j.csi.2021.103595

Zuiderveen Borgesius, F. (2017). *Breyer Case of the Court of Justice of the European Union: IP Addresses and the Personal Data Definition (Case Note)* (SSRN Scholarly Paper 2933781). https://papers.ssrn.com/abstract=2933781 doi:10.21552/edpl/2017/1/21

About the Contributors

Kris Helge currently serves as Adjunct Faculty at Rutgers University and Texas A&M University School of Law. He also serves as Deputy Director of Information Management at Colorado Judicial. He holds a J.D. from South Texas College of Law Houston, a Ph.D. and an M.L.S. from the University of North Texas, and a B.A. from Baylor University. He frequently publishes books, book chapters, and articles regarding Information Governance, IP law, open access, knowledge management, leadership, management, and technology. He also presents topics related to Information Governance at national and international conferences.

***

Kirt Agarwal, working as an Assistant Professor at the School of Law, Governance and Citizenship, Dr. B.R. Ambedkar University, Delhi, obtained his undergraduate degree from Guru Gobind Singh Indraprastha University, New Delhi. He has completed his LL.M. from National Law University, Delhi, specialising in Constitutional and Criminal Law. He has worked as an Assistant Lecturer at Jindal Global Law School. His areas of interest are Constitutional, Criminal, and Environmental Law.

Munir Ahmad, Ph.D. in Computer Science, brings over 24 years of invaluable expertise in the realm of spatial data development, management, processing, visualization, and quality assurance. His unwavering commitment to open data, big data, crowdsourced data, volunteered geographic information, and spatial data infrastructure has solidified him as a seasoned professional and a trusted trainer in cutting-edge spatial technologies. With a profound passion for research, Munir has authored more than 30 publications in his field, culminating in the award of his Ph.D. in Computer Science from Preston University Pakistan in 2022. His dedication to propelling the industry forward and sharing his extensive knowledge defines his mission.

Asmat Ali is PhD in Remote Sensing & GIS. He is Director of Cartography and GIS at Survey of Pakistan. He is also Project Director Feasibility Study for Establishment of National Spatial Data Infrastructure (NSDI) for Pakistan. In, 1998 he earned Professional Master Degree in Geoinformatics from Faculty of Geo-Information Science and Earth Observation (ITC), University of Twente, Enschede The Netherlands. The title of his IFA was, "DIGITAL PRODUCTION LINE IN THE CONTEXT OF SURVEY OF PAKISTAN". Later on, he got MSc Degree in Geo-information Science and Earth Observation, with Specialization in Geo-Information Management from the same university. The title of his MSc thesis was, "POTENTIAL OF PUBIC PRIVATE PARTNERSHIP FOR NSDI IMPLEMEN-

TATION IN PAKISTAN". In 2022, he got PhD degree in Remote Sensing and GIS from PMAS-Arid Agriculture University Rawalpindi, Pakistan. The title of his dissertation was "SPATIAL DATA INFRASTRUCTURE AS THE MEANS TO ASSEMBLE GEOGRAPHIC INFORMATION NECESSARY FOR EFFECTIVE AGRICULTURAL POLICIES IN PAKISTAN". He has 35 years of experience in geospatial information production and management discipline as practitioner, trainer and educator. He has served on several operational, administrative and instructional appointments. He was in-charge of the team which started GIS mapping and digital cartography at Survey of Pakistan in 1999. His more than 30 research papers including four book chapters and articles on Spatial Data Infrastructure (SDI), GIS, Remote Sensing, E-governance, as well as Land Administration have been published in various internationally renowned journals and conferences. In 2008, SDI Asia-Pacific identified him as FOCAL POINT FOR SDI DEVELOPMENT IN PAKISTAN. GSDI in 2016, acknowledged and awarded him as SDI IMPLEMENTER FROM PAKISTAN. He is on the visiting faculty of Bahria University Islamabad and PMAS- Arid Agriculture University Rawalpindi, Pakistan.

Luh Putu Sri Ariyani is an assistant professor in the Undergraduate Program of Library and Information Science under the Department of History, Sociology and Library, Faculty of Law and Social Sciences (FHIS) Universitas Pendidikan Ganesha, Bali. She holds a Master of Library and Information Science (MLIS) from the University of Indonesia in 2013. Her Doctoral education was completed in 2021 in the Cultural Studies Program at Udayana University, Bali. Her academic career began in 2003 as an academic librarian at IKIP Negeri Singaraja, Bali. In 2013, She began as a lecturer. Her research interests include knowledge management, knowledge and media preservation, and cultural heritage management.

Aniesa Samira Bafadhal is an assistant professor in the Tourism Program under the Department of Business Administration, Faculty of Administrative Science, University of Brawijaya, Indonesia. Since 2018, she has served as vice head of the Tourism Research Laboratory in the Faculty of Administrative Science at the University of Brawijaya. She was a certified drone pilot by the Indonesian Drone Pilot Federation, an augmented reality (AR) educator by Assemblr, and a virtual reality (VR) creator by Millealab. She is the author of several books in the tourism field, published in Indonesia and globally, consisting of encyclopedias, book chapters, and monographs. Her multifaceted role reflects his commitment to academic excellence and significant contribution to the scientific field. Her research interests currently focus on some areas, including information system management, virtual tourism, and cultural heritage tourism.

Amjath Fareeth Basha is working as Lecturer, College of computers and information Technology, Taif University, Taif, Saudi Arabia.

Kristin Clark has over a decade of experience working with digital materials in special and academic libraries. She holds a Masters in Library and Information Science from San Jose State University and a Bachelor of Arts in English from Sam Houston State University. Kristin currently serves as the Manager of Digital Collections at Texas Woman's University Libraries.

Balaji Gopalan is Assistant Professor at the CMS Business School in Bangalore, India. He has around 20 years of experience that includes working in academics, research and consulting and has worked at institutes and companies in Finland, USA and India. He holds a Doctor of Science in Industrial Management from the University of Vaasa, Finland. He has completed his M.Sc in Information Studies from Florida State University (USA). He has a M.E. in Manufacturing Systems from BITS-Pilani (Rajasthan, India) and a B.E. in Industrial and Production Engineering from SJCE, University of Mysore (India). His area of specialization includes production and operations management, logistics and supply chain management and value co-creation.

Muhammad Rosyihan Hendrawan is an assistant professor in the Department of Library and Information Science at the Faculty of Administrative Science, University of Brawijaya, Indonesia. In his administrative capacity, previously, he served as the vice head of university archives at the University of Brawijaya in 2016–2020 and memory institutions (library, archives, and museums/LAMs) for the Faculty of Administrative Science at the University of Brawijaya in 2020–2022. His scholarly contributions are also evident in his capacity as a board member of the Indonesian Library and Information Science Scholars Association (ISIPII). His research interests include knowledge management, knowledge organization systems, the organization of information, and cultural heritage information management. He is the author of twelve books in the library and information science (LIS) field, published in Indonesia and globally, consisting of encyclopedias, book chapters, and monographs. His multifaceted role reflects his commitment to academic excellence and significant contribution to the LIS field.

Sneha Hooda is working as a Lecturer and Assistant Dean (Research) at Jindal Global Law School, O. P. Jindal Global University. She is currently a doctoral candidate and researching in the field of Criminal Law. She obtained her LL.M. from National Law University Delhi, specialising in Criminal Law and Advanced Constitutional Law, LL.B. from University of Delhi and pursued B.Sc. (Hons.) Forensic Science from Amity University. She is a former practicing Advocate. Her areas of interest are Procedural Laws, Criminal Law, ADR methods and Gender Justice.

Hammad Hussain is a final year student of software engineering at COMSATS University Islamabad, Wah campus Pakistan. In 2023, he successfully completed an internship at Survey of Pakistan. During the internship, he worked on: i) Geospatial data development using GIS and Remote Sensing techniques. ii) Assessment of National Spatial Data Infrastructure (NSDI) websites and their improvement with respect to SDI services.

Gul Shaira Banu Jahangeer is working as Lecturer at College of computers and information Technology, Taif University, Taif, Saudi Arabia. She is Ph.D in Computer science and Engineering from Kalasalingam Academy of Research and Education .She also hold Master in Computer science and Engineering from Mepco Schlenk Engineering College, Anna university (2006) and Bachelor of computer science and Engineering from Mohammad Sadak Engineering College, Madurai Kamaraj University (2002). Her research interest includes Machine Learning, Deep Learning, Image Processing.

Ali Kavak is a assistant professor in the Department of Information and Document Management at Kırıkkale University in Turkey. In his academic work, he focuses more on issues in the field of library and information science. He has published articles in SSCI and field journals, especially on information security management, information literacy, transformation of libraries, library services, information access and technology. He regularly presents papers at national and international symposia. He has also published a book titled "Conceptual foundations of information security management: Information security in university libraries", he focused on information security in university libraries and made a significant contribution to the literature. She holds a PhD in Information and Document Management as well as an MA in Turkish Education. He also has undergraduate degrees in Turkish Language and Literature, Public Relations and Publicity, Aviation Management and Computer Programming.

Pranjal Khare is currently Faculty of Law at O.P. Jindal Gloabl University. He has completed his Master of Laws (LL.M.) in Corporate Laws and IPR from National Law Institute University, Bhopal; and his Bachelor's Degree from Rajiv Gandhi National University of Law, Punjab (2014-19).

Jennie Lee Khun is an adjunct professor for Purdue University Global. She currently works as an Applications Development Branch Chief with the United States Federal government and holds industry certifications including CISSP, PMP, PMI-ACP, and ITILv4. Prior to completing her Doctorate in Strategic Leadership she worked for Shepherd University as an IT Business Analyst and later IT Operations and Project Manager. Jennie received her MBA from Shepherd and her undergraduate IT degree from Kaplan University. She is passionate about bridging the gap between culture and leadership in the technology industry. Jennie grew up a military brat and cites that upbringing for her love of travel. She enjoys swimming, baking, and playing board games.

Kritika is a post graduate (Master of Technology(M.Tech)) in computer science and engineering and holds the position of an independent researcher, author and reviewer. She is the recipient of Young Researcher Award 2023, Gold Medallist in International Olympiad of Mathematics and holds accolades from Government of India for obtaining distinction during high school and senior school. The author is serving as Lifetime Member of International Association of Engineers(IAENG), Member of Women In Cybersecurity(WiCys) India Affiliate and and professional member of InSc Institute of Scholars. The author has obtained certifications in cyber security and is a top scorer in examinations like NTSE(India). The area of research includes cyber security, digital forensics, governance, and vulnerabilities.

Jason Merlo is a Forensic Scientist in the field of Friction Ridge who has been with the Texas Department of Public Safety Crime Laboratory's AFIS Section since 2009. His research interests include the history of knowledge about the friction ridge skin and the history of the use of friction ridge skin as a means of personal identification.

Tereza Raquel Merlo is a Professor and practitioner, currently teaching in the Department of Information Science at the University of North Texas and working for one of the top ranking Fortune Global 500 companies. She holds two Masters degrees in Information Sciences and a Ph.D in Business and Information Technologies. As an enthusiastic practitioner with more than twenty years of experience working for some of the world's leading companies in the fields of Information Technology and Management, she concentrates on business intelligence, data analytics, sales operations, business systems and process improvement. Her research has focused on knowledge management and information technologies in business settings. Her publications have included topics in the fields of Knowledge Management, Cloud Computing, Management and Data Analytics. Additionally, Dr. Merlo has over a decade of work in libraries and archives as well as in data management, having spent over ten years in the public sector, where she led programs designed to promote social/digital inclusion. Dr. Merlo was the keynote speaker for the XV ICKM, discussing international experiences in knowledge management.

Froilan Mobo is a Doctor of Public Administration graduate from the Urdaneta City University Class of 2016 and a graduate of the 2nd Doctorate Degree (Ph.D.) in Development Education program at the Central Luzon State University, Nueva Ecija, Philippines, Class of 2022. After obtaining his Doctorate Degree, he was promoted to the position of Associate Professor V in the Philippine Merchant Marine Academy (PMMA), and this allowed him to work with different international research institutions, such as the Director / Research Consultant of the IKSAD Research Institute, Turkey; At present, he is in the process of finishing his 3rd Masters's degree leading to Social Studies Education at Bicol University.

Adrian Shapiro serves as a librarian at Texas Woman's University.

Ahmad Tasnim Siddiqui is an Associate Professor at the Department of Computer Science & Engineering, Sandip University, Nashik, India. He is Ph.D. in Computer Science. He also holds a Master of Computer Applications, and an M. Phil (Computer Science) from Madurai Kamaraj University, Madurai, India. He has many publications in reputed journals indexed at SCI, SCIE, and SCOPUS. He has also published a book chapter in EMERALD insight, SPRINGER. and IGI Global His research interest includes e-commerce, e-learning, active learning, web mining, IoT, ICT, e-health, and cloud computing. He has a total of 15+ years of experience including 4.7 years of software industry experience. His favorite subjects are E-commerce and web Technologies using .net.

Hemendra Singh is a Lecturer of Law at Jindal Global Law School, situated within O.P. Jindal Global University, Sonipat. He pursued his LL.M. in Intellectual Property Rights from National Law University, Jodhpur, following his graduation with a B.A. LL.B. (Hons.) from Rajiv Gandhi National University of Law, Punjab. With a focus on corporate law, intellectual property law, criminal law, and constitutional law, he has authored numerous research articles published in both national and international journals.

Amand Zerangue serves as Assistant Dean at the University of North Texas Libraries.

Index

A

Ability to Pay 260, 267-268, 273-278, 282
Academic Discipline 309, 323
Andon 134, 153
Approweb 259, 267, 275-277, 279, 282
Archive 18, 39, 80, 118, 125, 192, 195
Artificial Intelligence 56-57, 62, 70-72, 106, 155-156, 159-160, 173, 175-178, 180, 183-184, 187, 199, 225, 227, 240, 263, 265-266, 268, 306, 310

B

Big Data 54, 56, 63, 65, 71-72, 103, 129, 155-156, 159-160, 173, 179, 181, 183, 187, 207, 214-215, 219, 257-260, 264-268, 271, 281-284, 287, 289-290, 300, 306-307
Big Data Analytics 72, 159-160, 215, 259-260, 264-267, 271, 281-282, 289
Business 13, 22, 30-33, 35-41, 43-44, 46-73, 75, 80, 88-89, 100, 102-103, 108, 116-117, 120, 125, 127, 129, 131, 133, 135, 141, 143, 145, 147, 150-152, 169-171, 175-178, 181, 185, 190, 207-208, 215, 217, 220-222, 228-229, 235, 258-259, 263, 266-276, 278-282, 284-287, 289, 291, 293-295, 297-298, 300-303, 309-310, 318-319, 321
Business Intelligence 55-59, 61-62, 64-65, 68-73, 259, 266-272, 275-276, 278-279, 281-282, 300, 302
Business operations 31, 38, 44, 51, 55, 57, 65, 70, 147, 229, 289

C

Cadillac 15-22
Cause–Effect Diagrams 153
Censorship 102, 106, 108, 114, 116, 119, 126, 129-130, 132
Cloud Computing 55-56, 155-156, 159, 175-178, 181, 184-185, 187, 289-290, 306
Compliance Risk Management 259, 266-267, 269, 271-279, 281-282
Consensus Mechanisms 78, 100, 104
Control Charts 135, 140-141, 146, 153
Cross-Border Data Transfers 106, 109, 132, 245
Customization 49, 136, 153, 302
Cybersecurity 25-26, 33, 40, 43, 45, 54, 170, 173-175, 177-181, 183-184, 187, 224-225, 231, 240-242, 246, 248-249, 253-254, 256

D

Data 1, 3-6, 8, 12-13, 16, 20, 22, 24-30, 32-33, 35-41, 43-47, 49-58, 60, 62-91, 93-109, 111, 113-129, 131-132, 135, 137, 152, 155-164, 166-169, 172-194, 196, 199-222, 224-228, 230-237, 239-260, 262-271, 274-308, 310-311, 314-321
Data Governance 20, 22, 37, 43-44, 46, 53-54, 56-73, 103, 131, 188-190, 198-202, 207-209, 212, 214, 216, 233, 245, 251, 253-254, 270, 283-287, 289-296, 298, 300-304, 306-307
Data governance framework 60, 198-199, 283-284, 290-292, 294-295
Data Governance tools 283
Data Intelligence 283, 287-288
data management 37, 46, 54-63, 65, 67-72, 98, 104, 135, 137, 152, 167, 178, 188-189, 192, 198-199, 203, 205-207, 233, 240-241, 264, 268, 270, 286, 288-291, 293, 298, 302, 315-316
data privacy 22, 61, 103, 128-129, 131, 155-159, 161-164, 167-169, 175-177, 179, 182, 187, 233, 235-236, 240, 242, 244, 250, 253-254, 287
data protection 46, 63, 71, 74-76, 79-80, 85-86, 88-90, 95-97, 99-104, 106-109, 111-116, 125, 127-129, 131-132, 158, 162-163, 168-169, 180-185, 187, 217-222, 225, 228, 232-234, 237, 240-243, 245-250, 253-258, 288, 290
data security 24, 46, 59-60, 62, 69, 155-156, 158-159, 161, 168-169, 176-178, 184-186, 224, 231, 241-

242, 245-248, 251, 253-254, 268, 285, 293, 304
Data Sharing 198, 203, 206, 209-212, 219, 257, 263, 286, 290, 306
data visualization 4, 6, 8, 55, 68
Decision Making 29, 48, 55, 57, 60, 63, 72, 136-137, 139, 142-143, 149, 156, 168, 194-195, 203, 240, 287, 291-292, 303
Deming 134-135, 140-142, 144-149, 152
Developing Countries 182, 201, 213, 259-261, 264-265
Dewey Decimal Classification 317, 321, 323
Digital age 24, 74, 102, 107, 125, 127-128, 130, 132, 167, 214, 218, 236-237, 240, 246-247, 250, 255-257
Digital Footprints 74-75, 104
Digital Preservation 188, 190, 196-198, 201-202
Digital Privacy Concerns 104
Directorate General of Taxes 259-260, 266-272, 274-282
Distributed Ledger Technology 74-75, 77, 100, 102, 104, 127, 176, 179
DMAIC Cycle 153

E

E-Discovery 218, 226-227, 229-230, 233-234
E-Government 203, 212, 214
Emotional Intelligence 36-37
Erasure of Information 105, 132
European Union 25, 74, 76, 100-101, 103, 106, 108-109, 111-112, 127-132, 158, 162-163, 168, 178, 180-182, 218, 220-221, 225, 253
executive 15-22, 31, 45, 49-50, 60, 71, 88

F

Faceted Classifications 323
Facial Recognition Technique 236

G

GDPR (General Data Protection Regulation) 74, 104, 132
General Data Protection Regulation 46, 71, 74, 96, 100-101, 103-104, 106, 109, 114, 128-129, 131-132, 158, 162, 168, 181-182, 184-185, 217-221, 225, 228, 232-234, 253, 288
Geo-fencing 236, 243-245
Geographical Information 203-204, 210, 215
Good Governance 48, 236-244, 247-248, 250-251, 253, 255
governance 14-16, 18, 20, 22-23, 32, 36-41, 43-50, 52-73, 78-79, 91, 99-103, 114-115, 127-131, 133, 136, 138, 140, 147, 149-150, 170, 173, 180, 185, 188-192, 195-202, 204, 206-209, 211-224, 226-245, 247-248, 250-251, 253-257, 264, 270, 283-287, 289-296, 298-307

H

Healthcare 28, 34, 61, 75, 133-138, 140, 142, 144-145, 147-149, 151-152, 162, 176, 185, 215, 218, 222-223, 228-229, 231-234, 239-242, 247, 249-250, 258
Hierarchical Classification 316-317, 323
Hiring 36, 42, 144

I

ICT 24
Indonesia 33, 259-260, 266-267, 271, 282, 308, 322
information 1-5, 8, 10-11, 13-41, 43, 45-77, 79-82, 84-85, 87-93, 95-98, 103-110, 112-127, 131-133, 137-138, 142-144, 147-150, 155-188, 190-216, 218-235, 237-238, 241-243, 245-247, 249-252, 256-258, 260-261, 264-268, 271, 275-280, 282, 284-286, 288-291, 295, 303, 306-313, 315-324
Information and Data Privacy 155-159, 161-163, 167, 169, 175-177, 187
Information Breach 217, 231
information governance 15-16, 18, 23, 36-41, 43-45, 47-50, 52-55, 57, 69-72, 133, 150, 188-192, 195-196, 198-200, 202-204, 207-208, 211-212, 214-215, 217-238
Information management 22, 33-34, 37, 39-40, 50, 52, 54, 67, 70, 72-73, 79, 133, 137-138, 150, 188-191, 200-202, 213, 215, 217, 220-221, 223-224, 226, 230-231, 237, 243, 266, 306, 324
Information Management and Retention 226
information privacy 56, 155, 157-159, 161, 184-185, 220, 224, 230, 232
Information Retrieval 192, 310, 319, 323
Information Security 24-35, 44, 46, 50, 155, 157-162, 164-177, 179, 181-187, 200, 221, 223-225, 228, 231
Information Security Policies 27, 30, 35, 44, 161, 164-165, 168-169, 182, 184
Information Security Standards 32, 35, 169-170
Information Society 87, 110, 310, 323
Information-Seeking Behavior 310, 323
Institutional Repository 188, 192, 195-197
Internet of Things 137, 150, 155-156, 159-160, 166, 173, 175, 177-180, 183-185, 187, 225
ISO 9000 147, 149, 153

J

Juran 133-135, 147-152

K

Kaizen 148-149, 153
knowledge management 14, 17-19, 22, 56, 60-61, 65, 67, 69-71, 136, 145, 149, 237, 268, 282, 308-309, 313, 315-316, 318-323
Knowledge Production 56, 65, 312, 319, 323

L

law enforcement 1-3, 11-13, 19, 254, 271-272, 274-275
Leadership 36, 38-42, 44-45, 47-49, 53-54, 59-60, 62, 66, 69, 134, 136, 138, 140, 145-147, 149, 190, 200
Lean 133-135, 140, 149-150, 152-153
Legal Analytical Method 76, 104
Legal Framework 108, 110, 117, 128, 217-218, 220, 232, 245
Legal Hold 226-228, 230, 233
Librarianship 182, 201, 308, 310-313, 315-316, 318-323
Library and Information Science 188-189, 200-201, 308-309, 311-313, 315, 318, 320-323

M

Manufacturing 32, 54, 133-136, 139-142, 144-147, 149-151, 153, 226, 256
Metadata 61, 188-190, 192-195, 197, 200-202, 205-206, 210, 213, 268, 286-287, 289, 296-298, 300-301, 303
modern era 24, 287

N

NSDI 208-209, 211-212

O

Organizational 17-19, 21, 25, 28, 30, 36, 38-40, 42, 47-49, 53-65, 68-70, 72, 96-97, 134, 136, 138, 160, 183, 189, 192, 196, 200, 202, 215, 229, 233, 283, 289-290, 296, 306, 310-311, 318-319

P

Pakistan 203-204, 208-213
Paradigm Classification 317, 324
Pareto Law 153
PDCA Cycle 153
Personal Data 75, 79-91, 93-99, 101-109, 111-113, 115, 118-120, 122-123, 126, 129, 132, 157-160, 162-163, 166-169, 174, 178-179, 182, 186-187, 218-219, 221, 237, 241-243, 245-246, 248-249, 252, 258
Poka-Yoke 153
Policy 13, 27-29, 33-35, 37, 41, 44, 50, 71, 99, 104, 114, 127, 129-131, 134, 151, 155-156, 161, 168, 177, 179, 182, 184, 187, 196-197, 201-202, 205-207, 209, 211-212, 226, 240-242, 247-249, 252, 255-257, 260-261, 264, 266-268, 270, 289, 302, 305-306
Policy Making 240, 257
Privacy 19, 21-22, 24, 26-27, 30, 33-34, 39-40, 49-50, 53, 56, 61-62, 71, 74-75, 88, 92-93, 96, 99-112, 114-117, 119-124, 126-132, 155-164, 167-169, 174-177, 179-187, 189-190, 199, 217-218, 220-224, 227-237, 240-257, 287-288, 293-294, 304
Privacy rights 105, 114-115, 117, 157, 232-233, 237, 241-242, 245
Procedure 112, 168, 179, 187, 230, 287, 292-293, 310, 323
Process Mapping 153

Q

Quality Function Deployment (QFD) 136, 140, 154
Quality Gurus 133, 135
Quality Management 73, 133-141, 143-154, 226

R

Restriction Of Access to Information 105, 132
Right to Be Forgotten 74-75, 80, 86-88, 90-97, 100-110, 112-132
Right to Privacy 74-75, 88, 92, 96, 106-110, 112, 119-124, 126-127, 132, 160, 186, 240, 243, 247-248, 255-257
Risk 16-18, 21, 24, 29-30, 32, 36, 39, 41, 44-46, 48-50, 52-54, 74-75, 79, 92, 95-96, 99, 124, 138-141, 143, 158, 160-161, 166, 168, 170, 173, 176-177, 180-185, 187, 197, 207, 215, 222, 224-225, 234, 242, 245, 252, 259, 264, 266-267, 269, 271-274, 276-277, 279, 281-282, 285, 287, 289, 293

S

sentiment analysis 1, 4-6, 8, 11
Six Sigma 134-135, 140-141, 143-147, 149-153
Smartweb 267, 274-280, 282

Social Engineering 25, 28, 159, 161, 163-165, 173, 179, 181, 185, 187
social epistemology 308, 311-316, 320-321
social media 1-4, 8, 12-14, 26, 80, 123, 157, 159-160, 162, 173-174, 177, 179, 183, 204, 248, 254, 256, 264
Spatial Data 203-206, 208-216
sponsor 15-22, 49, 60
Statistical process control (SPC) 141-142, 153

T

TADAT 267, 272, 282
Taguchi Method 147, 153
Tax Authorities 259-260, 263-265, 272
Teacher attendance 236, 242-245, 255
Technology 2, 17, 20, 24, 26-28, 32, 34-37, 39, 41, 45, 48, 50, 53-54, 56, 58-60, 62-63, 65-70, 72, 74-80, 82, 86-87, 91, 94, 96-107, 109-110, 116-118, 124, 127-128, 130, 132-133, 136-138, 143, 152, 155-156, 158, 160-161, 165, 169-172, 175-181, 184-187, 189, 192, 196, 198-199, 203, 207, 212, 218, 224-225, 227, 230, 232, 234-235, 237-240, 243-244, 246, 249-250, 252-254, 257, 261-262, 268, 282, 285, 287-290, 309-311, 318-323
Threat 25, 27, 30, 34, 99, 107, 124, 126, 159-161, 163-167, 172-173, 175, 180, 187, 257
Total Quality Management (TQM) 134, 136, 154
Toyota Production System 133-134, 151
Training 15-17, 28-30, 34, 36, 38, 41-43, 53, 67-68, 134-136, 139, 141, 145-147, 149, 151, 158, 162, 164-165, 179, 186, 189, 193, 198, 200, 223, 226, 238-239, 249, 254, 295, 304, 311
Tree Classification 317, 324

U

user behavior 1-2, 12

Z

Zero Defect 154

www.ingramcontent.com/pod-product-compliance
Lightning Source LLC
LaVergne TN
LVHW062120300926
849161LV00010B/2500